One Book/Five Ways

One Book/Five Ways

THE PUBLISHING PROCEDURES OF FIVE UNIVERSITY PRESSES

Foreword to the 1994 Edition by Joyce Kachergis

Introduction by Chandler Grannis

Afterword by William Kaufmann

THE UNIVERSITY OF CHICAGO PRESS   Chicago and London

The University of Chicago Press, Chicago 60637
The University of Chicago Press, Ltd., London

Copyright © 1977 by The Association of
American University Presses, Inc.
Copyright © 1978 by William Kaufmann, Inc.
Foreword © 1994 by The University of Chicago

Printed in the United States of America
01 00 99 98 97 96 95 94   6 5 4 3 2 1

ISBN 0-226-03024-5 (pbk.)

Library of Congress Cataloging-in-Publication Data

One book/five ways : the publishing procedures of five
university presses / foreword to the 1994 edition by
Joyce Kachergis ; introduction by Chandler Grannis ;
afterword by William Kaufmann.
     p.   cm.
     "Association of American University Presses"—
T.p. verso.
     1. University presses—United States—Case
studies.   I. Association of American University
Presses.   II. Title: 1 book/5 ways.
Z479.063   1994
070.5'94—dc20   93-41173
                                         CIP

Table of Contents

Foreword

The Manuscript Project

This book originated as the log of the "manuscript project" of the Association of American University Presses, in which five presses put *one* manuscript through their various publishing procedures from initial appraisal to production planning and the working out of a marketing program. Printed copies of the log were distributed for a workshop at the association's 1977 annual meeting in Asheville, North Carolina.

The log was intended for use at that meeting only. No one ever dreamed that it would later be published commercially, let alone that in 1993 I would be writing a Foreword to a new edition published by the University of Chicago Press. Had we known, we might have been too daunted to participate.

The project would not have been possible without an author, Purvis Mulch, who was "saintly enough to spar cheerfully with five different publishers over a period of many months." Mulch, as our colleagues learned at Asheville, was in fact Jerry Minnich, marketing manager of the University of Wisconsin Press. Another unexpected result of the Asheville meeting was that *No Time for Houseplants* was actually published by the University of Oklahoma Press.

The Value of This Book

When I was first asked to write this Foreword, I was doubtful: so much had changed since 1977. But a few minutes with the first edition changed my mind. The fact is that the procedures publishers now follow are the same; only the methods and the machines have changed. Publishers still acquire, edit, design, produce, and market books. The thinking behind publishing has not changed, nor has the basic sequence of events in bringing out a book. There are still manuscripts, though today they are much more likely to have been written on a computer and received by the publisher on a disk as well as in hard copy. Readers' reports are still obtained, though now they are more likely to be written on a computer and perhaps faxed rather than mailed. Manuscripts are still edited and copyedited with the same goals and thought processes, though now they are much more likely to be copyedited on a computer. Marketing people still think of strategies for selling a book, though now they may carry out their plans differently—for example, by typesetting their own ads and mailings.

If Flora Greenhouse (p. 63) has not retired from MIT Press, she is still writing the same kind of letters to authors and still lining up readers to review manuscripts.

One would hope that Agatha Q. Sigglesthwaite, editor (environmental arts), still holds forth at Toronto with an even bigger and bushier plant than Albert (pp. 269–70).

Letters like Gwen Duffey's (p. 156) are still being written to overdue authors. Contracts are still signed between authors and publishers. Launch meetings are still held for publishing projects. Cost estimates are still made by production departments. Sales managers still request an author information sheet. Designers still design books. Marketing managers still press for four-color jackets that will make their selling job easier.

One Book/Five Ways is still a viable introduction to publishing.

If *No Time for Houseplants* Were Published in 1993

In 1977 all five participating presses had some form of computerized in-house composition, in all cases recently introduced in an effort to save money. Different machines and methods were used; no one at that time knew what would replace Linotype. This question was soon answered with the introduction of the Mergenthaler Linotron 202, a powerful machine but too expensive for most publishers to purchase. The Linotron 202 is still the workhorse of the typesetting industry, but it now is being replaced by systems that support Postscript. In-house composition is reappearing today in the form of computers and page-makeup programs such as Quark Express and Pagemaker.

Today *No Time for Houseplants* would probably have been written on a computer or word processor (it is estimated that 90 percent or more of all manuscripts are now written by authors using DOS or Macintosh computers). Such manuscripts no longer have to follow the tedious and expensive routes of being pencil-edited in manuscript form and ultimately rekeyboarded by a typesetter. We can use the author's original keystrokes both to edit and to typeset the book.

Let us look at some of the implications of this fundamental change.

Acquisitions

Although the acquisitions editor's acceptance letter could be much the same as it was in 1977, now it would likely include a word processing questionnaire and a request for a sample disk along with one or more hard copies of the manuscript. The author may also be sent a form with the publisher's preferred style for electronic manuscript preparation.

Editing

Many copy editors edit a printout of the manuscript and ask the author to enter the changes. There are many sad tales told at publishers' meetings of situations in which the author did not make the changes properly, or made some but not others and left no clear indications of which were not made, or took the occasion to add new material (thus requiring further editing), or delegated the job to an incompetent secretary. Such complications can lead to months—sometimes a year or more—of the proof and disk going from author to publisher to author to publisher. It is usually better for editors to make the editing changes themselves on the disks and send the edited manuscript to the author for review. This is the way we assume that our copy editor in 1993 would edit *No Time for Houseplants*.

First, the author's disks would be converted to the publisher's editing program. This is not a complicated procedure. A number of programs are available that will convert disks from one program to another or from IBM disks to Macintosh disks. Our in-house editing program would probably be WordPerfect, MS-Word, or XyWrite.

The advantages of editing the original disk file on a computer are described by Jane Lago of the University of Missouri Press in *Scholarly Publishing*, January 1993:

> Although we had had some trepidation about surrendering our blue pencils, all our editors took to computer editing very quickly. In fact when each of us tried to edit a manuscript in the old way after having worked electronically, we all found working on paper far more laborious and time-consuming than we had remembered. When you copyedit on paper, for example, and come across a word you saw earlier with a different spelling but aren't quite sure where, it can take hours of rereading to locate its previous appearance. On the computer . . . it took only minutes to search through files for a specific word.

This search-and-change function, along with the spell-check function and the ease with which words, paragraphs, pages, and chapters can be moved from one place to another, adds to the efficiency of the editing process.

The author, of course, must be shown very clearly what changes the editor has made or is proposing to make. Here are some of the ways editors do this:

XyWrite's Redlining: XyWrite's "redlining" feature prints out deleted words with strikeovers and encloses inserted text within brackets (this can be modified). Editorial queries are made using XyWrite's footnote feature; the location of a query is marked in the text with either a number or a symbol, and the actual queries print at the foot of the page. The author reviews the edited printout, using the original manuscript as a check copy but making all corrections on the new printout. The copy editor then inputs additional corrections, deletes the queries, cleans up the redlined file, and makes any final necessary corrections to the code checklist.[1]

DocuComp and WordPerfect: DocuComp prepares a new file that also shows each of the changes made in the copyediting. That file then can be printed in WordPerfect, and all the formatting of the edited file be retained—including the placement of the queries at the bottom of the pages. It can show an editorial change by putting a line through the original wording and following it by the revised wording in bold. DocuComp also sets in italic passages that have been moved from one place to another.[2]

Queries in text: The copy editor does not print out the files or use a redlining program: he/she works in their familiar word processing environment, rewriting as necessary, and queries the author in bold all-caps type directly after any edited section.[3]

In addition, the 1993 copy editor would probably put in simple codes such as CN for chapter number, CT for chapter title, Hd1 for subhead 1, Hd2 for subhead

---

1. Pam Upton, University of North Carolina Press, "Editing at the Computer Terminal in XyWrite III," unpublished manuscript.
2. Jane Lago, "A Decade of Electronic Editing," *Scholarly Publishing*, January 1993.
3. Stanley Ivester, "Electronic Editing and Production at Tennessee," paper presented at the spring 1993 meeting of the Association of American University Presses.

2, <i> for italics, EXT for extract. A list of these codes would accompany the disk and a printout of the manuscript to design and production.

The copy editor would locate the illustrations in the file, either by noting the location on the printout or by actually typing it into the file and calling it to the compositor's attention. The illustrations and figures would be numbered and the numbers used to locate the illustrations in the text and to identify the illustration legends. The legends would be typed by the copy editor at the end of the file or in a separate file.

Design and Production

Here even more dramatic changes have taken place. Five years ago, I and my colleagues at Kachergis Book Design would have handled *No Time for Houseplants* by sending elaborate type specifications to a typesetter and receiving galleys in return. With such a heavily illustrated book we would have sized the illustrations and xeroxed them on a reducing/enlarging photocopier, preparing a detailed list of final dimensions and reduction percentages. When we received the galleys from the typesetter, we would have dummied the book (pasted up each page). When the proof was okayed by the author and the publisher, we would have either sent the dummy to the typesetter to follow in making up pages or paged the book ourselves, putting the xeroxes of the illustrations in place as a guide to the printer. This would have added four or five time-consuming and potentially error-producing steps to the procedures I describe below.

There are many ways that *No Time for Houseplants* could be designed and produced today. What follows is simply what we would do at Kachergis Book Design, first for the book, then for the jacket or cover.

The Book
1. Log in the manuscript, disk, and illustrations.
2. Pick up the character count from the disk and analyze the components of the manuscript, e.g. text, extracts, subheads, tables.
3. Read the publisher's memos and transmittals and do a preliminary design. This means establishing the trim, typeface, type size, general layout, and margins: no changes here since 1977. It also means looking ahead to the manufacturing stage. *No Time for Houseplants*, with its prospective 7,500 printing, would be a natural for a small web press. Because it is heavily illustrated, preference would be given to printers who can accept disks for final copy and can pre-scan illustrations.
4. Insert the preliminary specifications in the estimating program, which converts them to a page count chapter by chapter. If the overall page count is not desirable (ideally a multiple of 32 for most books), adjust the specifications to change it.
5. Do preliminary layouts on the computer in Quark Express.
6. Request preliminary estimates from printer-binders.
7. Once a printer is selected, send the printer the halftones to scan. The printer will make high-resolution scans that can be electronically stored, and will send low-resolution scans in the form of Quark libraries along with all of the original

photographs. (If we had not selected a printer with this capability, we would make our own low-resolution scans.)

8. Prepare the figures in Freehand. If any of the photographs need altering or touching up, scan them in at twice the resolution that they will be printed and alter them using Photoshop. Scan the line figures at a high resolution (depending on their final size) to put in place in the pages.

9. Make final style sheets in Quark, using the same codes that are used in the manuscript file.

10. Flow the text into the style sheet format, converting the word processing file into the chosen type style for each element.

11. Following the instructions from the copy editor, place the illustrations in the pages, cropping and sizing them, and put the legends in place.

12. Check a printout of the pages for bad breaks, loose lines, and other typographic flaws.

13. After making typographic corrections, print out the pages with the illustrations in place for the editor and author to check.

14. When the proof has been okayed, send the printer the disks along with a printout of the page proof and print-and-bind specifications.

15. The printer will go directly to negatives from the disks, picking up the size and cropping of the illustrations electronically and substituting the high-resolution scans of the illustrations for the low-resolution scans in the files that have been provided.

16. The printer will then send bluelines (proof of the negatives) for approval. Check these carefully for poorly handled illustrations, dirt, damaged type, incorrect margins, and so forth. Because there is no repro proof to get dirty and because the files are handled only electronically (untouched by human hands), bluelines produced directly from negatives generated by disks are very clean.

17. After the bluelines have been approved, the printer will send folded and gathered pages of the printed book before it is bound, as well as a sample case to okay; no change from 1977. The printer will then bind and ship the book.

What does this list of steps mean in the way of changes since 1977? It means that long, elaborate lists of composition specifications do not have to be made out and checked and looked up when questions arise. It means that the designer does not have to mark up the manuscript or prepare elaborate checklists of illustration sizes. It means that the designer does not have to check the page proof for typesetter errors, indicate corrections, write notes to the typesetter, and then check revised proof to see that all instructions have been properly carried out. It means that paging problems can be solved instantly by the designer as they arise, for example by cropping or altering the size of an illustration. It means that a designer who does not like the kerning combinations in the typeface—either in general or in specific display lines—can alter them on the spot.

The downside of all this is that there is no typesetter. Typesetting and paging skills are not easy to learn and are not learned overnight. Good typesetters know all the tricks: they make type look good in ways most designers never dream of. Wonderful as computers are, amazing as the software is, they cannot typeset and page a book without the guidance of someone experienced in typography.

The Jacket or Cover
Since *No Time for Houseplants* is a trade book, we would probably design the jacket before the book, so that the design could be used as early as possible by the publisher's marketing department.

Using any information supplied to us by that department (e.g., use such-and-such an illustration; or, the author hates green; or, this is a trade book and the jacket can be in four colors), we would design the face of the jacket or cover on the Macintosh, scanning in illustrations and altering them if necessary. When this design had been approved, it could be rendered in any one of several ways, depending on the publisher's needs. For *No Time for Houseplants* we could prepare a four-color sketch on the Macintosh and send the disk to a supplier, who would send us either negatives (one for each color) or a high-resolution color printout. If we requested negatives, we would send them to a supplier who could convert them into a very finished and accurate color sketch.

Finally, using a disk with the flap and back panel copy supplied by the publisher, we would assemble the complete jacket on the Macintosh, adding the spine, the flaps, and the back panel to the approved face design. This disk would be sent to the printer, who would send us either a color key or a chromalin for approval.

Marketing

The marketing department today would probably design and prepare its own ads and circulars on computers. With the ability to store data and retrieve information in many different forms, marketing departments can build lists of customers known to be interested in certain topics or areas and pinpoint their sales efforts accordingly. Sales and inventory figures have long been computerized, of course, but the ease with which such data are stored and retrieved now, and their accessibility in many different forms by anyone in the publishing house who is networked, has made the marketing effort more efficient.

Conclusion

One Book/Five Ways was first published at the beginning of this electronic revolution, when we were still searching for something that would replace Linotype. In 1993 we are at midstream. As Chuck Creesy of Princeton University Press wrote in the *AAUP Computer Newsletter*, May 1993: "The situation of the scholarly publishing community today resembles that of a person standing on a railroad track watching a train approach in the distance. That train is the new, digital information order, and though it is difficult to gauge precisely how far off it is or how fast it is coming, it will probably arrive sooner than we expect." We are at the beginning of instant books. CD-ROM publishing and interactive multimedia projects are imminent.

First, however, we need to learn how to take advantage of the capabilities that exist today, and to do this in a way that does justice to the honorable profession of publishing. There is always the temptation, whatever the tools, of doing things efficiently rather than well; always the danger that instead of taking advantage of the new control we have to do things better, we may just use the power and speed to do them faster. Maybe in another sixteen years *One Book/Five Ways* will be truly obsolete, the onrushing train will have knocked the scholarly publishing community galley west. More likely, I think, this book will even then have some useful things to tell us.

Joyce Kachergis
6 October 1993

Acknowledgments

These logs were planned and assembled over a two-year period by a special Project Committee of The Association of American University Presses comprised of

MURIEL COOPER, *The MIT Press*

RICHARD HENDEL, *University of Texas Press*

JOYCE KACHERGIS, *Chairwoman, The University of North Carolina Press*

HILARY S. MARSHALL, *University of Toronto Press*

CAMERON POULTER, *The University of Chicago Press*

BRUCE YOUNG, *The University of Chicago Press*

In addition to the Project Committee those individuals who contributed their particular talents to these logs are:

Chicago: Joseph Alderfer / Richard DeBacher / Penelope Kaiserlian / Catharine Seybold / Kimberly Wiar

MIT: Mary Collins / Robin Cruise / Mario Furtado / Nancy Greenhouse / Arthur Kaplan / Patricia A. Mahon / Donna Schenkel

North Carolina: Gwen Duffey / Martha Farlow / Anne Geer / Johanna M. Grimes / Rebecca Johnson / Malcolm MacDonald / Sally McMillan / John Rollins / Ann Sulkin

Texas: Dohn Barham / Nancy Burton / Suzanne Comer / Chris Gray / Shirley Knop / Kathryn Stevens / Eje Wray / Carolyn Cates Wylie

Toronto: Jean Jamieson / Audrey Livernois / Jean Melusky / Barbara Plewman / Pauline Potts / William Rueter

We acknowledge with appreciation the suggestions and assistance given by J. G. Bell, Stanford University Press, and Edward King, University of Missouri Press, at the inception of the project.

Support and counsel were given by Willard A. Lockwood, President of The Association of American University Presses; John B. Putnam, Executive Director of The Association of American University Presses; and Jerome J. Lewis, Managing Director of American University Press Services.

The completion and publication of these logs would not have been possible without the continuing advice, dedication, and work of Carol Franz, Assistant Director of The Association of American University Presses.

J.W.K.

Introduction

In this unusual book about publishing, five university presses show in step-by-step detail how each would proceed with an identical manuscript from first consideration up to the point of manufacturing. In doing so, they demonstrate that (1) there is more than one way to make a book and (2) the operating principles of several highly competent presses are rather similar. They show also that a group of publishers is willing to devote great amounts of time and effort to a cooperative project and that they can have some fun along the way. The AAUP's tradition of sedate spoofery continues to be a lively creative force.

Above all, the cooperating presses provide here a body of instruction that is at least as illuminating for general trade as for scholarly books. The **experimental** but wholly plausible manuscript in question presents a number of publishing problems: making partly technical materials attractive to a popular audience; copy-editing and dealing with an author; handling extensive illustrations; setting up special segments for useful reference; postulating markets and the channels to them; deciding on the optimum means of printing and binding; determining budgets and setting prices in line with cost estimates and sales projections; finally, planning an economical means of effective promotion.

The basic idea of the project was for each participating press to make a log of the entire day-to-day process, with all the supporting documents. In effect, the documents constitute the log. The steps are listed in the table of contents of each press's contribution to this volume.

Among the items are: the inquiries, memos, and forms leading to the decision to publish; contracts or letters of agreement; preliminary publishing schedules; transmittal forms; style instructions; editorial checklists; minutes of meetings; correspondence with the author; design specifications; orders regarding illustrations; production cost estimates; manufacturing orders and schedules; sales plans and budgets; promotional calendars; catalog, publicity, and jacket copy. Included by each press are Chapters II and IV of the proposed book, showing copy-editing and author's reactions, also layouts for typical pages and for jackets.

The five treatments have some elements in common. All call for a first printing of 7,500 copies (although alternative estimates are computed); all will employ the VIP composition system (that of The University of North Carolina Press is the model); and all involve standard arrangements for royalties, rights, and trade discounts.

To compare differences among the logs is especially interesting. Each plan looks as if it would work. Each one, however, contains its own points of emphasis. Among those worth examining might be:

★The different estimates of total pages, trim sizes, unit costs, and prices.

★North Carolina's paperback with slipcase, compared with Chicago's spiral-bound volume, Toronto's unjacketed book with preprinted cloth cover, and the jacketed hardcover books of MIT and Texas.

★The five contents pages—some detailed, some succinct.

★How the responsibility for supplying illustrations is decided.

★Doubts about the title: Is North Carolina right about wanting a question mark after the main title? Is Chicago right in wishing to emphasize that the book is for beginners?

*Conflicting views about the volume's book club possibilities.

Some of the participants provide narrative accounts of some areas. Texas precedes its collection of documents with an essay about the entire process and later describes correspondence, not documented, that would be conducted with the Library of Congress, the author, the illustrator, and others. North Carolina presents an example of copy prepared for Optical Character Recognition. All the presses write proposals for low-budget promotion programs. MIT suggests heavy advance distribution of reading copies; 500 will go to retailers.

The implied question "Who is Purvis Mulch?" pervades the logs. Each press has its own image of the author, described almost as if Anthony Trollope were describing some friend of the Pallisers. Most interesting, perhaps, is the view of Toronto, which imagines at first that Mulch is a man—a rather mossy type—and finally discovers the writer is a woman, "an attractive, articulate person in her early 40s." This greatly enhances the promotion program; Toronto will send her on tour for demonstrations and personal appearances—which will not be too expensive because she will stay with some of her many friends and relatives in cities en route.

One Book/ Five Ways will give working publishers many practical points on which to compare notes and will bring reality and a touch of humor into many an instructional workshop. It is a valuable contribution to the literature of education for publishing.

Chandler Grannis
17 April 1977

One Book/Five Ways

THE UNIVERSITY OF CHICAGO PRESS

Table of Contents

Acquisitions Procedures

When a manuscript is received, the editor's assistant sends an acknowledgement card to the author or the editor writes a personal note. The author's name, the author's address, the title of the manuscript, date received, number of copies received, and house (acquisitions) editor's initials are entered on two copies of a log card (p. 7), one for a master file and one for the house editor's file. The status of the manuscript is recorded on this card, names of readers, fees paid, etc. A book folder is prepared, and usually an Author and Manuscript Inquiry (pp. 5-6) is sent. The manuscript is walleted and labeled, with the author's name, the title, and date received.

Each manuscript is reviewed in the house, either by the editor, the editor's assistant, or a part-time reader. If the evaluation is favorable, the manuscript is sent to a scholar for review, usually with a page of suggestions (p. 7). Given a favorable first review, the house editor then must circulate a "house editor's statement," the reader's report, any response to the report, a preliminary cost estimate (p. 8) and a preliminary financial analysis (p. 9) to the senior editor, the editor-in-chief, and the director, requesting permission to obtain a second report. If the second report is approved and is also favorable, the earlier editorial reports, the second report and any response to it, a biographical note on the author, and the table of contents are circulated to the senior editor, the editor-in-chief, and the director, requesting approval to present the project to our faculty Board of University Publications. We do not present cost estimates or financial analyses to the Board, nor do we present projects that we do not wish to publish. The Board seldom rejects a project, but if there is doubt about the advisability of our publishing any manuscript submitted, it may request a third report, usually suggesting a reader's name.

If the Board approves publication, a contract abstract (p. 10) is circulated to the senior editor, the editor-in-chief, and the director for approval of the terms of the contract. The cost estimate and financial analysis accompany the abstract. If approved, the contract (pp. 11-13) is typed and sent to the author.

If necessary, the author may be asked to make final substantive revisions and to have the manuscript prepared according to the specifications in our Manual of Style. When the final version of the manuscript is in hand, the house editor completes a Book Transmittal form (p. 14) and the first (editorial) section of the Book Estimate and Release, eventually completed by the production controller, marketing manager, business manager, and director (p. 52). These forms and two copies of the manuscript are then transmitted to the managing editor.

THE UNIVERSITY OF CHICAGO PRESS

5801 ELLIS AVENUE
CHICAGO, ILLINOIS
60637

Author and Manuscript Inquiry

Would you be good enough to give us the following information in order to help us consider your manuscript for publication here?

Author and co-authors, if any:

-- , USA
Name   Address   Citizenship

Title of manuscript: NO TIME FOR HOUSE PLANTS: A Busy Person's Guide
                     to Indoor Gardening

Is this manuscript an unrevised version of your dissertation? **no**
Is this manuscript a revised version of your dissertation? **no**
If revised, what is the nature of the revision?

Has your manuscript or part of your manuscript been previously published (ie. distributed). Were these parts copyrighted by you, University Microfilms or any other party? **no**

Is your manuscript presently being considered for publication by another publisher? **no**

Characteristics of the final manuscript:

Estimated words per typewritten page: __250__

Total number of typewritten pages: __144__

Number of tables __15__ maps __0__ line drawings **undetermined**

photographs __38__

Are you prepared to submit the whole manuscript for review at this time? If not, what would remain to be submitted later? **whole ms submitted**

PR167-1M-6-75

Please summarize in a few sentences the essence or theme of your manuscript:

This is meant to be a book for the casual grower of house plants--
the home owner or apartment dweller who wants to raise several
dozen attractive house plants while spending only a few minutes a
day in caring for them. This book tells everything that is
necessary to know in order to achieve success. Most house plant
books are apparently written by enthusiasts who spend unending
hours in careful watering, potting, repotting, propagating, tying
up, inducing to flowering, humidifying, bathing, and even talking
to plants in an effort to get them to grow. This book cuts care
instructions to a bare minimum for the non-enthusiast who still
wants the company of healthy house plants.

Please name a few scholars working in your field and therefore competent to
read your manuscript. Indicate (*) if any of these scholars have already
read it.

1.
2.   (not applicable)
3.

Has your manuscript been read by others whose opinions you care to send us?

no

Please list any outstanding books on the subject of your work:

There are hundreds.

Please give us a brief curriculum vitae: your university affiliations, graduate
school, advanced degrees, and the titles of any previous books you have published.

University of Iowa, B.A., 1961; author, A Wisconsin Garden Guide,
Wisconsin House, Ltd., 1975, 362 pp., 15,000 copies in print,
3 printings; contributor, The Encyclopedia of Organic Gardening,
Rodale Press; book in progress, The Earthworm Book, Rodale Press
contract for 1977 publication; author of more than 50 articles
in Organic Gardening, House Beautiful, Mother Jones, Camping
Journal, other magazines; contributing garden editor & monthly
column (currently) in Countryside magazine.

What are your current research interests?

Organic gardening and farming; earthworms; solid waste management;
environmental issues

NOTE: If invited to submit your manuscript for review, you should retain
        a completed copy in case of loss or damage in the mails.

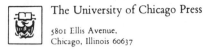

The University of Chicago Press

5801 Ellis Avenue,
Chicago, Illinois 60637

To the Reader:

Please be completely frank in giving us your critical judgment of this manuscript. Your report is solely for the guidance of the editors of the Press and the Board of University Publications, and your name will not be revealed to the author without your express permission. To protect you and us, as well as to avoid undue work and expense for the author, in case our decision is to decline publication of the manuscript, we ask you please to write any notes or queries on a separate sheet, not on the manuscript pages.

The questions below concern matters in which we are particularly interested. We shall be grateful if in the course of your comments you try to answer each of them for us.

1. Is the author's work original? Is his scholarship sound? What has he tried to accomplish, and to what degree has he succeeded? (A brief summary in your own words of the content and thesis, or argument, of the manuscript will be helpful.)

2. Is this a work of importance to specialists in its field? To what audience, or what particular groups, will it appeal?

3. What are the chief books already published on this subject, and how do they compare with this manuscript? (We should like as detailed a comparative bibliography as you can provide without inconvenience.)

4. Is the manuscript written in a clear, readable style? Is its organization suitable and effective? Does it contain unnecessary repetition? Could it be cut without loss of effectiveness, or is it about the right length for its essential content and purpose?

5. How could the manuscript be improved? (Please cite specific sections or chapters that need revision.)

Thank you for your helpful advice.

THE EDITORS

THE UNIVERSITY OF CHICAGO PRESS

Author: Purvis Mulch			Address: AAUP PROJECT		LOG CARD	
Title: NO TIME FOR HOUSE PLANTS						
Date MS recvd: 9/14/76			Editor: RI			

Date	Reader	Amt	Sent	Rpt In	Mss In	Paid
Out						
In	Transmitted 9/29					
Out						
In						
Out						
In						
Out						
In						
Out						
In						

PR151

SIMPLIFIED COST ESTIMATE FOR AN AVERAGE BOOK

1   Cast off: count the number of words in the manuscript. Include everything -- text, notes, extracts, bibliography. Estimate the extent of a missing preface or appendix. Divide the total by 400 to obtain printed text pages.

Number of printed text pages ... **90**
Display prelims (add 4 pages) ... **4**
Dedication or epigraph (2 each).. **2**
Contents (usually 2) ... **2**
Index (1/50 to 1/20 of text) ... **3**
+ 41 illus., 1 table
TOTAL PRINTED PAGES ... **143**

2   Figure the number of 32-page forms in the book. Divide total printed pages by 32. Ignore a remainder of 8 or less, but count any larger remainder as an additional form:

NUMBER OF FORMS ... **5**

3   Record the desired print run:

PRINT RUN ... **7,500**

These three figures are used below in making the cost estimate.

PLATE COSTS
41 illus. @ 10. ea.   **410**
1 table   **35**

Composition (total printed pages X $12.50*) **1263**
Other one-time costs (# of pages X $3 + $200) **629**

TOTAL PLATE COSTS........................   **2337**

STOCK COSTS

Paper

Number of sheets needed (print run X number of forms divided by 2) **18,750**
Spoilage (add 15 percent) **1,875**

Total number of sheets to be used **20,625**

COST OF PAPER (at $75.00 per 1,000 sheets) **1,547**

Presswork

Number of forms X print run + 15%. Divide by 4000 and multiply product by $100

TOTAL PRESSWORK **1,078**

Binding

Basic charge per copy ...... $ .75
Number of forms X .03 ...... .15

Binding cost per copy .90

TOTAL BINDING COST (print run X cost per copy)..... **6,750**

Jacket printing

Charge for first 1,000 jackets ...... $ 300.00
Additional 1,000s (at $50.00 per 1,000) ...... **325.**

TOTAL JACKET PRINTING **625**

TOTAL STOCK COSTS........................   **10,000**

TOTAL MANUFACTURING COST...   **12,337**

* or $15.00 for a more elaborate book

11/23/76

Financial Analysis

Date: 8 Sept 76   ☒ Original   ☐ Superseded Version

AUTHOR/EDITOR: Purvis Mulch   TITLE: The Time For House Plants

SERIES: ....   TRIM SIZE ....   NO. OF PAGES: est. 143 prtd

DISCOUNT CLASS: Cloth	Trade			
Paper				
ROYALTY TERMS:	10% NR	1st 2500; 12½% NR next 2500; 15% NR thereafter		

MANUFACTURING COST: Plate Cost	2337				**DISCOUNT** Actual Average %
Stock Cost	10 000				First year:
TOTAL MFG. COST	12 327				Second Year:
Unit Mfg. Cost	1.645				Add 1 % cushion to Highest Figure:
Subsidy					Reciprocal %:
TOTAL MFG. COST AFTER SUBSIDY					
Unit Mfg. Cost After Subsidy	1.645				

No. copies produced	7 500			
No. copies pre-sold				
No. frees	250			
No. on hand to sell	7250			

Pricing Without Subsidy

LIST PRICE	$ 7.50				
Average discount %	36%				
NET PRICE	$ 4.80				
Less unit cost	$ 1.645				
Less Average Royalty	$ .57				
GROSS MARGIN	$ 2.585				
% GROSS MARGIN	54%				

Unit $ required for overhead	$			
Unit $ available for overhead	$			
Unit (Loss) or Gain $	$			
NET SALES REVENUE (Multiply # units available for sale, + or (-))	$			
% Return on Investment				

	1973-74	This Year
Budgeted Overhead	48.7%	____ %
Gen'l Press Admin.	4.66%	____
Interest Rate on Borrowed Money	2.3%	____
Translation Expense	.2%	____
Write-Off Expense	4.6%	____
Total:	60.46%	____ %

CONTRACT ABSTRACT

Author: Purvis Mulch

Contract with (Author/~~Editor/Translator/Proprietor~~):

Address (and affiliation):

Box 1379

Title of work: NO TIME FOR HOUSE PLANTS: A BUSY PERSON'S GUIDE TO INDOOR GARDENING

Series title and editor:

Copyright by: University of Chicago

Rights limitations:

Market: World

Delivery date of MS: In hand

Illustrations: 41 photographs

Index: yes   Within ___15___ days

Subsidy:

Royalty terms: 10% NR first 2500; 12½% next 2500; 15% thereafter

Advance

Author's frees (clothbound/paperback): 10/5

Clauses to be deleted:

Special clauses/Remarks:

Type of contract:
- [X] Author
- [ ] Translator
- [ ] Import
- [ ] Proprietor (translation)
- [ ] Series
- [ ] Revised edition
- [ ] Letter of intent
- [ ] Other _____

BUP approval: ✔
Contract date: 15 Sept 76
Contract number: 9728

Length of MS: 156 pp. + 1 table

Author's alterations: 5%

Previous Contracts relating to this work (Series/Letter of intent/ _____)

Contract with: Contract number:

Royalty terms or fees:

House editor: KW
PR 114 rev. 71 5C 4-76

Approval: (MP) 9/15

Memorandum of Agreement made this   day of   ,
A.D. 19   , between THE UNIVERSITY OF CHICAGO, a corporation organized under the laws of the State of Illinois, of Chicago, Illinois, hereinafter referred to as the "University," its successors and assigns, and

Purvis Mulch

hereinafter referred to as the "Author," his heirs, executors, administrators, successors, and assigns, WITNESSETH:

In consideration of the covenants and agreements of the University hereinafter set forth, the Author covenants and agrees with the University as follows:

1 To grant and assign and he does hereby grant and assign exclusively to the University for its use any and all rights of whatsoever kind or nature now or hereafter protected by the Copyright Laws (common or statutory) of the United States and all foreign countries in all languages in and to a Work, the subject or title of which, subject to change by agreement of both parties, presently is: **Grant**

NO TIME FOR HOUSE PLANTS: A BUSY PERSON'S GUIDE TO INDOOR GARDENING

for any and all purposes, and by any means of communication and distribution, including the power to cause the same to be translated, abridged, dramatized, serialized and otherwise adapted, and other rights of every kind and nature now or hereafter during the term of this Agreement recognized as the property of the Author in said Work or in any parts thereof, for the United States of America and elsewhere for the respective term of the copyrights in the United States of America and elsewhere, and any permitted renewals thereof.

2 That the University shall have the exclusive right in its name, ~~or in the name of the Author~~, to secure   **Copyright**
copyright for said Work and all subsidiary rights therein in the United States and elsewhere, and the renewal of copyrights, and the University shall be the sole owner thereof; that the Author hereby irrevocably appoints the University, its successors and assigns, his attorney in fact with power of substitution in the name of the University to take out in his name or otherwise but for the exclusive use of the University any renewal or extension of original copyright and to execute in his behalf any and all documents necessary to secure to the University any renewal or extension; and said Author agrees to execute all papers necessary to secure to the University such renewals or extensions of such copyright.

3 That the Author warrants the Work is original and that he is the sole Author and owner of the said Work   **Warranty and**
and has full power to make this Agreement and grant; that the said Work or any part thereof has not   **Indemnity**
heretofore been published (except as may be set out in a rider annexed hereto and signed by the University) and no agreement to publish is now outstanding; that it contains no matter libelous or otherwise unlawful or which invades individual privacy or which infringes any proprietary right at common law or any statutory copyright; that he will hold harmless and indemnify the University, its licensees and distributees, or any of them, against any and all suits, claims, demands, or recoveries, including damages, costs, expenses, and attorneys' fees, which may be made, taken, or incurred at any time by or against the University, its licensees and distributees, or any of them, which are based upon any of the following allegations: invasion of privacy, violation of proprietary right or copyright, libelous or injurious matter contained in said Work.

4 To deliver to the University on or before 30 September 19 76 , time being of the essence, two   **Manuscript**
legible, double-spaced typewritten copies of the complete manuscript (with all illustrations, charts, graphs, and other material for the said Work, reproducible without redrawing or relettering), in a form and content and with subject matter satisfactory to the University for publication, it being understood that the length of the manuscript shall be approximately 156 typewritten pages ~~words~~ and the illustrations, etc., shall be as follows: approximately 41 photographs.

5 To read, correct, and return promptly galley and page proofs of the said Work submitted to the Author by the University, and that in the event of the Author's failure to return corrected proofs within sixty (60) days after the mailing thereof by the University, the University shall be free to proceed with the manufacture and publication of the said Work without waiting for the return of corrected proofs, and may deduct from royalties accruing to the Author or charge his account for any expense incurred by the University on this account.

Proofs

6 To pay the University within thirty (30) days after receipt of statement, at the current rates charged by its University Press, for all alterations made by or caused to be made by the Author in galley and page proofs in excess of ~~ten~~ five per cent ~~(10%)~~ (5%) of the cost of the original composition thereof.

Alterations

7 To revise the first and subsequent editions of the Work at the request of the University and to supply any new matter necessary from time to time to keep the said Work up to date, and provided that if the Author shall neglect or be unable to revise or supply new matter, the University may engage some other person or persons to revise or to supply such new matter and may deduct the expenses thereof from royalties accruing to the Author on such revised subsequent editions, it being understood that if such revisions be not made by the Author, the University shall cause such fact to be evident in the revised subsequent edition. The University shall have all of the rights in connection with all subsequent editions that it is entitled to in the original Work.

Subsequent Editions

8 To make the University the first offer of publication of his next full-length book. If the University fails to exercise this option by executing a publishing agreement within 90 days of receipt of the next completed manuscript, the Author shall be under no further obligation under this option and shall be free to cause its publication elsewhere.

Option

9 To prepare and deliver to the University index copy and such other similar matter as may be required by the University in connection with the publishing of the said Work, within fifteen (15) days after final page proofs are mailed to the Author by the University. In the event the University shall not receive such index copy and other matter in a form acceptable to it, within the time specified above, it may have such copy and other matter prepared at the expense of the Author. All permissions necessary to publish the Work are to be acquired by the Author at his own expense.

Index

Permissions

10 That the Author will not, during the continuance of this Agreement, furnish to any other publisher any work on the same subject of competing character or material therefor.

Competing Material

In consideration of the foregoing covenants and agreements on the part of the Author, the University covenants and agrees with the Author as follows:

11 As soon as practicable after receipt of the final manuscript, and following its formal acceptance by the University Board of Publications, to publish the said Work in the English language through its University Press, at its own cost and expense (except as otherwise provided in the memorandum annexed hereto), in such manner and style as the University deems best suited to the sale of the Work, and to reprint whenever in its judgment demand for the Work justifies reprinting, and, as long as the Work is in print and this Agreement is in effect, to offer the Work for sale at such prices as the University may from time to time determine.

Acceptance by Board

12 To pay to the Author, during the continuance of this Agreement, on the actual cash receipts or net price of the Work (net price being defined as list price less standard discounts), the following royalties from sales (less returns and refunds) of any one edition of the said Work published by the University:

Royalties

a.   10 % on the first   2500   copies sold; ~~thereafter~~ 12½% on next 2500; thereafter 15 % on all sales of any clothbound edition in the continental United States of America; and outside the United States, two-thirds thereof respectively;

b.   7½ % on sales of any paper-bound edition if published by the University;

c.   7½ % on sales by mail and coupon advertising outside regular bookstore channels;

d.   50% from the licensing by the University of any right in the Work protected by copyright, including the licensing of a cheap or paper-bound reprint or book-club edition, and the right to reprint portions thereof. In the event the Work be included in an omnibus edition and no specific sum be fixed for said use, then the University shall fix a pro rata reasonable sum therefor, 50% of which shall be paid to the Author.

e.   50% from the licensing by the University of any right in the Work or Revised Work not specifically in this paragraph set out.

Provided, however, that after two (2) years from date of first publication, the University shall be free to offer for sale, and to sell at reduced prices, retail or wholesale, any or all of the stock of this Work which in its judgment constitutes overstock, and, as become royalties and when payable hereunder, the rate of royalty payable to the Author on the sale of copies at such reduced prices shall be ten per cent (10%) of the actual receipts therefrom, except that on all copies sold at less than the manufacturing cost incurred or paid by the University, no royalty shall be payable to the Author; it being understood that no royalty shall be paid on free copies furnished to the Author, or on copies used for promotion of sales, review, advertising, samples, or like purposes, or on damaged copies, or on copies sold in any fiscal year of the University ending June 30th in which fewer than fifty (50) copies are sold, and that sales statements shall be made annually for the fiscal year ending as aforesaid, and that royalty payments due as set forth in such statements shall be made on or before August 15th following.

13 To present to the Author ___ten (10) clothbound & five (5) paperback___) free copies of   **Free Copies**
the said Work upon publication, and ___five (5)___ (...............)
free copies of any revised edition hereafter published; it being understood that additional copies will be supplied at the regular wholesale price prevailing at the time of such purchase.

It is mutually understood and agreed by and between the parties hereto as follows:

14 That the University shall have the right after three (3) years from the date of first publication of the said   **Termination of Contract**
Work to terminate this contract by giving the Author notice by registered mail of its intention to do so. The Author shall have the right within three (3) months from the date of the mailing of said notice to take and pay for the remaining stock and plates, if any, at cost, but the Author shall not in the sale and distribution of the said stock, or in printing from said plates, use the name of the said University. If the Author does not exercise this right, the University shall be free at the expiration of the said three (3) months' period to dispose of all stock and plates remaining on hand for waste paper or otherwise as it may determine, without incurring any obligation to the Author for payment of royalty thereon. This Agreement and the obligation of the parties hereunder shall terminate at the expiration of said three (3) months' period. The University will at any time after notifying the Author as provided above assign the copyright to the Author if he so requests subject to the exercise of any rights theretofore granted by the University.

15 That in every case where, under the provisions of this Agreement, it shall be required or permitted for   **Notices**
either party to give or serve any demand or notice to or upon the other party hereto it shall be sufficient: To deliver or cause to be delivered a written or printed copy of any such demand or notice to the said party, or to send a written or printed copy of such notice or demand by registered mail, with postage prepaid and duly addressed to "The University of Chicago Press, XXXXXXXXXXXXXXXX Ellis Avenue,   *5801
60637   Chicago XX, Illinois," and to the Author at

or at such other place as either party may designate to the other by written notice.

16 That the word "Author" as used herein, and the reference thereto by the masculine singular pronoun,   **Definition of Author**
shall be understood to include and designate all authors or editors who may be party to this Agreement.

17 That amendments to this Agreement shall not be valid unless in writing and signed by both parties.   **Amendments**

18 That the rights herein granted shall inure to the University, its successors, assigns and licensees.   **Succession**

19 That the submission by the University of unsigned copies of this document to the Author for his signature shall confer no rights on said Author, and this document shall not become effective unless and until it is executed by both parties hereto.

In Witness Whereof *the University has caused these presents to be signed under the hand of the Director of the University Press, and the Author has hereunto set his hand and seal the day and year first above written.*

THE UNIVERSITY OF CHICAGO

By...
Director of the University Press

....
Purvis Mulch

....
Soc. Security No.

Book Transmittal

Date: **29 Sept. 1976**
House editor: **KW**

Author: **Purvis Mulch**

XXXXXXXXXXXXX

Full title: **NO TIME FOR HOUSE PLANTS: A BUSY PERSON'S GUIDE TO INDOOR GARDENING**

General: Author's background and our reasons for publishing book: Mulch is a former editor of Organic Gardening, author of 50-odd articles on gardening, published in Org. Gardening, Mother Jones, HouseBeautiful, etc. His WISCONSIN GARDEN GUIDE sold 15,000 copies in 1½ years.

Mulch argues here that there are two basic secrets to raising house plants successfully: choosing the right plants in the first place and providing a "proper basic environment" for them. The right plant, he says, if given the right conditions for growth, will thrive even if the owner must necessarily be frequently inattentive. This is not a book that presents a wealth of new material on raising house plants: rather, the author has selected from the masses of material available on house plants those suggestions that are most helpful for the person with little time to spend on indoor gardening. The reader without much experience will find it especially helpful. Illustrated with some forty-one halftones, the book could be an attractive coffee table item and will make an excellent gift.

Checklist	Herewith [x]	To come [date]
Half title	X	
Series title		
Title page	X	
Copyright page	X	
Dedication		
Epigraph		
Contents	X	
List of illustrations		
List of tables		
Foreword		
Preface	X	
Acknowledgments		
Introduction		
Complete text	X	
Notes		
Appendix(es)		
Glossary		
Bibliography		
Index		w/p.prf.
All illustrations	X	
Tables	X	
Boxes	X	

Contract

Contract no.: 9728   Series: Series contract no.:

☒ Book represents all new work by one or more authors under contract to us.

☐ Category of book as follows:

Manuscript Editing

Manuscript and proof to:

Index to be done by: **Author**

Rights and Permissions

☒ We have world rights, all languages, all editions.   ☐ Rights specified below

☒ Author(s), editor(s), translator(s) citizens of U.S.   ☐ Specifics below

☒ No permissions needed   ☐ Permissions in, free to Press   ☐ Details below

Design and Production

☒ Duplicate MS attached   Words or MS pages: **156 pp.**   If reprint, no. pages:

No. line drawings: No. maps: No. photos: **41**

☒ All straight composition   ☐ Special sorts (see below)   No. tables: **1**

☐ Standard trim size OK   ☒ Special trim (see below)   ☐ Offprints needed

Proposed del. date: **March 77**

Marketing

Publishing season: **Fall 77**   Subject codes: **ODE, OJD** *

Proposed price and discount—   Cloth: **7.50 trade**   Paper:

Remarks/Explanations

Trim size: Depending on how we decide to handle the illustrations and market the book, a special oversize format may be needed.

(* NB: i.e. Botany, Horticulture, Floriculture, & Ornamentals)

PR 133-500-1/76

Editorial and Production Procedures

The managing editor on receiving a manuscript with its accompanying forms (see p. 4) obtains an ISBN, makes a first assessment of the editorial and production problems presented by the work, and sends the two copies of the manuscript to the chief manuscript editor and production manager, respectively. Copies of the Book Transmittal (p. 14) are sent to various persons throughout the Press at this time as a signal that the book is going into work, and the title is added to the agenda of the next preproduction meeting.

Preproduction meetings are held at intervals of one to four weeks to make decisions on such questions as trim size, binding, type of jacket, mode of composition, press run, and discount, to discuss preliminary marketing plans, and frequently to agree on a target delivery date. Persons concerned with the editing, production, and marketing of the book attend, as well as department heads and the director. Meetings are chaired by the managing editor. Minutes of the meeting on each book discussed (p. 17) are distributed to all who attend. Later, the managing editor, chief manuscript editor, assistant production manager, and chief designer--working back from the target delivery date if one has been assigned--assign other key target dates, and these are recorded on the schedule card (p. 51) from which preproduction and production schedules are made up.

Manuscript editing and design usually begin after the preproduction meeting, the editor using the ribbon copy and the designer the second copy. Edited manuscript (pp. 18-38) is always sent to the author for approval, and by the time it has come back, the book design (pp. 42-44) should have been completed and circulated, and the manuscript can be marked up for setting. With the design completed, the production controller also obtains a manufacturing estimate (p. 44), and if this is satisfactory, it is added to the Book Estimate and Release (p. 52), which is sent to the marketing manager for pricing, and the book is ordered.

Meanwhile, the promotion section of the marketing department has been furnished with prelim copy and other descriptive matter on the book and writes jacket or cover copy (p. 55) in time to meet production deadlines assigned earlier.

The progress of every book in work (100-150 titles) is checked every two weeks by a "tracking" committee consisting of the editor-in-chief, managing editor (chairman), senior editor, chief manuscript editor, production manager, assistant production manager, chief designer, and head of the in-house typesetting facility. If books have fallen behind, remedial action is agreed upon or future target dates are adjusted.

Author/TITLE   Purvis Mulch   **MS/pr pp.:** 36,040 words
                NO TIME FOR HOUSE PLANTS?: A BUSY PERSON'S   est. 143 Mid-Jan.
                GUIDE TO INDOOR GARDENING   **Target del. date:** June '77
KW/BY:CS

Description/Importance? KW: frustrated with title because it didn't really provide
time-savers. Felt photos were good. Boxes arranged by plant needs were the best
feature. CP: liked boxes that showed where things grew best and the provision of
English and Latin names.

Market? Limited to beginners. PK: many on market, most cloth at $7.95. Not a
bookclub possibility because it is a beginner's book, not coffeetable or library.

Title OK? Change subtitle: A BEGINNER'S GUIDE... (KW check with author). Other
suggestions: Dig This; Houseplants--Chicago Style; The Hows and Whys of House
Plants. Should clearly indicate that it is a book for beginners.
Jacket: Modular? Special points?   Use back as chart? Put design, not copy, on
the back cover since we have nothing like this to advertise.

Trim size? 5¼ x 8? Est. on spiral binding--like handbook of cat musculature.
Waterproof cover would look more practical. Consider plastic coating, large
pullout chart, paper over boards.
Special machinework?   No

Illustrations or Tables?   41 illustrations
                                      special boxes: straight prose & tabular

Anything missing in MS?   no list of illus.

Press run? 7500 Estimate on spiral book with bound-in pullout chart, also on 6 x 9
              trim. Part dividers are also possible.

Sugg. price & discount?   Aim for minimum cost: $1.50 unit or less; $7.50 or less, trade
                              discount. Price est. on our standard royalty terms.

Editorial Problems
                          Illus. interspersed or grouped?
                          CS to edit chapters 2 and 4.

Preproduction meeting: 14 October 1976

ital & cap for Latin   Style for Mulch)
lc & rom. for common   or Latin used
as common name
chap 2-3 heads after Soil are B's ⊗

stemlike II-lf
(like under-1 word)

potbound
white-striped
cream-colored
small-leaved
yellow-gold
slow-growing
cut-leaf
upright-growing

No Time for House Plants

Q

3½/48 (Garamond Headliner Light)

No Time for House Plants | A Busy Person's Guide to Indoor Gardening   18 pt ital / Gar Headliner light

Purvis Mulch   { 24 lk }

3 pt # | University of Chicago Press / Chicago and London   { 12 pt }

(iii)

(Author blurb here) ✗

The University of Chicago Press, Chicago 60637

The University of Chicago Press, Ltd., London

© 1977 by ~~The University of Chicago~~ Purvis Mulch

All rights reserved. Published 197

Printed in the United States of America

80 79 78 77   9 8 7 ...

(to come)

(iv)

(CIP data here
including ISBN and LC numbers)

CONTENTS

SPECIAL BOXES

1: The ABCs of Artificial Light

2: Should You Send Your Plants to Summer Camp?

3: Can Your Plants Survive Your Vacation?

4: Plants for Cool Conditions

5: Plants for Medium Temperatures

6: Plants for High Temperatures

7: Plants of Greatest Tolerance

8: Plants for Dry and Semi-Dry Conditions

9: Vines and Trailing Plants for Totem Poles

10: Plants for Hanging Baskets

11: Suggestions for Large-Tubbed Specimens

Guide to Plant Requirements

Bibliography

Suggested Symbols

Key to Symbols

Index

CHAPTER 2

UNDERSTANDING HOUSE PLANTS

Every plant has its own preferences and requirements
for soil type, light, temperature, ventilation, humidity,
and several other factors that are within our power to control, or at least to mitigate. It is vitally important for
you, as a busy indoor gardener, to understand the basics of
each, since a prior understanding will enable you to avoid
much work later on while achieving routine success in growing
plants.

In addition to understanding these basic needs, you
will want to know something about pots and other containers,
repotting plants, propagation, and a few other matters that,
while not vital to immediate success, will help you to gain
further enjoyment in raising better plants.

(A)

THE BASIC HOUSE PLANT

The major difference between a house plant and an outdoor plant is one of location. All house plants could live and flourish outdoors, in the proper climate. All are derived from forebears that lived, reproduced, and died in the outdoors, whether it was on a forest floor in Central Europe or in the bough of a tree in a South American rain forest. Over many centuries of adaptation and evolution, each plant species embraced those characteristics that enabled it to survive; and even today, every house plant carries within its genetic structure the characteristics of its distant progenitors. Thus the Maranta may lose some of its leaves each autumn, even though autumn's weather does not come to the top of the bookshelf where the plant rests, and a cactus, no matter how long we have been feeding and watering it with unfailing regularity, will continue to hoard food and water within its swollen stems. In plants, old habits might recede, but they are never forgotten.

At no time are these innate plant characteristics more noticeable than during the autumn and winter, when many plants--particularly those from temperate regions--enter a period of dormancy. Then, new growth ceases and the plant takes on a listless and washed-out appearance. Other plants, including many of tropical origin, will maintain their bright appearance but will stop growing completely for several months

each year, emulating the natural rest periods of their forebears. You will do well to watch for these signs of dormancy and rest, and respond to each plant's needs at that time. When any plant enters a dormant or rest period, water should be reduced and fertilizer withheld completely, until new growth once again begins, usually in the late winter or early spring. At that time, water the plant freely and give it normal doses of fertilizer once again, in order to encourage new growth. By your proper treatment of the plant at this time, you will emulate the advent of spring, working with the plant in carrying out its rhythmic cycles.

Some plants also are naturally short-lived and will last no more than a year or two in your home despite your careful attention, because their genetic structure dictates a finite life span. Garden annuals, for instance, will germinate, grow to maturity, flower, produce seeds, and die, all in as little as six months. For this reason, very few annuals are selected as house plants. Although a few short-lived plants are cultivated indoors for their unusual characteristics, such as the sensitive plant, which is easily grown from seed, the house plants that we have cultivated over the generations are most often those that will give years of pleasure. Some house plants, in fact, live to be literally hundreds of years old.

Still other house plants are attractive when young,

but grow ungainly or otherwise unattractive when they approach maturity. The only plants of this kind I have chosen for inclusion in this book are those that are very easy to propagate from cuttings, so that the parent plant may be discarded after a year or two, and to be replaced by its children.

From the hundreds of thousands of plant species in the world, those traditionally cultivated as house plants are the relatively few that have shown a wide tolerance to conditions of heat, light, moisture, humidity, and ventilation--in other words, those that can withstand a human environment. They are both attractive to the eye and they are tough. Still, if we are looking for success with house plants--and particularly success without working hard at it--then we should spend some time to learn the characteristics of each plant, recognizing its individual needs and fulfilling them to the best of our ability.

HOW A PLANT FEEDS

A plant manufactures nearly all of its food by itself--and not from the "plant food" that you buy for it. Commercial plant food is no more than a combination of certain chemicals (sometimes in an organic base) that are essential to the plant's basic functioning, much as vitamins are essential to human nutrition. But the bulk of a plant's food--the sugar it uses for energy and growth--is manufactured by the plant itself. In the presence of light, the leaves of the plant

draw carbon dioxide from the air and water from the roots, converting these into sugar that is then used for producing energy production or stored for future use.

During this sugar-manufacturing process, known as photosynthesis, several other things happen within the plant. While carbon dioxide is being absorbed, oxygen is being released from the pores of the leaf surface. (Plants produce not only all of the world's food but most of its atmospheric oxygen as well.) During darkness hours, the process is reversed; some of the atmosphere's oxygen is recaptured by the plant and used to convert stored sugar to energy for growth. Generally, a plant manufactures growth food during the day and does its actual growing at night.

Often, the plant converts its newly manufactured sugar to starch and stores it, reconverting it to sugar as the need arises. Although the starch can be stored in almost any area of the plant, certain plants have developed specialized storage areas just for this purpose. Cacti and succulents have enlarged stems and leaves for the greatest above-ground storage capacity of any house plant, while others have developed underground storage apparatus for this purpose, including bulbs, tubers, corms, and rhizomes. A bulb is simply an enlarged underground bud, such as is found with hyacinths, tulips, and onions. A tuber is nothing more than an enlarged root; a common potato is a tuber; gloxinias, caladiums, dahlias, and many other common plants are grown from tubers. →

A corm is the enlarged base of a stem. And a rhizome is
~~simply~~ a laterally growing, enlarged, underground stem. All
are used by the plant for food storage, and all can also be used
to propagate plants ~~too~~.

Water is constantly being drawn up through the plant.
As it transpires through the stomata (pores) of the leaves,
a "pulling" action draws more water up through the roots.
The water carries with it mineral salts, including all the
elements which the plant needs to carry out its complex chem-.
ical processes. The transpiration which takes place in the
leaves is similar to perspiration in humans and it serves a
similar purpose—to cool the plant. With house plants, it
would be difficult for you to notice this cooling effect. But
it is readily apparent when a group of large trees carry out
the transpiration process. The cool and fresh feeling you
enjoy in a thick woods in summer is not primarily the product
of the shade itself, but the transpiration of the millions of
leaves overhead.

A plant usually cannot absorb too much water, since its vessels
and cells can accommodate only so much at a given time; however, the overwatering of a plant can exclude oxygen from
the root system, ironically causing wilting of the top portion
of the plant. When water is withheld, the plant's cells will
gradually collapse, causing wilting of the entire plant. All
plants do have protective mechanisms that conserve water in
times of drought, however, and can withstand a temporary dry

spell. Most wilted house plants will quickly spring back to
a normal state when ~~water is again~~ they are watered provided.

PARTS OF THE PLANT

Stem. The stem serves to support the plant and to contain and direct the vessels that transport water from the
roots, and food from the leaves, to every other part of the
plant. Most house plants, including Philodendron, Ivy, and
Spider Plant, have soft stems. Such plants must either climb
or crawl, since their stems are not strong enough to support
an upward-growing structure of significant height. Other
plants have soft but thick stems that enable them to attain
good height, although their stems are apt to be subject to
breakage. Woody-stemmed plants, such as the Avocado, Poinsettia,
and Boxwood, are far more sturdy and are usually derived from
trees or shrubs of the temperate region. Canes are thick
stems with hollow or pithy centers. Bamboo is an example of
a cane with which we all are familiar; among house plants,
Dieffenbachia and Ti Plant are good examples.

Some plants have a distinct main stem, ~~while~~ while others
send up many stems, none dominant. A side shoot is a smaller
stem growing out from the main stem. A petiole is a leaf
stalk—the stem-like structure from which a leaf grows. A
node is a joint on the main stem from which a leaf or side
shoot grows.

Leaf. The major purpose of the leaf is, as we have

seen, to manufacture food for the plant's growth and reproduction. Considering its total mass, the leaf has a remarkably
large surface area, ideally designed for the efficient absorption and diffusion of gases through its thousands of stomata.

After the basic functions of the leaf are understood,
its proper care is not difficult to appreciate. The stomata
must be kept fairly clean, free of dust and oil that might
hinder their efficient operation. Leaves must also be given
the freest access to light and ventilation, according to the
individual preferences of each plant. Never crowd plants to
a point where they are competing for light and air.

Roots. Roots serve two main purposes—to anchor the
plant in the ground and to supply from the soil water and the
mineral salts which accompany water. Bulbs, corms, rhizomes,
and tubers serve much the same purposes, as well as acting
as food storage areas. Roots, just as the above-ground parts
of plants, may be pruned without injuring the plant in any
way. Roots are often trimmed to prevent a plant from growing
too large for the convenience of the grower, just as top growth
is cut back. If roots are cut back, however, be certain to
cut back top growth to about the same percentage, or the reduced roots might be unable to supply the plant with sufficient
amounts of water. The major precaution in caring for roots is,
as I will mention several times in these pages, to avoid overwatering.

Are these basic kinds of leaves? (Perhaps too complicated for this book)

YES—NO NEED TO GO INTO IT IN GREATER DETAIL

Flowers. The plant's flowers contain its sexual apparatus. Pollination occurs when male pollen is deposited onto
female stigmata, thus fertilizing the plant and allowing the
formation of seeds. The fruit of any plant is, in reality,
the ovary which swells to protect the seeds. In nature, most
plants produce flowers. For the purposes of cultivating
house plants, only certain ones—which in this book ~~are~~ listed
as flowering house plants—can be depended upon to produce,
under home conditions, blossoms of sufficient size, profusion,
and beauty to warrant our attention. The plants which we grow
for their attractive foliage often cannot produce flowers
indoors because of insufficient light or because of a pollination
failure. In nature, pollen is transferred either by insects
or wind, both of which are lacking in the home. Where indoor
pollinization is essential, it can be accomplished by transferring the pollen from one flower to another, using a soft
camel's hair brush. This process is described fully in ~~most~~
books devoted only to flowering house plants.

SOIL

Since the house plant you bring home from the shop
will already be rooted in soil (presumably the shop knows
its business), you might wonder why you have to consider
this need at all. The answer is that your house plant will,

assuming hoped-for longevity, someday need repotting, and you will want to provide it with a potting mixture that will serve its special needs. You might even wish to propagate some of your favorite house plants at some later time, to share with friends and to give as gifts. In any case, a basic knowledge of potting mixtures and soils is essential to a complete under-standing of all your plants.

Two simple definitions are in order here, to avoid any confusion later on. <u>Soil</u>, when mentioned here, refers to garden loam, that combination of mineral matter, organic matter, air, and water commonly found outside, in your garden or under your lawn. A <u>potting mixture</u> is soil with the addition of other materials, such as sand, compost, peat moss, limestone, and bone meal, that together form an ideal environment for the roots of your house plants.

The easiest way to assure your plants of a perfect loam is to buy prepackaged, sterile potting soil from your garden or flower shop. This soil will have not only the proper texture, but it will also be free of disease organisms, insects (some too small to be seen), and weed seeds. To this loam you will add the other ingredients which together will form an ideal potting mixture. You may also buy packaged potting mixture at the store, but if you do, read the package carefully to ascertain the ingredients, making sure that the mixture is right for your plants.

It is, of course, far less expensive to make your own potting mixture from your own garden loam (free), sand (free or next to free), and small amounts of purchased ingredients. If you choose this route, then it is important that you be able to make at least a cursory analysis of the garden loam that will form the basis of the potting mixture. Texture is important. A heavy clay soil will hold water for too long a time, encouraging disease and root rot, and it will bake cement-hard when dry. On the other hand, a coarse sand will not hold water well, nor will it hold nutrients long enough for the plant's roots to absorb them. Strive, then, for a happy medium—a good loam, containing both clay and sand, which will hold both water and nutrients, yet offer adequate drainage.

To this basic loam, we usually add one or more of other materials—peat moss, to increase water-holding capacity and to add organic matter; compost, for organic matter and nutrients; sand, to open up the soil to air; and some form of supplemental mineral fertilizer, usually bone meal and lime. Chemical fertilizer can be used, although it is not necessary to add it to the potting mixture, since the other ingredients will supply all the nutrients the plant can use for several months.

ACIDITY/ALKALINITY

A discussion of soils and potting mixtures would not be complete without some mention of acidity and alkalinity, and of the pH scale, which is the scientific measure of acidity and alkalinity. The midpoint on the pH scale is 7. A soil with a pH of 7 is neutral—neither acid nor alkaline. Numbers above 7 indicate an alkaline soil; those under 7, an acid soil. Most house plants, as most garden plants, will do best in a slightly acid soil (a pH of 6.0 to 7.0). Most garden soils are within this range, and so you should not worry unduly about the pH of the garden loam you dig for use in the potting mixture. In this book, all the house plants listed will do well in this normal range, unless special notations to the contrary are made.

If you have cause to worry about your soil's pH, or are simply curious, call your county agricultural agent and ask for directions on having a pH test made. The cost will be nominal. Any soil may be made more acid with the addition of peat moss, or less acid with the addition of ground limeste

POTTING MIXTURES

There are as many different basic potting mixtures as there are plant experts—probably more. Perhaps the most common one, however (and one which can be trusted), calls for two parts loam, one part finely screened compost (or a mixture of peat moss and compost) and one part builder's sand (not sea sand). To this is added a small amount of bone meal (about one teaspoon for a five-inch pot) and a pinch of ground limestone. Other recommendations call for more of one ingredient and less of another. Do a little experimenting of your own. After a while, you will doubtless come upon your own favorite mixture, which you can recommend to others.

And now that you have the basic mixture formula well in mind, we will consider the exceptions:

1. Acid-loving plants such as azaleas, camelias, gardenias, and heathers should have no lime, since they are acid-loving. They should, in fact, have some form of acid organic matter—acid peat moss or oak leafmold.

2. Foliage plants need somewhat more compost in the mixture, although half of this must be comprised of peat moss (which will not overstimulate the plant).

3. Fast-growing and hungry plants need more bone meal and lime, since they use them up so quickly.

4. Some plants, such as cacti, succulents, and orchids, have very special soil requirements; and these are described later in the discussions of individual plants.

NUTRIENT MAINTENANCE

The mineral nutrients contained in any fresh potting soil or mixture, whether it is home-made or a sterilized commercial brand, should be sufficient for your plant's needs for the first four to six months. After that, you should begin to replenish those nutrients on a regular and carefully-measured basis.

All plants need substantial amounts of three elements—nitrogen (N), phosphate (P_2O_5), and potash (K_2O)—and lesser amounts of a dozen or more others, called "trace minerals" or "trace elements." In grower's language, the three major elements are referred to as N, P, and K, and on the label of any commercial fertilizer, the percentages of each are given in N-P-K order. A 5-10-5 fertilizer, for instance, will contain 5 percent nitrogen, 10 percent phosphate, and 5 percent potash. A so-called "balanced" fertilizer contains a balance of all three in the amounts needed for the proper growth of most plants. The fertilizer may be either a chemical or an organic preparation, according to your preference. The chemical kind are quick-acting, easy to use, and tidy. Organic fertilizers, on the other hand, are slow to release their nutrients, providing a gentle and steady supply. Chemical mixtures come in liquid, tablet, and even spray form (the last applied directly on the foliage). Organic fertilizers may be purchased commercially in balanced formulas (fish emulsion, made from fish wastes, is a popular one for house plant use) or may be made at home from a combination of ingredients. Blood meal is a good choice for supplying substantial amounts of nitrogen (its NPK formula is 15.0∅-1.3∅-0.7∅), while bone meal (4.0∅-21.0∅-0.2∅) is good for phosphate and wood ashes (0.0∅-1.5∅-7.0∅) are high in potash content. A combination of one part blood meal, one partbone meal, and two parts wood ashes will make a 5-6-4 formula, which is a good one for house plants.

How often should plants be fertilized? There is wide disagreement on this point, some experts believing in weekly feedings of full strength (the dosage recommended on the label), others fertilizing no more than once a month, and even less often during the ~~plants dormant or rest period~~ winter. In the end, you will probably have to come to your own policy by way of experimentation. In the beginning, however, it is better to err on the conservative side, since far more plants have been injured from overfertilization than from nutrient starvation. If you use a commercial chemical or organic formula, I suggest that you feed your plants as often as recommended on the label, but only half the recommended dosage. (Manufacturers tend to overstate the need for their product.) If the plant shows a spurt of active growth in late winter or early spring, increase the dosage to the manufacturer's recommendation. During a dormant or rest period, withhold fertilizer entirely. If you are using a home-made organic fertilizer, such as the one suggested above, use it sparingly at first. A level teaspoon of the blood meal/bone meal/ wood ash formula, applied monthly, should be plenty for a plant in a five-inch pot. You may also put some of the mixture in a

bottle, fill the bottle with water, and use this "tea" to water your house plants. A mild tea solution, applied weekly, will give all your plants a continuing and gentle supply of the essential nutrients.

Last, remember never to apply a chemical fertilizer if the soil is dry. The quick action of the chemicals can easily injure the roots.

~~Balanced house plant fertilizer, which should be applied sparingly. Chemical preparations should be applied according to the manufacturer's directions.~~

CONTAINERS

Nearly any container that offers adequate drainage and (except from a drainage hole) doesn't leak is suitable for house plants. After checking a container ~~quickly~~ for leakage, consider drainage carefully. If ~~it~~ the container has a hole in its bottom, there is no problem. If not, then you should put coarse gravel or broken crockery in the bottom of the container to fill one-fourth to one-fifth its ~~height~~ depth. In this way, you will avoid the likelihood of waterlogging your plants and encouraging root rot.

The traditional terra cotta clay pot offers definite advantages. It is inexpensive, easily replaced, and—most important—allows air to be exchanged through its porous walls. This same porosity, however, allows water to evaporate ~~more~~ fairly quickly, necessitating ~~more~~ frequent watering. If ~~you have a plant in a spot which is awkward to water~~ a plant's location makes it (you as this) to put a plant where it will be difficult to water it, you will save yourself some effort by choosing a glazed or otherwise impervious container.

Some metal containers, notably copper, might really produce adverse chemical reactions with soil and fertilizer elements, injuring plants therein. Most Copper planters, however, are usually lacquered to ~~preventing~~ such reactions.

Wooden tubs and boxes are ideal for very large house plants. You can make any wooden container water-tight by lining it with

several sheets of heavy-~~gauge~~ plastic or, ~~if you are really serious about it,~~ for permanent results, sheet metal.

Last, if you want the best advantages of both a terra cotta pot and a decorative container, place the former inside the latter, leaving a ~~little room~~ quarter-inch or more of space for air circulation around the walls of the inner pot. Sometimes sphagnum moss is inserted here, to help preserve moisture A base of gravel in the decorative pot can provide good drainage while lifting the inner pot to the ~~proper height~~ level of the outer container.

WATERING

More house plants are killed by overwatering than by any other cause. This killing with kindness can be avoided, if you learn to understand just when your plants need water and when they ~~would prefer to~~ should be left alone.

The best rule of thumb is that a plant should be watered when the soil surface is dry to the touch. Then, water thoroughly, either by adding water to the soil surface, or by immersing the entire pot in a larger container of water.

Certain plants, such as the African violets and other woodsy varieties, need more water than most, while cacti and succulents need far less than the average. Aside from the specific preferences of individual varieties, there are many conditions which call for more or less water; these are ~~as~~ indicated in Table 1.

Immersion ~~is~~ provided the pot is porous, the best method of watering because it is the surest. The soil in any pot ~~might~~ may tend to form water channels which, upon receiving water from the surface, will rush it to

Table 1. WATERING NEEDS OF PLANTS UNDER VARIOUS CONDITIONS	
Plants will need more water when...	Plants will need less water when...
They are in a period of active growth	They are in a period of rest (usually during winter)
They are in bright light	They are in dim light or under artificial light
Room humidity is low	Room humidity is high
Room temperature is high	Room temperature is under 70°
They are contained in small pots	They are in large pots
They are in clay pots	They are in non-porous pots
They are fast-growing varieties	They are slow-growing varieties
They are planted in sandy soil	They are planted in heavy soil
They are in flower or about to go into flower	

the bottom of the pot and out the drainage hole, leaving large parts of the soil bone-dry. Then, some potting soil mixtures will shrink when drying, leaving many spaces along the wall of the pot where water can run past. Immersion is the one sure way to soak the soil thoroughly. You can do it in any large container, or even in a sink or bathtub. Set the pots in the water, but do not let the water flow over the lips of the pots. After the surface of the potting mixture has become moist—ten to thirty minutes—remove the potted plant, drain off any excess water, and put it back in its place. Never go out for the afternoon, leaving your plants standing in water.

If you water from the top, remember to remove any excess water from the saucer. Plants should never be allowed to stand in water for fear of root rot. In time, you should learn to give each plant just enough water to soak it thoroughly, with very little excess drainage.

Some other watering tips:

1. Do not let water into the crown of any plant; for this will encourage decay.

2. Never use very cold water, especially for tropical plants. Keep an open jar of water at room temperature for your house plants. Not only will the proper temperature be assured, but some of the chemicals in the water will have been dissipated by the time it is given to plants.

3. Water which is artificially softened may be detrimental to plant growth. If you can, use rainwater, or at

---

water that has not been softened. Fluorine and chlorine, on the other hand, are not thought to pose any problems.

4. If your water is especially hard, lime salts may cause trouble with such acid-loving plants as Orchids, Primulas, Rhododendrons, Azaleas, and other plants whose natural soil is woodsy (indicating a high organic content) and acid. Either choose plants which prefer a more neutral range in the pH scale, or plan to collect rainwater for your calcifuges (lime-haters).

HUMIDITY

Much of our trouble with house plants, especially in wintertime, can be traced to insufficient moisture in the air. Except for the cacti and succulents, nearly all house plants thrive best in a relative humidity of between 60 and 80 per cent, while that of most heated homes in winter is under 50 per cent—often, considerably under 50 per cent. House plants will virtually cry for moisture under these conditions, and it is incumbent upon you to answer that cry.

There are several ways to add moisture to the air in your home. The more expensive include the adding of a humidifying device to your furnace, if you live in a house, or installing an electric humidifier. This step will benefit not only the plants but everyone else living in the house, too. But there are less expensive ways of bringing moisture to the faces of your plants:

---

1. The pebble tray. Line the bottom of a waterproof tray with decorative pebbles and arrange your plants, in pots, on top of the pebbles. Keep the tray filled with water, being sure only that to avoid blocking the pots' drainage holes. Change the water weekly to keep it fresh.

2. Decorative containers. If you keep a clay pot inside a decorative container (double-potting), keep a pool of water in the bottom of the larger vessel. Again, provide some means of support for the clay pot so that it is not resting in water at any time.

3. Standing water devices. Water left standing in a room will gradually evaporate, meaning that the lost moisture is added to the room atmosphere. If your home is particularly dry during cold weather, take the trouble to place pans of water on tops of radiators; grow ivy, philodendron, or wandering Jew in containers of water; maintain an aquarium; rotate plants so that each can spend an afternoon in the bathroom each week, where the air is humid. Change standing water weekly.

4. Bathing and showering. Most house plants will respond favorably to a brief shower every day, or at least as often as you can manage to provide the treat. Little brass-plated atomizers are ubiquitous in mail order catalogs, but more dependable (albeit less decorative) are the plastic sprayers available in art supply stores. These hold perhaps a pint or quart of water, and they feature an adjustable shower head, affording an entire range of water action from a sharp jet capable of carrying twenty feet (the kids love this one) all the way to a fine mist. Your plants, of course, will like

the fine mist. Remember to fill the container after every use, so that the next day's spray will be at room temperature. Remember also to avoid spraying plants which have been standing in direct sunlight (the shock is great) and those which have been subjected to very cool temperatures (perhaps spending the autumn on a cold sunporch).

Rubber plants and others with large leaves should be cleaned thoroughly and gently with a damp cloth about once a week. The leaf polish sold commercially is permissible, if you want really stunning looking, large-leafed plants, but never use oil of any kind, *which can block the leaf's pores and impede respiration.* Ivies and other rugged small-leafed plants can be held under the gentle stream of a faucet for their weekly bath.

5. _Grouping._ Plants will maintain moist *surrounding air (leaves not touching)* with greater facility if they are grouped together rather than separated. During the coldest part of winter, you might want to group most plants on a pebble tray under a light window, to take advantage both of maximum light and greatest humidity.

Ⓐ
VENTILATION

Plants, like people, benefit from fresh air. Like people, also, they react badly to drastic changes in air movement and temperature. Provide adequate ventilation for your house plants, but do not subject them to sharp winds, winter drafts, or heat arising directly from a radiator. Think of your own comfort, in this respect, and you will

---

know what will *be best for* please your plants. If, in autumn, you bring your plants in from a summer outdoors, help them to adjust to indoor conditions gradually by placing them by an open window for the first several days. Gradually lower the window day by day, keeping *a* watchful eye on night temperatures.

Ⓐ
TEMPERATURE

The temperature requirements of house plants vary widely, according to the natural habitat of their forebears and also according to other conditions surrounding them. Many cool-weather plants prefer a range of 50°-60° F. and cannot tolerate temperatures above 70°, while tropicals may thrive in a moist 70°-75°. Know the temperature preferences of any house plant before you adopt it, and then place it in the best possible temperature location in your home. You might find, for instance, that a cool-loving aspidistra will do best in a back bedroom, while tropical plants thrive happily next to (but not above) a living room heat vent. The temperature needs of plants are included in their descriptions throughout this book. Heed them well, make liberal use of an indoor thermometer, and do not be afraid to experiment by placing different plants in different locations for a week at a time. You might notice in your plants distinct preferences for particular locations throughout the house, and their preferences will not always corroborate expert advice.

Ⓐ
LIGHT

Light and temperature needs are closely related. In their native surroundings, many tropical plants can thrive in higher temperatures because they receive long hours of sunlight. In the home, and especially during winter's short days, they *do* cannot receive enough light to enable them to stand high house temperatures.

Except for cacti and succulents, house plants should not be placed in windowsills where they will receive long periods of direct sunlight. Simply place a thermometer in this position and you will soon see that your plants can be literally cooked to death, even in the dead of a Minnesota winter. Strive, instead, for a bright spot with a few hours of filtered sunlight each day, at least for most plants.

Individual varieties vary, *differ* of course, in their light needs, and these needs are specified in the descriptions of individual plants in these *following* pages. Again, do not be afraid to experiment with different locations for different plants. I have a _Philodendron scandens_--*one of* the most popular and most common of all house plants--which has thrived for years in a *dim* dark corner, when actually it is supposed to require a bright spot out of direct sun. Plants, I am afraid, sometimes exhibit unmistakable individual characteristics which we have yet to understand.

Ⓐ
PRUNING AND TRAINING

Some plants should be pruned and pinched back occasion-

---

ally, in order to encourage bushy and stocky growth, while trailing plants such as philodendrons and ivies need gentle support to guide them into pleasing growth patterns.

Many people hesitate to prune at all, feeling somehow that they are hurting the plant or interfering with its natural development. Actually, plants will respond to judicious pruning with new and vigorous growth. Plants such as geraniums, coleus, and begonias should be pinched back routinely, in order to encourage lateral growth. The process is quite simple: With a sharp knife, cut back perhaps one-half inch of the central growing tip. The plant should respond by sending out side shoots below the central tip, and the main stem of the plant should then become thicker and sturdier. If this is done several times a year, the plant should eventually attain the vigorous and well-rounded form which you desire. Without this pruning, it might well grow "leggy" with a weak main stem requiring some kind of support. Many older plants, as well, will benefit from occasional pinching back or shearing of outside growth. Do not, however, prune or pinch back African violets, gloxinias, flowering bulbs, ferns, or cyclamen.

Vines and trailing plants often need some kind of support, unless you prefer to let them cascade from a hanging basket. The usual practice is to sink a slab of cork or tree bark into a pot, then to train the vines of the plant to grow around and up the support, eventually concealing it.

post? slab is a wide flat thing. Bad UC RIGHT- SLABS ARE COMMONLY USED.

Another effective device is the sphagnum moss cylinder. Pack the moss fairly tightly around a stake and secure it in a cylinder of the proper size for the pot. The cylinder can be made easily from either chicken wire or green plastic material made for this purpose. If you wish, sink a small clay pot into the top of the cylinder, so that you can add water regularly to keep the moss damp. (Otherwise, the moss will require regular spraying.) Tie the vines gently to the cylinder as they grow; eventually, philodendrons and similar plants will anchor themselves to the moss with their aerial rootlets, making other support unnecessary.

REPOTTING

The temptation to repot plants too readily and too often is a strong one, and should be resisted, with strong will. A plant needs repotting only when it has become potbound--when the roots have filled the entire container and are creeping out of the drainage hole. Only then is repotting indicated. Choose a new pot which is only one size larger than the old one, for a house plant will not do well in a pot which is too large. If the larger pot is a used one, scrub it thoroughly to remove any possibility of disease. If it is new, soak it for a few hours in water so that it is saturated. Then, with ample potting soil, gravel, and a tongue depresser or similar wood tool, set to work.

To remove the plant from its old pot, slide your hand over the top of the pot, index and second fingers cradling

the plant stem. Turn the pot upside down, thus supported, and tap the lip of the pot sharply on the edge of a bench or table. After a few taps the entire soil ball, ringed with plant roots, should come out easily, in one neat piece. Set it aside. Take the larger pot and line the bottom with a layer of coarse gravel or broken crockery, to provide good drainage. Then add potting soil on top of the gravel, placing the plant and soil ball on top of the new soil several times in order to see when it has reached the proper height. (The top of the soil should be about one-half inch below the lip of the new pot, in a four-inch pot, and one inch below the lip in an eight-inch pot, to leave room for watering.) When enough soil has been added to raise the plant to its proper height, center it well and begin to pack soil around the sides of the soil ball, using the tongue depresser. (A cork impaled with a stick handle is also effective.) Take your time in doing this, for it is the most crucial part of the entire operation. It is important to pack the soil firmly, so that no air spaces are left when the job is finished. Roots cannot draw nutrients in air spaces and many of them will thus be injured or die, affecting the health of the entire plant. When the new soil is finally brought up to a level even with the top of the soil ball, the job is finished. You might want to add just a little soil over the top of the root ball, especially if roots have been forced up to the soil surface, but don't add any more than you must, for you do not want to change the planting depth of the plant. Repotting is shock enough, for many plants, without altering the plant-

ing depth. Water it thoroughly and return the plant to its usual location.

How often should you repot? Obviously, only as each plant indicates a need. For slow-growers, this may be once every two or three years; a mature slow-grower may go for many years without repotting, if new growth is cut back. For fast-growing and very young plants, repotting may be needed once or twice a year for the first several years. Plants that do not need repotting after one year should have the top one-half to one inch of soil replaced annually, to keep the soil fresh.

PROPAGATION

There will come a time when you will want to start your own house plants--to increase your own plant population, to use as personal gifts for friends and family, or to replace a short-lived plant or one that has become ungainly with age. The propagation of most house plants is not difficult, and it is most rewarding.

There are two general methods of doing the job: by the collecting and planting of seeds, and by the cutting and rooting of plant parts--stems, leaves, or underground structures. The first way (sexual reproduction) is often difficult, always time-consuming, and likely to produce unsatisfactory results. Propagation from seed is ideal for garden annuals, but not for most house plants. Special equipment is required, and daily attention is essential, making the activity an unlikely one for

anyone who professes "no time for house plants." In addition, the seeds from hybrid plants are likely to produce plants vastly inferior to the parent plant. (A hybrid, incidentally, is any plant produced by cross-pollinating two plants of different species or genera.) Last, many house plants do not flower and produce seeds under home conditions, requiring the house plant gardener to purchase seeds from specialty houses. The one advantage of growing house plants from seed is that you can create new hybrids by the cross-pollination of plants. The excitement of this activity creates a fascinating hobby for some house plant enthusiasts, but is unlikely to appeal to those who cannot afford to devote a lot of it significant amounts of spare time to the activity.

Far more simple, and yielding far more reliable results, is the propagation of plants by the cutting and rooting of plant parts. Less care is required, and the offspring will look just like the parent, even when the parent is a hybrid.

Plants may be propagated at any time of year, although it is best to avoid tackling the job when the plant is going into a dormant period. In early spring, just before active

are most house plants hybrids? NO

growth begins, is perhaps the ideal time.

Cuttings. The most common method of propagating is by the taking of stem cuttings, which are then rooted in either water or some sterile rooting medium such as perlite, vermiculite, or sand. If you have never rooted a cutting before, then begin with African violets, coleus, Dracaena, Fuchsia, gardenias, geraniums, Impatiens, ivy, Philodendron, wandering Jew, or wax begonia. These are the easiest, because all can be rooted in water. Simply take a cutting from an actively growing tip of the plant, one containing four to six leaves, severing the stem cleanly just below a joint with a clean razor blade. Place the cutting (you may take several at a time, if you wish) so that the bottom portion is submerged in water-- a green wine bottle is fine--remembering only to keep the leaves above water. (Cut off the bottom leaf or two, if necessary, to get more of the stem into the water; about a third of the entire length should be in water.) Place the container in diffused light--not direct sun--and wait until vigorous roots appear. When they have, the little plants may then be removed from the water and potted in small pots, using the potting mixture recommended earlier in this chapter. Be sure to pack the potting mixture firmly around the roots of the plant, to avoid any air spaces, and water thoroughly afterwards.

Stem cuttings which cannot be rooted in water are rooted in perlite, vermiculite (both available wherever house plant

supplies are sold) or in builder's sand. The process is basically the same. The cuttings are inserted in the moist medium, which may be contained in a small clay pot or, for larger numbers of cuttings, a shallow plastic tray. The container is then placed in a plastic bag which is tied shut (the zip kind, used for food storage, is convenient, effective, and reusable) and placed in diffused light at a temperature of 65° to 70°. You can tell whether the cuttings have developed roots by testing them weekly. Open the bag and pull gently on a plant. If it moves easily, then the roots have not yet formed; if it resists your gentle tug fairly well, however, then the roots probably are mature enough to stand repotting. The process can take as little as two weeks, or as long as several months, depending upon the variety of the plant and the size of the cutting. When the roots are strong and vigorous, pot the plant in a small pot and treat it as you would any other plant.

Some plants which produce canes (including Chinese ever-

---

* You may by now be wondering why, throughout this book, builder's sand is recommended for potting purposes while sea sand is cautioned against. The answer is that builder's sand, which comes from inland locations, has irregular and sharp surfaces, allowing good soil drainage. Sea sand, having been washed smooth over the years, packs too snugly and leads to a compacted soil and resultant drainage problems.

green, Dracaena, and Dieffenbachia can be propagated by taking cuttings of the canes, which have discernible "eyes." Press each cane (containing one eye) into moist sphagnum moss, secure it with wooden clothes pins at each end so that it does not pop up, seal it in a plastic bag, and put it in a cool place out of direct sun. In six to eight weeks, move it into a warm place (70° to 90°), still out of direct sun. Soon, a shoot will grow from the eye. When the shoot has attained a respectable size, the cane may be cut close to the shoot on both sides, and the new plant may be lifted from the moss and potted.

Plants which have fleshy leaves are best propagated by taking leaf or leaf-petiole cuttings. (A petiole is a leafstalk, or stem.) Leaf cuttings work well when large and mature leaves are available. Cut the leaf close to the stem of the parent plant, using a razor blade for a clean cut without crushing the cells. The leaf may then be cut horizontally into smaller sections, so that the main vein runs from top to bottom along the center of the leaf section. Long-leaved plants such as Sansevieria and Streptocarpus may be cut into as many as ten sections, each of which will produce an individual plant. Each leaf section is then sunk halfway into the rooting medium, after which the process is the same as that described for stem cuttings.

Smaller leaves may be rooted by taking leaf-petiole cuttings. Cut one leaf stem close to the main stalk and sink the stem into the rooting medium, so that the leaf nearly, but

not actually touches the medium. African violets, begonias, piggy-back plants, and Peperomia respond well to leaf-petiole cuttings.

Underground division. Older plants which have thick main roots can be propagated by taking root cuttings. This is usually done when the plant is being repotted. Cut about one inch of the main root, making sure that it has at least one eye. Cover this with one-half of rooting medium and treat it as you would any other cutting.

Thick-rooted perennials may be propagated simply by the process of root division, in which the root mass is simply forced apart into two or more clumps, each of which is then repotted.

Plants which produce rhizomes (underground stems) may be propagated by dividing the rhizome, so that one leaf bud is contained on each piece, and planting the section under one-half inch of rooting medium. Plants which produce potato-like tubers can be propagated by cutting the tubers apart with a sharp knife, keeping one eye to each section, and planting the sections in the rooting medium, just as one would plant potatoes in the open field.

Some plants produce "suckers," small plants that grow up from an underground stem or root. These may be separated from the parent plant and potted in soil immediately.

Anyone who has seen strawberries grow outdoors knows what runners are--the baby plants that grow from a long stem coming

from the base of the parent plant. Among house plants, Boston
fern and spider plant both produce runners, which can be
severed from the parent and started in a rooting medium.

Other methods of underground division include the separation and replanting of baby bulbs and corms which are
produced by the mother bulb or corm.

Air layering. A fairly simple (and most impressive) way
of propagating larger or woody-stemmed plants is by air layering. Here, a sharp cut is made into the stem, perhaps a third
of the way in, into which a toothpick is placed horizontally
to keep the cut open. That stem section is then wrapped with
moist sphagnum moss and covered with clear plastic, tied top
and bottom so that moisture cannot escape. Roots will form
from the incision and will soon show through the plastic.
When a fair number of them have appeared, cut the stem below
the plastic wrap, remove both plastic and moss, and pot the
new plant immediately in potting soil.

As you might imagine, the propagation of plants can often
be integrated with the cutting back, pruning, and shaping of
older plants. It seems a shame to throw away plant parts
when they can be used to produce more plants, and it is precisely this attitude of thrift which, if not controlled, can
lead to a frightening multiplication of house plants. The
answer, of course, is to share plants with friends, thus encouraging still more enthusiasts and still more house plants.

How about moving IV-1-2-3-4 back
to the end of Chapter 2, and
inserting a new subhead--"Choosing
House Plants"--to begin this section? All this material applies
to Chapters 3, 4, & 5, and really
does fall under "understanding
house plants."   -jm

CHAPTER 4

FOLIAGE
INTRODUCING THE ~~HOUSE~~ PLANTS

CHOOSING HOUSE PLANTS

The number and variety of house plants available for
your consideration is staggering. For every combination of
conditions your home can offer--including heat, light, and
humidity--there are literally thousands of suitable house
plant varieties, offering almost limitless selection of
sizes, forms, colors, ~~patterns and~~ textures, growth patterns,
and flowering habits. You ~~have only to~~ survey the conditions
that your home can offer, and then make your plant selections,
within those limits, to suit your own tastes.

The house plants ~~which~~ I have selected for inclusion in
this chapter are only representative of their far greater
numbers. many available. I have included nearly all of the most common plants,
and I have tried to avoid those ~~that are very~~ difficult to
grow. ~~All~~ The old favorites are here, as well as some newer
varieties and unusual plants which can add zest to your
collection.

~~The plants listed~~ I have ~~been~~ divided into ~~four~~ three broad
groups: foliage plants, flowering plants, ~~fruiting plants,~~
and cacti and succulents. Within each group, individual
plants are listed alphabetically by their common names,
followed by (in parentheses) their ~~Latin or~~ scientific (or Latin)
designations. The ~~Latin~~ scientific name comprises both the genus and
species names. For example, the ~~Latin~~ scientific name for the common
boxwood is *Buxus* (the genus) *sempervirens* (the species).
After a genus name is introduced, it is thereafter abbreviated.
Thus *Buxus sempervirens*, if mentioned again, becomes *B. sempervirens*. Last, there may be a third part to the ~~Latin~~ scientific name
which designates a further subdivision of the species, usually
called a subspecies or a variety. The popular Japanese
boxwood, for example, is *B. microphylla japonica.*

Although I have attempted to maintain an informal tone in
these pages, by using common names whenever possible, the
scientific ~~Latin~~ nomenclature has obvious benefits. Many species are
known by different common names in different parts of the
country; different species of a genus are often called by a
single common name; and a single common name may be applied
even to varieties of completely different ~~genre~~ genera. The only
sure way to identify any plant, then, is by referring to its
scientific ~~Latin~~ name.

For each plant listed, you will find symbols ~~which~~ that
indicating its ~~individual~~ preferences for growing temperature,
light, soil moisture and air humidity, and window placement.

Please remember that these are rough guides and not inflexible
demands. Many plants have a wide range of tolerance, and ~~are tolerant of one or more of these
conditions, and~~ will thrive in a variety of ~~them.~~ Many plants
which are said to prefer an east window will do just as well
in a shaded south or a west location. Do not hesitate to try
a plant ~~of your liking~~ because you cannot provide its exact
needs--but neither should you attempt to grow a plant if you can provide none of them. Experimentation is both valuable and
enjoyable.

WHERE TO BUY HOUSE PLANTS

The best place to buy a house plant is from someone who
grows his own stock. He will know his plants and you will be able to rely on his advice. If there is no grower in your area,
the next best source is your local flower shop or nursery
center. Whichever place you choose, talk to the owner or his
representative about house plants. Ask for precise identification of a plant ~~which~~ that interests you. Ask for specifications
of the plant's needs for light, soil, temperature, and humidity.
Ask how large the plant is apt to become, and whether or not
it produces flowers, even if you know the answers to these
questions. If it becomes apparent that he doesn't know too
very much about the plant, or about house plants in general,
then ask to talk to someone who can answer your questions in
greater detail, or seek another source.

Plants found in supermarkets and discount houses are usually
not bad, although many ~~which are~~ you see flowering in the store may have
~~been~~ grown quickly and forced into bloom under ideal green-

house conditions that you cannot hope to match in your home. ←
~~However,~~ /Most plants offered by these sources *(however,)* are likely to
be common varieties that are quite tolerant of adverse conditions. It is hard to go wrong with grape ivy or a climbing
philodendron.

Plants stored outside at garden centers or in shopping
centers are *may* ~~more likely to~~ carry insects or disease, particularly if they are resting close to flats of outdoor
vegetable or flower seedlings. Examine them ~~very~~ closely
before purchasing, and isolate them for *one or* two weeks at home
before putting them with other house plants.

Wherever you buy your plants, look for young and sturdy
specimens with rich color and a generally healthy appearance.
Examine particularly carefully large and mature plants which
carry high price tags. These may have been growing for too
long a time in ideal conditions. Generally, you will have
better luck with a younger plant, and you will have the added
pleasure of bringing it along to maturity in your own home.

Larger plants offered at
bargain prices are often
severely under-rooted.

They need a chap title?- OK?
chap title 4
48 ★ (right)
folio IV [ ] 5
chapter ④
24 pt Headliner (light version)
If you move preceding section as suggested you do not need a heading here at all—

FOLIAGE PLANTS

check this with p.#2 - Combine to avoid repetition

←—In this chapter, we will survey many of the house plants
grown primarily for their foliage. Some of them, under favorable conditions, will flower from time to time, although few
should be selected for their flowering abilities. Nearly all
of these plants are fairly easy to grow and maintain, giving
even the beginner a wide variety of plants from which to choose.

The plants are listed in alphabetical order, according
to their common or popular names. If there is no popular name
for a plant, or if there ~~is~~ *are* more than one, *but no* ~~none~~ dominant, *name then*
the plant is listed by its scientific or Latin name. The
index, which includes both common and scientific names, provides
a convenient means of cross-checking names.

(?) The special symbols accompanying each plant name will
provide a quick and convenient guide to that plant's requirements. *(see key, pg 000)* Remember, however, that these are guides and not sharp
demands. Many of these plants are tolerant by nature, and
will take to an east window as well as a west window, and can
tolerate some direct sunlight even if none is recommended.
Most crucial, perhaps, are the guides to humidity and moisture,
since overwatering is one thing that ~~virtually~~ *almost* no plant will
tolerate.

11/13 Garamond w/ccx 21 pica ems —
flush L, ragged R
(aim for tight lines - ideally no more than 2 pica
em variation on R-hand edge)

---

bold, ital African Boxwood (Myrsine africana) ~~B-C-A-C~~
This slow-growing boxwood has red stems, but otherwise
is similar to regular Boxwood (q.v.). Many people think it
is even more graceful. African Boxwood is a good plant for
terrariums, if the atmosphere is not too hot.

bold, ital & throughout Aralia (Fatsia japonica) ~~C-B-D-C~~
Sometimes sold as Aralia sieboldii. Beautiful, bright
green, leathery, maple-like leaves highlight this cheerful
plant. In appearance, it is similar to the castor oil plant,
and in fact is sometimes called False Castor Oil Plant. It
thrives in a cool spot. Aralia can easily grow leggy, and so
it should be pruned annually in order to encourage it into
bushy growth. *It will attain a height of four feet at maturity.*

A striking hybrid, Fatshedera lizei, crosses F. japonica
and ivy (Hedera) forming a climbing plant with maple-shaped
leaves, which is tolerant of adverse conditions.

There is also a plant called False Aralia, which has
graceful and feathery foliage. It bears no resemblance to
the true Aralia and is difficult to grow.

Asparagus ~~A-B-B-B~~
There are two kinds of Asparagus suitable for growing
as house plants. Fern Asparagus (A. plumosus), with slender,
needle-like dark green leaves, forming a feathery appearance,
and A. sprengeri (Emerald Feather) which has thicker yellow-
green leaves and drooping stems. The latter makes a good

---

plant for hanging ~~plants~~ *baskets*, and produces red berries at Christmastime. Both like some sun in the summer and full sun in
the winter, *and both can grow to a height of about two feet.*

Australian Laurel (Pittosporum tobira) ~~C-B-A-B~~
A tolerant and slow-growing plant whose leaves, glossy
and leathery, resemble those of, *the* Rhododendron. Australian
Laurel will grow vigorously bushy and does not *require* ~~not~~ much
attention. Florists often use the leaves in floral arrangements.

An interesting variegated form is P. tobira variegata.

Australian Umbrella Tree (Schefflera actinophylla) ~~A-A-B-A~~
Here is a very attractive and vigorous-growing tree
with rich-looking and glossy leaves that radiate *like an* ~~umbrella like~~
from the ends of ~~several~~ *th* leaf stalks. It is a tough and
rewarding plant, ~~which~~ *Growing to six feet, and* can be propagated by air-layering.

Australian Umbrella Tree is also sold as Brassaia
actinophylla. A dwarf variety, B. actinophylla compacta, is
also available.

Baby's Tears (Helxine soleirolii) ~~B-B-A-B~~
This low creeper is also called Irish Moss. It likes
a constantly moist (but not soggy) soil, and higher than
average humidity. It makes a good ground cover for terrariums
but will also grow in a pot if adequate humidity is provided.
Baby's Tears may appear to die in the colder months, but after

an adequate rest period it will spring back to life.

#

Black Pepper (Piper nigrum) A-C-B-C

want to feeling plant? YES

    This is not a ~~terribly~~ *very* attractive plant, but it produces real peppercorns which you may use at the table, and is a good conversation piece for that reason. The plant's berries ~~begin as~~ green, later turn red, then dry up and turn black. Pick the dried-up black corns, dry them thoroughly for several weeks in an open spot, then use them in your pepper grinder. ~~The~~ Care for Black Pepper is the same as that required for Philodendron. It is not a demanding plant.

#

Boxwood (Buxus) C-A-B-B

    The same plant which grows the most prized hedges outdoors *with glossy, bright-green leaves* can make a very attractive house plant. Boxwood is slow-growing *the ancient Oriental art of growing dwarf trees and shrubs.* and dependable, a good subject for bonsai. *It has glossy,* ~~bright-green leaves.~~ B. sempervirens and B. microphylla japonica (Japanese Boxwood) are the two popular species.

2.
OK   *(Bromeliaceae)* #

Bromeliads A-B-B-C

    There are more than ~~1800~~ *eighteen hundred* varieties of this popular group, many of which are suitable for growing as house plants. Some of them produce attractive flowers, but most are grown for their striking and variegated leaf patterns. One distinctive feature of the Bromeliads is the rosette leaves ~~which~~ form a small water cup, which the plant uses to hold reserve

supplies of water in its natural habitat. ~~Since the plant lives in~~ the crotches of trees in Central and South America, ~~the water cup is an evolutionary survival characteristic.~~ In the home, keep the cup filled with water, changing it weekly to keep it fresh.

    A few of the more common Bromeliads are Aechmea, Ananas (Pineapple), Billbergia, Cryptanthus (Zebra Plant), Dyckia, Tillandsia (Spanish Moss), and Vriesia.

#

Caladium A-B-B-C

    Caladiums, with their spectacularly-colored and variegated leaves, are equally at home in the garden or on the window sill. They are ideal additions to plant groupings on porch or patio in the summer and early autumn. Give them bright light, but not long periods of direct sun, ~~especially~~ in summer, if you want the brightest leaf colors.

    Caladiums are grown from tubers, which can be divided easily to produce new plants. Start the tubers in regular potting soil at a very warm temperature--80° to 90°--and move the young plants to a cooler spot when they have appeared. *They will attain a height of about one foot.*

#

Cast Iron Plant (Aspidistra elatior) A-C-B-C

    This is perhaps the easiest plant in the world to grow, as its name suggests. It is virtually impossible to neglect it to death. It is also called Saloon Plant, since it was one of the few that could survive in Victorian taverns, and it was made immortal by George Orwell in his novel Keep the

Aspidistra Flying. If you cannot grow the Aspidistra, you may safely conclude that you have a purple thumb, hopelessly irredeemable *as a gardener*. *and all which grows about two feet tall,* The Cast Iron Plant seems to thrive even better when kept slightly pot-bound, and it will appreciate having its leaves washed occasionally. A white-striped species is called A. variegata.

Chamaeranthemum igneum A-B-A-C

    This low, spreading herb has attractive, dark green leaves with reddish-yellow veins. It is suitable for hanging baskets or as a low contrast in large plant groupings. It does like warm temperatures and high humidity, however, and might not be suitable for dry apartments.

Chinese Evergreen (Aglaonema) A-C-B-A

    Here is an attractive *and low-growing* plant that is very easy to grow. It will stand abuse almost as easily as its Cast Iron Plant.

    There are at least ten commonly-found species of the Aglaonema, the most popular of which, A. modestum, has interestingly mottled leaves. Perhaps the most attractive, however, is A. pseudobracteatum, which is sometimes difficult to find in stores and greenhouses.

#

Cissus A-B-B-C

    Cissus is a vine plant ~~which~~ *that* offers a number of interesting and attractive species. Most are vigorous climbers, suitable for training on a trellis or for adding to hanging baskets.

    Among the more popular species are C. rhombifolia (Grape Ivy), which is one of the most popular of all house plants; C. antartica (Kangaroo Vine), which prefers a small pot; C. antartica minima (Miniature Kangaroo Vine); C. rotundifolia; and C. discolor (Begonia Ivy), which is perhaps the most spectacular of the genus, although difficult to grow.

    Of all the Cissus, Grape Ivy is the easiest to grow, which doubtless accounts for a large share of its popularity.

#

Coleus A-A-A-B

    This old favorite has velvety leaves sporting bright splashes of reds, pinks, purples, and yellows. There is a seemingly endless number of varieties of Coleus, nearly all of them interesting, *most growing twelve to eighteen inches in height.*

    Coleus is equally happy outdoors, grown as an annual in the North, or in the window garden. It can be grown easily from seed, and stem tip cuttings can be taken from established indoor plants. If you grow Coleus outdoors in summer, take some cuttings before the first autumn freeze and root them for growing as house plants.

    The soil for Coleus should be kept damp, but not soggy. Pinch back plants often to encourage bushy growth.

#

Copper Leaf (<u>Acalypha wilkesiana</u>) ~~A-A-B~~ B

These ~~are~~ is members of the Spurge family, which feature copper-colored foliage. A close relative, <u>A. hispida</u>, is described ~~covered~~ in this book under flowering plants.

Copper Leaf may be propagated easily by taking cuttings late in the summer. The plant is susceptible to attack by spider mites, and proper precautions should be taken against this menace.

~~Croton (Codiaeum) A-A-B-B

Here is a genus that is not particularly easy to grow, but well worth the effort, since it is perhaps the most colorful of all the foliage plants. There are dozens of suitable varieties, nearly all of them sporting bright, variegated, and multi-colored leaves, in a variety of shapes.

Croton needs full sun, except in the heat of summer, and warm temperatures to keep it happy.~~

#

<u>Dichorisandra reginae</u>   ~~A-C-B-C~~

This is an attractive and slow-growing plant with interesting leaf markings. It resembles Wandering Jew, except that it grows upright. Give it warm temperatures and not too much direct light, but do watch room humidity.

#

Dieffenbachia   ~~A-C-B-C~~

There are many species of this popular plant, often called Dumbcane. It is prized for its large leaves with interesting markings, usually variations of cream and white on dark green. <u>Dieffenbachia</u> is a fairly tough plant, not too difficult to grow. Most varieties attain a height of eighteen to twenty-four inches, although growth is slow.

<u>D. arvida</u> 'Exotica' is very popular because it is even more durable than other members of the family. Other well-known species include <u>D. picta</u>, <u>D. amoena</u>, <u>D. sequina</u>, and <u>D. bowmannii</u>.

There are no special cultural requirements, although <u>Dieffenbachia</u> does like a warm spot and will appreciate having its foliage cleaned regularly. The plant may be propagated by taking stem cuttings and rooting them in moist and warm peat.

<u>Caution</u>: Eating or nibbling on the leaves of <u>Dieffenbachia</u> can cause severe swelling of the tongue and mouth tissues, hence its popular name, Dumbcane. It is not a plant to grow in a home with toddlers.

#

Dracaena   ~~A-B-B-C~~

There are many available species of <u>Dracaena</u>, which vary so greatly in appearance that some appear to be unrelated. Most grow tall--five feet or more--on sturdy stalks.

They are very tough plants, tolerant of a surprising amount of neglect, all in all one of our most dependable house plants.

Some varieties to investigate are <u>D. deremensis</u> 'Warnecki,' <u>D. fragrans</u> (which has corn-like leaves), <u>D. fragrans massangeana</u> (whose leaves feature yellow stripes), <u>D. marginata</u> (a truly exciting plant, with grass-like, cream-colored foliage, edged in red--sometimes sold as <u>D. marginata tricolor</u>), <u>D. sanderiana</u> (with white-banded leaves), <u>D. godseffiana</u>, <u>D. draco</u> (the Dragon Tree of the Canary Islands), and many others, some of which will doubtless be offered by any good supplier. Those mentioned, however, are some of the most attractive and also some of the easiest to grow.

Episcia   A-C-A-C

This genus, which offers many species and subspecies, is related to the African Violet and requires largely the same culture, although it does demand a little more light. <u>Episcia</u> is not really one of the easiest plants to grow successfully, and should be tried only after success ~~has been attained~~ with some of the others listed in these pages. The leaves are a rich green, most varieties tinged with copper, some ~~others~~ with variations of silver, blue, purple, and bronze. The veins often offer striking color contrasts. <u>Episcia</u> is a trailing plant, a natural selection for hanging baskets. It sends out runners that ~~which~~ may be used for propagation.

Most species of <u>Episcia</u> produce small and attractive flowers, in the color range of red-orange-yellow, but the plant is generally grown for its delightful foliage. If you do not wish to strive for blossoms, a north window will suit <u>Episcia</u> well enough.

The most popular species is <u>E. cupreata</u> (Flame Violet), which has soft and hairy copper-tinged leaves, and comes in several attractive varieties. Also investigate <u>E. dianthiflora</u>, which produces white flowers, and <u>E. lilacina</u> 'Cuprea,' with lavender-colored flowers. Many other species and subspecies are ~~easily~~ available, all of which have fascinating foliage variations and some of which will bloom quite profusely.

Fatshedra (<u>see</u> Aralia)

Fatsia japonica (<u>see</u> Aralia)

Ferns   A-C-A-C

The fern is the oldest plant, on the evolutionary scale, that you are likely to cultivate. Its family is predated only by the algae and the mosses. Everyone knows and admires ferns for their graceful and feathery fronds. They are one of the few house plants that reproduce themselves by spores rather than seeds. Some ferns grow regally upright, while others trail with modesty and grace. There are many sizes of ferns, from miniature plants suitable for the window sill, all the way to the seven-foot tub plants that can add a touch of class

Nephrolepis exaltata, which has long, sword-shaped fronds and is often called Sword Fern.

N. exaltata "Bostoniensis,' the ever-popular Boston Fern.

Platycerium bifurcatum (Staghorn Fern), whose fronds are usually attached to a piece of bark or other support, and which can become parched quite easily in a dry atmosphere.

The world of ferns is a large one, full of interest, and extremely rewarding. No house plant collection should be without at least one or two representatives of this proud family.

Ficus   B-C-C-C

This large group of indoor plants, whose best-known member is the Rubber Plant, offers species ranging from large, tree-like plants down to small-leafed trailers. Although they are not difficult plants to grow, the large species are especially sensitive to both overwatering and sudden temperature changes, and will react to either by dropping their leaves.

There has been much improvement in the Rubber Plant (F. elastica) since World War II. The best now is perhaps F. elastica 'Robusta,' which is remarkably trouble-free. There are many decorative varieties, as well, including F. elastica 'Doescheri,' which has light and dark green patched leaves and cream-colored leaf margins, and F. elastica

to entryways, patios, and conservatories.

The secret to the successful raising of ferns is in offering them an environment matching, as nearly as possible, that of their natural habitat. They need warmth, a decent degree of room humidity, and a moist and humusy soil (at least fifty per cent organic matter). They appreciate bright light, but will be affected adversely if allowed to stand for long periods of time in direct sun.

There are a great many ferns from which to choose. Among the smaller ones are:

Adiantum, the Maidenhair Fern, which is available in several varieties; it sends forth fragile-looking fronds in sprays; needs good light and high humidity.

Asparagus plumosus (Asparagus Fern), the most popular of the small "ferns," is really not a fern at all but a member of the lily family. It is treasured for its delicate, hair-like leaves.

Other smaller ferns of popularity include Asparagus medeoloides (Smilax), a trailer; A. sprengeri (Emerald Feather), a climber; Pteris multifida (Brake Fern); Woodwardia orientalis (Chain Fern), Polypodium aureum (Hare's Foot Fern); and many, many others.

Among the larger ferns are:

Cyrtomium falcatum (Holly Fern), which has holly-shaped fronds.

Asplenium nidus (Bird's Nest Fern), with broad lance-shaped fronds.

'Schryveriana,' another mottled-leafed variety. F. elastica 'Decora,' from which 'Robusta' was developed, is still a popular slow-growing variety. Rubber plants will grow as tall as any room, but may be cut back to encourage bushiness.
Chinese Banyan (F. retusa), another tree-like Ficus, showers forth with a profusion of small, leathery leaves. F. retusa nitida (Indian Laurel) resembles mountain laurel.

The Fiddle-Leaf Fig (F. lyrata) is a tough and attractive tree-like species, with large, dark green, fiddle-shaped leaves. It needs warmer conditions than other Ficus. Weeping Fig (F. benjamina) is another Ficus tree which has small, densely-growing foliage.

There are, as well, many small plants in the genus. Most popular, perhaps, is Creeping Fig (F. pumila), a small-leafed creeper that has been developed to include several variations--F. pumila minima (slower-growing and smaller), and F. pumila variegata, a variegated variety. All will adhere to rough surfaces, sending out aerial roots similar to those of ivy, and are thus easily trained.

The tree-type Ficus are propagated by air-layering, while the small-leafed climbers and trailers may be reproduced easily by simple division.

German Ivy (Senecio mikanioides)   C-B-B-C

Here is an easy-to-grow plant that is similar to the true ivies in both appearance and requirements. A handsome relative is S. macroglossus variegatus (Cape Ivy). Treat them in every way like Ivy (q.v.) for success.

Ginger (Zingiber officinale)   A-A-A-B

This is the same ginger that is used in cooking, which makes the plant even more interesting than its appearance would indicate. The untreated rhizomes which are sold in specialty food and gourmet shops can be planted directly in potting soil to produce plants--or, established plants may be divided easily. The plants have reed-like stems and interesting grassy foliage, truly exotic in appearance. Success as a house plant depends upon giving Ginger plenty of sunlight and warm temperatures. Keep the soil constantly damp but never soggy for long periods of time. As an added bonus, healthy plants will bear colorful clusters of flowers.

Golddust Plant (Aucuba japonica)   C-B-B-C

This modest plant features dark green leaves spotted with yellow-gold markings. Its main attribute is that it will withstand very cool temperatures, all the way down to freezing, and still come up smiling. It is good for unheated winter porches in all but the coldest parts of the country. Two popular varieties are A. japonica variegata and A. japonica goldeana.

Ivy (Hedra)   C-B-B-C

Here is surely one of the most popular of house plant species, both easy to grow and cheerful and attractive in appearance. There are a great number of varieties, with new improvements coming along all the time.

English Ivy (Hedra helix), is the most popular of the true ivies, and is available in more than fifty varieties to suit nearly any taste. There are varieties with large leaves and small, fast or slow growing habits, plain green or variegated. The best way to choose an English Ivy to your liking is to visit some flower shops and greenhouses, or to beg a few cuttings from a friend who has a plant that appeals to you.

Propagation of Ivy is easily, and in fact the plant does half of the job for you. Small rootlets will form on the stem of the plant, just below the leaves, which the Ivy uses to attach itself to rough surfaces, helping it to climb. Make cuttings just below the roots and plant these cuttings directly in potting soil or a sterile rooting medium.

It would be the sheerest folly to attempt to recommend all the good varieties of English Ivy. For a starter, however, you might investigate H. helix conglomerata (Japanese Ivy), an upright-growing plant with small and densely-growing leaves; "Curlilocks" and 'Ivalace' with curled leaf margins; 'Green Ripples,' 'Maple Queen,' 'Merion Beauty,' 'Needlepoint,' 'Pittsburgh,' 'Pixie,' 'Rochester,' H. helix cutifolia, and 'Shamrock,' the last of which likes more than average moisture and which is good for terrariums.

Among the variegated English Ivies, try 'Golddust,' 'Glacier,' and 'Goldheart,' the last of which has dark green leaves with sharply contrasting bright yellow centers.

Canary Islands Ivy (Hedera canariensis) is another easy-to-grow Ivy, which has larger leaves than English Ivy. It is often trained around a piece of bark, much like a Philodendron, to form a striking plant with a very bushy appearance. More popular than the basic green-leafed variety is the variant H. canariensis variegata, also known as 'Glorie de Marengo,' whose leaves are slate-green to cream in color.

Joseph's Coat (Alternanthera)   A-B-B-B
These are low-growing, dwarf plants that are good for terrariums. Their multicolored foliage adds interest to any plant grouping. Joseph's Coat needs warm temperatures and a moist soil to be happy.

(Note: Codiaeum is also called Joseph's Coat, because it, too, has colorful foliage. Codiaeum grows to a height of ten feet.)

Maranta   A-C-A-C
Here is a genus of plants that has striking foliage. It is easy to grow and impressive in appearance. Marantas will grow to about eight inches in height. M. leuconeura kerchoveana (Prayer Plant) is perhaps the most popular of the Marantas, and is so named because its leaves fold up at night, as if in prayer. The leaves are large and oval-shaped, and the plant requires a fairly humid atmosphere. In the autumn, the leaves may begin to die out.

If so, do not be alarmed. Cut off the affected leaves and reduce watering until late winter, when new growth begins; then water normally.

A red-veined variety, even more striking, is M. erythroneura. Another with red veins is M. leuconeura erythrophylla (Jungle Plant), which has olive-green leaves. Still another striking variation is offered by M. leuconeura massangeana.

Most house plant growers will want to include at least one Maranta among their collections. The key to success with this plant is in giving it lots of bright light, but no direct sun at all.

Miniature Holly (Malpighia coccigera)   C-B-B-B
This is not a true holly, but a bushy evergreen shrub with dense holly-like foliage. The leaves are shiny, dark green, and have spiny teeth. Miniature Holly does produce small flowers, but it is grown primarily as a foliage plant. It is propagated easily from cuttings.

Nephthytis (Arrowhead)   A-C-B-A
This is an attractive plant, but difficult to identify, since there is great confusion over what is and what is not a Nephthytis. Experts tell us that many Syngoniums are mistaken for Nephthytis. Other experts say that most plants sold as Nephthytis are really Syngoniums. Since the two plants are difficult to tell apart, however, no one cares very much except

or many varieties of Syngonium (no's) OK

the experts. Whatever they are, they are tough plants, able to withstand adverse conditions. Nephthytis have large, heart-shaped leaves, and are either trailers or climbers. Used as climbers, they will have to be offered some support, such as that used by Philodendron. Propagation may be achieved by taking stem cuttings.

Among several available species, the most popular is Syngonium podophyllum (Goosefoot Plant).

Norfolk Island Pine (Araucaria excelsa)   A-B-B-C
This popular evergreen, graceful and symmetrical, is seen with increasing frequency. It will hold up well under adverse conditions, although its branches will droop in dim light. Give it a damp, but not soggy, soil, for it is very susceptible to overwatering. It seems to do well when kept slightly potbound.

Norfolk Island Pine is a slow grower, and should never be pruned. It will grow gracefully to a height of about six feet, after which it tends to become ungainly.

Palms   B-C-B-B
Here is a plant family full of nostalgia for many of us. In Victorian times and right up through the 1930s and 1940s, the potted palm was a symbol of exotic elegance, bringing a bit of the tropics to shivering Northerners. No movie made before 1950 was complete without a detective peering out from behind a potted palm.

The elegant palms lost much of their allure after

World War II, but now they are making a modest comeback. You can achieve success with palms, by giving them bright light (even though they will endure shade), little water, and no plant food during the winter months. Palms/ actually/ seem to thrive on inattention, doing well when slightly potbound. They are slow-growing, in any case.

The palms are a plant family—Palmaceae is the scientific name—which comprises many genera and far more species. Few, however, are both attractive and manageable as house plants. Among the palms you might wish to investigate are:

Chamaerops (European Fan Palm) has fan-shaped leaves on long stalks, and will become quite large at maturity.

Cocos is an attractive dwarf coconut palm, the best species of which is C. wedelliana.

Howea is the Palm Court Palm, the most popular of all indoor large palms. H. belmoreana, the most attractive species, will eventually grow to ten feet or more in height.

Neanthe is an attractive and easy-to-grow dwarf which can tolerate a dry room.

Phoenix, the Date Palm, can be grown easily from the stone of a fresh date. Plant the stone in potting soil, keep it warm (70° to 80°) and it should germinate in about a month. It is slow-growing during the first year or so, but within ten or fifteen years it will reach the ceiling.

Pellonia   A-B-A-B

This is a colorful, slow-growing, creeping plant, fine for hanging baskets and a good filler plant for groupings. It features small, oval-shaped leaves with interesting variegated patterns. There are two popular varieties—P. daveauana and the more compact P. pulchra.

Pellonia is not difficult to propagate. As it creeps along the soil it sends down roots from the stems. Just cut the stems into sections and root them in potting soil.

Peperomia   A-C-B-C

There are many varieties of this popular and cheerful little plant (eight inches or less in height), most of which are low and upward-growing, with deeply ridged leaves. It is the ridging that gives Peperomia its distinction in a world of larger and more spectacular house plants. They are tough plants, tolerant of most conditions, although they will rot at the groundline if the top of the soil is not allowed to dry out between waterings. Peperomia like bright light, but not direct sun in the summer.

Among the more popular varieties are:

P. caperata (Emerald Ripple Peperomia) has deeply ridged heart-shaped leaves; the tops of the ridges are green and the valleys are brown, giving an interesting effect.

P. rotundifolia is a low grower with light green and thick leaves.

P. obtusifolia (Ovalleaf Peperomia) has solid green

leaves, while P. obtusifolia variegata is the variegated form of the same species.

P. sandersii (Watermelon Peperomia) is identified by its red petioles and silver-striped leaves.

P. griseo argentea hederaefolia has ridged, glossy leaves, silver-hued, and purple-olive veins.

There are many other varieties of the Peperomia, many of which may be found at your local flower shop or greenhouse.

Philodendron

These plants constitute what is probably the most popular group of house plants in America today. There are many, many species and varieties, with leaves ranging from small to very large, in an interesting variety of shapes offered by no other house plants. Most are climbers, and will appreciate a support that can be kept moist, such as that described on page 00.

The Philodendron are not difficult plants to grow, unless you disregard the rules. Growth will be stunted by poor light, and the leaves can turn yellow and drop from lack of water, or too much water, too small a pot, low temperatures, or poor drainage. They will appreciate a monthly washing with a mild soap (not detergent) solution. Cut back the growing tips if you wish to encourage bushy growth, and use the tip cuttings to form new plants.

Some of the more popular varieties include:

P. scandens (Sweetheart Vine), a very popular climber which can withstand the dry air of a typical apartment.

P. oxycardum, the most commonly grown form, which has heart-shaped leaves very similar to P. scandens. It is often grown in water or wet moss.

P. dubium (Cut-Leaf Philodendron) is a slow grower with star-shaped leaves.

P. panduraeforme (Fiddleleaf Philodendron) has irregularly shaped, olive-green leaves.

P. pertusum has perforated leaves, irregularly shaped. The adult form, known as Monstera deliciosa, has broad and thick leaves with many perforations.

P. squamiferum (Anchorleaf Philodendron) has leaves and petioles that are covered by red hairs. The leaves are shaped like daggers.

P. bipinnatifidum (Twice-Cut Philodendron) is a large-leafed variety; the leaves resemble the smaller P. dubium in shape, but are more deeply notched.

P. selloum is another cut-leaf variety, the cuts becoming more pronounced as the plant reaches maturity. This species will tolerate temperatures down to freezing with no apparent harm.

P. wendlandi is another large-leafed species, very tolerant of a wide range of temperature and humidity. Its leaves are long and narrow.

Piggy-Back Plant (<u>Tolmiea menziesi</u>)   B-B-A-A

    Here is a native to the West Coast of the United States, a modest sized plant that can be grown/in the warmer regions [*outdoors*] of the country. Its name is derived from its unusual habit of bearing young plantlets from the junction of the leaf and the petiole. These can be rooted easily to grow new plants. The leaves are toothed and lobed, covered in down. It is an easy plant to grow, although not considered especially attractive by some.

[*margin note: tsk! you should see mine! SORRY.*]

Pilea   A-B-B-B

    There are at least four cultivated house plants in this interesting group, none of which grows more than a foot in height. They are rather unusual looking plants, not liked by everyone. All like moist soil, warm temperatures, and full sun in the winter. The plants become less attractive as they grow older, but cuttings are easily made, so that older plants may be discarded when desired. Fertilize <u>Pilea</u> liberally when growth is active.

    P. cadierei (Aluminum Plant) has dark green leaves with striking aluminum-colored markings. A dwarf variety, <u>P. cadierei minima</u>, is preferred by many, as is <u>P. cadierei nana</u>, a compact variety.

    P. microphylla (Artillery Plant) is fine in texture with bright green, fern-like leaves. When its flowers are dry, pollen literally explodes from the blossoms, hence its common name.

    P. involucrata (South American Friendship Plant) is bushy in growth and has coppery leaves. It can be made to [*look even*] be more bushy, if several cuttings are taken, then rooted in the same pot, to [*at*] the sides of the parent plant.

    P. 'Silver Tree' has bronze-hued leaves with silver markings.

Plectranthus   A-C-A-B

    Various species of this genus are often called trailing Coleus or Swedish Ivy. Some are upright in growth, [*while*] others are trailers, making good subjects for hanging baskets.

    P. australis, a trailer, has waxy-green leaves, [*(Swedish ivy) round in shape with sawtooth edge*]

    P. australis variegatus, similar in [*leaf*] shape, has [*with*] added white leaf markings.

    P. purpuratus is an upright growing plant with purple coloring on the undersides of its leaves.

    There are other interesting varieties, including <u>P. oertendahlii</u>, a flowering trailer with bronze-hued leaves and silvery veins.

Pleomele   A-C-B-A

    This is an interesting group of plants with cultural requirements similar to those of <u>Philodendron</u>.

    P. reflexa variegata (Song of India) is now included in the genus <u>Dracaena</u>. Its attractive, spear-shaped leaves are gold and green striped, borne in clusters on branching stems. *It will grow to tree size in ten or fifteen years.*

    <u>P. reflexa gracilis</u> has dense foliage; its recurved leaves have translucent edges.

    <u>P. thalioides</u> has waxy green leaves, ribbed lengthwise.

Pothos (<u>Scindapsus</u>)   A-C-B-C

    Pothos is very similar in appearance and growth habits to the heart-leaf Philodendron, <u>P. scandens</u>, except that it needs less water and warmer temperatures--not below 65°. It likes bright light, but cannot stand direct sun. Pothos is a natural trailer, although it can be trained upward along a support, again like Philodendron. The leaves are heart-shaped, green, with pale yellow markings. *It is not as easy to grow as most plants listed in this book.* The most popular species is <u>S. aureus</u>, which offers several variegated varieties, some of which require even warmer temperatures.

Ruellia makoyana   A-C-A-C

    This is an old favorite, not seen as often today as in the 1930s. It is a free-spreading plant, with glossy and pale green leaves with silvery veins. It likes a warm and moist environment, shaded from the sun.

Sanchezia nobilis glaucophylla   A-C-A-B

    This is a member of the [*Acanthaceae*] Aphelandra family. It grows to a heighth of four feet and has large, glossy, sword-shaped leaves with yellow veins.

Screw Pine (<u>Pandanus</u>)   A-C-B-B

    This old favorite will withstand most adverse conditions. It is recognized by its long, arching, sword-like leaves, which have saw-toothed edges.

[*margin note: check-sp. BOTH ARE USED.*]

    P. veitchii has green and white striped leaves. Often preferred, however, is <u>P. veitchii compactus</u>, a dwarf variety with clearly variegated leaves. <u>P. baptistii</u> has no marginal spines, as do the other species. All Screw Pines like moist soil, but never soggy soil. They can take some direct sun, except in the heat of summer, although they do best in a bright location out of direct sun, altogether.

Selaginella   A-D-A-A

    Among these fern-like plants are some small creepers, some erect-growing species, and some trailers. All offer bright green, feathery foliage. The conditions they require are the same as those for ferns.

[*margin note: you use upright elsewhere mostly, I think. OK*]

    S. kraussiana is a low creeper, perfect for terrariums.
    S. emmeliana is an erect-growing plant.
    S. willdenovii is a vigorous climber with unusual blue leaves, while <u>S. apus</u> is a trailer, good for hanging baskets.

Sensitive Plant (<u>Mimosa pudica</u>)   B-C-*-B

    This is a fascinating plant for both adults and children

---

* Prefers dry soil but high room humidity.

because its delicate and feathery leaves and petioles droop and fold up instantly (and temporarily) whenever it is touched, or even if a *lighted* match is held close to it. Seeds are often available in stores, from which plants will grow easily. It becomes leggy and out of hand after about a year, but it is not difficult to grow more *plants* at any time.

Silk Oak (<u>Grevillea robusta</u>)   C-B-B-C

This is a pleasant plant with graceful and feathery foliage similar to that of the False Aralia. *It will grow to three feet in height. The* Silk Oak likes cool and moist conditions, and can spend the summer outdoors with benefit. It does tend to get leggy if unchecked, ~~and~~ so it should be cut back at the growing tip fairly regularly. *The* Silk Oak will react badly if its soil becomes very dry.

Snake Plant (<u>Sansevieria</u>)   A-C-B-A

The Snake Plant is actually a succulent, but *few of us* think of it as such, and so we include it among the foliage plants. It has long been very popular, probably because of its great tolerance to adverse conditions. It is also called Mother-in-Law Tongue and Bowstring. Like the Cast Iron Plant, it can grow perfectly well in hot, dry, and dim locations (including, it seems, most old hotel lobbies in the country). The leaves are thick and sword-shaped, usually upright, *growing to eighteen inches or more in height,* but in some varieties ground-hugging. It is propagated easily by

division of the rootstock or by taking leaf cuttings. (Be careful not to turn the leaf cutting upside down when setting it in the rooting medium, for roots grow only from the downward portion of the cutting.)

There are many varieties available, including:

<u>S. trifasciata laurenti</u> (Variegated Snake Plant) has handsome yellow bands along its leaf margins.

<u>S. trifasciata</u> is similar in form, but without the yellow bands.

<u>S. trifasciata laurenti</u> 'compacta' (Dwarf Congo Snake Plant) has shorter leaves and yellow margins.

<u>S. trifasciata</u> 'hahni' (Hahn's Dwarf Snake Plant) has light and dark green bands along the leaves.

There are many other interesting variegated varieties of this old standby.

Spathe Flower (<u>Spathiphyllum</u>)   B-D-A-A

Here is an easy-to-grow, tough plant, suitable for the homes of most novice green thumbs. It has sword-shaped and glossy green leaves. White blossoms will sometimes surprise you in the winter, but do not depend on ~~them~~ *their appearance.*

There are two popular species—<u>S. clevelandii</u> and <u>S. floribundum.</u>

Spider Plant (<u>Chlorophytum comosum</u>)   B-B-B-C

The Spider Plant is one of the most popular of house plants.

It has grassy leaves, variegated cream and green in color, which arch gracefully from either pot or hanging basket. Mature plants produce perfectly formed baby plants on the end of long runners, which resemble spiders hanging from a thread. Propagation is simply a matter of rooting one of the "baby spiders" in a rooting medium. The Spider Plant can store water in its tubers, and can take dry soil for a fairly long time because of this *characteristic* ~~foresight~~.

Strawberry Geranium (<u>Saxifraga sarmentosa</u>)   C-B-B-B

This trailing plant, also called Strawberry Begonia and Mother of Thousands, is good for both hanging baskets and terrariums. All its really asks is a woodsy soil, *containing plenty of organic matter,* and a cool location. Leaves of the Strawberry Geranium *resemble* ~~are very similar to~~ those of the true geranium, and it sends out runners just as strawberry plants do. The leaves of the standard variety are deep olive in color, with silver-gray markings. An interesting variant, <u>S. sarmentosa</u> 'tricolor,' has dark green leaves marked with white and pink, and is considerably more difficult to grow.

Sweet Flag (<u>Acorus gramineus</u>)   A-C-A-C

Here is a moisture-loving plant that grows only two inches tall. It is a pleasant little fellow, and will be most happy in a terrarium.

<u>Syngonium</u> (see <u>Nephthytis</u>)

Ti Plant (<u>Cordyline terminalis</u>)   A-B-A-B

<u>C. terminalis</u> is only one of many species of <u>Cordyline</u>, but is certainly the most popular. Also called Firebrand, it will last for only one to three years *and grow to two feet in height* before dying out, but its spectacular *short* ~~young~~ life is certainly worth your placing this plant on your list of house plant candidates. It has long, upward-reaching leaves, cerise, purple, and green, which grow from a cane trunk. Another popular species is <u>C. australis</u>, which features long and slender leaves. The Ti Plant is very popular in Hawaii, where its colorful grassy leaves are used in making grass skirts. It is sold there in tourist shops as a "Ti Log." In recent years, breeders have developed several variations of the original plant, including a dwarf and a variegated variety, which go under various names.

Umbrella Sedge (<u>Cyperus alternifolius</u>)   A-C-A-C

Here is a popular exotic plant with narrow, pointed, grasslike leaves *that* ~~which~~ grow in clusters. It will grow up to two feet tall in a pot. Constant moisture is essential, and propagation is a simple matter of root division.

Related species include <u>C. papyrus</u>, similar in appearance and requirements but which grows to seven feet in height, and a dwarf variety, <u>C. alternifolius gracilis.</u>

Velvet Plant (Gynura)   A-B-B-B

     This is a vigorous-growing plant with dark red, velvety
leaves. It will offer a fine contrast to your green plants.
It is best to train the Velvet Plant to some support, to keep
it in bounds, or to pinch it back often to encourage bushy
growth.

     There are two common varieties—G. aurantiaca, which is
upright in growth habit, and G. sarmentosa, a smaller and
loosely-twining plant. The flowers of both have a bad are horrible in
scent and should be removed immediately upon their appearance.

Yew (Podocarpus)   C-B-B-B

     Yews are prized outdoor plants in many parts of the
country, but can be made into attractive house plants anywhere.
These hardy evergreens can provide welcomed contrast to your
tropicals. They are slow-growing and very tolerant of adverse
conditions. They will take low temperatures without a whimper,
and may require frequent repotting because of vigorous growth.
They can become quite large and bushy.
     P. macrophylla angustifolia (Southern Yew) can be
pruned to a pleasing shape and will respond with even more
vigorous growth. Other similar species include P. macrophylla
'Nagai' and P. macrophylla 'Maki.'

Wandering Jew (Tradescantia)   C-C-B-C

     Tradescantia and Zebrina both claim the common name of
Wandering Jew, and the two genera are so similar that they are

commonly interchanged. All are easy-to-grow, tolerant, and
vigorous trailers of many varieties, perfect for hanging
baskets. Feed them regularly for good growth. Propagation
is simplicity itself. Simply take cuttings of growing tips
and root them in water.
     Among very many interesting species are:
     T. fluminensis, the original Wandering Jew, has silver
markings, but there are many variants of different markings
and colors available today.
     T. albiflora has bluish-green leaves with white stripes.
     Z. pendula is an excellent house plant whose leaves have
purple undersides. Again, there are several interesting
variegated varieties.

BIBLIOGRAPHY   24 pt headliner 11/11

ARTIFICIAL LIGHT GARDENING
6 M #
Bickford, Elwood D., and Stuart Dunn. Lighting for Plant
     Growth. Kent, Ohio: Kent State University Press, 1972.
     One of the best books on the subject; especially valu-
     able to those who have had some experience in the area.
6 M # between entries
Cherry, Elaine C. Fluorescent Light Gardening. New York:
     Van Nostrand Reinhold Co., 1965.

Elbert, George A. The Indoor Light Gardening Book. New York:
     Crown Publishers, Inc., 1975.

Fitch, Charles Marden. The Complete Book of Houseplants under
     Lights. New York: Hawthorn Books, 1975.

Kranz, Frederick H. and Jacqueline. Gardening Indoors under
     Lights. New York: Viking Press, rev. 1971.
13 M #
BEGONIAS
6 M #
Brilmayer, Bernice. All about Begonias. New York: Doubleday
     Publishing Co., 1960.

bibliography, add 1

Kramer, Jack. Begonias, Indoors and Out. New York: E. P.
     Dutton & Co., 1967.
13 M #
BONSAI
6 M #
Brooklyn Botanic Garden. Bonsai: Special Techniques. New
     York: Brooklyn Botanic Garden.

Chidamian, Claude. Bonsai: Miniature Trees. New York: Van
     Nostrand Reinhold Co., 1955.

BROMELIADS

Kramer, Jack. Bromeliads: The Colorful House Plants. New
     York: Van Nostrand Reinhold Co., 1965.

BULBS

Field, Xenia. Growing Bulbs in the House. New York: St.
     Martin's Press, Inc., 1966.

Peters, Ruth Marie. Bulb Magic in Your Window. New York:
     M. H. Barrows & Co., 1954.

Walker, Marion C. Flowering Bulbs for Winter Windows. New
     York: Van Nostrand Reinhold Co., 1965.

Key to Symbols   *Rough plate*
                                                  symbols will not be used in text

Explanation: Instead of saying, under each of 140 plants,
"This plant requires a moderate temperature of 50° to 70°,
will appreciate a bright spot out of direct sunlight, likes
a high degree of humidity and constantly moist soil, and
will do best in a west window," I suggest that we develop
a series of symbols indicating these preferences.

I have seen letters used in other books, something like
"A-B-A-C," and although this does save space, it is very
inconvenient for the reader, since he can never memorize the
symbols and must continually turn back to the explanation
of the letters (if he can remember what page it's on). I will
indicate the symbols in this way, in my ms copy, but better
symbols should be used in the book. Other books use a one-
or two-page chart, listing all the plants and then symbols
for their environmental preferences. This accomplishes the
same thing, but again the reader must flip back and forth to
get full information. Indeed, unless he is familiar with the
book, he might not even be aware that the chart is stuck in
the back pages.

The answer, I think, is to adopt some easily-memorized symbols
for use with each individual plant listing. I suggest:

TEMPERATURE PREFERENCE   BEST WINDOW

A. warm, 60° - 80°   A. north
B. moderate, 50° - 70°   B. south or east window
C. cool, 45° - 60°   C. west window

LIGHT NEEDS

A. full sun
B. tolerates some direct sun
C. bright spot with no direct sun
D. tolerates continuous shade

SOIL MOISTURE & HUMIDITY NEEDS

A. higher than room humidity,
    constantly moist soil
B. moderate humidity & soil moisture
C. tolerates dry conditions
D. low humidity & soil moisture
    required

In my copy, I will use the A-B-C indications, since I don't
want to spend hours drawing symbols, but the actual symbols
should be the job of the artist. Just for starters, I might
suggest the ones on the following page. The object, of
course, is that they should be immediately recognizable to
the reader--a visual touchstone. OK, then...

---

                                15 November 1976

Dear

Enclosed are chapters 2 and 4, copy-edited, of your
manuscript NO TIME FOR HOUSE PLANTS. I have made a
few changes to avoid word repetition or to attempt
further clarification for the layman, but no such change
is sacred, of course. Following current practice in
these matters, I have kept your italics and initial
capitals for scientific Latin names but have lowercased
common names and Latin names used as common names.

In chapter 2 I have suggested that the three subheadings
following "Soil" should be sub-subheadings because they
all relate to soil. Perhaps you would like to omit them
instead, or set them as run-in sideheads at the beginning
of a paragraph as you do similar headings under "Humidity."

In chapter 4 I suggest changing the title further by
eliminating "Introducing the"--leaving "Foliage Plants"
as the title, thus making it parallel with chapters 5
and 6. Also I have suggested moving the section "Where
to Buy House Plants" back to chapter 1, since it does not
seem to belong in this chapter devoted to foliage plants
alone. You will note in this chapter that what you say
on pages 2 and 5 is so similar that you will want to combine the material to avoid repetition.

Please check spelling of all scientific names carefully.
By comparing with other books in the field, I found a
number of errors, I think, in your typescript. I have not
checked every one of them.

Finally, now is the time for you to make any changes you
have in mind. Do not wait until you see proofs! We will
go straight to pages--omitting--galleys--and any alteration
other than correcting typographical errors will be enor-
mously expensive.

                - 2

Please return the manuscript to me by 1 December 1976,
with all questions answered and all your final changes
made. If this proves impossible for you, please let me
know when you plan to return it so that I can revise the
schedule for your book. My number is: 312 753 3326.

The designer is working on the problem of the symbols and
the boxes. We'll let you know what the decision is.

Since I am something of an indoor gardener myself, I
enjoyed reading your manuscript. And I learned something
from it.

Very sincerely yours,

Catharine Seybold
Senior Manuscript Editor

THE UNIVERSITY OF CHICAGO

Date 16 November 1976

To   BY   Department

From   KW   Department

In re   NO TIME FOR HOUSE PLANTS: A Busy Person's Guide to Indoor Gardening

I have just heard from   about the title change we proposed
for his book. He is quite emphatic in arguing for the above title and
subtitle. Any other suggestions from anyone? If not, we might as well
consider the above final.

    KW:rhm

The Association of American University Presses, Inc.
One Park Avenue, New York, N.Y. 10016 · 212 889–6040

November 23, 1976

Ms. Catharine Seybold
Senior Manuscript Editor
THE UNIVERSITY OF CHICAGO PRESS
5801 Ellis Avenue
Chicago, Illinois 60637

Dear Ms. Seybold:

Thank you for your letter of the 15th and for the copyedited manuscript. I have responded to the queries.
Any changes that I have not commented on are fine with
me.

I have suggested that the first four pages of chapter 4
be placed at the end of chapter 2. In this way, the
general information contained in those pages will not
be confined to the chapter on foliage plants but applied
to the section that deals with all house plants. I hope
that you agree with this suggestion.

I agree that, in chapter 2, the three subheadings following "Soil" should be run-in sideheads, since they all
deal with soil and potting mixtures. I would suggest
further that the subhead "Soil" be changed to "Potting
Media," which would then properly include all three
following sideheads.

I have checked scientific spellings as carefully as I
can. There are some instances in which even scientists
differ in their usage, and I don't suppose there is an
omnipotent authority for this nomenclature. In any case,
I do not think that any variances will interfere with
communication, and this, after all, is paramount.

There are no more changes I will want to make, and I do
thank you for an excellent job in copyediting. You have
made many passages clearer for the reader, without interfering with my basic style or message. I appreciate this.

Last, I apologize for slandering your piggy-back plant.
Please convey my sincere regret.

                    Sincerely.

UNIVERSITY OF CHICAGO PRESS
5801 S. Ellis Ave. / Chicago, Illinois 60637

AUTHOR:	Purvis Mulch	Date: 5 January 1977
TITLE:	NO TIME FOR HOUSE PLANTS	Manuscript Editor: CS
		House Editor: KW

GENERAL INFORMATION

Number of chapters	7
Total number of MS pages	
Front matter	
Text	
End matter	
Notes print at:	
Foot of page	
End of book	
Subheads (how many levels?)	2
Reduced material	
Halftones	
Print as figures on text paper	
Print as plates in special section(s)	
Text figures	x

HANDLING OF PROOF

Editor's Proofs

Galleys		sets
Pages	1	sets

Author's Proofs

Galleys		sets
Pages	2	sets
Allow ___ wks for galleys out & back		
Allow 3 wks for pages out & back		
Allow 2 wks for index after last pages out		

SPECIAL INSTRUCTIONS

EDITOR'S CHECK LIST / TRANSMITTAL INFORMATION

Items to be transmitted for this publication (√)	Here-with	To come (date)	For printer's use
GENERAL			
Spine & cover layout			
Prelim layouts			
Text layouts			
Spine copy (2 copies)	x		
Running head copy	x		
List spec. characters			
PRELIMS			
Half title			
Series title			
Frontispiece			
Title	x		
Copyright	x		
Dedication			
Epigraph			
Contents	x		
List of illustrations			
List of tables			
List of abbreviations			
Foreword			
Preface	x		
Acknowledgments			
Introduction			
BODY OF BOOK			
Second half title			
Part half titles			
Text (all or part?)	x		
Tables (how many?)			
Plates (how many?)			
Figures (how many?)	50		
Legend copy			
Footnotes			
END MATTER			
Appendix(es)			
Notes			
List of Abbreviations			
Glossary			
Bibliography	x		
Index		x	
Chart	x		

Preliminary specification from The University of Chicago Press

AUTHOR *MULCH, PURVIS*   Date: *25.*
TITLE *NO TIME FOR HOUSE PLANTS*   Printer:
Series: First Printing No.

FORMAT   **MARGINS**
Trimmed size: *6 X 8"*   Head (trimmed): *3½* pica ems
Size of paper: Back: *4* pica ems

PRELIMS   **OTHER MATTER**
Allowance for prelims and other material not yet supplied
* = copy supplied. Please cast off and add to total below

Half title and Title:	pp.	List of illustrations:	pp.	Tables:	
Dedication:	pp.	Introduction:	pp.	Appendixes:	
Epigraph:	pp.	Author's note:	pp.	Notes:	
Foreword:	pp.	Acknowledgments:	pp.	Bibliography:	
Preface:	pp.	Abbreviations:	pp.	Glossary:	
Contents:	pp.			Indexes:	

Total to come = pp.
Any text figures or plates will be allowed for separately by The University of Chicago Press

COMPOSITION: MONO/LINO/PHOTO *COMPUGRAPHIC*
Text typeface: *GARAMOND*   Display typeface: *GARAMOND*

Measure: *20* pica ems.   page depth: *36* lines text, excluding running heads and folios

PARTS   **CHAPTERS:**
New recto/recto or verso/separate half titles   New pages/run on/recto or verso
Part-opening pages start recto/verso   Allow   lines for heading

~~RUNNING HEADS~~ & FOLIOS *9//3 GARAMOND*
verso: Space between heading and text: pts.
recto:
Folios: Old Style/Modern/in running heads/at foot/centered/left/right/indented:
Number consecutively including prelims/Number prelims separately

TYPE SIZES   **QUOTES:** double quotes
Main text: *11/13*
Quoted matter:
Poetry:
Tables:
Footnotes: Aligning figs./superior figs. / * † ‡ § etc.   Number consecutively through: page/section/chapter/book
Appendixes:
Notes:
Bibliography:
Indexes: Flush and hang/run-on

HEADINGS All caps 14 pt. and above to be visually letterspaced. All smalls and caps below 14 pt. to be unit spaced: units

Part Nos: Chapter Nos: *42 PT.*
Part headings: Chapter headings: *24 PT.*
Part drop: Chapter drop: lines

SUB-HEADINGS
A to occupy   lines in text. Set in:
B to occupy   lines in text. Set in:
C to occupy   lines in text. Set in:
D to occupy   lines in text. Set in:
E to occupy   lines in text. Set in:
F to occupy   lines in text. Set in:

SPECIMEN
Please trim to correct size and show margins specified
Please return copy and layouts with specimens
Specimen to consist of   pp. showing:

Designer: The University of Chicago Press

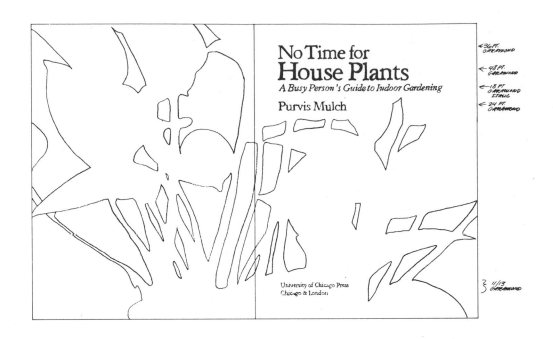

No Time for
House Plants
A Busy Person's Guide to Indoor Gardening

Purvis Mulch

University of Chicago Press
Chicago & London

← 36 PT.
GARAMOND

← 48 PT.
GARAMOND

← 18 PT.
GARAMOND
ITALIC

← 24 PT.
GARAMOND

} 11/13
GARAMOND

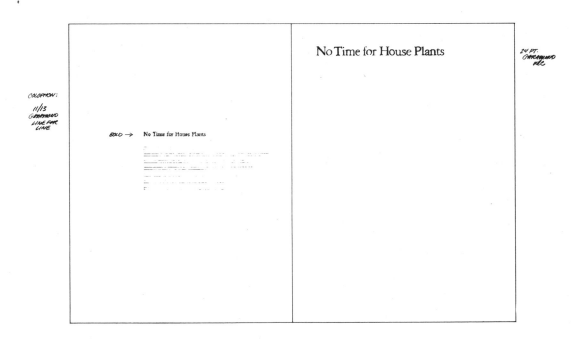

No Time for House Plants

24 PT.
GARAMOND
REG.

COLOPHON:

11/13
GARAMOND
LINE FOR
LINE

BOLD → No Time for House Plants

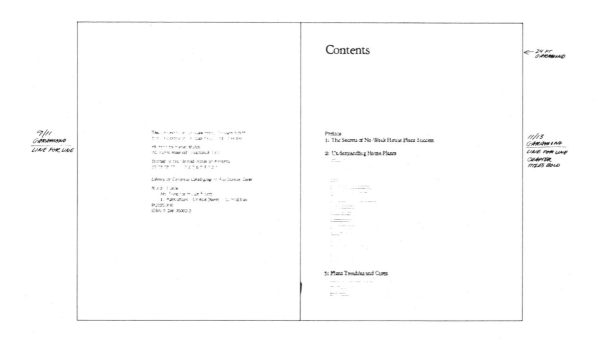

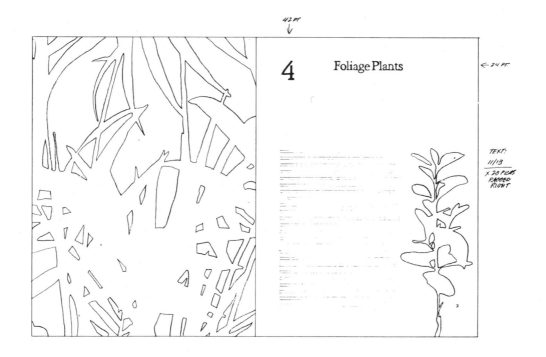

Contents

24 PT GARAMOND

9/11 GARAMOND LINE FOR LINE

11/13 GARAMOND LINE FOR LINE CHAPTER TITLES BOLD

Library of Congress Cataloging in Publication Data

42 PT

4 Foliage Plants

24 PT

TEXT: 11/13 X 20 PICAS RAGGED RIGHT

MANUFACTURING COST ESTIMATE

Author: *Mulch* Trim size: *6"X8"* No. pages: *160*

Title: *No Time for House Plants* Series:

Quantity: *7500* cloth paper: Compositor: *In house*

paper *50 W OS* Printer: } *P-D*

sheets *43125* Binder: }

PLATE COSTS

Text	Estimate	Estimate	Actual
Composition	1600		
5% Alterations	80		
*Addl Galley Proof			
*Addl. Page Proof			
Repros			
Negatives }			
Plates }	400		
Blues	30		

Illustrations

	Estimate	Estimate	Actual
Frontispiece			
Drawings/Photographs	1000		
Insert Plates			

Jacket/Cover

	Estimate	Estimate	Actual
Design			
Composition	150		
Plates	125		

Miscellaneous

	Estimate	Estimate	Actual
Printed Cloth Cover			
Dies			
3% Contingencies	102		
Total Plate Cost	3487		

*over two sets

Prepared by: *CP*

Date:

STOCK COSTS

Presswork	Qty Estimate	Qty Estimate	Qty Actual
Text	766		
Illustrations			

Paper

Text: Sheet size *25"x38"*

No. sheets: *43125* at *32.45* /M sheets

	Estimate	Estimate	Actual
Cost	1400		

Illustration: Sheet size

No. sheets: at /M sheets

	Estimate	Estimate	Actual
Cost			

Binding

	Estimate	Estimate	Actual
spiral at 230 /M	1725		

Jacket/Cover

	Estimate	Estimate	Actual
Printing	200		
Paper	250		

Miscellaneous

	Estimate	Estimate	Actual
coating Prntd Cloth Cover	100		

Freight

	Estimate	Estimate	Actual
local Costs	30		
Total Stock Cost	4471		

Unit Costs

Plate	.4649		
Stock	.5961		
Total	1.0610		

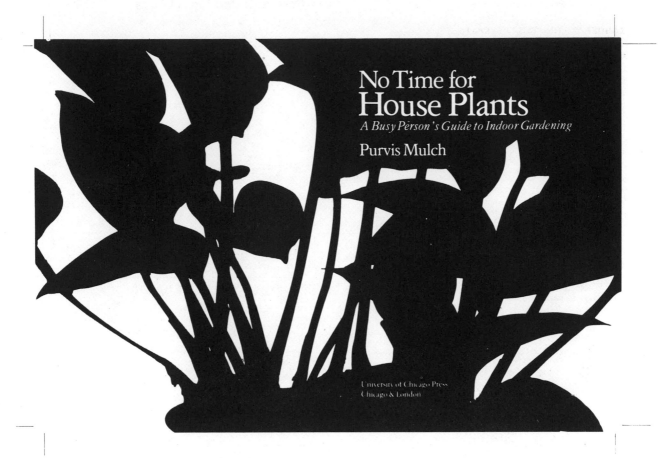

No Time for
House Plants
A Busy Person's Guide to Indoor Gardening

Purvis Mulch

University of Chicago Press
Chicago & London

No Time for House Plants

No Time for House Plants

Designed to a trim size of 6 x 8 inches
by the design staff of the University of Chicago Press.
Composed by the University of Chicago Press
in Compugraphic Garamond with display lines
in Compugraphic Headliner Garamond.
Printed by Kingsport Press, Inc. on
60# Springhill Offset, wove finish.

PAGE 16

PAGE 1

REPEAT ON PAGE 7

Contents

The University of Chicago Press, Chicago 60637
The University of Chicago Press, Ltd., London

© 1977 by Purvis Mulch
All rights reserved. Published 1977

Printed in the United States of America
80 79 78 77   9 8 7 6 5 4 3 2 1

Library of Congress Cataloging in Publication Data

Mulch, Purvis
      No Time for House Plants
          1. Agriculture—United States.   2. Hobbies.
PQ000.000
ISBN 0-266-00000-0

Preface
1: **The Secrets of No-Work House Plant Success**

2: **Understanding House Plants**
    The Basic House Plant
    How a Plant Feeds
    Parts of the Plant
    Soil
    Acidity / Alkalinity
    Potting Mixtures
    Nutrient Maintenance
    Containers
    Watering
    Humidity
    Ventilation
    Temperature
    Light
    Pruning and Training
    Repotting
    Propagation

3: **Plant Troubles and Cures**
    Improper Handling and Care
    Insect Foes
    Diseases

PAGE 4

PAGE 5

No Time for House Plants

REPEAT HALF TITLE,
PAGE 1

4   Foliage Plants

In this chapter, we will survey many of the house plants grown primarily for their foliage. Some of them, under favorable conditions, will flower from time to time, although few should be selected for their flowering abilities. Nearly all of these plants are fairly easy to grow and maintain, giving even the beginner a wide variety of plants from which to choose.

The plants are listed in alphabetical order, according to their common or popular names. If there is no popular name for a plant, or if there is more than one, but no dominant name, the plant is listed by its scientific or Latin name. The index, which includes both common and scientific names, provides a convenient means of cross-checking names.

The special symbols accompanying each plant name will provide a quick and convenient guide to that plant's requirements (see key, p. 000). Remember, however, that these are guides and not sharp demands. Many of these plants are tolerant by nature, and will take to an east window as well as a west window, and can tolerate some direct sunlight even if none is recommended. Most crucial, perhaps, are the guides to humidity and moisture, since overwatering is one thing that almost no plant will tolerate.

9

African Boxwood (*Myrsine africana*)

This slow-growing boxwood has red stems, but otherwise is similar to regular boxwood (q.v.). Many people think it is even more graceful. African boxwood is a good plant for terrariums, if the atmosphere is not too hot.

Aralia (*Fatsia japonica*)

Sometimes sold as *Aralia sieboldii*. Beautiful, bright green, leathery, maplelike leaves highlight this cheerful plant. In appearance, it is similar to the castor oil plant, and in fact is sometimes called false castor oil plant. It thrives in a cool spot. Aralia can easily grow leggy, and so it should be pruned annually in order to encourage it into bushy growth. It will attain a height of four feet at maturity.

A striking hybrid, *Fatshedera lizei*, crosses *F. japonica* and ivy (*Hedera*) forming a climbing plant with maple-shaped leaves, which is tolerant of adverse conditions.

There is also a plant called false aralia, which has graceful and feathery foliage. It bears no resemblance to the true aralia and is difficult to grow.

Asparagus

There are two kinds of asparagus suitable for growing as house plants—*Asparagus plumosus* (fern asparagus), with slender, needle-like dark green leaves, forming a feathery appearance, and *A. sprengeri* ("emerald feather") which has thicker yellow-green leaves and drooping stems. The latter makes a good plant for hanging baskets, and produces red berries at Christmastime. Both like some sun in the summer and full sun in the winter, and both can grow to a height of about two feet.

Australian Laurel (*Pittosporum tobira*)

A tolerant and slow-growing plant whose leaves, glossy and leathery, resemble those of the rhododendron. Australian laurel will grow vigorously bushy and does not require much attention. Florists often use the leaves in floral arrangements.

An interesting variegated form is *P. tobira variegata*.

Australian Umbrella Tree (*Schefflera actinophylla*)

Here is a very attractive and vigorous-growing tree with rich, glossy leaves that radiate like an umbrella from the ends of the leaf stalks. It is a tough and rewarding plant, which grows to six feet and can be propagated by air-layering.

Australian umbrella tree is also sold as *Brassaia actinophylla*. A dwarf variety, *B. actinophylla compacta*, is also available.

Baby's Tears (*Helxine soleirolii*)

This low creeper is also called Irish moss. It likes a constantly moist (but not soggy) soil, and higher than average humidity. It makes a good ground cover for terrariums, but will also grow in a pot if adequate humidity is provided. Baby's tears may appear to die in the colder months, but after an adequate rest period it will spring back to life.

Black Pepper (*Piper nigrum*)

This is not a very attractive plant, but it produces real peppercorns which you may use at the table, and is a good conversation piece for that reason. The plant's green berries later turn red, then dry up and turn black. Pick the dried-up black corns, dry them thoroughly for several weeks in an open spot, then use them in your pepper grinder. Care for the black pepper is the same as that required for philodendron. It is not a demanding plant.

Boxwood (*Buxus*)

The same plant which grows the most prized hedges outdoors can make a very attractive house plant. Boxwood with glossy, bright-green leaves is slow-growing and dependable, a good subject for bonsai, the ancient Oriental art of growing dwarf trees and shrubs. *B. sempervirens* and *B. microphylla japonica* (Japanese boxwood) are the two popular species.

Bromeliads (*Bromeliaceae*)

There are more than eighteen hundred varieties of this popular group, many of which are suitable for growing as house plants. Some of them produce attractive flowers, but most are grown for their striking and variegated leaf patterns. One distinctive feature of the bromeliads is the rosette leaves forming a small water cup which the plant uses to hold reserve supplies of water in its natural habitat—the crotches of trees in Central and South America. In the home, keep the cup filled with water, changing it weekly to keep it fresh.

A few of the more common bromeliads are *Aechmea*, *Ananas* (pineapple), *Billbergia*, *Cryptanthus* (zebra plant), *Dyckia*, *Tillandsia* (Spanish moss), and *Vriesia*.

Caladium

Caladiums, with their spectacularly colored and variegated leaves, are equally at home in the garden or on the window sill. They are ideal additions to plant groupings on porch or patio in the summer and early autumn. Give them bright light, but not long periods of direct sun in summer, if you want the brightest leaf colors.

Caladiums are grown from tubers, which can be divided easily to produce new plants. Start the tubers in regular potting soil at a very warm temperature—

80°–90°—and move the young plants to a cooler spot when they have appeared. They will attain a height of about one foot.

Cast Iron Plant (*Aspidistra elatior*)

This is perhaps the easiest plant in the world to grow, as its name suggests. It is virtually impossible to neglect it to death. It is also called saloon plant, since it was one of the few that could survive in Victorian taverns, and it was made immortal by George Orwell in his novel *Keep the Aspidistra Flying*. If you cannot grow the aspidistra, you may safely conclude that you have a purple thumb and are hopelessly irredeemable as a gardener.

The "cast iron plant," which grows about two feet tall, seems to thrive even better when kept slightly potbound, and it will appreciate having its leaves washed occasionally. A white-striped species is called *A. variegata*.

Chamaeranthemum igneum

This low, spreading herb has attractive, dark green leaves with reddish yellow veins. It is suitable for hanging baskets or as a low contrast in large plant groupings. It does like warm temperatures and high humidity, however, and might not be suitable for dry apartments.

Chinese Evergreen (*Aglaonema*)

Here is an attractive and low-growing plant that is very easy to grow. It will stand abuse almost as easily as the cast iron plant.

There are at least ten commonly found species of the *Aglaonema*, the most popular of which, *A. modestum*, has interestingly mottled leaves. Perhaps the most attractive, however, is *A. pseudo-bracteatum*, which is sometimes difficult to find in stores and greenhouses.

48 | *Chicago* | *Design* | *Production*

14

Cissus

Cissus is a vine plant that offers a number of interesting and attractive species. Most are vigorous climbers, suitable for training on a trellis or for adding to hanging baskets.

Among the more popular species are *C. rhombifolia* (grape ivy), which is one of the most popular of all house plants; *C. antarctica* (kangaroo vine), which prefers a small pot; *C. antarctica minima* (miniature kangaroo vine); *C. rotundifolia;* and *C. discolor* (begonia ivy), which is perhaps the most spectacular of the genus, although difficult to grow.

Of all the *Cissus,* grape ivy is the easiest to grow, which doubtless accounts for a large share of its popularity.

Coleus

This old favorite has velvety leaves sporting bright splashes of reds, pinks, purples, and yellows. There is a seemingly endless number of varieties of coleus, nearly all of them interesting, most growing twelve to eighteen inches in height.

Coleus is equally happy outdoors, grown as an annual in the north, or in a window garden. It can be grown easily from seed, and stem tip cuttings can be taken from established indoor plants. If you grow coleus outdoors in summer, take some cuttings before the first autumn freeze and root them for growing as house plants.

The soil for coleus should be kept damp, but not soggy. Pinch back plants often to encourage bushy growth.

Copper Leaf (*Acalypha wilkesiana*)

This is a member of the Spurge family, which features copper-colored foliage. A close relative, *A. hispida*, is described in this book under flowering plants.

Bibliography

Artificial Light Gardening

Bickford, Elwood D. and Stuart Dunn. *Lighting for Plant Growth.* Kent, Ohio: Kent State University Press, 1972. One of the best books on the subject; especially valuable to those who have had some experience in the area.

Cherry, Elaine C. *Fluorescent Light Gardening.* New York: Van Nostrand Reinhold Co., 1965.

Elbert, George A. *The Indoor Light Gardening Book.* New York: Crown Publishers, Inc., 1975.

Fitch, Charles Marden. *The Complete Book of Houseplants under Lights.* New York: Hawthorn Books, 1975.

Kranz, Frederick H. and Jacqueline. *Gardening Indoors under Lights.* New York: Viking Press, rev. 1971.

Begonias

Brilmayer, Bernice. *All about Begonias.* New York: Doubleday Publishing Co., 1960.

Kramer, Jack. *Begonias, Indoors and Out.* New York: E. P. Dutton & Co., 1967.

15

No Time for
House Plants
A Busy Person's Guide to Indoor Gardening

Purvis Mulch

Book Order　　　　The University of Chicago Press, Ellis Avenue and 58th Street, Chicago, Illinois 60637

Order No.	Date	Delivery
Composition & repros		
Printer		
Binder		

Author/Editor
Title
Series　　　　　　　　　　　　　　　Edition　　　　　　　Impression
Print Quantity　　　Cloth　　　　Bind　　　　　　　Flat
Print Quantity　　　Paper　　　　Bind　　　　　　　Flat

Plate Cost $　　　　　　　　　　Charge to 4-9002-30-0501
Stock Cost $　　　　　　　　　　Charge to 0-0134-01-0501
Alterations　　10% to composition; balance to suspense 0-0124-04-0501

Paper Stock: Body　　　　　　　　Sheet size　　　　　　Trim size
Paper Stock:Cover　　　　　　　　　　　　　　　　　Est. total pages
Inserts/Wraparounds/Frontispiece
Special/Labels

Typeface: Text　　　　　　　　　　Quoted Matter
Poetry　　　　　　　　　　　　　　　Tabular
Footnotes　　　　　　　　　　　　　Appendixes
Bibliography　　　　　　　　　　　　Legends
Index　　　　　　　　　　　　　　　Figs: OS/Mod.
Half titles　　　　　　　　　　　　　Chapters start　　　　Type page
Running heads:verso　　　　　　　　　　　　　　　　Columns　　　Lines
Running heads:recto　　　　　　　　　　　　　　　　Head margin
Artwork, photographs, etc.　　　　　　　　　　　　　Back margin
Printing process:(text):　　Offset/Letterpress/Other　　Printing process:(illustrations):　　Offset/Letterpress/Other
Please note:

Binding　　　　　　　　Rounded & backed　　Flatback　　　　　Perfectbound
Boards　　　　　　　　　　Staln　　　　　　　Headbands
Endsheets:Regular/Reinforced　Color　　　　　　　　　　　　　Printed
Cloth　　　　　　　　　　　　　　　　　　　1 Piece　　　　　2 Piece
　　　　　　　　　　　　　　　　　　　　　3 Piece
Stamping　　　　　　　　　Spine　　　　　　Front　　　　　　Back
Colors:Ink/Foil
Frontispiece　　　　　　　Wraparounds　　　Inserts　　　　　Tips
Jackets/Covers

Proofs
Sample Pages
Galleys　　　　　　　　　　　　　　　Pages
Repros　　　　　　　　　　　　　　　Blues
F & G's　　　　　　　　　　　　　　　Stamped sample case
Bound dummy for jacket art

Please note:　　　　　　　　　　　　　　　　　Page count:
　　　　　　　　　　　　　　　　　　　　　　Prelims
　　　　　　　　　　　　　　　　　　　　　　Text
　　　　　　　　　　　　　　　　　　　　　　Illustrations
　　　　　　　　　　　　　　　　　　　　　　Index
　　　　　　　　　　　　　　　　　　　　　　Total

Mulch　　NO TIME FOR HOUSEPLANTS　　　KW:CS : lj　　　　　PD　　　　75CD
0-226-00000-0　　　　　TRADE　Fall 77

MS rec'd	To MS ed	To author	From author	To prod	P'd for comp	Galleys rcv'd	Galleys back	Pages rcv'd	Pages back	Index to pr'st	Repros OK	Blues OK	Sheets printed	Delivery
	10/4	11/19	12/3	12/17				1/27	2/10	2/10	2/13	3/11	4/1	late
10/1	10/6	11/15	11/26	1/5	1/6			1/20	2/7					April

Des MS to prod.	Design finished	Estimate in	Sample pages					Ja'cover drawn	Ja'cover design	Ja'cover colored	Ja'cover delivered	Sample case ok
eP/JEA	12/15							12/21	1/6	2/13	3/25	Apr
10/1	12/29	1/3	1/13					12/27	1/6			

NOTE: The card above forms part of the preproduction and production schedules,
which are issued every three weeks and cover all books in work. The card is begun
and carried through the preproduction stage by the manuscript editor, then transferred to the production controller, who records the manufacturing events. The
upper rows of boxes are estimated target dates, the lower rows actual completion dates.

Early Fall '1977   Prod.

Book Estimate and Release

[x] New Book
[ ] Revision
[ ] Reprint

Author   Purvis Mulch   Editor/Trans.
Title   NO TIME FOR HOUSE PLANTS: A Busy Person's Guide to Indoor Gardening
Series   na   ISBN (cloth) 0-226- 00000-0 (paper) 0-226-

Editor's Release

Royalties 10% n.r. 1st 2,500; 12½% n.r. next 2,500; 15% n.r. thereafter on domestic cloth;
    2/3 thereof on foreign cloth; 7½% n.r. on paper and d.m.
Other fees or charges   none
Subsidy $ none   from   Copyright by University o f Chicago
Contract no.   9728   Market   world
Series contract no.   na   Target pub. date   (cloth)   June 1977
BUP approval na   (paper)
Remarks   Codes: ODE-OJD-

                            Editor   Kimberly Wiar   Date 9/29/76
                                                             (ANF) 9/30/76

Sales Release

	Print	Bind	Price	Discount	No. pages	Size	Pub. date
Cloth							
Paper -	spiral 7500	all	$5.95	Trade (40% av)	160	6 x 8"	Sept. 77

Remarks   Spiral bound with stiff covers. Suggest fall publication
           when interest in houseplants revives.

Main code: H-ODE   Marketing Manager   P. Kaiserlian   Date 2/10/77
                                            OK PK

Financial Release and Estimate

	Cloth	Paper		Cloth	Paper
Plate cost	$	$ 3,486	No. copies sold		7,250
Stock cost 7,500 copies	$	$ 4,471	Mfg. break even		2,228
Royalties	$	$ 3,262	Total break even		3,142
Less subsidy	$	$ –	Net price per copy	$	$ 3.57
Total cost	$	$ 11,219	Less mfg. cost per copy	$	$ 1.06
Sales revenue	$	$ 25,882	Less royalty	$	$ .45
Contribution to operation	$	$ 14,663	Gross margin	$	$ 2.06
			Gross margin %		57.7

Remarks

On the terms set forth above this book meets/does not meet current financial requirements of the Press

                            Business Manager   E.J. Hicani   Date   2/14/77

Director's Release
Remarks

                            Approved
                            Director   (NIP)   Date 2/15

                                                        DIRECTOR'S COPY

THE UNIVERSITY OF CHICAGO

DATE 15 November 1976

To PK   DEPARTMENT Marketing

FROM RD   DEPARTMENT Promotion

IN RE: Promotion plan for No Time for Houseplants

Despite its catchy title, we fear that NTFHP may appear to be only another "basic" houseplant book -- of which there are too many already. The "no time", "busy person's" handle helps distinguish it, but only to a point. Hawthorne Books has just published something called The Office Gardener and if the offices to which this book is intended are anything like ours, there's not much time for office plants either. NTFHP is entering a flooded market and may suffer (overwatering is the most common cause of ill health for houseplants) if an appropriate promotion strategy is not found.

Because we have chosen to enter these waters cautiously, a mass advertising campaign directed to consumers is out of the question. After all just about everyone considers him/herself busy these days, so the market is rather large. And nothing short of a fortune could buy NTFHP's way into the nation's consciousness as one of the basic houseplant books (such as The New York Times Book of Houseplants), or make it as ubiquitously resplendent as Sunset Books spinning racks of house and garden books.

Our promotional strategy is designed to capture those "busy houseplant novices" who take the time to go to a bookstore, looking for a basic guide and are confronted with an impossible number of books from which to choose. Overwhelmed, our customer turns to the friendly, informed clerk and inquires,"What would you recommend for someone who wants to grow a few plant but who really has no time for houseplants?" And our friendly, informed clerk will respond, "I have just what you're looking for," not only because NTFHP is just what the customer has in mind, but because our promotional plan has provided that clerk with good economic reasons to recommend our book above all others.

The aim, then of our promotional efforts is to make NTFHP attractive to booksellers to stock by making it easy for them to sell. The plan entails the following:
Total budget: $2,690
1. Space advertising: As I stated, one can go broke doing this sort of thing. We will place a single half-page ad in PW six to eight weeks before delivery of the book to announce its pub date and our special offers to booksellers (see below). Cost: $800

2. Statement stuffers. We will prepare 15,000 two color statement stuffers that can be imprinted with the bookseller's address at a later date. These will be offered to those who order 50 or more copies of the book. Minimum quantity of 500 statement stuffers for imprinting by the Press. Good booksellers know their customers and can direct these to likely buyers. They help generate larger bookstore orders and more frequent reorders. Cost: $450

3. Window posters: Since we planned to chart the Mulch "no time" system on a colorful wall poster, I shall ask the production department to overprint 1,000 posters for booksellers to use as window displays. Again, this makes our book stand out in the store. Always appreciated. Cost: $200

4. Ten copy pre-pack. We have offered our Spanish Dictionary in a 10-copy counter display pre-pack with good success and feel that a similar treatment would help NTFHP. A pre-pack can put the book in the spotlight in the store. This is especially important in a crowded field such as houseplant books. It makes it easy to display a title in other areas of the store, such as by the cash register, and pick up "impulse buyers" as they check out. (Just like the "supermarket trap"). One pre-pack qualifies the customer for full trade discount. They also make it easy for the warehouse to fill and ship orders quickly. Cost: $240

5. Co-op ads. $1,000 will be held in the advertising budget for co-op ads that will be arranged by the salesmen at their discretion. Once again, we're trusting the booksellers' knowledge of his/her area and customers.

THE UNIVERSITY OF CHICAGO

DATE 17 November 1976

To   RD
     cc: VH, GT   DEPARTMENT   Promotion

FROM   PK

                       DEPARTMENT   Marketing

IN RE   Promotion plan for NO TIME FOR HOUSEPLANTS

Thank you for your promotional plan for this spring title. I think you have covered everything we discussed in our marketing meetings about the book.

Since that time I have had the cost estimates. With our spiral binding and paper cover (which incidentally will be quite sturdy) we are able to come up with an attractive low price of $5.95. I think this will help it in competing with other titles in the stores; we are not expecting much in the way of library sales because of LJ's usually cool reception to more houseplant books.

Because of the low price, we do not have much to work with in the way of an advertising budget, and can make best use of our money with the kind of program you suggest.

Other possibilities we've thought of at our meetings I'll note here as a reminder to publicity and the sales department: a display at the spring Garden Show at McCormick place when many gardening aids are for sale; informing garden-supply wholesalers of the book and our promotional aids--by mail since we will not have time to call on them for this one title.

Mulch back cover

No Time for Houseplants
Purvis Mulch

Here is a beautifully-illustrated, complete guide to houseplant care designed for people who have "no time for houseplants."

Purvis Mulch, who has been writing about gardening and plant care for more than twenty years, has written this book for the novice indoor gardener who simply hasn't much time to spend caring for sensitive, exotic houseplants. He has brought together everything you need to know to grow interesting and beautiful houseplants without really working at it.

The Mulch "no time" system of houseplant care is built upon two fundamental rules: (1) Choose plants that will tolerate adverse conditions. (2) Provide your plants with conditions that will encourage growth without your constant attention.

No Time for Houseplants provides the busy indoor gardener with a beautiful wall poster that is as useful as it is attractive. It charts the light, watering, humidity, and temperature requirements for more than 100 "no time" indoor plants. The book contains all the essential information on topics such as

   *Choosing the right plant -- picking healthy specimens of
    those varieties that are easiest to grow
   *Potting mixtures, fertilizers, and containers
   *Pest control and other problems
   *Propagation and repotting
   *Terrariums, dish gardens, and even growing vegetables indoors

PURVIS MULCH is a graduate of the University of Iowa and a former editor of Organic Gardening. He is the author of The Wisconsin Garden Guide and some fifty articles on gardening.

Paper   ISBN:0-226-
The University of Chicago Press

Mulch catalog copy

No Time for Houseplants
A Busy Person's Guide to Indoor Gardening
Purvis Mulch

New books on houseplants and indoor gardening number in the dozens each publishing season. But most of these evermore specialized titles are written for green-thumbed enthusiasts who spend countless hours tending to their exotic flora. Until now no one has written a houseplant book for busy people -- and today, that includes most of us. Here is a beautifully illustrated guide to houseplant care designed for people who have "no time for houseplants."

Purvis Mulch, who has been writing about gardening and plant care for more than twenty years, has written this book for the busy, novice indoor gardener. He has brought together everything they need to know to grow interesting and beautiful houseplants without really working at it.

No Time for Houseplants includes a wall poster that is as useful as it is attractive. It charts the light, watering, humidity, and temperature requirements for more than 100 "no time" indoor plants. The book contains all the essential information on topics such as

   *Choosing the right plant -- picking healthy
    specimens of those varieties that are easiest
    to grow
   *Potting mixtures, fertilizers, and containers
   *Pest control and other problems
   *Propagation and repotting
   *Terrariums, dish gardens, and even growing
    vegetables indoors
   No Time for Houseplants may be ordered in a handsome 10-copy counter display pre-pack.

The University of Chicago Press
Marketing Department
Chicago, Illinois 60637
Since 1891 Publishers of Scholarly Books and Journals

Author Questionnaire

Your answers to the following questions will help us plan an effective advertising and promotion campaign for your work—and will be used in preparing jacket and catalogue copy and publicity releases, as well as in answering inquiries from libraries, booksellers, review media, and others. We urge you to expand upon your replies to any extent necessary to give us adequate information. Please return this questionnaire at the earliest possible date.

I. PERSONAL INFORMATION

Name (as you wish it to appear on title page):   Date: November 11, 1976

Jerry Minnich

Title of manuscript:
No Time for House Plants: A Busy Person's Guide to
Indoor Gardening
Your date and place of birth: Citizenship:
7/6/33; Allentown, Pa.   USA

Home address (please include Zip Code):
315 N. Franklin St., Madison, WI 53703
Home telephone number:
608: 255-6065

Office address (please include Zip Code):
Box 1379, Madison, WI 53701
Office telephone number:
608: 262-7756 (262-4928)

Married?   Spouse's name?   Children?
divorced   2

II. PROFESSIONAL INFORMATION

Present position: Asst. Dir., Univ. of Wisconsin Press, 1971-

Former positions:
Marketing Mgr., Univ. of Wisconsin Press, 1969-71
Journals Mgr., Univ. of Wisconsin Press, 1965-69
Editor, Vigor magazine, 1963-65
Assoc. Editor, Organic Gardening magazine, 1953-57; 1961-63
Colleges and universities attended, with degrees and dates, from most recent:

University of Iowa, B.A., 1961

Professional and other honors and offices:

PR 137-02-34

Principal countries, cities, and states in which you have lived, with approximate dates.:

Allentown, Pa., 1933-57; 1961-63
Iowa City, Ia., 1957-61
Newark, N.J., 1963-65
Madison, Wis., 1965-

Any other pertinent biographical data for use on book jackets, etc.:

(from jacket of my other book) Jerry Minnich has been gardening and writing about gardening for more than twenty years, the last ten in Wisconsin. He has published more than fifty articles on home gardening, most in Organic Gardening and Farming magazine, where he was formerly associate editor, but also in a number of other publications including House Beautiful. He has also contributed to several larger gardening books, including The Encyclopedia of Organic Gardening and The Complete Book of Compost (Rodale Press). Minnich was born and raised in Allentown, Pa., and was graduated from the University of Iowa. He is married [no longer], has two children, and has lived and worked in Madison since 1965.

Books published:
title (state whether author or editor)   publisher   year   approx. sales
(Please indicate book club adoptions, paperback reprints, serializations, and foreign editions)

A Wisconsin Garden Guide; Wisconsin House, Ltd.; 1975; 15,000

Other important published writings (journal articles, etc.):
title   where published   year

Am currently garden editor (contributing) for Countryside magazine; monthly column.

Currently working on The Earthworm Book (tentative title) to be published by Rodale Press in 1977.

Please enclose a glossy print of a recent photograph of yourself, if readily available. Be sure the photographer is willing to allow its reproduction without fee.

none available at present

III. MARKETING INFORMATION

Please describe the content of your manuscript and the *reasons for its importance* in 300 or more words. We hope you will bear in mind that *this information will be our primary source for preparing jacket, catalogue, and advertising copy*. Please do not refer us to your introduction, since this may not be available to us at the time information is needed. If it is available, we shall of course refer to it.

In 1973, with the purchase of a new house, I was determined to increase my house plant population. Still, I realized that, with my busy schedule, I would not have much time to devote to indoor plants. I was frequently gone for long periods of time, and many days, even while in town, I simply have no time to fuss with plants.

I therefore sought to find methods to raise interesting and beautiful house plants with the least amount of effort. All the house plant books I checked, however, were apparently written by enthusiasts who spent unending hours in careful watering, potting, repotting, propagating, tying up, inducing to flowering, humidifying, bathing, and even talking to their plants, in an effort to get them to grow. There was no book for the casual house plant grower.

There is now such a book. By researching many sources, and with the aid of personal experimentation and past experience, I have narrowed down the crucial requirements for a "no-time" indoor house plant population. The research yielded two cardinal rules: Choose plants that are tolerant of adverse conditions, and then give them the right conditions to grow without your constant attention.

The implementation of these rules form the crux of this book. I explain how to choose plants, tell which are the easiest to grow, and explain the conditions of light, soil moisture, humidity, and temperature that each of more than a hundred indoor plants requires. I explain, in short, how your house plants can live well without your constant attention and painstaking devotion.

The chapter on understanding house plants is critically important to the "no-time" system, since it details the initial requirements plants need for success, including potting mixtures, fertilizing, containers, watering, humidity, ventilation, temperature, light, and pruning. When these conditions are met at the very beginning, countless hours will be saved later in nursing plants or attempting to track down troubles.

There is a separate chapter devoted to plant troubles and cures, and special sections on artificial light, summer care, and lists of plants for various conditions of light and temperature. For those who wish to devote a little more time to raising house plants, there is detailed information on repotting, propagation, training, dish gardens, planters, bottle gardens and terrariums, kitchen scrap gardens, and growing vegetables indoors.

The bulk of the book, however, comprises listings of more than a hundred "easy" foliage plants, flowering plants, and succulents, including cacti, giving light, soil moisture, and humidity requirements for each.

For the home owner or apartment dweller who wants to raise several dozen attractive house plants while spending only a few minutes a day in caring for them, this book will tell everything that is necessary to know in order to achieve success.

Please list scholarly journals, magazines, and newspapers which you believe are most likely to carry a review of your book and be most suitable for possible space advertising:

(a) In the U.S.:

Organic Gardening and Farming
House Beautiful
Apartment Dweller
Mother Jones
Rolling Stone
Ms
(other general magazines going to single, affluent audience)

(b) Abroad:

Please list columnists, editorial writers, radio and television commentators, etc., who in your opinion would be interested in your book:

don't know of any

Please list, in order of importance, names and addresses of persons whose good opinion of the book might broaden its audience—those to whom, for instance, advance copies of the book might be sent by us for comments that could be quoted in advertising: *(Please be selective)*

Jeff Cox, Rodale Press, Inc.
Elvin McDonald, House Beautiful

Please list those professors and their institutions that should be approached with a view to the classroom adoption of the book:

/PAPER/ Review Distribution List

Date: June 1977
Attn. Langley:
--Charge to Acct. # 4-9010-48-0501
--Enclose review with each book
--Special instructions

TITLE   NO TIME FOR HOUSEPLANTS

AUTHOR/ED.   Purvis Mulch

Approved by   VH   Paper ISBN # 0-226- 00000-0

PLEASE SHIP AS SOON AS POSSIBLE   Virginia Heiserman 753-2594

Editor, Original Paperbacks
ALA BOOKLIST
Am. Library Assn.
50 East Huron
Chicago, IL 60611

Book Review Editor
AMERICAN HOME
641 Lexington Avenue
New York, NY 10022

Book Review Editor
AMERICAN HORTICULTURALIST
American Horticultural Society
Mt. Vernon, VT 22121

F. H. Hilner, Editor
AMERICAN NURSERYMAN
310 So. Michigan Avenue
Chicago, IL 60604

Bohdan S. Wynar, Editor
AMERICAN REFERENCE BOOKS ANNUAL
P. O. Box 263
Littleton, CO 80160

David Jordan, Editor
APARTMENT LIFE
Meredith Corp.
1716 Locust Street, Meredith Bldg.
Des Moines, IA 50365

Book Review Editor
APARTMENT LIVING
DeBare Publ. Co.
Box 1838
Wichita, KS 67218

Mr. John Barkham
JOHN BARKHAM REVIEWS
27 East 65th Street
New York, NY 10021

Book Review Editor
BETTER HOMES & GARDENS
1716 Locust Street
Des Moines, IA 50336

Book Review Editor
THE BOSTON PHOENIX
100 Mass. Avenue
Boston, Mass. 02115

Connie Dodds Devit, Editor
BUDGET DECORATING
Maco Publ. Co.
699 Madison Avenue
New York, NY 10021

Edith Proctor
CALIFORNIA SENIOR CITIZEN NEWS
2222 Albatros Drive
San Diego, CA 92101

Features Editor
CANADIAN HOMES MAGAZINE
Southstar Publ. Co.
401 Bay Street
Toronto, Ont. M5H 2Y8
CANADA

Book Review Editor
CANADIAN INTERIORS
Maclean-Hunter Ltd.
Toronto, Ont. CANADA M5W 1A7

The entire review mailing includes an additional five pages listing appropriate
publications. A generous review mailing, the cheapest form of advertising, is
consistent with our "less is more" approach to marketing this special book.

THE MIT PRESS

Table of Contents

Acquisition and Administration

Editorial

Production / Design

Sales and Promotion

THE PUBLISHING PROCESS

At the MIT Press acquisition is not a passive or rote process. Increasingly, successful acquisition is the result of an active search process. The formulation of an idea for a publishing program may find its origin within the Press, or through exchange of ideas with faculty. While today the Press conducts a growing part of the acquisition process through the development and implementation of publishing plans for each of its area programs, it would be misleading to say the the Press deliberately acquires all the properties it wishes to publish within the context of definitive plans. A significant part of our program grows out of our alertness to opportunities and possibilities for publishing successfully. The Mulch book presented such an opportunity.

The Acquisition Department screens approximately 1000 proposals, outlines or partial manuscripts each year. Perhaps 90% of the unsolicited manuscripts are rejected, most before outside scholarly or professional review. After initial screening, promising manuscripts and proposals are thoroughly read by outside reviewers, including members of the MIT faculty. In most cases two or three critical reviews are obtained before it is determined that a proposal to publish should be written and presented to the Editorial Board for consideration and approval.

The proposal to publish presents a complete profile of the book: it identifies and informs about special considerations for the editorial, design, production, marketing, and financial staff at the Press. The Acquisition Editor reviews the proposal with departments and with the Director, then finalizes the proposal, appends reviews and samples of the manuscript, and sends the proposal to each of the 10 members of the Editorial Board, in advance of the meeting. The Board meets for a half-day every third week to discuss the proposals on the agenda. After discussion of each proposal, the Board may accept it for publication, defer it for further consideration, or reject it. The Board's rejection rate is quite low, but the threat of rejection is effective in assuring quality submissions by the editors.

Following the Editorial Board meeting, projects are entered onto a seasonal Publishing Log, which along with copies of the proposal is distributed to all departments of the Press. In the interval between signature of the contract and delivery of a complete and satisfactory manuscript, Acquisition Editors and members of the Editorial, Marketing, and Design Departments might be involved in discussions with authors regarding the special needs of the manuscript.

After the manuscript is delivered, it is reviewed again before the Acquisition Editor launches it into the publishing process. By the time he has completed the manuscript, the author has also filled out an Author's Questionnaire which is reviewed both by Marketing and Acquisition. By providing the Press with the author's view of the market and specific interested segments of it, where he feels the book should be reviewed, publicity activities he will participate in, etc., this questionnaire helps the formulation of a marketing strategy for the book.

As the book is launched into the system, the Acquisition Editor prepares a Turnover document and a Release form which accompany the manuscript to the Editorial, Design, and Production Departments within the Press. The Turnover form is a means of updating all important information presented in the original proposal. Its preliminary review by the Editorial, Design, and Production Departments results in more accurate estimates of editorial difficulty, copyediting time, and any special design and production problems. The Marketing Department revises its estimate for print runs and prices at this stage, a bound book date is established, and the book is placed on a seasonal list. All this new information is brought to a formal Launch meeting for the book and after discussion is incorporated into a launch document and a Publication Information Sheet that becomes the basic control mechanism through which schedules, costs, and other variables of the publishing process are monitored.

The Turnover document also includes a preliminary Marketing Strategy prepared by the Acquisition Editor. This strategy is reviewed by various members of the Marketing and Promotion staffs, and following the Launch, at a time during the editing, design, and markup stage, before the manuscript is committed to composition, a marketing meeting is held to detail our approach to selling the book through a variety of channels: direct mail, promotion, publicity, exhibits, adoptions, subsidiary rights, book clubs, etc. Because of the necessary lead time, implementation of the marketing plan begins well in advance of the book's availability.

The Release/Publication Information document itself is reviewed by the Director at the Launch meeting, then when the book is sent to the compositor, again when the book is sent to the manufacturer, and before the book is actually released to the warehouse for shipping to buyers. MIT Press books take from six weeks to 18 months to publish, with an average of eight months for the typical book and 12 for those with more complex typographical and design demands.

At the production end, once a manuscript is launched into the system, copies of it are sent simultaneously to the Design and Editorial Departments. The Editorial Department will be responsible for working with the author on developmental editing, copyediting, and proofreading, and generally for monitoring the proofing cycle. While the work is in process in the Editorial Department, the Design Department is producing design specifications and sample pages for each book. When the manuscript is out of editing and after it is checked by the author, the Design Department then marks the manuscript against design specifications for the compositor. At this point the Production Department takes over the monitoring of the schedule as it releases the book for composition. Galley proofs or page proofs are circulated back through the Editorial Department for proofing and checking, and then on to the Design Department. In some cases books with multiple illustrations or complex typography will require both dummying and mechanical layout which in many cases is provided by the Design Department. Finally, repro copy is released to the printer for printing.

Finished bound copies of the books are shipped to the warehousing and fulfillment facility, UNISERV, in Littleton, Massachusetts, to IBD Warehouse in London, and to the Book & Film warehouse in Sydney. UNISERV was established by The MIT Press and Harvard University Press to supply present and future needs, and potentially to provide warehousing service to other university presses.

New books are featured in advance seasonal catalogs published twice each year which present books in display format. These catalogs are sent to our largest wholesale and reatil customers, including libraries. About 12,000 of these catalogs are distributed domestically twice each year and through the London office (Europe, the Middle East, Africa) and through agents in the Far East, India, South America, Australia, and New Zealand. Books are simultaneously listed in a variety of book-trade reference publications.

Our direct mail program concentrates on eight subject matter catalogs in Architecture and Urban Studies, Linguistics and Language, Management and Business, Life Sciences, Physical Sciences, Engineering, Humanities, and Political Science and Social Science. These subject matter catalogs feature new, recent, and important titles from the backlist and contain descriptive listing of the entire backlist in each area covered. Books are cross-listed as well. Approximately 1,000,000 of these direct mail pieces are mailed each year, mostly to the domestic and Canadian markets.

In addition to the emphasis on direct mail selling, the Press field sales staff, both here and abroad, make personal calls on our largest wholesale and retail book buyers. The Press covers the eastern United States and Canada from its Cambridge office and shares field representatives in the midwest and the west with other university presses.

Supporting our marketing campaign, especially for books aimed at general audiences, is our Advertising Department which places about 100 space advertisements each year. The Publicity Department is concerned with a variety of activities aimed at bringing visibility to the Press's recently published books, especially by way of ensuring that an adequate number of copies are placed with reviewers for journals, newspapers, magazines, and other periodicals around the world. MIT Press books generate from 800 to 1000 reviews each year.

The Subsidiary Rights Department is responsible for selling translation rights to our books and maintains an ongoing dialogue with interested publishers around the world. The Press places about two dozen of its book with foreign publishers each year. Book club sales are significant for many of the Press's books, not only producing income but also allowing larger print runs which reduce the unit cost and thereby increase the margin on books sold directly. When books are finally in stock, sales and shipping are traced on a daily basis so that we can closely monitor our inventory.

Orders from all of our market channels (except London and Sydney, where full inventories are maintained for direct shipping to those regions of the world) come to the Press offices in Cambridge where they are edited and processed through the Press's own Ultimacc electronic data processing system to generate packing lists as well as invoices then shipped daily to UNISERV for processing. Units shipped and sales are reported on a daily basis and are posted in the office. Ultimacc also supplies a variety of other Press needs, including the maintenance of customer files, accounts receivable processing, generation of mailing lists, and a wide variety of sales and inventory information on daily, weekly, and monthly bases. Similar electronic data processing services are available through our other warehousing and shipping facilities in London and Sydney.

The MIT Press

28 Carleton Street
Cambridge, Massachusetts 02142

Massachusetts Institute of Technology
617-253-5646

November 18, 1976

Purvis Mulch
PO Box 1379
USA

Dear Mr. Mulch:

Thank you for sending us your manuscript NO TIME FOR HOUSE PLANTS for publishing consideration.

As you may know, the MIT Press's list concentrates primarily on professional, scholarly, and reference books in the technical, scientific, business, and medical areas. As offshoots of those major interests, however, we have a small but significant trade list into which your work might well fit. Two of our titles related to NO TIME FOR HOUSE PLANTS -- both of which have enjoyed enormous success, I might add -- are Sauer's SEEDS, SPADES, HEARTHS AND HERDS (a history of gardening and farming on earth) and Preston's NORTH AMERICAN TREES (a complete, illustrated field handbook of all North American trees, now in its third edition).

We will, of course, have to submit your manuscript to outside referees for review and evaluation. We have a good retail network where there will be interest in NO TIME FOR HOUSE PLANTS, should it be evaluated as a good addition to our list. We would promote your work along with the two above titles from our backlist. All this, again, is contingent upon favorable review and approval by our faculty Editorial Board. In such a competitive market for plant books, I would like to rush along the decision process for the book. I'll put the work in the hands of reviewers as soon as possible, submit it to our Board if the reviews are favorable, and then I'll be in touch again.

Sincerely,

Flora Greenhouse
Acquisition Editor

FG/ddt

Author Purvis Mulch
Address

Title NO TIME FOR HOUSEPLANTS

Submitted by author

	Accepted	Date
	Declined	Date
	Returned for Revision	Date

Date Rec'd & Ack.	Editor	Copy Number	Pages	Miscellaneous
11/18/76	FG	1	147	Preface, VII chapts, Appendix, photos

READER INQUIRIES

Date Asked	Fee Off.	Reader's Name & Affiliation	Reply	Reply Date
11/20	$35	Cedric Crassula/MIT	yes	11/20
11/20	$35	Fern Boston/MIT	yes	11/20

MS ROUTING & CORRESPONDENCE

Sent	To (From)	Date Sent	Date Received Report	MS	Opinion	Date Paid
US mail	Crassula	11/20	11/30/76		yes, but in list?	11/30/76
US mail	Boston	11/20	11/28/76		yes & no	11/30/76

Ms. Flora Greenhouse
MIT Press
28 Carleton Street
Cambridge, MA 02142

Dear Ms. Greenhouse:

I have read and quite enjoyed Purvis Mulch's NO TIME FOR HOUSEPLANTS. I even revived a couple of my mysteriously ailing plants on Mr. Mulch's good advice.

One aspect of the book which is quite nice is the author's informal tone. He manages to impart his information by way of chatty, narrative instruction rather than formal, pedantic lesson-giving. One nice stylistic device is his frequent tone of address to the reader: "your plant" and "be sure that.." are examples.

He also engages in an appealing kind of personification of nature, which I think must appeal to the tender cultivator of little sprouts in Dixie cups on a kitchen windowsill. While referring to the plants as if they have energetic wills to thrive, to bear "children," Mr. Mulch gives just enough science to make it all legitimate. I would say that his technical level is exactly appropriate to the lay audience who have pretty much forgotten their post-sixth grade science.

Mr. Mulch does another handy and creative thing, which is to encourage the reader not to be taken in by plant-cult commercial gimmicks. For instance, he gives approximate recipes for mixing one's own potting soil.

I do hope the book is to be well indexed. One of the consistent problems with plant books is that in case of a problem with a particular plant the reader is unable to locate it in the plant book organized topically rather than by plant type. Mr. Mulch seems to cover his subject from both angles of organization (general issues and specific types) and the book will suffer if not well indexed. It will function best, after all, as a kind of handbook.

I do think this book is worth publishing, but I don't quite see how it fits the MIT list.

Yours truly,
Daisy Dirt for Cedric Crabula, MIT

Ms. Flora Greenhouse
MIT Press
28 Carleton Street
Cambridge, Mass. 02142

Dear Ms. Greenhouse:

My first reaction upon skimming the manuscript you sent to me was "What! Another book on houseplants!" Having examined the book more closely, I repeat that exclamation, with a few modifications.

Mulch's manuscript first examines the basic necessities of growing healthy houseplants -- soil, water, light, air, etc. -- before proceeding to a plant-by-plant description with much particulars on each plant. The first three chapters are useful but not in any sense of the word unique or special: there are at least ten books on the market, in all ranges of price, format, and intellectual demand, which cover this same material with equal or greater facility and inclusiveness. Time/Life, for instance, has covered this ground with an elegance of design that the MIT Press could certainly equal, but probably not surpass.

It is in the second part of the manuscript -- the detailed individual description of literally hundreds of different plants -- that Mulch takes on real interest and gains value as a useful, marketable guide. Very few plant books that I've seen are so encyclopedic in their scope, and those that do include as many different species usually become unwieldy by virtue of this very magnitude. Mulch, on the other hand, manages to cover the field with admirable brevity and concision.

One question that arose in my mind was that of illustrations. Are the illustrations included with the manuscript the only ones planned for the book? The usefulness of the book would certainly be increased almost arithmetically with the number of illustrations included.

Finally, I must wonder what place this book would fill on the MIT Press list. But I imagine that is your problem, not mine. My opinion is that this book is partly superfluous, partly useful; and that when it is useful it is very useful, but when it is redundant....

Sincerely,

Fern Boston
MIT Botany Dept.

The MIT Press
Publishing Proposal

Board Action: Date 12/8/76
Accepted ☑ Rejected ☐ Deferred ☐
Comments: _Full steam ahead!_

Author(s) and Editor(s)
Names and Addresses:

Purvis Mulch

Discipline Gardening/Botanical Science
Title NO TIME FOR HOUSE PLANTS
Subtitle A Busy Person's Guide to Indoor Gardening
Series/editor

Delivery Dates Complete Ms. in House 12/76   Recommended Pub. Date fall 1977

Type of Project:
X☐ New Manuscript ☐ Camera Ready ☐ Import ☐ Distribution ☐ Consignment ☐ Paperback ☐ Translation

Format Summary

Pages 176	Illustrations 38
Trim 4x6	Line Drawings
Binding hard	Half Tones

Recommendations for MIT Press to Publish (Basis and Reasons, Quantity, Retail Price, summation of P & L data)

It is recommended that the Press publish an edition of 7500 copies, paperback, priced at approximately $6.95T.

This book will be a useful and informative addition to the list of books on the plant lovers' market, no doubt crowding out much of the inferior work in this field. Moreover, this acquisition will fit into our burgeoning series on Home Crafts, thus strengthening the sales position of such new titles as BASKET WEAVING IN YOUR LIVING ROOM, THE BAYEUX TAPESTRY AT YOUR FINGERTIPS, and ISN'T MACRAME FUN?. I feel sure that the superb facilities of the MIT Press Design and Marketing Departments can turn this modest manuscript into the supersmash it deserves to be. It is hoped that the Board will concur.

Director [signature] 12/8/76 Date
Acquisitions Editor Flora Greenhouse 12/8/76 Date

The MIT Press
Publishing Proposal
Description of Project

Author Mulch

(1) Contract Terms:
10% net on first 3000, 12½% net on next 3000
15% net thereafter

Royalty Terms	Author Will Do	Author to Pay	Charge to Royalties	Charge to Edit.	Charge to Plant
Series Editor Override	--				
Advance $ --	Date				
Subsidy $ --	From whom	Purpose			
Art Work	XX				
Permissions					
Index	XX				
Translation					

Special Terms(Promotional Commitments, Possible Cooperative Arrangements, Scheduling Suggestions, Guaranteed Sales)

(2) The Author(s) or Editor(s) (Full Description of qualifications, degrees, professional affiliations, previously published books, achievements in field, etc.)

Purvis Mulch, Master of B.S. (Botanical Science) from Plant Univ., has long been a recognized authority in the field of indoor agriculture. He teaches Watering and Advanced Air-Layering at Plant U., and has authored several standard texts in this field, the most recent of which -- I LIKE PLANTS -- was awarded the "Thalassa Cruso plant book of the week" award. Mr. Mulch also writes a weekly column on plants in the New York Review of Books.

(3) List of Readers (Attach readers' reports or reviews to page 3)
A. Cedric Crassula, MIT Botany
B. Feu Boston, MIT Botany

(4) Describe Condition of Manuscript at Board Presentation

Manuscript is complete, and relatively clean. Some editing will be needed.

(5) General Description of the Book and Special Features (Collection, reprints, conference, thesis, original, etc.)

Mulch's book consists of seven (7) chapters. The first three describe the basic needs of house plants -- soil, water, containers, air, light, training, etc.-- as well as Mr. Mulch's radical suggestions as to plant care (e.g., "don't overwater").

After these introductory chapters come several specialized sections on foliage plants, cacti & succulents, flowering plants, and special gardens such as terraria, kitchen gardens, and dish gardens.

One unique and intriguing characteristic of this manuscript is the use of boxed-in special supplements to introduce more advanced or specialized data on "The ABC's of Artificial Light," "Plants for Cool Conditions," etc. Skillful design will surely make these boxes an eye-catching lure to potential buyers.

(6) Elaboration on Recommendation to Publish (Attach table of contents and reviews)

This work is grounded in the latest, most innovative and thought-provoking work in the complex field of plant relations. The author has drawn on the standard texts in this area, but breaks new ground in digging up new solutions to old knotty problems. Many thorny matters are considered with surprisingly fresh insight; indeed, he makes some of this old plant material seem positively green again with the vibrancy and fervor of his style.

Describe Primary Market (who will buy this book)

Plant enthusiasts of every shape and size; there should be a large trade market for this book. Perhaps some course adoptions in botany schools for a subsequent paperback edition.

Describe Secondary Market

Rich people and people who just love to buy books. People with hobbies, or who like to look at pictures.

MIT Press Related Books

Author	Title	Pub. Date	Quantity	Pages	Price	Sales History
Heinrich Dieffenbach/MY PLANT WORLD		11/71			$7.95	6000
Jerry Powers/PUSHING DAISIES		6/74			7.95	4589
Carl Sauer/SEEDS, SPADES,..		4/69			12.50	1422 hard
					3.45	15488 paper
Preston/N. AMERICAN TREES		7/77 3/e			5.95	2018

Competitive Books from Other Publishers

Publisher	Title	Pub. Date		Pages	Price	Sales History
many!						

Marketing Department (evaluation of publishing season, pricing for market, strategy for sales, costs, etc...)

Publicity [X]   Direct Mail [X]   Advertising [X]   Catalog [X]   Review Distr. [X]

I would recommend a first printing of 7500 and a list price of $6.95 with a trade discount.

This title is in a highly competitive market. While we might reasonably hope for a three-year sale of 10,000-15,000, we shouldn't count on it.

Marketing activities would be directed to the trade, with special emphasis on many reviews and moderate advertising. We will use our status as a university press to emphasize that this is an authoritative, though not stuffy, handbook.

It is unlikely that we would try to sell this title through the mail, although we might consider inserting inquiry/order cards into two related titles:
Preston/NORTH AMERICAN TREES, and Sauer/SEEDS, SPADES...

Marketing Director   TLM   Date 12/8/76

The MIT Press
Publishing Proposal
Title Profitability Analysis

Author/Title Mulch/NO TIME FOR HOUSEPLANTS

Suggested List Price/Discount $6.95 T / 38%   Print Size 7500   Total Mfg Unit 1.42

SALES ESTIMATES Source	Avg. Disc.	Avg. Net	1st yr sales Copies	$	2nd yr sales Copies	$	3rd yr sales Copies	$
Wholesalers & Jobbers	42 %	$ 4.03	1000	$ 4030	400	$ 1612	200	$ 806
College & Univ. Bkstores	41 %	$ 4.10	800	$ 3280	500	$ 2050	350	$1435
Retail Bkstores	41 %	$ 4.10	1000	$ 4100	900	$ 3690	600	$2460
Direct Mail	-- %	$ 6.95	100	$ 695	100	$ 695	30	$ 209
Libraries	10 %	$ 6.26	100	$ 626	100	$ 626	30	$ 188
Other Domestic	-- %	$		$		$		$
Foreign -- UK	35 %	$ 4.52	300	$ 1356	300	$ 1356	140	$ 633
Foreign -- Other	35 %	$ 4.52	200	$ 904	200	$ 904	150	$ 678
TOTALS	38 %	$ 4.28	3500	$14991	2500	$10933	1500	$6408

S.O.P.

	1st Printing	2nd Printing
(5) Print size, incl. Comp. Copies	7500	
(6) Plant costs	$ 1997	
(7) Less SUBV	$	
(8) Total plant (6-7)	$ 1997	
(9) Edition cost	$ 8663	
(10) MFG cost (8 + 9)	$ 10630	
(11) Unit cost (10 ÷ 5)	$ 1.42	
(12) MFG breakeven units (10 ÷ 2)	1947 copies	
(13) Royalty adv. breakeven units 17 ÷ 2 (% R)	copies	

The MIT Press
Publishing Proposal
Editorial and Media

Author Mulch

Editorial (Discuss editorial problems, time allocation, costs, directions to author)

About 30. editorial hours. No unusual difficulties.

Managing Editor HO/rc   Date 12/8/76

Media

Estimates based on

Manuscript pages 200 To make Book pages 176 Trim 4x6
Front matter 3 Text 19 Notes Footnotes
Chapter end Book end Bibliography 8 Appendixes
Tables 10 Equations displayed In text
Extracts Captions Heads 1 2 3 4 To be drafted
Line drawings Camera ready
Halftones 38 Color
Special Characteristics
Design In Out Dummy, full, partial, none
Scaling
Format
Composition Flat Hot metal Cold
Camera ready Partial Camera copy
Offset Letterpress
Estimates no. of hours No. of months

Comments

7500

Plant Costs	
Design	
Drafting	
Composition @$6	1056
Alterations	106
Engravings/prints	--
Repros	304
C. & S. Ills. @$8	226
Blues	62
Jacket Comp	100
Dies	30
Contingencies 6%	113
TOTAL PLANT	1997

Edition Costs	
Makeready	248
Presswork	261
Paper	1457
Binding 75 M@ .62	4650
M@	
M@	
Jacket pw/paper	1650
Freight	300
Plates	67
Total Edition	8663
Total plant	1997
TOTAL COST	10630
TOTAL UNIT	1.42

Media Director _____   Date _____

The Massachusetts Institute of Technology Press

MASSACHUSETTS INSTITUTE OF TECHNOLOGY, CAMBRIDGE, MASSACHUSETTS 02142

Letter of Agreement

December 11, 1976

Purvis Mulch

Dear Purvis Mulch:

We welcome the addition of your Work tentatively entitled: NO TIME FOR HOUSE PLANTS

to our list on the terms and conditions which follow, and we look forward to its publication.

1   By this letter you grant and assign to us exclusively for our use or disposition throughout the world, in all languages, during the term of copyright in each respective country (and renewal copyright where available), all rights in the Work and every part thereof, and any revisions thereof which you may make, protectible under each such country's respective common law and statutory copyright, for all purposes and adaptations, and by all means and methods of distribution and communication, be these graphic, audio-visual, or otherwise.

2   Upon its publication we will undertake to procure copyright for your Work, and any revisions thereof which you may make, in the United States and in all member countries of the Universal Copyright Convention in either our own or your name; and in order to protect copyright for the renewal term in the United States, you appoint us or our designee as your attorney-in-fact with power of substitution to renew copyright in your name or in the name of your executors; and upon such renewal, the grants made to us are to continue during the renewal copyright term.

3   You warrant: (a)   that the Work is original and that you are the sole author and owner of the Work and have full power to make the grants to us;   (b)   that neither the Work nor any part has been published before, nor is any agreement with respect thereto presently outstanding (except as you may set out in a rider that is attached to this letter and signed by both of us);   (c)   that the Work contains no unlawful or libelous material and does not invade the right of privacy or infringe upon the common law or statutory rights of anyone. You will hold us, our licensees, and our distributees harmless and indemnify us and them against liabilities, judgments, or decrees against us and them and against expenses and attorneys' fees that may be incurred by us or them resulting from any claim, action, or proceeding alleging facts that constitute a breach of any warranty enumerated in this paragraph.

4   You agree to deliver to us in substance, content, form, and style satisfactory to The M.I.T. Press Board, on or before   December 1976   , time being of the essence, two clean and legible double-spaced typewritten copies of the complete manuscript of the Work, including double-spaced footnotes and references, illustrations, charts, etc., ready for the printer, without requiring redrawing or relettering. It being understood that the length of the manuscript shall be approximately   words and that illustrations and other supplementary material shall be as follows:

5   When galley and page proofs of the Work are submitted to you, you are to correct and return them to us promptly; if by any chance you do not return corrected proofs within sixty (60) days after our mailing them to you, we shall be free to proceed with the manufacture and publication of the Work without waiting for the return of the corrected proofs. If we decide to have the proofs read and corrected by another because of your delay, then the expense incurred in that connection is to be charged to your royalty account. If, when correcting the galley or page proofs, alterations are required by you, or by us because of your delay in correcting them, and such alterations cost us more than 10% of the cost of original composition, then you will pay us or we will charge to your royalty account at our option such excess within thirty (30) days after we furnish you with a statement of such excess cost. If we request an index in connection with your Work, you are to deliver the copy for the index to us within   14   days after final page proofs are mailed to you. If you fail to deliver the index as requested, you authorize us to have the index copy prepared by another, and the cost of such preparation will be charged to your royalty account. If permissions are necessary in order to publish the Work, you will undertake to acquire them for us at your expense.

6   As soon as practical after receipt of the final and complete manuscript, and after formal approval of the Work by the M.I.T. Press Board, we will publish the Work in the English language at our own cost and expense in such manner and style and at such price as appears to us best suited for the sale of the Work, and we will reprint the Work as long as in our judgment demand justifies.

7   We will pay to you during the continuance of this agreement on our actual cash receipts the following royalties on our sales (less returns and refunds) of the Work as published by us:

a   No royalty shall be paid to you on the sale of the first   copies of any hard-bound edition;

b   10   % on sales of the first/next   3000   copies of any hard-bound edition;

    12.5 % on sales of the next   3000   copies of any hard-bound edition;

    % on sales of the next   copies of any hard-bound edition;

    15 % on all additional sales of this edition, in each case with respect to sales in the continental United States of America;

and on sales outside the continental United States, two-thirds thereof, respectively.

c   One-half the hard-bound royalty schedule (7b) shall be paid on sales of any paperback edition if published by us.

d   Five percent (5%) on all sales outside regular bookstore channels, by mail or coupon or other special solicitation advertising, in lieu of any other royalty.

e   The prevailing English-language hard-bound or paperback royalties shall be paid on sales of any translation published by us after first recouping the cost of the translation.

f   Ten percent (10%) of the amount we receive shall be paid on copies, bound or in sheets, sold for export at discounts of 50% or more.

g   Fifty percent (50%) from licensing by us to others to exercise any right in the Work protectible by copyright, after first recouping any costs incurred by us to effect the license.

h   In the event the Work is included in an omnibus edition and no specific sum is fixed for the use of this Work, we will fix a pro rata reasonable sum therefor, fifty percent (50%) of which will be your share.

i   We expect to distribute free copies of the Work for promotion of sales, review, advertising, samples, or like purposes; in such cases, and on copies furnished (or sold) to you, or damaged copies, no royalties shall be payable.

j   If at any time after two years from date of first publication of the Work, we find we are overstocked and sell your Work at reduced prices, either at retail or at wholesale, then the rate of royalty of such sales shall be calculated at five percent (5%) of our actual receipts from the sales, but if on such copies sold our receipts are less than our manufacturing cost, no royalty shall be payable, and no such royalty shall in any event reduce our receipts to less than our manufacturing cost.

8   Royalty statements and royalty payments in accordance with such statements will be made for each of our royalty years ending March 31 and will be mailed to you on or before the following thirtieth of June, except that, if the amount due you is less than $15.00, no payment will be required of us until a subsequent period ending March 31st when the amount has reached $15.00.

9   We will present to you   5   copies of your Work on publication by us. If you require additional copies for your own personal use, and not for resale, we will supply them to you at our wholesale price.

10   You grant permission for the use of your name, picture, and biographical data in connection with the distribution and publicizing of the Work and the exercise of other rights granted in paragraph 1 of this letter.

11   Any notice which either of us may desire to give to the other will be sufficient if addressed by prepaid certified or registered mail to our respective addresses above shown, or as last appearing on our records, or to such other place as either of us may designate by certified or registered mail notice to the other. Galley proofs and page proofs, statements, and remittances may be sent by ordinary mail. We should be addressed as The M.I.T. Press, Massachusetts Institute of Technology, Cambridge, Massachusetts 02142.

12   When requested by us, you are to revise the latest edition of the Work and provide us with any new matter necessary from time to time to keep the Work current and up to date. If for any reason you fail to do so, we may engage some other person or persons for that purpose and may deduct the cost of such revisions from royalties accruing to you on subsequent editions. If the revisions are made by others, such fact will be set forth in the revised edition. For all purposes the revised material will be deemed part of the original Work, except that the royalty provision on sales shall be calculated as if the revised Work were a new Work, unless the new material is less than 25% of the original Work.

13   As long as this contract is in force between us, it is understood that you may not contract for publication of a work that is competitive with the Work which is the subject of this agreement, unless our written consent is first obtained.

14   In order that there may be no misunderstanding between us, there are to be no amendments to this agreement unless in writing signed by both of us. All the rights granted to us under this agreement shall inure to us and our respective successors, assignees, licensees, and permittees. (Your interest in royalties hereunder may be assigned, but only as a whole, and no such assignment shall be binding upon us until you have first given us in writing due notice and evidence thereof.)

15.   The Press agrees to pay the cost of all alterations in galley proof made by the Author or his agent and varying from the manuscript as accepted for typesetting, up to an amount equal to ten (10) percent of the original cost of composition of the Work. Any amount in excess of the above allowance will be paid by the Author.

If the foregoing correctly reflects the agreement between us, will you please sign two copies in the place indicated below and return one to us within   7   days of the date hereof; upon your so doing, we will both be bound by the foregoing terms as an agreement.

Sincerely yours,

MASSACHUSETTS INSTITUTE OF TECHNOLOGY

by _____
Director, The M.I.T. Press

Accepted this ___15th___ day of ___December___, 19_____

PUBLISHING LOG (Board approved titles not yet turned over)
Season: Late Fall 1977
Routing date: 12/8/76

Author/TITLE	Board approved	contract signed	MS delivery projected	(MS) type	pp/ illust.	turnover projected
Editor: BHA						
Killian/SPUTNIK	12/8/76	pending	2/77	ms	300/10	2/15/77
Weaver/DECISION TO PROSECUTE	6/5/76	7/2/76	2/28/76	ms	250/0	3/5/77
Nelson/ZONING	3/11/76	3/20/76	4/15/77	most cc	175/18	4/20/77
Horowitz/SCIENCE, SIN...	1/8/76	2/1/76	2/15/77	ms	150/0	2/20/77
Greenberg/UNIVERSALS 2/e	1/74	2/74	3/15/77	cc+ms	218/0	3/10/77
Editor: FG						
Castells/URBAN QUESTION	7/6/76	8/10/76	books 9/1/77	import	215/27	to launch 1/77
Carr/PLANNING CITIES	12/8/76	pending	2/77	ms	350/30	2/15/77
Frieden/NEIGHBORHOODS	4/17/76	5/1/76	12/15/76	ms	400/22	12/20/76
Mulch/NO TIME FOR HOUSE PLANTS	12/8/76	pending	inhouse	ms	176/38	12/15/76
Editor: ABE						
Graves/RELATIVITY revised	10/71 & 11/8/76	1/72	new 3/1/77	ms+cc	180/9	3/5/77
Huxley/CRAYFISH	6/5/76	9/1/76	12/10/76	ms	360/30	12/12/76
Neyman/COPERNICUS	12/8/76	pending	2/7/77	ms	200/15	2/15/77
Shrock/GEOLOGY AT MIT	6/5/76	8/1/76	1/15/77	ms	400/0	1/25/77
Editor: FPS						
Harvey/ENVIRONMENT	11/8/76	pending	books 9/1/77	import	200/0	to launch 2/77
Hill/POWER GENERATION	8/1/76	9/16/76	2/1/77	ms	215/6	2/15/77
Kerrebrock/AIRCRAFT ENGINES	12/75	3/76	3/77	part cc	180/10	3/5/77
Wilson/ENERGY DEMAND STUDIES	10/5/76	11/6/76	2/1/77	ms	160/15	2/15/77
Zucker/CRISIS	7/6/76	8/3/76	1/15/77	ms	200/0	1/20/77

FINANCIAL PROJECTION

Date 12/8/76

Author/TITLE Mulch/NO TIME FOR HOUSEPLANTS Editor Greenhouse

Binding hard Size 4x6 Est. # bk pgs 176 Subject Area Botany

Suggested list price/discount $6.95 T Net price $4.28

Estimated print run 7500 Subsidy amount ___ Source ___

Estimated annual sales: 1st yr 3500 2nd yr 2500 3rd yr 1500 TOTAL 7500

	1978	1979	1980	TOTAL	% sales
1. Income	14991	10933	6408	32332	
Variable & Title-Related Costs					
2. Plant costs net of subsidy (Plant unit .27)	1997			1997	
3. Manufacturing cost of sales (Edition unit 1.15)	8633			8633	
4. Royalty expense	1499	1367	961	3827	
5. Complimentary copies	142			142	
6. Direct Title Promotion	500			500	
7. Total 2 thru 6	12771	1367	961	15099	
8. Contribution to Press Overhead (1-7)	2220	9566	5447	17233	
Shared Operating Expense					
9. Acquisitions	1700			1700	
10. Editorial	600			600	
11. Production	425			425	
12. Design	785			785	
13. Basic Marketing	3000	225	240	3465	
14. Fulfillment	2500	1500	1000	5000	
15. G&A Allocation	1050	270	290	1610	
16. Total Operating Expense (9 thru 15)	10060	1995	1530	13585	
17. Cost Inflation Adjustments 7%		139	214	353	
18. Total Shared Expense (16 + 17)	10060	2134	1744	13938	
NET PROFIT/(LOSS) (8-18)	(7840)	7432	3703	3295	

NET PRESENT VALUE/DISCOUNTED CASH FLOW ANALYSIS

	Prepub. yrs. 1977	Year 1 1978	Year 2 1979	Year 3 1980	TOTAL
Revenues					
1. Est. Sales Receipts		14991	10933	6408	32332
2. Subvention					
3. Total Revenues		14991	10933	6408	32332
Expenditures					
4. Author Advances/(Recovery)		1499	1367	961	2837
5. Royalty Expense	1997				1997
6. Plant Costs		8633			8633
7. Edition Costs		500			500
8. Direct Title Promotion					
9. Total Shared Expense (18 above)	4560	5500	2134	1744	13938
10. Total Expenditures	6557	16132	3501	2705	28895
Net Annual Cash Inflow/(Outflow) (3-10)	(6557)	(1141)	7432	3703	3437
Discount Factor @ 10 %	1.10	1.00	.909	.826	--
Net Present Value	(7212) 1.21	(1141)	6755	3058	1460

MIT PRESS

NEW PUBLICATION INFORMATION SHEET

Author or Editor ___ Purvis Mulch ___
Title (tentative) ___ NO TIME FOR HOUSEPLANTS ___
Title (final) ___

☒ Hard ☐ Paper   ☒ Press-owned ☐ Commission/Distrib. ☐ Import   Disc: Short ☐ Trade ☒ ☐ Text ☐
Discipline code ___ SD144 ___   Product line ___ Humanities ___   Series Ed. ___
Subsidy $ ___   Source ___   Contract date ___ 12/15/76 ___
Permissions cleared? ___ yes ___   Date ms. rec'd ___ 12/18/76 ___   Board approved ___ 12/12/76 ___   Series and Series No. ___
Translation required? ___ no ___   Trans. est cost $ ___   2nd copy ms.? ___ yes ___   charged to ___ author ___
                                                              Actual cost $ ___   How to be charged ___

Special sales anticipated ___
Royalties ☒ Net ☐ List   10 % 0 to 3000
                          12.5 % 3M to 6000   Payable to ☒ Author   Ed. override ___ % (Net or List)
                          15 % ___ to thereafter   — Other   Royalty advances ___

Remarks: ___

Acquisitions Ed. ___ Greenhouse ___   Date ___ 12/19/76 ___

Manuscript Data (Editorial Breakdown)
Type: (ms)/cc/pcc   207

Ms pages		No. Items		Illustrations	58		Scheduled dates
FM	13	tables	13	no. line drawings			1/15/77 edit, complete
text		lists		☐ camera-ready			1/21/? au, check complete
notes	9	equations	4	☐ draw and chg. auth.	all		ms to Prod.
bibliography	15	notes		no. halftones	38		Editor assigned
appendixes		extracts		no. in color (line ☐ HT)			☐ by freelance
Total ms pp.	207	legends					Cost: Est. 600 Actual $
		1 heads	3				Hours: Est. 30 Actual $
		2 heads					Proofreading ☐ None ☒ Editor
		3 heads	60				☐ Freelance
		4 heads					Index ☒ Author ☐ Freelance ☐ None
							Chg. to ☒ Royalty ☐ Plant

Remarks: ___

Managing Ed. ___   Date ___

Production and Design
Trim size ___ 6x8 ___   Total est. pp. ___ 176 ___   Design ☒ In-house ☐ Freelance   Cost Est $425 Actual $
Dummy ☐ Full ☒ Partial ☐ None ☐ Freelance   Cost Est $ Actual $ ___   Freelance chg. to: ___
Scaling: ☒ In-house ☐ Freelance   Cost Est $ Actual $ ___
Type comp: ☒ filmset ☐ hot metal ☐ cold type ☐ camera copy   ☐ in-house composition
Remarks: $M #425 production cost
         $M ?85 design cost

Design Mgr. ___   Date ___   Production Mgr. ___ DW ___   Date ___

APPROVAL OF MS. RELEASE TO COMPOSITION
Tentative Print Schedule
Print ___
Bind ___
Tentative Price ___
Director ___

APPROVAL OF FINAL PRICE AND PRINT QUANTITY
Final Print Schedule
Print ___   Hard ☐ Paper ☐
Bind ___   Discount Cat. ___
Final Price ___
Director ___   Date ___

Manufacturing Cost Estimates

Date of Estimate ___
Book Specifications at:

	Board		Launch	
Ms. pages	200		207	
Illustrations	38		38	
Book pages	176		176	
Trim size	4x6		4/8 × 8	
Type composition	VIP		VIP	
Est. comp. cost	1997		1997	

	Unit	Total	Unit	Total
Print 350 ☒ 75 (H) Plant	.27	1997	.27	1997
Edition	1.15	8633	1.15	1633
Total	1.42	10630	1.42	10630
Print ☐ Bind ☐ (H) Plant			50	1097
Edition			.24	4451
Total			.71	6451

Financial Projections
Sales copies (3 years) ___ 7500 ___
Suggested list price ___ 6.95 T ___   38%
Average discount ___
NET RECEIPTS ___ 32332 ___
Less controllable ___ 8633 ___
Royalties ___ 38.27 ___
CONTRIBUTION MARGIN ___ 19872 ___
Plant Expense (Net of SV) ___ 1997 ___
Free copies & spoilage ___ 142 ___
Direct promotion ___ 500 ___
NET CONTRIBUTION to OH ___ 17233 ___
Acquisition expense ___ 1700 ___
Editorial ___ 600 ___
Production ___ 425 ___
Design ___ 785 ___
Basic Marketing ___ 5000 ___
Fulfillment ___ 1610 ___
G&A Allocation ___ 13585 ___
Total Operating ___ 3648 ___
NET PROFIT/(LOSS) ___
CM% ___ 11.3% ___
Return on Sales ___

Acquisitions Department
Suggested Price ___ 6.95 T ___
Suggested Quantity ___ 7500 ___
Maximum Price ___ 8.95 T ___
← Sales Estimate ___ 7500 ___
Remarks: ___

Marketing Department
Suggested Price ___ 8.95 ___
Suggested Quantity ___ 4000 ___
Sales Estimate ___ 35700 ___
Remarks: Print 4000 and against 3500

Financial Approval ___
Date ___

MANUSCRIPT TURNOVER: EDITORIAL SPECIFICATIONS

Trim size 5-3/8 x 8 **

Cover X hard ____ paper ____ other

Docket: ____ Total MS pages: 200 Total book pages: 176 (est)

Turnover: 200 176 (est)

** this trim size may change after design has had a chance to look more carefully at material.

PERMISSIONS

File ____ copies with manuscript
____ missing

Charge to:
____ author royalty
____ book
____ other

FRONTMATTER
(in addition to title, copyright, and contents):
____ halftitle
____ frontispiece
____ series list
____ dedication
____ foreword
  8 preface

PROOF/MS CHECK

Author to check ____ edited MS XX galley proof XX page proof ____ other

Extra galleys needed: amount ____ by ____ for ____
Index XX author ____ other ____ charge to ____ au. royalty ____ book
Reference style (scholarly field) ____

Editorial Suggestions from Acquisition Editor:

The manuscript may need some copy-editing and probably some substantive editing, especially in the first parts.

Editorial Department Comments

(At launch): ____ level of difficulty ____ no. hours ____ freelance ____ in-house

Managing Editor ____
Date 12/20/76

IMPORTS

Foreign pub. price ____
Foreign pub. date ____
MIT territory ____

____ flat sheets ____ bound books
____ folded & gathered ____ jacketed
         sheets
Foreign publisher ____
Co-publisher ____

TRANSLATIONS

From ____
MIT trans. $ ____ charge: ____ manufacturing ____ other
Original publisher ____
Original provided? ____ yes ____ no
Translator's name & address ____

Co-publisher ____

CAMERA-READY MS
____ complete
____ running heads required
____ folios required
____ display composition required
____ drafting required
____ other

Author's alterations 10 % by contract

7/30/76 THE MIT PRESS TURNOVER FORM

PUB DATE WANTED Fall 1977 MS turnover date 12/20/76

XX New title ____ hard XX paper   Type of book: Acq. Ed. Greenhouse/ajk
____ Paperback number ____   XX Trade   ISBN # ____ (hard)
____ Translation ____   ____ Professional ISBN # ____ (paper)
____ Import ____   ____ Text   Series ____
____ Camera-ready ____   Board Approved '18/76   Series Ed. ____
____ Revision ____   Contract Signed 11/21/76

Principal Author/XXXX Purvis Mulch

Address ____
Telephone: Office ____
           Home ____

Title NO TIME FOR HOUSEPLANTS
Subtitle A Busy Person's Guide to Indoor Gardening
Copyright: XX MIT ____ author ____ other

TERMS
Royalty   XX net ____ list
           10 % to 300C
           12½% XX on next 3000   Editorial override royalty ____ net ____ list
           15 % thereafter   ____ % paid to ____
Paid to XX author ____ other   Total Advance Royalty: $ ____
Subvention $ -- ____ from ____   Date ____
Guaranteed sales # ____ @ ____ from ____

Brief description of content, market, and desired pub date:

This is a simple, comprehensive guide to growing and caring for indoor plants. It will be thoroughly and charmingly illustrated, and cover every conceivable aspect of this subject in a lucid but conversational style. As such, this book will be immensely salable to a wide variety of readers -- indeed, anyone who likes plants will want this book, and at $6.95 it will be quite a bargain. It is suggested that the book be ready by Spring 1978 to catch the yearly surge of interest in growing things.
This book will be an excellent entree for us into bookstores.

Acquisition Editor Greenhouse/ajk (Hack)
Date 12/20/76

Director ____
Date ____

MANUSCRIPT TURNOVER: MARKETING SPECIFICATIONS

	Acquisitions	Marketing (to be filled in at Launch)
Suggested price	$ 6.95	$ 6.95
Suggested Discount	T	T
Suggested Primary Market	___ Professional	___ Professional
	xx Trade	xx Trade
	___ Text	___ Text
Suggested Sales Estimate:	3500 # 1st year sales	2500 # 1st year sales
	2500 # 2nd year sales	2000 # 2nd year sales
	1500 # 3rd year sales	1500 # 3rd year sales
	TOTAL 7500	TOTAL 6000

LIST OF PRIMARY MARKET SPECIFCS (professional organizations, names of courses and enrollments, lists available, etc.)

Trade market, mainly bookstore sales. This effort should be directed through jobbers.

Comparable/Competitive Books Author/TITLE	Publisher (if different)	Pub Date	Price	Sales History
Cruso/MAKING THINGS GROW	Maple	7/77 (3/e)	5.95T	2018
Time/Life LIBRARY OF GARDENING T/L		h&p 1969	12.50, 3.45	1422 + 15488
Preston/N. AMERICAN TREES				
Sauer/SEEDS, SPADES...				

Suggested space advertising:

Any mass media newspapers, magazines, etc. Perhaps concentrating on women's magazines, Apartment Living, Pleasing Plants, and a variety of general-circulation media. We should stretch a $500 budget.
Suggested reviewers/journals:
See above.

MARKETING DEPARTMENT COMMENTS (at Launch meeting by Marketing Manager):

Design should reflect the authority of this university press book without seeming forbidding or too scholarly. Book club possibilities should be investigated thoroughly.

Marketing Manager TM
Date 12/20/76

MANUSCRIPT TURNOVER: DESIGN SPECIFICATIONS

ILLUSTRATIONS	# Line B/W	# HFT B/W	# Comb. L/HFT/BW	# Line Color (2-3-4)	#HFT Color
Camera-ready by author		38			

Camera-ready by author except for labeling

To be redrawn by us from roughs: suggestion to draft about 30 line drawings of plants

Use film from present edition (but if camera-ready art is available, list above)

List missing illustrations, itemized as above, with date due

SUGGESTED DESIGN (comparable book, etc.) _____

Suggested typeface/size/leading _____

Notes: ___ foot page ___ end chapter ___ end book
Jacket: ___ yes X no Suggested theme PRINTED COVER OVER BOARDS

PRODUCTION/DESIGN ANALYSIS AT LAUNCH (by Media Department at Launch)

# MS pages	Est. # Book Pages	Trim Size	# Illustrations	Composition	Est. Unit Costs
207	176	5-3/8x8 upright	38 ht's supplied (supplementary 30 line drawings to be drafted)	VIP (on in-house system)	4000 @ 1.74 5000 @ 1.60 7500 @ 1.42

Estimated time from editorial complete to bound book 7 months.

COMMENTS FROM MEDIA:

This manuscript seems to present few unusual problems to production/design. The typesetting is very straightforward. Because of the number of illustrations (38 halftones and about 30 to 50 line drawings to be drafted to correspond to text) and their importance to the text, we will get galleys, provide a dummy, and then see pages. Projected manufacturing time from edited ms in production until bound books is about seven months.

The above costs are based on a 5-3/8 x 8 format. This may change after Design has had a chance to look more carefully at the material. Also, the above costs are based on printers scales and could therefore change when we get actual costs from outside based on a real format and castoff.
PJM.
production
12/30/77

Media Director _____
Date 1-20-

MARKETING PLAN by Acquisition Editor   -- Flora Greenhouse

Author/Editor: Purvis Mulch

Title: NO TIME FOR HOUSEPLANTS: A Busy Person's Guide to Indoor Gardening
(Series)

List: Fall 1977   Pub. date: October 1977

List Price: Hard $6.95 (T)   Print size: (Trim 4x6
             Paper   Hard   7500
                                            Paper

I. Conceptual Outline of Book

This is a simple, comprehensive guide to growing and caring for indoor plants.
The book consists of seven chapters. The first three describe the basic needs
of house plants -- soil, water, containers, air, light, etc. -- and give
sound, easily understood suggestions on how to meet them.

After these introductory chapters come several specialized sections on
foliage plants, cacti & succulents, flowering plants, and special gardens
such as terraria, kitchen gardens, and dish gardens. Mulch provides a wealth
of usable material on these plants. One unique characteristic of this manuscript is the use of boxed special supplements to introduce more advanced or
specialized data on "The ABC's of Artificial Light," "Plants for Cool
Conditions," etc.

The book will appeal to plant lovers, more particularly to aspiring plant
lovers -- those who enjoy looking at, living and working among houseplants,
but who are either mystified by the process of care and feeding or misinformed
about time and techniques. The book presents a genuinely new approach to
keeping houseplants and will appeal to a significant part of a large but
amorphous market. We can expect an appealing layout from the Design Department
and an accessible text. The key to success will be getting this book on
the shelves in bookstores.

II. Primary Market Focus

Retail bookstores, college bookstores, wholesaler and jobber accounts.

III. Marketing Functions

1. Direct Mail. The book should be featured as a special item of
interest in all of the 8 subject matter catalogs and in season catalogs.
There should be some interest among the many people receiving these
catalogs, enough (it is hoped) to generate noticeable results. It'll be
an interesting experiment -- is there some correlation between purchasers
of professional and scholarly books, and plant lovers? No other direct
mail program is planned.

2. Catalogs. The book will be featured in the Fall general catalog for both
the domestic and London markets.

3. Space Ads. A budget of $500 has been allocated for specialty journals
like Apartment Life, Apartment World, Plants Alive, Happy Houseplants,
Plants & Gardens, Better Homes & Gardens, Avant Gardener,...

4. International Promotion. Graham reports that there will be excellent
opportunities to sell in London if we can keep the price down.

5. Publicity. We have allocated at least 100 copies for distribution to
reviewers in newspapers, popular magazines, and book review services. We
should explore local possibilities in some of the gardening programs.
Author might be willing to make appearances on local TV.

6. Endorsements. In the Boston area we have Jim Crockett and Thalassa
Cruso -- both famous plant popularizers (and competition). Their names
would be nice to emblazon boldly on jacket and/or ad, with a few kind words
from each.

7. Exhibits. ABA, Globe Book Fair, CBA, other general exhibits.

8. Subsidiary Rights. Excerpts in McCalls, Better Homes? (The boxes
lend themselves to magazine features.)

9. Field Sales. This should be the focus of our activity and we should
attempt to place about 1500 copies through college bookstores, retail
bookstores, and wholesaler and jobber accounts.

Launch report
12/30/76
Mulch/NO TIME FOR HOUSEPLANTS
Production/Design analysis

Ms.pages	Est.book pages	Trim size	Illustrations	Composition	Est.unit costs
207	176	5-3/8x8 upright	38 supplied (supplementary to be drafted)	VIP (on the in-house system)	4000 @ 1.74 5000 @ 1.60 7500 @ 1.42

General comments

This manuscript seems to present few unusual problems to production/design. The typesetting is very straightforward. Because of the number of illustrations and their importance to the text, we will get galleys, provide a dummy, and then see pages. Projected manufacturing time from edited manuscript in production until bound books is about seven months.

The above costs are based on a 5-3/8 x 8 format. This may change after Design has had a chance to look more carefully at the material. Also, the above costs are based on printer's scales and could therefore change when we get actual costs from outside based on a real format and castoff.

Launch Report
30 December 1976

No Time for House Plants: A Busy Person's Guide to Indoor Gardening, by Purvis Mulch,

Description: The author states in his preface that the book is "a guide to raising house plants for people who have no time to raise house plants." The opening chapters of the text discuss the basic needs of house plants--soil, water, containers, air, light, etc. Subsequent chapters deal with foliage plants, cacti and succulents, flowering plants, and unusual kinds of gardening. Special supplements illustrate more problematic topics such as the use of artificial light, special growing conditions, vines and trailing plants, large-tubbed specimens, etc. The simple, well-illustrated text makes the book a handy reference for all plant growers and will help them "to achieve house plant success without really working at it."

Contents: 12 pp. frontmatter, including half title, title, copyright, preface, content, symbols
            133 pp. text, including 7 chapters
                      31 no. 1 heads
                      19 no. 2 heads
                      80 no. 3 heads
                      13 lists
                       2 tables
                       4 notes (page end)
             38 pp. half tones with captions
             15 pp. special boxes (appendixes)
              9 pp. bibliography
             ____
            207 total manuscript pages

Comments: Manuscript appears to be in good shape. It will require light copy editing. Design will have to pay special attention the the "special boxes"; these should possibly be handled as appendixes. No text references are included for the thirty-eight figures.

Level of Difficulty: 3

Editorial Hours: 30

	bound books	notes
Allen/MANAGING THE FLOW OF TECHNOLOGY	July 1977	
Beck/HEMATOLOGY h & pb	July	
Preston/NORTH AMERICAN TREES rev'd	July	
Newman/MARINE HYDRODYNAMICS	August 1977	
SIPRI 1977	August	
Taylor/INTERNAL COMBUSTION ENGINE I & II	August	
WAES II & III	August	
Bathe/FORMULATIONS & COMPUTATIONAL ALGORITHMS	September 27 1977	
Bekefi & Barret/ELECTROMAGNETIC WAVES	September 15	
Bhagwati/NEW INTERNATIONAL ECONOMIC ORDER	September 16	
Bronowski/SENSE OF THE FUTURE	September 21	
Castells/URBAN QUESTION	September 15	
Douglass/HUMID LAND FORMS	September 29	
Fienberg/CROSSCLASSIFIED DATA	September 27	
Harvey & Hallet/ENVIRONMENT AND SOCIETY	September 27	
Hill/TOWER GENERATION	September 27	
Ivanaga/EDM	September 27	
Killian/SPUTNIK	September 19	
Mabbutt/DESERT LANDFORMS	September 29	
Nelson/ZONING	September 16	
Newman/COPERNICUS pb	September 28	
Shrock/GEOLOGY AT MIT	September 2	
Cantore/ATOMIC ORDER pb	October 4 1977	
Graves/RELATIVITY THEORY pb	October 7	
Greep & Koblinsky/FRONTIERS IN REPRODUCTION	October 23	
Huxley/CRAYFISH pb	October 7	
Kerrebrock/AIRCRAFT ENGINES	October 21	
Lynch/GROWING UP IN CITIES	October 3	
Mulch/NO TIME FOR HOUSEPLANTS	October 14	
Sherman/"MAMMALIAN EMBRYOGENESIS	October 28	
Solomon/HOUSING THE URBAN POOR pb	October 4	
Weaver/DECISION TO PROSECUTE	October 11	
Zucker/CRISIS IN ISRAEL pb	October 28	

Mulch/NO TIME FOR HOUSE PLANTS

Board approved 12/8/76
Contract signed 12/15/76
Turned over 12/20/76
Acq. Ed. FG

Author/TITLE 12/30/76
updates on:

	LAUNCH	2/1	3/1	4/1	6/1	8/1	9/1	FINAL
Edit. Complete	1/15/77	1/31						1/31
Design Samples	1/15	2/5						2/5
Release								
To Comp.	2/1	2/21	2/28					2/28
Galleys In	3/1	3/21	4/1	4/15				4/15
Galleys Out	3/15	4/7	4/15	6/1				6/1
Pp In	4/15	5/7	5/15	6/1	6/15			6/15
Pp Out	5/15	6/15	6/15	7/1	6/30			6/30
Mech./Repro In	6/1	6/21	7/1	7/15	7/5	7/30		7/30
To Manu.	6/15	7/7	7/15	8/1	7/15	8/15		8/15
Bound Books	9/1	9/21	10/1	10/15	10/1	11/1	10/14	10/14

COMMENTS: 12/30 - priority book! 1/1 - schedule OK. 3/1 - edited MS
late - author delay. 3L - MS late to comp, design pile up.
4/1 - galleys late - supplier overload. 5/1 - schedule OK.
6/1 - pages late. 7/1 - schedule OK 8/1 - repro delayed
by index. 10/1 - on schedule.

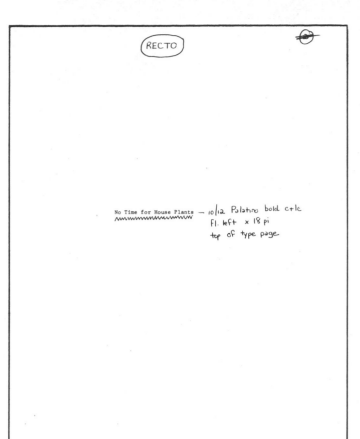

RECTO

No Time for House Plants — 10/12 Palatino bold c+lc
fl. left x 18 pi
top of type page

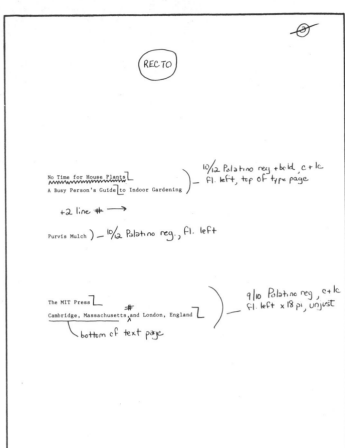

RECTO

No Time for House Plants
A Busy Person's Guide to Indoor Gardening — 10/12 Palatino reg + bold, c + lc
fl. left, top of type page

+2 line # →

Purvis Mulch — 10/12 Palatino reg., fl. left

The MIT Press
Cambridge, Massachusetts and London, England — 9/10 Palatino reg, c + lc
fl. left x 18 pi, unjust
bottom of text page

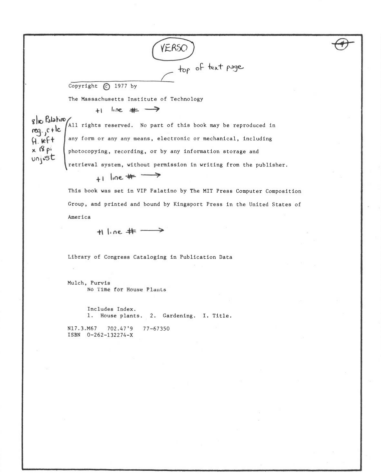

VERSO

top of text page

+1 line # →

Library of Congress Cataloging in Publication Data

Mulch, Purvis
    No Time for House Plants

    Includes Index.
    1. House plants. 2. Gardening. I. Title.

N17.3.M67   702.47'9   77-67350
ISBN 0-262-132274-X

8/10 Palatino reg., c + lc fl. left x 18 pi unjust

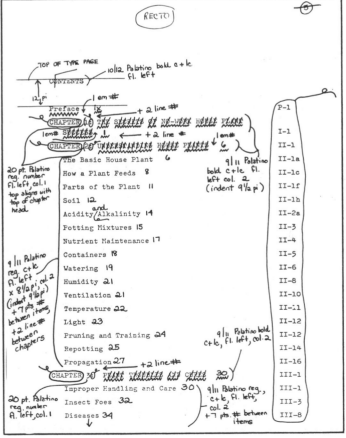

RECTO

TOP OF TYPE PAGE

CONTENTS — 10/12 Palatino bold c + lc fl. left

12 pi

+2 line #
1 em #
+2 line #
1 em #
+2 line #

20 pt. Palatino reg. number fl. left, col. 1 top aligns with top of chapter head

9/11 Palatino c + lc fl. left, col. 2 x 8 1/2 pi (indent 9 1/2 pi) + 7 pts # between items +2 line # between chapters

9/11 Palatino bold c + lc fl. left col. 2 (indent 9 1/2 pi)

9/11 Palatino bold c + lc, fl. left, col. 2

20 pt. Palatino reg. number fl. left, col. 1

9/11 Palatino reg., c + lc, fl. left, col. 2 + 7 pts # between items

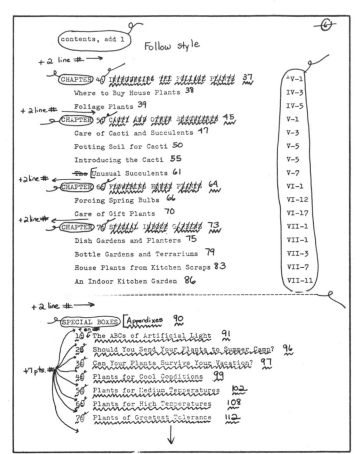

Follow style

+2 line #

CHAPTER 40 INTRODUCING THE FOLIAGE PLANTS 37 — IV-1
Where to Buy House Plants 38 — IV-3
Foliage Plants 39 — IV-5

+2 line #
CHAPTER 50 CACTI AND OTHER SUCCULENTS 45 — V-1
Care of Cacti and Succulents 47 — V-3
Potting Soil for Cacti 50 — V-5
Introducing the Cacti 55 — V-5
The Unusual Succulents 61 — V-7

+2 line #
CHAPTER 60 FLOWERING HOUSE PLANTS 64 — VI-1
Forcing Spring Bulbs 66 — VI-12
Care of Gift Plants 70 — VI-17

+2 line #
CHAPTER 70 SPECIAL INDOOR GARDENS 73 — VII-1
Dish Gardens and Planters 75 — VII-1
Bottle Gardens and Terrariums 79 — VII-3
House Plants from Kitchen Scraps 83 — VII-7
An Indoor Kitchen Garden 86 — VII-11

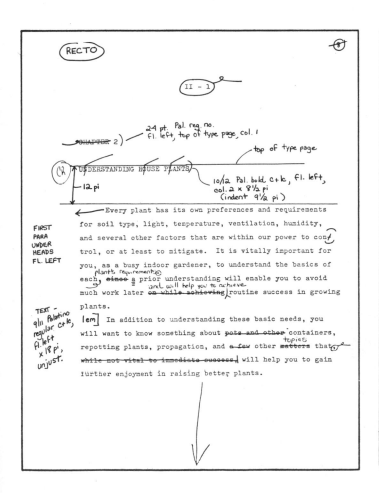

+2 line #
SPECIAL BOXES Appendixes 90
10 The ABCs of Artificial Light 91
20 Should You Send Your Plants to Summer Camp? 96
30 Can Your Plants Survive Your Vacation? 97
40 Plants for Cool Conditions 99
50 Plants for Medium Temperatures 102
60 Plants for High Temperatures 108
70 Plants of Greatest Tolerance 112

+7 pts. #

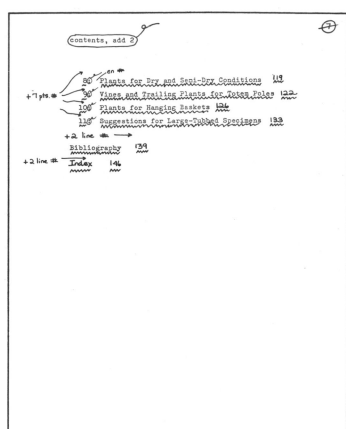

en #
+7 pts. #
80 Plants for Dry and Semi-Dry Conditions 119
90 Vines and Trailing Plants for Totem Poles 122
100 Plants for Hanging Baskets 126
110 Suggestions for Large-Tubbed Specimens 133

+2 line #
Bibliography 139

+2 line #
Index 146

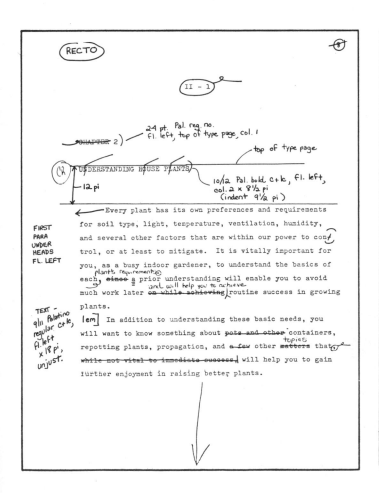

II - 1

CHAPTER 2 — 24 pt. Pal. reg. no. fl. left, top of type page, col. 1

UNDERSTANDING HOUSE PLANTS — top of type page

10/12 Pal. bold c+lc, fl. left, col. 2 × 8½ pi (indent 9½ pi)

12 pi

FIRST PARA UNDER HEADS FL. LEFT

Every plant has its own preferences and requirements for soil type, light, temperature, ventilation, humidity, and several other factors that are within our power to control, or at least to mitigate. It is vitally important for you, as a busy indoor gardener, to understand the basics of each plants requirements prior understanding will enable you to avoid much work later [on while achieving] and will help you to achieve routine success in growing plants.

TEXT — 9/11 Palatino regular c+lc, fl. left, × 18 pi, unjust.

[em] In addition to understanding these basic needs, you will want to know something about pots and other containers, repotting plants, propagation, and a few other topics that while not vital to immediate success will help you to gain further enjoyment in raising better plants.

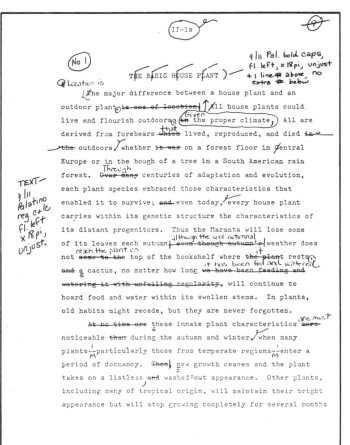

THE BASIC HOUSE PLANT — 9/11 Pal. bold caps, fl. left, × 18 pi, unjust +1 line # above, no extra # below

No 1

Location is

The major difference between a house plant and an outdoor plant is one of location. All house plants could live and flourish outdoors in the proper climate. Given All are derived from forebears which that lived, reproduced, and died in the outdoors whether it was on a forest floor in Central Europe or in the bough of a tree in a South American rain forest. Over many Through centuries of adaptation and evolution, each plant species embraced those characteristics that enabled it to survive; and even today, every house plant carries within its genetic structure the characteristics of its distant progenitors. Thus the Maranta will lose some of its leaves each autumn although the cool autumnal weather does not come to the top of the bookshelf where the plant rests it has been fed and watered and a cactus, no matter how long we have been feeding and watering it with unfailing regularity, will continue to hoard food and water within its swollen stems. In plants, old habits might recede, but they are never forgotten.

TEXT— 9/11 Palatino reg. c+lc fl. left × 18 pi, unjust.

At no time are these innate plant characteristics are most more noticeable than during the autumn and winter, when many plants—particularly those from temperate regions—enter a period of dormancy. Then new growth ceases and the plant takes on a listless and washed-out appearance. Other plants, including many of tropical origin, will maintain their bright appearance but will stop growing completely for several months

each year, thus emulating the natural rest periods of their
forebears. You will do well to watch for these signs of
dormancy and rest, and should respond to each plant's needs at
that time. When a plant enters a dormant or rest period,
water should be reduced and fertilizer withheld completely,
until new growth once again begins, usually in the late
winter or early spring. At that time, resume watering and fertilizing
in order to encourage the new growth. proper treatment of the
plant at this time will coincide with the advent of spring, and
will support the plant in carrying out its rhythmic cycles.

Some plants are naturally short-lived, and will
last no more than a year or two in your home despite
careful attention; their genetic structure dictates
a finite life span. Garden annuals, for instance, will
germinate, grow to maturity, flower, produce seeds, and die,
all in as little as six months. For this reason, very few
annuals are selected as house plants. Although a few short-
lived plants are cultivated indoors for their unusual characteristics, such as the Sensitive Plant which is easily
grown from seed, the house plants that we have cultivated
over the generations are most often those that will give
years of pleasure. Some house plants, in fact, live to be
hundreds of years old.

other house plants are attractive when young,

but grow ungainly or otherwise unattractive when they approach
maturity. The only plants of this kind I have chosen for
inclusion in this book are those that are very easy to propagate from cuttings; the parent plant may be discarded
after a year or two to be replaced by its children.
From the hundreds of thousands of plant species growing in the world,
those traditionally cultivated as house plants are the relatively few that have shown a wide tolerance to conditions of
heat, light, moisture, humidity, and ventilation—in other
words, those that can withstand a human environment. They
are both attractive to the eye and tough. However,
if we are looking for success with house plants—and particularly success without working hard at it—then we should spend
some time learning the characteristics of each plant, recognizing its individual needs, and fulfilling them to the best
of our ability.

No. 1   HOW A PLANT FEEDS

A plant manufactures nearly all of its own food and
not from the "plant food" that you buy for it. Commercial
plant food is no more than a combination of certain chemicals
(sometimes in an organic base) that are essential to the
plant's basic functioning, much as vitamins are essential to
human nutrition. But the bulk of a plant's food—the sugar
it uses for energy and growth—is manufactured by the plant
itself. In the presence of light, the leaves of the plant

draw carbon dioxide from the air and water from the roots,
converting them into sugar that is then used for energy
production or stored for future use.
During photosynthesis this sugar-manufacturing process is known as
photosynthesis several other processes are going on within the plant.
While carbon dioxide is absorbed, oxygen is re-
leased from the pores of the leaf surface. (Plants produce
not only most of the world's food, but most of its atmospheric
oxygen as well.) During the darkness hours, the entire process is
reversed; some of the atmosphere's oxygen is recaptured by
the plant and used to convert stored sugar to energy for
growth. Generally, a plant manufactures growth food during
the day and does its actual growing at night.

Often the plant converts its newly manufactured sugar
to starch and stores it, reconverting it to sugar as the
need arises. Although the starch can be stored in almost any
area of the plant, certain plants have developed specialized
storage areas. Cacti and succulents
The have enlarged stems and leaves of equip them with the greatest above-ground
storage capacity of any house plant
have developed underground storage apparatus for this purpose,
including bulbs, tubers, corms, and rhizomes. A bulb is (characteristic of hyacinths, tulips, and onions)
simply an enlarged underground bud. A tuber is nothing more than
an enlarged root; a common potato is a tuber, gloxinias, caladiums,
dahlias, and many other common plants are grown from tubers.

A corm is the enlarged base of a stem. a rhizome is
simply a laterally growing, enlarged, underground stem. Each
of these specialized structures is
used by the plant for food storage, and each can be used
to propagate new plants.
Water is constantly drawn up through the plant.
As it transpires through the stomata (pores) of the leaves,
a "pulling" action draws more water up through the roots.
The water carries with its mineral salts including all the
elements needed by the plant to carry out its complex chemical processes. The transpiration that takes place in the
leaves is similar to perspiration in humans and it serves a
similar purpose in cooling the plant. it is
difficult in house to notice this cooling effect, But plants;
however, the results of the process are
readily apparent when a group of large trees carry out
transpiration. The cool and fresh feeling you
enjoy in a thick woods in summer is not primarily the product
of the shade, but of the transpiration of the millions of
leaves overhead.

Because the capacity of
A plant cannot absorb too much water, its vessels
and cells is limited; how-
ever, the overwatering of a plant can exclude oxygen from
the root system, ironically causing wilting of the top portion
of the plant. When water is withheld, the plant's cells will
gradually collapse, causing wilting of the entire plant. All
plants do have protective mechanisms that conserve water in
times of drought, however, and all can withstand a temporary dry

spell. Most wilted house plants will quickly spring back to
a normal state when watering is resumed.

No.1 PARTS OF THE PLANT

No.2 Stem. The stem serves to support the plant and to contain and direct the vessels that transport water from the roots and food from the leaves to every other part of the plant. Most house plants, including Philodendron, Ivy, and Spider Plant, have soft stems. Such plants must either climb or crawl because their stems are not strong enough to support an upward-growing structure of significant height. Other plants have soft but thick stems that enable them to attain good height (susceptible to breakage). Woody-stemmed plants such as the Avocado, Poinsettia, and Boxwood, are far more sturdy and are usually derived from trees or shrubs of the temperate region. Canes are thick stems with hollow or pithy centers. Bamboo is an example of a cane familiar among house plants; Dieffenbachia and Ti Plant are good examples of cane.

Some plants have a distinct main stem while others send up many stems, none of which are dominant. A side shoot is a smaller stem growing out from the main stem. A petiole is a leaf stalk, the stem-like structure from which a leaf grows. A node is a joint on the main stem from which a leaf or side shoot grows.

No.2 Leaf. The major purpose of the leaf is, as we have

to manufacture food for the plant's growth and reproduction. Given its total mass, the leaf has a remarkably large surface area and is ideally designed for the efficient absorption and diffusion of gases through its thousands of stomata. Keeping in mind the basic functions of the leaf, its proper care is not difficult to appreciate. The stomata must be kept fairly clean, free of dust and oil that might hinder their efficient operation. Leaves must also be given easy access to light and ventilation according to the individual needs of each plant. Never crowd plants to a point where they are competing for light and air.

No.2 Roots. Roots serve two main purposes, to anchor the plant in the ground and to supply from the soil water and the mineral salts which accompany water. Bulbs, corms, rhizomes, and tubers serve much the same purposes while simultaneously acting as food storage areas. Roots, like the above-ground parts of plants, may be pruned without injuring the plant in any way. Roots are often trimmed to prevent a plant from growing too large for the convenience of the grower, just as top growth is cut back. If roots are cut back, however, top growth should be reduced by about the same percentage to assure that the reduced roots will be able to supply the plant with sufficient amounts of water. The major precaution in caring for roots is to avoid overwatering.

No.2 Flowers. The plant's flowers contain its sexual apparatus. Pollination occurs when male pollen is deposited onto female stigmata, thus fertilizing the plant and allowing the formation of seeds. The fruit of any plant is, in essence, the ovary that swells to protect the seeds. In nature, most plants produce flowers. For the purposes of cultivating house plants, only certain ones—which in this book are listed as flowering house plants—can be depended upon to produce, under home conditions, blossoms of sufficient size, profusion, and beauty to warrant our attention. The plants that we grow for their attractive foliage often cannot produce flowers indoors because of insufficient light or because of a pollination failure. In nature, pollen is transferred either by insects or wind. When indoor pollinization is essential, it can be accomplished by transferring the pollen from one flower to another, using a soft camel's hair brush. This process is described fully in most books devoted to flowering house plants.

No.1 SOIL

Since the house plant you bring home from the shop will already be rooted in soil, you might wonder why you have to consider this need at all. The answer is that your house plant will

someday need repotting, and you will want to provide it with a potting mixture that will serve its special needs. You might even wish to propagate some of your favorite house plants at some point, to share them with friends or to give them as gifts. In any case, a basic knowledge of potting mixtures and soils is essential to a complete understanding of all your plants. A clear understanding of two simple definitions will help here, to avoid confusion later. Soil, as mentioned here, refers to garden loam, that combination of mineral matter, organic matter, air, and water commonly found outside, in your garden or under your lawn. A potting mixture is soil combined with other materials such as sand, compost, peat moss, limestone, and bone meal; these together form an ideal environment for the roots of your house plants.

The easiest way to assure your plants of a perfect loam is to buy prepackaged, sterile potting soil from your garden or flower shop. This soil will have the proper texture and will also be free of disease organisms, insects (some are microscopic), and weed seeds. This loam, when combined with the other ingredients outlined above, will form an ideal potting mixture. You may also purchase packaged potting mixture at the store; however, the package should be read carefully to determine the ingredients included, making sure that the mixture is right for your plants.

It is, of course, far less expensive to make your own potting mixture from your own garden loam (free), sand (free or next to free), and small amounts of purchased ingredients. If you choose this route, it is important that you be able to make at least a cursory analysis of the garden loam that will form the basis of the potting mixture. Texture is important. A heavy clay soil will hold water for too long a time, thus encouraging disease and root rot, and it will bake cement-hard when dry. On the other hand, a coarse sand will not hold water well, nor will it hold nutrients long enough for the plant's roots to absorb them. Strive, then, for a happy medium, a good loam containing both clay and sand which will hold both water and nutrients, and will yet offer adequate drainage.

To this basic loam, we usually add one or more of the other ingredients--peat moss, to increase water-holding capacity and to add organic matter; compost, for organic matter and nutrients; sand, to open up the soil to air; and some form of supplemental mineral fertilizer, usually bone meal and lime. Chemical fertilizer can be used; however, it is not necessary to add such fertilizer to the potting mixture, since the other ingredients will supply all the nutrients the plant can use for several months.

ACIDITY AND ALKALINITY

A discussion of soils and potting mixtures would not be complete without some mention of acidity and alkalinity, and of the pH scale, which is the scientific measure for acidity and alkalinity. The midpoint on the pH scale is 7. A soil with a pH of 7 is neutral--neither acid nor alkaline. Numbers above 7 indicate an alkaline soil, those under 7, an acid soil. Most house plants (as well as most garden plants) will do best in a slightly acid soil (a pH of 6.0 to 7.0). Most garden soils are within this range, all the house plants discussed in this book will do well in this normal range unless special requirements are indicated.

If you are worried about your soil's pH level, or if you are simply curious, call your county agricultural agent and ask for directions on having a pH test made. The cost will be nominal. The acidity of any soil may be increased by the addition of peat moss, or decreased by the addition of ground limestone.

POTTING MIXTURES

There are as many different basic potting mixtures as there are plant experts--probably more. Perhaps the most common one (and one which can be trusted), calls for two parts loam, one part finely-screened compost (or a mixture of peat moss and compost), and one part builder's sand (not sea sand). A small amount of bone meal (about one teaspoon for a five-inch pot) and a pinch of ground limestone are added to this basic mixture. Other recommendations call for more of one ingredient and less of another. Do a little experimenting on your own; you will eventually determine your own favorite mixture, which you can then recommend to others. Now that you have a sense of basic mixture, we will consider the exceptions:

1. Acid-loving plants such as azaleas, camelias, gardenias, and heathers should have no lime. They should, in fact, have some form of acid organic matter--acid peat moss or oak leafmold.

2. Foliage plants need somewhat more compost in the mixture; half of it should be comprised of peat moss as it will not overstimulate the plant.

3. Fast-growing and hungry plants require more bone meal and lime because they use them up so quickly.

4. Some plants, such as cacti, succulents, and orchids, have very special soil requirements; these are mentioned later in the discussions of the individual plants.

NUTRIENT MAINTENANCE

The mineral nutrients contained in any fresh potting soil or mixture, whether it is home-made or a sterilized commercial brand, should be sufficient for your plant's needs for the first four to six months. After this initial period, you should begin to replenish those nutrients on a regular and carefully-measured basis.

All plants need substantial amounts of three elements-- nitrogen (N), phosphate (P_2O_5), and potash (K_2O), as well as lesser amounts of a dozen or more "trace minerals" or "trace elements." In grower's language, the three major elements are referred to as N, P, and K, the label of any commercial fertilizer includes the percentages of each given in N-P-K order. A 5-10-5 fertilizer, for instance, will contain 5 percent nitrogen, 10 percent phosphate, and 5 percent potash. A "balanced" fertilizer contains a balance of all three elements in the amounts needed for the proper growth of most plants. The fertilizer may be either a chemical or an organic preparation. The chemical varieties are quick-acting, easy to use, and tidy. Organic fertilizers, on the other hand, are slow to release their nutrients, thus providing a gentle and steady supply. These mixtures come in liquid, tablet, and even spray form (the last applied directly on the foliage). Organic fertilizers may be purchased commercially in balanced formulas (fish emulsion, made from fish wastes, is a popular one for house plant use) or may be made at home from a combination of ingredients. Blood meal is a good

choice for supplying substantial amounts of nitrogen (its NPK formula is 15.00-1.30-0.70), while bone meal (4.00-21.00-0.20) is good for phosphate, and wood ashes (0.00-1.50-7.00) are high in potash content. A combination of one part blood meal, one part bone meal, and two parts wood ashes will make a 5-6-4 formula, a good one for house plants.

How often should plants be fertilized? There is wide disagreement on this question, some experts believing in weekly feedings at full strength (the dosage recommended on the label), others suggest no more than once a month, during the winter. In the end, you will probably have to determine your own policy by way of experimentation. In the beginning, however, it is better to err on the conservative side, far more plants have been injured from overfertilization than from nutrient starvation. If you use a commercial chemical or organic formula, I suggest that you feed your plants as often as recommended on the label; however use only half the recommended dosage. (Manufacturers tend to overstate the need for their product.) If the plant shows a spurt of active growth in late winter or early spring, increase the dosage to the manufacturer's recommendation. During a dormant or rest period, withhold fertilizer entirely. If you are using a home-made organic fertilizer, use it sparingly at first. A level teaspoon of the blood meal/bone meal/ wood ash formula, applied monthly, should be plenty for a plant in a five-inch pot. You may also put some of the mixture in a bottle, fill the bottle with water, and use this "tea" to water your house plants. A mild tea solution, applied weekly, will give all your plants a continuing and gentle supply of the essential nutrients.

Finally, remember ~~never to apply~~ a chemical fertilizer should never be applied to dry ~~if the soil is dry~~. The quick action of the chemicals can easily injure the roots.

→ Continue to II-5

Balanced → house plant fertilizer, which should be applied sparingly. Chemical preparations should be applied according to the manufacturer's directions.

No. 1

CONTAINERS

Nearly any container that offers adequate drainage and doesn't leak is suitable for house plants. After checking a container ~~quickly~~ for leakage, consider drainage carefully. If ~~it~~ the container has a hole in its bottom, there is no problem. If not, then ~~you should put~~ should line coarse gravel or broken crockery ~~in~~ the bottom of the container to fill one-fourth to one-fifth of its ~~height~~ depth. In this way, ~~you will avoid~~ the liklihood of waterlogging ~~your~~ plants and ~~encouraging~~ encouraged root rot will be avoided.

The traditional terra cotta clay pot offers definite advantages. It is inexpensive, easily replaced, and—most important—allows air to be exchanged through its porous walls. This ~~same~~ porosity, however, allows water to evaporate fairly quickly, necessitating ~~more~~ frequent watering. If ~~you have a plant in a spot which is awkward~~ a plant's location makes it watering awkward ~~to water~~, you will save yourself some effort by choosing a glazed or otherwise impervious container.

Some metal containers (notably copper) ~~might~~ can produce adverse chemical reactions with soil and fertilizer elements, thereby injuring plants ~~therein~~ they contain. Copper planters, however, are usually lacquered, ~~preventing~~ to prevent such reactions.

Wooden tubs and boxes are ideal for very large house plants. ~~You can make~~ can be rendered any wooden container water-tight by lining it with

---

several sheets of heavy-gauge plastic or, ~~if you are really serious about it,~~ for more permanent results, sheet metal.

~~Finally, Last,~~ if you want the best advantages of both a terra cotta pot and a decorative container, place the former inside the latter, leaving a ~~little room~~ quarter-inch or more of space for air circulation around the walls of the inner pot. Sometimes, sphagnum moss is inserted here, to help preserve moisture. A base of gravel in the decorative pot can provide good drainage while lifting the inner pot to the ~~proper height~~ level of the outer container.

No. 1

WATERING

More house plants are killed by overwatering than by any other cause. ~~This~~ Such killing with kindness can be avoided if once you learn to understand ~~just~~ exactly when your plants need water and when they ~~would prefer to~~ should be left alone.

The best rule of thumb is that a plant should be watered when the soil surface is dry to the touch. Then, water the plant thoroughly, either by adding water to the soil surface, or by immersing the entire pot in a larger container of water.

Certain plants, such as ~~the~~ African violets and other woodsy varieties house plants, need more water than most, ~~while~~ cacti and succulents ~~need~~ require far less than ~~the~~ average watering. Aside from the specific preferences of individual varieties, there are many conditions which call for more or less water, ~~as~~ these are indicated in Table 1.

Table 1

Immersion is the best, surest, and therefore the method of watering ~~because it is the surest~~. The soil in any pot might tend to form water channels which, upon receiving water from the surface, will rush it to

---

the bottom of the pot and out the drainage hole, leaving large parts of the soil bone-dry. ~~Then~~ On the other hand, some potting soil mixtures will shrink when drying, leaving many spaces along the wall of the pot where water can run past. Immersion is the one sure way to soak the soil thoroughly. ~~Provided that the pot is porous,~~ Provided that the plant container is porous, a potted plant can be immersed ~~You can do it in any~~ in any large container, or even in a sink or bathtub. Set the pots in the water, but do not let the water flow over the lips of the pots. After the surface of ~~each pot~~ the potting mixture has become moist—ten to thirty minutes—remove ~~it~~ the potted plant, drain off any excess water, and put it back in its place. Never go out for the afternoon, leaving your plants standing in water.

If you water from the top, remember to remove any excess water from the saucer; ~~Plants should never be allowed~~ allowing plants to stand in water ~~for fear of~~ encourages root rot. In time, you should learn to give each plant just enough water to soak it thoroughly, with very little excess drainage.

Some other watering tips:

1. Do not ~~get~~ allow water ~~into~~ to stand the crown of any plant; ~~for~~ this will encourage decay.

2. Never use very cold water, especially for tropical plants. Keep an open jar of water at room temperature for your house plants. Not only will the proper temperature be assured, but some of the chemicals in the water will have been dissipated by the time it is given to plants.

3. ~~Water which is~~ Water artificially softened may be detrimental to plant growth. If you can, use rainwater, or at

list continued

water that has not been softened. Fluorine and chlorine, on
the other hand, ~~are~~ *do* not ~~thought~~ *seem* to pose any problems.

[lc] 4. If your water is especially hard, lime salts might
cause trouble with such acid-loving plants as Orchids, Primulas,
Rhododendrons, Azaleas, and other plants whose natural soil is
woodsy (indicating a high organic content) and acid. Either
choose plants which prefer a more neutral range in the pH scale,
or plan to collect rainwater for your calcifuges (lime-haters).

Insert Table 1 approximately here

① HUMIDITY *9/11 Pal. bold, caps, fl. left × 18 pi, + 1 line # above. No extra # below.*

Much of our trouble with house plants, especially in
wintertime, can be traced to insufficient moisture in the
air. Except for the cacti and succulents, nearly all house
plants ~~like~~ *thrive best in* a relative humidity of between 60 and 80 per cent,
while that of most heated homes in winter is under 50 per
cent--often, considerably under 50 per cent. House plants
will virtually cry for moisture under these conditions, and
it is incumbent upon you to answer that cry.

There are several ways to add moisture to the air in
your home. The more expensive include the adding of a
humidifying device to your furnace, if you live in a house,
or installing an electric humidifier. This step will benefit
not only the plants but everyone ~~else~~ living in the house,
too. But there are less expensive ways of bringing ∅ moisture
~~~~ to ~~the faces of~~ your plants:

list

1. The pebble tray. Line the bottom of a waterproof
tray with decorative pebbles and arrange *potted* ~~your~~ plants ~~in pots~~
on top of the pebbles. Keep the tray filled with water,
being sure only to avoid blocking the pots' drainage holes.
Change the water weekly to keep it fresh.
2. Decorative containers. If you keep a clay pot
inside a decorative container (double=potting), keep a pool
of water in the bottom of the larger vessel. Again, provide
some means of support for the clay pot so that it is not
resting in water at any time.

3. Standing water devices. Water left standing in a
room will gradually evaporate⊙ ~~meaning that the lost moisture
is added to the room atmosphere.~~ If your home is particularly dry during cold weather, take the trouble to place pans
of water on tops of radiators; grow ivy, philodendron, or
wandering Jew in containers of water; maintain an aquarium;
rotate plants so that each can spend an afternoon in the
bathroom each week⊙ where the air is humid. *Change standing
water* ~~weekly~~ *every week.*
4. Bathing and showering. ~~Your~~ *Most* house plants will *respond
favorably to* ~~appreciate~~ a brief shower every day, or ~~at least~~ as often
as ~~you can manage to provide the treat.~~ ~~Little~~ *Small* brass=plated
atomizers are ubiquitous in mail order catalogs, but more
dependable (albeit less decorative) are the plastic sprayers
available in art supply stores. These hold *roughly* ~~perhaps~~ a pint
of water⊙ ~~and~~ ~~they~~ feature an adjustable shower head,
affording an entire range of water action from a sharp jet
capable of carrying twenty feet ~~(the kids love this one)~~ all
~~the way~~ to a fine mist. ~~Your plants, of course, will like~~

list continued

~~the fine mist.~~ Remember to fill the container after every
use, so that the next day's spray will be at room temperature. Remember also to avoid spraying plants ~~which~~ *that* have
been standing in direct sunlight (the shock is great) and
those ~~which~~ *that* have been subjected to very cool temperatures⊙
~~(perhaps spending the autumn on a cold sunporch.)~~

Rubber plants and others with large leaves should be
cleaned thoroughly and gently with a damp cloth ~~about~~ once
a week. The leaf polish sold commercially is permissible ∅
for producing stunning, ~~if you want really stunning-looking,~~ large=leafed plants; *however,*
as it ~~which~~ *can block the leaf pores and impede respiration* ⊙
~~but~~ never use oil of any kind, ∧ Ivies and other rugged
small-leafed plants can be held under the gentle stream of a
faucet for their weekly bath.

5. Grouping. Plants will maintain ∅ moist ~~microclimate~~
surrounding air *(leaves not touching)*
with greater facility if they are grouped together ~~,~~ *rather*
than separated. During the coldest part of winter ~~you might
want to group most plants~~ *plants can be grouped*
on a pebble tray under a light
window⊙ to take advantage ⌐both of⌐ maximum light and greatest
humidity⌐

No.1 VENTILATION

Plants, like people, benefit from fresh air. ~~Like
people, also, they~~ *and* react badly to drastic changes in air
movement and temperature. Provide adequate ventilation for
your house plants, but do not subject them to sharp winds,
winter draughts, or heat ⌐rising directly from a radiator.
~~Think of your own comfort, in this respect, and you will~~

~~be best for~~
~~know what will please your plants.~~ If, in autumn, you bring
your plants in from a summer outdoors, help them to adjust
to indoor conditions gradually by placing them by an open
window for the first several days. Gradually lower the window
day by day, keeping ~~an ever~~ *a* watchful eye on night temperatures.

No.1 TEMPERATURE

The temperature requirements of house plants vary
widely, ∅ *in accordance with* ~~according to~~ the natural habitat of their forebears
and ~~also according to~~ other conditions ~~surrounding them.~~ Many
to
cool=weather plants prefer a range of 50/60° F. and cannot
tolerate temperatures above 70°, while tropicals may thrive in
to
a moist 70/75°. Know the temperature preferences of any
house plant before you adopt it, and then place it in the
best possible temperature location in your home. You might
find, for instance, that a cool=loving aspidistra will do
set
best in a back bedroom, while tropical plants thrive happily
Include in Intro.
~~next to (but not above)~~ a living room heat vent. ~~The temperature needs of plants are included in their descriptions~~
Pay attention to the temperature preferences specified for your plants, ~~throughout this book. Heed them well~~ make liberal use of
an indoor thermometer, and do not be afraid to experiment by
placing different plants in different locations for a week at
that
a time. You might notice ~~in~~ your plants ~~distinct~~ preferences
that
for particular locations throughout the house, and ~~(~~their
preferences will not always corroborate expert advice.

No.1

LIGHT

Light and temperature needs are closely related. In their native surroundings, many tropical plants can thrive in higher temperatures because they receive long hours of sunlight. In the home, and especially during winter's short days, they cannot receive enough light to enable them to withstand high house temperatures.

Except for cacti and succulents, house plants should not be placed in windowsills where they will receive long periods of direct sunlight. Simply place a thermometer in this position and you will soon see that your plants can be literally cooked to death, even in the dead of a Minnesota winter. Strive, instead, for a bright spot with a few hours of filtered sunlight each day, at least for most plants.

Individual varieties vary, of course, in their light needs and these needs are specified in the descriptions of individual plants in these pages. Again, do not be afraid to experiment with different locations for different plants. I have a Philodendron scandens--perhaps the most popular and most common of all house plants--which has thrived for years in a dark corner, when actually it is supposed to require a bright spot out of direct sun. Plants, I am afraid, sometimes exhibit unmistakable individual characteristics which we have yet to understand.

PRUNING AND TRAINING

No.1

Some plants should be pruned and pinched back occasion-

ally in order to encourage bushy and stocky growth, while trailing plants such as philodendrons and ivies need gentle support to guide them into pleasing growth patterns.

Many people hesitate to prune at all, feeling somehow that they are hurting the plant or interfering with its natural development. Actually, plants will respond to judicious pruning with new and vigorous growth. Plants such as geraniums, coleus, and begonias should be pinched back routinely in order to encourage lateral growth. The process is quite simple: with a sharp knife, cut back perhaps one-half inch of the central growing tip. The plant should respond by sending out side shoots below the central tip, and the main stem of the plant should then become thicker and sturdier. If this is done several times a year, the plant should eventually attain the vigorous and well-rounded form which you desire. Without this pruning, it might well grow "leggy" with a weak main stem requiring some kind of support. Many older plants as well will benefit from occasional pinching back or shearing of outside growth. Do not, however, prune or pinch back African violets, gloxinias, flowering bulbs, ferns, or cyclamen.

Vines and trailing plants often need some kind of support, unless you prefer to let them cascade from a hanging basket. The usual practice is to sink a slab of cork or tree bark into a pot, then to train the vines of the plant to grow around and up the support, eventually concealing it.

Another effective device is the sphagnum moss cylinder. Pack the moss fairly tightly around a stake and secure it in a cylinder of the proper size for the pot. The cylinder can be made easily from either chicken wire or green plastic material made for this purpose. If you wish, sink a small clay pot into the top of the cylinder so that you can add water regularly to keep the moss damp. (Otherwise, the moss will require regular spraying.) Tie the vines gently to the cylinder as they grow; eventually, philodendrons and similar plants will anchor themselves to the moss with their aerial rootlets, making other support unnecessary.

REPOTTING

No.1

The temptation to repot plants too readily and too often is a strong one, and should be resisted with strong will. A plant needs repotting only when it has become potbound--when the roots have filled the entire container and are creeping out of the drainage hole. Only then is repotting indicated. Choose a new pot which is only one size larger than the old one, for a house plant will not do well in a pot which is too large. If the larger pot is a used one, scrub it thoroughly to remove any possibility of disease. If it is new, soak it for a few hours in water so that it is saturated. Then, with ample potting soil, gravel, and a tongue depressor or similar wood tool, set to work.

To remove the plant from its old pot, slide your hand over the top of the pot, index and second fingers cradling

the plant stem. Turn the pot upside down, thus supported, and tap the lip of the pot sharply on the edge of a bench or table. After a few taps the entire soil ball, ringed with plant roots, should come out easily in one neat piece. Set it aside. Take the larger pot and line the bottom with a layer of coarse gravel or broken crockery to provide good drainage. Then add potting soil on top of the gravel, placing the plant and soil ball on top of the new soil several times in order to see when it has reached the proper height. (The top of the soil should be about one-half inch below the lip of the new pot in a four-inch pot, and one inch below the lip in an eight-inch pot, to leave room for watering.) When enough soil has been added to raise the plant to its proper height, center it well and begin to pack soil around the sides of the soil ball using the tongue depressor. Take your time in doing this, for it is the most crucial part of the entire operation. It is important to pack the soil firmly, so that no air spaces are left when the job is finished. Roots cannot draw nutrients in air spaces and many of them will thus be injured or die, affecting the health of the entire plant. When the new soil is finally brought up to a level even with the top of the soil ball, the job is finished. You might want to add just a little soil over the top of the root ball, especially if roots have been forced up to the soil surface, but don't add any more than you must, for you do not want to change the planting depth of the plant. Repotting is shock enough for many plants, without altering its plant

~~ing depth.~~ Water ~~it~~ the plant thoroughly and return ~~the plant~~ it to its usual location.

How often should you repot? ~~Obviously, only as each plant indicates a need.~~ The answer depends on the needs of each individual plant. For slow=growers, this might be once every two or three years; a mature slow=grower may go for many years without repotting if new growth is cut back. For fast=growing and very young plants, repotting might be needed once or twice a year for the first several years. Plants ~~which~~ that do not need repotting after one year should have the top one=half to one inch of soil replaced annually to keep the soil fresh.

No. 1

PROPAGATION

There will come a time when you will want to start your own house plants—to increase your own plant population, to use as personal gifts for friends and family, to replace a short=lived plant or one that has become ungainly with age. The propagation of most house plants is not a difficult task, and ~~it~~ is most rewarding.

There are two general methods of doing the job: by the collecting and planting of seeds, ~~and~~ or by the cutting and rooting of plant parts—stems, leaves, or underground structures. The first ~~way~~ method (sexual reproduction) is often difficult, always time=consuming, and likely to produce unsatisfactory results. Propagation from seed is ideal for garden annuals, but not for most house plants. Special equipment is required and daily attention is essential, ~~thus~~ making the activity an unlikely one for

anyone who professes "no time for house plants." In addition, (any plant produced by cross-polinating two plants of different species or genera) the seeds from hybrid plants are likely to produce plants vastly inferior to the parent plant. ~~(A hybrid, incidentally, is any plant produced by cross pollinating two plants of different species or genera.)~~ ~~Less~~ Finally, many house plants do not flower and produce seeds under home conditions; ~~requiring~~ thus the house plant gardener ~~to~~ must purchase seeds from specialty houses. The one advantage of growing house plants from seed is that ~~you can create~~ new hybrids can be created by the cross=pollination of plants. The excitement of this activity creates a fascinating hobby for some house plant enthusiasts, but is unlikely to appeal to those who cannot afford to devote significant amounts of spare time to the activity.

Plants can be propagated far more simply and reliably ~~Far more simple, and yielding far more reliable results, is the propagation of plants by the~~ by cutting and rooting ~~of~~ plant parts. Less care is required and the offspring will look ~~just like~~ identical to the parent, even when the parent is a hybrid.

Plants may be propagated at any time of year, although it is best to avoid tackling the job when the plant is going into a dormant period. ~~In~~ early spring, just before active

supplies are sold) or in builder's sand.* (fn)

The process is basically the same as for rooting in water. The cuttings are inserted in the moist medium, which may be contained in a small clay pot or, for larger numbers of cuttings, a shallow plastic tray. The planted container is then placed in a plastic bag which is tied shut (the zip kind often used for food storage is convenient, effective, and reusable) and placed in diffused light at a temperature of 65 to 70°. You can tell whether the cuttings have developed roots by testing them weekly. Open the bag and pull gently on a plant. If it moves easily, ~~then~~ the roots have not yet formed; if it resists your gentle tug, ~~fairly well~~ however, ~~then~~ the roots (probably are) mature enough to stand repotting. The process can take as little as two weeks, or as long as several months, depending upon the variety of the plant and the size of the cutting. When the roots are strong and vigorous, ~~pot the plant~~ plant the cutting in a small pot and treat it as you would any other plant.

Some plants ~~which~~ that produce canes (including Chinese ever— (hollow or pithy stems),

(fn) *1. ~~You may by now be wondering why~~ throughout this book, builder's sand is ~~recommended~~ suggested for potting purposes while sea sand is ~~cautioned against~~ not recommended. ~~The answer is that~~ builder's sand, which comes from inland locations, has irregular and sharp surfaces, ~~allowing~~ and allows good soil drainage. Sea sand, having been washed smooth over the years, packs too snugly and leads to a compacted soil ~~and~~ with resultant drainage problems.

growth begins, is perhaps the ideal time.

No. 2

Cuttings. The most common method of propagating is by the taking of stem cuttings, which are then rooted in either water or ~~some~~ a sterile rooting medium such as perlite, vermiculite, or sand. If you have never rooted a cutting before, ~~then~~ begin with African violets, coleus, Dracaena, Fuchsia, gardenias, geraniums, Impatiens, ivy, Philodendron, wandering Jew, or wax begonia. These are the easiest, ~~because all~~ since they can all be rooted in water. Simply take a cutting from an actively growing tip of the plant, ~~one~~ containing four to six leaves, severing the stem cleanly just below a joint with a clean razor blade. Place the cutting (several at a time can be taken from the same plant) ~~(you may take several at a time, if you wish)~~ so that the bottom portion is submerged in water while the leaves remain above water. ~~a green wine~~ colored or clear bottle is fine— ~~remembering only to keep the leaves above water.~~ Cut off the bottom leaf or two If necessary to get more of the stem into the water; about ~~a~~ one third of the entire length should be in water.) Place the container in diffused light—not direct sun. ~~and wait until~~ When ~~vigorous~~ roots appear, ~~when they have,~~ the ~~little~~ new plants ~~may~~ can be removed from the water and potted in ~~a~~ small pots, using the correct potting mixture ~~recommended earlier in this chapter.~~ Be sure to avoid air spaces by packing ~~to pack~~ the potting mixture firmly around the roots of the ~~plant; to avoid any air spaces, and~~ the plant and water potting ~~thoroughly afterwards.~~

Stem cuttings ~~which~~ that cannot be rooted in water are rooted in perlite, vermiculite (both available wherever house plant

green, Dracaena, and Dieffenbachia, can be propagated by taking cuttings of the canes, which have discernable "eyes." Press each cane section (containing one eye) into moist sphagnum moss, secure it with wooden clothes pins at each end so that it does not pop up, seal it in a plastic bag, and put it in a cool place out of direct sun. In six to eight weeks, move it into a warm place (70 to 90°), still out of direct sunlight. Soon, a shoot will grow from the eye. When the shoot has attained a respectable size the cane can be cut close to the shoot on both sides, and the new plant can be lifted from the moss and potted.

Plants that have fleshy leaves are best propagated by taking leaf or leaf-petiole cuttings. (A petiole is a leafstalk, or stem.) Leaf cuttings work well when large and mature leaves are available. Cut the leaf close to the stem of the parent plant, using a razor blade for a clean cut that does not crushing the cells. The leaf can then be cut horizontally into smaller sections so that the main vein runs from top to bottom along the center of the leaf section. (Long-leafed plants such as Sanseveiria and Streptocarpus can be cut into as many as ten sections, each of which will produce an individual plant.)

Each leaf section is then sunk halfway into the rooting medium; at this point the growing procedure previously described for stem cuttings can be applied to the leaf sections.

Smaller leaves can be rooted by taking leaf-petiole cuttings. Cut one leaf stem close to the main stalk and sink the stem into the rooting medium so that the leaf nearly (but

not actually) touches the medium. African violets, begonias, snake plants, piggy-back plants, and Peperomia respond well to leaf-petiole cuttings.

No. 2 Underground division. Older plants with thick main roots can be propagated by taking root cuttings. This is usually done when the plant is being repotted. Cut about one inch of the main root, making sure that it has at least one eye. Cover this with one-half inch of rooting medium and treat it as you would any other cutting.

Thick-rooted perennials can be propagated simply by the process of root division; the root mass is simply forced apart into two or more clumps, each of which is then repotted.

Plants that produce rhizomes (underground stems) can be propagated by dividing the rhizome so that one leaf bud is contained on each piece; the section is then planted under one-half inch of rooting medium. Plants that produce potato-like tubers can be propagated by cutting the tubers apart (one eye to each section) with a sharp knife, and planting the sections in the rooting medium just as one would plant potatoes in the open field.

Some plants produce "suckers," small plants that grow up from an underground stem or root. These can be separated from the parent plant and potted in soil immediately.

Anyone who has seen strawberries grow outdoors knows what runners are—the baby plants that grow from a long stem coming

from the base of the parent plant. Among house plants, Boston fern and spider plant both produce runners; these can be severed from the parent plant and started in a rooting medium.

Other methods of underground division include the separation and replanting of baby bulbs and corms which are produced by the mother bulb or corm.

No. 2 Air layering. A fairly simple (and most impressive) way of propagating larger or woody-stemmed plants is by air layering. In such layering a sharp cut is made into the stem, perhaps a third of the way in, into which a toothpick is placed horizontally, to keep the cut open. The stem section is then wrapped with moist sphagnum moss and covered with clear plastic and is tied at top and bottom so that moisture cannot escape. Roots will form from the incision and will soon show through the plastic. When a fair number of roots have appeared, cut the stem below the plastic wrap, remove both plastic and moss, and pot the new plant immediately in potting soil.

The propagation of plants can often be integrated with the cutting back, pruning, and shaping of older plants. It is a waste to throw away plant parts when they can be used to produce more plants, and it is precisely this thrifty attitude which, if not controlled, can lead to a frightening multiplication of house plants. The answer to such overwhelming plant production is to share plants with friends, thus encouraging still more enthusiasts and still more house plants.

TOP OF TYPE PAGE

(Appendix 1   THE ABCs OF ARTIFICIAL LIGHT)

The recent introduction of fluorescent tubes designed specifically for plant growing has been a great boon for indoor gardeners. With the aid of artificial light, we can now grow lush, green plants in areas where they would never grow before. A windowless bathroom, which might offer ideal humidity and temperature conditions, can now be made into an ideal plant-growing environment. Plants growing on a drab northern window sill can now receive supplemental light during winter's short and dark days. Dim corners of any room can be transformed into green showplaces. Cuttings and seedlings can now make faster and surer progress than ever, under artificial light, and we can even grow vegetables in the dead of winter in the bedroom or kitchen. Artificial lighting is not essential for house plant success, but it certainly broadens growing horizons and increases chances for maximum rewards.

The outdated incandescent bulb still offers some help to plant growers, although the heat it produces makes it impossible to offer plants the amounts of light they need without drying or burning them. Also, the short spectrum of light wavelengths emitted by incandescent bulbs, falling far short of simulating the beneficial rays of the sun. Ordinary daylight or cool white fluorescent lights are far better for growing plants since they have not only a wider and more effective light wavelength, but also produce light with three times as much efficiency as incandescent bulbs, thus reducing heat.

special box No. 1, add 2

turers) There are also some excellent books on artificial
light gardening *And some of these are probably* ~~which are most likely~~ in the collections of
your public library.

If you enjoy artificial light gardening and the gratifying results it brings, you will have no problem in expanding
your activities in this area. Manufacturers have introduced
a wide variety of special plant-growing stands, some with
several tiers capable of holding dozens of plants, others
decorative enough to enhance the beauty of any room. Your
choices are limited only by your imagination and your checkbook
balance.

special box No. 2

ch   Appendix 2)   *10/12 Pal. reg. c+lc*
Fl. left

12 pi   (SHOULD YOU SEND YOUR PLANTS TO SUMMER CAMP?)   *10/12 PAL.*
BOLD c+lc
indent 9½ pi
x 8½ pi

flourish

Nearly all house plants will ~~enjoy a summer~~ outdoors *in the summer* ~~where they will become rejuvenated and make very active growth.~~ *in so drastic a change*
There are dangers involved ~~here~~ however, *in environmental growing conditions* ~~not unlike those a sheltered city child will encounter in his first trip to a wilderness camp, and special precautions must be taken.~~

Shock, resulting from either sharp light or temperature
changes, is the first danger. *Shock can be avoided* ~~Avoid these~~ by placing ~~your~~ *do not dip*
plants outdoors only when ~~the~~ night temperatures ~~will go no~~ *below*
~~lower than~~ 55° (except for *plants that prefer cool conditions* ~~cool-loving plants~~). It might be
best to put them on a sheltered porch or breezeway for the
first few days *to acclimate them* ~~until they have become accustomed~~ to the
outdoors, or to put them out for only a few hours in the
morning, bringing them in again before the heat of the day
of gradual exposure
sets in. After a week or so, they may be placed outside for
the summer. Choose a spot shaded totally from the sun. After
that
a week of shade, those plants ~~which~~ can take some direct sun
can be moved to a place where they will receive diffused sun
light, perhaps under the protection of a large tree. Nearly
any house plant will be severely injured or killed by long
exposure to a hot summer sun.

Keep the plants in their pots, and do not sink them
directly into the ground for fear of soil insects and grubs.
provided that   *is lined*
You may sink them ~~if you line~~ the bottom of the hole with
two inches of gravel ~~or they may be kept above ground, in~~

CH   TOP OF TYPE PAGE
10/12 PAL. BOLD C+LC FL. LEFT
BIBLIOGRAPHY)

12 pi

No. 1   ARTIFICIAL LIGHT GARDENING)   *9/11 PAL. BOLD CAPS, FL. LEFT,*
NO EXTRA # BELOW

Bickford, Elwood D. and Stuart, Dunn. Lighting for Plant
Growth. Kent, Ohio: Kent State University Press, 1972.
~~One of the best books on the subject; especially valu-~~
9/11 PAL. REG. C+LC ~~able to those who have had some experience in the area.~~
FL. LEFT X 18 PI.,
RUNOVERS FL. LEFT
+5 PTS. # Cherry, Elaine C. Fluorescent Light Gardening. New York:
BETWEEN
ITEMS Van Nostrand Reinhold Co., 1965.

Elbert, George A. The Indoor Light Gardening Book. New York:
Crown Publishers, Inc., 1975.

Fitch, Charles Marden. The Complete Book of Houseplants under
Lights. New York: Hawthorn Books, 1975.

Kranz, Frederick H. and Jacqueline. Gardening Indoors under
Lights. New York: Viking Press, rev. 1971.

+1 LINE #
No. 1   BEGONIAS)   *9/11 PAL. BOLD CAPS*
FL. LEFT, +1 LINE # ABOVE,
NO EXTRA # BELOW.
Brilmayer, Bernice. All about Begonias. New York: Doubleday
Publishing Co., 1960.

bibliography, add 1

Kramer, Jack. Begonias, Indoors and Out. New York: E. P.
Dutton & Co., 1967.
9/11 PAL. BOLD CAPS
+1 LINE # ABOVE
No. 1   BONSAI)   *NO EXTRA # BELOW*

9/11 PAL. REG. Brooklyn Botanic Garden. Bonsai: Special Techniques. New
C+LC, FL. LEFT York: Brooklyn Botanic Garden.
X 18 PI,
UNJUST
+5 PTS. # Chidamian, Claude. Bonsai: Miniature Trees. New York: Van
BETWEEN Nostrand Reinhold Co., 1955.
ITEMS
9/11 PAL. BOLD CAPS
No. 1   BROMELIADS)   *+1 LINE # ABOVE*
NO EXTRA # BELOW

Kramer, Jack. Bromeliads: The Colorful House Plants. New
York: Van Nostrand Reinhold Co., 1965.
9/11 PAL. BOLD CAPS
No. 1   BULBS.)   *+1 LINE # ABOVE*
NO EXTRA # BELOW

Field, Xenia. Growing Bulbs in the House. New York: St.
Martin's Press, Inc., 1966.

Peters, Ruth Marie. Bulb Magic in Your Window. New York:
M. H. Barrows & Co., 1954.

Walker, Marion C. Flowering Bulbs for Winter Windows. New
York: Van Nostrand Reinhold Co., 1965.

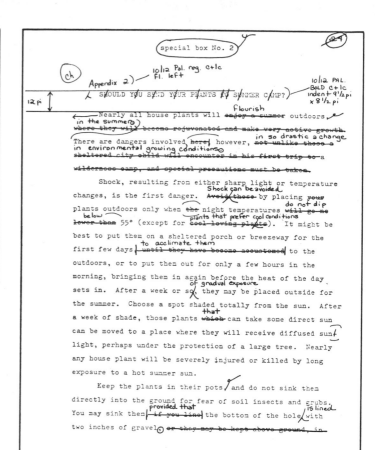
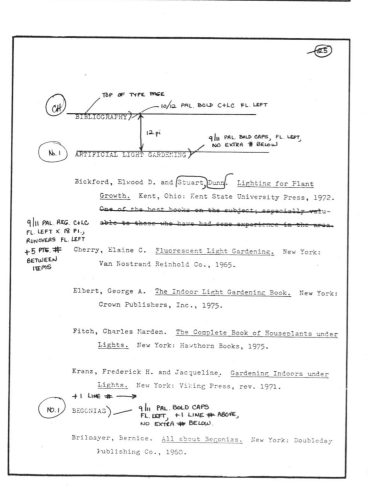
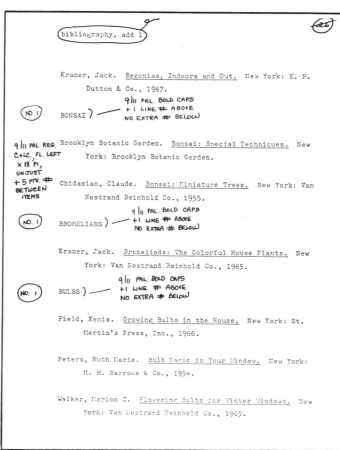

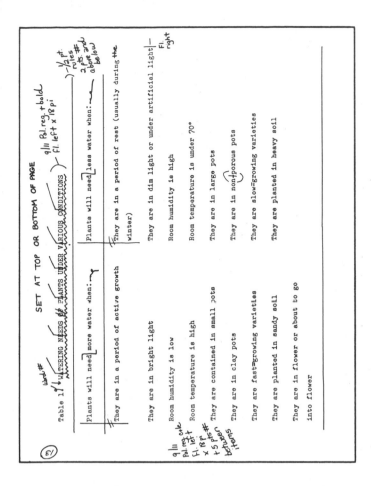

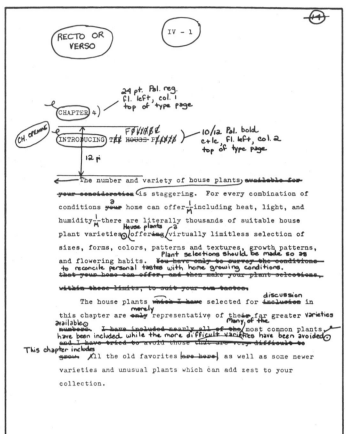

The plants ~~listed~~ have been divided into four broad categories ~~Groups~~: foliage plants, flowering plants, fruiting plants, and cacti and succulents. Within each group, individual plants are listed alphabetically by their common names, followed by (in parentheses) their ~~Latin or~~ scientific (or Latin) designations. The ~~Latin~~ scientific name comprises both the genus and species ~~names~~. For example, the Scientific name for the common boxwood is Buxes (~~the~~ genus) sempervirens (~~the~~ species). The genus is abbreviated after its original use in the text. ~~After a genus name is introduced, it is thereafter abbreviated.~~

Thus Buxes sempervirens ~~if mentioned again~~ becomes B. Sempervirens, in all subsequent text references. ~~Last~~, Finally, there may be a third part to the ~~Latin~~ scientific name which designates a further subdivision of the species, usually called a subspecies or a variety. The popular Japanese boxwood, for example, is B. microphylla japonica.

Although I ~~have attempted to maintain an informal tone~~ tried to keep the tone informal in these pages, by using common names whenever possible, the scientific ~~Latin~~ nomenclature has obvious benefits. Many species are known by different common names in ~~different~~ various parts of the country, different species of a genus are often called by a single common name, and a single common name may be applied even to varieties of completely different genera. Thus, the most accurate ~~sure~~ way to identify any plant ~~then~~ is by referring to its scientific ~~Latin~~ name. The listing for each plant includes ~~For each plant listed, you will find~~ symbols ~~which~~ that indicate its individual preferences for growing temperature, light, soil moisture and air humidity, and window placement.

~~Please remember that~~ these are rough guides and not inflexible requirements ~~demands~~. Many plants ~~are tolerant of one or more of these~~ have a wide range of tolerance, and conditions ~~and will thrive in a variety of them~~. ~~Many~~ While some plants ~~which~~ are said to prefer an east window will do just as well, many of them in a shaded south or a west location. Do not hesitate to try a plant ~~of your liking~~ because you cannot provide its exact needs, ~~but~~ however; neither should you attempt a plant if you can provide none of ~~them~~ its basic requirements. Experimentation is both valuable and enjoyable.

WHERE TO BUY HOUSE PLANTS

The best place to buy a house plant is from someone who grows his own stock. He will know his plants and you will be able to rely on his advice. If ~~there is~~ no grower ~~in your area~~ is available, the next best source is ~~your~~ local flower shop or nursery center. In either case, ~~Whichever place you choose~~ talk to the owner or his representative about house plants. Ask for precise identification of a plant ~~which~~ that interests you. Ask for specifications of the plant's needs for light, soil, temperature, and humidity. Ask how large the plant is apt to become, and whether or not it produces flowers, even if you know the answers to these questions. If it becomes apparent that ~~he doesn't know too~~ the owner is not thoroughly familiar with ~~very much about~~ the plant, or about house plants in general, then ask to talk to someone who can answer your questions in greater detail, or seek another source.

Plants found in supermarkets and discount houses are usually not bad, although many ~~which are~~ you see seen flowering in the store may have been grown quickly and forced into bloom under ideal green[house]

house conditions that you cannot hope to match in your home. ←
However, most plants offered by these sources are likely to
be common varieties that are quite tolerant of adverse conditions. It is hard to go wrong with grape ivy or a climbing
philodendron.

Plants stored outside at garden centers or in shopping
centers are ~~more likely to~~ *may* carry insects or disease, particularly if they are resting close to flats of outdoor
vegetable or flower seedlings. Examine them ~~very~~ closely
before purchasing, and isolate them for *one or* two weeks at home
before putting them with other house plants.

Wherever you buy your plants, look for young and sturdy
specimens with rich color and a generally healthy appearance.
Take particular care in examining ~~Examine particularly carefully~~ large and mature plants ~~which~~ *that*
carry high price tags. These may have been growing for too
long a time in ideal conditions. Generally, you will have
better luck with a younger plant, and you will have the added
pleasure of bringing it along to maturity in your own home.

Larger plants offered at bargain prices are often severely under-rooted.

(1) FOLIAGE PLANTS

9/11 Pal. bold caps, fl. left + 1 line # above no extra # below

←——In this chapter, we will survey many of the house plants
grown primarily for their foliage. Some of them, under favorable conditions, will flower from time to time, although few
should be selected for their flowering abilities. ~~Nearly all~~ *Most*
of these plants are fairly easy to grow and maintain, ~~giving~~ *thereby providing*
even the beginner a wide variety of plants from which to choose.

The plants are listed in alphabetical order, according
to their common or popular names. *The scientific (or Latin) name is used for plants with no popular names or for plants with more than one popular name.* ~~If there is no popular name for a plant, or if there are more than one, none dominant, then the plant is listed by its scientific or Latin name.~~ The
index, which includes both common and scientific names, provides
a convenient means of cross-checking names.

The ~~special~~ symbols accompanying each plant name ~~will~~
provide a quick and convenient guide to that plant's requirements. Remember, however, that these are guides and not ~~sharp~~ *strict*
demands. Many of these plants are tolerant by nature *and* will take to an east window as well as a west window; ~~and~~ *many* can
tolerate some direct sunlight even ~~if~~ *when* none is recommended.
Most crucial, perhaps, are the guides to humidity and moisture,
since ~~overwatering is one thing that~~ virtually no plant will
tolerate *overwatering*.

No.3 African Boxwood (Myrsine africana) B-C-A-C

DESIGN: USE SYMBOL (See Boxwood.)

This slow=growing boxwood has red stems ~~but otherwise~~ *but* is similar to regular Boxwood ~~(q.v.)~~. Many people think it
is even more graceful. African Boxwood is a good plant for
terrariums, if the atmosphere is not too hot.

No.3 Aralia (Fatsia japonica) C-B-B-C SYMBOLS

Aralia is characterized by
Sometimes sold as Aralia sieboldii, *beautiful, bright*
green, leathery, maple-like leaves highlight ~~this cheerful plant.~~
In appearance, it is similar to the castor oil plant,
and in fact is sometimes called *false castor oil plant*. It
thrives in a cool ~~spot~~ *environment*. Aralia can easily grow leggy; ~~and so~~
it should be pruned annually in order to encourage ~~it into~~
bushy growth. *It* ~~will~~ *can attain a height of four feet at maturity.*

A striking hybrid, Fatshedra lizei, crosses F. japonica
and ivy (Hedra), forming a *hardy* climbing plant with maple-shaped
leaves ~~which is tolerant of adverse conditions~~.

There is also a plant called *false* Aralia, which has
graceful and feathery foliage. It bears no resemblance to
the true Aralia and is difficult to grow.

No.3 Asparagus A-B-B-B SYMBOLS

There are two kinds of *Asparagus* suitable for growing
as house plants, *fern Asparagus* (A. plumosus), with slender,
needle=like, dark green leaves, ~~feeling~~ *which give the plant* a feathery appearance,
and A. sprengeri (*emerald feather*) which has thicker yellow=
green leaves and drooping stems. The latter makes a good

baskets
plant for hanging ~~plants~~, and produces red berries at Christmastime. Both like some sun in the summer and full sun in
the winter, *and both can grow to a height of about two feet.*

No.3 Australian Laurel (Pittosporum tobira) C-B-A-B SYMBOLS

A tolerant and slow=growing plant ~~whose leaves~~ *with* glossy,
~~and~~ leathery *leaves resembling* ~~resemble~~ those of Rhododendron. Australian
Laurel will grow vigorously bushy and does not ~~ask~~ *demand* much
attention. Florists often use the leaves in floral arrangements.

An interesting variegated form is P. tobira variegata.

No.3 Australian Umbrella Tree (Schefflera actinophylla) A-A-B-A SYMBOLS

Here is *an* ~~very~~ attractive and vigorous ~~growing~~ tree
with rich=looking ~~and~~ glossy leaves that radiate umbrella-like
from the ends of several leaf stalks. It is a tough and
rewarding plant, *growing to six feet,* which can be propagated by air=layering.
Australian *Umbrella Tree* is ~~also~~ *sometimes* sold as Brassaia
actinophylla. A dwarf variety, B. actinophylla compacta, is
also available.

No.3 Baby's Tears (Helxine soleirollii) B-B-A-B SYMBOLS

This low creeper is also called Irish Moss. It likes
a constantly moist (but not soggy) soil, and ~~higher~~ *more* than
average humidity. It makes a good ground cover for terrariums,
but will also grow in a pot if adequate humidity is provided.
Baby's Tears may appear to die in the colder months, but after

an adequate rest period it will spring back to life.

No.3 Black Pepper (Piper nigrum) A-C-B-C Symbols

While Black Pepper
This is not a terribly attractive plant, but it produces *can be used*
real peppercorns which you may use at the table, and *for this reason* is an
excellent good conversation piece for that reason. The plant's berries
begin as green, later turn red, *and eventually* then dry up and turn black.
Pick the dried-up black corns, dry them thoroughly for several
weeks in an open spot, then use them in your pepper grinder.
The care for Black Pepper is the same as that required for
Philodendron. It is not a demanding plant.

No.3 Boxwood (Buxus) C-A-B-B Symbols

used as *with glossy, bright-green leaves*
The same plant which grows the most prized hedges outdoors
can make a very attractive house plant. Boxwood is slow-growing
the ancient Oriental art of growing dwarf trees and shrubs.
and dependable, a good subject for bonsai. It has glossy,
bright-green leaves. B. sempervirens and B. microphylla
japonica (Japanese Boxwood) are the two popular species.

No.3 Bromeliads A-B-B-C Symbols

There are more than 1,800 varieties of this popular
group, many of which are suitable for growing as house plants.
Some of them produce attractive flowers, but most are grown
for their striking and variegated leaf patterns. One distinctive feature of the bromeliads is the rosette leaves which
form a small water cup; which *these leaves* the plant uses to hold reserve

supplies of water in its natural habitat. Since the plant
lives in the crotches of trees in Central and South America,
the water cup is an evolutionary survival characteristic.
In the home, keep the cup filled with water, changing it
weekly to keep it fresh.

A few of the more common Bromeliads are Aechmea, Ananas
(Pineapple), Billbergia, Cryptanthus (Zebra Plant), Dyckia,
Tillandsia (Spanish Moss), and Vriesia.

No.3 Caladium A-B-B-C Symbols

Caladiums, with their spectacularly-colored and variegated
leaves, are equally at home in the garden or on the window sill.
They are ideal additions to plant groupings on porch or patio
in the summer and early autumn. Give them bright light, but
for bright leaf colors avoid
not long periods of direct sun, especially in summer, if you
want the brightest leaf colors.

Caladiums are grown from tubers, which can be divided
easily to produce new plants. Start the tubers in regular
potting soil at a very warm temperature--$80°$ to $90°$--and move
the young plants to a cooler spot when they have appeared.
They will attain a height of about one foot.

No.3 Cast Iron Plant (Aspidistra elatior) A-C-B-C Symbols

one of
This is perhaps the easiest plants in the world to grow,
kill this plant
as its name suggests. It is virtually impossible to neglect
through neglect
it to death. It is also called Saloon Plant, since it was one
of the few that could survive in Victorian taverns, and it
was made immortal by George Orwell in his novel Keep the

Aspidistra Flying. If you cannot grow the Aspidistra, you
hopelessly
may safely conclude that you have a purple thumb. hopelessly
irredeemable.
,which grows about two feet tall, *best*
Cast Iron Plant seems to thrive even better when kept
slightly pot-bound, and it will appreciate having its leaves
washed occasionally. A white-striped species is called A.
variegata.

No.3 Chamaeranthemum igneum A-C-A-C Symbols

This low, spreading herb has attractive, dark green
leaves with reddish-yellow veins. It is suitable for hanging
baskets or as a low contrast in large plant groupings. It
does like warm temperatures and high humidity, however, and
might not be suitable for dry apartments.

No.3 Chinese Evergreen (Aglaonema) A-C-B-A Symbols

and low-growing
Here is an attractive plant that is very easy to grow.
It will stand abuse almost as easily as Cast Iron Plant.

There are at least ten commonly found species of the
Aglaonema, the most popular of which, A. modestum, has
interestingly mottled leaves. Perhaps the most attractive,
however, is A. pseudobractaetum, which is sometimes difficult
to find in stores and greenhouses.

No.3 Cissus A-B-B-C Symbols

that
Cissus is a vine plant which offers a number of interesting and attractive species. Most are vigorous climbers,
suitable for training on a trellis or for adding to hanging
baskets.

Among the more popular species are C. rhombifolia (Grape
Ivy), which is one of the most popular of all house plants;
C. antartica (Kangaroo Vine), which prefers a small pot; C.
antartica minima (Miniature Kangaroo Vine); C. rotundifolia;
and C. discolor (Begonia Ivy), which is perhaps the most spectacular of the genus, although difficult to grow.

Of all the Cissus, Grape Ivy is the easiest to grow,
which doubtless accounts for a large share of its popularity.

No.3 Coleus A-A-A-B Symbols

This old favorite has velvety leaves sporting bright
splashes of reds, pinks, purples, and yellows. There is a
seemingly endless number of varieties of Coleus, nearly all
of which
of them interesting, most growing twelve to eighteen inches in height.

Coleus is equally happy outdoors, grown as an annual in
the North, or in the window garden. It can be grown easily
from seed, and stem-tip cuttings can be taken from established
indoor plants. If you grow Coleus outdoors in summer, take
some cuttings before the first autumn freeze and root them
for growing as house plants.

The soil for Coleus should be kept damp, but not soggy.
Pinch back plants often to encourage bushy growth.

EDITORIAL STYLE SHEET

The M.I.T. Press
28 Carleton Street
Cambridge, Mass. 02142
Date:

Name of Author(s)/Editor(s): MULCH, PURVIS

Title of Book (Tentative/Final): NO TIME FOR HOUSE PLANTS

Press Editor (In-House/Free-Lance): ROBIN CRUISE

Spelling and Compounding of Words

1. Use Webster's Third New International Dictionary. (Webster's New Collegiate Dictionary, 7th ed., may also be used.)
2. For spelling and alphabetizing of personal names use Webster's Biographical Dictionary. Also consult the following:
3. For spelling of geographical names use Webster's Geographical Dictionary.
4. For spelling of technical terms use the following reference(s): — NONE —
5. For rules on compounding and hyphenating see A Manual of Style, 12th ed. (Chicago: University of Chicago Press, 1969).
6. Do not use hyphen with most prefixes (exceptions are before capitalized words, as in pre-Columbian; when two i's come together, as in semi-industrial; to distinguish homonyms as in re-cover).
7. See also Word List (attached) for examples, exceptions, and special terms.

Punctuation

1. Follow A Manual of Style for general rules.
2. Use a comma in a compound sentence unless both clauses are very short.
3. Use a comma before "and" or "or" in a series with three or more elements.
4. Use a comma after an introductory clause or a long introductory phrase.
5. Set off nonrestrictive phrases and clauses and parenthetical expressions by commas.
6. Do not use periods with abbreviations of units of measure. Two exceptions are inch (in.) and number (no.).
7. Periods and commas are placed inside quotation marks, semicolons and colons outside. Question marks and exclamation points are placed logically. Superscript references are placed outside all punctuation.
8. Do not separate a subject from a verb by a comma except to set off an intervening nonrestrictive clause or phrase.
9. Do not use an apostrophe to form the plural in dates (e.g., 1980s).

Capitalization

1. Follow A Manual of Style and/or Webster, but be consistent.
2. In most headings and titles capitalize the principal words, that is, first word and all others except articles, conjunctions, and prepositions. Capitalize first word of a subtitle.
3. Usually capitalize only the first word and proper names in legends.
4. In table headings and in stubs of columns, main words are capitalized; elsewhere within table only the first word in a cell is capitalized.

The MIT Press

28 Carleton Street
Cambridge, Massachusetts 02142

Massachusetts Institute of Technology
617-864-6900

January 20, 1977

Mr. Purvis Mulch

Dear Purvis:

I have sent to you today (under separate cover) a copy of the edited manuscript for NO TIME FOR HOUSE PLANTS for a check of editing. I have also included a copy of the editor's style sheet and word list to clarify the editing. Your manuscript was exceptionally well prepared and you will find only light copy editing for your review.

Please go through the manuscript carefully and answer all questions posed by the editor, using a red or green pencil to distinguish the marks. Do keep in mind that this is the last chance for substantive changes as we will be proceeding directly to page proof with your manuscript. Changes in the page proof stage are prohibitively expensive and could disrupt our production schedule.

We will expect to have the manuscript returned to us with your comments by February 19 unless we hear from you to the contrary. If you do have questions, please get in touch with us.

Yours sincerely,

Robin Cruise

Robin Cruise
Editorial Assistant

Editorial Style Sheet (Cont.)

Other Notes on Style

1. Follow H. W. Fowler, A Dictionary of Modern English Usage, 2nd ed., revised by Ernest Gowers (New York: Oxford, 1965), for standard English usage.
2. In most cases use "that" to introduce restrictive clauses and "which" to introduce nonrestrictive clauses.
3. Usually avoid the authorial "we"; instead use "I" or "one" or reconstruct sentence.

Editorial Style Sheet (cont.)

Use of Numbers

1. Follow recommendations in A Manual of Style or in (specify):
2. Use words for round numbers and most other numbers below (specify).
3. In most cases use arabic (rather than roman) numbers for chapters, tables, figures, appendixes, and, when necessary, sections.
4. When footnotes (or references) are numbered, start a new series in each chapter.
5. When many cross references are used, follow a double-numbering system for figures, tables, equations, sections, and subsections, using chapter number and number of item within chapter (e.g., Figure 1.2, Table 3.1, Equation 2.2).
6. In numbers containing four digits use (do not use) a comma. Please specify.
7. For consecutive page references repeat the second page number in full (e.g., 101-102, 234-239, 569-573).
8. Use figures for percentages (e.g., 15 percent).

References, Footnotes, Bibliography

1. Follow recommendations in A Manual of Style or in (specify):
2. When bibliographical references are repeated within a chapter, use a short form rather than op. cit. (see Chicago Manual for details).
3. Notes will be as follows (specify): (a) foot of page; (b) end of chapter; (c) end of book; (d) other: _None_
4. References will be handled as follows (specify): (a) as footnotes; (b) placed at end of chapter and arranged alphabetically (or in order of citation); (c) author's last name and date of publication in text or footnote and full reference in bibliography.
5. Samples of bibliographical style in footnotes for books and articles are:
a)
b)
6. Samples of style used in References or Bibliography are as follows:
a)
b)

Mathematics

1. Most algebraic letters, including subscripts and superscripts, are italic.
2. All physical units (g, cm, in., lb) are roman. Functions like sin, cos, log, exp, lim, det are roman.
3. All o, O, 0 are to be interpreted as zero unless otherwise noted.
4. Use sentence punctuation around displayed equations.
5. Do not use commas in expressions of apposition like "the energy E" or "the price P."
6. Use a comma after an introductory phrase ending with a mathematical expression.
7. Do not begin a sentence with an abbreviation or a figure; either spell out or recast sentence.

The MIT Press   28 Carleton Street
Cambridge, Massachusetts 02142   Massachusetts Institute of Technology
617-253-5646

April 16, 1977

Mr. Purvis Mulch

Dear Purvis:

I have sent to you today (under separate cover) the galley proof and original manuscript for NO TIME FOR HOUSE PLANTS for proofreading.

Please read through the galley proof, carefully noting all errors in red pencil in the margin. The galley proof will also be read here. We will need your proof returned to us by May 7 so that your corrections can be consolidated with those of our proofreader and the entire batch can be returned to the compositor by May 12.

If you have any questions, please feel free to call us.

Yours sincerely,

Robin Cruise
Editorial Assistant

The MIT Press   28 Carleton Street
Cambridge, Massachusetts 02142   Massachusetts Institute of Technology
617-864-6900

February 8, 1977

Mr. Purvis Mulch

Dear Purvis:

Enclosed you will find sample pages for NO TIME FOR HOUSE PLANTS for your review and comments. Please bear in mind in looking over the sample pages that they should be reviewed in terms of layout and design and not in terms of content -- i.e., do not be concerned with typographical errors, sentence structure, etc., since the sample pages are simply indications of the types of design problems inherent in the book.

We must have your approval of the sample pages February 15 in order to proceed with our production schedule.

If you have any questions, please feel free to contact our Design Department. Mario Furtado will be handling the design of your book and can bereached at 617-253-1961.

Yours sincerely,

Robin Cruise
Editorial Assistant

Encs.

The MIT Press

28 Carleton Street
Cambridge, Massachusetts 02142

Massachusetts Institute of Technology
617-864-6900

June 15, 1977

Mr. Purvis Mulch

Dear Purvis:

I am enclosing the page proof for NO TIME FOR
HOUSE PLANTS with all illustrations in place.
I will need these pages back by July 7.

You will notice that I have also enclosed
sample pages from an index as well as the
indexing chapter from the Chicago Manual of
Style; these are for your personal use and
need not be returned to us. We must have
your index no later than July 12. I realize
that you have been compiling the entries for
the index for some time now, so that filling in
the correct page numbers (taken from the page
proof) will not be terribly time consuming for
you.

Please phone if you have questions.

Yours sincerely,

Robin Cruise

Robin Cruise
Editorial Assistant

Encs.

The MIT Press
28 Carleton Street
Cambridge, MA 02142

4/15/77
RC

INDEXING INSTRUCTIONS

Instructions for preparing indexes can be found in A Manual of Style,
12th edition (Chicago: University of Chicago Press, 1969), pp. 399-
430, or in the booklet reprinted from this source. To a large extent
we follow the principles outlined in this booklet. However, there are
a few exceptions and a few preferences, which are listed here.

1 We prefer the indented form rather than the run-in style (see
sections 18.12 and 18.90) because it is easier to pick out the
subentries.

2 We use complete page numbers in inclusive references rather than
the somewhat complicated system suggested in the book (see section 8.36).
In other words, we would cite, for example, 3-10, 100-104, 107-108,
1002-1003, 321-325, 415-532 rather than as shown in the book.

3 We prefer to arrange subentries in alphabetical rather than chrono-
logical order (see section 18.76).

4 We like to have first names or initials as well as surnames listed
in the index even when persons have been referred to in the text only
by the surname. In the case of really obscure persons there can be a
brief description in parentheses following the name (see section 18.40).

5 Either the letter-by-letter or word-by-word alphabetical arrangement of entries is acceptable (see sections 18.49 and 18.50), as long
as one system is consistently followed.

6 We prefer not to use an adjective alone as a main entry. Therefore,
instead of using an entry such as the adjective "Indian" (see sections
18.3 and 18.4), we would use, for example, "Indian ceremonial dances"
and "Indian food" or we would use the noun "Indians" as a main entry
and use the subentries "ceremonial dances of" and "food of."

Important Note to Authors

The M.I.T. Press
MASSACHUSETTS INSTITUTE OF TECHNOLOGY
CAMBRIDGE, MASSACHUSETTS 02142

To DESIGN + PRODUCTION .... Date 2/20/77

We enclose the material listed below:

Author/Title: MULCH / NO TIME FOR HOUSE PLANTS

Manuscript pages ...201 pgs. COMPLETE AND COPY EDITED

Galley proof ....INCLUDING FRONT MATTER AND

Cut dummy ....LIST OF RUNNING HEADS

Foul galley proof ....

Page proof ....

Foul page proof ....

Plate proof ....

Blueprints ....

Other ....

Signed *ROBIN*

Author: when marking the master proof which is to be returned to us, please use a color different from that already used by the editor or printer.

AUTHOR'S ALTERATIONS
(Changes ordered in type matter which differ from original copy)

Correction of type, because of the hand work involved, is extremely expensive: a change in a single line may involve as many as five people in a composing room. At the present compositors' rate of more than $10 per minute, many changes will involve the author, if not in a bill for alterations, at least in a possible loss of sales through an increase in selling price. The author should, therefore, in his own and everyone else's interest, confine his alterations to those essential for accuracy.

The most expensive changes are those that cause overrunning of type from one line to another. At any time they should be avoided but more than ever on page proof. Lines may have to be carried over from one page to another, even to the end of a chapter. In so doing, running heads, extracts, and footnotes may have to be replaced or transposed, and changes may be necessary in the list of contents, list of illustrations, and index.

If insertions or deletions are inevitable, then the author should, wherever possible, make compensatory cuts and additions as close as possible to the point where the change has to be made. Only in this way will he avoid the greatest risks and the worst inflation of production costs.

QUERIES ON PROOF
(Questions to the author from editor or proofreader)

To answer a query affirmatively, cross out the question mark only. If you wish no change to be made, cross out the entire query.

FOUL MANUSCRIPT AND PROOF
(Ms. or proof superseded by a succeeding stage in production)

When you receive galley proof, please do not mark the foul manuscript in any way. Similarly, when you receive page proof, do not put any marks on the foul galleys.

Please return foul material to us.

Pages text		1	3 3
Notes (pg/ch/end)			
Bibliography			9
Glossary			
Appendixes			
~~Index~~ Illustrations			3 8
Other (Boxes)			1 5
Frontmatter			1 2
Captions			
Total ms. pp.			2 0 7

F.M.BREAKDOWNS

halftitle _x_ title _X_ copyright _X_ dedication __ epigraph __
foreword __ preface _X_ contents _X_ list of ~~illustrations~~ symbols _X_
introduction __ authors note __ acknowledgements __
abbreviations

Boxes

HEADINGS	1	2	3	4	5	6	7		TOTALS
Part									
Chapter	1	1	1	1	1	1	1		7
Number 1		16	3	2	4	2	4		3 1
Number 2		7				7	5		1 9
Number 3				60	3	15	2		8 0
Number 4									
Number 5									
pp. per chapt.	3	34	9	37	11	24	15	15	1 4 8
Lists		3		9		1			1 3
Tables		1			1				2
Equations									
Notes		1	1	1		1			4
Extracts									
Poetry									
Language									
Legends									
ILLUSTRATIONS									
No. line dwgs.									
camera ready									
draw & charge au.									
no. halftones									
no. color (1-h.t.)									3 8
placement in text									
grouped									
separate sig(s)									

THE M.I.T. PRESS Manufacturing Cost Estimate

Author/Title ____ PReMioUS ery   Date ___ 12/20/76
                    LAUNCH

Manuscript Description __ 20u __ No. halftones __ 38 __ est. to make _____ book pages
Ms total pages _____ No. line ills. __ 0 __ est. to make _____ book pages
No. tables _____ No. to be drawn _____ No. camera-ready _____

Remarks _____

Book Description (176)
Total pages _____ trim size __ 5¾ x 6 __
Type page size _____ ☐ Mono ☐ Lino No. forms __ 2/643,1/32,1/16 __ ☒ Film (_____) Type
Paper __ 4xb 60# white offset __   2.75/643
Binding: ☒ sewn (cloth) ☐-perle bd _____   ) ☐ sd. ☐ paper cover ☒ 10% ☐ -½- ☐L
        HARDCOVER

Plant Costs

	Estimated	Actual	supplier
Design			
Drafting			
Composition @ 1¢	1054		
Alterations	10¢		
Engravings/prints	-		
Repros			
C. & S. ills. @ 1¢	304		
Plates (+s	226		
Blues	62		
Jacket Comp	100		
Dies	30		
Contingencies 6%	113		

	TOTAL	PAPER	CLOTH
TOTAL PLANT	1997		
Edition Costs	4000	5000	7500
Makeready	246	248	248
Presswork	135	175	261
Paper	784	971	1457
Binding 4 M @ 165	3200		
5 M @ 64		3200	
7.5 M @ 62			4650
M @			
Jacket pw/paper	960	1150	1650
Freight	160	200	300
Plan	67	67	67

Total Edition	4454	6011	8633
Total plant	1997	1997	1997
TOTAL COST	6951	8008	10630
Plant unit	.50	.40	.27
Edition unit	1.24	1.20	1.15
TOTAL UNIT	1.74	1.60	1.42
sell at about	$5.75	$6.00	$7.00

ESTIMATE DETAIL:

Composition:
  pp PM @ _____
  pp text @ _____
  pp index @ _____
  pp ills @ _____

TOTAL _____ pages (as _____) $ _____
Draft _____ pp repros/negs @ _____ $ _____
C. + S. ills: _____ line ills @ _____ $ _____
   _____ halftone @ _____
   _____ loose prints @ _____
            TOTAL C. + S. $ _____

Plates: No. forms = _____
  First @ _____
  Second + subs. @ _____
  Work + turn @ _____
          TOTAL PLATES $ _____

MR: First @ _____
  Second + subs. @ _____
  Work + turn @ _____
          TOTAL MR $ _____

Run: No. forms: _____ x _____ M @ _____ /M = $ _____
  No. forms: _____ x _____ M @ _____ /M = $ _____
  No. forms: _____ x _____ M @ _____ /M = $ _____

Stock: Sheet size __ 2.75 __   4000   5000   7500
  No. forms _____ sheets/book x _____ M books =
  (or, no. forms = rms/M)   M (_____)   basis
  __ 2.75 ÷ 2 = 1.375 __ sheets/book
  plus _____ % spoil   Sheets
     6105   7563   11344
  TOTAL SHEETS =   347
  x M weight =   2240   2776   4163
  Total weight =   .35
  x cost/lb. =   971
  Total cost = $ 784   971   1457

Total Cost _____

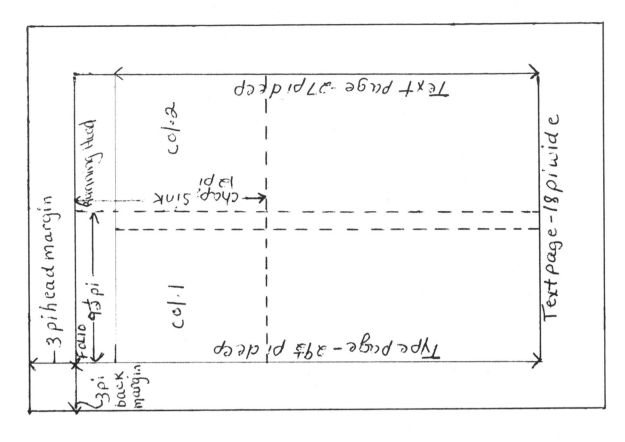

Mulch 4"×6"

The MIT Press

28 Carleton Street
Cambridge, Massachusetts 02142

Massachusetts Institute of Technology
617-253-5646

1 March 1977

M. Bradley
MIT In-House Media Computer Composition Group

Re: Mulch/NO TIME FOR HOUSEPLANTS

Enclosed is a marked edited manuscript of 176 pages, together with
composition specifications and a page layout. Also herewith are marked
sample pages (indicating any changes we have made in specifications).

There are 68 illustrations in this book. What we propose is that you
supply us with four sets of galleys(one marked set included). We will
prepare a dummy and return the dummy to you with marked galleys. You
will then provide us with three sets of page proof (one marked set
included). Finally, you will provide us with one set repro (with
holes where illustrations will go).

Our projected schedule is as follows:

manuscript to composition   3/2/77
galleys at MIT Press   4/15/77
galleys with dummy to comp   5/18/77
pages at MIT Press   6/15/77
pages to comp   7/13/77
repro to MIT Press   7/29/77

Please let me know immediately if you foresee any problems with this
schedule. We are looking for an October 1 book date and this schedule
allows that.

Thank you very much and please let me know if there are any questions.

pat mahon

MIT PRESS COMPOSITION SPECIFICATIONS

Author · Title Mulch/No Time for House Plants   Book code   Date 1/15/77

Composition In House   Linotype / Monotype / Film / Computer / IBM Composer / Typewriter

Format 4" x 6"   Trim size · 5 2/3 x 8 · 6 x 9 · 7 x 10 ·

Margin Head 3 picas · Back 3 picas.

Style

Typefaces · list by style, size, leading   Palatino bold + reg - 10/12, 9/11, 8/10

24 pt, 20 pt numbers

Makeup

Type page overall · wide 18 pi   deep 27½ pi

Text lines per page 30   excluding RH & folio

Text measure wide 18 pi   deep 27 pi

One column / Two column / Three column / Marginal column
1-2 column formats, as indicated

Space between columns 1 pi

Text column depth · full

Pages run long / short or long flush foot, 1 line only

Facing pages match / as they come · if possible. Do not add extra space.

Paragraphs · fl. / indent 1 em #   space between
First para under heads, fl. left

Style figures · lining / a, oc_lining

Spacing · French / between words / sentences tight

Unjustified · hyphenate to achieve good ragged right: x 18 pi

Word space tight

Text 9/11 Palatino reg. c+lc
fl. left x 18 pi, unjust.

Lists 9/11 Pal. reg. c+lc x 18 pi, unjust.
indent nos. 1 em #, runovers fl. left

Footnotes

    indent   / center /   turnovers

Bibliography 9/11 Pal. reg. c+lc
fl. left x 18 pi   Runovers fl. left   indent 5 p? space between items

Appendices 9/11 Pal. reg. c+lc fl. left x 18 pi, unjust.

Caption 9/11 Pal. reg. c+lc fl. left x 8.5 pi, unjust.

Headings

Parts none

Number

Headline   New recto / verso / 2 page spread

Text   Part sinkage   lines of text to part page
   Folio · RH / none
   Start text on new page R or V

Chapters

Number 24 pt. Palatino reg. fl. left, top of type page

Headings 19/21 Palatino bold c+lc, indent 9.5 pi,
top of type page, runovers indent 9.5 pi   Chapter sinkage 18 pi   lines of text to chapter page 20
   Start text on new page R or V

Text sinkage 4 18 pi   first words / first line   Folio · RH none

Front Matter

10/12, 9/11 Palatino reg. v. bold

Subheads

1 9/11 Palatino bold, all caps   +1 line space above 0 space below
fl. left x 18 pi, unjust.

2 9/11 Palatino bold c+lc   +1 line space above 0 space below
x 18 pi

3 9/11 Palatino bold c+lc   start new page · col. 3   space above 0 space below
indent 9.5 pi, x 8 pi

4   space above   space below

Running Heads

Verso 9/11 Pal. reg. c+lc, top of type page
indent 9.5 pi

Recto 9/11 Pal. reg. c+lc, top of type page
indent

Folios

Verso 9/11 Palatino reg.
top of type page

Recto 9/11 Palatino reg.
top of type page

Production / Design / MIT / 99

No Time for House Plants

No Time for House Plants
A Busy Person's Guide
to Indoor Gardening

Purvis Mulch

The MIT Press
Cambridge, Massachusetts, and London, England

Contents

2 Understanding House Plants

Every plant has its own preferences and requirements for soil type, light, temperature, ventilation, humidity, and several other factors that are within our power to control, or at least to mitigate. It is vitally important for you, as a busy indoor gardener, to understand the basics of each plant's requirements. A prior understanding will enable you to avoid much work later and will help you to achieve routine success in growing plants.

In addition to understanding these basic needs, you will want to know something about containers, repotting plants, propagation, and other topics that will help you to gain further enjoyment in raising better plants.

THE BASIC HOUSE PLANT

Location is the major difference between a house plant and an outdoor plant. Given the proper climate, all house plants could live and flourish outdoors. All are derived from forebears that lived, reproduced, and died outdoors, whether on a forest floor in central Europe or in the bough of a tree in a South American rain forest.

Roots

Roots serve two main purposes—to anchor the plant in the ground and to supply water and mineral salts from the soil. Bulbs, corms, rhizomes, and tubers serve much the same purposes while simultaneously acting as food storage areas. Roots, like the aboveground parts of plants, may be pruned without injuring the plant in any way.

If you water from the top, remember to remove any excess water from the saucer; allowing plants to stand in water encourages root rot. In time, you should learn to give each plant just enough water to soak it thoroughly, with very little excess drainage.

Some other watering tips:

1. Do not allow water to stand in the crown of any plant; this will encourage decay.

2. Never use very cold water, especially for tropical plants. Keep an open jar of water at room temperature for your house plants. Not only will the proper temperature be assured, but some of the chemicals in the water will have been dissipated by the time it is given to plants.

3. Artificially softened water may be detrimental to plant growth. If you can, use rainwater, or water that has not been softened. Fluorine and chorine, on the other hand, do not seem to pose any problems.

Table 1 **Watering Needs of Plants Under Various Conditions**

Plants will need more water when:	Plants will need less water when:
They are in a period of active growth	They are in a period of rest (usually during the winter)
They are in bright light	They are in dim light or under artificial light
Room humidity is low	Room humidity is high
Room temperature is high	Room temperature is under 70°
They are contained in small pots	They are in large pots
They are in clay pots	They are in nonporous pots
They are fast-growing varieties	They are slow-growing varieties
They are planted in sandy soil	They are planted in heavy soil
They are in flower or about to go into flower	

4 The Foliage Plants

The number and variety of house plants is staggering. For every combination of conditions a home can offer—including heat, light, and humidity—there are literally thousands of suitable house plant varieties. House plants offer a virtually limitless selection of sizes, forms, colors, patterns and textures, growth patterns, and flowering habits. Plant selections should be made so as to reconcile personal tastes with home growing conditions.

The house plants selected for discussion in this chapter are merely representative of the far greater varieties available. Many of the most common plants have been included while the more difficult varieties have been avoided. This chapter includes all the old favorites as well as some newer varieties and unusual plants which can add zest to your collection.

The plants have been divided into four broad categories: foliage plants, flowering plants, fruiting plants, and cacti and succulents. Within each group, individual plants are listed alphabetically by their common names, followed (in parentheses) by their scientific (or Latin) designations. The scientific name comprises both the genus and species.

FOLIAGE PLANTS

In this chapter, we will survey many of the house plants grown primarily for their foliage. Some of them, under favorable conditions, will flower from time to time although few should be selected for their flowering abilities. Most of these plants are fairly easy to grow and maintain, thereby providing even the beginner a wide variety of plants from which to choose.

The plants are listed in alphabetical order, according to their common or popular names. The scientific (or Latin) name is used for plants with no popular names, or for plants with more than one popular name. The index, which includes both common and scientific names, provides a convenient means of cross-checking names.

The symbols accompanying each plant name provide a quick and convenient guide to that plant's requirements. Remember, however, that these are guides and not strict demands. Many of these plants are tolerant by nature and will take to an east window as well as a west window; many can tolerate some direct sunlight even when none is recommended.

Dieffenbachia

There are many species of this popular plant, often called Dumbcane. It is prized for its large leaves with interesting markings, usually variations of cream and white on dark green. *Dieffenbachia* is a hardy plant and is not difficult to grow. Although growth is slow, most varieties attain a height of eighteen to twenty-four inches.

D. arvida "Exotica" is popular because it is even more durable than other members of the family. Other well-known species include *D. picta, D. amoena, D. sequina,* and *D. bowmannii.*

While Dieffenbachia has no special cultural requirements, it grows best under warm conditions and appreciates having its foliage cleaned regularly. The plant may be propagated by rooting stem cuttings in moist, warm peat.

Caution: Eating or nibbling on the leaves of *Dieffenbachia* can cause severe swelling of the tongue and mouth tissues, hence its popular name, Dumbcane. It should not be grown in a home with toddlers.

Many plants, such as this *Dieffenbachia pieta,* grow better when slightly potbound.

Dracaena

The many available species of *Dracaena* vary so greatly in appearance that some appear to be unrelated. Most grow tall—five feet or more—on sturdy stalks. They are very tough plants, tolerant of a surprising amount of neglect, all in all one of our most dependable house plants.

Some varieties to investigate are *D. deremensis* "Warnecki," *D. fragrans* (cornlike leaves), *D. fragrans massangeana* (yellow-striped leaves), *D. marginata* (an exciting plant with grasslike, cream-colored foliage edged in red—sometimes sold as *D. marginata tricolor*), *D. sanderiana* (white-banded leaves), *D. godseffiana, D. draco* (the Dragon Tree of the Canary Islands), and many others, some of which will doubtless be available from a good supplier. The dracaena mentioned, however, are some of the most attractive examples and are among the easiest to grow.

Dracaena sanderiana, D. fragrans, and Zebra Plant (*Aphelandra*).

Appendix 1

The ABCs of Artificial Light

The recent introduction of fluorescent tubes designed specifically for plant growing has been a great boon for indoor gardeners. With the aid of artificial light, we can now grow lush, green plants in areas where they would never grow before. A windowless bathroom, which might offer ideal humidity and temperature conditions, can now be made into an ideal plant-growing environment. Plants growing on a drab northern window sill can now receive supplemental light during winter's short and dark days. Dim corners of any room can be transformed into green showplaces. Cuttings and seedlings can now make faster and surer progress under artificial light, and we can even grow vegetables in the dead of winter in the bedroom or kitchen. Artificial lighting is not essential for house plant success, but it certainly broadens growing horizons and increases chances for maximum rewards.

The outdated incandescent bulb still offers some

Bibliography

ARTIFICIAL LIGHT GARDENING

Bickford, Elwood D. and Dunn, Stuart. *Lighting for Plant Growth.* Kent, Ohio: Kent State University Press, 1972.

Cherry, Elaine C. *Fluorescent Light Gardening.* New York: Van Nostrand Reinhold Co., 1965.

Elbert, George A. *The Indoor Light Gardening Book.* New York: Crown Publishers, Inc., 1975.

Fitch, Charles Marden. *The Complete Book of House-plants under Lights.* New York: Hawthorn Books, 1975.

Kranz, Frederick H. and Jacqueline. *Gardening Indoors under Lights.* rev. ed. New York: Viking Press, 1971.

BEGONIAS

Brilmayer, Bernice, *All about Begonias.* New York:

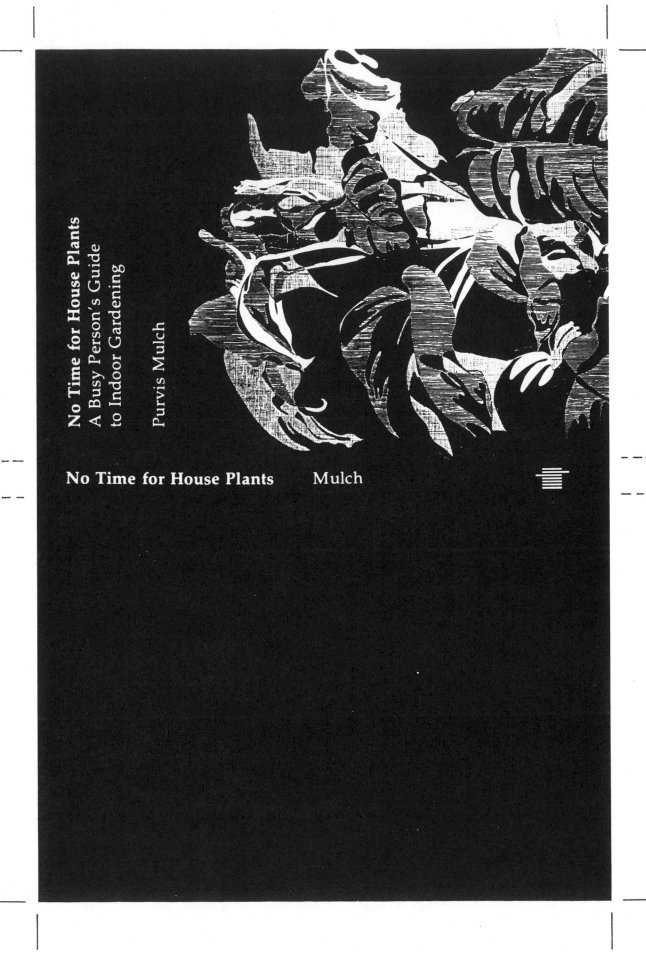

Background: PMS 354;   Illustration: Black overprinting green;   All type & colophon: Drop out white

No Time for House Plants
A Busy Person's Guide
to Indoor Gardening

Purvis Mulch

No Time for House Plants   Mulch

The MIT Press

28 Carleton Street
Cambridge, Massachusetts 02142

Massachusetts Institute of Technology
617-253-5646

March 15, 1977

Note:

If flaps are to be included, please add 2 1/8" (PMS 354) to each side of mechanical.

Thank you very much.

The MIT Press
Massachusetts Institute of Technology
Cambridge, Massachusetts 02142

Date March 14, 1977
Our PO No. _____
Job No. _____

Book Jacket Printing Order

To Arlington Lithograph
Author/Title Mulch/No Time for House Plants

See your quotation of Please call Pat Mahon 253-5640
Include breakdown with estimate

Quantity 4700

Dimensions
Spine 3/8"
Front 4 1/4" x 6 1/4"
Back 4 1/4" x 6 1/4"
Flaps 4"

☒ offset   ☐ letterpress

Trim size 12 7/8 inches wide x   6 1/4 inches deep   ☒ bleed, allow 1/8" for trim   ☐ no bleed)

Copy Herewith complete mechanical

Proofs _____ sets salt prints   1 sets 3M prints   imposition

Stock Grade offset coated   Color white   Basis 80 lb.
Size (1 side)   No. sheets
☒ supplied by printer   ☐ supplied by MIT

Ink ☐ black only   ☒ black and PMS 354   ☐ no black

Coating ☐ press varnish   ☐ plastic coat   ☐ none

Delivery
100   trimmed jackets to The MIT Press office
400   trimmed jackets to our warehouse at: The MIT Press
      c/o UNISERV, Inc.
      525 Great Road (Rte. 119)
      Littleton, Mass 01460

4200 untrimmed jackets to binder:
      Colonial Press
      Plant #2 Adams Road
      Clinton, MA

0   trimmed jackets to our London warehouse:
      P.A.G.E.S.
      17-21 Sunbeam Road
      London N.W. 10
      ENGLAND

Special Instructions Please ship jackets by 3/28
When the run is finished, please send us about 6 random press sheets that are representative of the run as a whole. Wait for our telephone OK before shipping sheets to the binder. Thank you.

Signed _Kenna Schenk_   The MIT Press

MIT Press

28 Carleton Street
Cambridge, Mass. 02142

BINDING SPECIFICATIONS

Date 3/16/77
Purchase Order
G-5678

See your quotation of

To Murray Printing Company
Author/Title Mulch/NO TIME FOR HOUSEPLANTS

From your pressroom

SHEETS
Quantity 4000   To come on
Sheet size 33 x 50   Imposition yours   supplied by Murray; please match
Quantity to bind 4000 (all)   Hold balance as F&G's folded sheets   color white of text stock as
closely as possible

OTHER MATERIALS
Endpapers printed plain   other
Headbands white black
Cloth
Board .080 binders .088 binders .040 red flex.   other .070
Foil
~~XXXXXXXXXXXXXXXXXXXXXXXXXXXXXXXXXXXXXXXXXXXXXXXXX~~
~~XXXXXXXXXXXXXXXXXXXXXXXXXXXXXXXXXXXXXXXXXXXXXXXXX~~
Covers printed paper nonwoven (to be adhered over boards)   supplied by MIT Press

BINDING
Trim size 5¼x8 6x9 7x10   other 4 x 6 upright   Head margin 3 picas Gutter margin 3 picas
(On adhesive bound books, trim size and gutter margin are given as the full dimensions, before trimming the spine)
Pages 224   No. signatures 3/64's, 1/32   Bulk 9/16"
Cancel or inserts none
Style Smyth sewn hardcover Smyth sewn paperback adhesive paperback
Reinforcing none paper cambric   Edges smooth rough   Line one super two supers paper
Cover one-piece two-piece three-piece   Spine round flat (Flat spines should not extend beyond front and back boards)

STAMPING none
Spine one hit two hits blind   color
Front one hit two hits blind   color
Back one hit two hits blind   color
Submit two sample cases for approval (with covers glued over boards)

SPECIAL INSTRUCTIONS

PACKING   SEE SEPARATE NOTICE ATTACHED
Pack books in 275-lb test, double-wall cartons. Mark each carton with:
Author MULCH
Title NO TIME
Code MNT   Books per carton please add

Pack cartons on skids which are to become the following dimensions:
and must not exceed the following dimensions:
3'6 x 2'8"
7' to 9' clearance from floor to underside

Bound books due our warehouse

Signed PAM 8/1/76
production manager

DELIVERY
23 copies to the MIT Press office
0 copies to T. D. Downing Co. for onward shipment to London
for our London office. See our Letter of July 1, 1970.
Author's copies as follows (shipping labels attached):
10 copies to:
Purvis Mulch

Balance to: Technical Impex Corp
Alexander Hamilton and Merrimack Streets
Lawrence, Massachusetts

---

28 Carleton Street
Cambridge, Mass. 02142

PRINTING SPECIFICATIONS

Purchase order

See your quotation of 11/30/76

To Murray Printing Company
Author/Title Mulch/NO TIME FOR HOUSEPLANTS

COPY
Text copy repros IBM Composer typewritten bound book negatives   other mechanicals with salts
Text reduction (% of original) 100%   in place for halftones and camera-
Illustration copy separate in text copy none   ~~copy in place for line drawings~~
You have already shot halftones and have negs on hand. '36 in all)
We will see these in place in book blues.
(There are also 30 line drawings which are in place in mechanicals.)
Text blueprints complete 1st signature only

PLATES
Offset surface   other
Letterpress plastic print from type   other
Trim size 5¼x8 6x9 7x10   other 4 x 6 upright   Head margin   Gutter margin
(On adhesive bound books, trim size and gutter margin are given as the full dimensions, before trimming the spine)
Pages 224   No. signatures   Imposition yours
Cancel or insert none

PRESSWORK
Quantity 4000   Ink color Black only other
Text stock size 33 x 50   basis 50# vellum   knit brand R&E Book
No. sheets about 7800 sheets   Supplied by MIT yes (on hand in lot   Supplied by printer
number G-567)

SPECIAL INSTRUCTIONS

SCHEDULE
Blues due MIT   Blues rel. to printer   Sheets due binder
(Cambridge)   (Cambridge)

DELIVERY
F&G's send 2 sets to The MIT Press with foul blues
(F&G's, with blueprints, must be sent immediately after job comes off press)

Flat sheets

Acceptance of this order will be considered as your agreement that the
negative flats produced as part of this order become the property of
The Massachusetts Institute of Technology Press.

Signed PAM 8/1/76
production manager

M.I.T. PRESS Manufacturing Cost Estimate

RELEASE COST SHEET   Date ___ 2/15/77

Author/Title ___ *No TIME FOR HOUSE PLANTS* ___

Manuscript Description

Ms total pages ___ 207 (b30 est) ___   No. halftones ___ 38 ___ est. to make ___ 38 ___ book pages

No. tables ___ 2 ___   No. line ills. ___ 0 ___ est. to make ___ book pages

No. to be drawn ___ 0 ___   No. camera-ready ___

Remarks ___

Book Description

Total pages ___ 224 ___ trim size ___ 4x6 upright ___   No. forms ___ 7/32's ___

Type page size ___ 33 x 50   60# offset ___   ☐ Mono   ☐ Lino   ☐ TW   ☒ Film (Copyright) Type

Paper ___ 33 x 50   60# offset   b-gone Playwright ___

Binding: ☒ sewn (cloth ___) bd.   ☐ ad. ☐ paper cover

Plant Costs	Estimated					Actual				supplier
Design	95									
Casting 38 M pp x 250 Composition 18#/c.	1116									
Alterations	121									
Engravings/prints	—									
Repros	—									
C. & S. ills. 38 x 3.72	142									
Plates	—									
Blues	67									
Jacket Comp	150									
Dies	30									
Contingencies 6%	103									
TOTAL PLANT	1824									
Edition Costs	4000	5000	7500							
Makeready	401	451	588							
Presswork	552	684	1012							
Paper	2400									
Binding 4/5 M @ .60 5/75 M @ .59 75 M @ .57		2950	4275							
M @						TOTAL	PAPER	CLOTH		
Jacket pw/paper	800	850	1125							
Freight	100	125	188							
Plate	387	387	387							
Total Edition	4640	5449	7575							
Total plant	1824	1824	1824							
TOTAL COST	6464	7273	9399							
Plant unit	.46	.36	.24							
Edition unit	1.16	1.09	1.01							
TOTAL UNIT	1.62	1.45	1.25							
Jacket @ 50¢ 2 col	1.59	1.43	1.23							

ESTIMATE DETAIL:

Composition: ___

pp FM @ ___

pp text @ ___

pp index @ ___

pp ills @ ___

TOTAL ___   pages (as ___)

pp repros/negs @ ___ $ ___

Draft ___   line ills @ ___ $ ___

C. + S. ills: ___   line @ ___

halftone @ ___

loose prints @ ___ $ ___

TOTAL C. + S. ___

Plates: No. forms = ___

First @ ___

Se-ond + subs. @ ___

Work + turn @ ___

TOTAL PLATES ___

MR: First @ ___

Se-ond + subs. @ ___

Work + turn @ ___

TOTAL MR ___

Run: Po. forms: ___ x ___ M @ ___   /M = $ ___

Po. forms: ___ x ___ M @ ___   /M = $ ___

No. forms: ___ x ___ M @ ___   /M = $ ___

Stock: Sheet size = 33 x 50   60#   4000 — 5000   7500

No. forms ___   sheets/book x ___ M books   M (basis)   sheets/book

(or, no. forms = rms/M)   plus $ spoil

TOTAL SHEETS = 7800   9700   14,300 (acc. to print)

60#   x M weight = .208 m   .208 m   .208 m   208 m

Total weight = 16324   20176   29744

x cost/lb. = .34   .34   .34   .34

Total cost = $ $ 558. $ 685.98 $ 1011.296

50#   .174 M   .174M   .174M   .174M

13572   16878   2488.2

.34   .34   .34

1461.   574.   846.

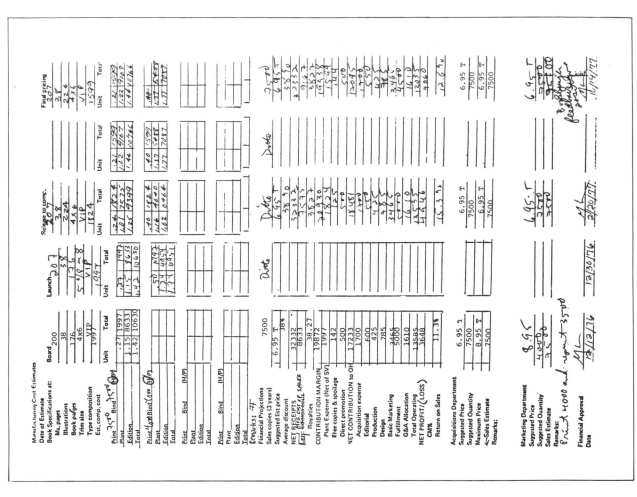

MIT PRESS

NEW PUBLICATION INFORMATION SHEET

Author or Editor ___ Purvis Mulch
Title (tentative) ___ NO TIME FOR HOUSEPLANTS
Title (final) ___

☒Hard ☐Paper
Discipline code ___ SD144
Subsidy $ ___
Permissions cleared? ___ yes
Translation required? ___ no
Special sales anticipated ___
Royalties ☒ Net ___ List

10 % 0 to 3000
12.5 % 3M to 6000
15 % to thereafter

Remarks:

Acquisitions Ed. ___ Greenhouse

☒ Press-owned ☐ Commission/Distrib. ☐ Import
Product line ___ Humanities
Series and Series No.
Source ___
Date ms. rec'd ___ 12/18/76
2nd copy ms.? ___ yes
Trans. est cost $ ___

Payable to ☒ Author ___ Other

Date ___ 12/19/76

Disc: Short ☐ Trade ☒ Text ☐
Contract date ___ 12/15/76
Board approved ___ 12/12/76
Actual cost $ ___
How to be charged ___
Ed. override ___ % (Net or List)
Royalty advances ___

Manuscript Data (Editorial Breakdown)
Type: ☒ms/cc/pcc
Ms pages
☐ FM
☐ text
☐ notes
☐ bibliography
☐ appendixes
Total ms pp.

Illustrations ___ 38
No. Items
tables
lists
equations
notes
extracts
legends
1 heads
2 heads
3 heads
4 heads

no. line drawings
camera-ready
draw and chg, auth.
no. halftones
no. in color (line, HT)

Scheduled dates
au, check complete
ms to Prod.
Editor assigned
☐ by freelance
Cost: Est. ___ Actual $
Hours: Est. ___ Actual ___
☐ Freelance
Proofreading ☐ None ☒ Editor
☐ Freelance
Cost: Est. ___ Actual ___
Index ☒ Author ☐ Freelance ☐ None
Chg. to ☐ Royalty ☐ Plant

Remarks:
Managing Ed. ___

Date ___

Production and Design
Trim size ___ 4x6 Total est. pp. ___ 176
Dummy: ☐ Full ☒ Partial ☐ None ☐ Freelance Cost Est. $
Scaling: ☒ In-house ☐ Freelance Cost Est. $
Type comp: ☐ filmset ☐ hot metal ☐ cold type ☐ camera copy ☐ in-house composition
Remarks:

Design ☒ In-house ☐ Freelance Cost Est. $425 Actual $
Actual $ ___ Freelance chg. to:
Actual $ ___

Design Mgr. ___ Date ___

Production Mgr. ___ Date ___

APPROVAL OF MS. RELEASE TO COMPOSITION
Hard ☒ Paper ☐ ___
Discount Cat. ___
Date ___ 2/20/77

APPROVAL OF FINAL PRICE AND PRINT QUANTITY
Final Print Schedule
Print ___ 7500 Hard ☒ Paper ☐
Bind ___ 7500 Discount Cat. ___
Final Price ___ 6.95 Date ___ 10/14/77
Director ___

Tentative Print Schedule
Print ___ 7500
Bind ___ 7500
Tentative Price ___ 6.95
Director ___

Manufacturing Cost Estimates

Book Specifications at:	Board	Launch	Release to comp.	Final pricing
Ms. pages	38	38	38	38
Illustrations	176	176	224	224
Book pages	4x6		4X6	176
Trim size	1997	VIP	1824	1599
Type composition				

	Unit	Total	Unit	Total	Unit	Total	Unit	Total
Print	.27	1997						
Edition	1.15	8633						
Total	1.42	10630						

Financial Projections
Sales copies (3 years) ___ 7500
Suggested list price ___ 6.95
Average discount ___ 38%
NET RECEIPTS ___ 32332
Less: cost of sales ___ 8633
Royalties ___ 38.27
CONTRIBUTION MARGIN ___ 19872
Plant Expense (Net of SV) ___ 1997
Free copies & spoilage ___ 142
Direct promotion ___ 500
NET CONTRIBUTION to OH ___ 17233
Acquisition expense ___ 1700
Editorial ___ 600
Production ___ 425
Design ___ 785
Basic Marketing ___ 5000
Fulfillment ___ 1610
G&A Allocation ___ 13585
Total Operating ___ 3648
NET PROFIT/(LOSS) ___
CM% ___ 11.3%
Return on Sales ___

Acquisitions Department
Suggested Price ___ 6.95
Suggested Quantity ___ 7500
Maximum Price ___ 8.95
← Sales Estimate ___ 7500
Remarks:

Marketing Department
Suggested Price ___ 8.95
Suggested Quantity ___ 7500
Sales Estimate ___
Remarks:

Financial Approval ___
Date ___ 12/30/76

The MIT Press   28 Carleton Street   Massachusetts Institute of Technology

Cambridge, Massachusetts 02142   617-253-5646

Purvis Mulch

8 January 1977

Dear Purvis Mulch,

We are enclosing a copy of our author questionnaire
which is essential to our overall marketing plans for
your book No Time for House Plants. As far as you are
able to, please provide suggestions about advertising,
the names of professional groups and/or industrial
concerns whose mailing lists may be useful in promoting
the book, the names of periodicals which are likely to
review the book, in addition to your curriculum vitae.

We would appreciate it if you would fill out the enclosed
questionnaire as completely and as soon as possible.
Please return it to me at the above address.

Thank you for your prompt attention to this matter.

Sincerely,

Mary E. Collins

Mary E. Collins
Marketing Department

Previous Books. Please give titles, publishers, and dates.

The Earthworm Book (contract, Rodale Press, Inc., 1977)

Affiliations. Please separate present from past, giving pertinent academic, business, and governmental affiliations; include professional and other honors, and relevant offices held.

President, Dane County ( ) chapter, American Gourd Society (1974-present)
Affiliate, Smithsonian Institution, 1972-73
Member, National Geographic Society, 1970-71
Member, Book-of-the-Month Club, 1969 (revoked)
Close friend of former Phi Beta Kappa member (1939)
Life member, American Red Cross Gallon Club (1957)

Other Biographical Information. Place of birth, marital status, children, principal foreign countries lived in, etc., any notable information that may help fill out the picture.

Born of wealthy but honest parents in Allentown, Pa., 1933. Still bear scars of Great Depression. Ate insects in father's victory garden 1942-45. Grew first house plant in 1948 (eggplant). Average student in public school, brilliant but undisciplined in college, only history undergraduate at Univ. of Iowa to ever pass Advanced Bridge and Crown course in dental school. Became intensely interested in gardening when, in post-college rooming house in Emmaus, Pa., mushrooms grew under bed. Investigation into causes led to general gardening inquiry, also clear understanding of Emmaus, Pa. housing code. From that point on, it was one thing after the other.

AUTHOR QUESTIONNAIRE

When completed, please return to:

Mary E. Collins
THE MIT PRESS
28 Carleton St.
Cambridge, Mass. 02142

TITLE OF BOOK AS IT IS TO APPEAR IN PRINT:

No Time for House Plants: A Busy Person's Guide to Indoor Gardening

The promotion of a book is necessarily a mutual effort: the author has the information, the publisher the promotional organization. The effectiveness of our promotional copy -- for jacket, catalogue, publicity releases, flyers, brochures and space advertising -- depends directly upon the thoroughness with which you complete this questionnaire. We urge you to develop your replies to whatever extent necessary to give us adequate and useful information.

PLEASE RETURN THIS QUESTIONNAIRE AT THE EARLIEST POSSIBLE DATE.

Date: January 29, 1977

ABOUT THE AUTHOR:
Your name as you wish it to appear in print Purvis Mulch

Home address and phone number

Present title and position
freelance garden writer, lecturer, and plant exorcist
Copyright information required:

Your legal address

Nationality U.S.

Education. Please list college, concentrations, degrees (with dates), and honors

Allentown Business College; certificate, payroll, accounting, 1952
University of Iowa; B.A. (history), B.S. (repotting), 1961 (no honors)

Research. Please list any research, discoveries, and inventions, and publications reporting such work.

Research is not my forte. In 1958, I grew two coleus for a period of eight months, one of which was shut in a dark closet and given no water or food; the other in a sunny window where it was watered regularly and fertilized with a balanced formula according to directions. Both died.

Artwork. Specify illustrations, figures, photos, etc., by figure or cut number if possible, that can be used in advertising to stimulate interest.

Any of the photographs or drawings submitted with the manuscript may be used for advertising purposes.

Endorsements. Who are considered leaders in the field (names and addresses) from whom we might solicit endorsements of your book after publication? Both foreign and domestic leaders should be considered.

M. C. Goldman, Managing Editor, Organic Gardening & Farming magazine
Jeffrey Klein, Editorial Board, Mother Jones magazine
Elvin MacDonald, Senior Editor, House Beautiful magazine
Heather Tischbein, Managing Editor, Countryside magazine

Reviews. List periodicals, domestic and foreign, which are most likely to review the book. Please star major journals.

The four listed above, plus NYTBR, Apartment Ideas, Apartment Life, Ms, Esquire, Better Homes & Gardens, Playboy, other magazines geared to the single and/or working life.

Description. In describing what your book is about, please cover these areas: PURPOSE, SUBJECT MATTER, WHAT MAKES YOUR BOOK UNIQUE? INTENSITY or EXTENSIVENESS OF TREATMENT, THE AUDIENCE INTENDED, APPROACH TO THE SUBJECT AREA COVERED, SPECIAL NEED FULFILLED BY THE BOOK, CONCLUSIONS.

Your response will provide us with our primary source of reliable information for use in all our advertising and promotional efforts on behalf of the book. WE URGE YOU, THEREFORE, TO BE AS COMPLETE AS POSSIBLE.

In 1973, with the purchase of a new house, I was determined to increase my house plant population. Still, I realized that, with my busy schedule, I would not have much time to devote to indoor plants. I was frequently gone for long periods of time, and many days, even while in town, I simply have no time to fuss with plants.

I therefore sought to find methods to raise interesting and beautiful house plants with the least amount of effort. All the house plant books I checked, however, were apparently written by enthusiasts who spent unending hours in careful watering, potting, repotting, propagating, tying up, inducing to flower, humidifying, bathing, and even talking to their plants in an effort to get them to grow. There was no book for the casual house plant grower.

There is now such a book. By researching many sources, and through past personal experience and experimentation, I have narrowed down the crucial requirements for a "no-time" indoor house plant population. The research yielded two cardinal rules: Choose plants that are tolerant of adverse conditions, and then give them the right conditions to grow without your constant attention.

The implementation of these rules forms the crux of this book. I explain how to choose plants, tell which are the easiest to grow, and explain the conditions of light, soil moisture, humidity, and temperature that each of more than a hundred indoor plants requires. I explain, in short, how your house plants can live well without your constant attention and painstaking devotion.

The chapter on understanding house plants is critically important to the "no-time" system, since it details the initial requirements plants need for success, including potting mixtures, fertilizing, containers, watering, humidity, ventilation, temperature, light, and pruning. When these conditions are met at the very beginning, countless hours will be saved later in nursing plants or attempting to track down troubles.

There is a separate chapter devoted to plant troubles and cures, and special sections on artificial light, summer care, and lists of plants for various conditions of light and temperature. For those who wish to devote a little more time to raising house plants, there is detailed information on repotting, propagation, training, dish gardens, planters, bottle gardens and terrariums, kitchen scrap gardens, and growing vegetables indoors.

The bulk of the book, however, comprises listings of more than a hundred "easy" foliage plants, flowering plants, and succulents, including cacti, giving light, soil moisture, and humidity requirements for each.

For the home owner or apartment dweller who wants to raise several dozen attractive house plants while spending only a few minutes a day

Advertising. Please list magazines and scholarly journals which accept advertising, where notice of your book might be especially effective.

The same magazines previously cited for review

Mailing lists. Please list the professional groups and industrial concerns whose mailing lists may be useful in promoting this book. Your efforts in this area can be especially valuable. Can you help us to secure the lists of any of these organizations? If so, please specify.

Subscription lists to the above magazines would be effective; also numerous garden clubs, e.g., African-Violet Society of America, American Fern Society, American Horticultural Society, Cactus and Succulent Society of America, etc.

Newspapers. Please list hometown or other newspapers to whom you or your books are news.

Competition with other books: Please give titles and dates of publication.

There are too many house plants books in print to attempt a listing here. However, there is none competing directly--none that instructs the busy working person in specific methods of caring for house plants with a minimum of time expended.

Courses. Please list courses for which your book might be used as text or collateral reading.

Probably extension or short courses in growing indoor plants.

The MIT Press   28 Carleton Street   Massachusetts Institute of Technology
Cambridge, Massachusetts 02142   617-253-5646   Telex 92-1497

Purvis Mulch

Dear Purvis Mulch,

Enclosed is the draft of an announcement of
your book. This will be used on the flaps of
the jacket and in our catalogue. Please return
it with your corrections of fact and suggestions
at your earliest convenience. If you have no
changes, or only very minor ones, you may want
to call either Randall Goff or myself at (617)
253-2884.

Sincerely,

Mary E. Collins
Mary E. Collins
Marketing Department
June 15, 1977

Enc.

Jacket copy -- Purvis Mulch/NO TIME FOR HOUSEPLANTS

Here at last is THE definitive, busy person's guide to raising,

feeding, caring for, and loving houseplants -- a book so

comprehensive and so comprehensible that no one who reads it

need ever exclaim, "I have no time for houseplants!"

Three introductory chapters explain carefully and thoroughly

the basic needs of your house plants -- soil, water, air, light --

and how you can meet those needs simply yet fully. Then come

several specialized sections which show the best and easiest ways

to make your particular plant healthy and happy -- whether it's a

colorful flowering plant, a beautiful lush foliage plant, or a

miniaturized terrarium collection.

Throughout the book, many photographs and sketches give you an

exact idea of what to do and how best to do it.

Purvis Mulch is a   columnist and houseplant lover,

author of such books as I LIKE PLANTS and PLANTS ARE A LOT LIKE

PEOPLE IN SOME WAYS.

Sketch of marketing plan

Direct mail

A sample copy would be sent to each of our 500 best retail accounts accompanied by a special order form quoting appropriate endorsements.

We would also compile a list of people in the trade (e.g. nurseries) to mail to.

An offer of a sample copy would be sent to all our bookseller customers.

Advertising

An announcement of the book would be included in our fall catalog.

This title would also be included in seasonal announcement ads in publications such as Publisher's Weekly and Library Journal.

Since we usually group books for ads, and this title could not be grouped with others on our list, individual advertisements would be very few, placed in horticultural magazines.

Review copies

We maintain our review list on a computer system such that we can order labels of publications based on subject matter and importance. In the case of this book we would choose review media coded as major newspapers, major general magazines, general science publications, including newspaper science writers, general biology publications, publications on botany, ecology horticulture, and phytopathology.

In addition to these, we would send additional copies to review media not on our standing review file, such as gardening magazines, home magazines, and women's magazines.

The approximate total number dispatched would probably be in the range of 180-240, probably closer to the latter.

PROMOTION AND DIRECT MARKETING FALL 1977

Promotion Expense '3070

Book

Bound date   Edition

NO TIME FOR HOUSEPLANTS
by Purvis Mulch
4x6-- 176 pp. -- $6.95T

10/77   7500

Publication date

11/15/77

Direct Mail 18 00 (@ '200)

Although this is primarily a trade title, it will also be featured in all 8 subject
matter catalogs. In addition, it will play a prominent role in the Christmas Gift
Treasury Catalog.

Space Advertising "500

Given the limitations of budget, we must stretch our advertising as far as possible.
Ads will be placed in as many as of the following as is feasible:

PW   Plants Alive
New York Times   Boston magazine
Home Garden Magazine   Countryside
Apartment Life
Apartment World
Boston Globe
McCall's
House & Garden
Avant Gardener

Exhibits "50

MIT Booth: ABA
            CBA
Montreal Book Fair
Globe Book Fair

Seasonal Catalog "70

Announced in the Fall 1977 catalog mailed to bookstores, libraries, wholesalers,
and the MIT community.

Review Copies 150

100 or so complimentary copies will include magazines listed under "Space Ads"
above, plus:

    Esquire   Ms
    Cosmo   Mother Jones
    Playboy   Organic Gardening & Farming
    Countryside   House Beautiful
Boston Herald American   American Nurseryman
    Phoenix, Real Paper, etc.
    and to 10-20 plant "experts"

Table of Contents

MEMO: Acquisitions / Administration

The Mulch manuscript was logged in by our editorial department in December 1975. At first our staff was skeptical at best about the appropriateness of a university press publishing, or even hypothetically publishing, a trade title like the Mulch. Our readers, two botanists and a plant store owner, were mixed in their reactions to the manuscript and shared some of our skepticism, but despite the divergent opinions of our readers and our initial misgivings, we soon warmed to the project and to the charm of Purvis.

The manuscript was returned twice to the author for revisions suggested by our readers and the editor-in-chief. Once revisions were completed, the next step was to prepare our decision-to-publish form, including the title budget, and present the project to our board of governors.

NO TIME FOR HOUSEPLANTS? is not a typical university press publication. In publishing the Mulch we were obviously entering a very crowded and highly competitive market in which an attractive price and a well-planned marketing approach would be critical to success. A low unit manufacturing cost, under $1.50, was a necessity.

Our manufacturing estimates were based on a print run of 7,500 copies, a figure that the director, editor-in-chief, marketing manager, and business manager nervously settled on after admitting that our resources and list of trade publications would limit our marketing effort to the southeast.

The completed decision-to-publish form, accompanied by the readers' reports and a statement from the sponsoring editor, was presented to our board of governors, whose editorial and finance committees consider the merit and financial factors associated with each project. Following acceptance by the board, a contract was drawn up with Ms. Mulch and the manuscript was sent for copyediting.

MEMO: Editorial Procedures

The managing editor was first exposed to the houseplant MS when the comptroller asked for an estimate for editorial overhead. The figure given was based on an average editorial cost figured from one year's experience in working with free-lance editors and was for the entire MS, not just the portion to be edited for the project. We had averaged $1.50 per MS page, which included the free-lance editing, the free-lance proofreading, and the in-house time spent on transferring marks, jacket preparation, and correspondence. In the few years immediately before working exclusively with free-lance editors, our editorial overhead had been approximately $4.00 per MS page.

The managing editor selected an experienced free-lance editor, and, when the MS was returned to the press, a photocopy was sent to the author for review. A covering letter was sent explaining that this was the appropriate time to make final changes, as he would see only page proof. Although we allow 5% of composition cost for author's alterations, this figure was not mentioned in the letter although it had appeared in the contract. The log reveals interesting differences in the percentage allowed for AAs: MIT allows 10%; Chicago 5%; Texas none; and Toronto budgets 20% of composition. When the photocopy was returned to the managing editor, she transferred the author's answers to queries and other changes to the original MS and, after preparing the editorial checklist, copy for running heads, and the frontmatter, gave the MS to the production manager for design and composition. The managing editor approved sample pages, and a production schedule was sent to the author. The original MS and two sets of proof were sent to the author for corrections, and the proof was also read by both production and editorial proofreaders. Revised pages and repros were checked by the managing editor, and the rest is history-- the history of One Book / Five Ways.

MEMO: Production / Design

In an effort to design and produce something that would compete in the book store with other trade titles--and, of course, we wanted the book to be attractive and readable--we did many things with this book that we would not ordinarily do with our usual scholarly monograph. One was the use of a photograph taken by the son of the production and design manager of a pathetic plant, a photo that demonstrates in its poignancy the theme of NO TIME FOR HOUSEPLANTS? Other factors in our planning had to do with the use of halftones, which are now so inexpensive to print, and the suggestion of a legibility study that a short measure containing just the phrase that the reader perceives with one eye movement is the most readable. Since it was impossible to produce a four-color trade jacket on our budget, we opted for a little bright green subliminal package that we hoped would attract the curious, sophisticated, busy, professional reader.

After layouts and specs were completed by the designer, the MS was turned over to a senior compositor who worked up the sample pages, and then the book went to the keyboard for corrections and line justification. Although the ragged right phrasing proved interesting, there were problems with ideal breaks. After galleys had been run through the VIP, they were pasted up, allowing a flexible column length for smoother layout work in placement of photos and headings. After paging, the book was proofread, line corrections were made, a quality check was made by four people in production and one in editorial, and the repros were off to the printer. Normally the book would have gone through a similar check in blues, and since this step was bypassed for the project, we failed to notice that the photo on the title page, which is also on the cover, was flopped. Our struggling plant must simply be reaching for the sun--wherever it may be.

MEMO: Sales/Promotion

In this project, North Carolina is the only press without sales representation. This was the controlling factor in our initial printing decision. It also controlled our promotion plans. We decided to focus our marketing effort on North Carolina, South Carolina, and Virginia, where our relationships with booksellers are well established, and in the author's home area--where she says she's well established. Our rather small marketing area is the major difference between North Carolina's promotion plan and those of other presses. We scheduled two "regional" ad campaigns, one on publication and the second during the Christmas season. Our only national ads are for Publishers Weekly. National advertising did not make much sense, we felt, because of the slim chance of having books available across the country. We have used "pre-pub" quotes in our sample ads to emphasize that we would secure advance quotes for this book. Our efforts would be directed to well-known and busy people, not houseplant experts.

Rather important, but not emphasized in the log, is our decision to send a majority of the newspaper review copies and news releases to lifestyle editors rather than book review editors. We have a better chance of getting publicity this way. Major buyers in our marketing area and wholesalers would receive reading copies. Advertising schedules (where relevant) and a brochure on the book would accompany reading copies. The brochure is important since the design of the book does not include jacket copy.

Finally, a comment on the title change. I did not like NO TIME FOR HOUSEPLANTS. Neither did anyone else at The UNC Press or the booksellers we queried. The title is negative and it is not clear. Adding the question mark seemed an appropriate solution and, to me, represents a real improvement.

Date: October 22, 1976

To: Johanna Grimes

From: John Rollins

Request for Marketing Estimates

Title and Author: No Time For House Plants-Purvis Mulch

Number of Pages: 222

Potential Market(s): Urban and Suburban adult reading public. Primarily Professional + Business People + families

Suggested Discount Classification: Trade

Initial Price Suggestions coupled with estimates of associated demand: Book is price Sensitive

Suggest range of 5.95 to 7.95

Marketing Cost Estimates:

Demand in units: 7500

Advertising: $3,500

Direct Mail: $ 500

Direct Time: 3 weeks $1,500

Comps Review Copies $ 400

Other Direct Costs: $ —

To: Gwen Duffey

Date: October 22, 1976

EDITORIAL ESTIMATES REQUEST

Title and Author: NO TIME FOR HOUSE PLANTS-Purvis Mulch

Number of Pages: 222

Inhouse editing _____ or Freelance editing ✓

Estimate of ___ hours needed to edit the manuscript: 53

Special editorial considerations: Many illustrations

Editorial Cost Estimates: #332   Editing: $ 266

Proof: $ 66

Please estimate for entire manuscript

Page 2

DECISION TO PUBLISH: *page 2*

The University of North Carolina Press
P.O. Box 2288
Chapel Hill, North Carolina 27514
(919) 933-2105

Title Budget

Title: NO TIME FOR HOUSEPLANTS ?   Author: Purvis Mulch

Printing: Initial printing and binding 7,500

		Unit Figures
Retail price		$ 7.95
Avg. discount		$ 3.34
Avg. net proceeds		$ 4.61

INCOME FROM SALES:

$ 4.61 × 7,100 copies = net proceeds $ 32,731 $ 4.61

COST OF SALES:

Manufacturing:
Plant Costs	$ 2,027		
Running Costs	3,448		
Binding Costs	4,058	$ 9,533	$ 1.34

Royalties:
10% of retail on all copies sold $ 5,645 $ .80

GROSS MARGIN ON SALES: $ 15,178 $ 2.14

SALE OF SUBSIDIARY RIGHTS: none foreseen $ -- $ --

   $ 17,553 $ 2.47

MARGINAL (OUT OF POCKET) DEPARTMENTAL EXPENDITURES:
Editorial	$ 332		
Marketing	4,000		
Order	(700		
Shipping	(		
Other		$ 5,032	$ .71

CONTRIBUTION TO ADMINISTRATIVE AND FIXED OH: $ 12,521 $ 1.76

PRORATED SHARE OF ADMINISTRATIVE AND FIXED OH:
Editorial	$ 1,000		
Production	350		
Marketing	3,800		
Administrative	6,400	$ 11,550	$ 1.63

TITLE SURPLUS OR (DEFICIT):   971 $ .13

SUBSIDY: $ $

SUBSIDIZED SURPLUS OR (DEFICIT): $ $

Page 1

DECISION TO PUBLISH: *page 1*

The University of North Carolina Press
P.O. Box 2288
Chapel Hill, North Carolina 27514
(919) 933-2105

Date: December 21, 1976

Author: Purvis Mulch

Title: NO TIME FOR HOUSEPLANTS?

Edition size: 7,500   Trim size: 5" x 7 3/8"   Number of Pages: 192

Cloth or Paper: cloth   Illustrations: 7 linecuts   30 halftones

Acquisition Editor: PETE MOSS

Projected Markets: General adult reading public, with special emphasis on urban and suburban population in the southeast.

Discount Classification: Trade   Expected Discount: 42%

Special Funding Considerations: none

Sales Forecasts, in $ and in units:

Time Period	Estimated Sales for Period	Estimated Cumulative Sales
6 months	$10,142 - 2,200	$10,142 - 2,200
6 –12 months	6,454 - 1,400	16,596 - 3,600
2nd year	9,220 - 2,000	25,816 - 5,600
3rd year	5,915 - 1,500	32,731 - 7,100
4th year		
5th year		

Expected Publishing Season: Fall 1977

MEMORANDUM OF AGREEMENT

Purvis Mulch

whose address is   13 Mouldering Way, Pemigewasett, Kansas
hereinafter described as the Author, and referred to by the masculine singular pronoun, and the University of North Carolina Press, Incorporated, of Chapel Hill, North Carolina, hereinafter described as the Press, agree as follows with respect to the publishing of a literary work, approximately

55,500   words in length and tentatively entitled

NO TIME FOR HOUSEPLANTS?

hereinafter described as the Work:

ARTICLE I. THE AUTHOR'S GUARANTEE

1. *Guarantee of Proprietorship.* The Author guarantees that the Work has not heretofore been published in book form, and that he is the Author Editor and, for the purpose of making this agreement, the sole proprietor of the Work.

2. *Guarantee Against Violation of Property Rights, Libel, or Unlawful Matter.* The Author guarantees that the Work is in no way whatever a violation of any existing copyright or other property right, and contains nothing libelous or otherwise unlawful; and that he will hold harmless and defend the Press from all manner of claims on the ground that the Work contains such violation, or anything libelous or otherwise unlawful; and that he will compensate the Press for any sums, including its attorney's fees, which it may find it necessary to pay in settlement of any claim or judgment against it, by reason of any violation of copyright or other property right or publication of libel or unlawful matter.

3. *Guarantee Against Conflicting Books by Author.* The Author agrees that during the life of this agreement he will not, without the consent of the Press, furnish to any other publisher any work on the same subject, of similar extent and character, which may conflict with the sale of the Work.

4. *Suits Against Others for Infringement.* The Author shall divide equally with the Press the expenses of any suit the Press may bring against any other party for infringement of copyright or violation of other property right, and shall receive one-half of any damages or profits, less attorney's fees and disbursements, that may be recovered in any such suit; or the Author may, at his option, decline to participate in the risks and proceeds of any such suit, leaving both open to the Press.

ARTICLE II. CONDITIONS OF PUBLICATION

1. *Extent of the Press's License.* The Author grants to the Press and its successors, representatives, and assigns full, sole, and exclusive license to print, publish, and sell the Work in book form throughout the world, and to sell or lease such other rights as are enumerated in Article V hereunder, during the full term of the copyright of the Work, and any renewals thereof. Rights not specifically granted to the Press are reserved to the Author.

2. *Publication of the Work.* The Press shall within a reasonable time publish the Work, at its own expense (except as provided for in Articles III and IV), in such style and manner, and shall keep it in print as long, and at such times, as it shall deem expedient.

3. *Copyright.* The Press agrees to take out copyright in its own name in the United States, but it shall not be obligated to take out any copyright elsewhere. The Press shall also have the right to effect any renewals of copyright that may be provided for by law, and the right to any assistance from the Author or his executor, administrator, heirs, or next of kin essential thereto.

ARTICLE III. AUTHOR'S RESPONSIBILITY FOR DELIVERY AND PREPARATION OF MANUSCRIPT, PROOF READING, AND NEW EDITIONS

1. *Delivery of Manuscript.* If the complete manuscript of the Work has not been delivered, the Author agrees to deliver a complete manuscript satisfactory to the Press not later than   January 1, 1977

2. *Preparation of Manuscript.* If, in the judgment of the Press, the manuscript is not furnished properly prepared for composition, the Author shall have the option of preparing it properly or commissioning the Press to do so at the Author's expense.

3. *Illustrations.* If the Author and the Press agree that the Work requires illustrations, the Author agrees to deliver to the Press within a reasonable time such photographs, drawings, diagrams, maps, graphs, or charts as are necessary in a condition suitable to the Press for reproducing without retouching, redrawing, or additional art work.

4. *Permissions for Use of Copyright Material.* Pursuant to the guarantee of Article I, the Author agrees to deliver promptly to the Press written authorizations for the use of any copyright material included in the Work, or any other material for which an authorization is necessary; and the Author agrees to pay all fees required for the use of such material.

5. *Proof Corrections.* The Press shall submit to the Author such proofs as it and the Author agree are necessary. The Author agrees to read, revise, correct, and promptly return all proof sheets of the Work, and to pay the cost of alterations in proof required by the Author, other than printers' errors, in excess of ____ 5% ____ of the cost of original composition. However, the Author shall pay the full cost of any changes which are necessary for the correction of actual errors, after the Press has made correction in conformity with the Author's directions on the last proof that the Press has agree to submit to him.

6. *Index.* The Author shall promptly furnish copy for an index satisfactory to the Press, if it considers one desirable; or at his option the Author may commission the Press to prepare an index at his expense.

7. *New Editions.* Whenever the Press and the Author agree that it is necessary, the Author shall prepare material for new editions of the Work. In case of desiring a new edition, or new editions, after the Author's death and disability, the Press may engage competent persons to prepare them, and charge the expense against the Author's royalty.

ARTICLE IV.

The Press shall pay the author a royalty of 10% of the retail price on all copies sold of the regular edition except for such royalties as are specified in Article V hereinunder.

ARTICLE V. SPECIAL RIGHTS AND ROYALTIES

1. *Special Royalties on the Regular Edition.* In lieu of such royalties as may be specified in Article IV on the Press's regular editions of the Work, the following royalties shall be paid to the Author under the conditions specified:

a. On books, whether bound or in sheets, sold at a discount greater than forty-six per cent (46%) from the list price, the Press shall pay the Author ten per cent (10%) of the actual price received.

b. On books sold for export, whether bound or in sheets, the Press shall pay the Author a royalty of ten per cent (10%) of the actual price received.

engravings of illustrations (if any), at one-half their cost to the Press, including the composition. If the Author fails to exercise this option by paying for the same in cash, this agreement shall terminate, and the Press shall have the right to dispose of the property as it sees fit, free of any commission or royalty to the Author.

ARTICLE X. ASSIGNMENT

This agreement shall be binding upon the assigns, heirs, executors, or administrators of the Author, and upon the assign or successors of the Press.

ARTICLE XI.

In consideration of the respective undertakings herein set forth, the Author and the Press agree to all the provisions of this agreement, and in testimony thereof affix their signatures, this ___1st___ day of ___January___, 19 _77_, at Chapel Hill, North Carolina.

Witness to signature of _____

                           Purvis Mulch

Witness to signature of _____

                      AUTHOR

                THE UNIVERSITY OF NORTH CAROLINA PRESS, INC.

           Matthew Hodgson, Director

Memorandum of Agreement

Between

      Purvis Mulch

and

THE UNIVERSITY OF NORTH CAROLINA PRESS

Made ___January   1,___ 19 _77_

at Chapel Hill, North Carolina

---

c. *After two years* from the date of the original publication, if the Press, in order to reduce an overstock of the Work, reduces the list price of its regular edition of the Work by fifty per cent (50%) or more, it shall pay the Author a royalty of five per cent (5%) of the list price of each copy sold at the reduced price.

2. *Cheap Editions.* The Press shall have the right to publish under its own imprint cheap editions of the Work at a list price not less than two-thirds of the original list price, and the Press agrees to pay the Author a royalty of 3½ per cent (6___%) of the net price of each copy sold of such editions. The Press shall also have the right to license the cheap edition rights of the Work to a regular publisher of cheap editions, and in this case it shall pay the Author one-half of the sums received from the cheap edition publisher.

3. *Copies Exempt from Royalties.* No royalty shall be paid on free copies furnished to the Author, or on copies for review, sample, or other similar purpose, or on copies sold below manufacturing cost, or on books sold in any accounting period, as defined in Article VII, in which no more than five copies are sold.

4. *Permission to Reprint Selections from the Work.* The Press may permit others to publish such selections from the Work, for publicity, educational, or scholarly purposes, as it may consider appropriate, without charge; but if any fee is charged, the Press shall pay one-half of the fee to the Author.

5. *Second Serial, Syndication, Anthology, and Digest Rights.* The Press shall control second serial, syndication, anthology, and digest rights, and if such rights are sold or leased, the Press shall pay the Author one-half of the net sums received.

6. *Book Clubs.* If the Press sells the book-club rights of the Work to a recognized book club which pays a royalty or outright sum for a license to distribute the Work to its members or subscribers, the Press shall pay to the Author one-half the net sums received.

7. *Foreign and Translation Rights.* The Press shall have exclusive right to arrange for publication of the Work in all foreign countries and for translations of the Work, on a royalty basis or for an outright fee, and it shall pay the Author three-fourths of the net proceeds of any such sale or license.

8. *Non-Book Rights.* The Press shall control dramatic, motion picture (sight and sound), radio, television, electrical recording, and microfilm rights, and if such rights are sold or leased the Press shall pay the Author three-fourths of the net proceeds of any such sale or lease.

ARTICLE VI. AUTHOR'S COPIES

The Press shall give to the Author on publication __12__ copies of the Work, and the Author shall have the right to purchase further copies for personal use but not for resale at a discount of thirty-three and one-third per cent (33⅓%) from the list price.

ARTICLE VII. SETTLEMENT OF ACCOUNTS

The Press shall render a statement of account annually, on August 1, as of June 30th of each year, and shall make settlement in cash within three months after the date of the statement.

ARTICLE VIII. THE PRESS'S LIABILITY FOR LOSS OR DAMAGE

Except for loss or damage due to its own negligence, the Press shall not be responsible for loss or damage to any property of the Author in its possession or in the possession of its independent contractors, or in the possession of anyone else to whom delivery is made by the Press in the normal course of its operations.

ARTICLE IX. TERMINATION

If, at any time after two years from the date of publication, the Press shall be satisfied that the public demand does not justify a continued publication of the Work, or if for any other cause it shall deem the further publication of the Work improper or inexpedient, the Press shall have the right to terminate this agreement by sending written notice to the latest address given by the Author to the Press. Thereupon the Author shall have the right within ninety (90) days to take from the Press, as an entirety, the copyright, all bound copies and sheets on hand, and the stamps, electrotype plates, and engravings of illustrations (if any), at one-half their cost to the Press, including the composition. If the

THE UNIVERSITY OF NORTH CAROLINA PRESS

Box 2288, Chapel Hill, N. C. 27514

4 December 1975

Dear

Joyce Kachergis gave me yesterday the original copy of your manuscript on house plants, together with your letter to her of November 25. I have had an opportunity to read quickly through the manuscript, and to discuss it with both Joyce and Matt Hodgson.

As you know, the Governors of the Press stipulate that we obtain two supportive readings, by disinterested senior specialists, of each complete manuscript that we recommend to them for acceptance. In your letter to Joyce you stated that you consider the manuscript to be in an unfinished state, and that you will be revising it. In my opinion, it would be prejudicial to the manuscript's chances for acceptance by the Press for us to obtain outside readings until you are satisfied that the manuscript is as good as you can make it.

Aside from your "suggested symbols," no illustrations accompanied the manuscript, although you did refer, in your letter to Joyce, to photographs and captions. Before we obtain our outside readings it will be necessary for us to have all the illustrations (in final form, if possible) that you plan to include.

I have taken the liberty of making a xerox copy of the manuscript, and I am returning the original to you separately. During the next three or four days I should like to read through (and mark up) the xerox copy in some detail, and I shall send it to you with my general observations.

I look forward to working with you on this project. May I suggest that all your correspondence about this project, for the time being, be directed to me? I shall make copies for Joyce's AAUP file.

With best wishes,

Sincerely yours,

Malcolm M. MacDonald
Assistant Director and Editor

MMM:kt

Received...3.December.1975.........   No. 09050

The University of North Carolina Press

I. MANUSCRIPT RECORD

Author ....

Title....THE SCHOLARLY HOUSE PLANT by Pruvis Mulch

141 pages   rec'd and acknowledged by MM

Returned to author for revision 1.24

Sent to for reading	Date sent	Date ret'd

Form No. A-649

8 December 1975
Page Two

We recommend that you include an annotated bibliography, in which you list five or six books in each of your categories (foliage plants, plants grown for their flowers, cacti and other succulents, and perhaps florescent light gardening and indoor vegetable gardening). Please prepare the annotated bibliography according to the style recommended in the Chicago Style Manual; and we recommend that you include the pagination of each book.

An index will be essential for the book, and I hope you will be prepared to provide the index manuscript at the proper time.

In your "special boxes" you refer exclusively to a publication by Widmer. May I suggest that you obtain similar lists from other authors (there must be dozens of such lists available), as excessive reliance on a single authority may convey a misleading impression.

When you send us the final draft, please include an extended table of contents (one that incorporates your principal subheadings).

May I have your best estimate about when I may expect to receive the complete, final draft of your manuscript? As we are looking toward publication in the spring of 1977, time is a factor: would it be possible for you to have the manuscript to me by mid January?

I do not wish to conclude without telling you that I have derived both pleasure and information from going through your manuscript. As it happens, I have a few indoor plants, which I have grown only with common sense to guide me. Your graceful manuscript has already given me a greater appreciation for, and understanding of, these special friends; and I am looking forward to working further with you toward its ultimate publication.

With very best wishes,

Sincerely yours,

Malcolm M. MacDonald
Assistant Director and Editor

MMM:kt

THE UNIVERSITY OF NORTH CAROLINA PRESS
Box 2288, Chapel Hill, N.C. 27514
8 December 1975

Dear

As I promised in my letter of December 4, I am returning separately the xerox copy of your manuscript on house plants. You will find a number of queries and suggestions in the margins of the manuscript, which are in addition to those on the attached sheets. As you plan to recast both your preface and first chapter, I began my annotations with chapter two.

In general, the manuscript reads well, although I believe chapters two and three are not as strong as chapters four-seven. In the earlier chapters you seem not to have your audience firmly in mind. I judge from your letter of November 25 that your book is intended for rank beginners: that is, for people who may have one or two plants (and no books on the subject) around the house. The main thrust of my annotations and separate comments is toward a clearer definition of your prospective reader and modifying the manuscript to meet his needs.

I agree with you that the preface and first chapter must be recast entirely. In the case of books, such as your own, intended for a broad general audience, the preface should be regarded as a selling tool. It should be brief (two or three double-spaced typewritten pages), and it should state clearly the audience for whom the book is written and how you have gone about helping that audience meet its plant-growing needs.

As my separate comments convey, I would like to see you introduce some elementary plant biology concepts into chapter one. Here, too, I think you would be wise to distinguish between indoor plants and outdoor plants. Such a distinction would enable you to lead right into the heart of the book, which deals with the special requirements of indoor plants. We are agreed, are we not, that references to scholarly publishing are not appropriate in a book of this kind?

As I mentioned in my earlier letter, it is essential that we receive all the illustrations with the final manuscript, as they form an integral part of the proposed book.

The following comments and suggestions are intended to help you sharpen the focus of the book and, in some cases, to make it more precise. In each case, I refer to check marks in the left margins of manuscript pages.

II-1: I think you might amplify on the difference between house plants and plants found in nature. Are all house plants found in the wild, somewhere?

II-2: I confess to a long-standing personal bias against anthropomorphism, and I have flagged several examples throughout the manuscript (while leaving some others). I think you could take it out without violating your style, and I think further that your manuscript would be stronger as a result.

II-3: (top of page) Why treat potting mixtures and soils under separate headings?

II-4: (top of page) I believe all the potting soils I have bought are advertised as "sterile": do they contain nutrients? You do not say enough about the methods of fertilizer application.

(middle & bottom of page) You sound as though you would like to launch into the chemical vs. organic controversy. Surprisingly, perhaps, some of us are vaguely aware of the "controversy," but don't really care much about it one way or the other. We look to this book for advice about growing house plants; why not recommend specific fertilizers for specific classes of plants. This entire brief section is in need of revision, for it is not informative.

II-7: You refer here, and at many other places in the manuscript, to a particular plant part. Somewhere in the book (I would prefer to see it in a first chapter) you should present enough botany (anatomy, physiology, and ecology) to enable the house-plant grower to understand, at a working level, what goes on in his indoor garden. A diagram showing the parts of plants is a must.
At several places in the manuscript, for example, you refer to periods of dormancy and periods of rapid growth. These references cry out for greater explanation.

II-8: (first check) See comment under II-1.

(second check) I suggest you either explain pH or not use it. But if you introduce a technical term, you owe your reader a working definition.

II-9: Is it wise to encourage the use of standing-water devices, which may provide a habitat for organisms harmful to humans? I understand some hospitals prohibit the introduction of cut flowers into the rooms of patients because the water in which they are kept has been found to harbor alarming numbers of disease-causing bacteria. If one does grow plants in containers of water, should the water be changed periodically?

II-10: The term "microclimate." This could be a useful unifying concept to tie together everything you present under the headings of containers, watering, humidity, ventilation, temperature, and light. At the very least, you should define "microclimate."

II-13: See comment under II-7.

II-16: What is a "worn out plant"? Please reword.

(second check) Why dismiss propagation from seeds, which affords delight to many house plant growers? If you don't wish to discuss it,

perhaps you could refer the reader to a book that does.

II-17: (third check) See comment under II-7.
Can you obtain vigorous roots this way? I had bad luck with coleus, as they developed long trailing roots that matted together when I removed them from the bottle. On the other hand, mine did well when rooted in moist vermiculite, which appeared to give the new roots something to "grab."

II-18: This sounds awkward. An illustration would help greatly here.
At bottom of page: the term "canes" brings me back to my earlier appeal for a section on the anatomy of plants.

II-19: Again, anatomical terms. You have referred earlier to the stem, or stalk of the plant; I believe you have used those terms interchangeably. Here you refer to leaf stems. It is confusing.

II-21: Anatomy again.

III-2: See comment under II-4.

III-5: (first check) Why single out government and university bulletins?
(second check) Another reference to the "organic-chemical controversy."

III-9: How does one Pasteurize potting soil? Do you Pasteurize yours? Really?!
(second check) Obviously, you live in a university community! Why not suggest a place people can mail their plants (or infected parts)? For example, to the county agent, or to the Department of Plant Pathology at any university within one's state that has a college of agriculture.

IV-3: Here you mention the mature size of plants, something you ought to stipulate in your discussions of the individual varieties. I expect the sizes will vary according to the treatment the plants receive; still the plant-grower should be given some indication about whether his plant will attain a height of eight inches, or three feet.

IV-13: Here you do give the size range of the mature plant. It is welcome information for the beginner!

V-5: If grafting is easy, perhaps the house-plant grower would like to try his hand. Is an explanation within the scope of your book?

"special box #1": What are the "special boxes" for? Where ought they to go in the finished book?

"special box #3, add 1": This procedure requires an illustration or sequence of illustrations. I simply cannot visualize the process from your description.

THE UNIVERSITY OF NORTH CAROLINA PRESS
Box 2288, Chapel Hill, N.C. 27514

19 December 1975

Dear

I was pleased to receive your letter of December 12, and to have your initial, general response to mine of December 8.

I like your new Preface. It not only defines your audience, but it tells the prospective reader what the remainder of the book is about.

I am sure you have already anticipated my reaction to the revised first chapter. I like your brief discussion of the natural environment and the home environment, and I shall look forward to seeing your extention of that chapter, where you will deal with some basic plant biology.

As you revise your manuscript, perhaps you could keep in mind that North Carolina is a southern university press, and that plants common to the South should not be excluded for that reason alone.

You state in your Preface that the book might serve as a useful companion when one visits his local florist or garden center. I agree thoroughly, and even in the brief period of time since I returned the manuscript to you, I have wished that I could refer to it while chosing plants to give as Christmas gifts. I believe that portability should be designed into the book, and we shall bring that to the attention to the designer at the appropriate time.

I am delighted that you are pushing ahead so well on this project, and I shall look forward to receiving the completed manuscript, with its illustrations, around the middle of next month.

With best wishes,

Sincerely yours,

Malcolm M. MacDonald
Assistant Director and Editor

MMM:kt

December 12, 1975

Mr. Malcolm M. MacDonald
Assistant Director and Editor
THE UNIVERSITY OF NORTH CAROLINA PRESS
Box 2288
Chapel Hill, North Carolina 27514

Dear Malcolm:

Thank you for your letter of the 8th, for the return of the manuscript, and for your detailed comments which I found very helpful.

Over the past several days I have recast entirely the preface and first chapter. I feel much better about the manuscript after having done this. As it stands now, the book is a straight-forward guide for the beginner, with no references to scholarly publishing. But now you present me with more work. Your recommendations regarding the preface have, I think, been carried out. The first chapter is improved, although it still needs a little more explanation of general biological concepts, as you point out. I will revise this further. Then, of course, I will address myself to the detailed comments, work up the bibliography, etc. I will be happy to prepare an index at the appropriate time.

I am sending my revised preface and first chapter to you at this time--not as final copy, but to give you an indication of the direction I am moving. As I said, these were revised without the benefit of your counsel, and they now are in for further revision.

I can see immediately that you are going to make me write a good book, and I am thankful for that. I will plan to send you the completed and revised ms. by January 15. After the readers' reports come in, there will doubtless be more revision in store, for which I am prepared.

Last, I might say that for the first time I am beginning to feel good about this whole project, especially knowing that you will be there to keep the train on the track.

Sincerely,

3505 Hampton Hall Way NE
Atlanta, Georgia 30319
August 2, 1976

Gwen Duffey, Managing Editor
University of North Carolina Press
Box 2288
Chapel Hill, North Carolina 27514

Dear Gwen:

Both your letter and the package containing the house plants manuscript have arrived safely. What an interesting project for the AAUP to do--seeing the results will be fun.

I'm going to try to have this in the mail back to you by August 25 (I'm allowing a little time off for a one-week visit from my brother and his wife, or I'd have it back sooner) and I can't imagine that this would be more than $150 dollars, maybe less.

Maybe working on this will help me save the maidenhair fern I am now in the process of destroying. I'm known in my neighborhood as The Purple Thumb (not quite black--for philodendrons and one neanthebella palm are known to be thriving in my house--but certainly not green, as this year it took three plantings in my window boxes before I could get marigolds to survive and everybody knows that you can't kill marigolds!) I live amongst dozens of young suburbanites whose houses are immaculate and whose house plants are exotic, numerous, and healthy. I keep hoping their children will turn out to be dope fiends or something, so that I can feel a little less inadequate.

Affectionately,

Barbara B. Reitt

---

28 July 1976

Mrs. Barbara Reitt
3505 Hampton Hall Way NE
Atlanta, Georgia 30319

Dear Bobbie:

The manuscript that I mentioned to you on the phone this morning has now been shipped to you. After looking over the material to be edited, please let me know about when you might be able to get it back to us and approximately how much the editing fee will be.

Yours sincerely,

(Mrs.) Gwen Duffey
Managing Editor

House Plants MS   28 July 1976

Mrs. Barbara Reitt   FIRST CLASS
3505 Hampton Hall Way NE   Registered (rrr)
Atlanta
Georgia   30319

AUTHOR'S MEMORANDUM

TO:
FROM: Barbara Reitt (copyeditor)
RE: No Time for House Plants, chapters II and IV

The text of your book reads well; directions and descriptions are concise, clear, and easy to follow. The overall organization of subjects is sensible and the use of symbols in the plant descriptions is particularly good.

The copyediting that has been done on the manuscript of your book has two purposes: to locate and correct any errors that might remain in the copy or in the organization of the book and to instruct the printer and his typesetter as to the details of the printing of the book. This reading has been intended to be as thorough as possible since corrections past this point are prohibitively expensive, as they would have to be made in type after it had been set.

Most of the marks you see on the manuscript pages are of a technical nature, instructing the typesetter, but some are corrections or queries to you, and all of these should be carefully reviewed by you at this time so that the Press can be assured that the manuscript as it now stands has your approval. Please feel free to question anything that has been done.

The few queries that need your attention have been signaled by a red check mark and should be easy for you to locate.

I have followed as many of your style choices as possible ("style" in this sense refers to such choices as which of two alternate spellings to use, word compounding, use of figures or words for number amounts, capitalization, etc.). The Press follows the style recommended in the Chicago Manual of Style, which has been the guide used in the copyediting of your book. Webster's New Collegiate Dictionary is the authority used for spelling.

The few revisions that have been suggested have to do with the coherence and overall structure of the book; content has not been changed, only the order of some of the elements. In each case, logic and the reader's ease dictated the change.

First, the footnote on p. 36, about builder's sand, seemed better placed on p. 18, where the reader is first instructed to use it.

Second, the opening section of chapter IV seemed to need some reworking. The explanations of symbols and nomenclature were repeated; these are now combined into one explanation for each instead of two. The section on buying plants seemed more appropriately placed early in chapter I, where one of the repeated ideas is that plant selection is a crucial part of plant-growing success. Moreover, as this material concerns all plants, not just foliage plants, it seemed wrong to place it in the chapter on foliage plants.

3505 Hampton Hall Way NE
Atlanta, Georgia 30319
August 24, 1976

Gwen Duffey, Managing Editor
University of North Carolina Press
Box 2288
Chapel Hill, North Carolina 27514

Dear Gwen:

I am sending today, by first class mail, the manuscript for the book and the accompanying notes. I am enclosing my statement with this letter.

I was not sure that any revisions of the organization of the book fell under the copyeditor's duties (it was the description of the project that boggled me a bit here) but I went ahead as I would have normally anyway. The two revisions in these chapters that I have recommended really were called for and I felt that the project's rather strict distinction between "editor" and "copyeditor" (maybe the distinction is more apparant than real anyway) need not be observed religiously.

I might add (nobody asked, but that isn't stopping me!) that if the whole book were to be undertaken by the Press for actual publication that quite a bit of revision would be necessary. A fair number of little pieces like the two I've suggested in these two chapters.

Hope this fills your bill. If you need anything else of me, let me know. Incidentally, it turns out to be hard to copyedit just a part of a book!

As ever,

Billie

Account #22

3505 Hampton Hall Way NE
Atlanta, Georgia 30319
August 24, 1976

University of North Carolina Press
Box 2288
Chapel Hill, North Carolina 27514

For copyediting chapters II and IV $150.00
of   NO TIME FOR HOUSE PLANTS

Thank you,

Barbara B. Reitt
Barbara B. Reitt

air layering (no hyphen)

central Europe

dates: 1930s

depressor

draft

homemade

life span

-like: fernlike, maplelike

North, the; northerner

numbers: 5-inch pot

18 inches

5 feet tall

5 percent

50-60° F.

overfertilization

potbound

q.v.

rainwater

repotting

short-lived

subdivision

table 1 (textual reference)

watertight

windowsill

World War II

PLANT NAMES

A. Common and family names, others that are set in roman type:

African violet, avocado, Boston fern, boxwood, bromeliads, Chinese evergreen, false castor oil plant, geraniums, gloxinia, ivy, orchids, piggy-back plant, poinsettia, primulas, sensitive plant, snake plant, spider plant, spurge, ti plant, wandering Jew

B. Scientific names; genus or genus and species usually; all set in italic type:

Aspidistra, Azalea, Begonia, Caladium, Camellia, Coleus, Cyclamen, Dieffenbachia, Dracaena, Ficus, Fuchsia, Gardenia, Hedera, Impatiens, Maranta, Peperomia, Philodendron, Rhododendron

Philodendron scandens is abbreviated P. scandens in a second mention, for example.

Cultivated species are referred to as follows: D. arvida 'Exotica' and as 'Exotica' in subsequent references.

Editing Notes   No Time for House Plants, II and IV

1. Plant names: the style follows that prescribed by the Chicago Manual backed up, for details, by the Style Manual for Biological Journals of the Conference of Biological Editors. I have used Webster's and Kathryn Arthurs, ed., How to Grow House Plants as sources for doublechecking some of the spellings.
The author tended to be inconsistent in his treatment of generic names. In casual speech or writing, "philodendron" would be acceptable, but in a work of this nature, the use of both "philodendron" and "Philodendron" would be slipshod and even confusing. The use of caps and itals for generic names has been applied consistently; likewise, the use of lc for common names (except elements within them that are normally capped--"Chinese" for example) has been applied consistently. The specific names, or at least many of them, are listed in the style sheet under "plant names."

2. The author was imprecise in his use of "that" and "which" and I have followed the recommendations of usage books in having him use "that" exclusively for the restrictive clauses and "which" with a comma for nonrestrictive.

3. I've explained carefully to the author in his memo why I am suggesting the revised order of a few passages in these chapters. The changes do improve the coherence greatly, and I hope he is pleased with the revision. No content has been deleted or altered in meaning.

4. An index will be essential to the book's usefulness, especially as a tool for cross-checking scientific and common names. Please note that the author refers to an index on p. 51; if you decide not to have an index, be sure to omit this sentence.

No Time for House Plants

A Busy Person's /Guide to/ Indoor Gardening

The University of North Carolina Press /:

Chapel Hill

*CONTENTS

contents, add 1

SPECIAL BOXES

1. The ABCs of Artificial Light
2. Should You Send Your Plants to Summer Camp?
3. Can Your Plants Survive Your Vacation?
4. Plants for Cool Conditions
5. Plants for Medium Temperatures
6. Plants for High Temperatures
7. Plants of Greatest Tolerance

contents, add 2

8. Plants for Dry and Semi-Dry Conditions
9. Vines and Trailing Plants for Totem Poles
10. Plants for Hanging Baskets
11. Suggestions for Large-Tubbed Specimens

Bibliography

Index

PREFACE

This is a guide to raising house plants for people who have no time to raise house plants.

Many of us—single people, working couples, harassed mothers, college students, anyone whose daily living pattern leaves precious little time for indoor gardening—would enjoy the beauty and companionship of bright, green house plants, especially through the drab winter months. Past failures, however, have led us to believe that we cannot raise indoor plants without giving them more time and attention that we can provide. Beautiful gift plants may have quickly withered and perished. The bright little English ivy, bought on impulse at the supermarket, may never have made it past childhood at home. Then the books and articles written by house plant experts present, in loving and extended detail, the special methods they use to achieve success—and it seems as though house plant growing must be a consuming hobby if it is to produce gratifying results.

Not so! The gift plant you received probably would not have survived in your home, no matter how much attention

it received. The first secret of house plant success is in choosing the right plants in the beginning, and gift plants from the florist are very often the wrong plants entirely for home conditions. The English ivy was perhaps given too little sun, or an atmosphere much too warm and dry, or too little growing room. Secret number two is in providing the proper basic environment for your plants. The right plant, given the right conditions for growth, will thrive despite your frequent inattention.

This book is meant not only for busy people, but also for busy people who have no long or extensive experience in growing house plants. The green-thumb grower with a collection of two hundred thriving exotic specimens will see at a glance that there are no revolutionary breakthroughs revealed in these pages, no closely guarded secrets unveiled, but simply a collection of solid and practical information, trimmed of excess detail and shaped for a single purpose: to help you to achieve house plant success without really working at it.

Last, we have created this book to be a pleasant companion in itself, one which can provide a pleasant few hours of reading and also one which you may refer to time and time again for the answers to many questions about your house plants. It might even be your travelling companion, for it will serve as a guide to your choosing plant varieties at the florist shop or garden center. However it is used, I

hope that this volume, modest in both size and scope, will lead you to success with house plants, and eventually to a love for them. Should that happen, it will have more than achieved its purpose.

---

*indicates reader's suggested change

CHAPTER 2

UNDERSTANDING HOUSE PLANTS

Every plant has its own preferences and requirements for soil type, light, temperature, ventilation, humidity, and several other factors that are within our power to control, or at least to mitigate. It is vitally important for you, as a busy indoor gardener, to understand the basics of each factor, since a prior understanding will enable you to avoid much work later on while achieving routine success in growing plants.

In addition to understanding these basic needs, you will want to know something about pots and other containers, repotting plants, propagation, and a few other matters that, while not vital to immediate success, will help you to gain further enjoyment in raising better plants.

Ⓐ

THE BASIC HOUSE PLANT

The major difference between a house plant and an outdoor plant is location. All house plants could live and flourish outdoors, in the proper climate. All are derived from forebears that lived, reproduced, and died in the outdoors, whether it was on a forest floor in Central Europe or in the bough of a tree in a South American rain forest. Over many centuries of adaptation and evolution, each plant species embraced those characteristics that enabled it to survive; even today, every house plant carries within its genetic structure the characteristics of its distant progenitors. Thus the Maranta will lose some of its leaves each autumn, even though autumn's weather does not come to the bookshelf where the plant rests, and a cactus, no matter how long we have been feeding and watering it with unfailing regularity, will continue to hoard food and water within its swollen stems. In plants, old habits might recede, but they are never forgotten.

At no time are these innate plant characteristics more noticeable than during the autumn and winter, when many plants—particularly those from temperate regions—enter a period of rest or dormancy. Then, new growth ceases and the plant takes on a listless and washed-out appearance. Other plants, including many of tropical origin, will maintain their bright appearance but will stop growing completely for several months each year, emulating the natural rest periods of their forebears. You will do well to watch for these signs of dormancy and respond to each plant's needs at that time. When any plant enters a dormant period, water should be reduced and fertilizer withheld completely, until new growth once again begins, usually in the late winter or early spring. At that time, water the plant freely and give it normal doses of fertilizer once again, in order to encourage new growth. By your proper treatment of the plant at this time, you will emulate the advent of spring, working with the plant in carrying out its rhythmic cycles.

Some plants also are naturally short-lived and will last no more than a year or two in your home despite your careful attention, because their genetic structure dictates a finite life span. Garden annuals, for instance, will germinate, grow to maturity, flower, produce seeds, and die, all in as little as six months. For this reason, very few annuals are selected as house plants. Although a few short-lived plants are cultivated indoors for their unusual characteristics, such as the sensitive plant which is easily grown from seed, the house plants that we have cultivated over the generations are most often those that will give years of pleasure. Some house plants, in fact, live to be literally hundreds of years old.

Still other house plants are attractive when young,

but grow ungainly or otherwise unattractive when they approach maturity. The only plants of this kind I have chosen for inclusion in this book are those that are very easy to propagate from cuttings, so that the parent plant may be discarded after a year or two, to be replaced by its children.

From the hundreds of thousands of plant species in the world, those traditionally cultivated as house plants are the relatively few that have shown a wide tolerance to conditions of heat, light, moisture, humidity, and ventilation—in other words, those that can withstand a human environment. They are both attractive to the eye and they are tough. Still, if we are looking for success with house plants—and particularly success without working hard at it—then we should spend some time to learn the characteristics of each plant, recognizing its individual needs and fulfilling them to the best of our ability.

HOW A PLANT FEEDS

A plant manufactures nearly all of its food by itself—and not from the "plant food" that you buy for it. Commercial plant food is no more than a combination of certain chemicals (sometimes in an organic base) that are essential to the plant's basic functioning, much as vitamins are essential to human nutrition. But the bulk of a plant's food—the sugar it uses for energy and growth—is manufactured by the plant itself. In the presence of light, the leaves or other green parts of the plant

draw carbon dioxide from the air and water from the roots, converting these into sugar that is then used for energy production or stored for future use.

During this sugar-manufacturing process, known as photosynthesis, several other things happen within the plant. While carbon dioxide is being absorbed, oxygen is being released from the pores of the leaf surface. (Plants produce not only all of the world's food but most of its atmospheric oxygen as well.) During darkness hours, the process is reversed; some of the atmosphere's oxygen is recaptured by the plant and used to convert stored sugar to energy for growth. Generally, a plant manufactures growth food during the day and does its actual growing at night.

Often, the plant converts its newly-manufactured sugar to starch and stores it, reconverting it to sugar as the need arises. Although the starch can be stored in almost any area of the plant, certain plants have developed specialized storage areas just for this purpose. Cacti and succulents have enlarged stems and leaves for the greatest above-ground storage capacity of any house plant, while others have developed underground storage apparatus for this purpose, including bulbs, tubers, corms, and rhizomes. A bulb is simply an enlarged underground bud, such as is found with hyacinths, tulips, and onions. A tuber is nothing more than an enlarged a common potato is a tuber; gloxinias, caladiums, dahlias, and many other common plants are grown from tubers.

A corm is the enlarged base of a stem. And a rhizome is simply a laterally growing, enlarged, usually underground stem. All are used by the plant for food storage, and all can be used to propagate plants, too.

Water is constantly being drawn up through the plant. As it transpires through the stomata (pores) of the leaves, a "pulling" action draws more water up through the roots. The water carries with it mineral salts, including all the elements that the plant needs to carry out its complex chemical processes. The transpiration that takes place in the leaves is similar to perspiration in humans and it serves a similar purpose—to cool the plant. With house plants, it would be difficult for you to notice this cooling effect. But it is readily apparent when a group of large trees carry out the transpiration process. The cool and fresh feeling you enjoy in a thick woods in summer is not primarily the product of the shade itself, but the transpiration of the millions of leaves overhead.

It is virtually impossible for a plant to absorb too much water, since its vessels and cells can accommodate only so much at a given time; however, the overwatering of a plant can exclude oxygen from the root system, ironically causing wilting of the top portion of the plant. When water is withheld, the plant's cells will gradually collapse, causing wilting of the entire plant. All plants do have protective mechanisms that conserve water in times of drought, however, and can withstand a temporary dry spell. Most wilted house plants will quickly spring back to a normal state when water is again provided.

PARTS OF THE PLANT

Stem. The stem serves to support the plant and to contain and direct the vessels that transport water from the roots, and food from the leaves, to every other part of the plant. Most house plants, including *Philodendron*, *Ivy*, and *Spider Plant*, have soft stems. Such plants must either climb or crawl, since their stems are not strong enough to support an upward-growing structure of significant height. Other plants have soft but thick stems that enable them to attain good height, although their stems are apt to be subject to breakage. Woody-stemmed plants such as the *Avocado*, *Poinsettia*, and *Boxwood* are far more sturdy and are usually derived from trees or shrubs of the temperate region. Canes are thick stems with hollow or pithy centers. Bamboo is an example of a cane with which we all are familiar; among house plants, *Dieffenbachia* and *Ti Plant* are good examples.

Some plants have a distinct main stem, while others send up many stems, none dominant. A side shoot is a smaller stem growing out from the main stem. A petiole is a leaf stalk—the stem-like structure from which a leaf grows. A node is a joint on the main stem from which a leaf or side shoot grows.

Leaf. The major ~~purpose~~ *function* of the leaf is, as we have

seen, to manufacture food for the plant's growth and reproduction. Considering its total mass, the leaf has a remarkably large surface area, ideally designed for the efficient absorption and diffusion of gases through its thousands of stomata.

After the basic functions of the leaf are understood, its proper care is not difficult to appreciate. The stomata must be kept fairly clean, free of dust and oil that might hinder their efficient operation. Leaves must also be given the freest access to light and ventilation, according to the individual preferences of each plant. Never crowd plants to a point where they are competing for light and air.

Roots. Roots serve two main ~~purposes~~ *functions*—to anchor the plant in the ground and to supply from the soil water and the mineral salts which accompany water. Bulbs, corms, rhizomes, and tubers *(all modified stems)* serve much the same purposes, as well as acting as food storage areas. Roots, just as the above-ground parts of plants, may be pruned without injuring the plant in any way. Roots are often trimmed to prevent a plant from growing too large for the convenience of the grower, just as top growth is cut back. If ~~roots are cut~~ *you cut* back, however, be certain to cut back top growth to about the same percentage, or the reduced roots might be unable to supply the plant with sufficient amounts of water. The major precaution in caring for roots is, as I will mention several times in these pages, to avoid overwatering.

Flowers. The plant's flowers contain its sexual apparatus. Pollination occurs when ~~male~~ pollen is deposited onto ~~female~~ stigmas, thus ~~fertilizing the plant and~~ allowing the formation of seeds. The fruit of any plant is, in reality, the ovary, which swells to protect the seeds *mature or ripened*. In nature, most plants produce flowers. For the purposes of cultivating house plants, only certain ones—which in this book are listed as flowering house plants—can be depended upon to produce, under home conditions, blossoms of sufficient size, profusion, and beauty to warrant our attention. The plants ~~which~~ we grow for their attractive foliage often cannot produce flowers indoors because of insufficient light ~~or because of a pollination failure~~ *or other conditions*. In nature, pollen is transferred either by insects or wind, both of which are lacking in the home. Where indoor pollinization is essential *for seed or fruit production*, it can be accomplished by transferring the pollen from one flower to another, using a soft camel's hair brush. This process is described fully in most books devoted to flowering house plants.

SOIL

Since the house plant you bring home from the shop will already be rooted in soil (presumably the shop knows its business), you might wonder why you have to consider this need at all. The answer is that your house plant will,

assuming hoped-for longevity, someday need repotting, and you will want to provide it with a potting mixture that will serve its special needs. You might even wish to propagate some of your favorite house plants at some later time, to share with friends and to give as gifts. In any case, a basic knowledge of potting mixtures and soils is essential to a complete understanding of all your plants.

Two simple definitions are in order here, to avoid any confusion later on. *Soil*, when mentioned here, refers to garden loam, that combination of mineral matter, organic matter, air, and water commonly found outside, in your garden or under your lawn. A *potting mixture* is soil with the addition of other materials, such as sand, compost, peat moss, limestone, and bone meal, that together form an ideal environment for the roots of your house plants.

The easiest way to assure your plants of a perfect loam is to buy prepackaged, sterile potting soil from your garden or flower shop. This soil will have not only the proper texture, but it will also be free of disease organisms, insects (some too small to be seen), and weed seeds. To this loam you will add the other ingredients which together will form an ideal potting mixture. You may also buy packaged potting mixture at the store, but if you do, read the package carefully to ascertain the ingredients, making sure that the mixture is right for your plants.

It is, of course, far less expensive to make your own potting mixture from your own garden loam (free), sand (free or next to free), and small amounts of purchased ingredients. If you choose this route, then it is important that you be able to make at least a cursory analysis of the garden loam that will form the basis of the potting mixture. Texture is important. A heavy clay soil will hold water for too long a time, encouraging disease and root rot, and it will bake cement-hard when dry. On the other hand, a coarse sand will not hold water well, nor will it hold nutrients long enough for the plant's roots to absorb them. Strive, then, for a happy medium—a good loam, containing both clay and sand, ~~which~~ *that* will hold both water and nutrients, yet offer adequate drainage. Be sure, also, to sterilize the soil by spreading it out in a shallow pan and placing it in an oven (medium heat) for one hour.

To this basic loam we usually add one or more of
other materials--peat moss, to increase water-holding capacity
and to add organic matter; compost, for organic matter and
nutrients; sand, to open up the soil to air; and some form of
supplemental mineral fertilizer, usually bone meal and lime.
Chemical fertilizer can be used, although it is not necessary
to add it to the potting mixture, since the other ingredients
will supply all the nutrients the plant can use for several
months.

ACIDITY/ALKALINITY

A discussion of soils and potting mixtures would not
be complete without some mention of acidity and alkalinity,
and of the pH scale, which is the scientific measure for
acidity and alkalinity. The midpoint on the pH scale is 7.
A soil with a pH of 7 is neutral--neither acid nor alkaline.
Numbers above 7 indicate an alkaline soil, those under 7 an
acid soil. Most house plants, as most garden plants, will
do best in a slightly acid soil (a pH of 6.0 to 7.0). Most
garden soils are within this range, and so you should not
worry unduly about the pH of the garden loam you dig for use
in the potting mixture. In this book, all the house plants
listed will do well in this normal range, unless special
notations to the contrary are made.

If you have cause to worry about your soil's pH, or
are simply curious, call your county agricultural agent and
ask for directions on having a pH test made. The cost will
be nominal. Any soil may be made more acid with the addition of
peat moss, or less acid with the addition of ground limestone.

POTTING MIXTURES

There are as many different basic potting mixtures as
there are plant experts--probably more. Perhaps the most
common one, however (and one that can be trusted), calls
for two parts loam, one part finely-screened compost (or a
mixture of peat moss and compost), and one part builder's
sand (not sea sand). To this is added a small amount of bone
meal (about one teaspoon for a 5-inch pot) and a pinch of
ground limestone. Other recommendations call for more of
one ingredient and less of another. Do a little experimenting of your own. After a while, you will doubtless come upon
your own favorite mixture, which you can recommend to others.

And now that you have the basic mixture formula well in
mind, we will consider the exceptions:

1. Acid-loving plants such as azaleas, camellias, gardenias, and heathers should have no lime, since they are
acid-loving. They should, in fact, have some form of acid
organic matter--acid peat moss or oak leafmold.

2. Foliage plants need somewhat more compost in the mixture, although half of it should be composed of peat moss
(which will not overstimulate the plant).

3. Fast-growing and hungry plants need more bone meal
and lime, since they use them up so quickly.

4. Some plants, such as cacti, succulents, and orchids,
have very special soil requirements; these are mentioned
later in the discussions of individual plants.

See note P. 18A

* 1. You may by now be wondering why, throughout this book,
builder's sand is recommended for potting purposes while sea
sand is cautioned against. The answer is that builder's sand,
which comes from inland locations, has irregular and sharp surfaces, allowing good soil drainage. Sea sand, having been
washed smooth over the years, packs too snugly and leads to a
compacted soil and resultant drainage problems.

NUTRIENT MAINTENANCE

The mineral nutrients contained in any fresh potting
soil or mixture, whether it is home-made or a sterilized commercial brand, should be sufficient for your plant's needs for
the first four to six months. After that, you should begin to
replenish those nutrients on a regular and carefully-measured
basis.

All plants need substantial amounts of three elements--
nitrogen (N), phosphate (P_2O_5), and potash (K_2O), and lesser
amounts of a dozen or more others, called "trace minerals" or
"trace elements." In grower's language, the three major elements are referred to as N, P, and K, and on the label of any
commercial fertilizer, the percentages of each are given in
N-P-K order. A 5-10-5 fertilizer, for instance, will contain
5 percent nitrogen, 10 percent phosphate, and 5 percent potash.
A so-called "balanced" fertilizer contains a balance of all
three in the amounts needed for the proper growth of most
plants. The fertilizer may be either a chemical or an organic
preparation, according to your preference. The chemical kind
are quick-acting, easy to use, and tidy. Organic fertilizers,
on the other hand, are slow to release their nutrients, providing a gentle and steady supply. Chemical mixtures come in
liquid, tablet, and even spray form (the last applied directly
on the foliage). Organic fertilizers may be purchased commercially in balanced formulas (fish emulsion, made from fish
wastes, is a popular one for house plant use) or may be made at
home from a combination of ingredients. Blood meal is a good

choice for supplying substantial amounts of nitrogen (its $N_N^1 P_N^1 k$
formula is $15.00_N^1 1.30_N^1 0.70$), while bone meal ($4.00_N^1 21.00_N^1 0.20$)
is good for phosphate and wood ashes ($0.00_N^1 1.50_N^1 7.00$) are high
in potash content. A combination of one part blood meal, one
part bone meal, and two parts wood ashes will make a $5_N^1 6_N^1 4$
formula, which is a good one for house plants.

How often should plants be fertilized? There is wide
disagreement on this point, some experts believing in weekly
feedings of full strength (the dosage recommended on the label),
others fertilizing no more than once a month, and even less often
during the ~~plant's dormant or rest period~~. winter. In the end, you will
probably have to come to your own policy by way of experimentation. In the beginning, however, it is better to err on the
conservative side, since far more plants have been injured from
overfertilization than from nutrient starvation. If you use a
commercial chemical or organic formula, I suggest that you feed
your plants as often as recommended on the label, but only half
the recommended dosage. (Manufacturers tend to overstate the
need for their product.) If the plant shows a spurt of active
growth in late winter or early spring, increase the dosage to the
manufacturer's recommendation. During a dormant or rest period,
withhold fertilizer entirely. If you are using a home-made
organic fertilizer, such as the one suggested above, use it
sparingly at first. A level teaspoon of the blood meal/bone meal/
wood ash formula, applied monthly, should be plenty for a plant
in a ~~five~~-inch pot. You may also put some of the mixture in a

bottle, fill the bottle with water, and use this "tea" to
water your house plants. A mild tea solution, applied weekly,
will give all your plants a continuing and gentle supply of
the essential nutrients.

Last, remember never to apply a chemical fertilizer
if the soil is dry. The quick action of the chemicals can
easily injure the roots.

balanced
house plant fertilizer, which should be applied sparingly.
Chemical preparations should be applied according to the
manufacturer's directions.

(A)

CONTAINERS

Nearly any container that offers adequate drainage and
does not ~~doesn't~~ leak is suitable for house plants. After checking a
container ~~quickly~~ for leakage, consider drainage carefully.
the container
If ~~it~~ has a hole in its bottom, there is no problem. If not,
then you should put coarse gravel or broken crockery in the
bottom of the container to fill one-fourth to one-fifth of
depth
its ~~height~~. In this way, you will avoid the liklihood of
waterlogging your plants and encouraging root rot.

The traditional terra cotta clay pot offers definite advantages. It is inexpensive, easily replaced, and--most
important--allows air to be exchanged through its porous walls.
fairly
This same porosity, however, allows water to evaporate ~~most~~
a plant's location
quickly, necessitating ~~more~~ frequent watering. If ~~you have a~~
makes it
~~plant in a spot which is~~ awkward to water, you will save
yourself some effort by choosing a glazed or otherwise impervious container.

Some metal containers, notably copper, might produce
adverse chemical reactions with soil and fertilizer elements,
injuring plants therein. Copper planters, however, are usually
to
lacquered, preventing ~~such~~ such reactions.

Wooden tubs and boxes are ideal for very large house plants.
You can make any wooden container water-tight by lining it with

several sheets of heavy-gauge plastic or, for permanent results,
sheet metal.

Last, if you want the best advantages of both a terra cotta
pot and a decorative container, place the former inside the latter,
leaving a quarter-inch or more of space for air circulation around
the walls of the inner pot. Sometimes sphagnum moss is inserted
here, to help preserve moisture. A base of gravel in the decorative pot can provide good drainage while lifting the inner pot to
the level of the outer container.

(A)

WATERING

More house plants are killed by overwatering than by any
other cause. This killing with kindness can be avoided, if
you learn to understand just when your plants need water and
should
when they ~~would prefer to~~ be left alone.

The best rule of thumb is that a plant should be watered
when the soil surface is dry to the touch. Then, water
thoroughly, either by adding water to the soil surface or by
immersing the entire pot in a larger container of water.

Certain plants, such as the African violets and other
woodsy varieties, need more water than most, while cacti and
succulents need ~~far~~ less than the average. Aside from the
specific preferences of individual varieties, there are many
conditions which call for more or less water, as indicated
in Table 1.

Immersion is the best method of watering because it is the
surest. The soil in any pot might tend to form water channels
which, upon receiving water from the surface, will rush it to

Table 1. WATERING NEEDS OF PLANTS UNDER VARIOUS CONDITIONS

(handwritten: please place near list on p. 23, bottom)

Plants will need more water when:
- They are in a period of active growth
- They are in bright light
- Room humidity is low
- Room temperature is high
- They are contained in small pots
- They are in clay pots
- They are fast-growing varieties
- They are planted in sandy soil
- They are in flower or about to go into flower

Plants will need less water when:
- They are in a period of rest (usually during winter)
- They are in dim light or under artificial light
- Room humidity is high
- Room temperature is under 70°
- They are in large pots
- They are in non-porous pots
- They are slow-growing varieties
- They are planted in heavy soil

---

the bottom of the pot and out the drainage hole, leaving large parts of the soil bone-dry. Then, some potting soil mixtures will shrink when drying, leaving many spaces along the wall of the pot where water can run past. Immersion is the one sure way to soak the soil thoroughly, provided that the pot is porous. You can do it in any large container, or even in a sink or bathtub. Set the pots in the water, but do not let the water flow over the lips of the pots. After the surface of the potting mixture has become moist-- ten to thirty minutes--remove the potted plant, drain off any excess water, and put it back in its place. Never go out for the afternoon, leaving your plants standing in water.

If you water from the top, remember to remove any excess water from the saucer. Plants should never be allowed to stand in water for fear of root rot. In time, you should learn to give each plant just enough water to soak it thoroughly, with very little excess drainage.

Some other watering tips:

1. Do not get water into the crown of any plant, for this will encourage decay.

2. Never use very cold water, especially for tropical plants. Keep an open jar of water at room temperature for your house plants. Not only will the proper temperature be assured, but if you use tap water, some of the chemicals will have been dissipated by the time it is given to plants.

3. Water that is artificially softened may be detrimental to plant growth. If you can, use rainwater, or

---

water that has not been softened. ~~Fluorine and chlorine, on the other hand, are not thought to pose any problems.~~

4. If your water is especially hard, lime salts might cause trouble with such acid-loving plants as Orchids, Primulas, Rhododendrons, Azaleas, and other plants whose natural soil is woodsy (indicating a high organic content) and acid. Either choose plants that prefer a more neutral range in the pH scale, or plan to collect rainwater for your calcifuges (lime-haters).

HUMIDITY

Much of our trouble with house plants, especially in winter, can be traced to insufficient moisture in the air. Except for the cacti and succulents, nearly all house plants thrive best in a relative humidity of between 60 and 80 per cent, while that of most heated homes in winter is under 40 per cent--often, considerably under 40 per cent. House plants will virtually cry for moisture under these conditions, and it is incumbent upon you to answer that cry.

There are several ways to add moisture to the air in your home. The more expensive include the adding of a humidifying device to your furnace, if you live in a house, or installing an electric humidifier. This step will benefit not only the plants but everyone living in the house, too. But there are less expensive ways of bringing moisture to your plants:

---

1. The pebble tray. Line the bottom of a waterproof tray with decorative pebbles and arrange your plants, in pots, on top of the pebbles. Keep the tray filled with water, being sure only to avoid blocking the pots' drainage holes. Change the water weekly to keep it fresh.

2. Decorative containers. If you keep a clay pot inside a decorative container (double-potting), keep a pool of water in the bottom of the larger vessel. Again, provide some means of support for the clay pot so that it is not resting in water at any time. (Or, fill the space between the walls of the two pots with sphagnum moss, and keep it constantly moist.)

3. Standing water devices. Water left standing in a room will gradually evaporate, meaning that the lost moisture is added to the room atmosphere. If your home is particularly dry during cold weather, take the trouble to place pans of water on tops of radiators; grow ivy, philodendron, or wandering Jew in containers of water; maintain an aquarium; rotate plants so that each can spend an afternoon in the bathroom each week, where the air is humid. Change standing water weekly.

4. Bathing and showering. Most house plants will respond favorably to a brief shower every day, or at least as often as you can manage to provide the treat. Little brass-plated atomizers are ubiquitous in mail order catalogs, but more dependable (albeit less decorative) are the plastic sprayers available in art supply stores. These hold a pint or quart of water, and they feature an adjustable shower head, affording an entire range of water action from a sharp jet ~~capable of carrying twenty feet, (the kids love this one) all the way~~ to a fine mist. Your plants, of course, will do best with

the fine mist. Remember to fill the container after every use, so that the next day's spray will be at room temperature. Remember also to avoid spraying plants that have been standing in direct sunlight (the shock is great) and those that have been subjected to very cool temperatures (perhaps spending the autumn on a cold sunporch).

Rubber plants and others with large leaves should be cleaned thoroughly and gently with a damp cloth about once a week. The leaf polish sold commercially is permissible, if you want really stunning looking, large-leafed plants, *which can block the leaf's pores and impede respiration.* but never use oil of any kind. Ivies and other rugged small-leafed plants can be held under the gentle stream of a faucet for their weekly bath.

Grouping. Plants will maintain a moist surrounding air (leaves not touching) with greater facility if they are grouped together, rather than separated. During the coldest part of winter, you might want to group most plants on a pebble tray under a light window, to take advantage both of maximum light and greatest humidity.

VENTILATION

Plants, like people, benefit from fresh air. Like people, also, they react badly to drastic changes in air movement and temperature. Provide adequate ventilation for your house plants, but do not subject them to sharp winds, winter drafts, or heat arising directly from a radiator. Think of your own comfort, in this respect, and you will

know what will be best for your plants. If, in autumn, you bring your plants in from a summer outdoors, help them adjust to indoor conditions gradually by placing them by an open window for the first several days. Gradually lower the window day by day, keeping a watchful eye on night temperatures.

TEMPERATURE

The temperature requirements of house plants vary widely, according to the natural habitat of their forebears and also according to other conditions. Many cool-weather plants prefer a range of 50-60° F. and cannot tolerate temperatures above 70°, while tropicals may thrive in a moist 70-75°. Know the temperature preferences of any house plant before you adopt it, and then place it in the best possible temperature location in your home. You might find, for instance, that a cool-loving aspidistra will do best in a back bedroom, while tropical plants thrive happily next to (but not above) a living room heat vent. The temperature requirements or tolerances of plants are included in their descriptions throughout this book. Heed them well, make liberal use of an indoor thermometer, and do not be afraid to experiment by placing different plants in different locations for a week at a time. You might notice in your plants distinct preferences for particular locations throughout the house, and their preferences will not always corroborate expert advice.

LIGHT

Light and temperature needs are closely related. In their native surroundings, many tropical plants can thrive at higher temperatures because they receive long hours of sunlight. In the home, and especially during winter's short days, they cannot receive enough light to enable them to stand high house temperatures.

Except for most cacti and succulents, house plants should not be placed in windowsills where they will receive long periods of direct sunlight. Simply place a thermometer in this position and you will soon see that your plants can be literally cooked to death, even in the dead of a Minnesota winter. Strive, instead, for a bright spot with a few hours of filtered sunlight each day, at least for most plants.

Individual varieties vary, of course, in their light needs, and these needs are specified in the descriptions of individual plants in these pages. Again, do not be afraid to experiment with different locations for different plants. I have a Philodendron scandens—one of the most popular and most common of all house plants that has thrived for years in a dim corner, when actually it is supposed to require a bright spot out of direct sun. Plants, I am afraid, sometimes exhibit unmistakable individual characteristics that we have yet to understand.

PRUNING AND TRAINING

Some plants should be pruned and pinched back occasion-

ally, in order to encourage bushy and stocky growth, while trailing plants such as philodendrons and ivies need gentle support to guide them into pleasing growth patterns.

Many people hesitate to prune at all, feeling somehow that they are hurting the plant or interfering with its natural development. Actually, plants will respond to judicious pruning with new and vigorous growth. Plants such as geraniums, coleus, and begonias should be pinched back routinely in order to encourage lateral growth. The process is quite simple: with a sharp knife, cut back perhaps one-half inch of the central growing tip. The plant should respond by sending out side shoots below the central tip, and the main stem of the plant should then become thicker and sturdier. If this is done several times a year, the plant should eventually attain the vigorous and well-rounded form you desire. Without this pruning, it might grow "leggy" with a weak main stem, requiring some kind of support. Many older plants, as well, will benefit from occasional pinching back or shearing of outside growth. (Do not, however, prune or pinch back African violets, gloxinias, flowering bulbs, succulents, ferns, Norfolk Island Pine, or cyclamen.)

Vines and trailing plants often need some kind of support, unless you prefer to let them cascade from a hanging basket. The usual practice is to sink a slab of cork or tree bark into a pot, then to train the vines of the plant to grow around and up the support, eventually concealing it.

Another effective device is the sphagnum moss cylinder. Pack wet the moss fairly tightly around a stake and secure it in a cylinder of the proper size for the pot. The cylinder can be made easily from either chicken wire or green plastic material made for this purpose. If you wish, sink a small clay pot into the top of the cylinder, so that you can add water regularly to keep the moss damp. (Otherwise, the moss will require regular spraying.) Tie the vines gently to the cylinder as they grow; eventually, philodendrons and similar plants will anchor themselves to the moss with their aerial rootlets, making other support unnecessary.

REPOTTING

The temptation to repot plants too readily and too often is a strong one, and should be resisted with strong will. A plant needs repotting only when it has become potbound--when the roots have filled the entire container and are creeping out of the drainage hole. Only then is repotting indicated. Choose a new pot which is only one size larger than the old one, for a house plant will not do well in a pot that is too large. If the larger pot has been used before, scrub it thoroughly to remove any possibility of disease. New clay pots, soak them for a few hours in water so that they become saturated. Then, with ample moist potting soil, gravel, and a tongue depressor or similar wood tool, set to work.

To remove the plant from its old pot, slide your hand over the top of the pot, index and second fingers cradling

the plant stem. Turn the pot upside-down, thus supported, and tap the lip of the pot sharply on the edge of a bench or table. After a few taps the entire soil ball, ringed with plant roots, should come out easily, in one neat piece. Set it aside. Take the larger pot and line the bottom with a layer of coarse gravel or broken crockery, to provide good drainage. Then add potting soil on top of the gravel, placing the plant and soil ball on top of the new soil several times in order to see when it has reached the proper depth. (The top of the soil should be about one-half inch below the lip of the new pot, in a four-inch pot, and one inch below the lip in an eight-inch pot, to leave room for watering.) When enough soil has been added to raise the plant to its proper height, center it well and begin to pack soil around the sides of the soil ball, using the tongue depressor. Take your time in doing this, for it is the most crucial part of the entire operation. It is important to pack the soil firmly, so that no air spaces are left when the job is finished. Roots cannot draw nutrients in air spaces and many of them will thus be injured or die, affecting the health of the entire plant. When the new soil is finally brought up to a level even with the top of the soil ball, the job is finished. You might want to add just a little soil over the top of the root ball, especially if roots have been forced up to the soil surface, but don't add any more than you must, for you do not want to change the planting depth of the plant. Repotting is shock enough, for many plants, without altering the plant

please place illustration II-15 near this page

ing depth. Water the plant thoroughly and return it to its usual location.

How often should you repot? Obviously, only as each plant indicates a need. For slow-growers, this might be once every two or three years; a mature slow-grower may go for many years without repotting, if new growth is cut back. For fast-growing and very young plants, repotting might be needed once or twice a year for the first several years. Plants that do not need repotting after one year should have the top one-half to one inch of soil replaced annually, to keep the soil fresh.

PROPAGATION

There will come a time when you will want to start your own house plants--to increase your own plant population, to use as personal gifts for friends and family, to replace a short-lived plant or one that has become ungainly with age. The propagation of most house plants is not a difficult task, and it is most rewarding.

There are two general methods of doing the job: by the collecting and planting of seeds, and by the cutting and rooting of plant parts--stems, leaves, or underground structures. The first way (sexual reproduction) is usually less satisfactory than the second. Propagation from seed is ideal for garden annuals, but not for most house plants. Special equipment is required, and daily attention is essential, making the activity an unlikely one for

anyone who professes "no time for house plants." In addition, the seeds from hybrid plants are likely to produce plants vastly inferior to the parent plant. (A hybrid, incidentally, is any plant produced by cross-pollinating two plants of different species, varieties, or genera.) Last, many house plants do not flower and produce seeds under home conditions, requiring the house plant gardener to purchase seeds from specialty houses. The one advantage of growing house plants from seed is that you can create new hybrids by the cross-pollination of plants. The excitement of this activity creates a fascinating hobby for some house plant enthusiasts, but is unlikely to appeal to those who cannot afford to devote significant amounts of spare time to the activity.

Far more simple, and yielding far more reliable results, is the propagation of plants by the cutting and rooting of plant parts. Less care is required, and the offspring will look just like the parent, even when the parent is a hybrid.

Plants may be propagated at any time of year, although it is best to avoid tackling the job when the plant is going into a dormant period. In early spring, just before active growth begins, is perhaps the ideal time.

(B)   Cuttings. The most common method of propagating is by the taking of stem cuttings, which are then rooted in either water or some sterile rooting medium such as perlite, vermicu- lite, or sand. If you have never rooted a cutting before, then begin with African violets, coleus, Dracaena, Fuchsia, gardenias, geraniums, Impatiens, ivy, Philodendron, wandering Jew, or wax begonia. These are the easiest, because all can be rooted in water. Simply take a cutting from an actively growing tip of the plant, one containing four to six leaves, severing the stem cleanly just below a joint with a clean razor blade. Place the cutting (you may take several at a time, from the same plant if you wish) so that the bottom portion is submerged in water-- a colored or clear green wine bottle is fine--remembering only to keep the leaves above water. (Cut off the bottom leaf or two, if necessary, to get more of the stem into the water; about a third of the entire length should be in water.) Place the con- tainer in diffused light--not direct sun--and wait until vigorous roots appear. When they have, the little plants may be removed from the water and potted in a small pots, using the potting mixture recommended earlier in this chapter. Be sure to pack the potting mixture firmly around the roots of the plant, to avoid any air spaces, and water thoroughly afterwards.

Stem cuttings that which cannot be rooted in water are rooted in perlite, vermiculite (both available wherever house plant

What is a node?

Be sure that at least one node is below the surface of the potting medium.

supplies are sold), or in builder's sand. *as for rooting in water*

The process is basically the same. The cuttings are inserted in the moist medium, which may be contained in a small clay pot or, for larger numbers of cuttings, a shallow plastic tray. The planted container is then placed in a plastic bag which is tied shut (the zip kind, used for food storage, is convenient, effective, and reusable) and placed in diffused light at a temperature of 65 to 70°. You can tell whether the cuttings have developed roots by testing them weekly. Open the bag and pull gently on a plant. If it moves easily, then the roots have not yet formed; if it resists your gentle tug fairly well, however, then the roots probably are mature enough to stand repotting. The process can take as little as two weeks, or as long as several months, depending upon the variety of the plant and the size of the cutting. When the roots are strong and vigorous, pot the plant in a small pot and treat it as you would any other plant.

Some plants that which produce canes (hollow or pithy stems), (including Chinese ever-

or eye

*A node is a point of the stem at which a leaf or root will emerge. It will appear as a little spot and may be slightly swollen, protruded, indented, or otherwise distinguished by coloration.

green, Dracaena, and Dieffenbachia, can be propagated by taking cuttings of the canes, which have discernable "eyes." Press each cane section/(containing one eye) into moist sphagnum moss, secure it with wooden clothes pins at each end so that it does not pop up, seal it in a plastic bag, and put it in a cool place out of direct sun. In six to eight weeks, move it into a warm place (70 to 90°), still out of direct sun. Soon, a shoot will grow from the eye. When the shoot has attained a respectable size, the cane may be cut close to the shoot on both sides, and the new plant may be lifted from the moss and potted.

What is an "eye"?

Plants that which have fleshy leaves are best propagated by taking leaf or leaf-petiole cuttings. (A petiole is a leafstalk, or stem.) Leaf cuttings work well when large and mature leaves are available. Cut the leaf close to the stem of the parent plant, using a razor blade for a clean cut without crushing the cells. The leaf may then be cut horizontally into smaller sections, so that the main vein runs from top to bottom along the center of the leaf section. (Long-leafed plants such as Sansevieria and Streptocarpus may be cut into as many as ten sections, each of which will produce an individual plant.) Each leaf section is then sunk halfway into the rooting medium, after which the process is the same as that described for stem cuttings. Patience is required here, for this method is often a very slow one to produce results.

Smaller leaves may be rooted by taking leaf-petiole cuttings. Cut one leaf stem close to the main stalk and sink the stem into the rooting medium, so that the leaf nearly (but

not actually) touches the medium. African violets, begonias, snake plant, piggy-back plant, and Peperomia respond well to leaf-petiole cuttings.

(B)   Underground division. Older plants that which have thick main roots can be propagated by taking root cuttings. This is usually done when the plant is being repotted. Cut about one inch of the main root, making sure that it has at least one inch eye. Cover this with one-half of rooting medium and treat it as you would any other cutting. Coleus, ivy, Philodendron, and wandering Jew may be easily propagated in this

give examples

Thick-rooted perennials may be propagated simply by the thinner process of root division, in which the root mass is simply forced apart into two or more clumps, each of which is then repotted.

Plants that which produce rhizomes (underground stems) may be propagated by dividing the rhizome so that one leaf bud is contained on each piece, and planting the section under one-half inch of rooting medium. Plants that which produce potato-like tubers can be propagated by cutting the tubers apart with a sharp knife, keeping one eye to each section, and planting the sections in the rooting medium just as one would plant potatoes in the open field.

Some plants produce "suckers," small plants that grow up from an underground stem or root. These may be separated from the parent plant and potted in soil immediately.

Anyone who has seen strawberries grow outdoors knows what runners are--the baby plants that grow from a long stem coming from the base of the parent plant. Among house plants, Boston fern and spider plant both produce runners, which can be severed from the parent and started in a rooting medium.

Other methods of underground division include the sep- aration and replanting of baby bulbs and corms ~~which~~ that are produced by the mother bulb or corm.

(B)   _Air layering._ A fairly simple (and most impressive) way of propagating larger or woody-stemmed plants is by air layer- ing. Here, a sharp cut is made into the stem, perhaps a third of the way in, into which a toothpick is placed, horizontally, to keep the cut open. That stem section is then wrapped with moist sphagnum moss and covered with clear plastic, tied top and bottom so that moisture cannot escape. Roots will form from the incision and will soon show through the plastic. When a fair number of them have appeared, cut the stem below the plastic wrap, remove both plastic and moss, and pot the new plant immediately in potting soil.

As you might imagine, the propagation of plants can often be integrated with the cutting back, pruning, and shaping of older plants. It seems a shame to throw away plant parts when they can be used to produce more plants, and it is pre- cisely this attitude of thrift which, if not controlled, can lead to a frightening multiplication of house plants. The answer, of course, is to share plants with friends, thus en- couraging still more enthusiasts and still more house plants.

CAN YOUR PLANTS SURVIVE YOUR VACATION?

What shall you do with your plants while you are gone ~~away~~ for a long weekend, for a week, for a month?

The best solution is to have someone come in to water your plants for you. Be sure to give the volunteer specific instructions, however, since anyone unfamiliar with the needs of house plants might easily kill them with kindness by over- watering them.

A long weekend should present no problem whatsoever, except perhaps for vegetable ~~plants~~ and the few others ~~which~~ that need daily watering. Simply soak your plants thoroughly by immersion, drain them, and they should last for four days with no problem. If you will be gone for a week, enclose each pot in a plastic bag and tie it snugly around the base of the plant stem. This device will cut surface evaporation greatly. ~~enabling you to stay away longer~~ Smaller plants can be enclosed completely in plastic bags, ~~so~~ as long as some support is provided so that the plastic does not ~~actually~~ touch the foliage.

Water wicks will keep a plant happy for an even longer ~~period. There a week~~ Wicks and pots are sold as units, usually called self-watering pots, but you can make your own easily ~~for~~ at far less expense. Buy several yards of broad lamp wick. Cut off a ~~six~~ 6 to ~~ten~~ 10-inch section for each potted plant, depending on the pot size. Invert ~~an~~ the empty pot ~~of the same size~~ in a

---

larger container of water, the water level coming to just below the top (well, the bottom, actually) of the inverted pot. Knock out the soil ball of the potted plant, insert the wick ~~up~~ into the drainage hole, and flare out the end of the wick so that it covers as much of the bottom of the pot as possible. (The wick should spread out above the drainage gravel, just under the soil ball.) Replace the soil ball and plant. The bottom of the wick then goes through the drainage hole of the inverted bottom pot and into the water. Water the plant once, from above, and the action should be continuous from then on. Test this method on several plants while you are still at home, in order to determine just how well it works for you, and how long you can afford to be away from home without worry. It is a most effective method.

NB. I am suggesting that the introductory part of this chapter be reorganized because the material explaining the symbols and the nomenclature of plants was repeated and the section of buying plants seemed more appro- priate in the first chapter and not here under foliage plants (the advice concerns all plants and fits nicely with the theme of ch. 1). The insertions on pp. 51 and 52 came from the passages that were deleted as being redundant. Pp. 52-54 were retyped as one page after the removal of one section and revisions to eliminate repetition.

CHAPTER 4

INTRODUCING THE ~~HOUSE~~ FOLIAGE PLANTS

The number and variety of house plants available for your consideration is staggering. For every combination of conditions your home can offer--including heat, light, and humidity--there are ~~literally~~ hundreds or thousands of suitable house plant varieties, offering virtually limitless selection of sizes, forms, colors, patterns and textures, growth patterns, and flowering habits. You have only to survey the conditions that your home can offer, and then make your plant selections, within those limits, to suit your own tastes.

The house plants ~~which~~ I have selected for inclusion in this chapter are only representative of their far greater numbers. I have included nearly all of the most common plants, and I have tried to avoid those ~~that are very~~ difficult to grow. All the old favorites are here, as well as some newer varieties and unusual plants ~~which~~ that can add zest to your collection.

If there is no popular name for a plant, or if there is more than one, none dominant, the plant is listed by its scientific name.

The plants are listed alphabetically by their common or popular names, followed by (in parentheses) their scientific (or Latin) names. The scientific name comprises both the genus name and the specific epithet. For example, the scientific name for the common boxwood is <u>Buxus</u> (the genus) <u>sempervirens</u> (the specific epithet). After a genus name is introduced, it is thereafter abbreviated. Thus <u>Buxus sempervirens</u>, if mentioned again, becomes <u>B. sempervirens.</u> Last, there may be a third part to the scientific name which designates a further subdivision, usually called a subspecies or variety. The popular Japanese boxwood, for example, is <u>B. microphylla japonica.</u>

Although I have attempted to maintain an informal tone in these pages, by using common names whenever possible, the scientific nomenclature has obvious benefits. Many species are known by different common names in different parts of the country; different species of a genus are often called by a single common name; and a single common name may be applied even to varieties of completely different genera. The only sure way to identify any plant, then, is by referring to its scientific name. The index, which includes both common and scientific names, provides a convenient means of cross-checking names.

For each plant listed, you will find symbols that indicate its individual preferences for growing temperature, light, soil moisture and air humidity, and window placement.

Please remember that these are rough guides and not inflexible demands. Many plants have a wide range of tolerance and will thrive in a variety of conditions. Many plants said to prefer an east window will do just as well in a shaded south or west location. Most crucial, perhaps, are the guides to humidity and moisture, since overwatering is one thing that virtually no plant will tolerate. Do not hesitate to try a plant of your liking because you cannot provide its exact needs--but neither should you attempt growing a plant if you can provide none of them. Experimentation is both valuable and enjoyable.

In this chapter we will survey many of the house plants grown primarily for their foliage. Some of them, under favorable conditions, will flower from time to time, although few should be selected for their flowering abilities. Nearly all of these plants are fairly easy to grow and maintain, giving even the beginner a wide variety of plants from which to choose.

Ⓒ African Boxwood (<u>Myrsine africana</u>) B-C-A-C
This slow-growing plant has red stems, but otherwise is similar to Boxwood (q.v.). Many people think it is even more graceful. African Boxwood is a good plant for terrariums, if the atmosphere is not too hot.

Ⓒ Aralia (<u>Fatsia japonica</u>) C-B-B-C
Sometimes sold as <u>Aralia sieboldii</u>. Beautiful, bright green, leathery, maple-like leaves highlight this cheerful plant. In appearance, it is similar to the castor oil plant, and in fact is sometimes called False Castor Oil Plant. It thrives in a cool spot. Aralia can easily grow leggy, and so it should be pruned annually in order to encourage it into bushy growth. _It will attain a height of 4 feet at maturity._

A striking hybrid, <u>Fatshedra lizei</u> (a cross between <u>F. japonica</u> and ivy (<u>Hedera</u>) forms a climbing plant with maple-shaped leaves, which is tolerant of adverse conditions.

There is also a plant called False Aralia (<u>Dizygotheca elegantissima</u>), which has graceful and feathery foliage. It bears no resemblance to the true Aralia and is difficult to grow.

Ⓒ <u>Asparagus</u> A-B-B-B
There are two common kinds of <u>Asparagus</u> suitable for growing as house plants--Fern Asparagus (<u>A. plumosus</u>), with slender, needle-like dark green leaves, forming a feathery appearance, and <u>A. sprengeri</u> (Emerald Feather) which has thicker yellow-green leaves and drooping stems. The latter makes a good

---

plant for hanging baskets, and produces red berries at Christmastime. Both like some sun in the summer and full sun in the winter, and both can grow to a height of about two feet. <u>A. meyeri</u>, less common but equally attractive, has tiny fern-like leaves that arch out on long stems from the center of the plant.

Ⓒ Australian Laurel (<u>Pittosporum tobira</u>) C-B-A-B
A tolerant and slow-growing plant whose leaves, glossy and leathery, resemble those of <u>Rhododendron</u>. Australian Laurel will grow vigorously bushy and does not ask much attention. Florists often use the leaves in floral arrangements.

An interesting variegated form is <u>P. tobira variegata</u>, which grows quite large.

Ⓒ Australian Umbrella Tree (<u>Schefflera actinophylla</u>) A-A-B-A
Here is a very attractive and vigorous grower, a tree-like plant with rich-looking and glossy leaves that radiate like umbrellas from the ends of several leaf stalks. It is a tough and rewarding plant, growing to six feet, which can be propagated by air-layering.

Australian Umbrella Tree is also sold as <u>Brassaia actinophylla</u>. A dwarf variety, <u>B. actinophylla compacta</u>, is also available.

Ⓒ Baby's Tears (<u>Helxine soleirollii</u>) B-B-A-B
This low creeper is also called Irish Moss. It likes a constantly moist (but not soggy) soil, and higher-than-average humidity. It makes a good ground cover for terrariums, but will also grow in a pot if adequate humidity is provided. Baby's Tears may appear to die in the colder months, but after

an adequate rest period it will spring back to life. It is most sensitive to fertilizer burn and salt accumulation.

Ⓒ Black Pepper (Piper nigrum)   A-C-B-C

This is not a ~~terribly~~ attractive plant, but it produces real peppercorns ~~which~~ that you may use at the table, and is a good conversation piece for that reason. The plant's berries ~~begin as~~ green, later turn red, then dry up and turn black. Pick the dried-up black corns, dry them thoroughly for several weeks in an open spot, then use them in your pepper grinder. The care for black pepper is the same as that required for Philodendron. It is not a demanding plant. (Be sure that you have this plant and not one of the so-called black peppers of the deadly nightshade family!)

Ⓒ Boxwood (Buxus)   C-A-B-B

The same plant ~~which~~ that grows the most prized hedges outdoors can make a very attractive house plant. Boxwood is slow-growing _with glossy, bright-green leaves_ and dependable, a good subject for bonsai, _the ancient Oriental art of growing dwarf trees and shrubs._ ~~It has glossy, bright-green leaves.~~ B. sempervirens and B. microphylla japonica (Japanese boxwood) are the two popular species.

Ⓒ Bromeliads   A-B-B-C

There are more than 1,800 varieties of this popular group, many of which are suitable for growing as house plants. Some of them produce attractive flowers, but most are grown for their striking and variegated leaf patterns. One distinctive feature of the bromeliads is the rosette of leaves ~~which~~ that form a small water cup, which the plant uses to hold reserve

supplies of water in its natural habitat. Since the plant lives in the crotches of trees in Central and South America, the water cup is an evolutionary survival characteristic. In the home, keep the cup filled with water, changing it weekly to keep it fresh.

A few of the more common bromeliads are Aechmea, Ananas (pineapple), Billbergia, Cryptanthus ~~(Zebra Plant)~~, Dyckia, Tillandsia (Spanish moss), and Vriesia.

Ⓒ Caladium   A-B-B-C

Caladiums, with their spectacularly colored and variegated leaves, are equally at home in the garden or on the window sill. They are ideal additions to plant groupings on porch or patio in the summer and early autumn. Give them bright light, but not long periods of direct sun, ~~especially~~ in summer, if you want the brightest leaf colors. They will not last through the year and should be treated as annuals.

Caladiums are grown from tubers, which can be divided ~~easily~~ to produce new plants. Start the tubers in regular potting soil at a very warm temperature—80° to 90°—and move the young plants to a cooler spot when they have appeared. _They will attain a height of about ~~one~~ foot._

Ⓒ Cast Iron Plant (Aspidistra elatior)   A-C-B-C

This is perhaps the easiest plant in the world to grow, as its name suggests. It is virtually impossible to neglect it to death. It is also called saloon plant, since it was one of the few that could survive in Victorian taverns, and it was made immortal by George Orwell in his novel Keep the

Aspidistra Flying. If you cannot grow the Aspidistra, you may safely conclude that you have a purple thumb, hopelessly irredeemable.

Cast Iron Plant, _which grows about two feet tall,_ seems to thrive even better when kept slightly pot-bound, and it will appreciate having its leaves washed occasionally. A white-striped species is called A. variegata.

Ⓒ Chamaeranthemum igneum   A-C-A-C

This low, spreading herb has attractive, dark green leaves with reddish-yellow veins. It is suitable for hanging baskets or as a low contrast in large plant groupings. It does like warm temperatures and high humidity, however, and might not be suitable for dry apartments.

Ⓒ Chinese Evergreen (Aglaonema)   A-C-B-A

Here is an attractive plant that is very easy to grow. It will stand abuse almost as ~~easily~~ well as Cast Iron Plant.

There are at least ten commonly found species of the Aglaonema, the most popular of which, A. modestum, has interestingly mottled leaves. Perhaps the most attractive, however, is A. pseudobracteatum, which is sometimes difficult to find in stores and greenhouses.

Ⓒ Cissus   A-B-B-C

Cissus is a ~~vine plant which~~ _viny genus that_ offers a number of interesting and attractive species. Most are vigorous climbers, suitable for training on a trellis or for adding to hanging baskets.

Among the more popular species are C. rhombifolia (grape ivy), which is one of the most popular of all house plants; C. antartica (kangaroo vine), which prefers a small pot; C. antartica minima (miniature kangaroo vine); C. rotundifolia; and C. discolor (begonia ivy), which is perhaps the most spectacular of the genus, although difficult to grow.

Of all the Cissus, grape ivy is the easiest to grow, which doubtless accounts for ~~a large share of~~ its popularity.

Ⓒ Coleus   A-A-A-B

This old favorite has _velvety_ leaves, _(some)_ sporting bright splashes of reds, pinks, purples, and yellows. There is a seemingly endless number of varieties of Coleus, nearly all of them interesting, _most growing_ ~~twelve to eighteen~~ _12 to 18_ inches in height.

Coleus is equally happy outdoors, grown as an annual in the North, or in the window garden. It can be grown easily from seed, and stem tip cuttings can be taken from established indoor plants _almost any time of the year._ ~~If you grow Coleus outdoors in summer,~~ take some cuttings before the first autumn freeze and root them for growing as house plants.

The soil for Coleus should be kept damp, but not soggy. Pinch back plants often to encourage bushy growth.

Ⓒ Copper Leaf (<u>Acalypha wilkesiana</u>) A-A-A-B

These are members of the Spurge family, which feature copper-colored foliage. A close relative, <u>A. hispida</u>, is described in this book under flowering plants.

Copper Leaf may be propagated easily by taking cuttings late in the summer. The plant is susceptible to attack by spider mites, and proper precautions should be taken against this menace.

Croton (<u>Codiaeum</u>) A-A-B-B

Here is a genus that is not particularly easy to grow, but well worth the effort, since it is perhaps the most colorful of all the foliage plants. There are dozens of suitable varieties, nearly all of them sporting bright, variegated, and multi-colored leaves, in a variety of shapes.

Croton needs full sun, except in the heat of summer, and warm temperatures to keep it happy.

Ⓒ <u>Dichorisandra reginae</u> A-C-B-C

This is an attractive and slow-growing plant with interesting leaf markings. It resembles Wandering Jew, except that it grows upright. Give it warm temperatures and not too much direct light, but do watch room humidity.

Ⓒ Dieffenbachia A-C-C-C

There are many species of this popular plant, often called Dumbcane. It is prized for its large leaves with interesting markings, usually variations of cream and white on dark green. <u>Dieffenbachia</u> is a fairly tough plant, not too difficult to grow. Most varieties attain a height of 18 to 24 inches, although growth is slow.

<u>D. arvida</u> 'Exotica' is very popular because it is even more durable than other members of the family. Other well-known species include <u>D. picta</u>, <u>D. amoena</u>, <u>D. sequina</u>, and <u>D. bowmannii</u>.

There are no special cultural requirements, although <u>Dieffenbachia</u> does like a warm spot and will appreciate having its foliage cleaned regularly. The plant may be propagated by taking stem cuttings and rooting them in moist and warm peat.

<u>Caution</u>: Eating or nibbling on the leaves of <u>Dieffenbachia</u> can cause severe swelling of the tongue and mouth tissues, hence its popular name, Dumbcane. It is not a plant to grow in a home with toddlers.

Ⓒ <u>Dracaena</u> A-B-B-C

There are many species of <u>Dracaena</u>, which vary so greatly in appearance that some appear to be unrelated. Most grow tall—five feet or more—on sturdy stalks.

They are very tough plants, tolerant of a surprising amount of neglect, all in all one of our most dependable house plants.

Some varieties to investigate are <u>D. deremensis</u> 'Warnecki,' <u>D. fragrans</u> (which has corn-like leaves), <u>D. fragrans massangeana</u> (whose leaves feature yellow stripes), <u>D. marginata</u> (a truly exciting plant, with grass-like, cream-colored foliage, edged in red—sometimes sold as <u>D. marginata tricolor</u>), <u>D. sanderiana</u> (with white-banded leaves), <u>D. godseffiana</u>, <u>D. draco</u> (the Dragon Tree of the Canary Islands), and many others, some of which will doubtless be offered by any good supplier. These mentioned, however, are some of the most attractive and also some of the easiest to grow.

Ⓒ Episcia A-C-A-C

This genus, which offers many species and subspecies, is related to the African Violet and requires largely the same culture, although it does demand a little more light. <u>Episcia</u> is not really one of the easiest plants to grow successfully, and should be tried only after success has been attained with some of the others listed in these pages. The leaves are a rich green, most varieties tinged with copper, some with variations of silver, blue, purple, and bronze. The veins often offer striking color contrasts. <u>Episcia</u> is a trailing plant, a natural selection for hanging baskets. It also sends out runners that may be used for propagation.

Most species of <u>Episcia</u> produce small and attractive flowers, in the color range of red-orange-yellow, but the plant is generally grown for its delightful foliage. If you do not wish to strive for blossoms, a north window will suit <u>Episcia</u> well enough.

The most popular species is <u>E. cupreata</u> (Flame Violet), which has soft and hairy copper-tinged leaves, and comes in several attractive varieties. Also investigate <u>E. dianthiflora</u>, which produces white flowers, and <u>E. lilacina</u> 'Cuprea,' with lavender flowers. Many other species and subspecies are easily available, all of which have fascinating foliage variations and some of which will bloom quite profusely.

Ⓒ <u>Fatshedra</u> (see <u>Aralia</u>)

Ⓒ <u>Fatsia japonica</u> (see <u>Aralia</u>)

Ⓒ Ferns A-C-A-C

The ferns are the oldest plants on the evolutionary scale that you are likely to cultivate. The ferns are predated only by the algae and the mosses. Everyone knows and admires ferns for their graceful and feathery fronds. They are one of the few house plants that reproduce themselves by spores rather than seeds. Some ferns grow regally upright, while others trail with modesty and grace. There are many sizes of ferns, from miniature plants suitable for the window sill, all the way to the seven-foot tub plants that can add a touch of class to entryways, patios, and conservatories.

The secret to the successful raising of ferns is in offering them an environment matching, as nearly as possible, that of their natural habitat. They need warmth, a decent degree of room humidity (not under thirty percent), and a moist and humusy soil (at least 50 per cent organic matter). They appreciate bright light, but will be affected adversely if allowed to stand for long periods of time in direct sun.

There are a great many ferns from which to choose. Among the smaller ones are:

Adiantum, the Maidenhair Fern, which is available in several varieties; it sends forth fragile-looking fronds in sprays and needs good light and high humidity. It is a rather difficult plant.

Asparagus plumosus (Asparagus Fern), the most popular of the small "ferns," is really not a fern at all but a member of the lily family and reproduces by seeds rather than spores. It is treasured for its delicate, hair-like leaves.

Other smaller "ferns" of this group include Asparagus medeoloides (Smilax), a trailer; A. sprengeri (Emerald Feather), a climber; Pteris multifida (Brake Fern); Woodwardia orientalis (Chain Fern); Polypodium aureum (Hare's Foot Fern); and many, many others.

Among the larger ferns are:

Cyrtomium falcatum (Holly Fern), which has holly-shaped fronds.

Asplenium nidus (Bird's Nest Fern), with broad lance-shaped fronds.

Nephrolepis exaltata, which has long, sword-shaped fronds and is often called Sword Fern.

N. exaltata 'Bostoniensis,' the ever-popular Boston Fern.

Platycerium bifurcatum (Staghorn Fern), whose fronds are usually attached to a piece of bark or other support, and which can become parched quite easily in a dry atmosphere.

The world of ferns is a large one, full of interest, and extremely rewarding. No house plant collection should be without at least one or two representatives of these proud families.

Ficus   B-C-C-C

This large group of indoor plants, whose best-known member is the Rubber Plant, offers species ranging from large, tree-like plants down to small-leafed trailers. Although they are not difficult plants to grow, the large species are especially sensitive to both overwatering and sudden temperature changes, and will react to either by dropping their leaves.

There has been much improvement in the Rubber Plant (F. elastica) since World War II. The best now is perhaps F. elastica 'Robusta,' which is remarkably trouble-free. There are many decorative varieties, as well, including F. elastica 'Doescheri,' which has light and dark green patched leaves and cream-colored leaf margins, and F. elastica

---

'Schryveriana,' another mottled-leafed variety. F. elastica 'Decora,' from which 'Robusta' was developed, is still a popular slow-growing variety. Rubber plants will grow as tall as any room, but may be cut back to encourage bushiness.

Chinese Banyan (F. retusa), another tree-like Ficus, showers forth with a profusion of small, leathery leaves. F. retusa nitida (Indian Laurel) resembles mountain laurel.

The Fiddle-Leaf Fig (F. lyrata) is a tough and attractive tree-like species, with large, dark green, fiddle-shaped leaves. It needs warmer conditions than other Ficus. Weeping Fig (F. benjamina) is another Ficus tree that has small, densely-growing foliage.

There are, as well, many small plants in the genus. Most popular, perhaps, is Creeping Fig (F. pumila), a small-leafed creeper that has been developed to include several variations—F. pumila minima (slower-growing and smaller), and F. pumila variegata, a variegated variety. All will adhere to rough surfaces, sending out aerial roots similar to those of ivy, and are thus easily trained.

The tree-type Ficus are propagated by air-layering, while the small-leafed climbers and trailers may be reproduced easily by simple division or cuttings.

German Ivy (Senecio mikaniodies)   C-B-B-C

Here is an easy-to-grow plant that is similar to the true ivies in both appearance and requirements. A handsome relative is S. macroglossus variegatus (Cape Ivy). Treat them in every way like Ivy (q.v.) for success.

Ginger (Zingiber officinale)   A-A-A-B

This is the same ginger that is used in cooking, which makes the plant even more interesting than its appearance would indicate. The untreated rhizomes which are sold in specialty food and gourmet shops can be planted directly in potting soil to produce plants—or, established plants may be divided easily. The plants have reed-like stems and interesting grassy foliage, truly exotic in appearance. Success as a house plant depends upon giving Ginger plenty of sunlight and warm temperatures. Keep the soil constantly damp but never soggy for long periods of time. As an added bonus, healthy plants will bear colorful clusters of flowers. A rest period is required for this plant.

Golddust Plant (Aucuba japonica)   C-B-B-C

This modest plant features dark green leaves spotted with yellow-gold markings. Its main attribute is that it will withstand very cool temperatures, all the way down to freezing, and still come up smiling. It is good for unheated winter porches in all but the coldest parts of the country. Two popular varieties are A. japonica variegata and A. japonica goldeana.

Ivy (Hedera)   C-B-B-C

Here is surely one of the most popular of house plant species, both easy to grow and cheerful and attractive in appearance. There are a great number of varieties, with new improvements coming along all the time.

English Ivy (Hedera helix) is the most popular of the true ivies, and is available in more than fifty varieties to suit nearly any taste. There are varieties with large leaves and small, fast or slow growing habits, plain green or variegated. The best way to choose an English Ivy to your liking is to visit some flower shops and greenhouses, or to beg a few cuttings from a friend who has a plant that appeals to you.

Propagation of Ivy is easy, and in fact the plant does half of the job for you. Small rootlets will form on the stem of the plant, just below the leaves, which the Ivy uses to attach itself to rough surfaces, helping it to climb. Make cuttings just below the roots and plant these cuttings directly in potting soil or a sterile rooting medium.

It would be the sheerest folly to attempt to recommend all the good varieties of English Ivy. For a starter, however, you might investigate H. helix conglomerata (Japanese Ivy), an upright-growing plant with small and densely growing leaves; 'Curlilocks' and 'Ivalace' with curled leaf margins; 'Green Ripples,' 'Maple Queen,' 'Merion Beauty,' 'Needlepoint,' 'Pittsburgh,' 'Pixie,' 'Rochester,' H. helix scutifolia, and 'Shamrock,' the last of which likes more than average moisture and which is good for terrariums.

Among the variegated English Ivies, try 'Golddust,' 'Glacier,' and 'Goldheart,' the last of which has dark green leaves with sharply contrasting bright yellow centers.

Canary Islands Ivy (Hedera canariensis) is another easy-to-grow Ivy, which has larger leaves than English Ivy. It is often trained around a piece of bark, much like a Philodendron, to form a striking plant with a very bushy appearance. More popular than the basic green-leafed variety is the variant H. canariensis variegata, also known as 'Glorie de Marengo,' whose leaves are slate-green to cream in color.

Joseph's Coat (Alternanthera)   A-B-B-B
These are low-growing, dwarf plants that are good for terrariums. Their multicolored foliage adds interest to any plant grouping. Joseph's Coat needs warm temperatures and a moist soil to be happy.

(Note: Codiaeum is also called Joseph's Coat, because it, too, has colorful foliage. However, Codiaeum grows to a height of 10 feet.)

Maranta   A-C-A-C
Here is a genus of plants that has striking foliage. It is easy to grow and impressive in appearance. Marantas will grow to about eight inches in height. M. leuconeura kerchoveana (Prayer Plant) is perhaps the most popular of the Marantas, and is so named because its leaves fold up at night, as if in prayer. The leaves are large and oval-shaped, and the plant requires a fairly humid atmosphere. In the autumn, the leaves may begin to die out.

If so, do not be alarmed. Cut off the affected leaves and reduce watering until late winter, when new growth begins; then water normally.

A red-veined variety, even more striking, is M. erythroneura. Another with red veins is M. leuconeura erythrophylla (Jungle Plant), which has olive-green leaves. Still another striking variation is offered by M. leuconeura massangeana.

Most house plant growers will want to include at least one Maranta among their collections. The key to success with this plant is in giving it lots of bright light, but no direct sun at all.

Miniature Holly (Malpighia coccigera)   C-B-B-B
This is not a true holly, but a bushy evergreen shrub with dense holly-like foliage. The leaves are shiny, dark green, and have spiny teeth. Miniature Holly does produce small flowers, but it is grown primarily as a foliage plant. It is propagated easily from cuttings.

Nephthytis (Arrowhead)   A-C-B-A
This is an attractive plant, but difficult to identify, since there is great confusion over what is and what is not a Nephthytis. Experts tell us that many Syngoniums are mistaken for Nephthytis. Other experts say that most plants sold as Nephthytis are really Syngoniums. Since the two plants are difficult to tell apart, however, no one cares very much except

the experts. Whatever they are, they are tough plants, able to withstand adverse conditions. Nephthytis have large, compound at maturity but simple before that, arum-shaped leaves, and are either trailers or climbers. Used as climbers, they will have to be offered some support, such as that used by Philodendron. Propagation may be achieved by taking stem cuttings.

Among several available species, the most popular is Syngonium podophyllum (Goosefoot Plant).

Norfolk Island Pine (Araucaria excelsa)   A-B-B-C
This popular evergreen, graceful and symmetrical, is seen with increasing frequency. It will hold up well under adverse conditions, although its branches will droop in dim light. Give it a damp, but not soggy, soil, for it is very susceptible to overwatering. It seems to do well when kept slightly potbound.

Norfolk Island Pine is a slow grower, and should never be pruned. It will grow gracefully to a height of about 6 feet, after which it tends to become ungainly.

Palms   B-C-B-B
Here is a plant family full of nostalgia for many of us. In Victorian times and right up through the 1930s and 1940s, the potted palm was a symbol of exotic elegance, bringing a bit of the tropics to shivering Northerners. No movie made before 1950 was complete without a detective peering out from behind a potted palm.

The elegant palms lost much of their allure after

World War II, but now they are making a modest comeback. You can achieve success with palms, by giving them bright light (even though they will endure shade), little water, and no plant food during the winter months. Palms, actually, seem to thrive on inattention, doing well when slightly potbound. They are slow-growing, in any case.

The palms are a plant family--Palmae is the scientific name--that comprises many genera and far more species. Few, however, are both attractive and manageable as house plants. Among the palms you might wish to investigate are:

Chamaerops (European Fan Palm) has fan-shaped leaves on long stalks, and will become quite large at maturity.

Cocos is an attractive coconut palm, the best species of which is the dwarf C. wedelliana.

Howeia is the Kentia palm, the most popular of all indoor large palms. H. belmoreana the most attractive species, will eventually grow to 10 feet or more in height, given many years and sufficient room.

Neanthe is an attractive and easy-to-grow dwarf that can tolerate a dry room.

Phoenix, the Date Palm, can be grown easily from the stone of a fresh date. Plant the stone in potting soil, keep it warm (70° to 80°) and it should germinate in about a month. It is slow growing during the first year or so, but within ten or fifteen years it will become as tall as any room.

Pellonia   A-B-A-B

This is a colorful, slow-growing, creeping plant, fine for hanging baskets and a good filler plant for groupings. It features small, oval-shaped leaves with interesting variegated patterns. There are two popular varieties--P. daveauana and the more compact P. pulchra.

Pellonia is not difficult to propagate. As it creeps along the soil it sends down roots from the stems. Just cut the stems into sections and root them in potting soil.

Peperomia   A-C-B-C

There are many species and varieties of this popular and cheerful little plant (eight inches or less in height), most of which are low and upward-growing, some with deeply ridged leaves. They are tough plants, tolerant of most conditions, although they will rot at the groundline if the top of the soil is not allowed to dry out between waterings. Peperomia like bright light, but not direct sun in the summer.

Among the more popular varieties are:

P. caperata (Emerald Ripple Peperomia) has deeply ridged heart-shaped leaves; the tops of the ridges are green and the valleys are brown, giving an interesting effect.

P. rotundifolia is a low grower with light green and thick leaves.

P. obtusifolia (Ovalleaf Peperomia) has solid green

leaves, while P. obtusifolia variegata is the variegated form of the same species.

P. sandersi (Watermelon Peperomia) is identified by its red petioles and silver-striped leaves.

P. grieseo-argentea hederaefolia has ridged, glossy leaves, silver-hued, and purple-olive veins.

There are many other varieties of the Peperomia, many of which may be seen at your local flower shop or greenhouse.

Philodendron   B-C-B-C

These plants constitute what is probably the most popular group of house plants in America today. There are many, many species and varieties, with leaves ranging from small to very large, in an interesting variety of shapes offered by no other house plants. Most are climbers, and will appreciate a support that can be kept moist, such as that described on page XX.

Philodendron are not difficult plants to grow, unless you disregard the rules. Growth will be stunted by poor light, and the leaves can turn yellow and drop from lack of water, too small a pot, low temperatures, or poor drainage. They will appreciate a monthly washing with a mild soap (not detergent) solution. Cut back the growing tips if you wish to encourage bushy growth, and use the tip cuttings to form new plants.

Some of the more popular varieties include:

P. scandens (Sweetheart Vine), a very popular climber that can withstand the dry air of a typical apartment.

P. oxycardum, the most commonly grown form, which has heart-shaped leaves very similar to P. scandens. It is often grown in water or wet moss.

P. dubium (Cut Leaf Philodendron) is a slow grower with star-shaped leaves.

P. panduraeforme (Fiddleleaf Philodendron) has irregularly shaped, olive-green leaves.

P. pertusum has perforated leaves, irregularly shaped. The adult form, known as Monstera deliciosa, has broad and thick leaves with many perforations.

P. squamiferum (Anchorleaf Philodendron) has leaves and petioles that are covered by red hairs. The leaves are shaped like daggers.

P. bipinnatifidum (Twice-cut Philodendron) is a large-leafed variety; the leaves resemble the smaller P. dubium in shape, but are more deeply notched.

P. selloum is another cut-leaf variety, the cuts becoming more pronounced as the plant reaches maturity. This species will tolerate temperatures down to freezing with no apparent harm.

P. wendlandi is another large-leafed species, very tolerant of a wide range of temperatures and humidity. Its leaves are long and narrow.

Piggy-Back Plant (<u>Tolmiea menziesi</u>)   B-B-A-A

Here is a native to the West Coast of the United States, a modest-sized plant that can be grown outdoors/in the warmer regions of the country. Its name is derived from its unusual habit of bearing young plantlets from the junction of the leaf and the petiole. These can be rooted easily to grow new plants. The leaves are toothed and lobed, covered in down. It is an easy plant to grow, although not considered especially attractive by some.

Pilea   A-B-B-B

There are at least four cultivated house plants in this interesting group, none of which grows more than a foot in height. They are rather unusual looking plants, not liked by everyone. All like moist soil, warm temperatures, and full sun in the winter. The plants become less attractive as they grow older, but cuttings are easily made, so that older plants may be discarded when desired. Fertilize <u>Pilea</u> liberally when growth is active.

<u>P. cadiere</u> (Aluminum Plant) has dark green leaves with striking aluminum-colored markings. A dwarf variety, <u>P. cadiere minima</u>, is preferred by many, as is <u>P. cadiere nana</u>, a compact variety.

<u>P. microphylla</u> (Artillery Plant) is fine in texture with bright green, fern-like leaves. When its flowers are dry, pollen literally explodes from the blossoms, hence its common name.

<u>P. involucrata</u> (South American Friendship Plant) is bushy in growth and has coppery leaves. It can be made to be even more bushy, if several cuttings are taken, then rooted in the same pot, to the sides of the parent plant.

<u>P. 'Silver Tree'</u> has bronze-hued leaves with silver markings.

Plectranthus   A-C-A-B

Various species of this genus are often called Trailing Coleus or Swedish Ivy. Some are upright in growth, while others are trailers, making good subjects for hanging baskets.

<u>P. australis</u>, a trailer, has waxy-green leaves, round in shape with saw-tooth edges.

<u>P. australis variegatus</u>, similar in leaf shape, with added white markings.

<u>P. purpuratus</u> is an upright plant with purple coloring on the undersides of its leaves.

There are other interesting varieties, including <u>P. oertendahlii</u>, a flowering trailer with bronze-hued leaves and silvery veins.

Pleomele   A-C-B-A

This is an interesting group of plants with cultural requirements similar to those of <u>Philodendron</u>.

<u>P. reflexa variegata</u> (Song of India) is now included in the genus <u>Dracaena</u>. Its attractive, spear-shaped leaves are gold and green striped, borne in clusters on branching stems. It will grow to tree size in ten or fifteen years.

<u>P. reflexa gracilis</u> has dense foliage; its recurved leaves have translucent edges.

<u>P. thalioides</u> has waxy-green leaves, ribbed lengthwise.

Pothos (<u>Scindapsus</u>)   A-C-B-C

Pothos is very similar in appearance and growth habits to the heart-leaf <u>Philodendron</u>, <u>P. scandens</u>, except that it needs less water and warmer temperatures—not below 65°. It likes bright light, but cannot stand direct sun. Pothos is a natural trailer, although it can be trained upward along a support, again like <u>Philodendron</u>. The leaves are heart-shaped, green, with pale yellow markings.

The most popular species is <u>S. aureus</u>, which offers several variegated varieties, some of which require even warmer temperatures.

Ruellia makoyana   A-C-A-C

This is an old favorite, not seen as often today as in the 1930s. It is a free-spreading plant, with glossy and pale green leaves with silvery veins. It likes a warm and moist environment, shaded from the sun.

Sanchezia nobilis glaucophylla   A-C-A-B

This is a member of the <u>Aphelandra</u> family. It grows to a height of four feet and has large, glossy, sword-shaped leaves with yellow veins.

Screw Pine (<u>Pandanus</u>)   A-C-B-B

This old favorite will withstand most adverse conditions. It is recognized by its long, arching, sword-like leaves, which have saw-toothed edges.

<u>P. veitchii</u> has green and white striped leaves. Often preferred, however, is <u>P. veitchii compactus</u>, a dwarf variety with clearly variegated leaves. <u>P. baptistii</u> has no marginal spines, as do the other species. All Screw Pines like moist soil, but never soggy soil. They can take some direct sun, except in the heat of summer, although they do best in a bright location out of direct sun altogether.

Selaginella   A-D-A-A

Among these fern-like plants are some small creepers, some erect-growing species, and some trailers. All offer bright green, feathery foliage. The conditions they require are the same as those for ferns.

<u>S. kraussiana</u> is a low creeper, perfect for terrariums.

<u>S. emmeliana</u> is an erect-growing plant.

<u>S. willdenovii</u> is a vigorous climber with unusual blue leaves, while <u>S. apus</u> is a trailer, good for hanging baskets.

Sensitive Plant (<u>Mimosa pudica</u>)   B-C-A-B

This is a fascinating plant for both adults and children

Prefers dry soil but high room humidity.

because its delicate and feathery leaves and petioles droop
and fold up instantly (and temporarily) whenever it is touched,
or even if a [lighted] match is held close to it. Seeds are often
available in stores, from which plants will grow easily. It
becomes leggy and out of hand after about a year, but it is
not difficult to grow more [plants] at any time. *It is very sensitive,
also, to mealybugs.*

Silk Oak (<u>Grevillea robusta</u>)   C-B-B-C

This is a pleasant plant with graceful and feathery
foliage similar to that of the False Aralia. *It will grow to ~~three~~ feet in height.* Silk Oak likes
cool and moist conditions, and can spend the summer outdoors
with benefit. It does tend to get leggy if unchecked, ~~and~~
so it should be cut back at the growing tip fairly regularly.
Silk Oak will react badly if its soil becomes very dry.

Snake Plant (<u>Sansevieria</u>)   A-C-B-A

The Snake Plant is actually a succulent, but ~~nobody~~ *few of us*
thinks of it as such, and so we include it among the foliage
plants. It has long been very popular, probably because of
its great tolerance to adverse conditions. It is also called
Mother-in-Law Tongue and Bowstring. Like the Cast Iron Plant,
it can grow perfectly well in hot, dry, and dim locations
(including, it seems, most old hotel lobbies in the country).
The leaves are thick and sword-shaped, usually upright, *growing to ~~eighteen~~ inches or more in height,* but
in some varieties ground-hugging. It is propagated easily by

division of the rootstock or by taking leaf cuttings. (Be
careful not to turn the leaf cutting upside-down when setting
it in the rooting medium, for roots grow only from the downward
portion of the cutting.)

There are many varieties available, including:

<u>S. trifasciata laurenti</u> (Variegated Snake Plant) has
handsome yellow bands along its leaf margins.

<u>S. trifasciata</u> is similar in form, but without the yellow
bands.

<u>S. trifasciata laurenti</u> 'compacta' (Dwarf Congo Snake
Plant) has shorter leaves and yellow margins.

<u>S. trifasciata</u> 'hahni' (Hahn's Dwarf Snake Plant) has
light and dark green bands along the leaves.

There are many other interesting variegated varieties
of this old standby.

Spathe Flower (<u>Spathiphyllum</u>)   B-D-A-A

Here is an easy-to-grow, tough plant, suitable for the
homes of most novice green thumbs. It has sword-shaped and
glossy green leaves. White blossoms will sometimes surprise
you in the winter, but do not depend on ~~them~~ *their appearance*.

There are two popular species—*S.* clevelandii and
<u>S. floribundum</u>.

Spider Plant (<u>Chlorophytum comosum</u>)   B-B-B-C

Spider Plant is one of the most popular of house plants.

It has grassy leaves, variegated cream and green in color,
which arch gracefully from either pot or hanging basket.
Mature plants produce perfectly-formed baby plants on the end
of long runners, ~~which~~ *that* resemble spiders hanging from a thread.
Propagation is simply a matter of rooting one of the "baby
spiders" in a rooting medium. The Spider Plant can store
water in its tubers, and can take dry soil for a fairly long
time because of this ~~foresight~~ *characteristic*.

Strawberry Geranium (<u>Saxifraga sarmentosa</u>)   C-B-B-B

This trailing plant, also called Strawberry Begonia and
Mother of Thousands, is good for both hanging baskets and
terrariums. All its really asks is a woodsy soil *, containing plenty of organic matter,* and a cool
location. Leaves of the Strawberry Geranium *resemble* ~~are very similar~~
~~to~~ those of the true geranium, and it sends out runners just
as strawberry plants do. The leaves of the standard variety
are deep olive in color, with silver-gray markings. An interesting variant, <u>S. sarmentosa</u> 'tricolor,' has dark green
leaves marked with white and pink, and is considerably more
difficult to grow. *Strawberry Geranium can be easily
harmed by overfertilization.*

Sweet Flag (<u>Acorus gramineus</u>)   A-C-A-C

Here is a moisture-loving plant that grows only ~~two~~ [2]
inches tall. It is a pleasant little fellow, and will be
most happy in a terrarium.

Syngonium (see <u>Nephthytis</u>)

Ti Plant (<u>Cordyline terminalis</u>)   A-B-A-B

<u>C. terminalis</u> is only one of many species of <u>Cordyline</u>,
but is certainly the most popular. Also called Firebrand, it
and grow to ~~two~~ feet in height
will last for only one to three years, before dying out, but
its spectacular young life is certainly worth your placing
this plant on your list of house plant candidates. It has
long, upward-reaching leaves, cerise, purple, and green, which
grow from a cane trunk. Another popular species is <u>C. australis</u>,
which features long and slender leaves. The Ti Plant is very
popular in Hawaii, where its colorful grassy leaves are used
in making grass skirts. It is sold there in tourist shops as
a "Ti Log." In recent years, breeders have developed several
variations of the original plant, including a dwarf and a
variegated variety, which go under various names.

Umbrella Sedge (<u>Cyperus alternifolius</u>)   A-C-A-C

Here is a popular exotic plant with narrow, pointed,
grasslike leaves ~~which~~ *that* grow in clusters. It will grow up to
~~two~~ [2] feet tall in a pot. Constant moisture is essential, and
propagation is a simple matter of root division.

Related species include <u>C. papyrus</u>, similar in appearance and requirements but which grows to ~~seven~~ [7] feet in height,
and a dwarf variety, <u>C. alternifolius gracilis</u>.

C   Velvet Plant (<u>Gynura</u>)   A-B-B-B

   This is a vigorous-growing plant with dark red, velvety leaves. It will offer a fine contrast to your green plants. It is best to train the Velvet Plant to some support, to keep it in bounds, or to pinch it back often to encourage bushy growth. The plants tend to become spindly and leggy with age.

   There are two common varieties—<u>G. aurantiaca</u>, which is upright in growth habit, and <u>G. sarmentosa</u>, a smaller and loosely twining plant. The flowers of both are horrible in scent and should be removed immediately upon appearance. The plant also tends to harbor mealybugs.

C   Yew (<u>Podocarpus</u>)   C-B-B-B

   Yews are prized outdoor plants in many parts of the country, but can be made into attractive house plants anywhere. These hardy evergreens can provide welcomed contrast to your tropicals. They are slow-growing and tolerant of adverse conditions. They will take low temperatures without a whimper, and might require frequent repotting because of vigorous growth. *They can become quite large and bushy.* <u>P. macrophylla angustifolia</u> (Southern Yew) can be pruned to a pleasing shape and will respond with even more vigorous growth. Other similar species include <u>P. macrophylla</u> 'Nagai' and <u>P. macrophylla</u> 'Maki.'

C   Wandering Jew (<u>Tradescantia</u>)   C-C-B-C

   <u>Tradescantia</u> and <u>Zebrina</u> both claim the common name of Wandering Jew, and the two genra are so similar that they are

commonly interchanged. All are easy-to-grow, tolerant, and vigorous trailers of many varieties, perfect for hanging baskets. Feed them regularly for good growth. Propagation is simplicity itself, take cuttings of growing tips and root them in water.

   Among very many interesting species are:

   <u>T. fluminensis</u>, the original Wandering Jew, has silver markings, but there are many variants of different markings and colors available today.

   <u>T. albiflora</u> has bluish-green leaves with white stripes.

   <u>Z. pendula</u> is an excellent house plant whose leaves have purple undersides. Again, there are several interesting variegated varieties.

Special Boxes: eleven of these highlighted topics are gathered at the end of the manuscript, and some might well be placed in these two chapters somewhere. I am assuming that the eleven will be fairly evenly distributed throughout the book. Numbers 1, 2, and 3 might go well in chapter II, as they directly concern plant-growing methods. Boxes 4-11 all list plants in various kinds of groups--those that have a predominance of foliage plants would be appropriate for chapter IV. The author can advise best the precise locations for these lists.

Tables: Table 1 should be placed near the text on p. 23. The table itself is on the sheet following that page, which contains a specific reference to it. The table has a title and a number; you might want to consider dropping the number, as the book contains only a handful itself. Reference in the text, in that case, would have to be changed from number to title. Note that the column heads had to be so marked so that they could be more easily distinguished from column items.

Display Lines: all chapter titles, headings, tables titles, etc. have been marked for u & lc as a guide for the designer in the event that he or she does not choose to use all caps or sc in these places.

Heads and Subheads: all are keyed by letter in manuscript margins, as follows:
1. A-level heads mark the major divisions of the text in chapter II (and other chapters in the manuscript); see pp. 8, -0, 13, 15, 17, 18, 19, 22, 23, 25, 27, 28, 29 (twice), 31, 33
2. B-level heads mark subdivisions of the major divisions of chapter II (and others in the manuscript); see pp. 13 (twice), 14, 26 (four times), 27, 35, 38, 39
3. C-level heads, which occur in chapter IV (and others in the manuscript),could be treated as A levels or as a completely separate series. They mark the descriptions of individual house plants and are quite numerous--often several per page. Each line includes not only the plant name(s) but also the set of four symbols described by the author in the "Key to Symbols" at the end of the manuscript. The symbols are here represented by the caps A,B, C, and D. These headings occur on pp. 55-86.

Extracts: none

Footnotes: all are signaled by asterisks and occur on pp. 18 and 80. None are citations of sources.

Unusual Characters and Accents:
degree sign: pp. 28, 36, 37, 58, 73, 79, all in text; ff. p. 23, in the table
subscript numbers: p. 19, in text

Cross-References: One by page number on p. 75; this will have to be filled in during the reading of page proofs.

Illustrations: suggestions for the placement of illustrations (those suggested by the author have been gathered in a separate section at the beginning of the manuscript) are written in the margins beside the relevant text. See pp. 13, 22, 24, 26, 30, 31, 32

EDITORIAL DEPARTMENT
The University of North Carolina Press
BOOK PLAN

Author _____
Date ___ 3 September 1976

Front Matter
Title page (copy to appear in print, check carefully)

Title ___ No Time for House Plants

Subtitle ___ A Busy Person's Guide to Indoor Gardening

Author or Editor _____

Special imprint ___ None

Copyright page ___ UNC Press 1977

Permissions notice ___ We may need permissions for illustrative material not yet received

Dedication page ___ None

Foreword ___ None

Preface ___ Yes, copy supplied

Acknowledgments ___ None

Table of Contents ___ Yes, copy supplied

List of Illustrations ___ To be prepared when all illustrations have been provided

List of Tables ___ None

Introduction ___ None

Other _____

Text
Part titles ___ None

Chapter divisions ___ 1-7

Tables ___ None

Other ___ 11 special boxes

Illustrations
Linecuts ___ Finished art work to be supplied

Halftones ___ 38 received; more to come

Other _____

Back Matter
Appendixes ___ None

Notes ___ Symbol notes to be set at the bottom of the page; not in backmatter

Bibliography ___ Yes, copy supplied

Index ___ To be prepared by author; approximately 6 finished pages

Other _____

THE UNIVERSITY OF NORTH CAROLINA PRESS

Box 2288, Chapel Hill, N. C. 27514

3 September 1976

Dear

We are sending you today by first class mail the edited manuscript of NO TIME FOR HOUSE PLANTS.

Please review it with care, answering all editorial queries, and make certain that the text now stands exactly the way you wish to see it in type. You will see only page proof, and making changes at that time—other than the correction of typographical errors—can be costly. If changes are made at that time, beyond the barest minimum, the author will be charged. So please review the edited manuscript with the care you would give to first proof.

The copy of the edited manuscript you will receive is a xerox, and your changes will be transferred to the original manuscript, so please make all marks in a bright color for high visibility.

You will also find with the manuscript a style sheet that will come in handy during the process of author review and also later when you are reading the proof.

Accompanying the manuscript you will find two copies of our book plan. This form is only a record for both of us, indicating the elements that are to appear in the finished book. Please check this form, initial one copy, and return it to us with the manuscript. The other copy is for your files.

We would like to have the reviewed manuscript back in this office no later than 20 September. Please feel free to call me (919-933-2105) if you have any questions concerning the review of your manuscript.

Yours sincerely,

(Mrs.) Gwen Duffey
Managing Editor

P.S. I noted that 6 of the 38 halftones accompanying the manuscript have no credits stamped on the back. Are these also USDA photos?

The Association of American University Presses, Inc.

One Park Avenue, New York, N.Y. 10016 · 212 889-6040

November 11, 1976

Mrs. Gwen Duffey
Managing Editor
THE UNIVERSITY OF NORTE CAROLINA PRESS
Box 2288
Chapel Hill, NC 27514

Dear Mrs. Duffey:

Please excuse this extreme delay in responding to your letters of September 3 and October 11. I hope that I have not inter-fered too seriously with your production plans.

In any case, I enclose the manuscript with this letter, with my appreciation to Barbara Reitt for a superb job of copy-editing. She struck a very fine balance that I appreciate greatly. I hope that I have responded properly to all of her queries.

I also enclose the Book Plan, initialed.

The biographical form was returned yesterday.

This should bring us up to date on the project, at least so far as I am concerned. If there is anything further I may do, please do not hesitate to write or call at

Thank you again, and best wishes.

Sincerely,

P.S. All the photos are USDA photos.

THE UNIVERSITY OF NORTH CAROLINA PRESS

Box 2288, Chapel Hill, N. C. 27514

11 October 1976

Dear

On 3 September we sent you copyedited chapters 2 and 4 of No Time for House Plants for review, with the request that the manuscript be returned to us by 20 September. Since we have not received it, I am concerned that it might have been lost in the mails. We were planning to start composition by mid-October, and this delay may well affect the scheduling of our other titles for spring. Please let me know at your earliest convenience when we may expect to receive the manuscript.

Yours sincerely,

(Mrs.) Gwen Duffey
Managing Editor

EDITORIAL CHECKLIST

Author (as name should appear on title page): _____

Mailing address for galleys and pages: _____

Title: No Time for House Plants: A Busy Person's Guide to Indoor Gardening

Number of pages in manuscript: 144

Check the kinds of typesetting: (If the kinds checked occur infrequently, please list MS pages)

			Part titles
X	Text		Poetry
X	Quoted matter	X	Bibliography
	Footnotes		Appendix
	Endnotes	X	Tabular (p. 23)
X	Index		Other
	Formula		

List special characters: math, foreign language, etc.; if infrequent, list MS pages

degree sign; subscript number _____

Front matter: (Please cross out any items not included)

~~Other of special imprint~~   Table of Contents
~~Verso blank~~   ~~Foreword~~
Half title   Preface
Verso blank   ~~Acknowledgments~~
Title page   ~~List of illustrations~~
Copyright page   ~~List of Maps, Tables, etc.~~
~~Dedication page~~   Introduction
Verso blank

How many levels of subheads? 3 (A,B,C)

What copy is to come? _____ finished artwork; additional halftones

Will there be illustrations? yes   How many? ?   What kind? halftones

and linedrawings _____   Frontispiece? no

Special problems of comment: (i.e., British spelling or punctuation, erratic spelling, special indents, etc.)

M E M O

TO: Joyce

FROM: Gwen

RE:

17 November 1976

Here is the _____ title ready for composition. Included you will also find the following:

editorial checklist   illustrations
copy for running heads   copy for legends
style sheet   author's key to symbols
production notes from editor
copy for spine

Jacket copy will be prepared later--if we decide to have a jacket.

May I please see sample pages that include the following:

text
chapter opening
subheads A, B, C
footnote
bibliography
special box (if we are going to treat this material in this fashion)

Finished art work has not been provided by the author. May I assume that the production department will take care of this?

Since we shall not have color in this title, have you considered the possibility of printing in dark green on pale green stock? Would there be any advantage in doing this with a ring binder?

UNC PRESS   Editorial Department
The University of North Carolina Press
Chapel Hill, N. C. 27514

Memo

To Joyce
From Gwen

The free-lance editor suggested that Species Boxes 1, 2, and 3 move up in Chap. II.

It seems to me that Boxes 4-11 should be grouped at the back of the book.

Design decisions will make change in Table of Contents necessary.

legends for ___ illustrations with MS locations

(handwritten note: Repetition have been marked for possible cutting)

22 A terrarium or bottle garden can be grown in nearly any clear glass container, as long as a top can be found to prevent moisture from escaping. Here a plastic coffee-can lid has been placed over a brandy snifter. (USDA Photo)

23 A good example of double potting. The sphagnum moss between the two pots reduces the need for watering. (USDA Photo)

26 Decorative containers without drainage holes can be used successfully if the plant is double potted. This prayer plant (Maranta) has been potted in a clay pot, which was then inserted into the decorative container or a layer of gravel. Moss occupies the space between the two pots, helping to assure constant moisture for the plant's roots. (USDA Photo)

26 Smaller house plants should be sprayed weekly for good health and a sparkling appearance. A strong spray will also remove many smaller insects from plants. (USDA Photo)

26 Large-leafed plants will appreciate an occasional bath. Use a mild soap solution and rinse thoroughly with clear water—both at room temperature. (USDA Photo)

27 Decorative planters are available in many shapes and sizes, many of them equipped with lighting of the correct intensity for stimulating vigorous plant growth. (USDA Photo)

30 Stem cuttings should be made just below a node—the point at which the leaf originates—since many plants have embryonic root systems at the nodes which develop rapidly when placed in water. For this purpose, a sharp pair of pruning shears is adequate, although a sharp single-edged razor blade is even better / since it will not crush the stem. (USDA Photo)

31 Any plant and soil ball may easily be separated from its pot by turning it upside-down and rapping the rim of the pot sharply against ~~the edge of the kitchen sink the potting bench~~. If the plant is not sufficiently potbound to require repotting—and this one is not—the soil ball may easily be replaced with no harm and little mess. (USDA Photo)

35 The cuttings of many house plants can be rooted easily in water. The roots of this aluminum plant are at a stage at which the plant can be potted. Many of these plants, including this one, can also be grown permanently in water. (USDA Photo)

57 A selection of bromeliads: left, living vase plant (Aechmea chantinii); center top, Vriesia carinata; center bottom, earth star (Cryptanthus zonatus); right, Neoregelia hybrid. (USDA Photo)

58 Cast iron plant (Aspidistra). (USDA Photo)

60 Coleus blumei, Dracaena sanderiana, and Iresine herbstii. (USDA Photo) *(handwritten: Coleus ref.)*

62 Many plants, such as this Dieffenbachia picta, grow better when slightly potbound. (USDA Photo)

62 Dracaena sanderiana, D. fragrans, and zebra plant (Aphelandra). (USDA Photo) *(handwritten: Dracaena ref.)*

62 Dieffenbachia picta 'Rudolph Roehrs,' Dieffenbachia amoena, and Ficus pandurata. (USDA Photo)

72 Palm (Phoenix), fern (Nephrolepsis), and Scindapsus (S. aureus). (USDA Photo)

72 Moses-in-the-cradle (Rhoeo spathacea 'discolor'), Norfolk Island pine (Araucaria excelsa), and Philea coderie. (USDA Photo)

74 A bromeliad, earth star (Cryptanthus zonatus), Peperomia floridii, and Bromelia serra. (USDA Photo)

75 Philodendron dubium, P. pertusum, and P. panduraeforme. (USDA Photo) *(handwritten: repetition unit next entry)*

(handwritten circled notes: repetition, repetition)

THE UNIVERSITY OF NORTH CAROLINA PRESS

Box 2288, Chapel Hill, N. C. 27514

16 December 1976

Dear

At a recent staff meeting, it was suggested that the present title of your book is somewhat negative in tone. Our sales manager suggested that the addition of a question mark would give it more appeal. We are all in favor of this change, and I believe that our production department is already planning the title page with the question mark included. How does No Time for Houseplants? strike you? (We are also following Webster's Third on the preferred usage of one word for "houseplant.") If I do not hear from you to the contrary, we shall proceed with this variation on your original title.

Yours sincerely,

(Mrs.) Gwen Duffey
Managing Editor

---

legends, p. 3

75   Philodendron squamiferum and umbrella tree (Schefflera actinophylla.)

(USDA Photo)

81   The snake plant (Sansevieria), in several interesting varieties, is one

of the easiest of all house plants to grow.

81   Snake plant (Sansevieria tricaciata), croton (Codiaeum varigatum),

rubber plant (Ficus elastica). (UDSA Photo)

85   Calathea ornata, southern yew (Podocarpus macrophylla), ard Chinese

everygreen (Aglaonemas commutatum). (USDA Photo)

running heads for   HOUSE PLANTS

verso   recto

Preface   Preface

No Time for House Plants   The Secrets of No-Work House Plant Success

No Time for House Plants   Understanding House Plants

No Time for House Plants   Plant Troubles and Cures

No Time for House Plants   Introducing the Foliage Plants

No Time for House Plants   Cacti and Other Succulents

No Time for House Plants   Flowering House Plants

No Time for House Plants   Special Indoor Gardens

Bibliography   Bibliography

Index   Index

February 3, 1977

Mrs. Gwen Duffey
Managing Editor
The UNIVERSITY OF NORTH CAROLINA PRESS
Box 2288
Chapel Hill, North Carolina 27514

Dear Gwen:

It was nice talking with you just now, and I must apologize once again for mixing up your sample pages with the Toronto material. I hope that I have not delayed things.

I enclose the pages, with the corrections we discussed.

Sincerely,

(answering for Purvis Mulch, who is out of sorts today)

THE UNIVERSITY OF NORTH CAROLINA PRESS
Box 2288

Chapel Hill, North Carolina 27514

Editorial Department

Date: 19 January 1977

To:

Author:

Title: HOUSEPLANTS

We have mailed to you today by

___ educational materials, insured
___ educational materials, special delivery, insured
_X_ first class mail
___ air mail
___ air parcel post, insured

2 sets of page proof (pages 1 - 14_____) and the edited manuscript.

One set is to be corrected and returned to us with the manuscript. The other set of proof is for your own use.

___ our index style memo, with attached specifications for your index.

Remarks:

Please have the proof back in this office no later than 27 January.

Signed: _Gwen Duffey_
(Mrs.) Gwen Duffey

Managing Editor

Contents

---

false castor oil plant. It thrives in a cool spot. Aralia can easily grow leggy, and should be pruned annually in order to encourage it into bushy growth. It will attain a height of 4 feet at maturity.

A striking hybrid, *Fatshedra lizei* (a cross between *F. japonica* and ivy or *Hedra*) forms a climbing plant with maple-shaped leaves that is tolerant of adverse conditions.

There is also a plant called false aralia (*Dizygotheca elegantissima*), which has graceful and feathery foliage. It bears no resemblance to the true aralia and is difficult to grow.

Asparagus

There are two common kinds of *Asparagus* suitable for growing as house plants—fern asparagus (*A. plumosus*), with slender, needle-like, dark-green leaves, forming a feathery appearance, and *A. sprengeri* (emerald feather) which has thicker yellow-green leaves and drooping stems. The latter makes a good plant for hanging baskets, and produces red berries at Christmastime. Both like some sun in the summer and full sun in the winter, and both can grow to a height of about 2 feet. *A. meyeri*, less common but equally attractive, has tiny fernlike leaves that arch out on long stems from the center of the plant.

14

MANUSCRIPT CASTOFF

date 10/25/76

Author/Title _____ MULCH _____

Number of ms. pages _____

Trim _____

Text page _____

Type _____

Text _____ 190747 _____

Extracts _____

Bibliography _____ 119 lines 150 -595C _____

Appendix _____

Index _____

Notes _____ table ~ 354 _____

Odd characters _____

Physical quality of ms. and comments _____

Tables _____ 10 - total of 107?/lines _____

Halftones _____ 6 1/1? _____

quality? _____

Linecuts _____ ~15 /page? (punctuation?) _____

camera-ready _____

no. to be drawn _____

Frequency _____

PRINTER #2 — PRODUCTION COST ESTIMATE

Author: Mulch   Title: NO TIME FOR HOUSEPLANTS?

Print 5000/7500   Bind 5000/7500   Paper/cloth   Trim size 5 x 7 3/8   Pages 192

Paper 60 lb. Publisher's Eggshell   Illustrations: lincuts 7, halftones 30, maps, etc.

	5000	7500
PLANT: Composition	1,023.28	1,023.28
AAs	102.32	102.32
Negatives/Plates	1,113.00	1,113.00
Illus. Prep. and Engravings		
Dixxxx Photographer	250.00	250.00
Lock-up		
Blues		
Extra proof/xeroxes		
Sample pages		
Miscellaneous	100.00	100.00
TOTAL PLANT:	2588.60	2588.60
RUNNING: Printing – text	371.00	468.00
– illustrations		
Paper – text	1124.50	1686.75
– illustrations		
Freight	500.00	750.00
Jackets		
Paperback covers (print and paper)	534.50	666.00
Endsheets		
TOTAL RUNNING:	2530.00	3570.75
SHEET COST:	5118.60	6159.35
Fold, gather...		
BINDING: xxxx Slipcases- stock & print	519.00	685.50
Paper	2781.00	4074.00
TOTAL ESTIMATED MANUFACTURING COST:	8418.60	10,918.85
	1.684	1.456

Date 12/20/76

PRINTER #1 — PRODUCTION COST ESTIMATE

Author: Mulch   Title: NO TIME FOR HOUSEPLANTS?

Print 5000/7500   Bind 5000/7500   Paper/cloth   Trim size 5 x 7 3/8   Pages 192

Paper 60 lb. Publishers white   Illustrations: lincuts 7, halftones 30, maps, etc.

	5000	7500
PLANT: Composition	1,023.28	1,023.28
AAs	102.32	102.32
Negatives/Plates	498.00	498.30
Illus. Prep. and Engravings		
Dixxx Photographer	250.00	250.00
Lock-up		
Blues	53.40	53.40
Extra proof/xeroxes		
Sample pages		
Miscellaneous	100.00	100.00
TOTAL PLANT:	2027.00	2027.00
RUNNING: Printing – text	382.00	487.00
– illustrations		
Paper – text	1135.00	1701.00
– illustrations		
Freight	500.00	750.00
Jackets		
Paperback covers (print and paper)	270.00	375.00
Sxxxxxxxxxx Shrinkwrap	90.00	135.00
TOTAL RUNNING:	2377.00	3448.00
SHEET COST:	4404.00	5475.00
Fold, gather...		
BINDING: xxxxh slipcases- manufacturing	2050.00	3075.00
slipcases-insert books	145.00	217.50
Paper	565.00	765.00
TOTAL ESTIMATED MANUFACTURING COST:	7164.00	9532.50
	1.433	1.271

Date 12/20/76

MATERIAL TO BE SCANNED   DATE: 11/30/76

TO: Interstate Graphics
       P.O. Box 1163
       Charlotte, North Carolina 28201

       Attn. Bill Evans

FROM: UNC PRESS PRODUCTION DEPARTMENT
       P.O. Box 2288
       305 Bynum Hall, UNC Campus
       Chapel Hill, N. C. 27514

Title: Mulch, NO TIME FOR HOUSEPLANTS?   Typescript pages: 1-160

Return 6 level TTS paper tape to us as soon as possible. Use
key optics. Use our code sheet as follows:
                        NO INDENT
Standard code sheet: _____ 1 em _____ 2 em _____ 3 em paragraph indent
                                        Helvetica
                     kern_ng: xxxxxxxxxxxxxXxxDembx xx or Sabon _____
                     Roman/Italic position: (1/2)   3/4 (circle one)

Please notify us of projected shipping date immediately upon receipt
of copy.

_____

11/17 Mulch

Estimated for Helvetica, no A indent — 1 line sp.

Frontmatter, tables, legends to be set at AEI
All text (+ preface) typed for scanner

— symbols to be put in after setting

(typist will indent A, scanner will output
no indent and extra line space)

===============================

CUSTOMER _____ JOB NO. _____ TYPIST _____ SHEET NO. _____ DATE _____
▸ ALIGN FIRST CHARACTER UNDER THIS ARROW

1 MULCH Galley 23/1/1

Chapter 2

Understanding House Plants

Every plant has its own preferences and requirements for soil type, light, temperature, ventilation, humidity, and several other factors that are within our
power to control, or at least to mitigate. It is vitally importa⌐nt for you.
as a busy indoor gardener, to understand the basics of each factor, since a
prior understanding will enable you to avoid much work later on wi⌐hile achieving routine success in growing plants.

     In addition to understading these basic needs, you will want to know
something about pots and other containers, repor⌐ting plants, propagation, and
a few other matters that, while not vital to immediate success, will help you
to gain further enjoyment in raising better plants.

The Basic House Plant

The major difference between a house plant and an outdoor plant is location.
All house plants could live and flourish outdoors, in the proper climate. All
are derived from forebears that lived, reproduced, and died in the outdoors,
whether it was on a forest floor in central Europe or in the bough of a tree
in a South American forest. Over many centuries of adaptation and evolution,
each plant species embraced those characteristics that enabled it to survive;
even today, every house plant carries within its genetic structue⌐re the characteristics of its distant progenitors. Thus the ¶Maranta¶r will lose some
of its leaves each autumn, even though autumn's weather does not come to the
bookshelf where the plant rests, and a cactus, no matter how long we have been
feeding and w⌐Hatering it with unfailing regularity, will continue to hoard

DO NOT TYPE BELOW THIS LINE

PRODUCTION DEPARTMENT
The University of North Carolina Press
P.O. Box 2288
Chapel Hill, North Carolina 27514
(919) 933-2163

COMPOSITION SPECIFICATIONS

Title NO TIME FOR HOUSEPLANTS?   **Author** Mulch·

Trim size 5" x 7³/₈"   **Text page** (incl. r. head/feet) 24 x 40 1/2   **Margins:** Head 1¹/₂pi. Gutter 3 pi

Typography Face Helvetica   ~~2 col. per page (11 pi ea.)~~ lire #   Paragraph indent

Text In 10 / 13pt Editor used A.B.C.

A. Subheads in text:
1   10 pt. B.F. lc anc c fl. left
    Space above 3 lines   Space below 2 lines
B. 2   10 pt. ital runon
    Space above 1 line #   Space below no extra
C. 3   9 pt. bf lc and c fl. left
    Space above 1 line #   Space below no extra
4   Space above   Space below

Extracts In / pt   Measure
    Style fl left   ctr   fl rt   indent

Poetry In / pt
    Style fl left   ctr   fl rt   indent

Tables Heads As marked   Subheads
    Body   Rules
    Style fl left   ctr   fl rt   indent

Legends Figures In 9 / 10 pt. bf. fl. left
    Illustrations In 9 / 10pt rom. and 6 pt. ital.

Appendixes In / pt None
    Subheads in appendices A
    B

Bibli-ography In 9 /10 pt 24 pi measure
    Subheads in bibliography: A
    B
    Hanging indent 1 em

Footnotes Foot of page In 8 /9 pt. measure 11 pi
    Standard paragraph indent
    Back of book In / pt. measure

Index In 8 / pt Set to 11   picas, 2 columns to page
    Initial letter Cap. fl. l.   space above 1 line   space below no extra
    Hanging indent 1 em

Running Heads / Feet Recto   Verso none
    With rule / without rule
    Space between runninghead/foot and text

Folios In 9 pt. Old style figure / Modern figure. Bracketed bf.   Dropped?   Outside / Inside / Centered
    In running head/foot? 1 pi from outside trim, 1 pi from bottom trim

Chapter Openings Chapter no in press type
    Titles in 24 pt. De Vinne Ornamented
    Sink 1 pi
    Sub chapter title

Other to be ragged ri.

Method Set at keyboard   Justified x *   Unjustified
    Paging keyboard   strip x   combination
    During setting   first proof corrections   second proof corrections x
    * This does not mean lines are justified (they are ragged) but that
      the compositor makes line ending decisions at the keyboard

No Time for Houseplants?

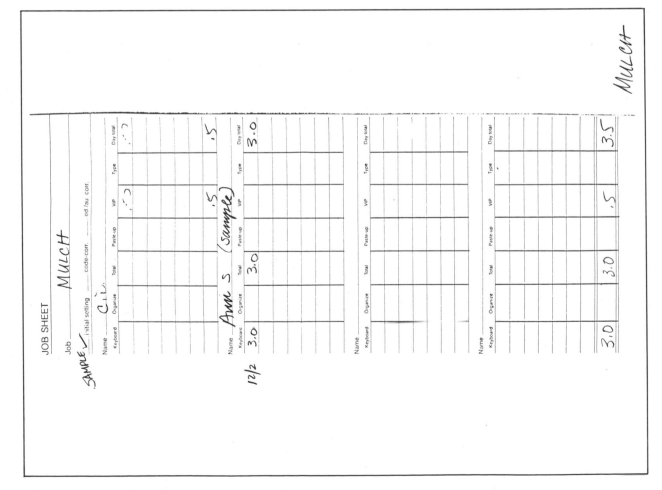

JOB SHEET

Job _MULCH_

SAMPLE — initial setting ____ code-corr. ____ ed /au corr.

Name _Gil._						
Keyboard	Organize	Total	Paste-up	VIP	Type	Day total
				(.)		.5

Name _Ann s (sample)_						
Keyboard	Organize	Total	Paste-up	VIP	Type	Day total
12/2	3.0		3.0	.5		3.0

Name						
Keyboard	Organize	Total	Paste-up	VIP	Type	Day total

Name						
Keyboard	Organize	Total	Paste-up	VIP	Type	Day total
	3.0	3.0		.5		3.5

MULCH

Preface

The recent introduction of fluorescent tubes meant especially for plant growing has been a great boon to indoor gardeners. With the aid of artificial light, we can now grow lush, green plants where they would never grow before. A windowless bathroom, which might offer ideal humidty and temperature conditions, can now be made into an ideal plant-growing environment. Plants growing on a drab northern windowsill can now receive supplemental light during winter's short and dark days. Dim corners of any room can be transformed into green showplaces. Cuttings and seedlings can now make faster and surer progress than ever under artificial light, and we can even grow vegetables in the dead of winter in the bedroom or kitchen. Artificial lighting is not essential for house plant sucess, but it certainly does broaden our horizons and increase chances for maximum rewards.

The old incandescent bulb offers some help to growing plants, although the heat it produces makes it impossible to offer plants the amounts of light they need without drying or burning them. Also, incandescent bulbs offer a very short spectrum of light wavelengths, falling far short of simulating the beneficial rays of the sun. Ordinary daylight or cool white fluorescent lights are far better for growing plants, since they have not only a wider and more effective light wavelength but also produce light with three times as much efficiency as incandescent bulbs, thus reducing heat by fully two-thirds. Not until the past decade, however, have we had fluorescent tubes made to meet exactly the needs of growing plants. These lights, sold under such names as Gro-Lux, Plant-Gro, and Plant-Light, cost more than ordinary fluorescent tubes, but they are long-lasting and they can solve virtually any light

2. Understanding Houseplants

The old incandescent bulb offers some help to growing plants, although the heat it produces makes it impossible to offer plants the amounts of light they need without drying or burning them. Also, incandescent bulbs offer a very short spectrum of light wavelengths, falling far short of simulating the beneficial rays of the sun. Ordinary daylight or cool white fluorescent lights are far better for growing plants, since they have not only a wider and more effective light wavelength but also produce light with three times as much efficiency as incandescent bulbs, thus reducing heat by fully two-thirds. Not until the past decade, however, have we had fluorescent tubes made to meet exactly the needs of growing plants. These lights, sold under such names as Gro-Lux, Plant-Gro, and Plant-Light, cost more than ordinary fluorescent tubes, but they are long-lasting and they can solve virtually any light problem for the indoor gardener. By attaching them to a twenty-four-hour timer, you can control light exposure perfectly, even for such tricky operations as forcing plants to bloom out of season.

Should You Send Your Plants to Summer Camp?

Nearly all houseplants will enjoy a summer outdoors, where they will become rejuvenated and make very active growth. There are dangers involved here, however, not unlike those a sheltered city child will encounter on his first trip to a wilderness camp, and special precautions must be taken.

Roots. Roots serve two main functions—to anchor the plant in the ground and to supply from the soil water and the mineral salts which accompany water. Bulbs, corms, rhizomes, and tubers (all modified stems) serve much the same purposes, as well as acting as food storage areas. Roots, just as the above-ground parts of plants, may be pruned without injuring the plant in any way. Roots are often trimmed to prevent a plant from growing too large for the convenience of the grower, just as top growth is cut back. If you cut roots back, however, be certain to cut back top growth to about the same percentage, or the reduced roots might be unable to supply the plant with sufficient amounts of water.

The old incandescent bulb offers some help to growing plants, although the heat it produces makes it impossible to offer plants the amounts of light they need without drying or burning them. Also, incandescent bulbs offer a very short spectrum of light wavelengths, falling far short of simulating the beneficial rays of the sun. Ordinary daylight or cool white fluorescent lights are far better for growing plants, since they have not only a wider and more effective light wavelength but also produce light with three times as much efficiency as incandescent bulbs, thus reducing heat by fully two-thirds. Not until the past decade, however, have we had fluorescent tubes made to meet exactly the needs of growing plants. These lights, sold under such names as Gro-Lux, Plant-Gro, and Plant-Light, cost more than ordinary fluorescent tubes, but they are long-lasting and they can solve virtually any light problem for the indoor gardener. By attaching them to a twenty-four-hour timer, you can control light exposure perfectly, even for such tricky operations as forcing plants to bloom out of season.

PRINTING AND BINDING SPECIFICATIONS

PRODUCTION DEPARTMENT
The University of North Carolina Press
P.O. Box 2288
Chapel Hill, North Carolina 27514
(919) 933-2163

Date: 10 December 1976

Title NO TIME FOR HOUSEPLANTS

Author Mulch
Print 5000/7500 **Binc** 5000/7500 Case _____ Paper All _____ F & G's _____

Specifica-
tions
Print by ___ Offset ___ Color black (one color) ___ X ___ others _____ Trim size 5 x 7 3/8 ___ Text page size 24 x 38 ___

Margins (after trim) head 2 1/2 ___ gutter 3 ___
No of pages 192 ___ Inserts _____
Halftones 30 ___ Linecuts 7 ___ Bleeds _____
Printed book _____ Repros X ___ Negatives _____ Other _____

Copy We will supply linecuts and text in place; halftones will be
sized with windows.

Text stock 60 lb. white offset
supplied by you to supply
Illustration stock same
supplied by you to supply
Endsheet stock no endsheets
supplied by _____
printed _____ color(s) _____

Reprints No changes _____ Frontmatter changes _____ Changes throughout _____

Binding material _____
Boards _____ binders _____ pasted _____
Smyth sew _____ Perfect bind _____
Case Inserts outside tip _____ inside tip _____ center insert _____ wrap _____
Binding Edges smooth ___ plain ___ rough cut. ___ stain _____
Backing rounded and backed ___ flat back (reinforced) _____
Lining crash and paper ___ headbands _____
Stamping spine only ___ face and spine _____
foil ___ ink _____

Perfect bind X ___ Smyth sew _____ Saddle stitch _____
We will supply negatives ___ original art X ___ You to print covers X ___
Paper Cover stock see sample
Binding supplied by you to supply others ___ will be on bright green background
Colors black X ___ spine _____ back _____ inside _____
face _____
Varnish covers _____ Plastic coat covers _____
Also, estimate box separately - see sample

Wrap Shrink wrap X ___ in multiples of 6 ___
Kraft wrap _____

Jackets
We will supply: Original art _____ Negatives _____ Finished jackets _____
Jacket stock _____
Stock supplied by _____
Varnish _____ Laminate _____
Color(s) black _____ others _____
Print _____ jackets; Ship _____ trimmed to us

Blues of cover X ___ Blues of illustrations _____ Complete set of blues X ___
Blues of the following pages _____

3M color key of jacket X ___ 3 M color key of cover _____
Set of 8 g's X ___ Stamped sample case _____

Proof
We Want
To OK

**Special
Instructions**

We need this estimate immediately. Please call in your estimate
before Christmas if at all possible.

Please note - no endsheets.

We would like a somewhat sturdier box - please suggest.

Please return sample.

To: _____
From: Rebecca Johnson
Re: Project
Date: 10 December 1976

Enclosed please find specifications for the above project.
Please submit your estimate as soon as possible.

Please return the enclosed sample.

UNC PRESS PRODUCTION DEPARTMENT

SCHEDULE

Author __Mulch__   Date __Dec. 21, 1976__
No. of MS pages __136__   Title __NO TIME FOR HOUSEPLANTS?__
Editor __Gwen Duffey__   MS to prod __Nov. 17, 1976__
    Sample pages _____
First proofreader __Jane__   Compositor __Martha Farlow__

Proof Information

Proofreader (1st proof) __1__ sets with MS   Editor __4__ sets with MS   Sales __1__ sets

Scanner

FIRST PART __ALL__   SECOND PART

Nov. 22, 1976	to typist
Nov. 30, 1976	to OCR
Dec. 7, 1976	to proofreader
Dec. 21, 1976	to production

First Proof

FIRST PART   THIRD PART
____ to xerox
____ to proofreader
____ to proofreader
SECOND PART
____ to xerox
____ to proofreader
____ to production

Green (corrected) Proof

FIRST PART __All__   THIRD PART

Jan. 17, 1977	to xerox	____	to xerox
Jan. 18, 1977	to editor & sales	____	to editor & sales

SECOND PART
____ to xerox
____ to editor & sales

Index

Feb. 21, 1977	MS to production
Feb. 28, 1977	page proof to editor & sales
March 7, 1977	page proof to production

Revises

Feb. 28, 1977	all page proof (green) to production with list of revises
March 14, 1977	revises and foul proof to editor
March 25, 1977	repros OK

Printing and Binding

March 25	repros to Printer		
April 20	blues to UNC Press	May 13	J & g's to printer
April 22	blues to printer	May 4	sample case to UNC Press
May 11	J & g's to UNC Press	July 1, 1977	**BOOKS IN**

DATE: __1/18/77__

TO: __Gwen__

FROM: PRODUCTION

TITLE: __Mulch__

NO. OF PAGES: __192__

1st PROOFREADER: __Jan McInroy__

DATE DUE BACK
TO PRODUCTION: __2/28__

____ 1st PART   __X__ 2nd PART   ALL

PRODUCTION DEPARTMENT Transmittal Form

DATE: 2/7/77

TO: Gwen

FROM: Martha

RE: Mulch cover a slipcase   DATE NEEDED: 2/7/77

Please return this form with the above proof and check the proper space below.

____ Proof OK for paste-up
____ Paste-up OK to print
____ Jacket comprehensive OK
____ Please make corrections as marked and let me see revised proof.

____ Browns (blues) OK to print
____ Gathers OK to bind
____ Stamping die proof OK

____ Sample case OK
____ Color key OK

Comments: _____

Date returned to Production Department: _____

FINAL JOB COST ESTIMATES

Author: Mulch   Title: NO TIME FOR HOUSEPLANTS

Budgeted for Composition   F.P.P. Mellon

Date Composition started   Ended

Operators   Ms, pages   Book pages 192

Operators' hourly rate   Total hourly rate

Composition

Month	Time	Cost
November	Scan/82.88	82.88
December	AKI/29.00 VIP/16.88 PU/34.38	80.26
January	AKI/290.00 VIP/124.89 PU/54.69	469.58
February	AKI/41.69 VIP/30.38 PU/18.75	90.82
March	AKI/52.56 VIP/20.23 PU/12.49	85.28

Total: Total: 808.82

Other costs:
Graphic Repro
XXXXXXXXXXType   14.00
Proofreader   53.04
Xeroxes   48.00
Other
Scanner   91.42
Letraset   8.00
Total   1023.28

No. of lines corrected:

PEs
AAs   less author's AAs
EEs
Total AAs and EEs   subtotal
Author charged   less ___ % AAs
Difference between amount budgeted and actual cost   actual cost   1023.28
Difference between budgeted plant cost and actual plant cost

Per page cost 5.33
Rates: Type- $6.50/hour   VIP- $13.50/hour
AKI- $7.25/hour   PU- $6.25/hour

REPROS AND BLUES CHECK   file

Date: 2/7/77
Author: Mulch   Title: No Time for Houseplants?
Compositor: Martha   Editor: Gwen
Date scheduled to go to the printer: 2/8/77

REPROS: Please put an X after the item after you have checked.
          The lines below are to list the pages which need
          correcting in that particular category.

EDITOR: √ 1. Check each page for obvious blobs of black or obvious
              white spots in the lettering
              Sample page OK - gd 2/7/77

          2. Check contents page against chapter titles and folios

          3. Check running heads (or running feet) and folios

          4. Record any other flaws that leap from the page

ANN: 1. Check typography throughout: Clean it!
             Opaque & clean around "Preface" - lc. f is broken
             last pages need cleaning - cap.13
          2. Check page length
          √ VIII - looks funny - is it OK? (column lengths)

          3. Check chapter openings for clear definition of type
             and for sinkage need [illegible] black sink (or trim) all
             Any marks on all display pages - for "e" in "TIME" p.iii)
             Window f.iii/ not cut straight upper left side
             Opaque "white" counter p.v - right side & window (p. vi) doesn't run parallel
          LESLIE: Opaque in frontmatter; see that it is there and complete. to trim
             1. Check [illegible]   (over)

          2. Return to compositor to correct. Items corrected should
             be checked off when complete.

JUDGE/PROOFR: Check all windows -
          1. Final check   lc. [illegible] sequence.

Purchase Order Form (top):

IMPORTANT
PLACE THIS NUMBER
1256
ON ALL PACKAGES, INVOICES
AND CORRESPONDENCE

THE UNIVERSITY OF NORTH CAROLINA PRESS
Box XX/2288
CHAPEL HILL, N. C. 27514

DATE 2-11-77

To   Dalton Press

PLEASE FURNISH AND DELIVER THE FOLLOWING, RENDERING INVOICE IN DUPLICATE.

FORM 196 MT

Mulch: NO TIME FOR HOUSEPLANTS?

Negatives/plates	498.00
Printing 7500	487.00
Paper	1701.00
Paperback covers	375.00
Shrinkwrap	135.00
Slipcases - manu.	3075.00
Slipcases-insert books	217.50
Paper	765.00

Please ship by motor freight to our warehouse, Airport Rd., Chapel Hill, NC

_____
John Rollins, Controller

PURCHASING AGENT

Form No. A-836

Print Order Request (bottom):

PRINT ORDER REQUEST

To: Ann

From: Joyce

Re: Mulch- NO TIME FOR HOUSEPLANTS?

Date: February 11, 1977

Please issue a purchase order to:

   Printer #1

for:

   items 1-8

Delivery or shipping instructions:

UNC Press Warehouse
Chapel Hill, NC 27514

November 3, 1976

To JK

From JG, SM

Re: Mulch

There are a lot (too many??) of books on houseplants. The book buyer at Rich's (Atlanta) said we would have to be nuts to do another. Books with full-color illustrations are available from $2.95 up.

Generally, we found some oversized books but most were 6 x 9. All cloth books had full color on jackets. Some of the books had only black and white illustrations. We were not particularly impressed with the photographs.

There is one book organized much like the Mulch : INDOOR GARDENING, by Krockmal and Krockmal (Drake, 186 pp., approx. 100 illus--b & w photos and line drawings). Chapter arrangement is similar to Mulch but this book does not share the time theme. It would be easy to top this book, but difficult to complete with others we saw at comparable prices.

I have serious doubts about our being able to market a book on houseplants unless ours has some characteristic that makes it stand out from its shelfmates. Even then, most people will prefer color.

Our preference is a 6 x 9 trim size, color on jacket or cover, and some "gimmick" that will help make our book different.

Finally, I object to the title, NO TIME FOR HOUSEPLANTS. It is negative. It is also not clear.

October 11, 1976

To: Johanna

From: John

Edition size for Mulch must be decided. Matt and I think 5,000 is a good edition. Talk to Matt, and then send memo to JK. I think everyone should know that price must be under $10.00, hence cost in the $2.50 to $3.00 range.

October 13, 1976

To JK

From JG

Re: Mulch estimates

Joyce, our alternate edition size will be 5,000 (p&b)

To GD

From JG

Re: Mulch

Gwen, I think we should add a question mark to the Mulch title--

No Time for House Plants?

This way, it seems less negative and even a bit clearer. Can we discuss this at next week's meeting?

Mulch: Some Competing Titles

Trim	Publisher	Pages	Price	Illustrations	Jacket or Cover	Title	Edition
	A&W Visual Library	*274*	~~$5.95~~	over 100	Paper, Watercolors	New York Times Book of Houseplants	225,000
	Quadrangle		9.95	" "	Cloth, " "	" "	
	Frederick Fell		1.95	35 pages color	Paper, Four color	Be Yuor Own Houseplant Expert	
	Alfred Knopf	*xv, 257, viii*	4.95	*sparse, b/w line drawings*	Paper, Color	Making Things Grow Indoors *very textual*	
	" "		8.95		Cloth, Color	" "	
	Sunset		2.45		Paper, Color	How To Grow Houseplants	
	McGraw Hill		4.95		Paper,	First Aid For Houseplants	
	" "		8.95		Cloth,	" "	
7 X 9	Scribners	*170 tight type*	8.95	*1200 photos, few color*	Cloth, *slick color jacket*	Exotic Houseplants	
	Better Homes and Gardens	96	2.95	140 / 97 in color	Full color Coated Cardboard	Better Homes and Gardens Favorite Houseplants	*150,000*
	S + S	*128*	6.95	*watercolor, loaded*	Cloth	Women's Day Book of Houseplants	
8 X 9	Doubleday	*vi, 179*	7.95	*line, photos b+w 4 pg insert of color*	Cloth	Houseplants Are For Pleasure	
	Deribooks		3.95		Paper	Houseplants and Indoor Gardening	
	B & N		3.95		Paper	Houseplants and Indooe Landscaping	
	A.B. Morse		6.95		Cloth	" "	" "
	Delacorte		14.95		Cloth	Houseplants of the World	

Memorandum of meeting between JG, PM, JR, and MH to set edition size for NO TIME FOR HOUSEPLANTS

November 23, 1976

An edition size of 7,500 copies has been decided upon after a discussion that focused upon the capability of the Press to market NO TIME FOR HOUSEPLANTS? and the economics of the book.

Since we do not have a strong national trade list and do not use sales representatives it would be difficult to market this book nationwide. It was the consensus of those attending the meeting that we could be more effective by restricting our active marketing effort to the Southeast. In the Southeast our regional trade publications are well known and our relationships with booksellers well established. By restricting our geographic market the Press can concentrate its resources on outlets that are already aware of our existence.

Our recent experience with THE CAROLINA HOME GARDENER indicates that a printing of 7,500 copies should last us three to four years. A print run of 7,500 will allow us to price the book reasonably without incurring unacceptable risk.

jr/aj

Memo

To: JK
From: Jg
Date: November 23, 1976
Re: Edition size for the Mulch:NO TIME FOR HOUSE PLANTS

Please obtain complete manufacturing estimates for a run of 7,500 books. We will want to bind the entire printing.

If employed by an educational or research institution, please give the name and address of the news bureau and/or public relations officer:

University of
News & Publications Office

List all honors, prizes, awards, etc., that you have received:

no rewards at all

List your other books (in addition to title, please give the publisher's name, the year of publication, and the type of book, e.g., history, literary criticism, poetry, fiction, etc.):

A _____ Garden Guide, _____ House, Ltd., 1975 (regional trade)

Periodicals to which you regularly contribute (including those for which you frequently review books):

Organic Gardening and Farming
Countryside

If any of the material in your book has been published previously in a copyrighted form (such as a scholarly journal) or if your book was derived from or forms a part of a copyrighted dissertation, give full details:

The University of North Carolina Press
Box 2288

Chapel Hill, North Carolina 27514

AUTHOR'S BIOGRAPHICAL RECORD
And Publicity Questionnaire

The information supplied by you will be used in connection with the publication and publicizing of your book. Please be as accurate as possible and do not supply any information that you do not want made public. Please use a typewriter or print legibly. If more space is needed please use the back of the sheets.

Also, please return the completed sheets with two prints of a recent photograph of yourself--preferably a glossy, black-and-white, 5" x 7" photograph.

Date: November 11, 1976   Telephone:

Full name: Purvis Mulch

Name as it is to appear on title page of book: Purvis Mulch

Address: 19 Mouldering Way, Remigwasett, Kansas

Present position: Assistant Director

Date and place of birth: July 6, 19__ , _____ Pennsylvania
Citizenship: USA
(The above two lines of information will be used for copyright purposes only.)

Education (schools, colleges, and universities attended, with dates of attendance and degrees earned):

University of   1957-61, B.A.

Principal occupations, with approximate dates (if teaching, list institutions, with dates and positions held):

Names and addresses of organizations to which you belong whose members will be interested in your book:

List any specialized mailing lists that you can make available for the promotion of your book. (To be usable all sizable lists should be available on labels):

none that I know of

Names and addresses of specialized reviewing media in the fields to which your book contributes:

The most likely reviewing media would be magazines whose audiences are largely single and affluent. These would include publications such as Apartment Ideas, Ms, Mother Jones, Rolling Stone, and others. I would not recommend garden magazines or shelter magazines.

Names and addresses of leading professional associates and other individuals engaged in work in your field who might influence the sales of your book:

Indicate the media you believe will be the most effective in advertising your book:

The same magazines mentioned for review purposes.

Note: We regularly send review copies of most of our new books to such publications as the New York Times, Saturday Review, North Carolina and major metropolitan area newspapers, etc.

Please give a summary in 200 words ~~or so~~ of the contents of your book:

This book will give the casual grower of house plants all the information he needs to know to achieve indoor gardening success while spending the absolute minimum of time in caring for those plants. It is not essentially for "beginners," although beginners can use the book to great benefit; rather it is for those who might have had much experience, much of it bad. Most house plant books are written by enthusiasts who spend much time with house plants--careful watering, potting, repotting, propagating, tying up, training, inducing to flowering, humidifying, bathing, and in other ways nursing their plants to peaks of perfection. These authors seem to assume that the reader is willing or able to spend a similar amount of time in caring for their plants. This book makes no such assumption, but realizes that the reader wants the company of healthy indoor plants but does not want to spend more than a few minutes a day in the pursuit. This book tells how that may be done, in three different steps: (1) in explaining the workings of plants, so that the reader can have this basic understanding; (2) in establishing the proper conditions at the very beginning, in order to avoid later troubles; and (3) in listing more than a hundred house plants that will grow with little trouble. For the home owner or apartment dweller who wants to raise several dozen attractive house plants while spending only a few minutes a day in caring for them, this book tells all that is necessary to know.

Please specify the special contributions made by the book to its area of study. Also indicate the purpose(s) of the book and its advantages over competing books in its field.

I think these questions are answered in the foregoing statement.

December 9, 1976

Mulch Project

JR, JG, SM attending

1. Publication date will be September 15, 1977. (Stock date is July.) We are satisfied with this timing—people begin to think about indoor plants in the fall, and the book would make a grand Christmas gift.

2. We will distribute 375 review and comp copies--250 books to book review and "lifestyle" editors, and 125 to book buyers. Because there are so many houseplant books, quite a few book review editors will probably ignore this one. We hope to get good exposure in the lifestyle sections of newspapers. Also, it is important for book buyers to see this book. Sending comp copies to major buyers in our area is about the only way we can handle this.

3. Our major bookstore/promotion effort will be in North Carolina, South Carolina, Virginia and _____ (using Mulch's advice here). We also will make a special effort with some stores in New York, Atlanta, Washington, and Chicago.

4. We will distribute flyers to bookstores in the areas mentioned above. Where relevant, bookstores will also receive an advertising schedule.

5. Wholesalers will get a special 50% discount on orders of 100 or more books.

6. We will contact some plant stores in North Carolina. Probably, Mulch could help with some plant stores in his area.

7. News release will be sent to lifestyle editors in generally the same areas as mentioned above.

8. No Time for Houseplants? will be included in our Christmas '77 gifts books promotion for North Carolina bookstores. This campaign has a $1,800 budget and involves 12 titles--so $150 will be charged against the Mulch budget. Nationally, we will advertise No Time for Houseplants? and Marion Brown's Southern Cook Book around Christmas.

9. Autographing parties will be restricted to the _____ area, because of a lack of funds.

NO TIME FOR HOUSE PLANTS?

Memo, Phone Conversation with Mulch, mid-November

For the most part, we discussed publicity in and around Mulch's home area.

He is willing to autograph books, and will send us a list of key stores. We will make the arrangements.

He likes the idea of an interview with the _____ newspaper--I prefer the lifestyle section. We will attempt to set this up.

Mulch will send a list of the important _____ newspapers and magazines. This will help with review copies and news releases.

We will send review copies fo Univ. of _____. News Bureau and to Alumni Office at University of _____. News Bureau may do a story--if pushed.

Mulch does not think advertising in _____ newspapers is important. We probably can get good publicity from our news releases and the interview.

He does think the PW ads are a good idea, since we do not have salesmen.

He promised to send a photograph of himself.

"For people who love plants--but love other things better."--Rogue

No Time for Houseplants?

A Busy Person's Guide to Indoor Gardening

by Purvis Mulch

A stunning collection of house plants does not have to take much time. One can, in fact, enjoy the company of nearly two dozen plants without spending more than two or three minutes with them every other day. No Time for Houseplants? gives only the essential information for house plant success. Purvis Mulch has two rules--choose plants that are easy to grow and give them the conditions they must have to thrive. Neither rule is difficult because he recommends more than one hundred easy-to-grow plants and plant groups, comprising several thousand varieties, and gives the conditions required for each recommended plant. Mulch also describes his "bit and snatch" method of house plant care and gives a brief description of the inner workings of plants.

Most house plant books suggest that growing plants indoors must be a consuming hobby. Mulch disagrees. "The right plant, given the right conditions for growth, will thrive despite your frequent inattention," he says. His book is for busy people and for people who have had little experience growing house plants.

LC 77-0000   192 pp., illus.,boxed

ISBN 0-8078-1300-1 $7.95

Memo to: JK, JR

From: SM

RE: Marketing and Design meeting on the Mulch--Notes taken

Date: 6 January 1977

JK: Discussed plans to leave case unillustrated in order to produce a surprise effect when book is taken out. Opinions all around were that this is somewhat risky but very well may attract the eye when placed with garden & houseplant books and will make an attractive gift item.

JR: Cost of case is high compared to overall cost--approximately 1/3.

JK: Will get   to reduce former estimate on case, if at all possible. Is there any possibility of increasing the edition size?

JG: This is a problem because we don't have salesmen and unless the books are available in the bookstores, much of our advertising will be wasted.

SM: We can handle the regional sales, but national marketing will have to be limited to PW and a few others.

JG: Discussed ads written and ideas about "busy people" approach. Will send ads to JK Monday morning. Meanwhile, if we can get cost down, that means more for marketing or a more reasonable price.

JR: 40% of estimated cost for Mulch is manufacturing. Price probably cannot be lowered more than 45¢ or so. Discussed whether or not 7.50 is better gift price than 7.95.

JG: Suggested the idea of a gift card enclosed in some way. General agreement was that it was too costly, but some description was needed. Sticker?

SM: Shrink-Wrapping causes problems when no description of the book is on the outside--bookstores tend to leave books in the shrink-wrap. JK said this book will not be shrink-wrapped because of the case.

JR: Bookstores will be putting a price sticker on the book--could this mess up the design? Discussion. Put a price on the book? No, because gift item.

JK: Will set 2 or 3 lines of descriptive copy on the back and design a circle for the bookstore to use for price sticker.

9/15/77

For Immediate Release

SOME PLANTS PREFER BUSY PEOPLE!

NEW UNC PRESS BOOK TELLS HOW TO SELECT PLANTS THAT REQUIRE ALMOST NO CARE

CHAPEL HILL, N.C. --- A stunning collection of house plants doesn't have to take much of your time.

You can, in fact, enjoy the company of nearly two dozen plants without spending more than two or three minutes with them every other day.

In "No Time for House Plants? A Busy Person's Guide to Indoor Gardening," author Purvis Mulch provides only the essential information for house plant success. The book was just published by The University of North Carolina Press.

Mulch has only two rules of success---choose plants that are easy to grow and give them the conditions they must have to thrive.

Neither rule is difficult because more than 100 easy-to-grow plants and plant groups, comprising several thousand varieties, are recommended in "No Time for House Plants?" Also, the conditions required for each recommended plant are given.

-- more --

NEW UNC PRESS BOOK -2-2-2

"The right plant, given the right conditions for growth, will thrive despite your frequent inattention," says Mulch.

His book includes a section explaining how plants work--basic information that is easily understood in a few minutes. As for plant care, the author explains his own "bit and snatch" method of tending plants. Nearly all of the chores necessary to keep plants thriving are little ones, he says. If you work them into your daily schedule, you won't spend any time "tending house plants."

Most house plant books suggest that growing plants indoors must be a consuming hobby. Mulch disagrees with this approach and designed his book for busy people and for people who have had little experience growing house plants.

"Many of us---single people, working couples, harrassed mothers, college students, anyone whose daily living pattern leaves precious little time for indoor gardening---would enjoy the beauty and companionship of bright, green house plants," he says.

"No Time for House Plants?" is illustrated and *boxed and sells for* $7.95. It is available at bookstores or from The UNC Press, Box 2288, Chapel Hill, NC 27514.

####

NO TIME FOR HOUSE PLANTS?

NATIONAL

Publishers Weekly, mid-August, 1/3 page $555.00

REGIONAL NEWSPAPERS   (all 3 cols x 5")

Raleigh News & Observer/Times, Sept. 18/20   158.25
Charlotte Observer/News, Sept. 18/20   260.00
Greensboro Daily News/Record, Sept. 18/20   162.45
Richmond, Va., Times-Dispatch/News Leader, Sept. 18   294.00
Columbia, S.C., The State   234.36

REGIONAL MAGAZINES

N.C. * New East, Sept.-Oct. 1/3 page   116.00
  "   * The State, Sept., 1/3 page   135.00

S.C. Sandlapper, Sept., 1/3 page   225.00

Total: $2,140.06   all assigned to NO TIME FOR HOUSE PLANTS

* contract rate

NO TIME FOR HOUSE PLANTS? /Promotion Schedule

Stock Date: July

Pub date: September 15

July 25: Review copies out

August 8: Comp copies and flyers to book buyers (chiefly regional)
        Advertising schedule included if relevant

August 15: PW ad

August 29: Fall Announcement Ads

September: Regional ads and distribution of news release

October: Remainder of flyers to individuals

October 24: PW Christmas ad (with Southern Cook Book)

October and November: Regional ads (with Southern Cook Book)

November: Christmas books promotion (North Carolina only; 11 other titles)

MULCH PROMOTION BUDGET

Ad # 1 $2,140.06
Ad # 2 (with cookbook)   1,162.18
Ad composition & design (UNCP)   35.76
Ad repros, negs   31.00
Flyer composition and design (UNCP)   56.97
Printing (2,500)   235.00
Postage (2,000 at bulk rates)   38.00
Christmas Bookstore Promotion   150.00
Fall Announcement Ads   125.00
          $3,973.97

Gifts for All Seasons

Marion Brown's
SOUTHERN COOK BOOK

"Mrs. Brown shows in her selection from over 30,000 recipes the happy mixture of English, Continental and Mexican cooking with true Southern richness and downright goodness that makes for famous food."
—*New York Times Book Review*

Nearly one million copies sold

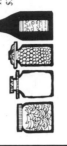

498 pp.
$7.95

No Time for Houseplants?
A Busy Person's Guide to Indoor Gardening
by PURVIS MULCH

"A must for people who love plants—but love other things better!"
—*Rogue*

"This little green book tells exactly how to select a stunning variety of houseplants that require almost no care."
—*Publishers Monthly*

192 pp., illus., boxed
$7.95

THE UNIVERSITY OF NORTH CAROLINA PRESS
Box 2288   Chapel Hill   27514

Ad #2

For:
Raleigh News & Observer
Charlotte Observer/News
Winston-Salem Journal/Sentinel

Greensboro Daily News/Record
Richmond Times-Dispatch
Columbia, S.C., The State

Advertising Schedule, Ad #2

NO TIME FOR HOUSE PLANTS?
Marion Brown's SOUTHERN COOK BOOK $555.00

NATIONAL
Publishers Weekly   116.00

REGIONAL MAGAZINES
*New East, Nov.-Dec., 1/3 page   .35.00
*The State, Oct., 1/3 page
*UNC University Report, Oct., 2" x 10"   99.00

REGIONAL NEWSPAPERS (all 3 cols x 6" except Charlotte)
Raleigh News & Observer/Times, Nov. 27/29   189.90
Charlotte Observer/News, Nov. 27/29 (2 cols x 6")   312.24
Winston-Salem Journal/Sentinel, Nov. 27/29 165.60
Greensboro Daily News/Record, Nov. 27/29   164.45
Richmond, Va., Times-Dispatch, Nov. 27   352.80
Columbia, S.C., The State, Nov. 27   234.36

Total: $2,324.35   one-half ($1,162.18) assigned to NO TIME FOR HOUSE PLANTS?
                   one-half ($1,162.17) assigned to SOUTHERN COOK BOOK

*contract rate

QUOTATION

meredith-webb printing company, incorporated

TELEPHONE 226-0363 AREA CODE 919 ☐ 116 E. HOLT STREET, BURLINGTON, NORTH CAROLINA

We, the undersigned, for the consideration hereinafter mentioned, covenant and agree with

Ms. Joyce Kachergis
UNC Press
Chapel Hill, N.C. 27514

to perform in a faithful and workman-like manner the following specified work.

2,500 8½x11 folders (Mulch circulars). Printed 2-colors ink -- 1-side. Fold to fit #10 Envelope. Camera-ready.
$235.00

2,500 Camera-ready Envelopes #10. Printed 2-color ink.
$105.00

Your acceptance in writing at the end of this agreement will complete the whole contract between us.

Dated at Burlington, N. C., this 3rd day of Feb. , 19 977

Accepted this _____ day of _____ , 19 _____

_____
Customer Signature

_____
meredith-webb printing co.

Sales Ad Transmittal Form

UNC PRESS SALES DEPARTMENT

Ad #: _____ Name: MULCH Brochure

From Sales to Production Date: 1/4/77   Finished Repros to Sales Date 1/18/77

Size: see below   Number of Repros: _____   ☒ Major ☐ Medium ☐ Minor Importance

Assigned to Compositor: _____

Paste-up xerox to Sales Date _____   Date: _____

OK Repro to Sales Date _____   Xerox to Production Date _____

Ad will be in the following:

distributed to bookstores and to some individuals

Special Instructions:

1. one page (8½x11) to fold type side out, top panel should be shiny

2. use sketch of book instead of photo

3. 2 colors, green & black

4. estimates for 2,000 & 2,500. Also, estimates for envelopes with sketch + quote on outside left, 2 color. (see our rough.)

end

Mulch Review list--Preliminary Plans

Southern Magazines

SOUTHERN EXPOSURE
SOUTHERN BOOKLORE
THE SOUTH MAGAZINE
SOUTHERN LIVING

Book Review Services & Syndicates

AB BOOKMAN'S WEEKLY
BEST-IN-BOOKS
CHOICE
KIRKUS REVIEWS
LIBRARY JOURNAL--BOOK REVIEW
PUBLISHERS WEEKLY--FORECASTS
JOHN BARKHAM REVIEWS
BOOK BEAT BY JOAN ORTH
LITERARY LANTERN

Television Programs Featuring Books (and/or Radio)

Critique (WITI-TV & WMVT-TV, Milwaukee)
Book Beat (WTTW-TV, Chicago)
Gamut (WFMT-FM, Chicago)
Peggy Mann Show (WTVD-TV, Durham, NC)
Ty Boyd Show(WBTV, Charlotte, NC)

Popular Magazines

AMERICAN HOME
APARTMENT LIFE
APARTMENT WORLD
BETTER HOMES AND GARDENS
FAMILY CIRCLE
FLOWER & GARDEN
GOOD HOUSEKEEPING
HOME LIFESTYLES
HOUSE BEAUTIFUL
HOUSE & GARDEN
HOUSE & HOME
HOME GARDEN MAGAZINE
INTERIORS
LADIES' HOME JOURNAL
McCALL'S MAGAZINE
MS.
SOUTHERN LIVING
SPHERE
WOMAN'S DAY
WOMEN'S LEAGUE OUTLOOK
MADEMOISELLE
GLAMOUR
TRAVEL & LEISURE
WORKING WOMAN
REDBOOK
WORKBASKET

NOTE: About 50 review copies
will be distributed in North Carolina,
and about 40 review copies, in the
author's home state.

Mulch--Preliminary Review List--Newspapers and Local Magazines

South Carolina

Columbia STATE
Columbia RECORD
Charleston NEWS & COURIER
Charleston EVENING POST
Greenville NEWS-PIEDMONT
Spartanburg HERALD-JOURNAL

SANDLAPPER Magazine

Georgia

Albany HERALD
Athens BANNER-HERALD
Atlanta JOURNAL CONSTITUTION
Augusta CHRONICLE HERALD
Columbus LEDGER-ENQUIRER
Gainesville TIMES
Macon TELEGRAPH & NEWS
Marietta JOURNAL
Savannah NEWS-PRESS

COASTAL QUARTERLY Magazine
GEORGIA LIFE Magazine
BROWN'S GUIDE TO GEORGIA

Florida

Miami HERALD
Miami NEWS
Orlando SENTINEL-STAR
St. Petersburg TIMES-INDEPENDENT
Tampa TRIBUNE & TIMES

Tennessee

Chattanooga NEWS-FREE PRESS
Chattanooga TIMES
Knoxville JOURNAL
Knoxville NEWS-SENTINEL
Memphis COMMERCIAL APPEAL
Nashville BANNER
Nashville TENNESSEAN

Virginia

Charlottesville PROGRESS
Norfolk VIRGINIAN-PILOT
Richmond TIMES-DISPATCH
Richmond NEWS LEADER
Roanoke TIMES

District of Columbia

The GEORGETOWNER
WASHINGTON POST BOOKWORLD
Washington STAR-NEWS

New York

TIMES - Home Editor
TIMES BOOK REVIEW
TIMES Daily Book Section
VILLAGE VOICE
New York DAILY NEWS

NEW YORK MAGAZINE

California

Los Angeles TIMES
San Francisco EXAMINER & CHRONICLE

MOTHER JONES
ROLLING STONE

Pennsylvania

Philadelphia INQUIRER
Pittsburgh PRESS
Philadelphia BULLETIN

Illinois

Chicago SUN-TIMES SHOW-BOOK WEEK
Chicago NEWS
Chicago TRIBUNE

UNIVERSITY OF TEXAS PRESS

Table of Contents

University of Texas Press

No Time for Houseplants

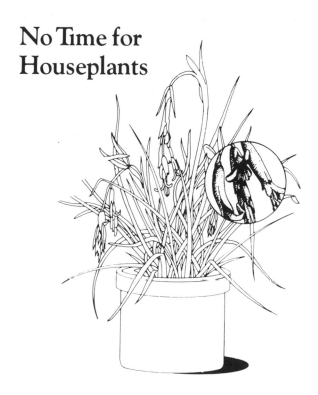

No Time for Houseplants is not representative of the kind of book the University of Texas Press normally publishes. For that reason we were at some disadvantage in attempting to show our *normal* procedures for publishing. Throughout we have tried to deal with the manuscript as if it were actually being published by us and have made our decisions recognizing our regular financial constraints. Our solutions have been the ones we would have used in reality and we have made no attempt to edit, design, produce and market in any special or ideal manner.

In our first review of the project we decided that we had to do something to distinguish our plant care book from the others on the market. Since we could not afford the use of color, and preferred not to use photographs because there was no one in our area we could afford or who could realistically complete the job in the time schedule we needed, we decided to commission line drawings. We felt that the artist we selected had a unique approach and hoped that buyers would be as attracted by the drawing style as by the clarity of information provided.

The book would have been typeset and pasted up in-house. The illustrations would have been sized on our stat camera and put into place on the repros by us.

Only in the preparation of the jacket design did we feel we compromised what might have been done differently had we actually published the book.

LOG OF ACQUISITIONS PROCESS: <u>NO TIME FOR HOUSE PLANTS</u>

Texas Press receives a letter from author Purvis Mulch, descriptive of the manuscript. Acquisitions editor decides manuscript might be a good trade book for Texas Press, but wants further information about the manuscript. (Note: This situation is of course hypothetical. If the initial inquiry had been "real," the Press would in fact have declined consideration, recommending a commercial publisher.)

Acquisitions editor sends author letter expressing interest, and encloses Author and Manuscript Inquiry form, from which she/he (in this case Iris Hill, who is also the Senior Editor) derives information about original form of manuscript (was it a dissertation?), length of manuscript, whether it is under consideration by another press (if so, we will not consider manuscript till it is free), whether the manuscript has tables, maps, photos, etc. (which, with the estimated length, aids the editor in determining whether the manu- script may be too expensive to produce), other books on the subject (has the subject been covered to too great an extent elsewhere?), the background of the author, and names of scholars in the field who may have read the manuscript or may be able to read it for us and give us an expert opinion of its worth.

Acquisitions editor receives AMI from author. Mulch has a good background in the field. There are a number of other books on the topic, but editor feels (in this hypothetical situation) that the topic is always popular. Manu- script is not long, and Mulch can provide his own line drawings for it. Editor invites the manuscript, with the condition that it not be simultaneously under consideration by another press.

Manuscript arrives, is logged in on file cards for Editorial Department's records and for acquisition editor's records, and receipt is acknowledged by secretary by postcard.

Manuscript is screened in house by acquisitions editor. The information seems to be well presented, clear to the general reader, though Mulch's drawings are not the best that can be obtained. Perhaps we will provide our own line drawings. Acquisition editor decides to send the manuscript out for a first reading, and chooses a reader after consulting with advisors in botany. Writes this person, offering an honorarium in payment for the reading. (Honorarium varies with length and complexity of manuscript.) The manuscript is sent to this reader, whose identity is kept confidential. (Such is always the case except for rare instances when a reader asks to have his/her identity re- vealed to the author.)

Manuscript returns from reader with report. At this point, if the report is negative, the Press usually rejects the project. If it is all praise, the acquisition editor directs a memo (see next step below) to the Director and with his/her (at Texas Press, Philip D. Jones) approval proceeds to a second reading. In Mulch's case, the first reader's report is mixed: The code he uses throughout for light and temperature conditions needs clarifying, the reader believes, and some reorganization is needed. The acquisition editor sends a copy of this report to the Press Director, with a description of the project, the AMI, and an initial cost estimate (a rough one which she has figured on the basis of figures and calculations provided the acquisition editors by the Press Production Department). The Director is asked his opinion about the mixed report--what step to take next (the acquisition editor suggests getting Mulch's response, and if this is adequate, going on for a second reading), who he considers a likely second reader (the editor suggests a regional "plant person," who conducts a weekly program on educational television advising viewers on plant care--this to get a slightly different angle of vision than the first reader's, a scholar in the Botany Department of a northern university), and in general whether the project seems suitable to pursue. The Director responds in agreement with the editor, suggesting a second reader's report if Mulch's response to the criticisms is adequate. In this case, since the revisions are not extensive, Director also suggests going on for a second reading without Mulch's revising the manuscript. (If suggested revisions are extensive but there is nevertheless sufficient praise to balance, the Press may ask the author to revise before seeking a second report, and may in fact go back to the original reader for an opinion on the revision.)

Mulch is sent a copy of the reader's report, with the acquisition editor's criticism of the line drawings included as a revision the Press would also wish to have made. He responds adequately, saying that he had feared the coding might not be completely clear, agreeing that the Press provide its own illustrations, and also agreeing to make some of the organization changes that the reader felt were necessary. He disagrees with a few of the reader's points and argues his case convincingly, so the acquisition editor phones the regional plant person, who does indeed read the manuscript for the Press and reports favorably, having been advised by the editor that Mulch would make certain revisions (the illustrations, the organizational problems, etc.) before the Press would publish the manuscript.

(A note: If for some reason--for example, competition with another press in the acquisition of a manuscript--there is a rush, the Press occasionally arranges for simultaneous readings by two experts at once.)

At this point the acquisition editor again directs a memo on the status of the project to the Press Director, including copies of this second report and the previous cost estimate; the editor recommends taking the project to the Press's next Faculty Advisory Committee meeting for the Committee's approval, but suggests first, because of the unusual nature of the project (its position as a trade book, with a large number of illustrations, etc.), a meeting with Business, Marketing, and Production Departments to discuss the viability of the manuscript's publication by the Press, the costs, and so on. Director agrees and meeting is held, at which a tentative arrangement for the new illustrations is discussed, a tentative number of illustrations set and an illustrator suggested, and suggestions of pricing, marketing methods, and general approach for the book are made. Given the print run tentatively decided on, the price can be set so as to be acceptable to a fairly extensive popular audience. The book can be made more distinctive and more attractive to buyers, the Production Manager suggests, by striking new line drawings.

Director and acquisition editor agree that the manuscript may be taken before the Press's next Faculty Advisory Committee meeting. The Committee, made up of eleven faculty members, must approve all new manuscripts and reprints originating from other presses.

Docket materials begin to be prepared for presentation to the FAC. Docket has a key which identifies readers for Committee members. Docket goes to the FAC before the meeting, so that they may read it in advance. Included in the docket for this book are the following:

1. House editor's statement describing the project and the Press's reasons for wishing to publish it-in this case, the manuscript is a good potential trade book for the Press (not an acceptable reason in the actual normal process)

2. Biographical note on author

3. Table of contents

4. First manuscript report

5. Author's response to criticisms and suggestions in first manuscript report

6. Second manuscript report

7. (optional) Supporting statement (from well-known botanist who says Mulch's work is reputable,this work useful for beginning plant raisers)

The acquisition editor presents the project before the FAC meeting, and after some discussion the manuscript is approved (unlikely in reality). The acquisition editor notifies Mulch that evening by phone that his project has passed, and the next afternoon prepares a Contract Abstract. Royalty terms are figured on the basis of the house editor's estimate corrected by the later tentative decision for the Press to provide its own illustrations for the book, and have been discussed by the acquisition editor with the Press business manager. Terms are okayed by the Press's director, who signs the Contract Abstract, and contracts are prepared by the Press secretary. (A post docket meeting of all department managers and acquisition editors to discuss marketing, editorial, and production strategy also occurs shortly after FAC.) 3 copies of the contract signed by press Director are sent to Purvis Mulch for signing. He keeps one copy, and the others are returned, one for a master file at the Press, another for University records. The Director's secretary assigns contract number which is the date of the last signature on the contract.

The Director's secretary sends to the acquisition editor a Notice of Contract Signed. Others who receive copies of this are the Press managers, and the advertising manager of the Marketing Department. Once this notice is distributed, the acquisition editor, the head of Production, and the Marketing Manager meet to plan a tentative schedule for the book.

Mulch in the meantime has been revising his manuscript and now sends it on to the Press by date stipulated in contract. At this point, the acquisition editor transmits the manuscript to the Senior Editor (though not in this case, since

here the acquisition editor is also the Senior Editor). (A note: Were the acquisition editor not also the senior editor, as here, all memos would pass
from the acquiring editor to the senior editor for comments, and then to the
Director, and the senior editor would be involved in all discussions of the
project.)

The transmittal material includes (1) the file card that has been kept on
the manuscript, listing the readers, the author's address, and so on; (2) the
manuscript itself and if possible a duplicate copy for Marketing*(if not, this
will come later); (3) the file the acquisition editor has kept on the manuscript; (4) the Transmittal Sheet, which is distributed to the Marketing
Manager, with a copy also of the front matter and preface or introduction,
the advertising manager, the direct mail manager, the production manager (who
received the original of the Transmittal Sheets), the business manager, and
the manuscript's copy editor; (5) the Fact Sheet, which is given to the
marketing manager, the advertising manager, the direct mail manager, the
production manager (again, the original), the business manager, the Press
Director, the senior editor, the proofreader, and the copy editor; (6) the
Estimate & Release form, which is distributed to the production manager (the
original) and the copy editor; (7) the Editorial Schedule (for the copy
editor); and (8) the Copyright Notice Form, also for the copy editor's use.
At this point the editorial secretary assigns an ISBN to the book.

The senior editor's transmittal of this material (by means of the editorial
secretary) is announced in the weekly Editorial Report, copies of which are
given to all in the Editorial Department as well as to the marketing manager
and the advertising manager, the business manager and two of his assistants,
the Press director, the production manager and the other designer at the Press.

The manuscript now enters the actual copy editing process, and the copy
editor's weekly progress on the manuscript is reported in the Editorial Report.

When the manuscript nears the time when it will enter the actual production
stage, a Preproduction meeting is called.

*and Production

University of Texas Press

P. O. Box 7819   Austin, Texas 78712

DEAR Purvis Mulch:

This letter is our contract with you. It sets down the terms of our agreement to publish your book, presently entitled NO TIME FOR HOUSE PLANTS

It also represents the convictions that govern our relations with authors. We believe that a book belongs to its author; that the chief function of a publisher is to publish the author's work in appropriate form and to get it to as many readers as possible; that the author should be consulted in the disposition of book club and reprint rights. Finally, although we hope and expect that our association with each of our authors will extend through the publication of many books, we do not believe in requiring commitments for the future and so do not ask for options.

1. You grant to us during the term of the United States copyright, and during any renewal or extension thereof, the exclusive right to publish and sell, including the right to permit others to publish and sell, your work in book form in the English language throughout the world.

2. You shall deliver to us no later than   (date)   a typed copy of your work in final form, complete and ready for the printer and accompanied by all necessary permissions, licenses, and consents. If we both agree that photographs, maps, charts, or other illustrations are necessary to the book, you will provide them in final form, ready for reproduction without additional art work (maps and charts will first be furnished in draft form for editing). When page proofs are ready you will prepare or cause to be prepared and deliver to us within 3 weeks of your receipt of such proofs an index to the work, unless we have agreed beforehand that one will not be needed.

If you do not so deliver your work to us in acceptable form by the date specified or at another date to be agreed to by us in writing, we may terminate this agreement by notice to you (unless failure to deliver is caused by circumstances beyond your control). When your work has been copy edited it will be returned to you so that you can discuss with the editor any changes which have been made with which you are not in agreement. Queries from the editor will be made on "flyers" attached to the typescript pages and you will make any queries or suggest any changes on flyers; you will not make changes directly on the edited copy. When you receive edited copy, this will be your last opportunity to make any substantive changes in your book without cost to you, so read it carefully. After the book has been set in type, you will read galley proofs, if any. Page proofs will be sent to you, and reading them will be your sole responsibility, although we will check all lines reset to make corrections. The cost of changes made on page proofs other than for the correction of actual errors made by the printer or our staff will be charged against your account.

(If your work is a collection of articles by several authors and you are its general editor, you will be responsible for distributing edited copy to the contributors and forwarding their suggested changes which you approve to the copy editor. You will also be responsible for reading page proofs or for getting the contributors to read them and, unless otherwise agreed upon, for providing an index.)

3. We shall publish your work at our expense in manner and style and at a price we believe appropriate as soon as circumstances permit.

4. We shall apply for copyright in our name in the United States (unless otherwise stipulated in writing) and you shall (though we may do so on your behalf) apply for renewal or extension of such copyright if this agreement is then in effect. We may apply for copyright in our name in other countries. We shall publish your work in the United States in a way that complies with the provisions of the Universal Copyright Convention. In general, it is agreed that both you and we shall take all steps necessary to secure and preserve a valid United States copyright in your work.

5. You represent and warrant to us, and to those to whom we may license or grant rights hereunder, that you are the sole owner of your work and that it has not previously been published in book form; that it is original, is not in the public domain, and does not infringe upon or violate any personal or property rights of others; that it contains nothing scandalous, libelous, in violation of any right of privacy, or contrary to law; and that you have all necessary permissions, licenses, and consents and the full power to enter into this agreement and to grant us the rights herein provided for.

6. You agree to indemnify and hold us harmless against any loss, damage, liability, or expense (including counsel fees reasonably incurred) arising out of any claim, action, or proceeding asserted or instituted on any ground which, if established, would be a breach of any of the warranties made by you in this agreement.

7. We shall pay to you:

A. On each copy of the trade edition or microfiche sold by us, less returns, a royalty of

    5% net receipt proceeds 1-3000
    7 1/2% net receipt proceeds 3001-5000
    10% net receipt proceeds beyond 5000

B. On copies sold by us, at a special discount of 50% or more from the publisher's retail price through channels outside of the ordinary wholesale and retail trade (other than remainders as described in paragraph E), a royalty of 10% of the amount we receive. Such sales shall be accounted for separately and not included in other sales totals.

C. On copies sold by us for export (except as provided in paragraph F), a royalty of 10% of the amount we receive.

D. On copies of a paperback edition issued by us, a royalty of 6% of the publisher's retail price of such paperback edition.   7 1/2% of the net proceeds

E. On copies sold at a remainder price (any sale at a price at or below manufacturing cost, whether through normal trade channels or otherwise, being deemed a remainder sale for purposes of this clause), no royalty shall be paid.

F. On copies, bound or in sheets, sold for export at discounts of 60% or more, a royalty of 10% of the amount we receive.

G. On copies furnished without charge or for review, advertising, sample, promotion, or other similar purposes, no royalty.

8. We may publish or permit others to publish or broadcast without charge and without royalty such selections from your work for publicity purposes as may, in our opinion, benefit the sale of your work. We shall also be authorized to license publication of your work without charge and without royalty in Braille or by any other method primarily designed for the physically handicapped.

9. You grant to us the exclusive right on your behalf to license, sell or otherwise dispose of the following rights in your work: publication or sale of your work by book clubs; publication of a reprint edition of your work by another publisher; condensations; serializations in magazines or newspapers (whether in one or more installments and whether before or after book publication); dramatic, motion picture, phonograph, and broadcasting rights and electronic, mechanical, or visual reproduction rights; publication of your work in the British Commonwealth; publication of your work in foreign languages; publication of your work and selections therefrom in anthologies, compilations, and digests; picturized book versions; and microprint and microfilm versions. In order to afford you the opportunity to consult with us on book club or reprint rights before we dispose of these rights, we shall notify you before making any disposition of same.

In the case of each of the rights specified in this paragraph 9, the net proceeds of its disposition (after all commissions, foreign taxes, and other charges) shall be shared equally between us except that as to first serial, dramatic, motion picture, phonograph, and broadcast uses the division of net proceeds shall be 90% to you and 10% to us. (If this work is a collection of contributions, we may permit others to publish or make use of separate contributions from it, as described above, but not without approval of the individual contributor, with whom proceeds from such permissions will be divided on the same basis as described above in this article.)

10. During the life of this agreement you will not, without our written consent, furnish to any other publisher any book on the same subject and of the same extent and character as the book covered by this agreement, publication of which would clearly conflict with the sale of our book. When in doubt about application of this article to a new work, you will confer with us to receive the necessary clearance.

11. On publication of your work we shall deliver to you ten copies without charge and you shall have the right to purchase further copies, for your personal use but not for resale, at a discount of 40% from the publisher's retail price. (If this work is a collection of contributions edited by you, we shall deliver to you five copies without charge and you shall have the right to purchase further copies, for your personal use but not for resale, at a discount of 40% from the publisher's retail price. We shall deliver to each contributor one copy without charge if there are more than five contributors, two copies if there are five or fewer contributors.)

12. A. We shall render to you in October of each year an annual statement of account as of the preceding August thirty-first. Each statement shall be accompanied by payment of all sums due thereon. If in any yearly period the total payments due are less than $10.00, we may defer the rendering of statements and payments until such time as the sum of $10.00 or more shall be due.

B. You may, upon written request, examine our books of account insofar as they relate to your work.

13. A. In case we fail to keep your work in print (and for all purposes of this paragraph the work shall be considered to be in print if it is on sale by us in any edition or if it is on sale in any edition licensed by us during the term of this agreement) and you make written request of us to keep it in print, we shall, within sixty days after the receipt of your request, notify you in writing whether or not we intend to do so, and if we elect to do so, we shall have six months thereafter in which to comply. If we fail to comply (unless the failure is due to circumstances beyond our control), or if we do not desire to keep your work in print, then this agreement shall terminate and all of the rights granted to us shall revert to you.

B. In case of such termination you shall have the right for thirty days thereafter on prior written notice to us to purchase negatives and plates, if any, of your work at one third of their manufacturing cost, including composition, and any remaining copies or sheets of your work at the manufacturing cost. If you fail to do so, we may dispose of all of them as we see fit, subject to the provisions of paragraph 7 of this agreement.

C. Nothing contained herein shall affect our right to sell remaining copies of your work on hand at the date of termination of this agreement, nor shall such termination affect any license or other grant of rights, options, or contracts made to or with third parties by either of us prior to the termination date, or the rights of either of us in the proceeds of such agreements.

14. Prior to remaindering your work under paragraph 7E, we shall make reasonable effort to notify you and afford you the opportunity to purchase all or part of such overstock at the remainder price.

15. You shall execute and deliver to us whatever documents and assignments of copyright or other papers as may be necessary to fulfill the terms and intent of this agreement.

16. Any rights in your work not specifically granted to us hereunder are reserved to you. You agree, however, not to exercise or dispose of any of your reserved rights in such a way as to affect adversely the value of any of the rights granted to us under this agreement.

17. No waiver or modification of this agreement shall be valid unless in writing and signed by both of us.

18. This agreement shall inure to the benefit of and be binding upon you and your heirs, personal representatives, and assigns and upon us and our successors and assigns. We shall not assign this agreement without your consent.

If the foregoing correctly states your understanding of our agreement, please sign the enclosed copy of this letter where indicated below and return it to us, whereupon it will constitute a binding agreement between us.

Very truly yours,

By UNIVERSITY OF TEXAS PRESS

Accepted and Agreed to:

Date

Home Address

Social Security Number

CONTRACT ABSTRACT

Type of contract:
- ☒ Author
- ☐ Translator
- ☐ Import
- ☐ Proprietor (translation)
- ☐ Series
- ☐ Revised edition
- ☐ Letter of intent
- ☐ Other

Author: Mulch, Purvis

Contract with (Author/Editor/Translator/Proprietor):

Address (and affiliation):

FAC approval: July 15, 1976
Contract date:
Contract number:

Title of work: NO TIME FOR HOUSE PLANTS

Series title and editor: n/a

Copyright by: UT Press

Rights limitations: None

Market: world

Delivery date of MS:

Length of MS: 170 ms. pp., not incl. index and illustrations

Illustrations: to be supplied by Press

Index: yes   Within 21   days

Subsidy: no

Author's alterations: no

Royalty terms: 5% net receipt proceeds 1-3000
7 1/2% net rec. proceeds 3001-5000
10% net receipt proceeds beyond 5000

Advance: no

Author's frees (clothbound/paperback)   10/10

Clauses to be deleted: none

Special clauses/Remarks: none

Previous Contracts relating to this work (Series/Letter of intent)

Contract with:

Contract number:

Royalty terms or fees:

Approval:

House editor:

PR 114 rev. 71 5C 11-71

NOTICE OF CONTRACT SIGNED
University of Texas Press

Author: Purvis Mulch

Contract with (Author/Editor/Translator/Proprietor):

Address (an affiliation): n/a

Title of work: NO TIME FOR HOUSE PLANTS

Series title and editor: n/a

Copyright by: UT Press

Rights limitations: none

Market: world

Delivery date of MS: August 1, 1976   Length of MS: 170 ms. pp. not including index & illustrations

Illustrations: yes, to be supplied by Press

Index: yes   Within 21   days

Subsidy: none   Author's alterations: none

Clauses to be deleted:

Special clauses/Remarks:

Previous Contracts relating to this work (Series/Letter of intent/

Contract with: Contract number:

Royalty terms or fees:

House editor: ITH   Approval: (Director)

Type of Contract:

XX Author
   Translator
   Import
   Proprietor (translation)
   Series
   Revised edition
   Letter of intent
   Other

FAC approval: July 15, 1976
Contract date:(last date on
Contract no.:   0000   contract)

Book Estimate and Release

New Book [X]
Revision [ ]
Reprint [ ]

Author: Mulch, Purvis
Title: NO TIME FOR HOUSE PLANTS
Series: n/a

Editor/Trans.
ISBN (cloth) 0-292-   (paper) 0-292-
Copyright by UT Press
Market: world

Editor's Release
Royalties: 5% net rec. proceeds 1-3000, 7 1/2% net rec. proceeds 3001-5000, 10% net rec. proceeds beyond 5000

Other fees or charges: none
Subsidy $: n/a   from
Contract no.
Series contract no.
FAC approval: July 15, 1976
Target pub. date: (cloth) (paper)
Remarks

Editor   ITH   Date Aug. 1, 1976
Pub. Date

Sales Release

	Print	Bind	Price	Discount	No. pages	Size
	7,500		6.95	Trade	128	6 x 9"
Cloth	7,500					
Paper						

Remarks
Marketing Manager CDS   Date 8/17/76

Financial Release and Estimate

	Cloth	Paper
Plant cost	$ 4400	$
Running cost 7500 copies	$ 8875	$
Royalties	$ 2275	$
Less subsidy	$ ---	$
Total cost	$15570	$
Sales revenue	$ 31275	$
Contribution to operation	$15705	$

	Cloth	Paper
No. copies sold	3184	3735
Mfg. break even		
Total break even		
Net price per copy	$	$
Less mfg. cost per copy	$	$ SEE WORKSHEETS
Less royalty	$	$
Gross margin	$	$
Gross margin %		

Remarks: Due to royalty increases, overall edition return at 50%. Should be safe. Savings in composition & illustrations on reprint should cover maximum royalty.

On the terms set forth above this book meets/~~does not meet~~ current financial requirements of the Press

Business Manager   Date 8/17/76
Approved Director [signature]   Date 8/23/76

Director's Release
Remarks

PRICING WORKSHEET

August 4, 1976

Royalty rate—5% net	1-3000	7½% net 3001-5000	10% net 5001 up	1st Prtg. Total
$6.75				
Gross	$20,250	$13,500	$16,875	$50,625
Discount	40%	40%	40%	40%
Net	$12,150	$8,100	$10,125	$30,375
Cost	5,310	3,540	4,425	13,275
Royalty	608	608	1,013	2,229
Revenue	$6,232	$3,952	$4,687	$14,871
				49%
$6.95				
Gross	$20,850	$13,900	$17,375	$52,125
Discount	40%	40%	40%	40%
Net	$12,510	$8,340	$10,425	$31,275
Cost	5,310	3,540	4,425	13,275
Royalty	626	626	1,043	2,295
Revenue	$6,574	$4,174	$4,957	$15,705
				50.2%

# pages	128	128	128	128	128
per page	4¢	4.5¢	5¢	5.5¢	6¢
list	$5.12	$5.76	$6.40	$7.04	$7.68

unit cost	$1.77	$1.77	$1.77	$1.77
x	4	4½	5	3½
	$7.08	$7.97	$8.85	$6.20

List	$6.95	$6.75	$6.50
Discount	40%	40%	40%
Net	4.17	4.05	3.90
Unit	1.77	1.77	1.77
Royalty 5%	.21	.20	.20
Return	2.19	2.08	1.93
%	53%	51%	49%

4 August 1976

Dear

I am happy to have been chosen as the copy editor for Texas Press for No Time for House Plants and will be starting immediately on the editing of Chapters 2 and 4. I expect to have edited copy ready to send to you for checking and any final revisions by August 9 and will need to have it back again by August 23 if at all possible. Please let me know if there is any reason that you will be unable to check the edited copy at this time.

On preliminary reading the manuscript seems to be in very good shape. The notes will need to be retyped on separate pages from the text, but, since there are so few, we will be able to handle that here at the Press. Also, since there are so few notes, we will be able to set them as footnotes at the bottoms of the pages. (If there were more than one or two notes per chapter, we would put them all at the end of the book, just before the bibliography.)

There is one structural problem that I noticed in looking over the manuscript. The book seems to fall into two rather different parts: a discussion of house plants in general, consisting of Chapters 1-3, and a listing of detailed information on specific kinds of plants and plants for specific purposes, consisting of Chapters 4-7. The first sections of Chapter 4 are actually an introduction to the whole second part. I think it would be helpful to the reader to label the two parts and provide titles for them, in addition to the Chapter titles. The introductory sections now on pages 1-4 of Chapter 4 could then come after the part title for Part 2 but before the Chapter title, thus making it clear that they refer to all types of house plants, not just foliage plants. Chapter 4 would then begin on page IV-5 with the section now headed "Foliage Plants." Does this suggestion seem reasonable to you? What titles would you suggest for the two parts?

I'll hold any further questions until I send the edited copy.

I am enclosing a copy of our Guide for Authors for your information about

---

- 2 -

Texas Press style and policies, as well as our Author Information form. Please fill out and return the Author Information form as soon as possible, as the requested information will be needed by people in several departments of the Press.

                    With best wishes,

                    Carolyn Cates Wylie
                    Associate Editor

CCW:pj

Enclosures

Note:

Normally this first letter to the author would also include a reminder that the contract calls for the author to provide an index at the page-proof stage and a discussion of any obvious problems with the illustrations. If we were going to use the illustrations provided with the copy, we would have to have glossy prints of photos and originals of drawings, rather than xerox copies. The author would be asked to provide a typed list of captions (captions are now on the backs of the Xerox copies) and to number the illustrations for purposes of identification.

The time required for editing and for checking edited copy would of course be greater if the whole book were being edited rather than just two chapters. The suggested dates allow only one week for him to check the copy, plus one week for mailing time both ways (an optimistic estimate).

The Guide for Authors would normally have been sent earlier, by the acquiring editor.

                    August 9, 1976

Ms. Carolyn Cates Wylie
Associate Editor
UNIVERSITY OF TEXAS PRESS
P.O. Box 7819
Austin, TX 78712
                    Re: No Time for House Plants
Dear Ms. Wylie:

Thank you for your letter of the 4th, and for the author information form, which I enclose, completed.

Yes, I agree that the structural suggestion you propose will strengthen the manuscript. It seems obvious to me, now, and I thank you for making the suggestion.

The titles I propose for the two sections are "Understanding House Plants" and "Introducing the House Plants."

I look forward to your queries and to working with you in the completion of this project.

Best wishes.

                    Sincerely,

11 August 1976

Mr.

Dear

The editing took a little longer than I had expected, as a result of interruptions due to other projects, but the edited copy is now ready for you to check. Please read through it carefully and indicate any changes that may be needed. (This review of the edited copy is the last stage at which Texas Press authors can make stylistic or substantive revisions; at the proof stage no changes are allowed except correction of typesetter's errors.)

My questions about the book are written on gummed flyers attached to the pages, and a supply of blank flyers is enclosed for your use in answering the questions and adding any corrections, comments, or suggestions of your own. Please use flyers or separate pages to indicate any disagreement with the editing, add additional material, or make changes of any sort. We ask that you not write or erase anything on the edited pages themselves.

One of the readers had suggested editorial checking of common and scientific plant names in the book. I have edited the spelling of common names in accordance with Webster's Third International Dictionary and have checked the scientific names, insofar as possible, against Standardized Plant Names, ed. Harlan P. Kelsey and William A. Dayton, 2d ed., indicating on flyers where the SPN system disagrees with yours. Please recheck your own sources in these cases.

You will find a few flyers in Chapter 2 which suggest possible illustrations. The Texas Press plans for the book will include a list of illustrations we would use in the two edited chapters--probably a number of line drawings and perhaps some photographs. Because of the special nature of this project, the matter of illustrations is being handled at a later time than would be normal; ordinarily the number, type, and source of illustrations would be agreed on at the acquisitions stage, although some modifications might be introduced during copy-editing. (Any such changes would require the approval of both the Press and the author.) In this case, you don't need to do anything about my suggestions other than comment on whether you consider them appropriate.

I need to have the edited copy back by August 25--sooner if possible. Please call me if for any reason you will be unable to return it by that date, or if you have any questions about the editing. The editorial department number is 512-471-4278.

The editing has been a very pleasant assignment, and I'll be looking forward to getting the copy back again.

                         With best wishes,

                         Carolyn Cates Wylie
                         Associate Editor

CCW:pj

Enclosures

UNIVERSITY OF TEXAS PRESS
P.O. BOX 7819 • AUSTIN, TEXAS 78712 • (512) 471-7233

10 September 1976

Mr.

Dear

Thanks for returning the edited copy so quickly. I'm sorry to be so slow in answering your letter but have been tied up with a couple of urgent projects these past few weeks.

The second edition of _Standardized Plant Names_ was published by the J. Horace McFarland Company of Harrisburg, Virginia, in 1942. The authors (editors?) are Harlan P. Kelsey and William A. Dayton. I don't know whether there is a newer edition that might still be in print. This was the only source I could find in the U.T. Biology Library that had names for a reasonable percentage of the plants in the book. Your own source is probably as good or better, and I haven't made any changes except the ones you authorized on the flyers.

So far there is no definite schedule for the plant project. If it were a regular Texas Press book, it would be in production by now, and I would be telling you when to expect galleys, indexing proofs, etc. But, since we aren't doing the whole book, things are happening somewhat out of the normal order, and in fact the copy is still awaiting a final reading, although I have removed the flyers and made the changes you suggested on them. I'll let you know when there are further developments.

With best wishes,

Carolyn Cates Wylie
Associate Editor

CCW:pj

August 18, 1976

Ms. Carolyn Cates Wylie
Associate Editor
UNIVERSITY OF TEXAS PRESS
Box 7819
Austin, Texas 78712

Dear Ms. Wylie:

Let me congratulate you on a keen bit of editing. I was amazed at the number of errors you picked up along the way, and I do appreciate the structural changes you suggested. I have no doubt that the manuscript is now stronger.

If I have one regret, it is that all my anthropomorphisms have been purged. Malcolm MacDonald plucked most of them during an earlier draft, and now you have flushed out the last remaining ones, poor fellows. I feel that most people who grow plants do impart human characteristics to them; they talk about _their_ plants as if they were friends; they even talk to their plants; I even know one woman who insists that her plants talk back to her, in language that only she understands. With this attitude rampant among growers, I would think that my anthropomorphism friends might find a good home in the pages of a book on house plants. Alors.

I am returning the edited manuscript to you before leaving for a short camping trip to Rock Island, a pinpoint in Lake Michigan/Green Bay where there are no telephones, no TV, and no publishers. I will return on August 25.

Again, thank you for your careful and sympathetic work. I hope to hear from you soon.

Sincerely,

P.S.   Can you give me the publisher and (if available) the current price of _Standardized Plant Names_?

18 Goudy Bold clc
22

InternationStandard Book Number 0-292-FANTAS-Y
al
Library of Congress Catalog Card Number 76-PLANT
Copyright © 1977 by the University of Texas Press
All rights reserved
Printed in the United States of America

11/22 goudy old style
Flush left
line for line
sink to align with first
text line

No Time for Houseplants 18/22 GOUDY BOLD CLC
A Busy Person's Guide to Indoor Gardening 18/22 GOUDY OLD STYLE CLC
by Purvis Mulch 18/22 Goudy old style clc
University of Texas Press Austin & London 1/22 goudy old style clc

---

II - 1

CHAPTER 2   △ 10 goudy old style italic

Basic Needs of   △ 16 goudy old style clc
~~UNDERSTANDING~~ HOUSE PLANTS

Flush left

Every plant has its own preferences and requirements
for soil type, light, temperature, ventilation, humidity,
and several other factors that are within our power to control, or at least to mitigate. It is vitally important for
you, as a busy indoor gardener, to understand the basics of
each, since a prior understanding will enable you to avoid
much work later on while achieving routine success in growing
plants.

In addition to understanding these basic needs, you
will want to know something about pots and other containers,
repotting plants, propagation, and a few other matters **which**
while not vital to immediate success, will help you to gain
further enjoyment in raising better plants.

11/11 goudy old style
RAGGED RIGHT
14 PI MAX approx
12 PI min
OK TO hyphenate

Basic Needs of House Plants

30 pts#

THE BASIC HOUSE PLANT   14 GOUDY OLD STYLE ITALIC clc

11 pts#

The major difference between a house plant and an outdoor plant is one of location. All house plants could live and flourish outdoors, in the proper climate. All are derived from forebears which lived, reproduced, and died outdoors, whether on a forest floor in Central Europe or in the bough of a tree in a South American rain forest. Over many centuries of adaptation and evolution, each plant species embraced those characteristics that enabled it to survive; and even today, every house plant carries within its genetic structure the characteristics of its distant progenitors. Thus the Maranta will lose some of its leaves each autumn, even though autumn's weather does not come to the top of the bookshelf where the plant rests, and a cactus, no matter how long it has been and watered with unfailing regularity, will continue to hoard food and water within its swollen stems. In plants, old habits may recede, but they are never forgotten.

At no time are these innate plant characteristics more noticeable than during the autumn and winter, when many plants—particularly those from temperate regions—enter a period of dormancy. Then new growth ceases and the plant takes on a listless and washed-out appearance. Other plants, including many of tropical origin, will maintain their bright appearance but will stop growing completely for several months

each year, emulating the natural rest periods of their forebears. You will do well to watch for these signs of dormancy and rest and respond to each plant's needs at that time. When any plant enters a dormant or rest period, water should be reduced and fertilizer withheld completely until new growth begins, usually in the late winter or early spring. At that time, water the plant freely and give it normal doses of fertilizer once again, in order to encourage new growth. By your proper treatment of the plant at this time, you will emulate the advent of spring, working with the plant in carrying out its rhythmic cycles.

Some plants also are naturally short-lived and will last no more than a year or two in your home despite your careful attention, because their genetic structure dictates a finite life span. Garden annuals, for instance, will germinate, grow to maturity, flower, produce seeds, and die, all in as little as six months. For this reason, very few annuals are selected as house plants. Although a few short-lived plants are cultivated indoors for their unusual characteristics, such as the sensitive plant, which is easily grown from seed, the house plants that have been cultivated over the generations are most often those that will give years of pleasure. Some house plants, in fact, can live to be hundreds of years old.

Still other house plants are attractive when young

but grow ungainly or otherwise unattractive when they approach maturity. The only plants of this kind I have chosen for inclusion in this book are those that are very easy to propagate from cuttings, so that the parent plant may be discarded after a year or two, to be replaced by its children.

From the hundreds of thousands of plant species in the world, those traditionally cultivated as house plants are the relatively few that have shown a wide tolerance to conditions of heat, light, moisture, humidity, and ventilation—in other words, those that can withstand a human environment. They are both attractive to the eye and tough. Still, if you are looking for success with house plants—and particularly success without working hard at it—then you should take some time to learn the characteristics of each plant, recognizing its individual needs and fulfilling them to the best of your ability.

30 pts#

HOW A PLANT FEEDS   14 clc ital

11 pts#

A plant manufactures nearly all of its food by itself—and not from the "plant food" that you buy for it. Commercial plant food is no more than a combination of certain chemicals (sometimes in an organic base) that are essential to the plant's basic functioning, much as vitamins are essential to human nutrition. But the bulk of a plant's food—the sugar it uses for energy and growth—is manufactured by the plant itself. In the presence of light, the leaves of the plant

draw carbon dioxide from the air and water from the roots, converting these into sugar that is then used for energy production or stored for future use.

During this sugar-manufacturing process, known as photosynthesis, several other things happen within the plant. While carbon dioxide is being absorbed, oxygen is being released from the pores of the leaf surface. (Plants produce not only all of the world's food but most of its atmospheric oxygen as well.) During darkness hours, the process is reversed; some of the atmosphere's oxygen is recaptured by the plant and used to convert stored sugar to energy for growth. Generally, a plant manufactures growth food during the day and does its actual growing at night.

Often, the plant converts its newly manufactured sugar to starch and stores it, reconverting it to sugar as the need arises. Although the starch can be stored in almost any area of the plant, certain plants have developed specialized storage areas just for this purpose. Cacti and succulents have enlarged stems and leaves for the greatest above-ground storage capacity of any house plant, while other plants have developed underground storage apparatus for this purpose, including bulbs, tubers, corms, and rhizomes. A bulb is simply an enlarged underground bud, such as is found with hyacinths, tulips, and onions. A tuber is nothing more than an enlarged stem or root; a common potato is a tuber; gloxinias, caladiums, dahlias, and many other common plants are grown from tubers.

A <u>corm</u> is the enlarged base of a stem. And a <u>rhizome</u> is simply a laterally growing, enlarged ~~stem~~ *usually underground* stem. All are used by the plant for food storage, and all can be used to propagate plants, too.

Water is constantly being drawn up through the plant. As it transpires through the stomata ~~of the leaves,~~ of the leaves, a "pulling" action draws more water up through the roots. The water carries with it mineral salts, including all the elements which the plant needs to carry out its complex chemical processes. The transpiration which takes place in the leaves is similar to perspiration in humans, and it serves a similar purpose to cool the plant. With house plants, it would be difficult for you to notice this cooling effect. But it is readily apparent when a group of large trees carry out the transpiration process. The cool and fresh feeling you enjoy in a thick woods in summer is primarily the product *not* of the shade itself but *of* the transpiration of the millions of leaves overhead.

A plant can *seldom* absorb too much water, since its vessels and cells can accommodate only so much at a given time; however, the overwatering of a plant can exclude oxygen from the root system, causing wilting of the top portion of the plant. *If* water is withheld, *on the other hand,* the plant's cells will gradually collapse, causing wilting of the entire plant. All plants do have protective mechanisms that conserve water in times of drought, however, and can withstand a temporary dry

spell. Most wilted house plants will quickly spring back to a normal state when water is again provided.

PARTS OF THE PLANT

<u>Stem.</u> The stem serves to support the plant and to contain and direct the vessels that transport water from the roots, and food from the leaves, to every other part of the plant. Most house plants, including Philodendron, Ivy, and Spider Plant, have <u>soft stems.</u> Such plants must either climb or crawl, since their stems are not strong enough to support an upward-growing structure of significant height. Other plants have soft but thick stems that enable them to attain good height, although their stems are apt to be subject to breakage. <u>Woody-stemmed</u> plants, such as the Avocado, Poinsettia, and Boxwood, are far more sturdy and are usually derived from trees or shrubs of the temperate region. <u>Canes</u> are thick stems with hollow or pithy centers. Bamboo is an example of a cane with which we all are familiar; among house plants, Dieffenbachia and Ti Plant are good examples.

Some plants have a distinct main stem, while others send up many stems, none dominant. A <u>side shoot</u> is a smaller stem growing out from the main stem. A <u>petiole</u> is a leaf stalk—the stemlike structure from which a leaf grows. A <u>node</u> is a joint on the main stem from which a leaf or side shoot grows.

<u>Leaf.</u> The major purpose of the leaf is, as *mentioned* above,

to manufacture food for the plant's growth and reproduction. Considering its total mass, the leaf has a remarkably large surface area, ideally designed for the efficient absorption and diffusion of gases through its thousands of stomata.

After the basic functions of the leaf are understood, its proper care is not difficult to appreciate. The stomata must be kept fairly clean, free of dust and oil that might hinder their efficient operation. Leaves must also be given the freest access to light and ventilation, according to the individual preferences of each plant. Never crowd plants to a point where they are competing for light and air.

<u>Roots.</u> Roots serve two main purposes—to anchor the plant in the ground and to supply from the soil water and the mineral salts which accompany water. Bulbs, corms, rhizomes, and tubers serve much the same purposes, as well as acting as food storage areas. Roots, *like* the above-ground parts of plants, may be pruned without injuring the plant in any way. Roots are often trimmed to prevent a plant from growing too large for the convenience of the grower, just as top growth is cut back. If roots are cut back, however, be certain to cut back top growth to about the same percentage, or the reduced roots *may* be unable to supply the plant with sufficient amounts of water. The major precaution in caring for roots is, as will *be* mentioned several times in these pages, to avoid overwatering.

<u>Flowers.</u> The plant's flowers contain its sexual apparatus. Pollination occurs when male pollen is deposited onto female stigmata, thus fertilizing the plant and allowing the formation of seeds. The fruit of any plant is, in reality, the ovary, which swells to protect the seeds. In nature, most plants produce flowers. *But only a small percentage of house plants* which in this book are listed as flowering house plants can be depended upon to produce, under home conditions, blossoms of sufficient size, profusion, and beauty to warrant attention. The plants which *are* grown for their attractive foliage often cannot produce flowers indoors because of insufficient light or because of a pollination failure. In nature, pollen is transferred either by insects or wind, both of which are lacking in the home. Where indoor pollination is essential, it can be accomplished by transferring the pollen from one flower to another, using a soft camel's-hair brush. This process is described fully in most books devoted to flowering house plants.

SOIL

Since the house plant you bring home from the shop will already be rooted in soil *(unless you are growing a plant from seed),* (you *might* wonder why you have to consider this need at all. The answer is that your house plant will,

assuming hoped-for longevity, someday need repotting, and you
will want to provide it with a potting mixture that will serve
its special needs. You might even wish to propagate some of
your favorite house plants at some later time, to share with
friends and to give as gifts. In any case, a basic knowledge
of potting mixtures and soils is essential to a complete understanding of all your plants.

Two simple definitions are in order here, to avoid any
confusion later on. Soil, when mentioned here, refers to garden
loam, that combination of mineral matter, organic matter, air,
and water commonly found outside, in your garden or under your
lawn. A potting mixture is soil with the addition of other
materials, such as sand, compost, peat moss, limestone, and
bone meal, that together form an ideal environment for the roots
of your house plants.

The easiest way to assure your plants of a perfect loam
is to buy packaged sterile potting soil from your garden or
flower shop. This soil will have not only the proper texture
but will also be free of disease organisms, insects (some too
small to be seen), and weed seeds. To this loam you will add the
other ingredients which together will form an ideal potting mixture. You may also buy packaged potting mixture at the store,
but if you do, read the package carefully to ascertain the ingredients, making sure that the mixture is right for your plants.

It is, of course, far less expensive to make your own
potting mixture from your own garden loam (free), sand (free or
inexpensive), and small amounts of purchased ingredients. If
you choose this route, then it is important that you be able to
make at least a cursory analysis of the garden loam that will
form the basis of the potting mixture. Texture is important.
A heavy clay soil will hold water for too long a time, encouraging disease and root rot, and it will bake cement-hard when dry.
On the other hand, a coarse sand will not hold water well, nor
will it hold nutrients long enough for the plant's roots to absorb them. Strive, then, for a happy medium, a good loam, containing both clay and sand, which will hold both water and
nutrients, yet offer adequate drainage.

To this basic loam, one usually add one or more
other materials, peat moss, to increase water-holding capacity
and to add organic matter; compost, for organic matter and
nutrients; sand, to open up the soil to air; some form of
supplemental mineral fertilizer, usually bone meal and lime, if the soil is overly acid.
Chemical fertilizer can be used, although it is not necessary
to add it to the potting mixture, since the other ingredients
will supply all the nutrients the plant can use for several
months.

ACIDITY/ALKALINITY

A discussion of soils and potting mixtures would not
be complete without some mention of acidity and alkalinity
and of the pH scale, which is the scientific measure for
acidity and alkalinity. The midpoint on the pH scale is 7.
A soil with a pH of 7 is neutral—neither acid nor alkaline.
Numbers above 7 indicate an alkaline soil; those under 7, an
acid soil. Most house plants, like most garden plants, will
do best in a slightly acid soil (a pH of 6.0 to 7.0).

In this book, all the house plants
listed will do well in this normal range, unless special
notations to the contrary are made.

If you have cause to worry about your soil's pH, or
are simply curious, call your county agricultural agent and
ask for directions on having a pH test made. The cost will
be nominal. Any soil may be made more acid with the addition of
peat moss, or less acid with the addition of ground limestone.

POTTING MIXTURES

There are as many different basic potting mixtures as
there are plant experts—probably more. Perhaps the most
common one, however (and one which can be trusted), calls
for two parts loam, one part finely screened compost (or a
mixture of peat moss and compost), and one part builder's
sand (not sea sand). To this is added a small amount of bone
meal (about one teaspoon for a five-inch pot) and, unless the soil is alkaline, a pinch of
ground limestone. Other recommendations call for more of
one ingredient and less of another. Do a little experimenting of your own. After a while, you will doubtless come upon
your own favorite mixture, which you can recommend to others.

And now that you have the basic formula well in
mind, we will consider the exceptions:

1. Acid-loving plants such as azaleas, camelias, gardenias, and heathers should have no lime. In fact, they should
have some form of acid
organic matter—acid peat moss or oak leafmold.

2. Foliage plants need somewhat more compost in the mixture, although half of the total mixture should be comprised of peat moss
(which will not overstimulate the plant).

3. Fast-growing and hungry plants need more bone meal
and lime, since they use them up often more quickly.

4. Some plants, such as cacti and succulents,
have very special soil requirements. these are mentioned
later in the discussions of individual plants.

NUTRIENT MAINTENANCE

The mineral nutrients contained in any fresh potting
soil or mixture, whether it is home-made or a sterilized commercial brand, should be sufficient for your plant's needs for
the first four to six months. After that, you should begin to
replenish those nutrients on a regular and carefully measured
basis.

All plants need substantial amounts of three elements—
nitrogen (N), phosphate (P_2O_5), and potash (K_2O)—and lesser
amounts of a dozen or more others, called "trace minerals" or
"trace elements." In grower's language, the three major elements are referred to as N, P, and K, and on the label of any
commercial fertilizer the percentages of each are given in
N-P-K order. A 5-10-5 fertilizer, for instance, will contain
5 percent nitrogen, 10 percent phosphate, and 5 percent potash.
A "balanced" fertilizer contains a balance of all
three in the amounts needed for the proper growth of most
plants. The fertilizer may be either a chemical or an organic
preparation, according to your preference. The chemical ones
are quick-acting, easy to use, and tidy. Organic fertilizers,
on the other hand, are slow to release their nutrients, providing a gentle and steady supply. Chemical mixtures come in
liquid, tablet, and even spray form (the last applied directly
on the foliage). Organic fertilizers may be purchased commercially in balanced formulas (fish emulsion, made from fish
wastes, is a popular one for house-plant use) or may be made at
home from a combination of ingredients. Blood meal is a good

choice for supplying substantial amounts of nitrogen (its NPK formula is 15.00-1.30-0.70), while bone meal (4.00-21.00-0.20) is good for phosphate, and wood ashes (0.00-1.50-7.00) are high in potash content. A combination of one part blood meal, one part bone meal, and two parts wood ashes will make a 5-6-4 formula, which is a good one for house plants.

How often should plants be fertilized? There is wide disagreement on this point, some experts believing in weekly feedings of full strength (the dosage recommended on the label), others fertilizing no more than once a month, and even less often during the *winter* ~~_____~~ In the end, you will probably have to come to your own policy by way of experimentation. In the beginning, however, it is better to err on the conservative side, since far more plants have been injured from overfertilization than from nutrient starvation. If you use a commercial chemical or organic formula, I suggest that you feed your plants as often as recommended on the label, but only half the recommended dosage. (Manufacturers tend to overstate the need for their product.) If the plant shows a spurt of active growth in late winter or early spring, increase the dosage to the manufacturer's recommendation. During a dormant or rest period, withhold fertilizer entirely. If you are using a home-made organic fertilizer, such as the one suggested above, use it sparingly at first. A level teaspoon of the blood meal-bone meal-wood ash formula, applied monthly, should be plenty for a plant in a five-inch pot. *Or* You may *use some of the mixture to fill a bottle*

about one-fourth full, add water to the top of the bottle, and use the resulting ~~_____~~ "tea" to water your house plants. A mild tea solution, applied weekly, will give all your plants a continuing and gentle supply of the essential nutrients.

Last, remember never to apply a chemical fertilizer if the soil is dry. The quick action of the chemicals can easily injure the roots.

CONTAINERS

Nearly any container that offers adequate drainage and doesn't leak is suitable for house plants. After checking a container ~~____~~ for leakage, consider drainage carefully. If *the container* has a hole in its bottom, there is no problem. If not, then you should put coarse gravel or broken crockery in the bottom of the container to fill one-fourth to one-fifth of its *depth*. In this way, you will avoid the liklihood of waterlogging your plants and encouraging root rot.

The traditional terra cotta clay pot offers definite advantages. It is inexpensive, easily replaced, and—most important—allows air to be exchanged through its porous walls. This same porosity, however, allows water to evaporate *fairly* quickly, necessitating ~~____~~ frequent watering. If *a plant's location makes it* ~~_____~~ awkward to water, you will save yourself some effort by choosing a glazed or otherwise impervious container.

Some metal containers, notably copper, *may* ~~____~~ produce adverse chemical reactions with soil and fertilizer elements, injuring plants therein. Copper planters, however, are usually lacquered *to* prevent ~~__~~ such reactions.

Wooden tubs and boxes are ideal for very large house plants. You can make any wooden container watertight by lining it with

natural sheets of heavy-gauge plastic or, for permanent results, in sheet metal.

To gain the best advantages of both a terra cotta pot and a decorative container, place the former inside the latter, leaving a quarter inch or more of space for air circulation around the walls of the inner pot. Sometimes sphagnum moss is inserted here to help preserve moisture. A base of gravel in the decorative pot can provide good drainage while lifting the inner pot to the level of the outer container.

Plastic containers are ideal for house plants. They do not allow air exchange through their walls, but, for this reason, they reduce the need for watering. Their light weight also suits them for hanging.

Nearly any container can be used for hanging plants, if you consider possible drainage problems. A cork can stop up a drainage hole to prevent floor and furniture damage, but then the advantage of the drain will be lost. Those hanging plastic pots that include a drip pan are ideal. You might also think of wire baskets, which are to be lined with sphagnum moss and then filled with the potting mixture. If possible, gather live sphagnum moss in a nearby bog and use that. It will continue to thrive in its natural green state, in sharp contrast to the dead, brown moss that your florist offers.

WATERING

More house plants are killed by overwatering than by any other cause. This killing with kindness can be avoided, if you learn to understand just when your plants need water and when they should be left alone.

The best rule of thumb is that a plant should be watered when the soil surface is dry to the touch. Then, water thoroughly, either by adding water to the soil surface or by immersing the entire pot in a larger container of water.

Certain plants, such as African violets and other woodsy varieties, need more water than most, while cacti and succulents need far less than the average. Aside from the specific preferences of individual varieties, there are many conditions which call for more or less water, as indicated in Table 1.

Immersion is the best method of watering because it is the surest. The soil in any pot may tend to form water channels which, upon receiving water from the surface, will rush it to

---

Table 1. WATERING NEEDS OF PLANTS UNDER VARIOUS CONDITIONS

Plants will need more water when:	Plants will need less water when:
They are in a period of active growth	They are in a period of rest (usually during winter)
They are in bright light	They are in dim light or under artificial light
Room humidity is low	Room humidity is high
Room temperature is high	Room temperature is under 70°
They are in small pots	They are in large pots
They are in clay pots or wire baskets	They are in nonporous pots
They are fast-growing varieties	They are slow-growing varieties
They are planted in sandy soil	They are planted in heavy soil
They are in flower or about to go into flower	

---

the bottom of the pot and out the drainage hole, leaving large parts of the soil bone-dry. Moreover, some potting soil mixtures will shrink when drying, leaving many spaces along the wall of the pot where water can run past. Immersion is the one sure way to soak the soil thoroughly, provided that the pot is porous. You can do it in any large container, or even in a sink or bathtub. Set the pots in the water, but do not let the water flow over the lips of the pots. After the surface of the potting mixture has become moist, ten to thirty minutes, remove the pot, drain off any excess water, and put it back in its place. Never go out for the afternoon, leaving your plants standing in water.

If you water from the top, remember to remove any excess water from the saucer. Plants should never be allowed to stand in water for fear of root rot. In time, you should learn to give each plant just enough water to soak it thoroughly, with very little excess drainage.

Some other watering tips:

1. Do not get water into the crown of any plant (the portion where stem and roots meet, usually at the soil surface) for this will encourage decay.

2. Never use very cold water, especially for tropical plants. Keep an open jar of water at room temperature for your house plants. Not only will the proper temperature be assured, but some of the chemicals in the water will have dissipated by the time it is given to plants.

3. Water which is artificially softened may be detrimental to plant growth. If you can, use rainwater or

---

water that has not been softened. Fluorine and chlorine, on the other hand, are not thought to pose any problems.

4. If your water is especially hard, lime salts may cause trouble with such acid-loving plants as orchids, primulas, rhododendrons, azaleas, and other plants whose natural soil is woodsy (indicating a high organic content) and acid. Either choose plants which prefer a more neutral range in the pH scale, or plan to collect rainwater for your calcifuges (lime-haters).

HUMIDITY

Much trouble with house plants, especially in winter in the northern states, can be traced to insufficient moisture in the air. Except for the cacti and succulents, nearly all house plants thrive best in a relative humidity of between 60 and 80 percent, while that of most heated homes in winter is often considerably under 40 percent. In much of the West, the humidity is constantly lower than the range best for house plants. Where the problem is severe, it must be solved before general success with house plants can be expected.

There are several ways to add moisture to the air in your home. The more expensive include the adding of a humidifying device to your furnace, if you live in a house, or installing an electric humidifier. This will benefit not only the plants but everyone living in the house as well. But there are less expensive ways of bringing moisture to your plants:

1. <u>The pebble tray.</u> Line the bottom of a waterproof tray with decorative pebbles and arrange your plants, in pots, on top of the pebbles. Keep the tray filled with water, being sure only to avoid blocking the pots' drainage holes. *Change the water weekly to keep it fresh.*

2. <u>Decorative containers.</u> If you keep a clay pot inside a decorative container (double-potting), keep a pool of water in the bottom of the larger vessel. Again, provide some means of support for the clay pot so that it is not resting in water at any time.

3. <u>Standing water devices.</u> Water left standing in a room will gradually evaporate, meaning that the lost moisture is added to the room atmosphere. If your home is particularly dry during cold weather, take the trouble to place pans of water on tops of radiators *or on stands placed above heat registers;* grow ivy, philodendron, or wandering Jew in containers of water; maintain an aquarium; rotate plants so that each can spend an afternoon in the bathroom each week, where the air is humid. *Change standing water weekly.*

4. <u>Bathing and showering.</u> *Most* house plants will respond *favorably to* a brief shower every day, or as often as you can manage to provide the treat. Little brass-plated atomizers are ubiquitous in mail-order catalogs, but more dependable (albeit less decorative) are the plastic sprayers available in art-supply stores, *garden shops, and many supermarkets.* These hold perhaps a pint of water, and they feature an adjustable shower head, affording an entire range of water action from a sharp jet capable of carrying twenty feet to a fine mist. Your plants, of course, *should have*

the fine mist. Remember to fill the container after every use, so that the next day's spray will be at room temperature. Remember also to avoid spraying plants which have been standing in direct sunlight (the shock is great) and those which have been subjected to very cool temperatures (perhaps spending the autumn on a cold sunporch).

Rubber plants and others with large leaves should be cleaned thoroughly and gently with a damp cloth about once a week. The leaf polish sold commercially is permissible, if you want really stunning looking large-leafed plants, *which can block the leaf pores and impede respiration.* but never use oil of any kind; ivies and other rugged small-leafed plants can be held under the gentle stream of a faucet for their weekly bath.

5. <u>Grouping.</u> Plants will maintain a moist *surrounding air (leaves not touching)* with greater facility if they are grouped together, rather than separated. During the coldest part of winter, you might want to group most plants on a pebble tray under a light window, to take advantage both of maximum light and greatest humidity.

<u>VENTILATION</u>

Plants, like people, benefit from fresh air. Like people, also, they react badly to drastic changes in air movement and temperature. Provide adequate ventilation for your house plants, but do not subject them to sharp winds, winter draughts, or heat arising directly from a radiator. Think of your own comfort, in this respect, and you will

know what will *be best for* your plants. If, in autumn, you bring your plants in from a summer outdoors, help them to adjust to indoor conditions gradually by placing them by an open window for the first several days. Gradually lower the window day by day, keeping a watchful eye on night temperatures. *Reverse the process in spring.*

<u>TEMPERATURE</u>

The temperature requirements of house plants vary widely, according to the natural habitats of their forebears and also according to other conditions. Many cool-weather plants prefer a range of 50-60° F. and cannot tolerate temperatures above 70°, while tropicals may thrive in a moist 70-75°. Know the temperature preferences of any house plant before you adopt it, and then place it in the best possible temperature location in your home. You may find, for instance, that a cool-loving aspidistra will do best in a back bedroom, while tropical plants thrive happily next to (but not above) a living-room heat vent. The temperature needs of plants are included in their descriptions throughout this book. Heed them well, make liberal use of an indoor thermometer, and do not be afraid to experiment by placing different plants in different locations for a week at a time. You may notice in your plants distinct preferences for particular locations throughout the house, and their preferences will not always corroborate expert advice.

<u>LIGHT</u>

Light and temperature needs are closely related. In their native surroundings, many tropical plants can thrive at a high temperatures because they receive long hours of sunlight. *Indoors,* especially during winter's short days, they cannot receive enough light to enable them to stand high house temperatures.

Except for cacti and succulents, house plants should not be placed on windowsills where they will receive long periods of direct sunlight. Simply place a thermometer in this position and you will soon see that your plants can be literally cooked to death, even in the dead of a Minnesota winter. Strive, instead, for a bright spot with a few hours of filtered sunlight each day, at least for most plants.

Individual varieties vary, of course, in their light needs, and these needs are specified in the descriptions of individual plants in these pages. Again, do not be afraid to experiment with different locations for different plants. I have a <u>Philodendron scandens</u>, one of the most popular and most common of all house plants, which has thrived for years in a *dim* corner, *although* it is supposed to require a bright spot out of direct sun. Plants sometimes exhibit unmistakable individual characteristics which we have yet to understand.

<u>PRUNING AND TRAINING</u>

Some plants should be pruned and pinched back occasionally

ally, in order to encourage bushy and stocky growth, while
trailing plants such as philodendrons and ivies need gentle
support to guide them into pleasing growth patterns.

Many people hesitate to prune at all, feeling somehow
that they are hurting the plant or interfering with its
natural development. Actually, plants will respond to
judicious pruning with new and vigorous growth. Plants such
as geraniums, coleus, and begonias should be pinched back
routinely, in order to encourage lateral growth. The process
is quite simple: With a sharp knife, cut back perhaps one-half
inch of the central growing tip. The plant should respond
by sending out side shoots below the central tip, and the
main stem of the plant should then become thicker and sturdier.
If this is done several times a year, the plant should eventually attain the vigorous and well-rounded form you
desire. Without this pruning, it might grow "leggy"
with a weak main stem, requiring some kind of support. Many
older plants, as well, will benefit from occasional pinching
back or shearing of outside growth. Do not, however, prune
or pinch back African violets, gloxinias, flowering bulbs,
ferns, or cyclamen.

Vines and trailing plants often need some kind of
support, unless you prefer to let them cascade from a hanging
basket. The usual practice is to sink a slab of cork or
tree bark into a pot, then to train the vines of the plant
to grow around and up the support, eventually concealing it.

Another effective device is the sphagnum-moss cylinder. Pack
the moss fairly tightly around a stake and secure it in a
cylinder of the proper size for the pot. The cylinder can
be made easily from either chicken wire or green plastic
material made for this purpose. If you wish, sink a small
clay pot into the top of the cylinder, so that you can add
water regularly to keep the moss damp. (Otherwise, the moss
will require regular spraying.) Tie the vines gently to the
cylinder as they grow; eventually, philodendrons and similar
plants will anchor themselves to the moss with their aerial
rootlets, making other support unnecessary.

REPOTTING

The temptation to repot plants too often
is a strong one and should be resisted with strong will. A
plant needs repotting only when it has become potbound—when
the roots have filled the entire container and are creeping
out of the drainage hole. Indeed, some plants seem to thrive best when
slightly potbound, these will be indicated in the section on
individual plants.) When repotting is indicated, choose a new pot
only one size larger than the old, for a house plant will not do well
in a pot that is too large. If the larger pot has been used before,
scrub it thoroughly to remove any possibility of disease. Soak new
clay pots for a few hours in water so that they become saturated. Then,
with ample potting soil, gravel, and a tongue depressor or similar
wood tool, set to work.

To remove the plant from its old pot, slide your hand
over the top of the pot, index and second fingers cradling

the plant stem. Turn the pot upside down, thus supported, and
tap the lip of the pot sharply on the edge of a bench or
table. After a few taps the entire soil ball, ringed with
plant roots, should come out easily, in one neat piece. Set
it aside. Take the larger pot and line the bottom with a
layer of coarse gravel or broken crockery, to provide good
drainage. Then add potting soil on top of the gravel, placing
the plant and soil ball on top of the new soil several times
in order to see when it has reached the proper depth. (The
top of the soil should be about one-half inch below the lip
of the new pot, in a four-inch pot, and one inch below the
lip in an eight-inch pot, to leave room for watering.) When
enough soil has been added to raise the plant to its proper
height, center it well and begin to pack soil around the sides
of the soil ball, using the tongue depressor. Take your time
in doing this, for it is the most crucial part of the entire
operation. It is important to pack the soil firmly, so that
no air spaces are left when the job is finished. Roots
cannot draw nutrients in air spaces and many of them will
thus be injured or die, affecting the health of the entire
plant. When the new soil is finally brought up to a level
even with the top of the soil ball, the job is finished. You
might want to add just a little soil over the top of the root
ball, especially if roots have been forced up to the soil
surface, but don't add any more than you must, for you do not
want to change the planting depth of the plant. Repotting
is shock enough, for many plants, without altering the plant.

ing depth. Water the plant thoroughly and return it to its
usual location.

How often should you repot? Obviously, only as each
plant indicates a need. For slow-growers, this might be once
every two or three years; a mature slow-grower may go for
many years without repotting, if new growth is cut back. For
fast-growing and very young plants, repotting may be needed
once or twice a year for the first several years. Plants that
do not need repotting after one year should have the top
one-half to one inch of soil replaced annually, to keep the
soil fresh.

PROPAGATION

There will come a time when you will want to start your
own house plants—to increase your own plant population, to
use as personal gifts for friends and family, to replace a
short-lived plant or one that has become ungainly with age.
The propagation of most house plants is not a difficult task,
and it is most rewarding.

There are two general methods of doing the job: by the
collecting and planting of seeds, and by the cutting and rooting of plant parts—stems, leaves, or underground structures.
The first way (sexual reproduction) is often difficult, always
time-consuming, and likely to produce unsatisfactory results.
Propagation from seed is ideal for garden annuals, but not for
most house plants. Special equipment is required, and daily
attention is essential, making the activity an unlikely one for

anyone who professes "no time for house plants." In addition,
the seeds from hybrid plants are likely to produce plants
vastly inferior to the parent plant. (A hybrid
is any plant produced by cross-pollinating two plants of different species or genera.) Last, many house plants do not
flower and produce seeds under home conditions, requiring
the house-plant gardener to purchase seeds from specialty
houses. The one advantage of growing house plants from seed
is that you can create new hybrids by the cross-pollination
of plants. The excitement of this activity creates a fascinating hobby for some house-plant enthusiasts but is unlikely
to appeal to those who cannot afford to devote significant
amounts of spare time to the activity.

Far more simple, and yielding far more reliable results,
is the propagation of plants by the cutting and rooting of
plant parts. Less care is required, and the offspring will
look just like the parent, even when the parent is a hybrid.

Plants may be propagated at any time of year, although
it is best to avoid tackling the job when the plant is going
into a dormant period. In early spring, just before active

growth begins, is perhaps the ideal time.

Cuttings. The most common method of propagating is by
the taking of stem cuttings, which are then rooted in either
water or some sterile rooting medium such as perlite, vermiculite, or sand. If you have never rooted a cutting before,
then begin with African violets, coleus, Dracaena, fuchsia,
gardenias, geraniums, impatiens, ivy, philodendron, wandering
Jew, or wax begonia. These are the easiest, because all can
be rooted in water. Simply take a cutting containing four to six leaves, from an actively
growing tip of the plant, severing the stem cleanly just below a joint with a clean razor
blade. Place the cutting (you may take several at a time, from the same plant, if
you wish) so that the bottom portion is submerged in water,
a colored or clear bottle is fine, remembering only to keep the
leaves above water. (Cut off the bottom leaf or two, if
necessary, to get more of the stem into the water; about a
third of the entire length should be in water.) Place the container in diffused light, not direct sun, and wait until
vigorous roots appear. When they have, the little plants may
be removed from the water and potted in a small pot, using the
potting mixture recommended earlier in this chapter. Be sure
to pack the potting mixture firmly around the roots of the
plant, to avoid any air spaces, and water thoroughly afterwards.

Stem cuttings which cannot be rooted in water are rooted
in perlite, vermiculite (both available wherever house-plant

supplies are sold), or builder's sand.
(You may by now be wondering why, throughout this book,
builder's sand is recommended for potting purposes, while sea
sand is cautioned against. The reason is that builder's sand,
which comes from inland locations, has irregular and sharp surfaces, allowing good soil drainage. Sea sand, having been
washed smooth over the years, packs too snugly and leads to a
compacted soil and resultant drainage problems.)

run in The process is basically the same as for rooting in water. The cuttings are
inserted in the moist medium, which may be contained in a
small clay pot or, for larger numbers of cuttings, a shallow
plastic tray. The planted container is then placed in a plastic bag
which is tied shut (the zip kind, used for food storage, is
convenient, effective, and reusable) and placed in diffused
light at a temperature of 65-70° F. You can tell whether the
cuttings have developed roots by testing them weekly. Open
the bag and pull gently on a plant. If it moves easily, then
the roots have not yet formed; if it resists your gentle tug
fairly well, however, then the roots probably are mature enough
to stand repotting. The process can take as little as two
weeks or as long as several months, depending upon the variety
of the plant and the size of the cutting. When the roots are
strong and vigorous, pot the plant in a small pot and treat it
as you would any other plant.

Some plants which produce canes, including Chinese ever-

green, Dracaena, and Dieffenbachia, can be propagated by taking
cuttings of the canes, which have discernable "eyes." Press
each cane (containing one eye) into moist sphagnum moss, secure
it with ⬛⬛ clothes pins at each end so that it does not
pop up, seal it in a plastic bag, and put it in a cool place
out of direct sun. In six to eight weeks, move it into a warm
place (70° – 90°), still out of direct sun. Soon, a shoot will
grow from the eye. When the shoot has attained a respectable
size, the cane may be cut close to the shoot on both sides, and
the new plant may be lifted from the moss and potted.

Plants that have fleshy leaves are best propagated by
taking leaf or leaf-petiole cuttings. ⬛⬛⬛⬛⬛⬛
Leaf cuttings work well when large and mature leaves
are available. Cut the leaf close to the stem of the parent
plant, using a razor blade for a clean cut without crushing the
cells. The leaf may then be cut horizontally into smaller
sections, so that the main vein runs from top to bottom along
the center of the leaf section. (Long-leafed plants such as
Sansevieria and Streptocarpus may be cut into as many as ten
sections, each of which will produce an individual plant.)
Each leaf section is then sunk halfway into the rooting medium,
after which the process is the same as that described for stem
cuttings.

Smaller leaves may be rooted by taking leaf-petiole
cuttings. Cut one leaf stem close to the main stalk and sink
the stem into the rooting medium, so that the leaf nearly (but

not quite ⬛⬛) touches the medium. African violets, begonias,
snake plant, piggyback plant, and Peperomia respond well to
leaf-petiole cuttings.

Underground division. Older plants which have thick main
roots can be propagated by taking root cuttings. This is
usually done when the plant is being repotted. Cut about one
inch of the main root, making sure that it has at least one
eye. Cover this with one-half inch of rooting medium and treat it
as you would any other cutting.

Thick-rooted perennials may be propagated ⬛⬛ by the
process of root division, in which the root mass is simply
forced apart into two or more clumps, each of which is then
repotted.

Plants which produce rhizomes ⬛⬛⬛⬛⬛ may
be propagated by dividing the rhizome so that one leaf bud is
contained on each piece and planting the section under one-half
inch of rooting medium. Plants which produce potato-like
tubers can be propagated by cutting the tubers apart with a
sharp knife, keeping one eye to each section, and planting the
sections in the rooting medium just as one would plant potatoes
in the open field.

Some plants produce suckers, small plants that grow
up from an underground stem or root. These may be separated
from the parent plant and potted in soil immediately.

Anyone who has seen strawberries grow outdoors knows what
runners are — the baby plants that grow from a long stem coming

from the base of the parent plant. Among house plants, Boston
fern and spider plant both produce runners, which can be
severed from the parent and started in a rooting medium.

Other methods of underground division include the separation and replanting of baby bulbs and corms which are
produced by the mother bulb or corm.

Air layering. A fairly simple (and most impressive) way
of propagating larger or woody-stemmed plants is by air layering. Here, a sharp cut is made into a stem, perhaps a third
of the way in, ⬛⬛ and a toothpick is placed in the cut horizontally,
to keep it ⬛⬛ open. That stem section is then wrapped with
moist sphagnum moss and covered with clear plastic, tied top
and bottom so that moisture cannot escape. Roots will form
from the incision and will soon show through the plastic.
When a fair number of them have appeared, cut the stem below
the plastic wrap, remove both plastic and moss, and pot the
new plant immediately in potting soil.

As you might imagine, the propagation of plants can often
be integrated with the cutting back, pruning, and shaping of
older plants. It seems a shame to throw away plant parts
when they can be used to produce more plants, and it is precisely this attitude of thrift which, if not controlled, can
lead to a frightening multiplication of house plants. The
answer, of course, is to share plants with friends, thus encouraging still more enthusiasts and still more house plants.

[Chapter 3 would come here]

18 *grundy old style.*
Cic

Part Two. Introducing the House Plants

(fl.) ⎯The number and variety of house plants available for
your consideration is staggering. For every combination of
conditions your home can offer, including heat, light, and
humidity, there are literally thousands of suitable house=
plant varieties, offering a virtually limitless selection of
sizes, forms, colors, patterns and textures, growth patterns,
and flowering habits. You have only to survey the conditions
that your home can offer. and then make your plant selections,
within those limits, to suit your own tastes.

The house plants ⬛ selected for inclusion in
this book are only representative of ⬛ far greater
numbers. I have included nearly all of the most common plants,
and I have tried to avoid those ⬛ difficult to
grow. All the old favorites are here, as well as some newer
varieties and unusual plants which can add zest to your
collection.

51

IV - 2

The plants ⬛ have been divided into *three main* ⬛
groups: foliage plants, *other* ⬛ *and flowering plants.*
⬛ (cacti and succulents. Within each group, individual
plants are listed alphabetically by their common names,
followed [by (in par*e*ntheses)] their ⬛ scientific *(or Latin)*
designations. The *scientific* name *usually* comprises both the genus and
species names. For example, the ⬛ *scientific* name for the common
boxwood is Bux*u*s (the genus) semṕervirens (the species).
After a genus name is introduced, it is thereafter abbreviated.
Thus Bux*u*s sempervirens, if mentioned again, becomes B. semper- /
virens. ⬛ there may be a third part to the ⬛ *scientific* name
which designates a further subdivision of the species, usually
called a subspecies or a variety. The popular Japanese
boxwood, for example, is B. microphylla japonica. ⟶

52

IV-2a

(turn to) In addition, some breeders have given their creations patented
variety names, such as English ivy 'Pixie'; ⎯ in this book,
all such names will be indicated by single quotes.

Although I have attempted to maintain an informal tone in
these pages by using common names whenever possible, the
scientific nomenclature has obvious benefits. Many species are
known by different common names in different parts of the
country; different species of a genus are often called by a
single common name; and a single common name may be applied
even to varieties of completely different *genera*. ⬛ The only
sure way to identify any plant, then, is by referring to its
scientific name.

For each plant listed, you will find *information on* ⬛
⬛ its individual preferences for growing temperature,
light, soil moisture and air humidity, and window placement.

Please remember that these are rough guides and not inflexible
demands. Many plants *have a wide range of tolerance and* ~~will thrive in a variety of~~ *conditions.* ~~Many plants
which are said to prefer an east window will do just as well
in a shaded south or a west location.~~ Do not hesitate to try
a plant of your liking because you cannot provide its exact
needs—but neither should you attempt a plant if you can provide none of them. Experimentation is both valuable and
enjoyable.

WHERE TO BUY HOUSE PLANTS

It is best to buy house plants from growers who know their own
plants and who will be able to offer sound advice on their
culture. If there is no grower in your area,
the next best source is your local flower shop or nursery
center. Whichever place you choose, talk to the owner or *the owner's*
representative about house plants. Ask for precise identification of a plant *that* ~~that~~ interests you. Ask for specifications
of the plant's needs for light, soil, temperature, and humidity.
~~Ask how large the~~ plant is apt to become and whether or not
it produces flowers, even if you know the answers to these
questions. If it becomes apparent that *the person you are talking to* doesn't know
very much about the plant or about house plants in general,
then ask to talk to someone who can answer your questions in
greater detail, or seek another source.

Plants found in supermarkets and discount houses are *usually*
not bad, although many, *that you see* ~~flowering in the store~~ *may* have
been grown quickly and forced into bloom under ideal green-

---

house conditions that you cannot hope to match in your home,
and ~~large~~ plants offered at bargain prices are often severely underrooted.
However, most plants offered by these sources are likely to
be common varieties that are quite tolerant of adverse conditions. It is hard to go wrong with grape ivy or a climbing
philodendron.

Plants stored outside at garden centers or ~~at~~ shopping
centers ~~~~ *may* carry insects or disease, particularly if they are resting close to flats of outdoor
vegetable or flower seedlings. Examine them ~~~~ closely
before purchasing, and isolate them for *one or* two weeks at home
before putting them with other house plants.

Wherever you buy your plants, look for young and sturdy
specimens with rich color and a generally healthy appearance.
Examine particularly carefully large and mature plants which
carry high price tags. These may have been growing for too
long a time in ideal conditions. Generally, you will have
better luck with a younger plant, and you will have the added
~~pleasure of~~ bringing it along to maturity in your own home.

Chapter 4/5 FOLIAGE PLANTS

In this chapter, we will survey many of the house plants
grown primarily for their foliage. Some of them, under favorable conditions, will flower from time to time, although few
should be selected for their flowering abilities. Nearly all
of these plants are fairly easy to grow and maintain, giving
even the beginner a wide variety of plants from which to choose.

The plants are listed in alphabetical order, according
to their common or popular names. If there is no popular name
for a plant, or if there are *two or* more, ~~~~ none dominant, ~~~~
the plant is listed by its scientific or Latin name. The
index, which includes both common and scientific names, provides
a convenient means of cross-checking names.

The special symbols accompanying each plant name will
provide a quick and convenient guide to that plant's requirements. Remember, however, that these are guides and not sharp
demands. Many of these plants are tolerant by nature, ~~~~
will take to an east window as well as a west window, and can
tolerate some direct sunlight even if none is recommended.
Most crucial, perhaps, are the guides to humidity and moisture,
since overwatering is one thing that virtually no plant will
tolerate.

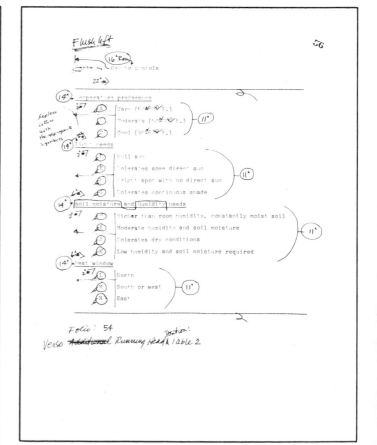

Folio: 54
Verso ~~Additional~~ *Running Head* | *Position:* Table 2

 *(Replace circled letters with symbols throughout)* 57

African Boxwood (Myrsine africana) B-F-H-N DO NOT SET THROUGHOUT

A slow-growing plant with red stems, but otherwise similar to regular Boxwood (q.v.). Many people think it is even more graceful. African Boxwood is a good plant for terrariums, if the atmosphere is not too hot.

Aluminum plant. See Pilea.

Aralia (Fatsia japonica) C E I N

Sometimes sold as Aralia sieboldii. Beautiful bright green, leathery, maple-like leaves highlight this cheerful plant. In appearance, it is similar to the castor-oil plant, and in fact it is sometimes called False Castor-oil Plant. It thrives in a cool spot. Aralia can easily grow leggy and so should be pruned annually in order to encourage it into bushy growth. *It will attain a height of four feet at maturity.*

F. japonica crosses with ivy (Hedera) to form a striking hybrid. Fatshedera lizei, a climbing plant with maple-shaped leaves, which is tolerant of adverse conditions.

There is also a plant called False Aralia (Dizygotheca elegantissima), which has graceful and feathery foliage. It bears no resemblance to the true Aralia and is difficult to grow.

Artillery plant. See Pilea.

Asparagus A E I N

There are three kinds of Asparagus suitable for growing as house plants: Fern Asparagus (A. plumosus), with slender, needle-like dark green leaves, forming a feathery appearance; A. asparagoides (smilax), a trailer; and A. sprengeri (Emerald Feather) a climber which has thicker, yellow-green leaves and drooping stems. The latter makes a good

---

58

plant for hanging *baskets* and produces red berries at Christmas time. These plants like some sun in the summer and full sun in the winter and can grow to a height of about two feet.

Aspidistra. See Cast-iron plant.

Australian Laurel (Pittosporum tobira) C E H M

A tolerant and slow-growing plant whose leaves, glossy and leathery, resemble those of Rhododendron. Australian Laurel will grow vigorously bushy and does not ask much attention. Florists often use the leaves in floral arrangements.

An interesting variegated form is P. tobira variegata.

Australian Umbrella Tree (Schefflera actinophylla) A D I L

a very attractive and vigorous-growing tree with rich-looking glossy leaves that radiate like umbrellas from the ends of several leaf stalks. It is a tough and rewarding plant, growing to six feet, which can be propagated by air-layering.

Australian Umbrella Tree is also sold as Brassaia actinophylla. A dwarf variety, B. actinophylla compacta, is also available.

Baby's Tears (Helxine soleirollii) B E H M

A low creeper, also called Irish Moss. It likes a constantly moist (but not soggy) soil and higher than average humidity. It makes a good ground cover for terrariums but will also grow in a pot if adequate humidity is provided. Baby's Tears may appear to die in the colder months, but after

---

Foliage Plants

59

an adequate rest period the plant will spring back to life.

Black Pepper (Piper nigrum) A E I N

not an especially attractive plant, but one which produces real peppercorns which may used at the table and is a good conversation piece for that reason. The plant's green berries later turn red, then dry up and turn black. Pick the dried-up black corns, dry them thoroughly for several weeks in an open spot, then use them in your pepper grinder. The care for Black Pepper is about the same as that required for Philodendron. It is not a demanding plant.

Boxwood (Buxus) C D I M

The same plant which grows the most prized hedges outdoors can make a very attractive house plant which has glossy, bright green leaves. Boxwood is slow-growing and dependable, a good subject for bonsai, the ancient Oriental art of growing dwarf trees and shrubs. B. sempervirens and B. microphylla japonica (Japanese Boxwood) are the two popular species.

Bromeliads A E I N

There are more than eighteen hundred varieties of this popular group, many of which are suitable for growing as house plants. Some of them produce attractive flowers, but most are grown for their striking and variegated leaf patterns. One distinctive feature of the Bromeliads is the rosette leaves which form a small water cup, which the plant uses to hold reserve

---

60

supplies of water in its natural habitat. the crotches of trees in Central and South America the water cup is an evolutionary survival characteristic. In the home, keep the cup filled with water, changing it weekly to keep it fresh.

A few of the more common genera of Bromeliads are Aechmea, Ananas (Pineapple), Billbergia, Cryptanthus, Dyckia, Tillandsia (Spanish Moss), and Vriesia.

Caladium A E I N

Caladiums, with their spectacularly colored and variegated leaves, are equally at home in the garden or on the window sill. They are ideal additions to plant groupings on porch or patio in the summer and early autumn. Give them bright light, but not long periods of direct sun in summer, if you want the brightest leaf colors.

Caladiums are grown from tubers, which can be divided easily to produce new plants. Start the tubers in regular potting soil at a very warm temperature—80° to 90° F.—and move the young plants to a cooler spot when they have appeared. *They will attain a height of about one foot.*

Cast-Iron Plant (Aspidistra elatior) A F I N

perhaps the easiest plant in the world to grow, as its name suggests. It is virtually impossible to neglect it to death. It is also called Saloon Plant, since it was one of the few that could survive in Victorian taverns, and it was made immortal by George Orwell in his novel Keep the

Aspidistra Flying. If you cannot grow the Aspidistra, you may safely conclude that you have a purple thumb, hopelessly irredeemable.

The Cast Iron Plant (which grows about two feet tall,) seems to thrive even better when kept slightly pot-bound, and it will benefit from having its leaves washed occasionally. A white-striped species is called A. elatior variegata.

① Chamaeranthemum igneum ⟨A E H N⟩

A low, spreading herb that has attractive dark green leaves with reddish-yellow veins. It is suitable for hanging baskets or as a low contrast in large plant groupings. It does like warm temperatures and high humidity, however, and may not be suitable for dry apartments.

Chinese banyan. See Ficus.

① Chinese Evergreen (Aglaonema) ③ ⟨A E I L⟩ and low-growing

an attractive plant that is very easy to grow. It will stand abuse almost as easily as Cast-Iron Plant.

There are at least ten commonly found species of the Aglaonema, the most popular of which, A. modestum, has interestingly mottled leaves. Perhaps the most attractive, however, is A. pseudobractaetum, which is sometimes difficult to find in stores and greenhouses.

---

① Cissus ⟨A E I N⟩

a vine plant that offers a number of interesting and attractive species. Most are vigorous climbers, suitable for training on a trellis or for adding to hanging baskets.

Among the more popular species are C. rhombifolia (Grape Ivy), which is one of the most popular of all house plants; C. antartica (Kangaroo Vine), which prefers a small pot; C. antartica minima (Miniature Kangaroo Vine); C. rotundifolia; and C. discolor (Begonia Ivy), which is perhaps the most spectacular of the genus, although difficult to grow.

Of all the Cissus, Grape Ivy is the easiest to grow, a fact that doubtless accounts for a large share of its popularity.

① Coleus ⟨A D H m⟩

An old favorite with velvety leaves sporting bright splashes of reds, pinks, purples, and yellows. There are a seemingly endless number of varieties of Coleus, nearly all of them interesting, most growing twelve to eighteen inches in height
Most garden varieties are varieties of C. blumei. Coleus is equally happy outdoors, grown as an annual in temperate areas, or in the window garden. It can be grown easily from seed, and stem tip cuttings can be taken from established indoor plants. If you grow Coleus outdoors in summer, take some cuttings before the first autumn freeze and root them for growing as house plants.

The soil for Coleus should be kept damp but not soggy. Pinch back plants often to encourage bushy growth.

For "trailing coleus" see Plectranthus.

---

① Copper Leaf (Acalypha wilkesiana) ③ ⟨A D H m⟩

A member of the Spurge family which features (chenille plant), copper-colored foliage. A close relative, A. hispida, is described as a flowering plant in Chapter 60.

Copper Leaf may be propagated easily by taking cuttings late in the summer. The plant is susceptible to attack by spider mites, and proper precautions should be taken against this menace.

no extra #

① Dichorisandra reginae ⟨A E I N⟩

an attractive, slow-growing plant with interesting leaf markings. It resembles Wandering Jew, except that it grows upright. Give it warm temperatures and not too much direct light, but do watch room humidity.

---

① Dieffenbachia ⟨A F J N⟩
A popular plant with many species, often called Dumbcane. It is prized for its large leaves with interesting markings, usually variations of cream and white on dark green. Dieffenbachias are fairly tough plants not too difficult to grow. Most varieties attain a height of eighteen to twenty-four inches, although growth is slow.

D. arvida 'Exotica' is very popular because it is even more durable than other members of the family. Other well-known species include D. picta, D. amoena, D. sequine, and D. bowmannii.

There are no special cultural requirements, although the Dieffenbachia does best in a warm spot and should have its foliage cleaned regularly. The plant may be propagated by taking stem cuttings and rooting them in moist and warm peat.

Caution: Eating or nibbling on the leaves of the Dieffenbachia can cause severe swelling of the tongue and mouth tissues; hence the popular name, Dumbcane. It is not a plant to grow in a home with toddlers.

① Dracaena ⟨A E I N⟩
many available species, which vary so greatly in appearance that some appear to be unrelated. Most grow tall, five feet or more, on sturdy stalks.

They are very tough plants, tolerant of a surprising amount of neglect, all in all one of the most dependable house plants.

Some varieties to investigate are D. deremensis Warneckj, D. fragrans (which has corn-like leaves), D. fragrans massangeana (whose leaves feature yellow stripes), D. marginata (a truly exciting plant, with grass-like, cream-colored foliage, edged in red—sometimes sold as D. marginata tricolor), D. sanderiana (with white-banded leaves), D. godseffiana, D. draco (the "Dragon Tree" of the Canary Islands), and many others, some of which will doubtless by offered by any good supplier. These mentioned, however, are some of the most attractive and also some of the easiest to grow. See also Pleomele.

Dumb cane. See Dieffenbachia.

① Episcia A-F H N

A genus, offering many species and subspecies, which is related to the African Violet and requires largely the same culture, although it does demand a little more light. Episcias are not really among the easiest plants to grow successfully and should be tried only after success has been attained with some of the others listed in these pages. The leaves are a rich green, most varieties tinged with copper, some with variations of silver, blue, purple, and bronze. The veins often offer striking color contrasts. Episcias are trailing plants, a natural selection for hanging baskets. They send out runners that may be used for propagation.

Most species produce small and attractive flowers, in the color range of red-orange-yellow, but the plant is generally grown for its delightful foliage. If you do not wish to strive for blossoms, a north window will suit an Episcia well enough.

The most popular species is E. cupreata (Flame Violet), which has soft, hairy, copper-tinged leaves and comes in several attractive varieties. Also investigate E. dianthiflora, which produces white flowers, and E. lilacina 'Cuprea,' with lavender-colored flowers. Many other species and subspecies are easily available, all of which have fascinating foliage variations and some of which will bloom quite profusely.

Fatshedera, see Aralia.

Fatsia japonica, see Aralia.

① Ferns A-F H N

ferns the oldest plants on the evolutionary scale, that you are likely to cultivate. They are predated only by the algae and the mosses. Everyone knows and admires ferns for their graceful and feathery fronds. They are among the few house plants that reproduce by spores rather than seeds. Some ferns grow regally upright, while others trail with modesty and grace. There are many sizes of ferns, from miniature plants suitable for the window sill, all the way to the seven-foot-tub plants that can add a touch of class

to entryways, patios, and conservatories.

The secret to the successful raising of ferns is in offering them an environment matching, as nearly as possible, that of their natural habitat. They need warmth, a decent degree of room humidity (not under 30 percent) and a moist and humusy soil (at least 50 per cent organic matter). They appreciate bright light but will be affected adversely if allowed to stand for long periods of time in direct sun.

There are a great many ferns from which to choose. One of the smaller ones is

Adiantum, the Maidenhair Fern, which is available in several varieties; it sends forth fragile-looking fronds in sprays; needs good light and high humidity.

Other smaller ferns include

Pteris multifida (Brake Fern), Woodwardia orientalis (Chain Fern), and Polypodium aureum (Hare's-Foot Fern). There are many, many others. For asparagus fern, emerald feather, and smilax, see Asparagus. Among the larger ferns are the following:

Cyrtomium falcatum (Holly Fern), which has frond leaflets reserbling the shape of Holly and with a similar gloss.

Asplenium nidus (Bird's-Nest Fern), with broad, lance-shaped fronds.

Nephrolepis exaltata, which has long, sword-shaped fronds and is often called Sword Fern.

N. exaltata Bostoniensis, the ever-popular Boston Fern.

Platycerium bifurcatum (Staghorn Fern), whose fronds are usually attached to a piece of bark or other support, and which can become parched quite easily in a dry atmosphere.

The world of ferns is a large one, full of interest, and extremely rewarding. No house-plant collection should be without at least one or two representatives.

① Ficus B-F J N

large family of indoor plants, whose best-known member is the Rubber Plant. Ficus species range from large, tree-like plants to small-leafed trailers. Although they are not difficult plants to grow, the large species are especially sensitive to both overwatering and sudden temperature changes and will react to either by dropping their leaves.

There has been much improvement in the Rubber Plant (F. elastica) since World War II. The best now is perhaps F. elastica 'Robusta,' which is remarkably trouble-free. There are many decorative varieties, as well, including F. elastica 'Doescheri,' which has light and dark green patched leaves and cream-colored leaf margins, and F. elastica

'Schryveriana,' another mottled-leafed variety. <u>F. elastica</u> 'Decora,' from which 'Robusta' was developed, is still a popular slow-growing variety. Rubber plants will grow as tall as any room but may be cut back to encourage bushiness. Chinese Banyan (<u>F. retusa</u>), another tree-like <u>Ficus</u>, showers forth with a profusion of small, leathery leaves. (<u>F. retusa nitida</u>) (Indian Laurel) resembles mountain laurel.

The Fiddle-Leaf Fig (<u>F. lyrata</u>) is a tough and attractive tree-like species, with large dark green, fiddle-shaped leaves. It needs warmer conditions than other <u>Ficus</u>. Weeping Fig (<u>F. benjamina</u>) is another <u>Ficus</u> tree which has small, dense-growing foliage.

There are, as well, many small plants in the genus. Most popular, perhaps, is Creeping Fig (<u>F. pumila</u>), a small-leafed creeper which has been developed to include several variations, such as <u>F. pumila minima</u> (slower-growing and smaller), and <u>F. pumila variegata</u>, a variegated variety. All will adhere to rough surfaces, sending out aerial roots similar to those of ivy, and are thus easily trained.

The tree-type <u>Ficus</u> are propagated by air-layering, while the small-leafed climbers and trailers may be reproduced easily by simple division.

Firebrand See Ti plant.
Flame violet. See Episcia.
Friendship plant. See Pilea.

German Ivy (<u>Senecio mikaniodies</u>) an easy-to-grow plant that is similar to the true ivies in both appearance and requirements. A handsome relative is <u>S. macroflossus variegatus</u> (Cape Ivy). Treat them in every way like Ivy (q.v.) for success.

Ginger (<u>Zingiber officinale</u>) the same ginger used in cooking, a fact that makes the plant even more interesting than its appearance would indicate. The untreated rhizomes sold in specialty food and gourmet shops can be planted directly in potting soil to produce plants (root in water, as for an avocado, then plant with just the tip of the root showing) or established plants may be divided easily. The plants have reed-like stems and interesting grassy foliage, truly exotic in appearance. Success as a house plant depends upon giving Ginger plenty of sunlight and warm temperatures. Keep the soil constantly damp but never soggy for long periods of time. As an added bonus, healthy plants will bear colorful clusters of flowers.

Golddust Plant (<u>Aucuba japonica</u>) modest plant features dark green leaves spotted with yellow-gold markings. Its main attribute is that it will withstand very cool temperatures, all the way down to freezing It is good for unheated porches in all but the coldest parts of the country. Two popular varieties are <u>A. japonica variegata</u> and <u>A. japonica goldeana</u>. Indian laurel. See Ficus. Irish moss. See Baby's tears.

Ivy (<u>Hedra</u>) Surely one of the most popular of house-plant species, both easy to grow and cheerful and attractive in appearance. There are a great number of varieties, with new improvements coming along all the time.

English Ivy (<u>Hedra helix</u>) is the most popular of the true ivies and is available in more than fifty varieties to suit nearly any taste. There are varieties with large leaves or small, with fast or slow growing habits, plain green or variegated. The best way to choose an English Ivy to your liking is to visit some flower shops and greenhouses, or to beg a few cuttings from a friend who has a plant that appeals to you.

Propagation of Ivy is easy, and in fact the plant does half of the job for you. Small rootlets will form on the stem of the plant, just below the leaves (the Ivy uses the rootlets to attach itself to rough surfaces, helping it to climb.) Make cuttings just below the roots and plant these cuttings directly in potting soil or a sterile rooting medium.

It would be the sheerest folly to attempt to recommend all the good varieties of English Ivy. For a starter, however, you might investigate <u>H. helix conglomerata</u> (Japanese Ivy), an upright-growing plant with small, densely growing leaves; 'Curlilocks' and 'Ivalace' with curled leaf margins; 'Green Ripples,' 'Maple Queen,' 'Merion Beauty,' 'Needlepoint,' 'Pittsburgh,' 'Pixie,' 'Rochester,' <u>H. helix scutifolia</u>, and 'Shamrock,' the last of which likes more than average moisture and is good for terrariums.

Among the variegated English Ivies, try 'Golddust,' 'Glacier,' and 'Goldheart,' the last of which has dark green leaves with sharply contrasting bright yellow centers.

Canary Islands Ivy (<u>H. canariensis</u>) also known as Algerian ivy is another easy-to-grow Ivy, which has larger leaves than English Ivy. It is often trained around a piece of bark, much like a Philodendron, to form a striking plant with a very bushy appearance. More popular than the basic green-leafed variety is the variant <u>H. canariensis variegata</u>, also known as 'Globe de Marengo,' whose leaves are slate-green to cream in color.

For grape ivy and begonia ivy, see Cissus; for German ivy and cape ivy, see German ivy; for Swedish ivy, see Plectranthus.

① Japanese sweet flag (Acorus gramineus) A-F-H-N

A moisture-loving plant that grows only two inches tall. It will do best in a terrarium.

① Joseph's coat (Alternanthera) A E I M

low-growing dwarf plants *that* are good for terrariums. Their multicolored foliage adds interest to any plant grouping. Joseph's coat needs warm temperatures and a moist soil. *(leaf color)* *sometimes*

Codiaeum is also called Joseph's coat, because it, too, has colorful foliage. However, Codiaeum grows to a height of ten feet. The name "Joseph's coat" is also applied to various other plants.

Jungle plant. See Maranta.

Kangaroo vine. See Cissus.

① Maranta A F H N

a genus of plants that has striking foliage. *They are* easy to grow and impressive in appearance. *Marantas will grow to about eight inches in height.*

Marchaviana M. leuconeura kerchoveana (Prayer Plant) is perhaps the most popular of the Marantas and is so named because its leaves fold up at night, as if in prayer. The leaves are large and oval-shaped, and the plant requires a fairly humid atmosphere. In the autumn, the leaves may begin to die out.

If so, do not be alarmed. Cut off the affected leaves and reduce watering until late winter, when new growth begins; then water normally.

A red-veined variety, even more striking, is M. erythroneura. Another with red veins is M. leuconeura erythrophylla (Jungle Plant), which has olive-green leaves. Still another striking variation is offered by M. leuconeura massangeana.

Most house-plant growers will want to include at least one Maranta among their collections. The key to success with this plant is in giving it lots of bright light, but no direct sun at all.

① Miniature Holly (Malpighia coccigera) C E I m

not a true holly but a bushy evergreen shrub with dense, holly-like foliage. The leaves are shiny, dark green, and have spiny teeth. Miniature Holly does produce small flowers, but it is grown primarily as a foliage plant. It is propagated easily from cuttings.

① Nephthytis A E I L

an attractive plant, but difficult to identify, since there is great confusion over what is and what is not a Nephthytis. Experts *say* that many plants sold as Nephthytis are really *from the genus* Syngonium. Since the two *genera* are difficult to tell apart, however, no one cares very much except

the experts. Whatever they are, they are tough plants, able to withstand adverse conditions. Nephthytis *and Syngoniums* have large, arum-shaped leaves and are either trailers or climbers. Used as climbers, they will have to be offered some support, such as that used *for* Philodendrons. Propagation may be achieved by taking stem cuttings.

Among several available species, the most popular is Syngonium podophyllum (Goosefoot Plant).

① Norfolk Island Pine (Araucaria excelsa) A E I N

A popular evergreen, graceful and symmetrical, seen with increasing frequency. It will hold up well under adverse conditions, although its branches will droop in dim light. Give it a damp, but not soggy, soil, for it is very susceptible to overwatering. It seems to do well when kept slightly potbound.

Norfolk Island Pine is a slow grower and should never be pruned. *It will grow gracefully to a height of about six feet, after which it tends to become ungainly.*

① Palms B F I m

a plant family full of nostalgia for many *people*. In Victorian times and right up through the 1930s and 1940s, the potted palm was a symbol of exotic elegance, bringing a bit of the tropics to shivering Northerners. No movie made before 1950 was complete without a detective peering out from behind a potted palm.

The elegant palms lost much of their allure after

World War II, but now they are making a modest comeback. You can achieve success with palms by giving them bright light (even though they will endure shade), *water*, and no plant food during the winter months. Palms, actually, seem to thrive on inattention, doing well when slightly potbound. They are slow-growing, in any case.

The palms are a plant family. *Palmae* is the scientific name, which comprises many genera and far more species. Few, however, are both attractive and manageable as house plants. Among the palms you might wish to investigate are *the following*:

Chamaerops (Fan Palm) has fan-shaped leaves on long stalks *and will become quite large at maturity.*

Cocos is an attractive coconut palm, the best species C. weddelliana, on its proper name is actually

Howea is the Palm Court Palm, the most popular of all indoor large palms. H. belmoreana, the most attractive species, will *eventually grow to ten feet or more in height.*

Neanthe is an attractive and easy-to-grow dwarf which can tolerate a dry room.

Phoenix, the Date Palm, can be grown easily from the stone of a fresh date. Plant the stone in potting soil, keep it warm *(70° to 80° F)*, and it should germinate in about a month. *It is slow-growing during the first year or so, but within ten or fifteen years it will become as tall as any room.*

① Pellionia 〔EHM〕

a colorful, slow-growing, creeping plant, fine
for hanging baskets and a good filler plant for groupings.
It features small, oval-shaped leaves with interesting
variegated patterns. There are two popular varieties: P.
daveauana and the more compact P. pulchra.

Pellionia is not difficult to propagate. As it creeps
along the soil it sends down roots from the stems. Just cut
the stems into sections and root them in potting soil.

① Peperomia 〔A F I V〕

There are many varieties of this popular and cheerful
little plant (eight inches or less in height) (most of which are low and upward-growing, with
deeply ridged leaves. It is the ridging that gives these peperomias
their distinction in a world of larger and more spectacular
house plants. They are tough plants, tolerant of most conditions, although they will rot at the groundline if the top
of the soil is not allowed to dry out between waterings.
Peperomias like bright light, but not direct sun in the summer.

Among the more popular varieties are these:

P. caperata (Emerald-Ripple Peperomia) has deeply ridged,
heart-shaped leaves; the tops of the ridges are green and the
valleys are brown, giving an interesting effect.

P. rotundifolia is a low grower with thick, light green
leaves.

P. obtusifolia (Oval-leaf Peperomia) has solid green

leaves, while P. obtusifolia variegata is the variegated form
of the same species.

P. Sandersii (Watermelon Peperomia) is identified by its
red petioles and silver-striped leaves.

P. grieseo argentea hederaefolia has ridged, glossy,
leaves, silver-hued, and purple-olive veins.

There are many other varieties of Peperomia, many
of which may be seen at your local flower shop or greenhouse.

① Philodendron 〔B-F-I-M〕

probably the most
popular group of house plants in America today. There are
many, many species and varieties, with leaves ranging from
small to very large, in an interesting variety of shapes
offered by no other house plants. Most are climbers and
will appreciate a support that can be kept moist, such as
that described in Chapter 2.

Philodendrons are not difficult plants to grow, unless
you disregard the rules. Growth will be stunted by poor
light, and the leaves can turn yellow and drop from lack of
water, too small a pot, low temperatures, or poor drainage.
The plants will benefit from a monthly washing with a mild soap (not
detergent) solution. Cut back the growing tips if you wish
to encourage bushy growth, and use the tip cuttings to form
new plants.

Some of the more popular varieties include:
P. scandens (heart-leaf philodendron), a very popular climber
which can withstand the dry air of a typical apartment.

P. oxycardum, the most commonly grown form, which has
heart-shaped leaves very similar to those of P. scandens. It is often
grown in water or wet moss.

P. dubium (Cut-leaf Philodendron) a slow grower with
star-shaped leaves.

P. panduraeforme (Fiddle-leaf Philodendron) which has irregularly shaped, olive-green leaves.

P. pertusum, also known as Monstera deliciosa, has perforated leaves, irregularly shaped.
The older plants have broad,
thick leaves with many perforations.

P. squamiferum (Anchor-leaf Philodendron) which has leaves and
petioles that are covered by red hairs. The leaves are shaped
like daggers.

P. bipinnatifidum (Twice-cut Philodendron) a large-
leafed variety; the leaves resemble those of the smaller P. dubium in
shape but are more deeply notched.

P. selloum, another cut-leaf variety, the cuts becoming
more pronounced as the plant reaches maturity. This species
will tolerate temperatures down to freezing with no apparent
harm.

P. wendlandii is another large-leafed species, very tolerant of a wide range of temperature and humidity. Its leaves
are long and narrow.

① Piggyback Plant (Tolmiea menziesii) 〔B〕

native to the West Coast of the United States;
a modest-sized plant that can be grown outdoors in the warmer regions
of the country. Its name is derived from its unusual habit of
bearing young plantlets from the junction of the leaf and the
petiole. These can be rooted easily to grow new plants. The
leaves are toothed and lobed, covered with down. It is an easy
plant to grow.

① Pilea 〔E I m〕

A genus that includes at least four cultivated house plants,
none of which grows more than a foot in
height. They are rather unusual-looking plants,
all like moist soil, warm temperatures, and full
sun in the winter. The plants become less attractive as they
grow older, but cuttings are easily made, so that older plants
may be discarded when desired. Fertilize liberally when
growth is active.

P. cadiere (Aluminum Plant) has dark green leaves with
striking aluminum-colored markings. A dwarf variety, P. cadiere
minima, is preferred by many, as is P. cadiere nana, a compact
variety.

P. microphylla (Artillery Plant) is fine in texture with
bright green, fern-like leaves. When its flowers are dry,
pollen literally explodes from the blossoms, hence its common
name.

P. involucrata (South American Friendship Plant) is bushy in growth and has coppery leaves. It can be made to appear even bushier if several cuttings are taken, then rooted in the same pot, to the sides of the parent plant.

P. 'Silver Tree' has bronze-hued leaves with silver markings.

Pineapple. See Bromeliads.

Plectranthus [A-F H m]

Various species of this genus are often called trailing coleus or Swedish Ivy. Some are upright in growth, while others are trailers, making good subjects for hanging baskets.

P. australis, a trailer, has waxy-green leaves, round in shape with saw-tooth edges.

P. australis variegatus is similar in leaf shape, with added white markings.

P. purpuratus is an upright-growing plant with purple coloring on the undersides of its leaves.

There are other interesting varieties, including P. oertendahlii, a flowering trailer with bronze-hued leaves and silvery veins.

Pleomele [A-F I L]

an interesting group of plants with cultural requirements similar to those of Philodendrons.

P. reflexa variegata (Song of India) is now included in the genus Dracaena. Its attractive, spear-shaped leaves are gold-and-green striped, borne in clusters on branching stems. It will grow to tree size in ten or fifteen years.

P. reflexa gracilis has dense foliage; its recurved leaves have translucent edges.

P. thalioides has waxy-green leaves, ribbed lengthwise.

Pothos (Scindapsus) [A-F I N]

Pothos is very similar in appearance and growth habits to the heart-leaf Philodendron, P. scandens, except that it needs less water and warmer temperatures—not below 65° F. It likes bright light but cannot stand direct sun. Pothos is a natural trailer, although it can be trained upward along a support, again like Philodendron. The leaves are heart-shaped and green, with pale yellow markings. Pothos is not as easy to grow as most plants listed in this book.

The most popular species is S. aureus, which offers several variegated varieties, some of which require even warmer temperatures.

Prayer plant. See Maranta.

Rubber plant. See Ficus.

Ruellia makoyana [A-F H N]

an old favorite, not seen as often today as in the 1930s. It is a free-spreading plant that has glossy pale green leaves with silvery veins. It likes a warm, moist environment, shaded from the sun.

Sanchezia nobilis glaucophylla [A-F H M]

a member of the Aphelandra family. It grows to a height of four feet and has large, glossy, sword-shaped leaves with yellow veins.

Screw Pine (Pandanus) (3) [A-F I M]

An old favorite that will withstand most adverse conditions. It is recognized by its long, arching, sword-like leaves, which have saw-toothed edges.

P. veitchii has green-and-white-striped leaves. Often preferred, however, is P. veitchii compactus, a dwarf variety with clearly variegated leaves. P. baptistii has no marginal spines, as do the other species. All Screw Pines like moist, but never soggy soil. They can take some direct sun, except in the heat of summer, although they do best in a bright location out of direct sun altogether.

Selaginella [A-G H L]

fern-like plants, including some small creepers, some erect-growing species, and some trailers. All offer bright green, feathery foliage.

S. kraussiana is a low creeper, perfect for terrariums.

S. emmeliana is an erect-growing plant.

S. willdenovii is a vigorous climber with unusual blue leaves. S. apus is a trailer, good for hanging baskets.

Sensitive Plant (Mimosa pudica) [B-F M] (prefers dry soil but high room humidity)

a fascinating plant for both adults and children

because its delicate and feathery leaves and petioles droop and fold up instantly (and temporarily) whenever it is touched, or even if a lighted match is held close to it. Seeds from which plants will grow easily are often available in stores. The plant gets leggy and out of hand after about a year, but it is not difficult to grow more plants at any time.

Silk Oak (Grevillea robusta) (3) [C-E I N]

a pleasant plant with graceful, feathery foliage similar to that of the false Aralia. It will grow to three feet in height. Silk Oak likes cool, moist conditions and can spend the summer outdoors with benefit. It does tend to get leggy if unchecked, so it should be cut back at the growing tip fairly regularly. Silk Oak will react badly if its soil becomes very dry.

Snake Plant (Sansevieria) (3) [A-F I L]

actually a succulent but seldom thought of as such. It has long been very popular, probably because of its great tolerance to adverse conditions. It is also called Mother-in-Law Tongue and Bowstring. Like the Cast-Iron Plant, it can grow perfectly well in hot, dry, and dim locations (including, it seems, most old hotel lobbies in the country). The leaves are thick and sword-shaped, usually upright, growing to eighteen inches or more in height, but in some varieties ground-hugging. It is propagated easily by division of the rootstock or by taking leaf cuttings. (Be careful not to turn the leaf cutting upside down when setting it in the rooting medium, for roots grow only from the downward portion of the cutting.)

There are many varieties available, including:

S. trifasciata laurenti (Variegated Snake Plant), with handsome yellow bands along its leaf margins.

S. trifasciata, similar in form, but without the yellow bands.

S. trifasciata laurenti compacta (Dwarf Congo Snake Plant), with shorter leaves and yellow margins.

S. trifasciata hahni (Hahn's Dwarf Snake Plant), with light and dark green bands along the leaves.

There are many other interesting variegated varieties of this old standby.

line #

Song of India. See Pleomele.

South American friendship plant. See Pilea.

Spanish moss. See Bromeliads.

Spathe Flower (Spathyphyllum) an easy-to-grow, tough plant, suitable for the homes of most novice green thumbs. It has glossy, sword-shaped green leaves. White blossoms will sometimes surprise you in the winter, but do not depend on their appearance.

There are two popular species, S. clevelandii and S. floribundum.

Spider Plant (Chlorophytum comosum)

Spider Plant is one of the most popular of house plants.

It has grassy leaves, variegated cream and green in color, which arch gracefully from either pot or hanging basket. Mature plants produce perfectly formed baby plants on the end of long runners, which resemble spiders hanging from a thread. Propagation is simply a matter of rooting one of the "baby spiders" in a rooting medium. The Spider Plant can store water in its tubers and can take dry soil for a fairly long time because of this characteristic.

Strawberry Geranium (Saxifraga sarmentosa)

A trailing plant, also called Strawberry Begonia and Mother-of-Thousands, good for both hanging baskets and terrariums. All it really asks is a woodsy soil containing plenty of organic matter, and a cool location. Leaves of the Strawberry Geranium resemble those of the true geranium, and it sends out runners just as strawberry plants do. The leaves of the standard variety are deep olive in color, with silver-gray markings. An interesting variant, S. sarmentosa tricolor, has dark green leaves marked with white and pink and is considerably more difficult to grow.

---

line #

Syngonium. see Nephthytis.

Ti Plant (Cordyline terminalis)

C. terminalis is only one of many species of Cordyline, but it is certainly the most popular. Also called Firebrand, it will last for only one to three years and grow to two feet in height before dying out, but its spectacular young life is certainly worth your placing this plant on your list of house-plant candidates. It has long, upward-reaching leaves, cerise, purple, and green, which grow from a cane trunk. Another popular species is C. australis, which features long, slender leaves. The Ti Plant is very popular in Hawaii, where its colorful grassy leaves are used in making grass skirts. It is sold there in tourist shops as a "Ti Log." In recent years, breeders have developed several variations of the original plant, including a dwarf and a variegated variety, which go under various names.

Umbrella flatsedge (Cyperus alternifolius) a popular exotic plant with narrow, pointed, grasslike leaves that grow in clusters. It will grow up to two feet tall in a pot. Constant moisture is essential, and propagation is a simple matter of root division.

Related species include C. papyrus, which is similar in appearance and requirements but grows to seven feet in height, and a dwarf variety, C. alternifolius gracilis.

Velvet Plant (Gynura)

This is a vigorous-growing plant with dark red, velvety leaves. It will offer a fine contrast to your green plants. It is best to train the Velvet Plant to some support, to keep it in bounds, or to pinch it back often to encourage bushy growth.

There are two common varieties, G. aurantiaca, which is upright in growth habit, and G. sarmentosa, a smaller and loosely-twining plant. The flowers of both have a horrible scent and should be removed immediately upon appearance.

Wandering Jew (Tradescantia; Zebrina)

Tradescantia and Zebrina both claim the common name of Wandering Jew, and the two genera are so similar that they are →

commonly interchanged. *Both include* ~~easy~~ to-grow, tolerant, ~~___~~
vigorous trailers of many varieties, perfect for hanging
baskets. Feed them regularly for good growth. Propagation
is simplicity itself. Simply take cuttings of growing tips
and root them in water.

Among very many interesting species are *the following*:

T. fluminensis, the original Wandering Jew, has silver
markings, but there are many ~~___~~ *species* of different markings
and colors available today.

T. albiflora has bluish-green leaves with white stripes.

Z. pendula is an excellent house plant whose leaves have
purple undersides. Again, there are several interesting
variegated varieties.

Yew (Podocarpus) c——m

Yews are prized outdoor plants in many parts of the
country *and* ~~___~~ can be made into attractive house plants anywhere.
These hardy evergreens can provide *a* welcome contrast to ~~___~~
tropical *plants*. They are slow-growing and ~~___~~ tolerant of adverse
conditions. They will *withstand* ~~___~~ low temperatures ~~___~~
and ~~___~~ *may* require frequent repotting because of vigorous growth.
They can become quite large and bushy.
P. macrophylla angustifolia (Southern Yew) can be
pruned to a pleasing shape and will respond with even more
vigorous growth. Other similar species include P. macrophylla
Nagai and P. macrophylla Maki.

<u>Note</u>: If we were really publishing this book, the following correspondence would ensue.

1. CIP form to the Library of Congress, as soon as manuscript is in production. New copyright page, with LC number and other CIP information, as soon as CIP slip returned by LC.

2. Letter to author explaining production schedule, as soon as schedule is available, with request for notification if he will be unable to meet given deadlines. (Follow-up letter or phone call if any changes in schedule become necessary at this end.)

3. If illustrations prepared here, Xerox copies to author for his approval before they go to printer.

4. One set of galleys to author, with the attached proofreading instructions. Phone call to author to say that galleys are coming and be sure he can still meet deadline for returning them. Check-up phone call near deadline to be sure they are coming on time, if there is any reason for doubt. (Proofreading against copy done by Press proofreader since this is a trade book. Author's changes, if allowable, transferred to master proofs by Press proofreader or editor. If this were a scholarly monograph rather than a trade book, author would be expected to read galleys against copy.)

5. Pages to author for indexing, with <u>Chicago</u> indexing guide (if not sent earlier). Phone call to author to say pages are coming and be sure he can meet schedule. Index in this case would need to include common and scientific names of all plants discussed in book, with cross referencing. Index would be checked by editor against style cards prepared during editing. Index proofs checked here.

6. If illustrations not included in indexing pages, Xerox copies of repros with illustrations to author for approval when ready. Approval by phone if possible. (Except in unusual cases, authors don't see vandykes or blues.)

All the above-mentioned correspondence with author, by letter and telephone, would be handled by the manuscript editor and progress reported in weekly editorial report.

TRANSMITTAL SHEET (Editorial Checklist)   House Editor: ITH
                                                 Date: 8/1/76

Author/~~Editor/Translator:~~ Pruvis Mulch

Title: NO TIME FOR HOUSEPLANTS: A Busy Person's Guide to Indoor Gardening

Series: None   FAC Approval Date: July 15, 1976

Length of MS. 170 ms. pp, not including index & illustrations	One-edition book: yes/no For discussion
Trim size: ~~5¼x8"~~ ~~5½x8½"~~ 6x9" ~~For discussion~~	Paperback possibility: yes/~~no~~ For discussion

Release attached: yes/~~no~~	Duplicate MS herewith: yes/~~no~~	Original to MS Editor: yes/~~no~~

Prelims & end matter: Check items now in manuscript. If items are to follow,
mark each with estimated MS pages. Cross out those items not to be included.

Half title	Illustrations in text:
~~Series title~~	Number of line drawings: 100
Title	Number of halftones:
Copyright	No. of charts, graphs, maps:
~~Dedication~~	No. of separate plates:
~~Foreword~~	
Preface	
Contents	Binding: Cloth: one/two/three piece
List of Illustrations	stamping: one/two hits
List of tables	
~~Introduction~~	
Acknowledgements	Jacket: Number of colors: 3
Appendix(es) 11	Line drawing/~~halftone/type~~
~~Glossary~~	Good varnish/laminate/plain
Bibliography	
~~Notes~~	
Index? : yes	Paperback: Number of colors:
Index to be done by: author	

Quantity - first printing: Cloth: 5000 min.	Paper:	2nd prtg. probable: yes/~~no~~
Proposed publishing price: $6 - $7	Required return, 1st prtg.:	%
Discount: trade	Required return, 2nd prtg.:	%

Market: World rights: yes	Limited territory (specify):

No. of free copies: 10/10	Offprints: yes/no No. per contributor:

Royalty terms: 5% net receipt proceeds 1-3000, 7½% net receipt proceeds 3001-5000,
10% net receipt proceeds beyond 5001

Permission/other fees: none	Subsidy: none
Target pub. month: March 1977	MS, proofs to: author

Copies: (1) Production   (2) MS-Editing   (3) Bookfolder

Present: Acquisition and Copy Editors, Production Manager and Staff, Business Manager, Marketing Manager and Staff, and Director

Title: NO TIME FOR HOUSE PLANTS
Subtitle: A Busy Person's Guide to Indoor Gardening
Author: Purvis Mulch

Press ed.: CW	Acqu. ed.: ITH
Designer: RH	ISBN: 0-292-FANTAS-Y
Fund: uncertain (Corrie Herring Hooks?)	Series: No
Category B (inexpensive trade book)	Subsidy: No

No. of pp.: 170 ms. pp., not including index & illustrations; castoff 128

Size 6 x 9	Jacket: yes, trade

Ads on jacket: no, descrip. of book instead with possible blurb from someone like Thalassa Cruso (in catalog, book should be placed with *Roadside Flowers of Texas*).

Illustrations: yes—opinion expressed by ITH and agreed to by others that the book is not "cute" as are many similar books, and while in some ways this works to its advantage, at the same time it needs the distinction that good new illus. would add—BNS also points out that more illus. are needed to help the reader identify plants—therefore we will do our own new illus.—mostly line drawings (Ed Lindlof will do sample). Designer to discuss no. and type of illus. needed with copy editor. The point was made, however, that in dealing with a book of this type a decision would have been made and settled in the acquisition phase.

Proofreading: in house	Typesetting: in house
Index: yes, necessary	AA's/blue pencil changes: no

Direct to pp.: no

Books in warehouse: (edited copy to author this week or early next wk.) ca. 7 months from time edited copy goes to author

Print: tent. 7500 cloth only

Cost estimate: $13,275	Unit cost: $1.77
Price: $6.95	Discount: trade

Author information: Author bio. has been requested by CCW; to come.

Editorial comments: CCW described contents and distributed copies of a table of contents. A trade book. PDJ points out that in the case of a trade book the audience must be defined before making production, marketing, etc., plans. Need to check prices of similar books, size of audience, etc., to make it competitive with the many others on the market. RH and CCW define this as a general trade book for the beginner, ordinary people raising house plants. To be treated as a national trade book. Large no. of very low-cost mass market paperbacks in this field emphasized by several. CT and others point out that in actuality this press would not do this book—this will be pointed out in the project log.

Marketing plans: Sell rights to paperback ed., book club also (CA will do sample letters). Market as if this were the lead title in our catalog in any season. Ads in suitable gardening mags., *Better Homes and Gardens*, perhaps organic gardening mags. Point out that Mulch describes both organic and inorganic methods. Marketing to circulate a sheet descriptive of ad methods, as usual.

Discussion: Question of omitting subtitle raised. Decided to retain subtitle lest the book be mistaken for a humorous book a la Erma Bombeck. Possibility of humorous cover described by RH, however; by Sally Blakemore, of a busy person attempting to deal with flourishing house plants.

EDITORIAL FACT SHEET

Date 8/1/76

To: All concerned

From (House Editor): ITH

You are hereby officially notified that

(x) The following book has been contracted, and the manuscript has been transmitted to Manuscript Editing and Production.

( ) The following book has been contracted will be imported from (foreign publisher):

Author: Purvis Mulch

Title: NO TIME FOR HOUSE PLANTS

Series: Not applicable   Translation: No

Author's background:
Purvis Mulch received his B.A. from the University of Iowa in 1961. He is the editor of _Vigor_ magazine and an associate editor of Organic Gardening & Farming. His books include the _____ Garden Guide and _The Earthworm Book_.

Description of book--reason for publishing:

This is a basic book on house plant care; it is directed to the busy person who has little or "no time" for attending to his/her plants. The book must be distinguished from others on the market by striking illustrations throughout which we will commission.

Production information

Number of (MS/printed) pages: 170 ms. pp. not incl. index & illustrations

Number of illustrations: 100

    Halftones _____ Line cuts _____

Binding:

Marketing information

Proposed month of publication: March 1977

Proposed price: under $7.00

Proposed discount: Trade/Specialist/Text

Rights: World/Other

Special marketing prospects (book club, Overseas, etc.):
Gardening book clubs, magazine excerpts. We might consider a calendar using the illustrations.

Ed.: CCW

EDITORIAL/PRODUCTION TRANSMITTAL SHEET

170 ms. pp.
Category A B C D

Author Purvis Mulch   ~~Illustrator~~

Title No Time for House Plants

Subtitle A Busy Person's Guide to Indoor Gardening

~~Translator~~

~~Series/sub/joint pub/new ed~~   ~~Intro or Foreword author~~

Date to Production 9-14-76   ISBN number: 0-292-FANTAS-Y

Proofreading time: galleys 10 working days   pages 5 working days
              (Includes mailing time)

Index to be done by author (x) _____ 15 _____ working days (Includes mailing time)

Proofreading time for index page proofs 2 working days

Number of proofs needed (total) galleys 3 sets, pages 4 sets
galleys: master, author, shelf; pages: master, indexer, sales, shelf
Cross out items which do not apply. Check items submitted with manuscript and indicate which are to come and when. Indicate position in book if possible:

    Halftitles 3
    Subheads: No. of levels 1
    Line illusts: ~~No~~ yes
    Halftones: ~~No~~
    ~~Color plates: No.~~   number to be determined
    ~~Frontispiece: No.~~   in production
    ~~Maps: No.~~
    Tables: No. 3

~~Series~~

~~Dedication~~

~~Foreword~~

Preface X

~~Acknowledgments~~

~~Introduction~~

~~Epigraph~~

~~From note~~

~~Abbreviations~~

Appendices (no.) 11

~~Glossary~~

Bibliog X

~~Notes~~

Index to come

~~Other~~

Extracts ( ) yes   (x) no

~~Notes: ( ) end of book   ( ) end of article   ( ) at foot of page~~

Foreign language: no

Special characters needed: 4 symbols, to be created in production.

Special instructions: If designer prefers, the 11 appendices may be treated as "special boxes" and placed throughout the text. If this is done, "Appendices" in Contents should be changed to "Boxes."

ESTIMATED COSTS   Date: 8/4/76   By: NB

Title: NO TIME FOR HOUSEPLANTS

Author: Purvis Mulch

Quantity: HB 7500   PB

Pages: Castoff 128   Actual _____   Trim size 6 x 9

Paper: 60# Warrens Old Style

Binding costs based on: A grade cloth, plain endsheets, stamping one hit on spine, individual shrinkwrapping

Additional binding costs for: multicolor endleaf

Suppliers: Composition: In-house
           Printing: Kingsport
           Jacket/Covers: P.D.
           Binding: Kingsport

Plant Costs:

Composition:	$ 750
10% A.A.'s & misc. type:	$ 75
Illustrations:	$ 2625
Photographs: stats	$ 150
Paste-up:	$ 750
Re-design of artwork:	$
Stamping dies:	$ 50
Subtotal:	$ 4400

Manufacturing Costs:

Quantity:	7500 HB		
Printing:	$ 2500	$	$
Paper:	$	$	$
Halftones/Illustrations:	$	$	$
Color Section:	$	$	$
Jackets/Covers:	$ 525	$	$
Binding:	$ 5175	$	$
Freight:	$ 675	$	$
Subtotal:	$ 8875	$	$
Total:	$ 13,275	$	$
Unit cost:	$ 1.77	$	$

Comments: This includes 100 illustrations.

Title/Author	NO TIME FOR HOUSEPLANTS/Mulch

Halftitle 18 Goudy Bold clc, lead 4 pts, flush left.

Series title None

Title page 18/22 Goudy Bold, 18/22 Goudy Old Style, 11/22 Goudy Old Style. See layout.

Copyright 11/22 Goudy Old Style, flush left.

Dedication None

Contents 11/22 Goudy Old Style ragged right 29 pi max. Folios one word space from titles. Part titles 14/22 Goudy italic.

List of Illusts 11/22 Goudy Old Style ragged right 14 pi max. Folios one word space from titles.

Preface Same as main text.

Introduction None

Part titles 18 Goudy Old Style clc, flush left at top.

Notes None

Bibliography 11/11 Goudy Old Style, ragged right 29 pi max. Turnovers indent one em.
10/10 Goudy Old Style, ragged right, 14 pi max, OK to hyphenate.
Runover lines indent one em. Lead 10 pt between alphabetic sections

Index ☐ Oldstyle figures ☒ Lining figures

Other instructions No widow lines at the top of page.
All display matter to be set with tight word spacing.

Appendices: 11/11 Goudy Old Style, double column. Each 14 pi max.

Publisher will supply complete makeup instructions on dummy.

Manuscript to compositor   September 20, 1976

Galleys complete to Texas Press October 15, 1976

Galleys returned to compositor November 1, 1976

Pages complete to Texas Press

Pages and Index manuscript to compositor   SEE ATTACHED SCHEDULE

Index pages to Texas Press

Index pages returned to compositor

Repros complete to Texas Press January 7, 1977

Galleys:	3 sets
Corrected galleys:	3 sets
Pages:	4 sets (Xeroxes of dummy)
Repros:	1 sets

University of Texas Press Box 7819, Austin Texas 78712

COMPOSITION SPECIFICATIONS   Date September 17, 1976

Author/Title   Purvis Mulch   NO TIME FOR HOUSEPLANTS

Trim size   6 x 9"   Overall text page   29x46   picas

Margins: top 7/8"
gutter 5/8"

Main text: In justified setting use thin space bands. In ragged right setting use tight and uniform word spacing.

11/11 Goudy Old Style (VIP). Ragged right. Double column. 14 picas maximum, a-prox 12 picas minimum. OK to hyphenate. One pica column space

Text 47 lines per page   OK 1 line long/short facing pages

Paragraph indent one em, except flush left after heads.   Figures ☐ Oldstyle ☒ lining

Folios 10/10 Goudy Old Style lining figs, flush outside at bottom.

Running heads 10/10 Goudy Old Style italic clc, flush left bottom recto pages only.

Lead to first text line   --

Extract None

Lead above   Lead below

Chapter openings

Begin ☐ recto or verso as it falls   ☒ recto only

Folios ☒ will show on chapter opening pages   ☐ will not show on chapter opening pages

Chapter number: 10/10 Goudy Old Style italic, clc, flush left bottom (same position as running head).

Chapter title: 16/16 Goudy Old Style clc, flush left. Align with base of first text line.

Sink first text line 55 points from top margin.

Subheads

Level 1: 14/14 Goudy Old Style italic clc, flush left. 28 picas maximum. Do NOT hyphenate

Lead above 30 points   Lead below 11 points

Begin first text line following   flush left.

Level 2: 11/11 Goudy Old Style italic clc, flush left. Run in.

Lead above 11 points   Lead below --

Begin first text line following run in.

Level 3: (captions) 9/9 Goudy Old Style italic clc, flush left.

Lead above cutting space   Lead below cutting space

Begin first text line following --

University of Texas Press

Date January 14, 1977

SPECIFICATIONS FOR PRINTING

Book title   NO TIME FOR HOUSEPLANTS   Author PURVIS MULCH

Quantity   7500   Trim size 6 x 9"   Pages 128

Margins: top   7/8"
         gutter 5/8"

Ink   Black throughout

Stock 60# Warrens Old Style white wove   ☒ supplied by printer   ☐ supplied by Texas Press

Illustrations   100 line illustrations in place on repros

Special Instructions

Bound books needed in Austin not later than April 1, 1977

One set of silverprints folded and trimmed for approval before printing.

Provide   3   sets folded and gathered sheets as soon as ready

☐ for approval before casing in ☒ for Texas Press use only, do not wait for OK

Please provide a schedule for shipping silverprints, F&G's, bound books as soon as possible.

BINDING SPECIFICATIONS

Casebound books

Quantity 7500   ☐ perfect bind   ☒ smyth sewn   Sew in ☐ 32's   ☒ 16's   ☐ round back   ☒ flat back

Crash & paper, no stain, square edges, headbands in _green & white_

Endleaf: Multicolor Carioca Green

Cloth: One piece Columbia Bayside Linen BSL 4647

80   point genuine binders boa'd

Stamping: Black foil on spine only

Repro for stamping die provided by Texas Press. Bindery to provide dies.

Jackets supplied by Texas Press as flat untrimmed printed sheets.

☐ sample case to Texas Press for approval before casing in   ☒ sample case not necessary

Paperback books

quantity NONE   ☐ perfect bound   ☐ smyth sewn in ☐ 32's   ☐ 16's

Covers provided as flat, untrimmed printed sheets by Texas Press. If books are combined run (smyth sewn casebound and perfect bound paperbacks), the paperbacks may be slightly narrower to allow for loss in binding.

ALL BOOKS TO BE INDIVIDUALLY SHRINK WRAPPED.

Shipping

Pack in 275 lb. test cardboard cartons. Mark each carton with title and number of copies contained. Ship skid packed via prepaid motor freight to Austin, Texas. Have driver call 471-3634 or 471-7233 upon arrival in Austin for further delivery instructions.

6 advance copies to be sent as soon as books are bound (6 casebound and 6 paperbacks if combined run).

Manuscript to compositor	September 20
Galleys to Texas Press	October 15
Galleys returned to compositor	November 1
Corrected galleys to Texas Press	November 5
Dummy to compositor for page makeup	November 19
Xerox of dummy to indexer	November 19
Index manuscript to compositor	December 14
Index pages to Texas Press	December 20
Index pages to compositor	December 23 (allow 1 week extra because of holiday)
Complete repros to Texas Press	January 7, 1977
Illustrations due from illustrator	November 5
Illustration photostats ready	December 14
Complete repros to printer with line illustrations in place	January 14
Book blues due from printer	February 11 (ca.)
Books due in Austin	not later than April 1

Author __MULCH__   Title __NO TIME FOR HOUSEPLANTS_____   Bound bks due   Pub date

April 1, 77   May 77

	Manuscript to prod	to comp	Galleys to ed	from ed	to comp	Pages to ed	from ed	to comp	Index to prod	to comp	to ed	from ed
due			10/15	11/1	11/1	11/19	12/14	12/14	12/14	12/14	12/20	12/23
in	9/14	9/20										

	OK pgs/repros to ed	fm ed	to printer	Blues OK	F&Gs recd	Ja/cover copy recd	Art to printer	Vandyke OK	Ja/cover shipped	Die art sent	Category: A ⒷC D
due	1/11	1/12	1/14			12/14	1/28		2/18	1/14	
in											

Corrected galleys due from comp.: 11/5
Complete dummy made up by: 11/19 (xeroxes to editor for indexer, to comp for pasteup)
Illustrations due from Lindlof: 11/5
Illustration photostats done: 12/14

Editor CCW   Designer EW   Illustrator Lindlof   Trim size 6 x 9"   Pages ca 128   Print run: HB 7500   PB --

Compositor In house (Manley)   Printer Kingsport   Binder Kingsport

Typefaces and leading 11/11 Goudy Old Style (VIP)   Stock 60# Warrens Old Style

Binding cloth Bayside Linen BSL 4647   Endleaves Multicolor Carioca Green

Illustrations ca. 100 line illusts

Jackets: quantity 7800   printer PD   Designer EW   Price $6.95   Discount trade Fund --

Series --   ISBN NO: 0—292— FANTAS-Y   Estimated manufacturing cost $13,275

**No Time for
Houseplants**

University of Texas Press

Austin & London

A Busy Person's Guide
to Indoor Gardening

**No Time for
Houseplants**

by Purvis Mulch

International Standard Book Number 0-292-FANTAS-Y

Library of Congress Catalog Card Number 76-PLANT

Copyright © 1977 by the University of Texas Press

Contents

Basic Needs of House Plants

Every plant has its own preferences and requirements for soil type, light, temperature, ventilation, humidity, and several other factors that are within our power to control, or at least to mitigate. It is vitally important for you, as a busy indoor gardener, to understand the basics of each, since a prior understanding will enable you to avoid much work later on while achieving routine success in growing plants.

In addition to understanding these basic needs, you will want to know something about pots and other containers, repotting plants, propagation, and a few other matters which, while not vital to immediate success, will help you to gain further enjoyment in raising better plants.

The Basic House Plant

The major difference between a house plant and an outdoor plant is one of location. All house plants could live and flourish outdoors, in the proper climate. All are derived from forebears which lived, reproduced, and died outdoors, whether on a forest floor in Central Europe or on the bough of a tree in a South American rain forest. Over many centuries of adaptation and evolution, each plant species embraced those characteristics that enabled it to survive; and, even today, every house plant carries within its genetic structure the characteristics of its distant progenitors. Thus the maranta will lose some of its leaves each autumn, even though autumn's weather does not come to the top of the bookshelf where the plant rests, and a cactus, no matter how long it has been fed and watered with unfailing regularity, will continue to hoard food and water within its swollen stems. In plants, old habits may recede, but they are never forgotten.

At no time are these innate plant characteristics more noticeable than during the autumn and winter, when many plants—particularly those from temperate regions—enter a period of dormancy. Then new growth ceases and the plant takes on a listless and washed-out appearance. Other plants, including many of tropical origin, will maintain their bright appearance but will stop growing completely for several months each year, emulating the natural rest periods of their forebears. You will do well to watch for these signs of dormancy and rest and respond to each plant's needs at that time. When any plant enters a dormant or rest period, water should be reduced and fertilizer withheld completely until new growth begins, usually in the late winter or early spring. At that time, water the plant freely and give it normal doses of fertilizer once again, in order to encourage new growth. By your proper treatment of the plant at this time, you will emulate the advent of spring, working with the plant in carrying out its rhythmic cycles.

Chapter 2

Aechmea
fasciata

Cryptanthus
zonatus

Ananas
comosus

Billbergia
nutans

Some plants also are naturally short-lived and will last no more than a year or two in your home despite your careful attention, because their genetic structure dictates a finite life span. Garden annuals, for instance, will germinate, grow to maturity, flower, produce seeds, and die, all in as little as six months. For this reason, very few annuals are selected as house plants. Although a few short-lived plants are cultivated indoors for their unusual characteristics, such as the sensitive plant, which is easily grown from seed, the house plants that have been cultivated over the generations are most often those that will give years of pleasure. Some house plants, in fact, can live to be hundreds of years old.

Still other house plants are attractive when young but grow ungainly or otherwise unattractive when they approach maturity. The only plants of

this kind I have chosen for inclusion in this book are those that are very easy to propagate from cuttings, so that the parent plant may be discarded after a year or two, to be replaced by its children.

From the hundreds of thousands of plant species in the world, those traditionally cultivated as house plants are the relatively few that have shown a wide tolerance to conditions of heat, light, moisture, humidity, and ventilation—in other words, those that can withstand a human environment. They are both attractive to the eye and tough. Still, if you are looking for success with house plants—and particularly success without working hard at it—then you should take some time to learn the characteristics of each plant, recognizing its individual needs and fulfilling them to the best of your ability.

How a Plant Feeds

A plant manufactures nearly all of its food by itself—and not from the "plant food" that you buy for it. Commercial plant food is no more than a combination of certain chemicals (sometimes in an organic base) that are essential to the plant's basic functioning, much as vitamins are essential to human nutrition. But the bulk of a plant's food—the sugar it uses for energy and growth—is manufactured by the plant itself. In the presence of light, the leaves of the plant draw carbon dioxide from the air and water from the roots, converting these into sugar that is then used for energy production or stored for future use.

During this sugar-manufacturing

process, known as *photosynthesis*, several other things happen within the plant. While carbon dioxide is being absorbed, oxygen is being released from the *stomata* (pores) of the leaf surface. (Plants produce not only all of the world's food but most of its atmospheric oxygen as well.) During darkness hours, the process is reversed; some of the atmosphere's oxygen is recaptured by the plant and used to convert stored sugar to energy for growth. Generally, a plant manufactures growth food during the day and does its actual growing at night.

Often, the plant converts its newly manufactured sugar to starch and stores it, reconverting it to sugar as the need arises. Although the starch

can be stored in almost any area of the plant, certain plants have developed specialized storage areas just for this purpose. Cacti and succulents have enlarged stems and leaves for the greatest above-ground storage capacity of any house plant, while other plants have developed underground storage apparatus for this purpose, including bulbs, tubers, corms, and rhizomes. A *bulb* is simply an enlarged underground bud, such as is found with hyacinths, tulips, and onions. A *tuber* is nothing more than an enlarged stem or root: a common potato is a tuber; gloxinias, caladiums, dahlias, and many other common plants are grown from tubers. A *corm* is the enlarged base of a stem. And a *rhizome* is simply a laterally growing, enlarged stem, usually underground. All are used by the plant for food storage, and all can be used to propagate plants, too.

Water is constantly being drawn up through the plant. As it transpires through the stomata of the leaves, a "pulling" action draws more water up through the roots. The water carries with it mineral salts, including all the elements which the plant needs to carry out its complex chemical proc-

esses. The transpiration which takes place in the leaves is similar to perspiration in humans, and it serves a similar purpose—to cool the plant. With house plants, it would be difficult for you to notice this cooling effect. But it is readily apparent when a group of large trees carry out the transpiration process. The cool and fresh feeling you enjoy in a thick woods in summer is primarily the product not of the shade itself but of the transpiration of the millions of leaves overhead.

A plant can seldom absorb too much water, since its vessels and cells can accommodate only so much at a given time; however, the overwatering of a plant can exclude oxygen from the root system, causing wilting of the top portion of the plant. If water is withheld, on the other hand, the plant's cells will gradually collapse, causing wilting of the entire plant. All plants do have protective mechanisms that conserve water in times of drought, however, and can withstand a temporary dry spell. Most wilted house plants will quickly spring back to a normal state when water is again provided.

Parts of the Plant

Stem. The stem serves to support the plant and to contain and direct the vessels that transport water from the roots, and food from the leaves, to every other part of the plant. Most house plants, including philodendron, ivy, and spider plant, have *soft stems*. Such plants must either climb or crawl, since their stems are not strong enough to support an upward-growing structure of significant

height. Other plants have soft but thick stems that enable them to attain good height, although their stems are apt to be subject to breakage. *Woody-stemmed* plants, such as the avocado, poinsettia, and boxwood, are far more sturdy and are usually derived from trees or shrubs of the temperate region. *Canes* are thick stems with hollow or pithy centers. Bamboo is an example of a cane with

Spider mite

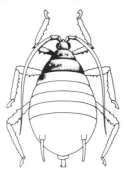

Spider mites, or red spiders, are probably the most virulent attackers of house plants. They thrive in the warm and dry atmosphere of your home and will readily take up residence among your prize plants. Spider mites are too small to be seen with the naked eye. Small white spots on plant leaves may be evidence of spider mite activity, the result of the mites having sucked juices from the leaf surface. If the infestation is sizeable, leaves will gradually take on a fine webbed appearance, have a vaguely fuzzy feeling on their undersides, and eventually feel crumbly. The attack, if unchecked, can prove fatal.

Since spider mites thrive on warmth and dryness, control rests on making them cold and wet. At least in the early stages, they can be elimi-

nated by washing the plant with a mild soap (not detergent) solution, then spraying the entire plant vigorously with cold water, being sure to hit the undersides of leaves where the mites are usually harbored. Repeat this process weekly until the infestation has ceased, and in the meanwhile spray plants daily with a fine mist, preferably in the morning, again being sure to reach the undersides of leaves. If the infestation is truly severe, a solution of rotenone and/or pyrethrum may be used. Both are of low toxicity to warm-blooded creatures, including children, dogs, and cats. (Caution—rotenone is very toxic to fish.) As a last resort, you might choose to use malathion or some other powerful chemical.

43

Key to symbols

Temperature preference

▮ Warm (60–80F.)

▮ Moderate (50–70° F.)

▯ Cool (45–60° F.)

Light Needs

○ Full sun

◐ Tolerates some direct sun

◑ Bright spot with no direct sun

● Tolerates continuous shade

Humidity and soil moisture needs

◆ Higher than room humidity, constantly moist soil

◆ Moderate humidity and soil moisture

◇ Tolerates dry conditions

◇ Low humidity and soil moisture required

Best window

▲ North

➚ South or west

◄ East

Table 2 /Foliage Plants   54

Bromeliads

There are more than eighteen hundred varieties of this popular group, many of which are suitable for growing as house plants. Some of them produce attractive flowers, but most are grown for their striking and variegated leaf patterns. One distinctive feature of the bromeliads is the rosette leaves which form a small water cup, which the plant uses to hold reserve supplies of water in its natural habitat—the crotches of trees in Central and South America. The water cup is an evolutionary survival characteristic. In the home, keep the cup filled with water, changing it weekly to keep it fresh.

A few of the more common genera of bromeliads are *Aechmea, Ananas* (pineapple), *Billbergia, Cryptanthus, Dyckia, Tillandsia* (Spanish moss), and *Vriesia*. ▮○◆◄

Caladium

Caladiums, with their spectacularly colored and variegated leaves, are equally at home in the garden or on the window sill. They are ideal additions to plant groupings on porch or patio in the summer and early autumn. Give them bright light, but not long periods of direct sun in summer, if you want the brightest leaf colors.

Caladiums are grown from tubers, which can be divided easily to produce new plants. Start the tubers in regular potting soil at a very warm temperature—80–90° F.—and move the young plants to a cooler spot when they have appeared. They will attain a height of about one foot. ▮◑◆➚

62

Plants for Cool Conditions
50°–60° at night

Aloe
Aspidistra
Australian Laurel
Azalea
Baby's Tears
Black Pepper
Boxwood
Bromeliads
Cacti
Calceolaria
Camellia
Cape Ivy
Christmas Begonia
Chrysanthemum
Cineraria
Citrus
Creeping Fig
Cyclamen
Easter Lily
English Ivy
Fatshedera
Fiddle-Leaf Fig
Flowering Maple
Freesia
Fuchsia
Geranium
German Ivy

Honeysuckle
Hyacinth
Jasmine
Jerusalem Cherry
Kalanchoe
Kangaroo Vine
Lily-of-the-Valley
Lithops
Miniature Holly
Mother of Thousands
Narcissus
Oxalis
Primrose
Sensitive Plant
Silk Oak
Snake Plant
Spindletree
Tulip
Vinca
Wandering Jew
White Calla Lily

Appendix 4   153

No Time for Houseplants

A Busy Person's Guide to Indoor Gardening

Purvis Mulch

PMS 139

PMS 368

Black

Black

Drawing in black. pot in PMS 139. Plant in PMS 368

Texas Press

University of Texas Press

Date   January 28, 1977

DUST JACKETS/PAPERBACK COVERS PRINTING SPECIFICATIONS

Title   NO TIME FOR HOUSEPLANTS

Job must ship not later than   February 18, 1977

Dust Jackets

Quantity   7800
Trim Size   20 x 9 1/4"
Stock   80# Lustro Offset Enamel Gloss Text
Ink   PMS 139, PMS 368, Black   plus full bleed varnish

Paperback Covers

Quantity   NONE
Trim Size
Stock
Ink   plus full bleed varnish

Description

    Front panel: First line of title and flower pot in PMS 139
                Second line of title and flower in PMS 368
                All else in black including drawing outline.
    Spine: Pressmark in PMS 368
    Back panel: Pot in PMS 139, flower in PMS 368
    Flaps in black

Provide a ☐ vandyke or blue print   ☒ 3M or equivalent

☒ Not necessary to check color with University Press. Match PMS color exactly.

☐ Call   to check color

Allow approximately 1/4" all around for copies sent to bindery.

We have allowed 1/8" on artwork for bleeds.

Ship _____7500_____ flat and untrimmed to bindery

Ship _____300_____ trimmed to size to University Press as soon as job is ready.

Call for labels and shipping instructions.

BA300V   TEXAS PRESS, UNIVERSITY OF TEXAS AT AUSTIN   WORK-IN-PROGRESS   DATE   1/31/78   PAGE   1

REVOLVING PUB. FUND

ISBN   10-999997   NO TIME FOR HOUSEPLANTS

SUNR   104-600   CARD AN   DSCNT   1   LIST PRICE   6.95   NET PR   4.93
            CARD AU   SUB-TITLE   NO TIME FOR HOUSEPLANTS   AUTHOR OR EDITOR   PURVIS MULCH
                       SUBSIDY   0 SOURCE   SERIES
            CARD AK   CAT YEAR   577   PAGES   128   PRINT   7,500   BIND   7,500   MFG COST   13,275

WORKS-IN-PROGRESS   NO TIME FOR HOUSEPLANTS

    NUMBER UNITS   P   7,500   B   7,500   EST MFG COST   13,275.00   EST SUBSIDY   0.00

DATE	JOURNAL	DESCRIPTION	CDE TC	MFG EXP	OTH EXP	TOT EXP	SUB REC
12/15/76	159	ED LIDLOF STUDIOS	551 1	2,658.79	.00	2,658.79	.00
12/29/76	176	EMPRESSION	551 1	752.00	.00	3,410.79	.00
1/11/77	252	WALLACE ENGRAVING	551 1	20.00	.00	3,430.79	.00
1/08/77	357	WALLACE ENGRAVING	551 1	54.00	.00	3,484.79	.00
1/12/77	382	CATHERINE LENOX	551 1	148.00	.00	3,632.79	.00
2/25/77	1229	KINGSPORT PRESS	551 1	9,110.75	.00	12,743.54	.00
12/14/77	5669	UNIVERSITY PRINTING DIV	551 1	525.00	.00	13,268.54	.00

1/31/78   TOTAL PRODUCTION EXPENSE   13,268.54   .00   13,268.54   .00

              EDITORIAL EXPENSE   .00
              PRODUCTION EXPENSE   .00
              MANUFACTURING EXPENSE   13,268.54
              PROMOTION EXPENSE   .00
              OTHER EXPENSE   .00
              AUTHORS EXPENSE   .00

TOTALS   EST MFG COSTS   13,275.00   ACT MFG COSTS   13,268.54   EST SUBS   .00   SUB REC   .00

FUND TOTALS   EST MFG COSTS   13,275.00   ACT MFG COSTS   13,268.54   EST SUBS   .00   SUB REC   .00

XXX END-OF-REPORT XXX

Summary of Promotion Plan: No Time for House Plants

No Time for House Plants will be the lead title in the
catalog the season it is published. It will be treated as a
general audience trade book. We will try to reach "busy"
young singles and professionals as well as the more traditional
home gardening market through our promotional efforts. We
will emphacize the "no-time" aspect of this book in an effort
to differentiate it from the hundreds of other plant books
on the market.

ROUTE SLIP--SPACE ADVERTISING

Job Number _7700 SP_

Journal & Issue _Texas Monthly_

Specifications _4 5/8" X 4 7/8" CRC_

Date Needed _a.s.a.p._

Route: Advertising Manager _CS 12/1_

Marketing Manager _CVS 12/1_

Senior Editor _dot 12/1_

Director _QI 12/2/76_

Advertising Manager _CS 12/2_

Manuscript Editor _QCI 12/2_

Advertising Manager _____

Special Instructions to Production:

— Treat "No Time for House Plants" as headline.

7700 SP

No Time for House Plants

A Busy Person's Guide to Indoor Gardening

By Purvis Mulch

The "no-time" gardener can raise ~~as many as twenty different house~~ _a houseful of healthy, interesting_ plants without spending more than five minutes daily and a half hour every other week caring for them. No Time for House Plants tells you exactly how to do it.

(bibliographic material to come)

University of Texas Press

Post Office Box 7819

Austin 78712

Direct Mail

Copy for mailing piece will be drawn from catalog copy with emphasis on busy people market and information about author's background.

It will offer 46% discount if the establishment orders the tabletop display dump (holds 20 books). The order blank will have no provision for charge cards.

Mailer cost:

$500   production
$195   mailing
$695   total

print 5,000

Mail to:

900 to Texas Assn. of Nurserymen (test mailing)
2000 to selected bookstore (Bowker list)
1000 to selected department store book departments (Bowker list)

Dump Display
Order 500 initially at $1.50 ea.
cost: $750

Direct Sales

Bookstores and major plant stores in major Texas cities

Major bookstores in major cities in New Mexico, Arizona, California, Washington, Oregon and the Northeast.

University of Texas Press
Post Office Box 7819
Austin, Texas 78712
512-471-7233

11/29/76

D̶S̶, I̶T̶H̶ (et al), P̶D̶J̶, B̶S̶, CG

Catalog copy for NO TIME FOR HOUSE PLANTS.

. Same copy for jacket
. no ads on jacket

No Time for House Plants
A Busy Person's Guide to Indoor Gardening
By Purvis Mulch

No matter what color your thumb and no matter how hectic your
schedule, you can brighten your home with healthy, growing
plants.

There are two crucial rules the "no-time" indoor gardener
must follow: ¢hoose tolerant, hardy plants↲ and then give them
the right conditions to grow without your constant attention.
No Time for House Plants tells you exactly how to do it. Purvis
Mulch begins by explaining how plants work and what they need
for success, including potting mixtures, fertilizing (either
organic or chemical), containers, watering, humidity, ventilation,
temperature, light, and pruning. When these conditions are met
at the beginning, countless hours will be saved later in nursing
plants or attempting to track down troubles.

The book lists over (100) beautiful and interesting no-time
plants, including foliage plants, flowering plants, and succulents.
Each listing is accompanied by a description, a finely detailed
line drawing, and a set of read-at-a-glance symbols indicating
temperature, light, moisture, and window placement preferences.
There are graphic illustrations of processes like potting and
pruning which might be unfamiliar to the beginning gardener, and
the chapter devoted to plant ailments and cures includes drawings
of the most common insect pests. There are also special sections on

summer care, artificial light, and maintaining plants while
you're away.

The no-time gardener can raise as many as twenty different
house plants without spending more than five minutes daily and
a half hour every two weeks caring for them. For those who
enjoy a little fussing, there is detailed information on repotting,
propagation, training, dish gardens, planters, bottle gardens
and terrariums, kitchen scrap gardens, and indoor vegetable
gardening.

Purvis Mulch is a very ~~busy~~ person who has been gardening
and writing for over twenty years. He is
the author of _____

<u>Garden Guide</u> and <u>The Earthworm Book</u>.

For catalog:

6 x 9 in., ca. 000 pp., 000 line drawings, 00 black-and-white photographs.
Pub. date LC 00-000 (00000-0) $00.00.

For jacket front:

No Time for House Plants
A Busy Person's Guide to Indoor Gardening
Purvis Mulch

For jacket spine:

No Time for House Plants
Purvis Mulch
Texas Press

Advertising

<u>Texas Monthly</u>

4 5/8 x 4 7/8 $660 - 15% agency discount $561

<u>Apartment Life</u> (mail order section)

2 1/4 x 5 $1200 - 15% $1020

<u>Better Homes & Gardens</u> (mail order section)

2 1/4 x 2 1/2 $463

<u>Saturday Evening Post</u> (classified)

25 words @ $2 per word $50

<u>Publishers Weekly</u>

Will share full page with other trade titles

in announcement issue $250

Newspaper advertising in major dailies in conjunction with

author parties and television appearances $600

TOTAL: $2944

Title _No Time for House Plants_

Author or editor _Mulch_

Publication date _0/0/77_

Date to Business Office _0/0/77_

Date shipped _0/0/77_   Postage _____

Total number of books _132_

Special Instructions:

Send one book each unless otherwise indicated on label.

All books outside U.S. and Canada should be sent Air Mail.

— Review cards as usual
       $00.00 cloth

— news release w/ each book

Authorized by _____Chris Gray_____
                    0/0/77

Flower & Garden	House Beautiful
Ms.	Mademoiselle
Playboy	House & Garden
Sphere	Town & Country
Vogue	Cosmopolitan
Esquire	Glamour
Good Housekeeping	Avant Gardener
National Observer	Home & Country
New Woman	National Gardener
Plants Alive	Plants & Gardens
News & Information Service-UT Austin	(Brooklyn Botanical Garden)

Cumulative Book Index
Citizen Journal, Arlington, Tx
The El Paso Times
San Antonio Light
Albuquerque Tribune
Chicago Sun-Times
Hartford Times
Memphis Commercial Appeal
Pittsburgh Press
Seattle Times
Mr. John Dawson, AUPG, London
Abilene Reporter News
Corpus Christi Caller-Times
Houston Chronical
Victoria Advocate
Texas Monthly
Scrooge & Marley, Gene Shalit
The Arizona Republic
Chicago Tribune
Indepen. Press-Telegram
Miami Herald
The Plain Dealer
San Francisco Chronicle
Blackwell North America
A L A Booklist
Amarillo News-Globe
Courier-Times-Telegraph
Fort Worth Star-Telegram
San Angelo Standard Times
Waco News Tribune
Mother Earth News
Charlotte Observer
Detroit News
Los Angeles Times
The News, Birmingham, Alabama
San Francisco Examiner
Bro-Dart Books
The Kirkus Service, Inc.
Daily Texan
El Paso Herald-Post
San Antonio Express & News
Books West
Baltimore Sun
Christian Science Monitor
Kansas City Star
Minneapolis Tribune
Richmond Times-Dispatch
Tulsa World

Austin American-Statesman
Dallas News
Pasadena News-Citizen
Atlantic Monthly
Boston Globe
Denver Post
LA Herald-Examiner
The New Mexican
Rocky Mountain News
Washington Post
Choice
Austin Citizen
Fort Worth Press
Saunders Book Store
John Barkham Reviews
Book Review Critics, NY Times
United Press International
Boston Herald American
Detroit Free Press
Little Rock Gazette
New Orleans Times-Picayune
Southern Exposure
The Baker & Taylor Co.
Library of Congress
Library Journal
Avalanche-Journal
Dallas Times Herald
Houston Post
Southwest Books
Bookletter
Atlanta Journal-Constitution
Cleveland Press
Oklahoma City Oklahoman
Milwaukee Journal
Portland Oregonian
Star-Tribune Publications
Publisher's Weekly
Beaumont Enterprise
Galveston News
Palestine Herald-Press
American Scholar
Universal Features
Chicago Daily News
Hartford Courant
Louisville Courier-Journal
Philadelphia Inquirer
Seattle Post-Intelligencer
Book People

University of Texas Press

POST OFFICE BOX 7819, AUSTIN, TEXAS 78712, (512) 471-7233

AUTHOR INFORMATION

The promotion of a book is necessarily a mutual effort. The effectiveness of our promotional copy—for jacket, catalogue, publicity releases, flyers, brochures, and space advertising—depends directly upon the thoroughness with which you complete this questionnaire. We urge you to develop your replies to whatever extent necessary to give us adequate information. Please fill out this form on the typewriter if possible. If for any reason you cannot supply portions of the requested information, please indicate your omission so we will know you have not overlooked the item. Return the completed form as soon as possible. Thank you.

Date   August 9, 1976

1. Name (a) in full (required for copyright registration)

   (b) as you wish it to appear on title page

2. If the title page is to carry the names of any other authors, editors, or contributors, please supply their names here as used on title page

3. Title of book (or manuscript)

   No Time for House Plants: A Busy Person's Guide to Indoor Gardening

4. Series (if applicable)   none

5. Required for copyright registration: legal address, citizenship, and place of birth. Please indicate which address is to be used for correspondence concerning this book.

   (a) Office address and zip code   Office phone

   (b) Home address and zip code   Home phone

(c) Citizenship   USA
   If not native, when did you come to the USA?
   Naturalized citizen?   When?

(d) Place and date of birth

6. Social Security number

7. Present academic connection, position, or occupation

8. Previous positions (with dates)

9. Education (please include dates of degrees) and honors

10. Learned and honorary societies to which you belong. Please separate present from past and include all relevant offices held.

11. Special research, experience, or travel for this book; relevant military, government, or other official positions. Also include countries, cities, and states in which you have lived, with approximate dates.

    No field research for this book.   Lived in Pennsylvania, 1933–1957; Iowa, 1957–1961; Pennsylvania, 1961–1963; New Jersey, 1963–1965;

12. Special fields of interest. Any other pertinent biographical data for use on book jackets, etc.

    Organic gardening; solid waste recycling; environmental issues

[14, continued]

The chapter on understanding house plants is critically important to the "no-time" system, since it details the initial requirements plants need for success, including potting mixtures, fertilizing, containers, watering, humidity, ventilation, temperature, light, and pruning. When these conditions are met at the very beginning, countless hours will be saved later in nursing plants or attempting to track down troubles.

There is a separate chapter devoted to plant troubles and cures, and special sections on artificial light, summer care, and lists of plants for various conditions of light and temperature. For those who wish to devote a little more time to raising house plants, there is detailed information on repotting, propagation, training, dish gardens, planters, bottle gardens and terrariums, kitchen scrap gardens, and growing vegetables indoors.

The bulk of the book, however, comprises listings of more than a hundred "easy" foliage plants, flowering plants, and succulents, including cacti, giving light, soil moisture, and humidity require-ments for each.

For the home owner or apartment dweller who wants to raise several dozen attractive house plants while spending only a few minutes a day in caring for them, this book will tell everything that is necessary to know in order to achieve success.

---

13. Titles of your publications (including forthcoming) and publishers. Indicate (with *) which two or three of your books and articles are most important. Attach list if lengthy. (Please indicate book club adoptions, paperbeck reprints, serializations, and foreign editions).

Title	Publisher	Year	Approx. Sale
* WISCONSIN GARDEN GUIDE, Wisconsin House, Ltd., 1975; 15,000 in print			
* THE EARTHWORM BOOK, Rodale Press, Inc., scheduled for 1977			
"The Earthworm Czar," Organic Gardening & Farming, Sept. 1976			
"Gardening for the Late Bloomer," Mother Jones, June 1976			
"To Garden in the City, Organize Community Plots," House Beautiful, April 1976			
Other articles in Camping Journal, Mobile Life, other magazines			

14. Description of your book that might be used to inform its potential readers (literate nonspecialists as well as students in the field) about its subject matter, the reasons for its importance, your method of approach to that subject matter, and your conclusions (300 or more words). *We hope you will bear in mind that this information will be our primary source for preparing jacket, catalogue, and advertising copy.* Please do not merely refer us to your preface or other parts of your manuscript, for the manuscript is often unavailable at the time the information is needed.

I have been gardening and writing about gardening for more than twenty-three years. In this time, my major emphasis has been on indoor plants, particularly vegetables. I have always had a few outdoor plants, but never took much interest in them and, so, had very limited success.

In 1973, with the purchase of a new house, I was determined to increase my house plant population. Still, I realized that, with my busy schedule, I would not have much time to devote to indoor plants. I was frequently gone for long periods of time, and many days, even while in town, I simply have no time to fuss with plants.

I therefore sought to find methods to raise interesting and beautiful house plants with the least amount of effort. All the house plant books I checked, however, were apparently written by enthusiasts who spent unending hours in careful watering, potting, repotting, prop-agating, tying up, inducing to flowering, humidifying, bathing, and even talking to their plants, in an effort to get them to grow. There was no book for the casual house plant grower.

There is now such a book. By researching many sources, and with the aid of personal experimentation and past experience, I have narrowed down the crucial requirements for a "no-time" indoor house plant population. The research yielded two cardinal rules: Choose plants that are tolerant of adverse conditions, and then give them the right conditions to grow without your constant attention.

The implementation of these rules form the crux of this book. I ex-plain how to choose plants, tell which are the easiest to grow, and explain the conditions of light, soil moisture, humidity, and temper-ature that each of more than a hundred indoor plants requires. I explain, in short, how your house plants can live well without your constant attention and painstaking devotion.

(more, separate sheet attached)

15. Particular points to be emphasized in promotion, including details on new material or new interpretation of old material as compared with previously published studies in the field. (This is very important for a variety of sales and promotional purposes.)

There are hundreds of house plant books in print; this is, so far as I know, the first to take this approach.

16. Does any section of your book lend itself to excerpting? Have any sections been previously published? If so, by whom?

Chapter 2 could be excerpted, as a short guide to the care of house plants in general.

17. Artwork. Specify illustrations, figures, photos, etc. that might be used in advertising to stimulate interest.

The photos on hand are not spectacular. The ones depicting bottle gardens are perhaps the most interesting.

18. Audiences for your book: *be as specific as possible* and list in order of importance. Also list names and addresses of persons whose good opinion of the book might broaden its audience—those to whom, for instance, advance copies of the book might be sent by us for comments that could be quoted in advertising. Endorsements from both foreign and domestic scholars and critics should be considered.

Single people, working people, apartment-dwellers would constitute the major audience for the book.

19. Other books on the same subject (with dates of publication and publisher if possible; compare with yours if possible).

There are dozens of books on house plants published each year. It would serve no purpose to list them all, even if I could.

20. Courses for which your book might be used as a text or collateral reading. Please list those professors and their institutions that should be approached with a view to the classroom adoption of the book.

The only course for which I could foresee this book's adoption is a short course in growing house plants. It is meant for a lay audience and not suitable for students in botany and/or horticulture, who will have advanced far beyond this book's scope.

21. Special groups to circularize. Please give us the names and addresses of professional societies and organizations that will be interested in the book. Include, if possible, the names and addresses of persons to whom we can apply for very specialized lists; indicate (with *) which lists you can supply yourself. *Your efforts in this area can be especially valuable to our marketing success.*

Apartment Ideas subscription list; other general magazines with a young, professional, and largely single audience--Mother Jones, Esquire, Ms, Rolling Stone, Playgirl, etc.

22. Individuals to circularize. Attach to this form. You may supply as many names and addresses of individuals as you wish.   none

23. At which association conventions might it be appropriate to exhibit your book? Which conventions do you normally attend?

ALA, ABA

24. How many circulars could you use for your own purposes?
100

25. Suggested advertising media. Please list magazines and scholarly journals that accept advertising, where notice of your book might be especially effective. List in order of importance. (Include publications outside the USA—especially Canada and Europe.)

Professional Journals   General Magazines

NYTBR
Apartment Ideas
Mother Jones
Organic Gardening & Farming
Ms
Esquire
Better Homes & Gardens
House Beautiful

26. Reviewing media. List the most important scholarly and general publications that might review your book. You may attach a list of publications of secondary importance if you wish.

Scholarly Publications   General Publications

Organic Gardening & Farming   Milwaukee Journal
Horticulture   Chicago Tribune
Flower & Garden   Los Angeles Times
Better Homes & Gardens   Village Voice
House Beautiful   Mother Jones
House & Garden   Rolling Stone

27. Hometown or other newspapers (and editors, columnists) to whom you or your book is news.

28. Bookstores and/or radio/TV commentators to whom you or your book is known.

29. Prizes and awards for which your book might be eligible.

don't know of any

30. Photograph. Please supply one or more copies of whatever recent black-and-white photograph (preferably 5 x 7 inches or larger) that you would prefer we use for promotion purposes. Note: Many prizes and award competition entries must be accompanied by photograph. Photograph will not be returned. Photo enclosed _____ (or date when we can expect one).

call when needed

Thank you,

Marketing Department
University of Texas Press

NO TIME FOR HOUSE PLANTS

Book Club Rights

After receiving docket material, the editorial fact sheet, and other pertinent information on the book (through various discussions with the acquisitions editor and marketing), the rights and permissions manager would decide if book club rights should be sought.

As a trade title with a projected large audience, the book seems a likely candidate. At the earliest possible date, I (the r&p manager) would request extra sets of galleys to be ordered by the production department. Then, inquiries would be sent to the appropriate book clubs when galleys are received. A covering letter would accompany the (bound) set of galleys explaining the general content of the ms. with a brief note about the author and why we feel it would appeal to the book club membership. Since this manuscript is a basic introduction to house plants, I would stress its simplistic style and easy comprehensible nature as well as elaborating on the excellent quality of the book's illustrations which most plant enthusiasts find to be useful and desireable. I would also emphasize its potential value for the working man or woman with an interest in plants but a heavy schedule which leaves little time to devote to plant care. Finally, the letter would include the list price, bound book date, publication date, and the (deadline) date by which we would need a response from the book club if they intend to print with us. Although a response might take six to eight weeks, a follow-up letter or phone call would be made perhaps two weeks before the actual deadline (if no response has been received at that time).

Possible book clubs to investigate would be the American Garden Guild Book Club, Better Homes & Gardens Crafts Club, Woman Today Book Club, Organic Gardening Book Club, and, perhaps, one of the subsidiary clubs from, say, Prentice Hall, Inc.

In actuality, I would not be too hopeful of selling these rights. The field is already flooded with books on most every aspect of growing house plants and acceptance by a book club would require a very strong and distinguished manuscript. This particular manuscript does not seem to be especially unique or enlightening from what has previously appeared on the market.

AUTHOR PARTY

We assume for our purposes that Mulch is willing to pay
his way to Texas in order to promote the book.

The author appears in major plant stores (those that stock
plant books) in Houston, San Antonio, Dallas, Fort Worth, and
Austin. He will be available at the store all day Saturday
to autograph books and to give plant buyers advice on how to
care for their plants the "no-time" way. The announcement
will stress that Mulch will be there to give his expert advice
to anyone who has questions about plants. The plant stores
will use their lists for the announcements, and the Press will
pay for printing and postage.

We will also send news releases to local media. We will try
to get Mulch on noon time chat shows the Friday preceeding the
autograph day to talk about the book, the autograph party and
to demonstrate some of the processes explained in the book.

UNIVERSITY OF TORONTO PRESS

Table of Contents

Some Notes on Toronto's Log

<u>No Time For House Plants</u> would not have been seriously considered by Toronto for publication in real life, and we would have recommended to Purvis Mulch that he approach a commercial house. As a result, and also because of the constraints imposed by the limited number of pages available for the log, certain steps in our procedures are omitted altogether.

When a manuscript first arrives in house it is immediately logged and a preliminary publications docket opened for it. It is then placed with the house editor into whose area of responsibility it falls, who is responsible for acknowledging to the author its arrival and giving a first indication of what will follow. Frequently a manuscript is rejected outright after an editorial reading for any of a number of valid reasons and the author so informed. If the house editor sees possibilities for us in the manuscript it will be sent to a first outside reader for a report. Depending on the nature of this report and on whether subsidy is to be sought for the work from one or other of the sources of such subsidy, a second reader may be sought or the manuscript sent to one of the subsidizing councils for their scrutiny and report.

When the house editor is satisfied with the reports, a decision to publish form is started (page 254) and this is sent, together with the manuscript and the readers' reports, to the sales and promotion departments. The sales manager makes a marketing assessment of the book, usually in more than one combination of price, discount and quantity, notes the special requirements if any, and passes to the promotion manager who notes if any special promotional costs may be involved and also any special promotional requirements.

The manuscript and copies of the decision to publish form are then circulated to the internal committee (representing management, sales, promotion, editorial, production and design) for approval. The Production Manager obtains an estimate and the last page of the decision to publish form is completed so that the full picture of the marketing possibilities and costs can be seen in the one form. The house editor presents the manuscript, the reports and the financial picture to the Manuscript Review Committee. If the work is approved, the house editor draws up a contract with the author, and editing and production proceed.

Numerous internal forms are not to be seen in the log. Such forms include the production record, the form circulated with the jacket design, blurb, the final proofs and etc. and the card controlling the final quantity to be printed, bound, or held unbound, and the complete promotion record.

A final word about the change in sex of the author, a thoroughly 'unreal' event. In this case it was occasioned by a memo from the University of North Carolina Press which gave the author's sex as female, and it was accepted happily by our promotion manager as a means of greatly expanding the promotional possibilities of the book at minimum expense.

Editorial comments (including strengths, weaknesses, special features, origins, of ms)

Author is a plain practical person who knows how to choose house plants that are easy to look after and is confident, as I am, that there are a great many people who would benefit from her knowledge. The main problem is that she cannot express herself clearly, mostly because her knowledge of grammar is faulty. But we have here a short, practical book which with severe editing should enjoy a long life and have a reasonable share of a large market.

Information about the author (notable qualifications, honours, previous publications, etc.)

Previous outdoor gardening book very well received.

Readers' names and present affiliations (with date report received)
T.H. Everett, Senior Horticulture specialist, New York Botanical Gardens
D. Levine, Owner, The Potted Plant, Chapel Hill, N.C.

Physical description of manuscript   Number of manuscript pages 136
Illustrations supplementary to text [XX] essential [XX] can be grouped [ ] must be through text [XX]
number of halftones ____   number of line illustrations 15
special artwork required ____
Tabular material number of tables ____   Formula setting none [ ] limited [ ] extensive [ ]
Special design/production considerations (including any use of colour)

Markets expected for this book
Will appeal particularly to the well-educated and serious reader. Big city and college market particularly. Good library possibilities also.
Sales experience of comparable books published by UTP

Author	Title	ISBN	Pub date	Price	1st yr	2nd yr	3rd yr	Total to date
Not Applicable								

Competitive books from other publishers
(Author, title, publisher, publication date, page length, price, sales history if known)
Numerous, particularly from specialized publishers such as Sunset Books.

How does this manuscript differ from such competition?
This work will appeal to serious people as it is well organized and amusingly written and conveys much essential information in a short space.
Recommendations re subsidiary rights, special promotion, prepublication prices, etc.
Some opportunity for Book Club sales.

_____   _____
Date   Area editor

University of Toronto Press
Decision to Publish

Date started 25 Nov 1976
Docket 1234

Author(s)/~~Editor(s)~~ Purvis Mulch
with affiliations

Title [ ] tentative [XX] final No Time for House Plants: a Busy Person's Guide to Indoor Gardening
Series
Printed pages (per estimate) 136

Brief description
This is a sprightly short book clearly and amusingly written and the sub-title A busy person's guide to indoor gardening well explains its purpose. The market for the work covers all of North America but it will have a particular appeal to the well educated and should enjoy a particularly good sale in university communities. There are a number of books of a similar nature, of course, and it will be necessary to ensure that the promotion of the book is clearly aimed at the most likely elements of the market - such as university communities. This work is not like any other in our list but fits well into our general program of publishing good books for the general public on a commercial basis.

Projected schedule: manuscript complete in house now [XX] anticipated date _____
recommended publishing season Spring 1977

Outside assistance: subsidy available [ ] anticipated [ ] to be applied for [ ]
from HRCC [ ] SSRCC [ ] block grants [ ] other _____
amount (if firm) $_____
totally underwritten (sponsored) by _____
co-publication government [ ] import [ ] rights available all

On the basis of projections in this form, addition of this title to the List of Publications following Option _____ is recommended by:

Comments

_____ Date _____ Area editor

_____ Date _____ General Editor

_____ Date _____ Manager, Sales and Distribution

_____ Date _____ Associate Director

Approved by
Date _____ Director

Approved by Manuscript   Agreement concluded _____   ISBN cloth _____ paper _____
Review Committee
Date _____   Date _____   Subject classification _____

PUBLISHING BUDGET

MULCH

	CLOTH OPT. 1	OPT. 2	OPT. 3	PAPER OPT. 4	OPT. 5	OPT. 6
Suggested list price	$ 10.95	$ 9.95	$	$	$	$
Average discount	38 %	38 %	%	%	%	%
Net proceeds	$ 6.79	$ 6.17	$	$	$	$
Sales in units	7,250	9,500				
Sales	$49,220	$ 58,615				

	OPT. A	OPT. B	OPT. C
Sales income – cloth	49,220	58,615	
– paper			
Total	49,220	58,615	

Costs:

Production
	OPT. A	OPT. B	OPT. C
Copy editing (78 hrs @ $11.75)			
Design (40 hrs @ $15.00)	920	920	
Production (30 hrs @ $15.00)	600	600	
Mfg. cost – compilation	450	450	
– variable	5,244	5,244	
Other	11,837	15,466	
Total production	19,051	22,680	

Selling
	OPT. A	OPT. B	OPT. C
Special promotion	2,500	2,500	
Royalties @ % 10	4,922	5,862	
Overhead @ % 40	19,688	23,446	
Commission @ % of sales 5000/65000	3,285	3,881	
Mark-up 10	4,922	5,862	
Total selling	35,317	41,551	

	OPT. A	OPT. B	OPT. C
Total costs	54,368	64,231	
Net income (shortfall)	(5,148)	(5,616)	
Edition sale, if any			
Total net income (shortfall)	$	$	

Subsidy required, if any

Sources of subsidy
Subsidized publications budget
Other

	OPT. A	OPT. B	OPT. C
Overhead	$ 19,688	$ 23,446	
Less UTP subsidy	5,148	5,616	
Net contribution to overhead	$ 14,540	$ 17,830	

Date 25/1/77   Publications Co-ordinator

Appraisal of manuscript editing requirements, given current state of ms

Ms editing budget in-house hours 60   freelance fees _____

Projected schedule, assuming ms will be complete in house on anticipated date
editing to begin Dec. 1, 1976   edited ms ready for production Jan. 21, 1977
(Revised projected schedule to be circulated when complete ms received)

Extraordinary costs for ms editing: artwork [ ] to be absorbed by UTP [X] charged to author [ ]
charged against royalties [ ] other   Est. amount $

Date _____ Executive Editor

Date _____ General Editor

SALES-OPTIONS

	Cloth 1	2	3	Paper 4	5	6
Price/Discount	10.95	9.95				
	40	40				
Wholesalers	750	1,000				
Bookstores (incl. flower shops)	5,000	6,500				
College Bookstores	1,000	1,500				
Libraries	500	500				
Edition						
Export (other than U.S.)						
Other						
Total Sales	7,250	9,500				
Frees	250	500				
Printing run	7,500	10,000				

SALES FORECAST

	Cloth	Paper
First year	4,000	6,000
Second year	2,000	3,000
Third year	1,250	500
Fourth & Fifth year		
Total	7,250	9,500

Recommended publication date Spring 1977   published when 12 months - 2 years
Paperback prospects excellent   sewn copies 25   other
Need for advance jacket covers, 250   page proofs 6

Subsidiary markets [X] book clubs [X] serialization [ ] translation [ ] excerpts [ ] co-publication [ ]
Special plans and budget requirements

Promotion } Extra $2,500 (Total $5,000)
Advertising }
Direct Mail nil

Date _____ Manager, Promotion   Date _____ Manager, Sales & Distribution

WHEREBY IT IS MUTUALLY AGREED BETWEEN THE PARTIES HERETO for themselves and their respective executors, administrators, assigns, or successors as follows:

1. The Author hereby grants and assigns to the Publisher the sole and exclusive world rights to copyright, produce, and publish in book form and as hereinafter provided, subject to the following conditions, the literary work at present entitled and described as follows:

No Time for House Plants: A Busy Person's Guide to Indoor Gardening

2. The Author , if   not already done so, agree to deliver to the Publisher, within   from the date of this agreement the manuscript of the said work in its final form properly prepared for the press, including illustrative material as follows:

Receipt of the manuscript is hereby acknowledged.

3. The Author hereby undertakes that the material submitted for publication is (will be) original and free from any copyright restrictions, or where not original with the Author, that it will be free from copyright restrictions except as may be set forth in writing to the Publisher at the time of submission. The Author further guarantees that he will indemnify and hold harmless the Publisher from and against all claims, demands and actions that may be made against the Publisher, and against all costs, damages, expenses and liability sustained or incurred by the Publisher, by reason of any unlawful or libellous matter contained in the said work.

4. The Publisher undertakes, subject to his editorial approval, to publish the said manuscript at his own expense in such style or styles as he deems best suited to its sale, provided however that the cost of making Author's corrections or revisions in the text after typesetting may be charged against the Author's future royalties. However such charges shall not include those for correcting deviations from copy by the compositors, which shall remain the responsibility of the Publisher.

5. The Publisher agrees to deliver to   the Author on publication six (6) copies of the published work free of charge, and to supply additional copies for the Author's personal use at the full trade discount from the list price at which the book is currently being sold. Two free copies shall also be delivered by the Publisher to the National Library, Ottawa.

Title No Time for House Plants: A Busy Person's Guide to Indoor Gardening

Memorandum of Agreement

between

Purvis Mulch, ..., Box 1379, ...

Hereinafter referred to as the Author

OF THE ONE PART

and

UNIVERSITY OF TORONTO PRESS

Hereinafter referred to as the Publisher

OF THE OTHER PART

(i) On any income from rights not otherwise set forth in this agreement, fifty per cent (50%) of the amount received, said percentage to be distributed in the proportions indicated in 8(a) where there is more than one author.

9. The Publisher shall render annual statements of account to the Author for each year ending the thirtieth day of April or before the first day of September following, and shall at the same time make any payments due to the Author hereunder in respect of the preceding accounting period.

10. This agreement shall not be deemed to have been completed until two copies (or more if so provided for elsewhere in this agreement) have been duly completed by all parties to it and one copy has been actually received at the editorial and administrative offices of the Publisher.

11. Where the work referred to in this agreement has been approved for publication under subsidy from the Publications Fund of the Publisher, the Publisher's obligation to publish shall be conditional on such subsidy being available from the Publications Fund at the time of publication.

12. Should sales of the work referred to herein fail to justify, in the opinion of the Publisher, its re-publication, the Publisher may cancel this contract by forwarding a written notice to this effect by registered mail to the last known address of the Author. On receipt of such notice the Author shall have the right to purchase from the Publisher at half the cost of original production the plates of the said work if such are in existence and at the disposal of the Publisher. It is understood that cost of original production of the plates shall include the cost of typesetting. If the Author shall decide to exercise this right he must also purchase at the same time from the Publisher the bound stock of said work then on hand at one-third of the current catalogue or retail price of said work, and the sheet stock at one-fifth of such price. If there are no plates of said work in existence, but if the type of the said work is standing, then the Publisher shall make said type available to the Author at one-half the cost of setting and compilation plus the full cost of the type metal. If the Author has not exercised his rights under this provision within three months of the mailing of the notice as specified herein, the Publisher may destroy the plates and/or distribute the type and/or dispose of the stock as he sees fit without royalty or other compensation to the Author. If the Publisher for any reason should subsequently decide to reissue said work, he may do so, but only under the royalty provisions and other conditions specified in this agreement.

6. Should it at any time in the future, in the opinion of the Publisher, become necessary to offer a revised edition of the said work the Author agrees to prepare at his own expense the manuscript of such revision as may be necessary, and should the Author by reason of death or otherwise be unable or unwilling to prepare such a revision then the Publisher may charge any editorial payments he may have to make for such revision by another editor or editors against the Author's future royalties.

7. The Publisher will have the right to make such editorial revisions as in his opinion may be considered necessary to render the finished work suitable for publication.

8. In consideration of the rights herein granted, the Publisher agrees to pay to the Author or to his duly authorized representatives the following royalties on books sold by him except as otherwise provided in this contract:

(a) Ten per cent (10%) of the list price on the first 5,000 (five thousand) copies sold; twelve and one-half per cent (12 1/2%) of the list price on the next 5,000 (five thousand) copies sold; and fifteen per cent (15%) on all copies sold thereafter.

(b) Where bound copies or sheets are sold for export from Canada at less than the domestic booksellers' normal net price the total royalty payable under this agreement shall be calculated at ten per cent (10%) on the price actually received by the Publisher (after deduction of selling discounts and commissions,) said royalties to be divided in the proportions indicated in 8(a) where there is more than one author.

(c) On sales of all or parts or digests of the said work, subsequent to publication, to newspapers or periodicals for publication therein, fifty per cent (50%) of the amount received, said percentage to be divided in the proportions indicated in 8(a) where there is more than one author.

(d) On sales of the right to publish in countries outside Canada for a lump sum or royalty all or parts of said work fifty per cent (50%) of the amount received after commissions if any, said percentage to be divided in the proportions indicated in 8(a) where there is more than one author.

(e) On sales of all or parts of the said work, subsequent to publication, for reprint in other books, fifty per cent (50%) of the amount received, said percentage to be divided in the proportions indicated in 8(a) where there is more than one author.

(f) On sales of editions for a lump sum or a royalty to Book Clubs, fifty per cent (50%) of the amount received, said percentage to be divided in the proportions indicated in 8(a) where there is more than one author.

(g) On sales of dramatic, motion and talking picture, and broadcasting rights fifty per cent (50%) of the amount received, said percentage to be divided in the proportions indicated in 8(a) where there is more than one author.

(h) No royalties shall be payable on copies supplied free of charge by the Publisher in the course of promoting sales of the published work.

(i) On sales of the right to translate into foreign languages, fifty per cent (50%) of the amount received, said percentage to be divided in the proportions indicated in 8(a) where there is more than one author.

PROVISION FOR PAPERBOUND EDITION OF

Purvis Mulch, 'No Time for House Plants: A Busy Person's Guide to Indoor Gardening'

With respect to the publishing agreement for the above work dated it is further agreed as follows:

In the event that the Publisher issues in addition to a regular case-bound edition of the said work, and/or in addition to case-bound reprinted editions of the said work, whether or not the latter be similar in format to the original edition, a paperbound edition of the said work at a catalogue price of *less than one-half* the original catalogue price of the first case-bound edition of the said work, then the royalties and/or other income payable on the sales of copies or sheets *of the paperbound edition (only)* shall be calculated at one-half of the rates provided in this agreement with respect to sales of the first case-bound edition, it being further understood and agreed:

(*a*) that the numbers of copies or sheets sold in such a paperbound edition shall not be counted as part of any formula for accelerated royalty percentage payments on sales of the regular edition where such an accelerated royalty formula keyed to accumulated sales may have been provided for under the original agreement, and

(*b*) that all other terms and conditions respecting the first case-bound edition shall apply to the paperbound edition, and

(*c*) that "paperbound edition" as used in this supplementary agreement shall include any paperbound edition offered *bona fide* by the Publisher, his agents, or customers as a part of a series of generally similar paperbound books, whether or not acetate or similar transparent lamination is used on such paper bindings, provided however that case-bound editions, whether or not paper is used as the binding material, shall not be treated as "paperbound" editions for the purpose of this supplementary agreement.

IN WITNESS WHEREOF the parties hereto have hereunto set their hands and seals this 27th day of December 1976

.... AUTHOR

UNIVERSITY OF TORONTO PRESS

A. N. Oher
.... PUBLISHER

IN WITNESS WHEREOF the parties hereto have hereunto set their hands and seals this 27th day of December 1976

.... AUTHOR

UNIVERSITY OF TORONTO PRESS

A. N. Oher
.... PUBLISHER

Manuscript / Project Information Sheet   Date 12 Dec. 1976
                                          revised ____

author Mulch, Purvis   citizenship/residence U.S.
title No Time for House Plants: a busy person's guide to indoor working/final
                                          gardening ____   number ____
series n/a
subsidy: UTP ___ other ___   manufacture required: UTP ___ USA X other ___
total no of ms pages 168   no to come ____   expected run 7,500
other ____

Preliminary Pages

half title ____ title X frontis ____ copyright X dedication ____
series list ____ contents X list of illustrations X list of abbreviations ____
preface X foreword ____ acknowledgments ____
other ____   estimated no of printed prelim pages 6

Text

total no of chapters 7 no to come ____ no of parts ____ part titles ____
footnotes ____ notes: at end of chapter ____ at end of book X captions yes
headings 8 no of levels ____ tabular matter ____ mathematical setting ____
charts of graphs ____ maps ____ extracts ____ poetry ____
foreign language setting ____ kinds ____
special symbols X other ____

Further Comments

End Matter

total no of appendixes ____ to come (length) ____ notes ____ series list ____
bibliography X to come (length) ____ glossary ____ to come (length) ____
index ____ number ____ estimated no of printed pages ____
other ____

Illustrations
no of halftones 30 estimated no of pages ____ to come ____ colour ____
no of line cuts ____ estimated no of pages ____ to come ____
artwork required diagrams and line drawings
other ____

MS Pages with Special Problems ____   Other Notes ____

Editor ____

Mr. Marshall
re: No Time for House Plants

This experiment is proving to be more interesting than even I had expected it to be. At this stage it has indeed assumed a larger dimension. I greatly hope that this exchange of correspondence, containing the author's response to the readers' reports, will be shown to directors and accountants, for it illustrates a problem in appraisal which cannot be solved, and is in fact made far worse, by indiscriminate budgetary constrictions.

The author of "No Time for House Plants" is clearly a plain, practical man who knows how to choose house plants that are easy to look after and is confident that there are a great many people who would benefit from his knowledge. (He is right. There are, and I number myself among them.) His main problem is that he cannot express himself clearly, mostly because his knowledge of grammar is faulty. I have thought of him up to this point as a sensible, even-tempered fellow, not self-conscious about his knowledge but concerned rather to share it effectively, and I have assumed that he would be open to suggestions about his writing out of natural respect for a branch of knowledge which he does not command.

The editor at University of North Carolina Press who handled this appraisal has my sympathy. The second reader turned out to be a judge of the blunt and scornful sort. (I had supposed that these irascible persons were largely confined to the field of

bibliography, but I now see that I was naïve.) The appraising editor, left to his own devices, would undoubtedly have chosen to incorporate this reader's criticisms in a letter of his own composition, suggesting and persuading rather than challenging and denouncing. But if he had done that, he would have incurred severe criticism for running up the costs of appraisal. So he decided, resignedly, to send the author a copy of the report in its raw state. The result is an author so self-conscious and tetchy that it is going to be very difficult to get him to listen to suggestions about his writing. To make matters worse, the effect of the third report is to lend support to the notion that photographs and line drawings can compensate for lack of clarity in the text. They cannot, and the belief that they can is the reason why most hand-books are so frustrating to use. I would expect that a book published by a university press would set a new standard.

I have not got the manuscript beside me as I write, but I remember from my first reading that the account of double-potting was impossible to understand. Hence it is only too likely that readers would think the author meant them to sit out in the backyard waiting for the pail to fill with rainwater, as he so vehemently protests in this response. They will in fact interpret this as a humane suggestion, a lovely restful thing to do while trying to recover from the effort of carrying bathtubs around the house. I refer to the sentence beginning on page 2 of the response to the second reader: "Using the bathtub as the container, anyone can carry 20 to 25 plants into the bathroom and immerse them in five minutes." I remark, with some feeling, that even if I had a free-standing bathtub (but mine is built into the wall and floor) I would not be strong enough to carry it around my apartment even if it would go through the doors, but it wouldn't. Another confusing description is contained in the next sentence: "After a half-hour or so of soaking, the water is drained...." Water is by nature soaked; what does it need to be soaked some more for? To carry the care of plants to this extreme is only going to discourage people who would profit by this prospective book.

The result of skimping on the rightful costs of appraisal is plain to see. More money will be spent on the copyediting than would otherwise have been necessary. The appraisal editor knows that and feels bad about it. The copyeditor will soon know it and will feel bad too, but not quite so bad, for he knows he is just the PBI.

Respectfully submitted

AQS

CHAPTER 2

UNDERSTANDING HOUSE PLANTS

START HERE

① Every plant has its own preferences and requirements for soil type, light, temperature, ventilation, humidity, and several other factors that are within our power to control, or at least to mitigate. It is vitally important for
② you, as a busy indoor gardener, to understand the basics of *person interested in* *ing* each ~~plant you intend to grow if you are to be successful with~~ *needs* ~~since a prior understanding will enable you to avoid~~
③ ~~much work later on while achieving routine success in growing~~ *a minimum of time and work.* *a minimum* ~~plants~~

~~In addition to understanding these basic needs,~~ You *also need* will ~~want~~ to know something about pots and other containers,
④ repotting, ~~plants~~ propagation, and a few other *relevant practical* matters ~~that~~ *that* ~~while not vital to immediate success, will help you to gain further enjoyment in raising better plants.~~

---

① This sentence repeats information already given in the Preface, and so can safely be omitted.

OK

② The term 'busy indoor gardener' is confusing in the context of this book. Your prospective readers are busy at other things, and do not want to be busy at gardening.

③ The intention of the editing here is to suggest a more economical way of making these points.

④ Would not a knowledge of these matters be needed immediately – at the time of buying a plant? It might (although healthy so far) be in a poor container, or one that it was sure to outgrow very soon, or might (although small at the time it was bought) be due to grow very soon to a size too big for its window sill, etc. Hence the suggested rewording.

Good thinking OK

THE BASIC HOUSE PLANT

START HERE

① The major difference between a house plant and an outdoor plant is one of location. All house plants could live and flourish outdoors, in the proper climate. All are derived from forebears which lived, reproduced, and died in the outdoors, whether it was on a forest floor in Central Europe or in the bough of a tree in a South American rain forest. Over many centuries of adaptation and evolution, each plant species embraced those characteristics that enabled it to survive; and even today, Every house plant carries within its genetic structure the characteristics of *that lived out of doors ⊙* its distant progenitors. Thus the Maranta ~~will~~ loses some
② of its leaves each autumn, even though autumn's weather does not come to the top of the bookshelf where the plant *sits*, ②
③ and a cactus, no matter how long ~~we have~~ been ~~feeding~~ and *it has* *fed* *ed during its growing season keeps*
④ water~~ing it with unfailing regularity~~ will continue to ~~hoard~~ food and water within its swollen stems. ~~In plants~~ ⑤ *ing* Old habits ~~might~~ recede, but they are never forgotten. *may*

At no time are these innate ~~plant~~ characteristics more noticeable than during the autumn and winter, when many plants, particularly those from temperate regions, enter a
⑥ period of dormancy, ~~Then~~ New growth ceases, and ~~the~~ plants *or rest.* *some*
⑦ take~~s~~ on a listless ~~and washed-out~~ appearance. Other plants, including many of tropical origin, ~~will~~ maintain their bright appearance but ~~will~~ stop growing completely for several months ⑧

Sounds good to me

① This passage could be omitted with benefit for it repeats information given in Chapter I, pp. 1-2. The suggested insertion at the end of the next sentence should be a sufficient reminder of what has gone before. I'd be grateful, however, if you would improve upon the wording of my insertion. I haven't been able to get it quite right.

Well Taken

② This term might be taken to mean 'lies dormant' (see next par.) and might lead some literal-minded readers to deduce that a Maranta must always be placed on a bookshelf in the autumn. The misunderstanding could have economic implications - many of your readers may not own bookshelves, or, if they do, may have family pictures or geegaws on them. I feel sure you want to avoid an accusation of elitism.

OK

③ Best to avoid 'we' here (and in similar instances elsewhere). You will not be helping your readers with these chores, and the implication that you are may only annoy them, especially after a bad day at the office.

OK

④ Please reword more carefully re feeding and watering of cacti. The 'know it all' or 'smart aleck' type of reader will either accuse you of inconsistency (see V3 ff) or else treat his cacti the same as all his other plants, and so kill them.

BULLSHIT

⑤ It is quite natural to keep referring to plants specifically, but as the whole book is on that subject, the term may safely be used more sparingly. Also, at this point, by making the application more general, you may convey a moral lesson to your readers - a spiritual boon in these troubled times.

Good

⑥ Best to define all terms that need defining (and I agree that this one may be unknown to some readers) on the very first occasion on which they are used. Hence the transfer from II 1b (fourth line) to here.

OK

⑦ Again, a literal-minded reader might find in this an accusation of over-watering his plants. The adjective listless is sufficient.

Good point Well Taken

⑧ This use of 'will' becomes rather obtrusive. Does not the simple present tense convey this unreasonable behavior of plants even more pungently?

II-1b

(1) each year, [so] ~~emulating the natural rest periods of their forebears.~~ ~~You will do~~ [It is] well to watch for these signs ~~of dormancy and rest,~~ and ~~respond to each plant's needs at that time. When any plant enters a dormant or rest period,~~ [to make the appropriate response.] Water should be reduced and fertilizer withheld completely until new growth once again begins, usually in ~~the~~ late winter or early spring. ~~At that time, water~~ The plant [should then be] (2) ~~freely and~~ give[n] its normal doses of [water and] fertilizer once again ~~in order to encourage new growth.~~ By your [proper] treatment ~~of the plant at this time,~~ (3) ~~you will emulate~~ [in emulation of] the advent of spring, [so as to] work~~ing~~ with the plant in carrying out its rhythmic cycles.

Some plants ~~also are naturally short-lived, and will~~ (4) last no more than a year or two ~~in your home~~ [indoors] despite ~~your~~ careful attention, because their genetic structure dictates (5) a ~~finite~~ [short] life [of] span. [Very few] Garden annuals, ~~for instance, will~~ [because they] germinate, grow to maturity, flower, produce seeds, and die, all in as little as six months. ~~For this reason, very few annuals~~ are selected as house plants. Although a few short-[hyphen] lived plants are cultivated indoors for their unusual characteristics, such as the Sensitive Plant which is easily grown from seed, [most of] the house plants that ~~we~~ have [been] cultivated over the generations are ~~most often~~ those that ~~will~~ give years of pleasure. Some house plants, in fact, live to be literally hundreds of years old.

Still other house plants are attractive when young,

II - 1b

Right you are — (1) The term 'dormancy' having been defined on its first appearance (see pink slip on previous page) there is now no need to give it repeated stress - hence the suggested omissions. Also, the influence of forebears has been fully explained already.

OK - Good — (2) This word seems open to unfortunate misconstruction given the widely varying needs for water and the tendency of owners to over-water. The editorial suggestion is to put more weight on the word 'normal' in the same line.

Don't agree, but will accept — (3) The occasional use of 'you' and 'your' gives a warm human touch, but frequent use makes the impression that the author is giving orders - but that would be totally out of character. Would you agree that an impersonal tone is somewhat better in this passage (and below) as suggested?

(4) Not needed here - see lower in paragraph.

Good point — (5) True enough, but not the meaning you wish to convey in this passage. All spans of life are (to the best of our knowledge) finite, but in this instance you are concerned with plants whose span of life is too short to make it very rewarding to grow them indoors.

II-1c

but grow ungainly or otherwise unattractive when they approach maturity. The only plants of this kind I have chosen for inclusion in this book are those that are very easy to propagate from cuttings, so that the parent plant may be discarded after a year or two, to be replaced by its children.

~~From~~ [Of] the hundreds of thousands of plant [species] in the world, those traditionally cultivated as house plants are the relatively few that have shown a wide tolerance to conditions of (1) heat, light, moisture [in the ground and in the air], ~~humidity,~~ and ventilation; in other words, those [plants] that can withstand a human environment. They are both attractive to the eye and ~~they are~~ tough. Still, [their natural adaptability and resilience do need human fostering.] (2) If we are looking for success with house plants--and particularly success without working hard at it--then we should spend some time to learn the characteristics of each plant, recognizing its individual needs and fulfilling them to the best of our ability.

HOW A PLANT FEEDS

(3) A plant manufactures nearly all of its food by itself--and not from the "plant food" that you buy for it. Commercial (4) plant food is no more than a combination of certain chemicals (sometimes in an organic base) that are essential to the plant's basic functioning, much as vitamins are essential to human nutrition. But the bulk of a plant's food--the sugar it uses for energy and growth--is manufactured by the plant itself. In the presence of light, the leaves ~~of the plant~~

II - 1c

Good — (1) The terms 'moisture' and 'humidity' seemed to require clearer differentiation.

OK — (2) This point is weakened by repetition (see II 1), and should only be touched on very lightly here.

OK — (3) This same point is made at the bottom of the page. Better to delete this sentence.

Good point — (4) The distinction between chemical food and naturally grown food is not made clear in this passage. I would suggest omitting the sentence about chemical food because (1) it seems out of place here and (2) it is dealt with a length later in the book.

[boxed insertion: *a process which is known as photosynthesis⊙*]

draw carbon dioxide from the air and water from the roots,
converting them into sugar that is then used for energy
① production or stored for future use.

② During this ~~sugar manufacturing~~ process, ~~known as~~
something else is happening
~~photosynthesis, several other things happen~~ within the plant.
③ *the leaves are absorbing carbon dioxide through their stomata (or*
pores) they are also releasing oxygen.
~~While carbon dioxide is being absorbed, oxygen is being re-~~
~~leased from the pores of the leaf surface.~~ (Plants produce
not only all of the world's food but most of its atmospheric
oxygen as well.) During *of* darkness *the* hours, the process is
④ reversed; some ~~of the atmosphere's~~ oxygen is recaptured *from the atmosphere* ~~by~~
~~the plant,~~ and used to convert *the* stored sugar ~~to~~ *into* energy ~~for~~
~~growth~~ Generally, a plant manufactures ~~growth~~ food during
the day and does its actual growing at night.

⑤ Often, the plant converts its newly-manufactured sugar
into
~~to~~ starch and stores it, reconverting it ~~to~~ *into* sugar as the
need arises. ~~Although the~~ starch can be stored in almost any
part, but
~~part of the plant~~ certain plants have developed specialized
~~storage~~ areas ~~just for this purpose~~ Cacti and succulents *have*
in the form of
~~have~~ enlarged stems and leaves ~~for~~ the greatest above-ground
storage capacity ~~of any house plant~~ while others ~~have~~
~~have~~ developed underground storage apparatus ~~for this purpose~~
including bulbs, tubers, corms, and rhizomes. A bulb is
simply an enlarged underground bud, such as is found ~~with~~ *on*
hyacinths, tulips, and onions. A tuber is nothing more than
an enlarged root; a common potato is a tuber; gloxinias, *caladiums,*
dahlias, and many other common plants are grown from tubers. ⟶

OK   ① Repetition of previous sentence, and should be deleted. The reason for the insertion is to move the definition up to the first place where it is mentioned.

OK   ② The use of 'several' seems excessive, and is likely therefore to be confusing.

light   ③ Again, a definition moved back, this time from II 1c, line b.

OK   ④ Best to avoid using nouns as adjectives, because they make such a jolt in the natural rhythm of the sentence, as in this case.

light   ⑥ Hyphen not needed: 'newly' is an adverb which is already modifying 'manufactured' and so does not need a visual link.

---

that grows laterally⊙

⟶ A corm is the enlarged base of a stem. And a rhizome is
an
simply ~~a laterally growing~~ enlarged underground stem. All *these*
to store food⌃ *of them*
~~methods~~ are used by ~~the~~ plants ~~for food storage,~~ and all can be used
to propagate plants, too.
① ~~Water is constantly being drawn up through the plant.~~
water
② As ~~it~~ transpires through the stomata ~~(pores)~~ of the leaves,
a ~~"pulling"~~ action draws more water up through the roots.
The water carries with it mineral salts, including all the
elements which the plant needs to carry out its complex chemical processes. ~~The~~ Transpiration ~~which takes place~~ in the
of plants *the skin of*
leaves ~~of plants~~ is similar to perspiration in ~~humans~~ and ~~it~~ serves a
The cooling effect of
similar purpose ~~to cool the plant.~~ ~~With house plants, it~~
transpiration is difficult to detect in house plants
~~would be difficult for you to notice this cooling effect,~~ but
in
it is readily apparent ~~when~~ a group of large trees ~~carry out~~
~~the transpiration process~~ The cool and fresh feeling ~~you~~
of
~~enjoy in~~ a thick woods in summer is not primarily the product
of
of the shade itself, but ~~the transpiration of the millions of
leaves overhead.
more *than it needs because*
③ A plant cannot absorb ~~too much~~ water ~~since~~ its vessels
and cells can accommodate only so much at a given time; however, ~~the~~ overwatering ~~of a plant~~ can exclude oxygen from
the root system, ironically causing wilting of the top portion
no watering is done⌃
of the plant. When ~~water is withheld,~~ the plant's cells ~~will~~
and *wilts. Because*
gradually collapse, ~~causing wilting of~~ the entire plant. ~~All~~
plants do have protective mechanisms that conserve water in
they
times of drought, however, ~~and~~ can withstand a temporary dry

---

OK - Good   ① This statement seems to be a contradiction of the statement at the bottom of II 1c a and the top of II 1d - that water is only drawn up during the hours of light. I would suggest that the first statement be made comprehensive and that this statement be omitted, repetition being unnecessary.

OK   ② See comment on II 1d re moving definition back.

③ I suggest this change because in common speech nowadays, 'too' is misused to mean 'very,' and so your statement could be given a wrong meaning, even though it is correct.

Upon receiving new evidence, I now suggest: "A plant can rarely absorb more water than it can use profitably because its vessels...etc."

African Boxwood (<u>Myrsine africana</u>)   B-C-A-C

This slow-growing boxwood has red stems; but otherwise it is similar to regular Boxwood (q.v.). Many people think it is even more graceful. African Boxwood is A good plant for terrariums, if the atmosphere is not too hot.

Aralia (<u>Fatsia japonica</u>)   C-B-B-C

Sometimes sold as <u>Aralia sieboldii</u>. Beautiful, bright-green, leathery, maple-like leaves highlight this cheerful plant. In appearance, it is similar to the Castor Oil Plant and in fact is sometimes called False Castor Oil Plant. It thrives in a cool spot. Aralia can easily grow leggy, and too it should be pruned annually in order to encourage it into bushy growth. *It will attain a height of four feet at maturity.*

A striking hybrid, <u>Fatshedra lizei</u>, crosses <u>F. japonica</u> and Ivy /Hedra/ (Ivy) to produce a climbing plant with maple-shaped leaves, which is tolerant of adverse conditions.

There is also a plant called False Aralia, which has graceful and feathery foliage. It bears no resemblance to the true Aralia and is difficult to grow.

Asparagus   A-B-B-B

There are two kinds of Asparagus suitable for growing as house plants. Fern Asparagus (<u>A. plumosus</u>), with slender, needle-like, dark-green leaves, giving a feathery appearance, and <u>A. sprengeri</u> (Emerald Feather) which has thicker yellow-green leaves and drooping stems. The latter makes a good

---

What if someone refers to this species alone?
↓
The q.v. directs them

Good idea

① Not needed here because included in description of regular Boxwood (IV 8). It is best to mention only the characteristics that are different.

② Should you not supply the botanical name of the Castor Oil Plant for the sake of precision (and consistency)?

---

plant for hanging baskets and produces red berries at Christmastime. Both like some sun in the summer and full sun in the winter, *and both can grow to a height of about two feet.*

Australian Laurel (<u>Pittosporum tobira</u>)   C-B-A-B

A tolerant and slow-growing plant whose leaves, glossy and leathery, resemble those of Rhododendron. It will grow vigorously bushy and does not need much attention. Florists often use the leaves in floral arrangements.

An interesting variegated form is <u>P. tobira variegata</u>.

Australian Umbrella Tree (<u>Schefflera actinophylla</u>)   A-A-B-A

Here is a very attractive and vigorous-growing tree with rich-looking, glossy leaves that radiate umbrella-like from the ends of several leaf stalks. It is a tough and rewarding plant, growing to six feet, which can be propagated by air-layering. Australian Umbrella Tree is Also sold as <u>Brassaia actinophylla</u>. A dwarf variety, <u>B. actinophylla compacta</u>, is also available.

Baby's Tears (<u>Helxine soleirollii</u>)   B-B-A-B

This low creeper is also called Irish Moss. It likes a constantly moist (but not soggy) soil, and higher than average humidity. It makes a good ground cover for terrariums, but will also grow in a pot if adequate humidity is provided. Baby's Tears may appear to die in the colder months, but after

---

That is the botanical name There are many species

① Insert botanical name?

an adequate rest period it will spring back to life.

Black Pepper (<u>Piper nigrum</u>)   A-C-B-C

This is not a ~~horribly~~ very attractive plant, but it produces real peppercorns which you may use at the table, and is a good conversation piece for that reason. The plant's berries ~~begin as green~~ later turn red, then dry up and turn black. Pick the dried-up black corns, dry them thoroughly for several weeks in an open spot, then use them in your pepper grinder. ~~The care for Black Pepper is~~ the same *care* ~~as that required for~~ Philodendron. [It is not a demanding plant: it needs]

Boxwood (<u>Buxus</u>)   C-A-B-B

The same plant which grows the most prized hedges outdoors can make a very attractive house plant. Boxwood is slow-growing *the ancient Oriental art of growing dwarf trees and shrubs.* and dependable, a good subject for bonsai. *It has* ~~It has glossy, bright-green leaves.~~ *with glossy, bright-green leaves* *and* B. sempervirens and B. microphylla japonica (Japanese Boxwood) are the two popular species.

Bromeliads   A-B-B-C

There are more than 1,800 varieties of this popular group, many of which are suitable for growing as house plants. Some of them produce attractive flowers, but most are grown for their striking and variegated leaf patterns. One distinctive feature ~~of the Bromeliads~~ is the rosette leaves which form a small water cup *The* ~~which the plant uses to hold reserve~~

artificial habitat of a house · *used to hold reserve supplies of water.*

~~supplies of water in its~~ natural habitat *of* ~~Since the plant lives in~~ the crotches of trees in Central and South America, *and* the water cup is an evolutionary survival characteristic, *is* ~~In the home, keep~~ the cup/ *should be kept* filled with water/ *which is* ~~changing it~~ weekly *ed* ~~to keep it fresh~~

A few of the more common Bromeliads are <u>Aechmea</u>, <u>Ananas</u> (Pineapple), <u>Billbergia</u>, <u>Cryptanthus</u> (Zebra Plant), <u>Dyckia</u>, <u>Tillandsia</u> (Spanish Moss), and Vriesia.

Caladium   A-B-B-C

Caladiums, with their spectacularly *u* colored and variegated leaves, are equally at home in the garden or on the window sill. They are ideal additions to plant groupings on porch *es* or patios in ~~the~~ summer and early autumn. Give them bright light, but not long periods of direct sun ~~especially~~ in summer, if you want ~~the~~ *them to show their* brightest ~~leaf~~ colors *u*.

Caladiums are grown from tubers, which can be divided easily to produce new plants. Start the tubers in regular potting soil at a very warm temperature *(80° to 90°)* and ~~move~~ *when* *appear, move them* the young plants to a cooler spot ~~when they have appeared~~ *They will attain a height of about one foot.*

Cast Iron Plant (<u>Aspidistra elatior</u>)   A-C-B-C

This is perhaps the easiest plant ~~in the world~~ to grow, as its name suggests. ~~It~~ *is virtually impossible* to neglect it to death. It is also called Saloon Plant, since it was one of the few that could survive in Victorian taverns, and it was made immortal by George Orwell in his novel <u>Keep the</u>

<u>Aspidistra Flying</u>. If you cannot grow the <u>Aspidistra</u>, you may safely conclude that you have *an* ~~a~~ purple thumb ~~hopelessly~~ ① irredeemable. *, which grows about two feet tall,*

Cast Iron Plant/ seems to thrive even better when kept slightly pot-bound, ~~and~~ *but* it will appreciate having its leaves washed occasionally. ¶ A white-striped species is called <u>A.</u> <u>variegata</u>.

Chamaeranthemum igneum   A-C-A-C

This low, spreading herb has attractive, dark green leaves with reddish-yellow veins. It is suitable for hanging baskets or as a ~~low~~ contrast in large plants groupings ②. It does like warm temperatures and high humidity, however, and might not be suitable for dry apartments.

Chinese Evergreen (<u>Aglaonema</u>)   A-C-B-A ③
and low-growing

Here is an attractive plant that is very easy to ~~grow~~ *look after*. It will stand abuse almost as easily as Cast Iron Plant.

There are at least ten commonly found species of ~~the~~ Aglaonema, the most popular of which, <u>A. modestum</u>, has interestingly mottled leaves. Perhaps the most attractive, however, is <u>A. pseudobractaetum</u>, which is sometimes difficult to find in stores and greenhouses.

Good point   ① Not needed, because irredeemable means hopeless.

OK   ② The term 'low contrast' seemed awkward and its meaning obscure. As the plant has already been described as 'low' in the first line of the description, I thought it could be deleted here, thus solving the problem.

Must be a variety with which I am unfamiliar. Can we cut "low"?   ③ 1) Would not simply 'low' be just as expressive, and neater? 2) Would you consider qualifying this point? A friend of mine has a Chinese Evergreen that is two feet tall, and quite bushy. Perhaps height varies with species?

16   9/12 Sabon

<u>CAPTIONS</u>

12 #   <u>Cast Iron Plant (Aspidistra).</u>   en dash
12 #   A selection of succulents -- easy to grow and infinite in variety.
12 #   <u>Anthurium andreanum and A. crystalinum.</u>
12 #   A good example of double-potting. The sphagnum moss between
the two pots reduces the need for watering.

A selection of begonias for indoor growing.

Decorative containers without drainage holes can be used
sucessfully if the plant is double-potted. This Prayer Plant
(<u>Maranta</u>) has been potted in a clay pot, which was then inserted
into the decorative container on a layer of gravel. Moss occupies the
space between the two pots, assuring constant moisture for the
plant's roots.

Large-leafed plants will appreciate an occasional bath. Use a mild
soap solution and rinse thoroughly with clear water -- both at
room temperature.

Stem cuttings should be made just below a node--the point
where a leaf originates. The cut should be sharp without
damaging the stem, since many plants already have embryonic
root systems at the nodes which develop rapidly when placed
in water. For this purpose, a sharp pair of pruning shears
is adequate, although a sharp single-edge razor blade is
even better, since it will not crush the stem.

(CAPTIONS 2)   **17**

The cuttings of many house plants can be rooted easily in
water. The roots of this Aluminum Plant are at a stage
where the plant can be potted. Many of these plants, including this one, can also be grown permanently in water.

Any plant and soil ball may easily be separated from its
pot by turning it upside-down and rapping the rim of the
pot sharply against the end of a bench. If the plant is
not sufficiently potbound to require repotting--as this
one is not--then the soil ball may easily be replaced with
no harm and little mess.

Overwatering is the most common cause of house plant failure.
This device prevents overwatering. Use a pot with a hole in
the bottom. Then get a piece of plastic tubing one inch in
diameter. Stop up the end and drill 1/8-inch holes up and   FRACTION, IF POSSIBLE
down the tube. Set the tube vertically in the pot, add soil,
and fill the tube with sand. When watering, simply fill the
tube.

---

18   special box No. 1

THE ABCs OF ARTIFICIAL LIGHT   } 12/14 Sabon Bold ulc
10 #
The recent introduction of fluorescent tubes meant
especially for plant growing has been a great boon for
indoor gardeners. With the aid of artificial light, we can
now grow lush, green plants in areas where they would never
grow before. A windowless bathroom, which might offer ideal
humidity and temperature conditions, can now be made into
an ideal plant-growing environment. Plants growing on a
drab northern window sill can now receive supplemental light
during winter's short and dark days. Dim corners of any
room can be transformed into green showplaces. Cuttings and
seedlings can now make faster and surer progress than ever,
under artificial light, and we can even grow vegetables in
the dead of winter in the bedroom or kitchen. Artificial
lighting is not essential for house plant success, but it
certainly does broaden our horizons and increase chances for
maximum rewards.
The old incandescent bulb does offer some help to growing plants, although the heat it produces makes it impossible
to offer plants the amounts of light they need without drying
or burning the plants. Also, incandescent bulbs offer a very
short spectrum of light wavelengths, falling far short of
simulating the beneficial rays of the sun. Ordinary daylight
or cool white fluorescent lights are far better for growing
plants, since they have not only a wider and more effective

10/12 Sabon ulc < 15½

---

19   special box No. 1, add 1

light wavelength, but also produce light with three times as
much efficiency as incandescent bulbs, thus reducing heat by
fully two-thirds. Not until the past decade, however, have
we had fluorescent tubes made to meet exactly the needs of
growing plants. These lights, sold under names such as
Gro-Lux, Plant-Gro, and Plant-Light, cost more than ordinary
fluorescent tubes, but they are long-lasting and they can
solve virtually any light problem for the indoor gardener.
By attaching them to a twenty-four hour timer, you can control
light exposure perfectly, even for such tricky operations as
forcing plants to bloom out of season.
The best way to start out with artificial light is the
most simple way. Purchase two forty-watt plant-growing tubes
with the proper fixture, and hang it over a table where you
wish to begin your experiments. Be sure that you have some
method of raising and lowering the fixture, for you will want
to adjust the lighting intensity to meet different plant
requirements. Ferns and snakeplant, for instance, have low
light requirements, so that the tubes should be placed twelve
to eighteen inches above them, while succulents, ivy, most
flowering plants, and all vegetables have high light requirements, requiring the lowering of the tubes to eight inches or
less above the plants. The lowest you can bring the tubes
and still avoid injury from heat is three inches above the
plants. There are guidebooks giving the exact light requirements of most common plants, available from the tube manufac-

10/12 Sabon < 15½

special box No. 1, add 2

turers] There are also some excellent books on artificial
light gardening, *And some of these are probably* ~~which are most likely~~ in the collection/ of
your public library.

If you enjoy artificial light gardening and the gratifying results it brings, you will have no problem in expanding
your activities in this area. Manufacturers have introduced
a wide variety of special plant-growing stands, some with
several tiers capable of holding dozens of plants, others
decorative enough to enhance the beauty of any room. Your
choices are limited only by your imagination and ~~~r checkbook
balance.

special box No. 4

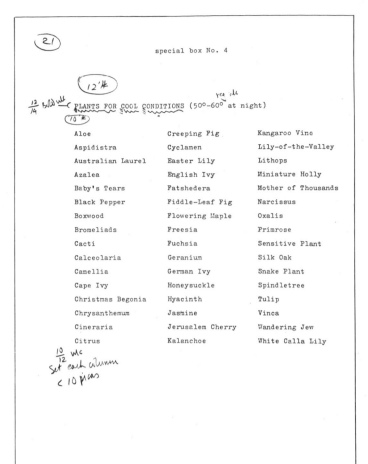

12/14 Bld wl< (12'#) PLANTS FOR COOL CONDITIONS (50°-60° at night) *rea ile*
(10'#)

Aloe	Creeping Fig	Kangaroo Vine
Aspidistra	Cyclamen	Lily-of-the-Valley
Australian Laurel	Easter Lily	Lithops
Azalea	English Ivy	Miniature Holly
Baby's Tears	Fatshedera	Mother of Thousands
Black Pepper	Fiddle-Leaf Fig	Narcissus
Boxwood	Flowering Maple	Oxalis
Bromeliads	Freesia	Primrose
Cacti	Fuchsia	Sensitive Plant
Calceolaria	Geranium	Silk Oak
Camellia	German Ivy	Snake Plant
Cape Ivy	Honeysuckle	Spindletree
Christmas Begonia	Hyacinth	Tulip
Chrysanthemum	Jasmine	Vinca
Cineraria	Jerusalem Cherry	Wandering Jew
Citrus	Kalanchoe	White Calla Lily

10/12 wlc
Set each column
< 10 picas

special box No. 5

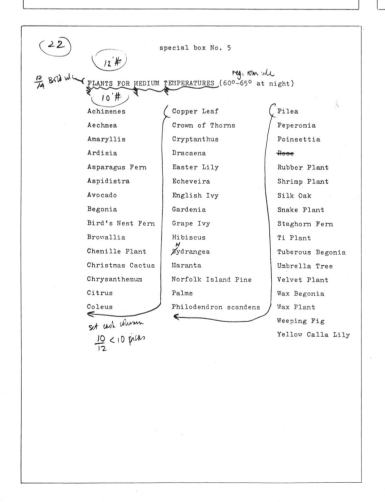

12/14 Bld wl< (12'#) PLANTS FOR MEDIUM TEMPERATURES (60°-65° at night) *reg, rom wlc*
(10'#)

Achimenes	Copper Leaf	Pilea
Aechmea	Crown of Thorns	Peperomia
Amaryllis	Cryptanthus	Poinsettia
Ardisia	Dracaena	~~Rose~~
Asparagus Fern	Easter Lily	Rubber Plant
Aspidistra	Echeveira	Shrimp Plant
Avocado	English Ivy	Silk Oak
Begonia	Gardenia	Snake Plant
Bird's Nest Fern	Grape Ivy	Staghorn Fern
Browallia	Hibiscus	Ti Plant
Chenille Plant	Hydrangea	Tuberous Begonia
Christmas Cactus	Maranta	Umbrella Tree
Chrysanthemum	Norfolk Island Pine	Velvet Plant
Citrus	Palms	Wax Begonia
Coleus	Philodendron scandens	Wax Plant
		Weeping Fig
		Yellow Calla Lily

set each column
10/12 < 10 picas

UNIVERSITY OF TORONTO PRESS

University of Toronto, Toronto, Canada M5S 1A6

EDITORIAL DEPARTMENT
1 December 1976

Professor Purvis Mulch
c/o Wisconsin University Press
Box 1379
Madison, WI 53701

Dear Professor Mulch

My last duty as appraisal editor of your manuscript, 'No Time for House Plants,' is to send you the two official forms which are enclosed with this letter. The first is the Memorandum of Agreement. I hope that you will find the terms agreeable, and if you do, please date and sign both copies, keeping one in your file and returning the other to me. The Author's Information Sheets which are also enclosed have been devised by our Promotion Department as a help to them in reaching the largest possible market for our books. They are rather a chore to fill out, but I suppose you will not mind that very much, especially as your book is expected to have an unusually wide appeal and therefore needs special promotion.

Ordinarily I would at this stage have handed the manuscript and its file to our Executive Editor, who would have arranged for it to be edited and shepherded through to publication by one of our copyeditors (someone keen about house plants,needless to say). But I had become so interested in your manuscript and had discussed it so thoroughly with my colleagues and other friends that to give it up seemed uneconomic and frustrating - so much explaining to fill in the background and what I had learned about this genre during appraisal. Besides, the explaining would not likely have been satisfactory anyway.

I still have a bad conscience over sending you the report of Reader B in its original state instead of selecting his important criticisms and suggestions and incorporating them in a letter of my own. To be faced with such abrasiveness and irascibility was upsetting for you, and the effects on the manuscript have been more far-reaching and subtle than I realized until I examined this latest version closely. On such a tight schedule, though, it seemed necessary to save time by taking any possible shortcuts.

..../2

Professor Purvis Mulch   -2-   1 December 1976

In one of his characteristics - his literal-mindedness - Reader B has to be reckoned with as being in a curious way representative of the prospective readers of your book. To be sure, they are not going to be wilfully dim (as I greatly suspect Reader B of being) but on the contrary receptive and keen to learn. For that very reason they will come close to B's literal-mindedness in their wanting a handbook of this kind to be direct and compact, and for the additional, equally strong reason that they are on your own definition very busy people who have very little time to spend on this hobby. They will want an efficient book - the book you describe in your Preface as 'a collection of solid and practical information, trimmed of excess detail and shaped for a single purpose,' and, as you mention in the next paragraph,portable, so that it can be carried on trips to florist shops and gardening centres. The damage done by B is to lead you to question your original confidence in the ready intelligence of your readers, and to use repetition as a method of making information stick in their heads.

This reaction, though understandable, is a grave mistake, for it will simply perpetuate the irritation caused by B. Most of the editing I have done is aimed at obviating the sharp retort, 'I caught that the first time; why are you telling me again?' and to work towards exactitude of expression as the best means of imparting information in a lasting way. A great many authors of handbooks and guidebooks obviously do think that repetition is necessary, but the sample testing I have done on a liberal cross-section of users of such books confirmed my impression that this method is a source of irritation and even resentment.

My markings are intended as suggestions for you to consider, not as cut and dried changes. When I have put a fence like this ⌐ over a word or passage, I mean to suggest that it be omitted. Suggested rewording is written above the fence. Explanations and questions are written on the pink slips attached to the pages; please write your answers and comments, sacred or profane, on the back of the slips. A simple yes, or no, or a note in the margin will be enough to show me your reaction to the changes, and I'd be grateful if you would leave all the tidying up for me to do rather than change my markings, for otherwise a considerable amount of confusion could result.

I have greatly enjoyed your manuscript and will certainly buy a copy of the book for my shelves when it is published. I wonder if there is any chance of your coming to Toronto when all this rush is over. I should very much like to meet you, and so would Albert, who sends you a leaf as a token of his affection. He was sold to me as a fruit sage, but I'm not sure if that is right, and I have no notion of his botanical name. I do not think I could honestly recommend him for inclusion in your book, for although he is immensely good-natured and a great sire - our Sales Manager has Son of Albert, our Editor (Modern Languages) has Albert II, and an author on the west coast has III and IV - he has a drinking problem,

..../3

Professor Purvis Mulch   -3-   1 December 1976

especially on weekends. No amount of soaking satisfies him, and practically
every Monday morning he is in a thoroughly dejected state of dehydration.
I am pretty sure he has never heard of storing food, or if he does store any
he uses it up right away - growing taller and bushier. Then he gets
claustrophobia and when he is repotted promptly gets agoraphobia. So,
altogether, and even though he is so handsome and sheds such a lovely scent
in my office, I must conclude, with sadness, that he is just a little
bit too temperamental to qualify.

Yours sincerely

Agatha Q. Sigglesthwaite
Agatha Q. Sigglesthwaite
Editor (Environmental Arts)

AQS:sm
Encl.

Ms. Agatha Q. Sigglesthwaite, December 28, 1976, page 2

Again, thank you for your enthusiasm and concern for my manuscript, and for the exceeding care that you have given it. I appreciate your efforts, and look forward, along with you and Mr. Marshall, to its swift and successful completion.

Best wishes.

Sincerely,

Purvis Mulch

Purvis Mulch

December 28, 1976

Ms. Agatha Q. Sigglesthwaite
Environmental Arts Editor
UNIVERSITY OF TORONTO PRESS
University of Toronto
Toronto, Canada M5S 1A6

Dear Ms. Sigglesthwaite:

Thank you for your good letter of December 1, for the Memorandum of Agreement, and for the Author's Information Sheets and the edited copy from my manuscript, No Time for House Plants. I return, herewith, the last three of these, properly completed.

I appreciate your acting not only as appraisal editor but also as executive editor and copyeditor for my work. (From your description, the only duty of the executive editor is to receive manuscripts from the appraisal editor and pass them along to the copyeditor. Should a vacancy ever occur in that position, please call me.)

I believe the less said about Reader B, the better.

I think you did a superb job of editing this section, operating along unshakeable principles of logic. My only concerns are that (1) some of the flow, the character, of the language—good or bad as it might have been—has been interrupted or clouded, and (2) some of the repetitions deleted might have served a good purpose when the reader turns to the work in order to seek the answer to a particular question. The editorial logic employed here appears to assume that each reader will read the entire work at a sitting, absorbing and retaining everything he reads. If that assumption were true, then there would be no need for repetition. In a reference work such as this, however, I do question the assumption. Nevertheless, the editing was the most thorough I have seen.

Last, I have become intrigued by Albert, whom I have as yet not identified. Could I ask that you cut a growing tip from him, wet it down thoroughly, seal it in a plastic bag, and send it to me? I would like to root it.

Page 1

University of Toronto Press, Publications Production Department (page 1)

BREAKDOWN OF PRODUCTION COSTS

Author MULCH
Title NO TIME FOR HOUSE PLANTS Docket 01676 Date Jan. 24/77
Anticipated date of receipt of edited MS ___ Mark-up for lapse of time ___
Trimmed page size 7x9 Length (pp) 136 Process VIP/OFFSET
Significant features of production and special circumstances to be noted:
30 H/T'S, APPROX. 55 SMALL DIAGRAMS, 15 LINE DRAWINGS

COMPILATION

Suppliers A ___ B ___

Copy preparation

	A	B
Editorial costs 78 hrs copy editing @ $1.75, appraisal ___ hrs @ ___	920.00	
Design costs 40 hrs @ $15.00	600.00	
Production costs 30 hrs @ $15.00	450.00	
Proofreading	150.00	
Charges for special artwork/photography (for 55 DIAGRAMS & 15 DRAWINGS)	400.00	
Other special requirements (___)		

Composition #1800

Typesetting 100 pp @ ___ per page (by VIP TO GALLEYS (ALPHA GRAPHICS)	1800.00	
Tabular, formulae or special setting to pages ☐ galleys ☐		
Page assembly 136 pp @ 4.00 per page (by ___)	544.00	
Proofing ___ copies @ ___ per copy		
Strip-up for offset		
Line negatives and offset plates	757.00	
Making blues		
Author's alterations (10 %)	180.00	

Purchases (one time)

Outside type or repros, stats, photo prints and binding stamps	400.00	
Line negs: ___ fine-line negs: ___ (from ___)		
Halftone or duotone film: ___ (from ___)	400.00	
Colour separations/colour proving: ___ (from ___)		

TOTAL COMPILATION 6601.00

Unit costs of compilation

7500 copies	10,000 copies	___ copies
.880 unit	.660 unit	___ unit

Page 2

University of Toronto Press, Publications Production Department (page 2)

BREAKDOWN OF PRODUCTION COSTS

Author MULCH
Title NO TIME FOR HOUSE PLANTS Docket 01676 Date Jan 24/77
Suppliers A ALPHA/T.H.BEST B

	A	(7500)	(10M)	B
COMPILATION (see page 1)	6601.00	.880	.660	6601.00
PRESS PREPARATION	525.00	.070	.053	525.00
RUNNING COSTS (per 7500 copies)				
Paper	2400.00			3325.00
Presswork	750.00			875.00
Bindery (to FLAT SHEETS)		.420	420	
SUBTOTAL	3150.00			4200.00
CASING-IN (Including SEWING SECTIONS & PAINTING CLOTH ROUND) (7500 copies)	875.00	1.170	1.135	1135.00
JACKET Compilation				
Running (___ copies)				
PAPERBINDING (___ copies)				
COVER Compilation				
Running (___ copies)				
OFFPRINTS (___ copies each of ___)				
SHIPPING (___ copies)				
TOTAL (7500 copies)	19051.00	2.54	2.27	22480.00

Prelim specs: Final specs: **x**   Date: **1 December 1976**

Author & Title   **Mulch: No Time for House Plants**

Prelim docket   **01676**   Typesetting/printing docket

Trim page size   **7" x 9"**   Margins: head **3 pica** gutter **3½ picas**

University of Toronto Press

TYPESETTING SPECIFICATIONS

Typeface: text **VIP Sabon**   display **Sabon, Vivaldi**

Type area: **32½** picas X **44** picas (plus r/h)   Text lines per normal column page: **44**

Running head: **x**   Sample r/h: left page **folio r/h**   } flush left   Foot folio:

Space below r/h: **1 pica**   right page **folio r/h** }   Space above foot folio:

Chapters start: right only **x** left or right   Lines per chapter opening page: **31**

Notes: end of chapter   end of book

SIZES OF TYPE AND LEADING

Text: **10 on 12 x 16 picas**   Title Page: **see ms**

Extracts: Part number:
Space above:
Space below: Half title:) **10/12 caps L space**
Footnotes: Part title:)   **1 unit**
End notes: Initial:
Bibliography: **10/12 x 16**   Chapter number: **10/12 caps**
Appendix: **10/12 x 16**   Chapter title: **42 pt Vivaldi 12'**
Index: Subheads (1): **Bold rom. ulc**
10/12 s.c. with o/s figs.   Space above: **18'**
Running head: Space below: **4'**
Tables: Sub-subs (2): **italic ulc. 12'**
    Space above: **see ms**
Captions: **9/12 x 16**   Space below: **see ms**
Folios: Sub-sub-subs (3): **10/12 s.c.**
Reference guide - see   Space above: **12 '**
Other: **appendix**   Space below: **12'**

| TIGHT WORD SPACING |
| REQUIRED THROUGHOUT |
| 4-to-em mono |
| thin bands lino |
| TIGHT VARIABLE |
| SPACING |

SPECIAL STYLE NOTES

Ellipses: En dash:

Figures: old style **x**   modern
Quotes: single **x**   double
Headings: centered   flush left **x**
Caps: letterspace **1 unit** s average
small caps: letterspace **1 unit** s average

Close up space around initials
(i.e. G.H. Smith)

Text setting - 16 picas tight ragged right throughout
     will appear as 15½ picas average line
     in final printing.

Editor: **A.Q.T.**   Designer: **W.R.**

BOOK SPECIFICATIONS   Prelim specs: final specs: **x**   date: 1 December 1976

Author & Title   Mulch: No Time for House Plants
_____

Trim page size   7" x 9"   Pages not known at time of estimate
_____

COMPOSITION: See separate sheet for typesetting specifications

ILLUSTRATIONS   Production to check)

line   halftone   colour
_____

print with text, or separate   print with text
_____

if separate, indicate tip-ins, wraps, inserts, sections, and number of pages

_____

PRINTING

letterpress   offset **x**
_____

Ink: text black   illustrations black   endpaper
_____

Paper: text   opaque offset stock of your choice
_____
                          "
Paper: illustrations
_____

Paper: endpaper   Multicolor Carioca Green
_____

X̶X̶X̶X̶X̶X̶X̶X̶X̶X̶X̶X̶X̶X̶ CASE   Duotone printing with foil stamping (front and spine)

No. of colours   2   letterpress   offset **x**
_____

p̶a̶p̶e̶r̶ ̶(̶j̶a̶c̶k̶e̶t̶)̶:   inks: (1)   black
_____   (2)   green - PMS 582
p̶a̶p̶e̶r̶ ̶(̶c̶o̶v̶e̶r̶)̶:   (3)
_____   (4)
Print duotone so that light to mid-grey areas
are predominantly green, and dark to black areas
B̶I̶N̶D̶I̶N̶G̶   are predominantly black. Minimum 150 line screen halftone.

Cloth Riverside Linen RL 334   Headbands x   tailbands   x   colour white
_____
                                       Back: rounded   x   square

Stamp: front & spine   x   spine only   foil glitter gold
_____

Print cloth: letterpress   offset   x   ink(s)
_____

Collate separate illustrations as
_____

FOR PRODUCTION USE:

Paper binding: perfect bound   sewn
_____

Trim size after perfect binding
_____

Production schedule form

Author MULCH
Title NO TIME FOR HOUSE PLANTS
Series

Editor
Docket
Delivery MAY 30/77

		SCHEDULED 1977	ACTUAL
MANUSCRIPT	to Production		
	to Design		
	to Editorial		
	to Supplier	14/1	
GALLEYS	to Editorial	31/1	
	to Design		
	to Production	7/2	
	to Supplier	8/2	
REVISED GALLEYS	to Editorial		
	to Design		
	to Production		
	to Supplier		
PAGE PROOFS	to Editorial	21/3	
	to Design	24/3	
	to Production	25/3	
	to Supplier	28/3	
REVISED PAGE PROOFS	to Editorial	5/4	
	to Design		
	to Production		
	to Supplier		
FINAL PROOFS OK'd	by Editorial	8/4	
	by Design	15/4	
	by Production	15/4	
	to Supplier	15/4	
CAMERA COPY	to Supplier	20/4	
BLUES OK'd	to Editorial	28/4	
	to Design	28/4	
	to Production	28/4	
	to Supplier	28/4	
SEWN COPY OK'd	by Design	19/5	
	by Production	19/5	
BOUND COPY OK'd		30/5	

MS & PROOF ROUTING

Date Sept. 30, 1976

Author MULCH
Title No Time for House Plants

Docket

(Circle present stage) MS GALLEYS FIRST PP REVISES/REPROS FINAL PP BLUES

FROM
Name Pru Potts

TO
Name HSM

Dept Production

Dept

FOR
Process

HEREWITH (list all accompanying material)

1. Manuscript
2. Preliminary specifications and layouts
3. Guesstimate
4. Rough schedule

COMMENTS

unless marked otherwise

These rules are based on the principle that legible typography depends upon the careful use of space. Strict adherence to these rules will not always be possible because of differences between the major keyboard systems. However, the principle remains as a constant, and the more rules that are followed the better will be the over-all composition.

TEXT COMPOSITION

WORD SPACING
All text composition must be closely word spaced. In mono setting, the average word space should be 4-to-the-em (minimum 5-to-the-em, maximum 3-to-the-em); in lino setting use minimum space bands. Divide words at the ends of lines in preference to loose word spacing. No more than normal word spacing should be used after punctuation and, in certain situations, the word spacing can be omitted (see *periods*). When setting unjustified material, line lengths should not fluctuate more than 1 pica. Never use an en-quad for spacing.

WORD DIVISION
Letters retained at the end of the line should forecast the portion of the word turned over. Do not divide the last word in a paragraph.

LOWER CASE ROMAN AND ITALIC
Text setting of roman or italic must never be letterspaced.

PARAGRAPHS
Do not indent the first line of the first paragraph of any text or separate section thereof. Indent following paragraphs 1 em of the text type size.

LEADING
No extra space should be placed between paragraphs. When extra space is required between sections of the text, such space should be ½, the same as, or a multiple of, the type size plus the leading. For example, space above and below set-down copy should be approximately ½ line each.

SMALL CAPITALS
Use small capitals in text setting for degrees / LL D, PH D, MA, P ENG, B SC, B PAED, D PHIL / abbreviations / BNA USA CBC MP / and Roman numerals / Richard III, George V, Chapter X.

FIGURES
Use old style, non-aligning figures with small caps and, wherever possible, in text settings. Use modern, aligning figures with capitals. Divide date and page sequences with an en dash without extra space. Always use the fewest possible figures / 306-9, 1946-7, but 1914–18.

PUNCTUATION

DASHES
Always use an en rule, preceded and followed by the word space of the line. Centre dashes and hyphens on capital height when used in conjunction with capitals or lining figures.

PERIODS
Use sparingly and omit after the following abbreviations and contractions / Mr / Mrs / Messrs / Dr / St / Co / Ave / Inc / 8vo / No / am / pm /. Spacing following the period must approximate the rest of the word space in the line. No word spacing is required after the period when it is followed by the capitals A J T V W Y. Equalize visual space around initials in names / H.C. Jones / John L. Smith.

APOSTROPHES
Not required in plural forms of such contractions as 1920s. Where small capitals are used for abbreviations insert hair space between final cap and s / MP s.

COLONS AND SEMI-COLONS
Should be preceded by a hair space only.

EXCLAMATION AND INTERROGATION MARKS
Should be preceded by a thin space only.

ELLIPSIS
This mark of omission consists of three periods set without spaces, but preceded and followed by the word spacing of the line. No further punctuation is required.

QUOTATIONS
Opening quotes must be followed by a hair space except before the capitals A, C, G, J, and the lower case a, c, d, e, g, i, j, m, n, o, p, q, r, s, u, v, w, x, y, z. Closing quotes must be preceded by a hair space except after a comma or a period. When a paragraph commences with a quotation, the quote mark must be considered part of the indentation space.
    Either single quote style [' "   " '] or double quote style [" '   ' "] should be used consistently through each book. UTP manuscripts will be marked at the front for style to be followed, and quote style will be indicated on manuscript style sheet. Punctuation goes inside or outside closing quotes, as marked on manuscript.

SPECIAL SETTING

CAPITALS
Words in full capitals will not appear within text setting, but may be used in headings or display. Words in capitals must always be visually letterspaced. The goal is to secure the appearance of even spacing. The same rule applies to small capitals used in headings or display setting.

TABLES
Avoid double rules. Use 1 or 2 pt rules for head and foot of table, hairline rules within. Avoid vertical rules.

FOOTNOTES
When footnote reference figures are required in text, use superior fraction figures preceded by a thin space. Either modern or old style fraction figures may be used provided they are in harmony with the face used for the text. Do not use modern fraction figures in any old style fount and vice versa. Use full figures, not superior fraction figures, for numbering of the footnotes themselves.

SET-DOWN QUOTATIONS, EXTRACTS
If possible, extracts should begin flush left, with subsequent paragraphs indented one em of text size. Spacing between text and set-down material should be approximately ½ line of text size plus leading.

PAGE MAKE-UP

FACING PAGES
Facing pages should be made equal in depth. Fractional differences should be corrected by varying slightly the space around subheadings or set down material, or between text and footnotes.

WIDOWS
Lines of less than half the full measure are considered to be widows, and should not appear as the first line of a page. This can usually be avoided by increasing or decreasing the number of lines of type on facing pages. A pair of facing pages may be one line longer or one line shorter than a standard text page, but should not vary more than one line from preceding or following pages.

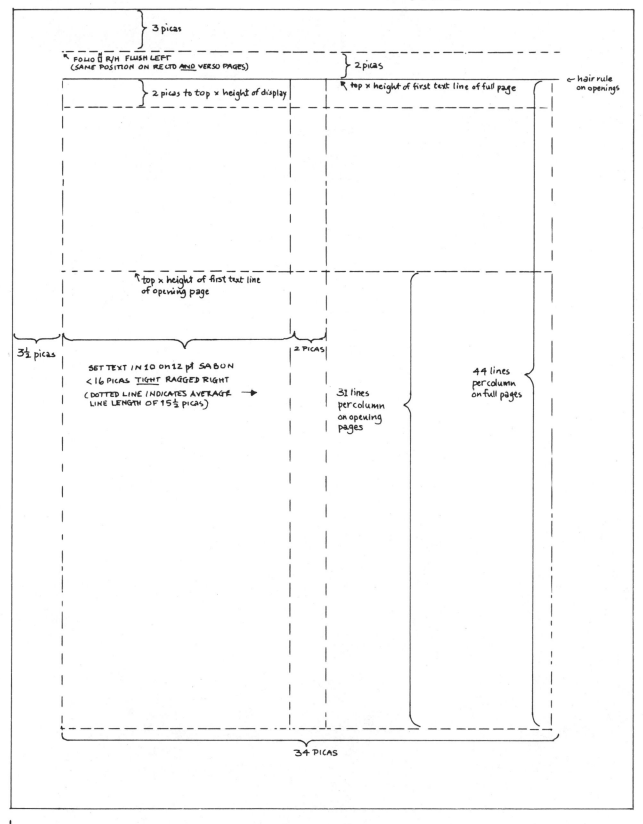

} 3 picas

FOLIO & R/H FLUSH LEFT
(SAME POSITION ON RECTO AND VERSO PAGES)

} 2 picas

} 2 picas to top x height of display

top x height of first text line of full page

← hair rule on openings

top x height of first text line of opening page

3½ picas

SET TEXT IN 10 on 12 pt SABON
< 16 PICAS TIGHT RAGGED RIGHT
(DOTTED LINE INDICATES AVERAGE →
LINE LENGTH OF 15½ PICAS)

2 PICAS

31 lines per column on opening pages

44 lines per column on full pages

34 PICAS

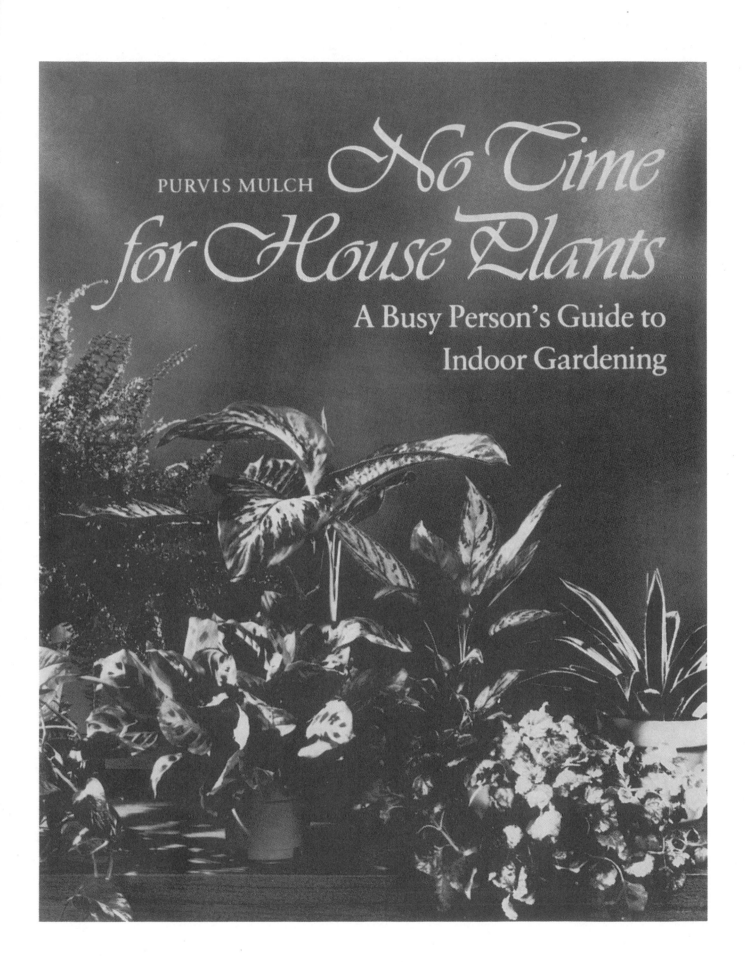

PURVIS MULCH *No Time for House Plants*

A Busy Person's Guide to
Indoor Gardening

Specifications

Trim page size: 7″ x 9″
Margins: head – 3 picas, gutter 3 ½ picas

TYPESETTING

Typeface: VIP Sabon with Sabon and Vivaldi display
Type area: 32½ by 44 picas (plus r/h)
44 lines per full column
Chapters start right only
31 lines per chapter opening column
Text: 10/12 x 15 ½ picas tight ragged right
Bibliography: 10/12 x 15 ½ picas
Running head: 10/12 s/c + o/s figures x 15½ picas
Captions: 9/12 x 15 ½ picas
Reference guide: 10/12 x 15 ½ picas
Title page: see ms
Half title: 10/12 caps + 12 upper and lowercase
Chapter number: 10/12 caps
Chapter title: 42 Vivaldi
Plant reference headings: 12/14 ulc
sub heads: 10/12 s/c

SPECIAL STYLE NOTES

Ellipses: [...]   En dash: [–]
Figures: old style
Quotes: single
Headings: flush left
Caps and small caps: letter space 1 unit

ILLUSTRATIONS: (Production to check)

Print with text

PRINTING

Offset: black ink
Paper: 70 lb Warren's 1854 (or similar opaque stock)
Endpaper: Multicolor Carioca Green

BINDING

Case printed two colours (duotone): black + PMS Green (colour to come)
Stamp glitter gold foil on front and spine
Cloth: Riverside Linen RL 334
Rounded back

This signature was printed by Kingsport Press, Kingsport, Tennesee.

PURVIS MULCH

No Time for House Plants

A Busy Person's Guide to Indoor Gardening

UNIVERSITY OF TORONTO PRESS Toronto and Buffalo

University of Toronto Press 1977
Printed in USA
ISBN 0-8020-2214-7

Library of Congress Cataloguing in Publication Data

Mulch, Purvis
No time for house plants: a busy person's guide to indoor gardening
Bibliography
Includes index
1. House plants I. Title
SB126.K7   635.9'54   76-26057

Contents

Understanding House Plants

It is vital for you as a busy person interested in indoor gardening to understand the basic needs of each plant you intend to grow if you are to be successful with a minimum of time and work. You will also need to know something about pots and other containers, repotting, propagation, and a few other relevant practical matters.

THE BASIC HOUSE PLANT

Every house plant carries within its genetic structure the characteristics of its distant progenitors that lived out of doors. Thus the Maranta loses some of its leaves each autumn, even though autumn's weather does not come to the top of the bookshelf where the plant sits, and a cactus, no matter how long it has been fed and watered during its growing season, keeps hoarding food and water within its swollen stems. Old habits may recede, but they are never forgotten.

At no time are these innate characteristics more noticeable than during the autumn and winter, when many plants enter a

period of dormancy, or rest. New growth ceases, and some plants, particularly those from temperate regions, take on a listless appearance. Other plants, including many of tropical origin, maintain their bright appearance but stop growing completely for several months each year. It is well to watch for these signs, and to make the response. Water should be reduced and fertilizer withheld completely until new growth once again begins, usually in late winter or early spring. The plant should then be given its normal doses of water and fertilizer once again in emulation of the advent of spring, so as to work with the plant in carrying out its rhythmic cycles.

Some plants last no more than a year or two indoors despite careful attention, because their genetic structure dictates a short span of life. Very few garden annuals are selected as house plants because they germinate, grow to maturity, flower, produce seeds, and die, all in as little as six months. Although a few short-lived plants are cultivated indoors for their unusual characteristics, such as the Sensitive Plant which is easily grown from seed, most of the house plants that have been cultivated over the generations are those that give years of pleasure. Some house plants, in fact, live to be literally hundreds of years old.

Large-leafed plants will appreciate an occasional bath. Use a mild soap solution and rinse thoroughly with clear water — both at room temperature.

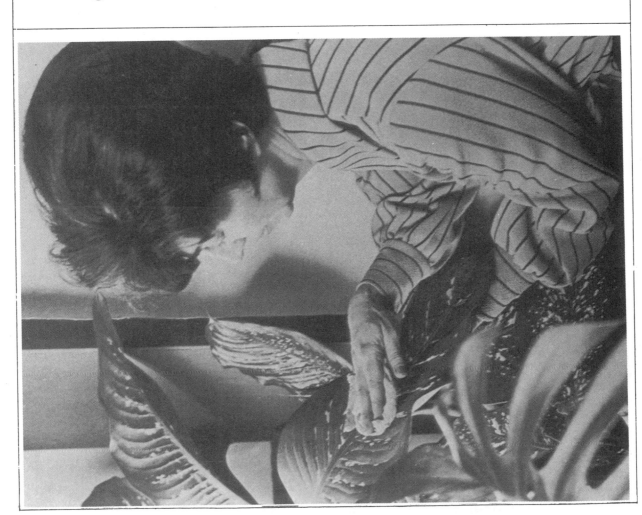

Still other house plants are attractive when young, but grow ungainly or otherwise unattractive when they approach maturity. The only plants of this kind I have chosen for inclusion in this book are those that are very easy to propagate from cuttings, so that the parent plant may be discarded after a year or two, to be replaced by its children.

Of the hundreds of thousands of plant species in the world, those traditionally cultivated as house plants are the relatively few that have shown a wide tolerance to conditions of heat, light, moisture in the ground and in the air, and ventilation; in other words, those plants that can withstand a human environment. They are both attractive to the eye and tough, and their natural adaptability and resilience do need human fostering.

HOW A PLANT FEEDS

The bulk of a plant's food – the sugar it uses for energy and growth – is manufactured by the plant itself. In the presence of light, the leaves draw carbon dioxide from the air and water from the roots, converting them into sugar, a process which is known as photosynthesis.

During this process, something else is happening within the plant. While the leaves are absorbing carbon dioxide through their stomata (or pores) they are also releasing oxygen. (Plants produce not only all of the world's food but most of its atmospheric oxygen as well.) During the hours of darkness, the process is reversed; some oxygen is recaptured from the atmosphere and used to convert the stored sugar into energy. Generally, a plant manufactures food during the day and does its actual growing at night.

Often, the plant converts its newly manu-

factured sugar into starch and stores it, reconverting it into sugar as the need arises. Starch can be stored in almost any part, but certain plants have developed specialized areas. Cacti and succulents have the greatest above-ground storage capacity in the form of enlarged stems and leaves, while others, including bulbs, tubers, corms, and rhizomes, have developed underground storage apparatus. A bulb is simply an enlarged underground bud, such as is found on hyacinths, tulips, and onions. A tuber is nothing more than an enlarged root: a common

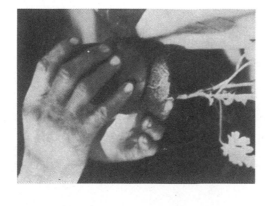

Any plant and soil ball may easily be separated from its pot by turning it upside-down and rapping the rim of the pot sharply against the end of a bench. If the plant is not sufficiently pot-bound to require repotting – as this one is not – then the soil ball may easily be replaced with no harm and little mess.

Decorative containers without drainage holes can be used successfully if the plant is double-potted. This Prayer Plant (Maranta) has been potted in a clay pot, which was then inserted into the decorative container on a layer of gravel. Moss occupies the space between the two pots, assuring constant moisture for the plant's roots.

potato is a tuber; gloxinias, caladiums, dahlias, and many other common plants are grown from tubers. A corm is the enlarged base of a stem. And a rhizome is simply an enlarged, underground stem that grows laterally. All these methods are used by plants to store food, and all of them can be used to propagate plants, too.

As water transpires through the stomata of the leaves, a 'pulling' action draws more water up through the roots. The water carries with it mineral salts, including all the elements which the plant needs to carry out its complex chemical processes. Transpiration in the leaves of plants is similar to

perspiration in the skin of humans and serves a similar purpose – to cool. The cooling effect of transpiration is difficult to detect in house plants but is readily apparent in a group of large trees. The cool and fresh feeling of a thick woods in summer is not primarily the product of the shade itself, but of the transpiration of the millions of leaves overhead.

A plant can rarely absorb more water than it can use profitably because its vessels and cells can accommodate only so much at a given time; however, overwatering can exclude oxygen from the root system, ironically causing wilting of the top portion of the plant. When no watering is done, the plant's cells gradually collapse, and the entire plant wilts. Because all plants do have protective mechanisms that conserve water in times of drought, however, they can withstand a temporary dry spell. Most wilted house plants quickly spring back to normal when water is again provided.

PARTS OF THE PLANT

Stem. The stem serves to support the plant and to contain and direct the vessels that transport water from the roots, and food from the leaves, to every other part of the plant. Most house plants, including Philodendron, Ivy, and Spider Plant, have soft stems. Such plants must either climb or crawl, since their stems are not strong enough to support an upward-growing structure of significant height. Other plants have soft but thick stems that enable them to attain a good height, although their stems are apt to break. Woody-stemmed plants, such as the Avocado, Poinsettia, and Boxwood, are far more sturdy, and are usually derived from trees or shrubs of the temperate region. Canes are thick stems with hollow or pithy centres: Bamboo is an

African Boxwood
(Myrsine africana)

Similar to regular Boxwood (q.v.) except that it has red stems. Many people think it is even more graceful. A good plant for terrariums, if the atmosphere is not too hot.

Aralia
(Fatsia japonica)

Beautiful, bright-green, leathery, maple-like leaves highlight this cheerful plant. In appearance, it is similar to *Ricinus communis* (Castor Oil Plant) and in fact is sometimes called False Castor Oil Plant. It thrives in a cool spot. Aralia can easily grow leggy, and should be pruned annually in order to encourage it into bushy growth. It will attain a height of four feet at maturity.

Sometimes sold as *Aralia sieboldii*.

A striking hybrid, *Fatshedra lizei*, crosses *F. japonica* and *Hedra* (Ivy) to produce a climbing plant with maple-shaped leaves which is tolerant of adverse conditions.

There is also a plant called False Aralia, which has graceful and feathery foliage. It bears no resemblance to the true Aralia and is difficult to grow.

Asparagus

There are two kinds of asparagus suitable for growing as house plants – *A. plumosus* (Fern Asparagus) with slender, needle-like, dark-green leaves, giving a feathery appearance, and *A. sprengeri* (Emerald Feather) which has thicker yellow-green leaves and drooping stems. The latter makes a good plant for hanging baskets, and produces red berries at Christmastime. Both like some sun in the summer and full sun in the winter, and both can grow to a height of about two feet.

Australian Laurel
(Pittosporum tobira)

A tolerant and slow-growing plant whose leaves, glossy and leathery, resemble those of Rhododendron. It will grow vigorously bushy and does not need much attention. Florists often use the leaves in floral arrangements.

An interesting variegated form is *P. tobira variegata*.

Australian Umbrella Tree
(Schefflera actinophylla)

Here is a very attractive and vigorous-growing tree with rich-looking, glossy leaves that radiate umbrella-like from the ends of several leaf stalks. It is a tough and rewarding plant, growing to six feet, which can be propagated by air-layering.

Also sold as *Brassaia actinophylla*.

A dwarf variety, *B. actinophylla compacta*, is also available.

Baby's Tears
(Helxine soleirollii)

This low creeper is also called Irish Moss. It likes a constantly moist (but not soggy) soil, and higher than average humidity. It makes a good ground cover for terrariums, but will also grow in a pot if adequate humidity is provided. Baby's Tears may appear to die in the colder months, but after an adequate rest period it will spring back to life.

Black Pepper
(Piper nigrum)

This is not a very attractive plant, but it produces real peppercorns which you may use at the table, and is a good conversation piece for that reason. The plant's green ber-

produce attractive flowers, but most are grown for their striking and variegated leaf patterns. One distinctive feature is the rosette leaves which form a small water cup. The natural habitat of the plant is in the crotches of trees in Central and South America, and the water cup is an evolutionary survival characteristic, used to hold reserve supplies of water. In the artificial habitat of a house the cup should be kept filled with water which is changed weekly.

A few of the more common Bromeliads are *Aechmea, Ananas* (Pineapple), *Billbergia, Cryptanthus* (Zebra Plant), *Dyckia, Tillandsia* (Spanish Moss), and *Vriesia*.

Caladium

Caladiums, with their spectacularly coloured and variegated leaves, are equally at home in the garden or on the window sill. They are ideal additions to plant groupings on porches or patios in summer and early autumn. Give them bright light, but not long periods of direct sun in summer, if you want them to show their brightest colours.

Caladiums are grown from tubers, which can be divided easily to produce new plants. Start the tubers in regular potting soil at a very warm temperature – 80° to 90° – and when the young plants appear, move them to a cooler spot. They will attain a height of about one foot.

Cast Iron Plant
(Aspidistra elatior)

This is perhaps the easiest plant to grow, as its name suggests. To neglect it to death is virtually impossible. It is also called Saloon Plant, since it was one of the few that could survive in Victorian taverns, and it was made immortal by George Orwell in his novel *Keep the Aspidistra Flying*. If you cannot grow the *Aspidistra*, you may safely

Cast Iron Plant (*Aspidistra*).

ries later turn red, then dry up and turn black. Pick the dried-up black corms, cry them thoroughly for several weeks in an open spot, then use them in your pepper grinder. It is not a demanding plant: it needs the same care as that required for Philodendron.

Boxwood
(Buxus)

The same plant which grows the most prized hedges outdoors can make a very attractive house plant. It has glossy, bright-green leaves and is slow-growing and dependable, a good subject for bonsai, the ancient Oriental art of growing dwarf trees and shrubs. *B. sempervirens* and *B. microphylla japonica* (Japanese Boxwood) are the two popular species.

Bromeliads

There are more than 1,800 varieties of this popular group, many of which are suitable for growing as house plants. Some of them

Handy Reference Guide

The ABCs of Artificial Light

The recent introduction of fluorescent tubes meant especially for plant growing has been a great boon for indoor gardeners. With the aid of artificial light, now grow lush, green plants in areas where they would never grow before. A windowless bathroom, which might offer ideal humidity and temperature conditions, can now be made into an ideal plant-growing environment. Plants growing on a drab northern window sill can now receive supplemental light during winter's short and dark days. Dim corners of any room can be transformed into green showplaces. Cuttings and seedlings can now make faster and surer progress than ever, under artificial light, and we can even grow vegetables in the dead of winter in the bedroom or kitchen. Artificial lighting is not essential for house plant success, but it certainly does broaden our horizons and increase chances for maximum rewards.

The old incandescent bulb does offer some help to growing plants, although the heat it produces makes it impossible to offer plants the amounts of light they need without drying or burning the plants. Also, incandescent bulbs offer a very short spectrum of light wavelengths, falling far short of simulating the beneficial rays of the sun. Ordinary daylight or cool white fluorescent lights are far better for growing plants, since they have not only a wider and more effective light wavelength, but also produce light with three times as much efficiency as incandescent bulbs, thus reducing heat by fully two-thirds. Not until the past decade, however, have we had fluorescent tubes made to meet exactly the needs of growing plants. These lights, sold under such names as Gro-Lux, Plant-Gro, and Plant-Light, cost more than ordinary fluorescent tubes, but they are long-lasting and they can solve virtually any light problem for the indoor gardener. By attaching them to a twenty-four hour timer, you can control light exposure perfectly, even for such tricky operations as forcing plants to bloom out of season.

The best way to start out with artificial light is the most simple way. Purchase two forty-watt plant-growing tubes with the proper fixture, and hang it over a table where you wish to begin your experiments. Be sure you have some method of raising and lowering the fixture, for you will want to adjust the lighting intensity to meet different plant requirements. Ferns and snake-plant, for instance, have low light requirements, so that the tubes should be placed twelve to eighteen inches above them, while succulents, ivy, most flowering plants, and

Plants for Cool Conditions (50° – 60° at night)

Aloe	Creeping Fig	Kangaroo Vine
Aspidistra	Cyclamen	Lily-of-the-Valley
Australian Laurel	Easter Lily	Lithops
Azalea	English Ivy	Miniature Holly
Baby's Tears	Fatshedera	Mother of Thousands
Black Pepper	Fiddle-Leaf Fig	Narcissus
Boxwood	Flowering Maple	Oxalis
Bromeliads	Freesia	Primrose
Cacti	Fuchsia	Sensitive Plant
Calceolaria	Geranium	Silk Oak
Camellia	German Ivy	Snake Plant
Cape Ivy	Honeysuckle	Spindletree
Christmas Begonia	Hyacinth	Tulip
Chrysanthemum	Jasmine	Vinca
Cineraria	Jerusalem Cherry	Wandering Jew
Citrus	Kalanchoe	White Calla Lilly

Plants for Medium Temperatures (60° – 65° at night)

Achimenes	Crown of Thorns	Peperomia
Aechmea	Cryptanthus	Poinsettia
Amaryllis	Dracaena	Rubber Plant
Ardisia	Easter Lily	Shrimp Plant
Asparagus Fern	Echeveira	Silk Oak
Aspidistra	English Ivy	Snake Plant
Avocado	Gardenia	Staghorn Plant
Begonia	Grape Ivy	Ti Plant
Bird's Nest Fern	Hibiscus	Tuberous Begonia
Browallia	Hydrangea	Umbrella Tree
Chenille Plant	Maranta	Velvet Plant
Christmas Cactus	Norfolk Island Pine	Wax Begonia
Chrysanthemum	Palms	Wax Plant
Citrus	Philodendron scandens	Weeping Fig
Coleus	Pilea	Yellow Calla Lily
Copper Leaf		

UNIVERSITY OF TORONTO PRESS

University of Toronto, Toronto, Canada M5S 1A6

November 24, 1976

Professor Purvis Mulch

Dear Professor Mulch:

We are all of us enthusiastic about No Time for House Plants and I have just come from the second conference devoted to it.

Our ambition is to produce your book initially in a clothbound edition priced at less than $10.00 in a format that will be as economical as possible and which will lend itself to a large run cheap edition in due course.

We recognize that your book is going to appeal to a very particular section of what is a large market and it is one which we are quite accustomed to reaching, for it is the market for good general scholarly books. We see the particular merit of your book being in the fact that it is amusingly and well written but, most particularly, that it condenses a very great deal of information into a short space. It should be an ideal book for literate people who want all the necessary information provided to them in the most compact and easily digested form possible. We think we can achieve this well with your excellent little work.

You will be receiving from the editorial department a form of contract and an author's information sheet which will be invaluable to us in planning the detailed promotion of the book. Naturally, we will see that a simple and inexpensive announcement about the book goes out very widely with our general direct mail program to scholars but we will also, of course, have to place appropriate advertisements in quite a variety of places. Your thoughts as to what will be most effective will be very helpful to us for we will be working with a budget that will be far from inexhaustible.

Professor Purvis Mulch   - 2 -   November 24, 1976

Our production department is anxious to have a set of the drawings that we know you can provide us and I would be grateful if you could send them to me at your earliest convenience.

I look forward to associating with you over the next few months and, particularly, when we publish in the spring of next year.

Yours sincerely,

Hilary S. Marshall,
Manager,
Sales and Distribution.

HSM:ir

2

A BIOGRAPHY Please fill in ALL the information requested below

Author, editor, translator, introducer. Please give your name here in exactly the form you wish it to appear in the book's advertising.

Purvis Mulch

Title (or working title) of book

No Time for House Plants: A Busy Person's Guide to Indoor Gardening

Working address (including postal code and telephone number)

University of Wisconsin Press
Box 1379, Madison, Wisconsin 53701 USA   608: 262-7756

Home address (including postal code and telephone number)

315 N. Franklin St.
Madison, Wisconsin 53703
608: 255-6065

Please indicate which is to be used for correspondence concerning your book

WE ARE REQUIRED BY LAW TO PROVIDE THE FOLLOWING INFORMATION TO
THE NATIONAL LIBRARY OF CANADA FOR COPYRIGHT PURPOSES

Name in full   Purvis Sphagnum Mulch

Maiden name if applicable   (current maiden)

Year and place of birth 1933, Crackersport, Pennsylvania, USA

Nationality U.S.

If Canadian, is it by birth or residence?

1 Present academic connections or occupation and official title.

Freelance garden writer, lecturer, and plant exorcist

2 Education and professional training, degrees, honorary degrees. Please give dates.

No professional training, no degrees, no honorary degrees

3 Prizes, honours, scholarships, fellowships, medals, membership in honorary societies. Please give name and purpose of award, name of organization awarding and year.   No recognition whatsoever

4 Reference books (i.e. Who's Who) in which you are listed.

Listed in no reference books

5 Titles, dates, and publishers of other books you have written, edited, or worked on in some capacity / magazines which have published your work.

A Crackersport Garden Guide (1975); Encyclopedia of Organic
Gardening (contributing editor, 1960); articles in House Beautiful,
Organic Gardening & Farming, Mother Jones, Camping Journal, etc.

6 Other writing you are engaged in at present.

The Earthworm Book (for Rodale Press, 1977)

7 Television and radio programmes you have appeared on.

No TV or radio

Author's Information Sheets

University of Toronto Press
Sales & Promotion Department
Toronto M5S 1A6, Ontario
Telephone (416) 928-2250

Author: Purvis Mulch

Title of Book: No Time for House Plants: A Busy Person's Guide to Indoor
                                                              Gardening

Form sent: 1 December 1976   Form received back:

Sponsoring Editor: Agatha Q. Sigglesthwaite   Manuscript Editor: the same
                   Editor (Environmental Arts)

The Sales and Promotion Department of the University of Toronto Press is responsible for finding the greatest possible market for your book. To do this, many different methods of promotion are used, the chief of which are:

1 Distribution of review copies to suitable media

2 Description in the appropriate seasonal catalogue and listing in our complete catalogue of books in print. These catalogues are distributed to librarians and booksellers throughout the world

3 Description in a brochure which will be mailed to librarians, scholars, booksellers and appropriate professional groups

4 Listing in Bowker's Publishers' Trade List Annual and Books in Print, two of the most important reference tools for booksellers and librarians

5 Book exhibits at meetings of academic, library and professional groups

6 Advertising in scholarly journals

7 Advertising in metropolitan daily newspapers, and mass-circulation magazines (for books of interest to the general reader)

8 In the case of a book with textbook possibilities, distribution of desk copies to appropriate department heads and instructors

9 Special promotions applicable to the individual book

It should be noted that not all these methods are necessarily used for every book, although with rare exceptions the first two are used for every book. As we believe that the author, with his intimate knowledge of the content and style of his book, is in an excellent position to assist us in reaching the largest possible market, we ask you to complete as fully as possible the information requested on the following sheets. Please note that while portions of your description of the book, and your biography, may be used verbatim in jacket and catalogue descriptions and in mailing pieces, this material will not be attributed to the author, and will be revised if necessary to suggest that it has been written by a member of the Press staff.

PLEASE return the attached sheets as soon as possible. If we have these details at an early stage, it ensures that the many people dealing with your book are fully and accurately informed.

ALTHOUGH SOME OF THE ITEMS MAY BE IRRELEVANT TO YOUR BOOK, PLEASE ANSWER ALL THOSE QUESTIONS YOU CAN.

1

(9-continued)

cents a pound in grocery stores, mangoes and guavas were going for a dime apiece. In 1948, he became convinced that a large greenhouse might be the answer to the recurring frost problem. He finished the greenhouse on August 12, 1950, the day before the greatest hail storm in local memory, and spent the next three years in constructing glass mobiles for the tourist trade. All this while, mother commanded top wages in the steel mill, commuting between the farm and Bethlehem six days a week. She organized the steel workers union at Bethlehem and is still remembered there for once dispatching four goons in an alley behind a tavern. A folk song about her exploits never sold well.

From this background, I developed a sensitivity to growing things as well as a respect for the inner toughness that often sees us through life's cloudy days. The fact that I once assaulted a six-foot dieffenbachia in the Brooklyn Botanical Gardens is not without developmental roots.

After childhood, my life's direction was fairly well set. I educated myself in both library and garden, and at the age of 28 developed a theory that organic fertilizer was the answer to communism. My first published article, "Marx or Manure: America's Choice for the 50s," appeared in the Philadelphia Inquirer Sunday garden supplement of March 2, 1955. On the strength of that piece, I began to write and lecture full-time, paying special attention to mangoes and left-wing bureaucrats at the U.S. Department of Agriculture.

With the waning of the communist scare, my interests turned more to companion planting, varieties of hairy vetch, bacterial control of brown rot on sour cherry trees, and earthworms as the guardians of modern civilization.

My first book, A Crackersport Garden Guide, was well received throughout Lehigh County, selling out its first edition of 114 copies within a year and a half. This latest effort, No Time for House Plants, was written in a desperate effort to make money quickly.

---

8 What is your attitude to personal publicity, i.e. are you prepared to be interviewed by journalists and broadcasters if your book lends itself to this treatment?

I'll try anything once.

9 Please give us a short autobiography. The Press, the booktrade, and the public are always interested in 'human interest' material concerning the lives of authors. (Childhood, travels, special interests, professional life, writing experience, and, in particular, activities connected with the subject of your book.) Attach a separate sheet if you require more space.

I was born in Crackersport, Pennsylvania during the Great Depression, of Pennsylvania Dutch parents. We were not poor, but honest—good country folk. My father, Marvin Mulch, was a farmer who specialized in mangoes and guavas. My mother Roxanne worked at the open hearth furnaces at Bethlehem Steel. I believe that I inherited my love for plants and my romantic streak from my father, and my intensely practical nature from my mother. Father's history still remains a frazzled thread in the family fabric. He spent twenty-three years in trying to grow tropical fruits in the middle of the best potato-growing land on the Eastern Seaboard. Naturally, his young trees died every year around Thanksgiving. During one unusually warm year, in 1939, he nursed a guava until three days before Christmas before it fell to mice. Dad's reasoning was that, while potatoes were selling for four   (continued)

10 Can you supply, if requested, a photograph of yourself suitable for book jacket or promotion?

Yes—available later.

B YOUR BOOK

1 What are the particular characteristics of your book which you think will help us in promoting it? What led you to write it? What is the single most significant point of this book? What is the first point we should emphasize in telling others about your book? This is the only book written for the working person or couple who wants to raise a few house plants successfully, but have little time to devote to the task. It is not for rank beginners, as many house plant books are, but for someone who might have some experience but wishes to learn short-cuts, proper plants to buy, etc.

2 Are there any circumstances connected with the book that may have possible news value? Are there any centenaries, festivals, exhibitions, or other occasions with which we could link our publicity?

It would make a dandy Christmas present for anyone who has half a dozen sickly house plants around the house.

3 Are there any forthcoming conferences or seminars to which the book has particular relevance?

No.

4 Please list recent books, with prices and publication dates if possible, (or any you know of that are in active preparation) that could be said to compete with yours, noting any significant differences.

There are many "beginning" house plants—but none competing directly.

5 For whom is your book intended?' Be as specific as possible, and if applicable please list professors and their institutions that might be approached with a view to classroom adoption of the book. Name courses to which it might apply.

(explained above)

C PROMOTION

Questions A.7 and A.8 are also relevant. Where you suggest the name of a contact, please mark with an asterisk if we may NOT say that we are telephoning/writing at your suggestion.

1 Local
a Have you any contacts with your local press, broadcasting, or television? Please give names and addresses.

I have no local contacts of value.

b Please list chronologically (with dates) any places where you have lived for any length of time; any places which might have a special interest in you or the subject of your book.

Crackersport, Pa. (1933-57)
Iowa City, Ia. (1957-61)
Emmaus, Pa. (1961-65)
Newark, N.J. (1963-65)
Madison, Wis. (1965-present)

2 National
a Please suggest any television or radio programmes you consider suitable for the promotion of your book.

Many local stations have weekly gardening programs. I have no list of them.

b Can you suggest any newspapers, magazines, periodicals (lay or specialized) which we might approach to do a feature on your book, print extracts from it, or interview you? Please give names of any contacts you have with these papers.

Try Organic Gardening & Farming (M. C. Goldman), Mother Jones (Jeffrey Klein), House Beautiful (Elvin MacDonald), and Countryside (Heather Tischbein), all of which I have written for.

3 Abroad
a Which countries might be *particularly* interested in your book?

Possibly Great Britain and Australia.

b Please give names of foreign publishers who have translated or bought rights of any work of yours not published by us. Please also give names of any contacts.

None.

c Please give similar information concerning any other foreign publishers who might be interested in publishing translations of this book.

None that I know of.

4 Please list scholarly journals, magazines, and newspapers which you believe are most likely to carry a review of your book and mark with an asterisk those most suitable for possible display advertising. (Attach another page if necessary.)

NYTRB, Apartment Ideas, Apartment Life, Mother Jones, Organic Gardening & Farming, Ms, Esquire, Better Homes & Gardens, Playboy, other magazines geared to the single and/or working life.

---

6 With these people' in mind, please describe your book.

a short description (20 to 50 words in one or two sentences)

This book explains how anyone can raise several dozen house plants with a minimum of care, by centering on two areas: How to choose easy-care plants to begin, and how to give them the proper conditions initially that will encourage them to grow successfully.

b long description (300 to 400 words). Your summary or précis will assist us in preparing a good description of your book for the jacket and for other promotional material. Please do not refer us to your preface or other parts of your manuscript, for this is often unavailable when the information is needed.

In 1973, with the purchase of a new house, I was determined to increase my house plant population. Still, I realized that, with my busy schedule, I would not have much time to devote to indoor plants. I was frequently gone for long periods of time, and many days, even while in town, I simply have no time to fuss with plants.

I therefore sought to find methods to raise interesting and beautiful house plants with the least amount of effort. All the house plant books I checked, however, were apparently written by enthusiasts who spent unending hours in careful watering, potting, repotting, propagating, tying up, inducing to flower, humidifying, bathing, and even talking to their plants in an effort to get them to grow. There was no book for the casual house plant grower.

There is now such a book. By researching many sources, and through past personal experience and experimentation, I have narrowed down the crucial requirements for a "no-time" indoor house plant population. The research yielded two cardinal rules: Choose plants that are tolerant of adverse conditions, and then give them the right conditions to grow without your constant attention.

The implementation of these rules forms the crux of this book. I explain how to choose plants, tell which are the easiest to grow, and explain the conditions of light, soil moisture, humidity, and temperature that each of more than a hundred indoor plants requires. I explain, in short, how your house plants can live well without your constant attention and painstaking devotion.

The chapter on understanding house plants is critically important to the "no-time" system, since it details the initial requirements plants need for success, including potting mixtures, fertilizing, containers, watering, humidity, ventilation, temperature, light, and pruning. When these conditions are met at the very beginning, countless hours will be saved later in nursing plants or attempting to track down troubles.

There is a separate chapter devoted to plant troubles and cures, and special sections on artificial light, summer care, and lists of plants for various conditions of light and temperature. For those who wish to devote a little more time to raising house plants, there is detailed information on repotting, propagation, training, dish gardens, planters, bottle gardens and terrariums, kitchen scrap gardens, and growing vegetables indoors.

The bulk of the book, however, comprises listings of more than a hundred "easy" foliage plants, flowering plants, and succulents, including cacti, giving light, soil moisture, and humidity requirements for each.

For the home owner or apartment dweller who wants to raise several dozen attractive house plants while spending only a few minutes a day in caring for them, this book will tell everything that is necessary to know in order to achieve success.

Memo to: H. S. Marshall   From: A. Livernois

OUTLINE OF SALES AND PROMOTION CAMPAIGN

No Time for House Plants

by Purvis Mulch

After closer examination of the manuscript, discussions amongst ourselves and with sales representatives, a sampling of the media and the trade, we concluded that No Time for House Plants has a wider market potential than originally anticipated. Our campaign therefore will be directed toward a general audience of intelligent, busy people; it will be aggressive but in good taste. We will not attempt to compete with the low-priced books which tend to provide only basic information, but will stress that No Time for House Plants provides complete information on the selection and care of appropriate house plants which will help the reader raise healthy plants with a minimum of time and care, and a maximum of pleasure.

April 1 has been chosen as publication date, after due consideration of production timing versus suitable release date. This will catch the market just prior to the outdoor planting season (in our area at least), in time for various gift periods, and will avoid the busy fall book season. Finished books will be ready two months in advance of publication. The following is a general outline of sales and promotion plans:

Book Clubs

Submissions for possible book club sale:

    American Garden Guild Book Club, New York,
    Organic Gardening Book Club, Emmaus, PA.

Excerpts

Approach the following magazines and journals for possible excerpting, those asterisked because Purvis Mulch has written articles for them, the others because of their large distribution to the potential market:

Author's Information Sheets

5 Please give the dates, places, and sponsoring organizations of any forthcoming speaking engagements.

None.

6 Are there any societies or other organizations likely to be interested in you or the subject of your book? Are mailing lists available from them and from whom?

None that I know of.

7 At which association conventions might it be appropriate to exhibit your book?

ALA, ABA.

8 If you feel it appropriate, please list in order of importance, names and addresses of individuals whose good opinion of the book might broaden its audience – those to whom, for instance, advance copies of the book might be sent by us for comments that could be quoted in advertising. Add a brief note of explanation where necessary.

Try M. C. Goldman, Managing Editor, Organic Gardening & Farming.

9 Give the name and address of any booksellers or librarians who might take a special interest in your book. Add a brief note of explanation where necessary.

All bookstores' know me through my first work.

10 Please list names and addresses of personal friends, relatives, and colleagues to whom you wish copies of your book sent (with' compliments of the author' cards) and charged to you at author's discount of 40% from the list price, plus mailing costs.

Mrs.   54 Farragut Dr., Palm Coast, Fla. 32037 (mother)
Mr.   2414 Fairview St., Allentown, Pa.

11 Please indicate how many copies of the mailing piece you will want for your own distribution to friends and colleagues.

100

PLEASE ADD ANY OTHER PROMOTION IDEAS AND FURTHER INFORMATION WHICH YOU THINK MIGHT BE USEFUL.

Thank you,

Sales and Promotion Department
University of Toronto Press

Excerpts (continued)

*Organic Gardening and Farming
*Mother Jones
*House Beautiful
*Countryside
Cosmopolitan)
Playboy) and to other similar magazines should
Canadian Homes Magazine) these not be interested
Today's Woman

Sales Particulars

1. We will concentrate on the areas in which we have sales representation: the northeast, middle west, and western states, as well as every province in Canada. (Promotion and distribution in the United Kingdom and Europe will be handled by our agent, Books Canada Limited.)

2. In addition to covering their regular book and department store accounts, sales representatives will call on the larger indoor plant shops and nurseries in their areas. They will recommend the most appropriate location for Author Demonstrations in the cities on the publicity tour, and provide a list of accounts for poster distribution. They will arrange their itineraries so that they will be available to assist Purvis Mulch when she visits the cities in their areas.

3. Co-operative advertising, on a 50/50 basis, will be offered to stores holding Author Demonstrations. It is necessary that stores liaise with the Promotion Department regarding timing and shared costs.

4. The following escalating discount schedule will apply to all trade orders:

1 - 24 copies	40%
25 - 99 copies	42%
100 - 249 copies	44%
250 - 999 copies	46%
1000 up	50%

.../3

These discounts should induce quantity buying and allow the sales representative to get the books into appropriate wholesalers.

5. Our plans envisage a paperback edition, but it will not appear until at least one year after publication.

Promotion Particulars

Purvis Mulch is an attractive, articulate woman in her early 40s - an expert on house plants, with a good sense of humour and a quick wit. She is fairly well known through her articles and lectures on gardening and she is willing to do all she can to promote her book.

The promotion budget has been set at roughly $5,000 -- made up of $2500 based on our usual calculations and another $2500 built into the price of the book, since we felt $5000 was the minimum amount required to promote No Time for House Plants. Should initial orders suggest a larger printing, or should reprinting be necessary at a later date, additional promotional dollars will be made available. Therefore we are including one or two extras, which we may or may not be able to finance. A breakdown of the budget is attached. (A)

The following is an outline of promotion plans:

Catalogues

No Time for House Plants will be announced in the spring and summer seasonal catalogue, with a photograph of the jacket. Copy is attached. (B) It will appear as well in the Complete Catalogue of Books in Print. Catalogues are distributed to booksellers (trade and college), libraries (public and university), and the media in the United States, Canada, the United Kingdom and Europe. They are also given away at exhibits and on request.

.../4

- 4 -

Advance Material

Pages will be sent to Publishers' Weekly and Kirkus Review. Since we have planned a two-month lead time, finished books can be sent to all other reviewers.

Release

Copy for a release is attached. (C) The release will be sent to all garden columnists prior to the review copy. Also to bookstores, indoor plant shops, and nurseries with the poster; to general columnists at time of publication; to radio and TV shows and columnists who are approached for interviews. (For the latter group, a biographical sheet (D) has been prepared as well.)

Review Copies

At a cost of $2.54 each, review and publicity copies will be our least expensive method of promotion and will be distributed generously. (The cost of frees does not come out of the book budget.) We toyed with the idea of being gimmicky and sending a pot containing one of the hardiest and healthiest of house plants to major garden columnists, but decided that this had been overdone, not to mention the difficulty of delivering the plants in a healthy condition.

The review list is attached (E); the publicity list has not been prepared in detail as yet, but a general plan is included as part of the review list. A clipping service will be retained for this book, since many of the columnists are likely to omit mention of the publisher.

Review copies will be sent in three groups:

(1) Journals and magazines - two months before publication date
(2) Newspapers - 5 weeks prior to publication date
(3) Publicity - 4 weeks prior to author's visit

.../5

- 5 -

Direct Mail

Initially, there will be no direct mail campaign for No Time for House Plants. Later, if more money becomes available, an inexpensive circular may be produced and included in mailings of other circulars. Costs therefore would be kept to a minimum, including only the cost of the circular and of the extra insertion.

Author's Publicity Parties

We do not plan to spend promotion dollars on publicity parties, thinking that little publicity would result from such parties that we cannot get in other less expensive ways.

Advertising

(Copy and layouts attached)

1. Announcement advertisements in: (F)

    Publishers' Weekly,
    Quill and Quire
    American Nurseryman
    Organic Gardening and Farming

2. Co-operative advertising with stores holding Author Demonstrations. (G)

3. Original plans called for small advertisements in such magazines as Apartment Life, House Beautiful, and New Yorker. Advertising rates proved prohibitive, however, and we had to abandon this plan. We would like to run a series of classified advertisements in these and other consumer magazines such as Playboy and Cosmopolitan, but even these prove too expensive for the initial promotion budget. Classified advertisements therefore become (H) part of the second stage of promotion which becomes possible if advance sales permit a larger printing and a concomitant increase in promotion budget.

Posters

Approximately 2500 will be distributed to popular bookstores, indoor garden

.../6

shops, and nurseries. While posters are a costly item, they are extremely

useful for this type of book, especially where the book cover design is

used for maximum recognition and impact. To avoid the expense and waste of

a large haphazard poster mailing, sales representatives will provide distri-

bution lists. Copy and layout attached. (I)

Publicity Tour

Purvis Mulch lives in   ; thus we plan a publicity tour that

will take her to seven major cities between there and New York City.

The cities on the itinerary, and tentative dates, are:

Home City	March 31
	April 3 & 4
Near-by City	April 6 - 8
Chicago, Illinois	April 10 - 12
Cleveland, Ohio	April 13 - 15
Toronto, Canada	April 17 - 19
Boston, Massachusetts	April 20 - 24
New York City	April 25 - May 2
Philadelphia, Pennsylvania	May 3 - 5
Home (via New York)	May 6

Fortunately, Purvis Mulch is a popular lady with friends in all of these

cities who have offered her their hospitality. Thus living expenses during

the publicity tour will be minimal. Much as I would like to accompany Purvis

Mulch on this tour, the budget will not allow it. However we will provide

detailed itineraries well in advance to the author, sales representatives,

stores in the particular area, and ABA Newswire. Sales representatives will

schedule their itineraries so that they can assist Ms. Mulch. They will not

have to spoon feed her of course; she is a competent woman, accustomed to

travel and interviews, and quite capable of getting herself from interview

to interview, when necessary. Sales representatives should be at the Author

Demonstrations, however.

.../7

Activities in each city will fall into the following areas:

1.   Television Interviews

These and the following interviews have yet to be set up. Early research

and contact will indicate who is likely to be interested in interviews.

To these we will send release, biographical sheet, photograph of Purvis Mulch,

and a copy of No Time for House Plants, accompanied by an individual letter.

Follow up and final arrangements will be made by telephone.

Television interviews, both national and regional, will be scheduled on

appropriate talk, garden, and general interest shows. In some cases, plants

and props, or possibly photographs, will be provided for demonstration and

discussion.

2.   Radio Interviews

Radio interviews will include garden and general interest shows, as well

as phone-in discussion and advice programs.

3.   Newspaper Coverage

In each city we will attempt to get feature articles in one or more of the

leading newspapers and magazines. These interviews are likely to be done

by by-line columnists. However, Ms. Mulch will talk to garden and book

columnists as time permits, following up the review copy sent in February.

Photographs of Author Demonstrations will be sent to newspapers and may get

some additional space.

4.   Author Demonstrations

So called for lack of a better description. In actual fact these demon-

strations will combine:

(i) Demonstration of plant selection and care
(ii) Clinic to which people are invited to bring their plant problems
     or even their sick plants if they wish
(iii) Autographing books.

.../8

One exorcism is all we plan since it is extremely exhausting for Purvis Mulch and the show will probably want an 'exclusive'.

Exhibits

No Time for House Plants will be shown at every exhibit which we ourselves attend; the people who visit our booth are as likely to be interested in house plants as in their own discipline. In addition, we will include it in major co-operative displays.

Lectures

Whenever Purvis Mulch speaks on the subject of indoor gardening in future we will arrange that her book is available for display and sale, if possible. Naturally she will refer to it herself at every opportunity.

With the help of sales representatives, demonstrations will be arranged at the best possible location in each city, which could be a department store with both book and plant departments, a major indoor gardening shop, or a large nursery. Alternatively, a Demonstration could tie in with a garden show or convention.

Demonstrations will be scheduled on the last day in each city if this is possible, in order to take advantage of newspaper, radio, and television publicity. Ms. Mulch will be instructed to mention Demonstrations whenever possible.

Demonstrations will be supported by:

(i) Co-operative advertising (50/50) which must be co-ordinated with the Promotion Manager, and the cost approved. Repros will be available. (Layout and copy attached.) (G)

(ii) Posters, those provided by us, and others announcing the Demonstration.

(iii) Prescription Slips (Layout and copy - see attached). (J) These prescription slips are double duty - to advertise No Time for House Plants and provide a space for Ms. Mulch's advice.

(iv) Plant stakes (See attached.) (K) This is an extra, and part of Stage 2, i.e. increased promotion budget. The sticks would be ideal for use both at Demonstrations and by plant shops afterwards. The idea of course is that the dye-cut plant stake sticks into the soil of the plant -- No Time for House Plants is advertised on one side, and the other side is left blank for plant identification.

(v) Each store will be encouraged to offer its own special inducement during the Demonstration, such as a particular hardy plant at discounted price with purchase of the book.

Special Television

One area in which Purvis Mulch has been very successful is in plant exorcism. We want to reserve this performance for a really big talk show, such as Mike Douglas, or if the 'Tonight Show' people could be persuaded to pay Ms. Mulch's expenses to Los Angeles, then that would be our first choice.

.../9

PROMOTION BUDGET

No Time for House Plants

by Purvis Mulch

3500 copies Release	
3500 copies Autobiographical Sheet	$ 200.00
Announcement ads	1,270.00
Purvis Mulch Travel Expenses	500.00
Meals and Miscellaneous (no accommodation and only some meals)	700.00
Posters 2500	800.00
Prescription Slips	60.00
Co-operative Advertising re Author Demonstrations	1,500.00
Miscellaneous	300.00
	$5,330.00

Stage 2

Classified Advertisements	$1,000.00
Plant Stakes	800.00
Direct Mail: Inexpensive Circulars plus small handling cost	700.00
	$2,500.00

NB

Cost of frees and mailing are not included in individual book budgets.

Outside Back Cover Copy

No Time for Houseplants

A busy person's guide to indoor gardening

Purvis Mulch

This delightful and entertaining book is the first guide to indoor gardening written specifically for the indoor gardener. It offers a recommended list of plants that will thrive under various conditions of light and temperature and explains the basic rules for caring for them without spending more than five minutes every other day. The busy homeowner or apartment dweller will find No Time for Houseplants an ideal guide.

'A simple and sensible guide to indoor gardening. It should demolish, once and for all, the myth of the green thumb.'   M.C. Goldman, Organic Gardening and Farming

'Refreshing and welcome ... a Mulch-needed publication.' Weekend Gardener

Purvis Mulch is the author of A Crackersport Garden Guide and has written numerous articles on gardening and related subjects. She is presently working on The Earthworm Book.

ISBN 0-8020- 2214-7

LC 76-10000

University of Toronto Press

Cover photograph by Ken Bell

B

<u>Catalogue copy</u>

<u>No Time for House Plants</u>

A busy person's guide to indoor gardening

Purvis Mulch

This delightful and entertaining book is the first guide to indoor gardening written specifically for the casual gardener. It explains the basic rules for selecting and caring for plants that need a minimum of attention.

Purvis Mulch, a busy person herself, has developed this successful approach to easy-care gardening through research, experience, and experimentation. The principles of the 'no-time' system are simple: first, choose plants that can tolerate some neglect, and then provide the right conditions for them to grow without constant attention. She outlines the initial requirements that plants need in order to thrive, requirements which, if met from the start, will save hours of identifying and correcting problems.

A separate chapter covers the diagnosis and treatment of plant ailments. Special sections are devoted to artificial light and summer care. The book lists over a hundred easy care foliage plants, flowering plants, and succulents, including cacti, giving light, soil moisture, and humidity requirements for each. Special lists of plants suited to various conditions of light and temperature enable indoor gardeners to select plants that will grow in any part of the country or in any corner of the house.

For those who find that this easy-care system leaves time for more ambitious adventures in gardening, Mulch provides detailed information on repotting, propagation, training, dish gardens, planters, bottle gardens and terrariums, kitchen scrap gardens, and growing vegetables indoors.

For the homeowner or apartment dweller who would like to raise several dozen attractive house plants without spending more than a few minutes a day in caring for them, <u>No Time for House Plants</u> is an ideal guide.

Purvis Mulch is the author of <u>A Crackersport Garden Guide</u> and has written numerous articles on gardening and related botanical subjects. She is currently working on <u>The Earthworm Book</u>.

University of Toronto Press

TORONTO / ONTARIO / CANADA M5S 1A6

For Immediate Release

PURVIS MULCH demolishes the myth that house plants require a lot of time, effort, and a very green thumb in her new book, No Time for House Plants.

Many people - singles, working couples, harassed mothers, college students, anyone whose daily living pattern leaves precious little time for indoor gardening - would enjoy the beauty and companionship of luxuriant green house plants. However, past failures and fruitless excursions into gardening books that confuse while trying to explain have convinced them that they had neither the time nor the expertise to raise plants successfully. 'Nonsense,' maintains Purvis Mulch, 'anyone can raise beautiful and healthy plants.'

'The secrets to success are simple,' Ms. Mulch continues. 'Choose plants that are easy to grow and give them the conditions they must have to thrive.' Explaining her approach to easy-care gardening in No Time for House Plants, she recommends and describes more than one hundred plants and plant groups (comprising several thousand individual varieties) which have demonstrated tolerance of the human environment.

Every plant has its own requirements for soil type, light, temperature, ventilation, humidity - factors that are within our power to control, or at least to mitigate. Purvis Mulch fully describes the preferences of each plant; also, through a system of unique symbols, she provides an at-a-glance profile of their needs.

Before growing any plant, however, Ms. Mulch advises the indoor gardener to take some time first to understand it, to learn what the plant needs and to decide whether that is easily provided, and to choose the spot in which the plant will be most comfortable. Then, as many as twenty different house plants can be raised by spending no more than five minutes with them every other day, and perhaps a half-hour every two weeks in pruning,

.../2

- 2 -

tying climbers, bathing leaves, spraying, and fertilizing.

The recommended plants are divided into four broad groups - foliage plants, cacti and other succulents, flowering house plants, and bulb plants. Amongst the known and lesser known varieties are Asparagus, Bromeliads, Cast Iron Plants, Dieffenbachia, Ferns, Ficus, Ivy, Umbrella Sedge (foliage plants) and the Aloes, Echeverias, Crassulas, Kalanchoes, Spider Plant, Snake Plant, and Sedums (succulents). Flowering house plants include Achimenes, African Violets, Amaryllis, Begonia, Chenille Plant, Gloxinia, Wax Plant, and Zebra Plant. The bulb plants are Crocuses, Hyacinths, Tulips, and Daffodils. Within each group, the plants are listed alphabetically by their common names, followed by their scientific (Latin) names in parentheses.

For those who find this easy-care system leaves time for more ambitious adventures in gardening, Purvis Mulch provides chapters on pots and other containers, repotting plants, propagation, problems and their cures, special gardens such as planters, bottle gardens and terrariums, and growing vegetables indoors.

Busy people will find No Time for House Plants the ideal guide for adapting indoor gardening to their lifestyles.

Purvis Mulch is well known for her articles and lectures on gardening and for her bestselling book, A Crackersport Garden Guide.

NO TIME FOR HOUSE PLANTS: A Busy Person's Guide to Indoor Gardening $9.95, publication date April 1, 19--, published by University of Toronto Press

Contact Audrey M. Livernois
416-978-2052

University of Toronto Press

TORONTO / ONTARIO / CANADA M5S 1A6

D

Autobiographical Sheet

PURVIS MULCH (Author of No Time for House Plants)

[Purvis Mulch tells her own story so well that we have decided to provide an Author's Autobiographical Sheet, rather than the usual Biographical Sheet.]

'I was born in Crackersport, Pennsylvania during the Great Depression, of Pennsylvania Dutch parents. We were not poor, but honest, good country folk.

'My father, Marvin Mulch, was a farmer who specialized in mangoes and guavas. My mother Roxanne worked at the open hearth furnaces at Bethlehem Steel. I believe that I inherited my love for plants and my romantic streak from my father, and my intensely practical nature from my mother. Father's history still remains a frazzled thread in the family fabric. He spent twenty-three years in trying to grow tropical fruits in the middle of the best potato-growing land on the Eastern Seaboard. Naturally, his young trees died every year around Thanksgiving. During one unusually warm year, in 1939, he nursed a guava until three days before Christmas before it fell to mice. Dad's reasoning was that, while potatoes were selling for four cents a pound in grocery stores, mangoes and guavas were going for a dime apiece. In 1948, he became convinced that a large greenhouse might be the answer to the recurring frost problem. He finished the greenhouse on August 12, 1950, the day before the greatest hail storm in local memory, and spent the next three years constructing glass mobiles for the tourist trade. All this while, mother commanded top wages in the steel mill, commuting between the farm and Bethlehem six days a week. She organized the steel workers' union at Bethlehem and is still remembered there for once dispatching four goons in an alley behind a tavern. A folk song about her exploits never sold well.

'From this background, I developed a sensitivity to growing things as well as a respect for the inner toughness that often sees us through life's cloudy days.

.../2

Purvis Mulch - Autobiographical Sheet -- Page 2

The fact that I once assailed a six-foot dieffenbachia in the Brooklyn Botanical Gardens is not without developmental roots.

'After childhood, my life's direction was fairly well set. I educated myself in both library and garden, and at the age of 28 developed a theory that organic fertilizer was the answer to communism. My first published article, "Marx or Manure: America's Choice for the 50s", appeared in the Philadelphia Inquirer Sunday garden supplement of March 2, 1955. On the strength of that piece, I began to write and lecture full-time, paying special attention to mangoes and left-wing bureaucrats at the U.S. Department of Agriculture.

'With the waning of the communist scare, my interests turned more to companion planting, varieties of hairy vetch, bacterial control of brown rot on sour cherry trees, and earthworms as the guardians of modern civilization.'

Publisher's Note

Purvis Mulch has become well known through her lectures and articles on gardening. Her tongue-in-cheek autobiography is typical of the humor for which she is also known. She has two previous books to her credit: A Crackersport Garden Guide (author) and Encyclopedia of Organic Gardening (contributing editor), and numerous articles in such magazines as House Beautiful, Organic Gardening and Farming, Mother Jones, Camping Journal, and Countryside. She is presently working on a new book to be entitled The Earthworm Book. Purvis Mulch has been married twice. Currently unmarried, she remains 'good friends' with her ex husbands. She has three children all of whom wholeheartedly support her earthy interests.

REVIEW COPIES LIST

(120)

CODE: SBN 8020 - 2214-7

TITLE: No Time for House Plants

AUTHOR: Purvis Mulch

PUB. DATE: April 1, 19---

PRICE: $9.95

Sheet No: 1 of _____ sheets.

DATE	State / Province	PUBLICATION
February 1		U.S. Newspapers
	California	Los Angeles Times, Carolyn Murray, Home Columnist
		San Francisco Chronicle, Ruth Miller, Women's Interest
		San Francisco Examiner, Marie Hammock, Garden Columnist
	Colorado	Denver Post, Clark Secrest, Garden Columnist
	Connecticut	Hartford Courant, John Massaro, Garden Columnist
		New Haven Register, Marion McDonald, Women's Interest
	DC	Washington Post, Tom Stevenson, Garden Columnist
	Florida	Miami Herald, Wilbur H. Youngman, Garden Columnist
	Illinois	Chicago Daily News, Peclice Dickson, Garden Columnist
		Chicago Sun Times, Richard Delano, Garden Columnist
		Chicago Tribune, Eldred E. Green, Garden Columnist
	Indiana	Indianapolis News, Arthur Kozelka, Garden Columnist
	Iowa	Des Moines Register, Richard Creem, Garden Columnist
	Massachusetts	Christian Science Monitor, Fleeta Woodruffe, Garden Columnist
		Boston Globe, Millicent J. Taylor, Garden Col.
		Boston Herald American, G. D'Alfonso, Women's Interest
	New Jersey	Worcester Telegram, Maureen Taylor, Women's Interest
		Newark Star Ledger, Nicholas Zook, Garden & Home Columnist
		Trenton Sunday Times, John Van de Water, Garden Columnist
	New York	Buffalo Evening News, Sally Lane, Garden & Home Columnist
		Rochester Democrat & Chronicle, Ed Collins, Garden & Home Columnist
		Syracuse Sunday Herald, Home & Family Department
		New York Times, Edward Sabine, Garden Columnist
		New York Times Book Review, Joan Lee Faust, Garden Columnist
		New York News, R. Marie Burke, Women's Interest (2 copies)
	Maryland	Baltimore Sun, Francis Rackemann, Garden & Home Columnist
		Baltimore News American, Tom Stevenson, Garden Columnist
	Michigan	Detroit Free Press, Dorothy Weddell, Garden Columnist
		Detroit News, June Hicks, Garden Columnist
		Grand Rapids Press, Charles Johnson, Garden Columnist
	Missouri	St. Louis Post-Dispatch, Joan Dames, Garden & Home Col.
		Kansas City Star, Mary Hobbs, Garden Columnist
	Minnesota	Minneapolis Tribune, Mary Hart, Women's Interest
		St. Paul Dispatch, Robert Phillips, Garden Columnist
	Ohio	Akron Beacon Journal, Kate Clapp, Garden Columnist
		Cincinnati Enquirer (Sun), Elliw Rawnsley, Garden Col.
		Cleveland Plain Dealer, Irma W. Bartell, Garden Columnist
		Cleveland Press, Paul Young, Garden Columnist
		Dayton Daily News, Linda Heffley, Home & Family Columnist

REVIEW COPIES LIST

CODE: SBN 8020 - 2214-7

TITLE: No Time for House Plants

AUTHOR: Purvis Mulch

PUB. DATE: April 1, 19---

PRICE: $9.95

Sheet No: 2 of _____ sheets.

DATE	State/Province	PUBLICATION
February 1		U.S. Newspapers Continued
	Pennsylvania	Philadelphia Sunday Bulletin, Patricia Spollen, Garden Col.
		Philadelphia Inquirer, Florence Bahar, Garden Columnist
		Pittsburgh Press, Newton Georg, Garden Columnist
	Texas	Dallas Morning News, Neil Sperry, Garden Columnist
		Dallas Times Herald, Edith McRoberts, Garden Columnist
		Houston Post, May Del Flagg, Garden Columnist
		Richmond Times Dispatch, Mrs. Jerry Williams, Garden Col.
	Virginia	Seattle Times, Clayton Hay, Garden Columnist
	Washington	Seattle Post Intelligencer, Ed Hume, Garden Columnist
		Madison Capital Times, Mary B. Hopkins
	Wisconsin	Madison State Journal, Carmen Elsner, Book Editor
		Madison Progressive, Mary Sheridan, Managing Editor
		Milwaukee Journal, Gerald Van Ryzin, Garden Columnist
		Milwaukee Sentinel, David Kitchen, Garden & Home Columnist
		U.S. Magazines, Journals, Book Review Service
		Publishers' Weekly (also pages)
		Kirkus Review (also pages)
		Library Journal
		Booklist
		John Barkham Reviews
		Chicago Seed
		New Home Books
		American Home
		American Nurseryman
		Apartment Ideas
		Apartment Life
		Better Homes and Gardens
		Budget Decorating
		Cosmopolitan
		Countryside
		Esquire
		Family Circle
		Harpers
		Home Lifestyles
		House and Garden
		House Beautiful
		The Homemaker
		Horticulture
		Interior Design
		Ladies' Home Journal
		Leisure Living

REVIEW COPIES LIST

CODE: SBN 8020 - 2214-7
TITLE: No Time for House Plants
AUTHOR: Purvis Mulch
PUB. DATE: April 1, 19--
PRICE: $9.95

Sheet No: 4 of _____ sheets.

DATE	State / Province	PUBLICATION
		Canadian Magazines, Journals, Miscellaneous (cont'd)
		Canadian Homes (supplement to Canadian Magazine)
		Chatelaine
		Homemaker's Magazine
		Nature Canada
		Quest
		Readers' Club of Canada
		Miscellaneous Additions

REVIEW COPIES LIST

CODE: SBN 8020 - 2214-7
TITLE: No Time for House Plants
AUTHOR: Purvis Mulch
PUB. DATE: April 1, 19--
PRICE: $9.95

Sheet No: 3 of _____ sheets.

DATE	State / Province	PUBLICATION
February 1		U.S. Magazines, Journals, Book Review Service (cont'd)
		McCall's
		Mother Jones
		Ms.
		National Gardener
		New York Magazine
		New Yorker
		New Woman
		Plants & Gardens
		Playboy
		Playgirl
		1000 + 1 Decorating Ideas
		Organic Gardening and Farming
		Todays Woman
		Vogue
		West Coast Review
		Women's Circle
		Workbasket
		Woman's Day
		Canadian Newspapers
	British Columbia	Vancouver Sun, R. Nicholson, Garden Columnist
	Alberta	Calgary Herald, Walter Webber, Garden Columnist
		Edmonton Journal, B. Andrews, Garden Columnist
	Saskatchewan	Regina Leader Post, Family Editor
		Saskatchewan Star Phoenix, Ted Hainworth, Family Living
	Manitoba	Winnipeg Free Press, M.W. Chestnut, Garden Columnist
	Ontario	Ottawa Citizen, Steve Jonescu, Garden Columnist
		Toronto Globe and Mail, Lenore MacDonald, Family Section Ed.
		Toronto Star, H. Fred Dale, Garden Columnist
		Toronto Sun, Joan Sutton, Women's Interest
	Québec	Montréal Star, Paul Pouliot, Garden Columnist
	Nova Scotia	Halifax Mail Star, Lorna Inness, Columnist
		Canadian Magazines, Journals, Miscellaneous
		Canadian Press
		John Bradshaw, syndicated horticulturalist
		Canadian Book Review Annual
		Canadian Field Naturalist
		Canadian Living

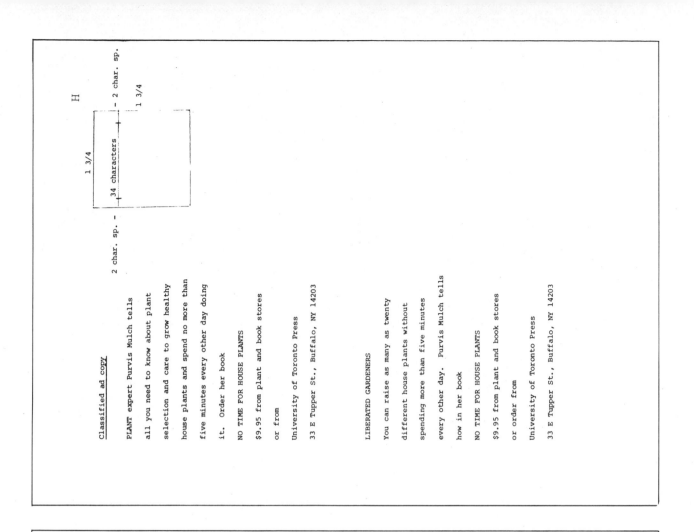

H

1 3/4

34 characters — 2 char. sp.

2 char. sp. —

1 3/4

Classified ad copy

PLANT expert Purvis Mulch tells
all you need to know about plant
selection and care to grow healthy
house plants and spend no more than
five minutes every other day doing
it. Order her book
NO TIME FOR HOUSE PLANTS
$9.95 from plant and book stores
or from
University of Toronto Press
33 E Tupper St., Buffalo, NY 14203

LIBERATED GARDENERS
You can raise as many as twenty
different house plants without
spending more than five minutes
every other day. Purvis Mulch tells
how in her book
NO TIME FOR HOUSE PLANTS
$9.95 from plant and book stores
or order from
University of Toronto Press
33 E Tupper St., Buffalo, NY 14203

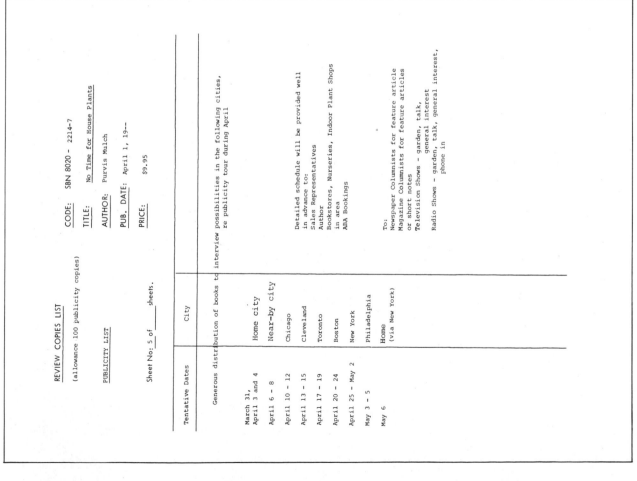

REVIEW COPIES LIST
(allowance 100 publicity copies)

PUBLICITY LIST

CODE: SBN 8020 - 2214-7
TITLE: No Time for House Plants
AUTHOR: Purvis Mulch
PUB. DATE: April 1, 19--
PRICE: $9.95

Sheet No: 5 of _____ sheets.

Generous distribution of books to interview possibilities in the following cities, re publicity tour during April

Tentative Dates	City
March 31, April 3 and 4	Home city
April 6 - 8	Near-by city
April 10 - 12	Chicago
April 13 - 15	Cleveland
April 17 - 19	Toronto
April 20 - 24	Boston
April 25 - May 2	New York
May 3 - 5	Philadelphia
May 6	Home (via New York)

Detailed schedule will be provided well in advance to:
Sales Representatives
Author
Bookstores, Nurseries, Indoor Plant Shops in area
ABA Bookings

To:
Newspaper Columnists for feature article
Magazine Columnists for feature articles or short notes
Television Shows - garden, talk, general interest
Radio Shows - garden, talk, general interest, phone in

You can raise as many as twenty different house plants by spending no more than five minutes with them every other day.

PURVIS MULCH

PURVIS MULCH *No Time for House Plants*
A Busy Person's Guide to Indoor Gardening

Lorem ipsum dolor sit amet, consectetur adipiscing elit, sed diam nonnumy eiusmod tempor incidunt ut labore et dolore magna a erat volupat. Ut enim ad minim veniam, quis nostrud exercitatio ut aliquip ex ea commcdo consequat. Duis autem vel eum irure in reprehenderit in volupante velit esse molestaie consequat, vel dolore eu fugiat nulla pariatur. At vero eos et accusam et iusto o dignissim qui blandit praesent luptatum delenit aigue duos dolor molestias excepteur sint occaecat cupiditat non provident, simil s culpa qui officia deserunt mollit anim id est laborum et dolor fug harund dereud facilis est er expedit distinct. Nam liber tempor c soluta nobis eligend optio comgue hinil impedit doming in quodr placeat facer possim omnis voluptas assumenda est. Omnis dolor aut tum rerum necessit atib saepe eveniet ut er repudiand sint et i Itaque earud rerum hic tenetury sapiente delectus au aut prefer dolorib asperiore repellat. Hanc ego cum tene senteniam, quid e

University of Toronto Press
otest fier ad augendas cum conscient to factor tum poen

F

Ad copy for

Publishers Weekly, Quill & Quire, American Nurseryman,

and Organic Gardening and Farming (minus the discount line)

"You can raise as many as

twenty different house plants

by spending no more than five

minutes with them every other day."

Purvis Mulch

No Time for House Plants is the first guide to indoor greenery

writter specifically for the casual gardener. Informative and

entertaining, it outlines a simple approach to easy-care gardening.

In it, Purvis Mulch recommends and describes more than one hundred

plants, comprising several thousand individual varieties, and

shows through a unique system of symbols the conditions required

for each. She discusses pots and potting, propagation, problems

and cures, and other matters that will increase the indoor gardener's

understanding and enjoyment of plant raising.

"Choose plants that are easy to grow, give them the conditions they

need to thrive," advises the author, "and you can grow house plants

anywhere in the country, any time of the year, in any corner of the

house."

$9.95

Generous discounts on quantity orders

UNIVERSITY OF TORONTO PRESS
Buffalo, NY   Toronto, Canada

Bring your plant problems and meet PURVIS MULCH, author of

as she demonstrates plant selection and care, advises on your ailing plants, and autographs copies of her book

---

Cooperative Ad

Date and time space block (large)

Bring your plant problems
and MEET plant expert

PURVIS MULCH

author of

```
┌─────────────┐
│             │
│     cut     │
│      of     │
│    book     │
│             │
└─────────────┘
```

as she

- demonstrates plant selection and care
- advises on your ailing plants
- autographs copies of her book

space block for name and address of
sponsoring store (large)

Instructions

2 cols. X
up to a maximum of 100 lines,
preferably 75
Strong ad please,
with border.

G

Plant Stake   (K)

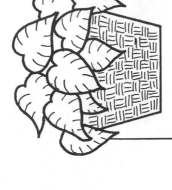

For easy plant care
consult
Purvis Mulch's
NO TIME
FOR HOUSE PLANTS

Poster   (I)

Size 10 1/4 x 15

2 colour, reverse title

jacket reproduced 9 3/4 x 12 3/4

Copy

If you can spare five minutes every other day

welcome to the pleasures of indoor gardening.

$9.95

University of Toronto Press

Prescription Slip (J)

Rx   PURVIS S. MULCH, P D

DATE

RE

Author of NO TIME FOR HOUSE PLANTS

Afterword

*What Do You Make
of a "Make-believe" Book?*

*One Book Six Ways:
The University of Oklahoma Press*

Afterword

ONE BOOK/FIVE WAYS has told its own story very well so far, but a number of things remain to be said. Clearly, as Chandler Grannis noted in his Introduction, "There is more than one way to make a book." But what may not be so clear (even though some of the harsh economic realities of publishing are evident, directly or indirectly, in the foregoing pages) is that book publishing is "a slow way to make a fast buck"—at least for the vast majority of publishers and authors. Furthermore, there are interesting and entertaining facts regarding the development and publication of ONE BOOK/FIVE WAYS which have not been presented elsewhere and which deserve to be shared. These and a number of other incidental topics that concern book publishing in general and education for publishing in particular are included here in the spirit of the rest of the book. It is our hope that many readers with differing interests will be provided with some additional insights and food for ongoing thought.

Critic Herbert Mitgang noted recently in *The New York Times* that "America's university presses do not publish just for college students and professors. Quite often these days, they are putting out books that almost any regular trade house would be proud to include on its list." I would add that for some time now, university presses have been publishing books that are far more interesting, imaginative, useful, and substantial in every way than are the largest numbers of books published by the regular trade houses. University presses also help conceive and develop good books that are published eventually by a trade house or by some other commercial publisher, rather than by one of their own number. ONE BOOK/FIVE WAYS is a case in point, to which all of the foregoing assertions apply.

In his Introduction to this book, which was written well before any plans for commercial publication were made, Chandler Grannis also noted, "It is a valuable contribution to the literature of education for publishing . . ." The opinions of Chandler Grannis, a lifelong observer of book publishing, are not to be taken lightly; Mr. Grannis has served as Editor-in-Chief of the leading trade journal, *Publishers Weekly*, to which he is now a Contributing Editor. He is also a book editorial consultant to the R. R. Bowker Company, "the publishers' publisher". He has written extensively on bookmaking, book design, and university presses, and he is also the editor of two books: HERITAGE OF THE GRAPHIC ARTS and WHAT HAPPENS IN BOOK PUBLISHING.

Given the importance of ONE BOOK/FIVE WAYS and the existence of so many excellent university presses as possible publishers, why has this book been published by William Kaufmann, Inc.—a commercial publisher—rather than by one of the participating presses; or, for that matter, by any one of the scores of others?

The answer to the question is simple. We are the publisher because we made a proposal for the book that was acceptable to the "author"—in this instance, the Association of American University Presses, Inc., which acted as "agent" in behalf of the participating presses and others in the Association who were involved in the project. This is the simple procedure by which most books get signed up by publishers in the first place. Publishers discover (or are shown) book proposals or manuscripts at various stages of completion. If they find any of these proposals appealing from the vantage point of their own editorial needs, the publishers offer the authors or their agents an agreement for publication. If the terms are found to be acceptable to all parties concerned, a formal contract for publication (much like any of those in this book) is concluded.

But, as may be imagined, there were unusual elements leading to the publication of ONE BOOK/FIVE WAYS. My own involvement with this extraordinary enterprise began with a telephone call in June 1976 from Walter Sears, the Director of the University of Michigan Press. He briefly described a project which was under way, which he called "The Manuscript Project", and invited me to speak about it from a commercial publisher's point of view at the Annual Meeting of the Association of American University Presses, scheduled to take place in Asheville, North Carolina, June 26–29, 1977. I accepted his invitation, but was not fully aware of what I had let myself in for until many months later.

Early in March 1977 I received a complete xerox copy of the press-ready pages (reproduction proofs) for what had by then become known as ONE BOOK/FIVE WAYS. It was to be printed for distribution as a "workbook" for all of the delegates to the upcoming Annual Meeting. Even in a small edition of fewer than 1,000 copies it would be less expensive per copy to print than to reproduce by xerox or other copying methods, and of course much more convenient to use.

By the time I had gone through all those xerox pages, I knew that here was something truly original, something remarkable, something that should be published for broader distribution. It seemed to me that this would be a unique book, completely unprecedented. Such a book is (as everyone in publishing knows) a rare and almost miraculous event. Who else but the university presses would be willing or able to assign the talent and make a comparable expenditure of the time and money and the multiple creative efforts that had so obviously gone into its development and production? (The "sedate spoofery", wit and good humor throughout that are characteristic of the entire venture come as sheer bonuses to the reader, even though the thorough and serious explication of the entire publishing process is the chief contribution of this superbly educational book.) And, from a competitive marketing point of view, it seemed clear to me that ONE BOOK/FIVE WAYS fulfilled its aims so well that it was unlikely that anyone else would even try to match its achievement for a long time to come.

Following the AAUP Meeting in Asheville, the Canadian Book Trade Journal *Quill and Quire* published a long account in which the reporter pointed out that there is ". . . much to learn from ONE BOOK/FIVE WAYS. The logs contain complete sets of forms for handling a mansucript from acquisition to printing and reveal methods of costing, contracts and royalty schemes that no trade publisher would let out of his office . . . a wealth of material on publishing procedures." It was just those aspects of this book that had "hooked" me as a publisher when I first saw it in xerox copy form. As "one of commercial publishing's strongest advocates for publishing education" (*Publishers Weekly's* designation), I have been active in the development of various courses, seminars and conferences about publishing, at

Stanford University, at campuses of the University of California, Berkeley, Davis and San Francisco, and in other West Coast educational centers. It has also been my privilege to serve on the Committee on Education for Publishing, which was established in 1975 by the Association of American Publishers in response to the growing recognition, among leaders in the regular trade, textbook, reference and other commercial publishing houses, of the vital importance of fostering better education for (and about) publishing. It is satisfying to see publishing education beginning to receive the attention it merits.

Different people concerned with publishing have their own, perhaps different, reasons for considering education for publishing to be so important. But there are two major reasons why I do. First, I regard the publishing of good books (or journals or magazines) as a very high calling indeed, one for which the opportunity for continuing education is highly desirable, if not absolutely necessary, with potential benefits for those who work in publishing as well as for many who do not—librarians, booksellers, teachers, and other "book consumers" of all sorts. In his book, *Dr. Johnson's Printer*, J. A. Cochrane said that publishing

> ". . . was and is no ordinary trade . . . It is practised by men no more intelligent than those engaged in other lines of business; its rewards are, commercially, trifling in relation to the industry and shrewdness it calls into play; as an occupation it entails fully as much of the humdrum drudgery, the pettiness of detail, as is exhibited in any manner of earning a living. But the book trade is distinguished from any other by the fact that its fundamental staple is ideas, even though the tangible expression o those ideas is bought and sold like other commodities. This is the reason for its intrinsic interest and for the fascination it exerts upon those who work in it and so rarely desert it; this is what gives the market place its curious atmosphere, in fluctuating proportions, of idealism and commercial practicality."

On the occasion of the 500th Anniversary of The Oxford University Press, John Russell commented, in *The New York Times Book Review*,

> "Publishing (ideally, at any rate) has to do with genius . . . It has to do with gambling of a lofty but nonetheless desperate kind. It calls for insight, imagination, great technical address and a superfine sense of social and political realities . . . To the layman, it might seem that a university press is the easiest thing in the world to run . . . These are delusions. A university press is, if anything, even more difficult to run than an independent publishing house. . ."

The second reason for placing so high a value on education is related to the first. Given the fundamental importance of reading and books in our society, it is essential that people involved in publishing be given the chance to keep up with the challenges that new techniques and technologies, new ideas, new legislation and social changes will inevitably bring to their work. If they can gain and maintain a broader understanding of the whole world of books they themselves, as well as the important commodities they deal in, can compete more successfully in an increasingly competitive world. Samuel S. Vaughan, Publisher and President of the publishing division of Doubleday and Company, noted in his 1976 Bowker Lecture:

"... forty of the finest people I know in publishing are at work today on education for publishing, education in publishing, and education about publishing. They believe that to help educate the world, we and those who follow had better educate ourselves further. . . . Publishers first have to understand better what it is we do and then take less time to gossip and more time to explain."

Fortunately, there is a growing (even if still terribly insufficient) appreciation of the importance of reading and books—including their economic importance—to contemporary society. The *mini-industries*, including film and television "tie-ins", that have literally been founded on some recent books, such as *Jaws* and *Roots*, as well as on various series such as those from Time-Life, Inc., the National Geographic Society, and others that could be mentioned, are astonishing. The combined economic impact of certain scholarly monographs and textbooks, not to mention various automotive books, cookbooks, craft books, survival books and other kinds of "how-to-be-successful-at-this-or-that" books is enormous. Incidentally, in 1975, "How-to-do-it" books occupied about 20 pages of *Books in Print*, the Bowker book trade "bible", representing some 1200 titles—and this includes only those whose titles begin with "How To. . ."! But of course economic power is hardly a new phenomenon in the world of books. For centuries, the Bible and other religious publications in many lands have provided countless people with their daily "bread", as well as with inspiration.

The distinguished publishing consultant, Datus C. Smith, Jr. (himself a former Director of the Princeton University Press and President of the AAUP, 1947-48) spoke eloquently of some of these issues (in a different context) in his 1977 report for UNESCO:

"Unawareness of the basic economic facts of book publishing is astonishingly prevalent among book people—even including book publishers themselves—in all countries. That lack of understanding is found not just in developing areas but also in the publishing industries of the countries preening themselves on their sophistication in both technology and economics . . .

"And if the publishers themselves are uninformed . . . it would be remarkable if the governments of their countries should have any better grasp of the facts and concepts. Yet the welfare of book institutions—publishing houses, printing plants, bookstores, libraries—can be powerfully affected for good or ill by those governments. The need for educating the government—and the public to which the government is supposed to be responsive—is overwhelming if there is to be any true understanding of the national interest in book development . . .

"The first step toward mobilizing public and governmental support for any program in book development is therefore full understanding of their own field by book people themselves. . ."

Amen. My own powerful convictions about the importance of publishing and publishing education are as an almost inevitable consequence of my background and training in educational publishing, especially under the gifted tutelage of William H. Freeman, founder of the San Francisco publishing company that bears his name, during the 1950's. Science education in particular was burgeoning then, and some of the world's leading scientists were writing introductory textbooks, monographs and other expository works (as distinguished from their research reports) in unprecedented numbers. To my surprise, many of these scientists reported that they were learning more about their own special subject matter whenever they undertook to write popularizations or introductory textbooks than they had in almost any other way. It turned out that this was an unexpected "dividend"—a by-product of the stringent requirement that they survey an entire field or discipline thoroughly, and at the same time explain it simply, clearly and accurately to readers who presumably knew little or nothing about the subject. Some authors even undertook to write books for the express purpose of learning. Dr. John R. Pierce, a professor of engineering at the California Institute of Technology in Pasadena, recently recalled just such an occasion, writing in *Science* magazine about Dr. Edward E. David Jr., President-Elect of the American Association for the Advancement of Science, who had served as science advisor to President Richard Nixon and as director of the U.S. Office of Science and Technology. Dr. Pierce relates that, when they first met, Dr. David was at Bell Laboratories, in charge of acoustics research, which included fundamental work on speech and hearing. "Because neither he nor I knew much about this," Pierce said, "we wrote a book . . . which taught us a great deal. . ."

But I later learned that this was hardly new. Nearly a century ago, one of America's earliest and most distinguished entomologists, Leland O. Howard, contributed the entomological terms to the *Century Dictionary*. Later on, he wrote regarding this task,

> "The whole work was extremely interesting and had a high educational value. Things that I learned then have been of service to me in many ways. Then, too, the extra money was a great help."

Fiction writers also have commented on this educational aspect of book writing. For example, California author Peter S. Beagle has observed:

> "There's a very odd relationship between me and a piece of paper . . . I'll start a chapter without knowing what's in it. Things come to flower that I have no idea I'm thinking about . . . I seem to write books to find out what it is I'm writing about. In each case, with every book I've done, I've been wrong about what I thought it was. About two-thirds of the way through, I find out what book I'm suppose to be doing . . ."

As my own publishing experience grew during the 1960's, I became increasingly aware of how narrowly trained many of the people I met in publishing seemed to be, and how circumscribed were their special jobs within their companies. They often seemed unnecessarily cut off from access to any overall view of the publishing process from beginning to end. Gradually I found myself assuming the role of an advocate for more effective communication among all people in publishing and for more and better channels for publishing education.

This, then, was some of the background that ensured the firing of my enthusiasm about ONE BOOK/FIVE WAYS when those xerox copies arrived. Coincidentally, our company had concluded publishing arrangements for a related book (see Bibliography) just a few months earlier, and it seemed to us that these two books would complement one another nicely. Although we could not be certain of the size of the market for either book, we were confident that they were both going to be valuable and important working tools for many individuals employed in the various departments of publishing companies, as well as for authors. They would also be useful references for many of the other "book people" mentioned earlier, who have either a professional interest in book publishing or merely some degree of curiosity about our profession. My enthusiasm for publishing these books and the different problems inherent in producing and selling them reminded me of a favorite passage from *Now, Barabbas*, William Jovanovich's delightful book:

> ". . . a publisher should commit himself only to those books that engage him most seriously and thus confine his excesses to his interests. This suggests that there are sound personal reasons for the existence of many different kinds of publishing, and it may explain why publishing does not tend to follow a uniform procedure. The uniqueness of a book, any book, argues against the refinement of those skills based on repetition of effort. It is for this reason that my colleagues and I seem to approach each book as if we had never made one before."

The observation that publishing does not tend to follow a uniform procedure is confirmed again and again in the pages of ONE BOOK/FIVE WAYS, where different approaches to the same project at so many stages of its development are demonstrated by the participating presses. It should be apparent to authors that the insights and comparative data contained in this book will be of great value to them, too—especially any who may be contemplating "self-publishing". As self-publication has become a more respectable and feasible alternative route to publication, more and more individual authors will need to avail themselves of the kinds of detailed knowledge offered here. (I can report from first-hand experience that anyone contemplating either self-publication or the launching of his or her own publishing company is going to find either experience an incomparably effective way—if an unexpectedly strenuous and expensive one—to obtain an education about publishing!)

From the outset of the meetings in Asheville, one of the questions that engaged the attention of most participants was, "Who *is* Purvis Mulch?" The true identity of Purvis Mulch, the pseudonymous author of *No Time for Houseplants*, the manuscript used for this unprecedented educational experiment with comparative publishing procedures, was not revealed until the second day of the Asheville meeting. The further adventures of his now-famous manuscript are related below, but before coming to those matters, further information regarding the background of the entire project is essential. I am indebted to Hilary Marshall of the University of Toronto Press for permission to borrow freely from the lively and informative remarks he presented at the AAUP Meeting in Asheville regarding the early evolution of ONE BOOK/FIVE WAYS. I only regret that space does not allow for a complete presentation of all the rich intellectual fare presented by Hilary and the others who participated in the program—particularly Jack Putnam, Executive Director of the AAUP, and J. G. Bell, Associate Director of the Stanford University Press, whose Introduction to the entire program at the Sunday Evening Plenary Session was a masterpiece of wit and wisdom.

In Hilary Marshall's words, then, here is how it all began:

"Ten years ago our annual meeting was held in Toronto. Approximately two years before that I was asked to be responsible for the arrangements for the Toronto convention. Perhaps it was while I was working on them that the idea that we now see realized as ONE BOOK/FIVE WAYS came to me.

The basic idea was quite simply that if you were to present exactly the same manuscript to a number of different publishing houses, each of them would see in it a different book and, quite possibly, a different market. I thought that different editors would probably treat the manuscript differently, I knew I could count on the designers to come up with different designs, and I was pretty certain that sales people would also see different ways of getting to the market, given the right manuscript.

There were a lot of things I did not consider, of course, and some of these come close to being impossible to achieve. How, for example, could one ever find an author prepared to deal with five or six different presses, fill in all their different forms, carry on correspondence with editors, sales and promotion people, read all the edited versions, make comments on them, and spend hundreds of hours of time, all for the good of the cause? How could one find five or six presses prepared to donate the time and effort and money to put through this purely experimental idea, in the hope that it would be educational?

Somehow this idea came to be mentioned at a meeting of the Education and Training Committee some five or six years ago, and, at a meeting soon after that, Joyce Kachergis told me that the 1977 convention would be taking place under the aegis of North Carolina—and they were going ahead with the project.

Immediately all the problems that one could possibly think of with a project like this began to come into my mind, but once Joyce picks up an idea, she is just about impossible to stop. In no time at all she had six presses agreeing to do the work. We lost only one of them subsequently, and that was for very good reasons.

By the middle of January 1976, the final version of a manuscript entitled "No Time for Houseplants," by a pseudonymous author known as Purvis Mulch, came into being. A great deal of the preparatory work on the manuscript, and the time and energy the author and many staff members of the presses gave to the project does not show up in ONE BOOK/FIVE WAYS . . . The manuscript was subjected to a normal critical appraisal both in-house and outside. Malcolm Macdonald, who was then executive editor of the University of North Carolina Press, read it in first draft and made many wise and constructive comments on it. These are to be found in the North Carolina log, but it should be understood that the other presses benefitted from them. Not many of the exchanges of the author and the Press can be included here, for reasons of space, but some excerpts may help give the flavor. For instance, on January 6 1976, the author sent the following information to North Carolina: "Did you know that, 200 years ago today my great-great-great-great-grandfather cooked schnitz and knep because his wife Emma had strained herself on the way to the outhouse? It all happened in Lehigh County, Pennsylvania. . ." (The importance of such information to a promotion department at the beginning of a bicentennial year can easily be discerned.)

The final version of the manuscript was sent to two outside readers by the University of North Carolina Press. Reader A, a very senior horticulturalist, liked the manuscript instantly and said so. He described it as generally meritorious, offering much sound information and advice, and having the makings of a good book. But he warned that good editing was going to be needed.

Reader B did not like the book. The owner of a large shop selling household plants, Reader B wrote a single-spaced, six page review in which he attempted to pull the book to pieces. The author's response ran to 16 pages and consisted of a line by line (literally word by word) refutation of about 90% of Reader B's comments and an acceptance of the balance. Reader B caused some anxiety at North Carolina so the manuscript went to a third reader.

Reader C was an academic in the Department of Botany at the University. He made a short report and a number of editorial comments. His main concern seemed to be the market for the book, a concern of the publisher just as much as the author. The author was grateful for the helpful suggestions but disturbed that Reader C apparently did not see the purpose of the book and responded "It is, I hope, brevity, directness and a sense of purpose that will distinguish this manuscript from others. I think that the reader to whom the book is directed will find this book of value."

It was with all this background that the four other presses concerned with this project started to work on their individual editions."

ONE BOOK/FIVE WAYS details most of the consequences of this work in the preceding pages, but in concluding his remarks, Hilary Marshall also revealed to us the "confidential" evaluations Purvis Mulch had made of each of the university presses on the basis of his own experiences with them throughout this exercise. With the initial diffident remark, "I know so little about design I hesitate to comment on any of the five, except to say that each is lovely in its own way." Mulch made the following observations:

One of the early communications I received from Chicago informed me that a meeting had just been held, among eleven top executives, discussing plans for my manuscript. I think of this as "The Chicago Meeting," and I had the idea that awsome and irresistible forces were at that time set into motion, over which I had no control. After that, each Chicago department went about its business in a perfectly routine and professional manner, and I felt that I shouldn't interfere in any way. Catherine Seybold's editing was assertive, reasonable, and free from needless tinkering. My style was preserved. I saw Chicago as an aspidistra—tenacious, fearless, strong, and utterly dependable.

The people at MIT exuded a spirit of self-confidence and pride bordering on cockiness. This attitude bothered me at first, but it was soon justified by their cool and professional execution in all areas. Of the five presses, they were the last in getting started; but, after having begun, they brought the task to fruition in short order. Their editing was crisp and reasonable, their marketing and production plans bold and assertive. The MIT staff is, in my mind, a fiddleleaf philodendron—strong, clean in line, fully assured, and reaching without doubt for the sky.

The North Carolina treatment of my manuscript was, it seems to me, fraught with grave concern for both the manuscript and my well being. Barbara Reitt's copyediting, arriving in the mail, was like a hand extended across the miles, offering a pat of encouragement, perhaps an apology, and, afterward, a warm handshake—probably in relief that I had agreed to most suggestions with a struggle. In the end, the Chapel Hill product was a thing of beauty, competent and graceful in every way. North Carolina was a paradise palm—slow-growing and occasionally uncertain, but, in the end, branching out strongly with more than a touch of grandeur.

Texas provided, I think, the most thorough job of editing of all the five presses—so thorough, in fact, that I feared for the very character of the manuscript. The structure was attacked, the anthropomorphisms plucked, the non sequiturs properly sequitured. My manuscript was returned, adorned with dozens of gummed tabs holding queries. I answered the queries on more gummed tabs, and stuck them onto the pages. I was most relieved finally to be finished with Texas—but I knew also that Carolyn Wylie's gentle persuasion had produced a better manuscript, and that her task was greater than mine. Texas was a morning glory—worrysome, but beautiful.

Toronto is a grape ivy—strong and deep-rooted, exploding forth unabashedly, slightly impish in its behavior. The enthusiasm of both the editorial and marketing staffs came through without reservation or hesitation. The forms were, in themselves, things of beauty. In working with Toronto, I felt that my worries were over, that these were professional publishers with enough self-confidence to laugh occasionally at themselves. I would enjoy, late on a Friday afternoon, having a glass of sherry with Toronto, perhaps exchanging some choice repotting stories.

Purvis Mulch then concluded his observations:

"My dream is to see my little book, in each of its five beautiful forms, displayed in every bookstore in the United States and Canada. The customer, then, could choose the design that best suits his or her personality—and I could built up oh-so-lovely a royalties account."

The expressed "dream" of Purvis Mulch was not to be, but there was a happy outcome after all. As a result of the Asheville meeting and the AAUP's "workbook" version of ONE BOOK/FIVE WAYS, the interest of the University of Oklahoma Press in *No Time for Houseplants* had been aroused, and arrangements for publication were concluded with "Purvis Mulch", who had by now—undoubtedly with great relief—reassumed his true identity: Jerry Minnich, Assistant Director of the University of Wisconsin Press. May his little book—and all good books—fulfill their authors' and their publishers' fondest dreams.

We are deeply grateful to the University of Oklahoma Press for its cooperation in providing information comparable to that of the other presses represented in this volume relating to the publication of *No Time for Houseplants*. The appearance of that book in the fall of 1978 under the Oklahoma imprint marks the ultimate realization of the visionary ideas of Hilary Marshall and Joyce Kachergis and the fulfillment of the greatest expectations of the other dedicated and generous participants in "The Manuscript Project". From beginning to end, this project stands as a benchmark in the developing field of education for publishing. It is a pleasure to record our gratitude to all of the other participants in this volume, to thank everyone involved for giving us the opportunity to become participants ourselves, and to express the hope that ONE BOOK/FIVE WAYS will serve the interests of our magnificent profession long and well.

William Kaufmann
21 April 1978

UNIVERSITY OF OKLAHOMA PRESS

Table of Contents

UNIVERSITY OF OKLAHOMA PRESS

General Statement:

Unlike the presses involved in the One Book Five Ways project, the University of Oklahoma Press was interested in the actual possibility of publishing No Time for Houseplants. We have always carried a number of general trade titles on our list, particularly the how-to-do-it types of books, and this seemed a natural addition.

ACQUISITION PROCESS

The idea of our publishing the book was first raised by our Marketing Manager at one of our July 1977 biweekly editorial board meetings. (Any one of our seven member editorial board may make acquisition recommendations.) At this meeting it was decided to ask Jerry Minnich to submit the manuscript to us for formal consideration.

The editor telephoned Mr. Minnich; the manuscript arrived, was logged in, and was immediately assigned to an in-house reader for evaluation of style, suitability for our list, and potential market. The in-house reader reported favorably on the manuscript; the editorial board decided to seek an outside expert's opinion; the outside reader was contacted; the manuscript was sent out accompanied by our standard Reader's Report form; and within a couple of weeks the reader's report arrived recommending publication pending some minor revisions.

At this point a cost estimate was requested from our Production Department, to be based on producing 5,000 copies, paperback only, in a 6x9 trim size. The estimate returned from production; the editor completed a preliminary pricing analysis; and the project, with in-house reader's report, outside reader's report, cost estimates, and preliminary pricing information, was again considered for a final publishing decision at our late August 1977 editorial board meeting.

It was agreed at this meeting that the Press should offer Mr. Minnich a contract to publish the book, pending the revision suggested by the readers. The editor sent a contract memorandum to the Director, detailing the terms of the contract as agreed upon by the editorial board. The Director prepared and signed the contracts, sent them to the Business Manager for second signature, and the Business Manager forwarded them to the Editor for negotiation with the author.

The Editor prepared a contract letter to the author, detailing the conditions of publication, and sent the contracts, relevant portions of reader's reports, and an Author Information form to the author. The author accepted the terms of contract, returned the contracts signed, and informed the Editor that the revision would be completed and the final manuscript submitted in mid-October 1977.

EDITORIAL

The final manuscript was received on November 16, 1977, and was assigned to a house editor to prepare a physical inventory of the manuscript; to note any missing materials (the illustrations--line drawings--were noted as missing at this point); to determine any potential editorial or production problems; to prepare the manuscript for copyediting; and to make recommendations on print quantities, binding, price, and preferred publication season.

The house **editor's** "Report on Contracted Manuscript Received" was considered at our early December 1977 editorial board meeting, and it was decided to publish the book early in the Fall of 1978. A first printing quantity of 5,000 copies, all paperback, and a price of $5.95 was set at this time, based on a second cost estimate from the Production Department, and a second pricing analysis by the Editor.
The Editor contacted the author to determine a date for receipt of final artwork, and contracted with a freelance editor for the copyediting of the manuscript. The manuscript was sent to the freelance editor with a set of detailed instructions on editorial preparation of the manuscript.

The edited manuscript returned from the freelance editor, and the finished artwork arrived from the author in late January 1978. A house editor checked the editing of the freelancer, prepared and placed the artwork, prepared frontmatter copy, and running head copy, and completed a transmittal form for design and production.

The manuscript, artwork, transmittal form and related materials were turned over to the Director for final analysis and approval of the publication plan. The Director then sent the manuscript to design and production.

SALES AND PROMOTION

Publication date: September 30, 1978

Bound Book arrival date: August 15, 1978

Summary:

The emphasis of our promotional effort on this publication will be through bookstores and trade wholesalers. We will rely heavily on our publicity department to see that consumers hear/read about No Time for Houseplants. There will be minor efforts made in advertising (mostly classified), subsidiary rights, and exhibits. The Marketing Manager has asked for estimates on print runs of 5000, 7500, and 10,000 paperbacks. While we feel there may be a market for some cloth, the competition in this field is very great (see UNC Press list of competition), thus a low-price paperback is in order. Marketing Assignments are listed in left column.

(SM)=Sales and Marketing Manager   (R&PM)=Rights & Permissions Manager
(PM)=Publicity Manager   (BM)=Business Manager
(TSM)=Trade Sales Manager   (RM)=Review Copy Manager
(DMM)=Direct Mail Manager

(PM) 1. Poster: colorful (2-or3-color), distribution to 2500 bookstores (including chain stores)

2. Circular:
(DM) (a) 15,000 with 1-page sales letter (with order blank) mailed in envelope to Nursery people. States: CA, CT, IL, MA, NY, NY BOROS, OH, OK, TX
(DM) (b) 3,000 with 1-page sales letter (with order blank) mailed in envelope to florist. States: CA, CT, IL, MA, NY, NY BOROS, OH, OK, TX
(TSM) (c) 100 stuffers to each account of B. Dalton, Waldens, Doubleday, Brentanos, and Coles.
(TSM) (d) 100 stuffers to each: top 250 O.U. Press accounts.
(BM) (e) Single stuffers inserted in each of our statements for 2 months (i.e. Sept/Nov)
(DMM) (f) 500 to author
(SM) (g) piggyback circulars in One Book Five Ways (Kaufman Publishing Company)
(SM) (h) 4,000 circulars to our exhibit program
(DMM) (i) 3,000 misc. use
TOTAL 152,500

(TSM) (3) Counter-pre-pack: 10 copies each. TOTAL: N/A at this time. Quantity depends on advance sales orders to bookstores.

(TSM) (4) Trade Sales efforts: (a) special approaches by Sales Representatives to B. Dalton, Brentanos, Coles, Doubleday, Hunters, etc. (Alpha order) (b) special emphasis on promotion plans to sales force (consist of 16 commission sales representatives in each of the 50 states.)

(TSM) (5) Complimentary copies: Sent to 250 bookbuyers. Selected on basis of total net business (1977) with OU Press. This will hopefully promote book store awareness of this publication in an already crowded field of houseplant books, thus increasing sales when a customer asks for suggestions.

(RPM) (6) Bookclub adoptions: These will be sought through appropriate book clubs. (i.e. Quality Paperback Club, American Garden Guild Book Club, Organic Gardening Book Club, etc.)

(SM) (7) Two quotes from famous (but busy) individuals will be sought. Examples might be Jane Pauley or Sylvia Porter. These will be used in promotional copy and back-cover copy. Unlikely but worth a small amount of effort.

(RPM) (8) Excerpts: We will approach selected magazines and journals for possible excerptions. (List available on request.) Examples: Organic Gardening and Farming, Mother Jones, House Beautiful, Cosmopolitan, Today's Woman.

(SM) (9) Exhibits: OU Press regularly attends 35-40 exhibits per year (discipline, Library, historical society, etc.). We will feature No Time for Houseplants at each of these as a "bonus" consumer item. In this manner we will reach many professional people (teachers, librarians, etc.) who have house plants but "no time". We will also emphasize that No Time for Houseplants would make a nice, inexpensive gift.

(AM) (10) colorfully announced in Publishers Weekly seasonal ad (fall announcement)

(AM) (11) Classified ads will be arranged in selected magazines. List available on request. Examples: New York, Los Angeles, New Times, Texas Monthly, New Yorker.

(AM) (12) Space advertising: ads will be arranged in selected magazines, journals, and newspapers. List available on request. Emphasis will go to magazines in the North (shortest outside growing season) and magazines read by professional people (rather than horticultural magazines). Examples: various apartment magazines, New Times, New West, New York.

(PM/RM)(13) Newsrelease plus book (for review purposes): These copies to selected Garden Editors and life style editors (newspapers and magazines). Emphasis on this being the perfect house plant book for professional people. Newspaper list selected from Editor and Publisher; available on request.

(RM) (14) Selected copies to book reviewers but not many. List available on request. Hold to 75 copies.

(PM) (15) Review copies (plus letter) to 25 selected TV shows covering plants, flowers, and horticulture in general. (This might boost sales representative results in 25 area markets.) List available on request.

(TSM) (16) Newsrelease circular to <u>selected paperback jobbers</u> (wholesalers) not on OU Press account listing. List available on request.

(PM) (17) Advance page proofs to 25 selected newspapers and magazines. List available on request. Examples: <u>Publishers Weekly</u>, <u>New York Times</u>, <u>Better Homes & Gardens</u>, <u>House & Garden</u>, <u>House Beautiful</u>, <u>New Times</u>, <u>New West</u>, <u>New York</u>, (selected), <u>Chicago Sun</u>.

(DMM) (18) <u>No Time for Houseplants</u> will be included in our Fall and Winter 1978 seasonal catalog (8½x11). Distribution to 40,000 institutions and individuals (previous OU Press book buyers).

Contract sent 8/30/77 *(noted to Helen 10-17-77*

MANUSCRIPT TITLE: NO TIME FOR HOUSEPLANTS

PHOTOGRAPHS AND ILLUSTRATIONS (Give number): ~~Being compiled~~ 180-p. MS; illust. to come

AUTHOR: Jerry Minnich (Purvis Mulch)   ADDRESS: P.O. Box 1379
Madison, WI   53701

DATE RECEIVED: 11-16-77 ACKNOWLEDGED 11-17-77 RETURNED:
Rejection
Revision
Correction
After publication

READERS:

Name: Doris Morris   Date taken: 11-17-77   Date returned: 12-7-77

Name: Su Emry   Date taken: 12-16-77   Date returned: 1-10-78

Name: Date taken: Date returned:

Name: Date taken: Date returned:

TO AUTHOR: Date taken: Date returned:

TO SHOP: Date taken: Date returned:

PROOF   Date taken: Date returned:

First Reader's Report On NO TIME FOR HOUSEPLANTS: A BUSY PERSON'S GUIDE TO INDOOR GARDENING
by Jerry Minnich

Summary of the Manuscript: 180 pages of manuscript, with perhaps as many as 50 pen and
ink drawings to come. The subtitle is pretty descriptive: this is a guidebook
for those people who want to have greenery in their living environment, but
do not have the time or inclination to spend a lot of time and effort caring
for plants. The first three chapters deal with general problems associated
with care of plants; the remaining four chapters treat specific types of
plants and plant environments: Foliage Plants; Cacti and other Succulents;
Flowering Houseplants; and Special Indoor Gardens. Chapters 4, 5, and 6,
list specific plants in alphabetical order, detailing their special characteristics, and providing through the use of special symbols the pertinent
information concerning the necessary temperature range, humidity, amount
of sunlight, and exposure.

Qualities of Style: The style is fine for its intended readership--the general trade.
There is little or no scientific detail. There are numerous typos; some
lapses in syntax; and much switching from singular to plural and back
creating some problems in subject-verb agreement.

Suitability for List: As suitable as any of our other guide books.

Adaptability to Series: Not adaptable.

Probable Reader Appeal: It should have a wide appeal, but the competition is pretty
stiff. It will need special promotion that points up its strengths over
competing titles (it _is_ simple, easy to follow, and specific plants or
specific problems are easy to find.)

Recommendations: That we get an opinion from an outside reader knowledgeable both
about houseplants, and about the potential market for the book. If the
reading is favorable, I would recommend offering to publish.

Date: 8/2/77

First Reader ___ Wilson ___ __ __ ___

READER'S REPORT
UNIVERSITY OF OKLAHOMA PRESS

AUTHOR Jerry Minnich   **TITLE** NO TIME FOR HOUSEPLANTS: A BUSY
                                    PERSON'S GUIDE TO INDOOR GARDENING

TO THE EDITOR:

In reply to the question—Is this manuscript a contribution to the field?—it is my opinion that
It is a contribution in the sense that it is well organized, complete, and
easy to follow. It should make a very handy reference for anyone who wants
to have attractive plants around the house, but do not want to go to the
kind of trouble necessary to grow the more exotic and sensitive sorts of
plants.

In reply to the question—Is the scholarship of this manuscript sound?—it is my opinion that
This question does not really apply, because this is not intended as a
scholarly work. However, within the framework of the intent of the manuscript,
it is certainly sound. The material on plant diseases, cures, and general
descriptions of plant environments and needs is quite accurate.

In reply to the question—Does this manuscript have a readable style?—it is my opinion that
The style is very good. It is a warm, personal style; there are numerous
anthropomorphisms that fit well with the sort of intimate relationship
the author obviously has with plants.

*In reply to the question—If you were a publisher of scholarly books, would you consider the publication of this
manuscript a worthy addition to your list?—I would say that*
It is not a scholarly book, but it is a useful book. It is certainly never
going to be considered a seminal work. It is, though, similar to other
books that the Oklahoma Press publishes for the general market.

My opinion of the market for such a work is The potential market is enormous, but so
is the competition. It will require a very special promotion effort on
your part, to get ahead of the rather elaborately illustrated competing
volumes.

Remarks:
This was really a pleasure to read, and has been helpful to me already; I
will look forward to receiving a bound copy.

My final reaction to this manuscript is that I would—would not—publish it. I would definitely
publish it.

(Signed) Duard Leafrot, Ph.D.

DATE

PLACE

For your information: PLEASE BE FRANK IN YOUR OPINION. IT WILL BE HELD STRICTLY CONFIDENTIAL. NEITHER
YOUR NAME NOR YOUR OPINION WILL IN ANY CASE BE REVEALED TO THE AUTHOR OF THE MANUSCRIPT UNDER CON-
SIDERATION. WHAT WE WANT IS YOUR HONEST OPINION OF THE MERIT OF THIS MANUSCRIPT AS A CONTRIBUTION TO
SCHOLARSHIP OR TO THE FIELD TO WHICH IT PERTAINS.

UNIVERSITY OF OKLAHOMA PRESS

PUBLISHING DIVISION OF THE UNIVERSITY

PUBLISHERS' CONTRACT

A contract is hereby entered into by and between the UNIVERSITY OF OKLAHOMA PRESS, SALES DIVISION, hereinafter referred to as the PUBLISHERS, and   Jerry Minnich (Purvis Mulch)   , of P.O. Box 1379, Madison, Wisconsin 53701   ,

hereinafter referred to as the AUTHOR, for the publication of a manuscript entitled NO TIME FOR HOUSEPLANTS   ,

according to the terms and conditions hereinafter set forth.

I. The PUBLISHERS promise:

1. To publish such manuscript, subject to the availability of funds, within a period of two years from the date of the receipt by the said PUBLISHERS of a completed copy thereof, ready for the editorial marking and printing thereof, in such book form and edition, or editions, and at such price as the PUBLISHERS deem best suited for the successful marketing thereof, and to keep such in print as long as the demand for such work reasonably justifies;

2. If such work be subject to copyright, to secure, in the name of the PUBLISHERS, a copyright in the United States, together with copyrights in such foreign countries as the PUBLISHERS deem necessary to protect all rights in such work, and to secure a renewal of such copyright or renewals of such copyrights as is or are necessary so long as this contract remains in force and effect;

3. Upon the publication and distribution of such work to:

a) supply said AUTHOR with five (5) copies thereof;

b) furnish, at the discretion of the PUBLISHERS, copies for review, publicity, or other business purposes;

c) pay to the said AUTHOR a royalty of 10 per cent of the retail (list) price of the said work on the cloth edition on the first five thousand (5,000) copies thereof sold and distributed; 12½ per cent of the retail (list) price of the said work on the next five thousand (5,000) copies sold and distributed; and 15 per cent of the retail (list) price on all further copies sold and distributed of the cloth edition; and, in addition, pay to the said AUTHOR a royalty on any paperback edition issued by said PUBLISHERS of 5 per cent of the retail (list) price on the first five thousand (5,000) copies sold and distributed; 6¾ per cent of the retail (list) price on the next five thousand (5,000) copies sold and distributed; and 7½ per cent of the retail (list) price on all further copies sold and distributed of any paperback edition issued by said PUBLISHERS; with the exception of copies of the said work which are sold outside the territorial limits of the fifty states of the United States, which shall be considered overseas sales, for which the royalties payable to the said AUTHOR shall be one-half of the foregoing rates;

provided, however, that no royalty shall be paid or payable upon such copies of said work as are distributed under subparagraphs a) and b) above, or upon such copies as are damaged or unsalable, or upon such copies as are distributed under the provisions of subparagraph d) below;

d) pay to the AUTHOR 50 per cent of the net profits accruing in the event any first or second serialization, motion picture, television, radio production or transcription, or dramatic or musico-dramatic production of such work for the stage is arranged or contracted for by the PUBLISHERS or the work is selected and contracted for by any book club, reprint house, or other agency of publication, for all of which purposes the said PUBLISHERS are hereby solely empowered by said AUTHOR to contract;

e) submit to the said AUTHOR on or before each May 1 following the publication of the said manuscript provided for herein, during the life of this contract, a statement of account of the sales made and contracts consummated by the said PUBLISHERS or account of the said publication for the annual period preceding as of   April 1   ;

f) remit to the said AUTHOR on or before each   May 1   following the publication of the said manuscript provided for herein, during the life of this contract, such royalties and profits as may have accrued in his favor on the basis provided in subparagraphs c) and d) hereof and as are shown by the aforesaid statement of account;

g) permit the said AUTHOR, upon written request, to examine by certified accountant the books of account of the PUBLISHERS in so far as they relate to the said publication, which examination shall be at the expense of the AUTHOR, unless errors adverse to the said AUTHOR shall be discovered in such accounting amounting to fifteen (15) per cent of the total sum properly payable to the AUTHOR in any annual accounting period commencing   April 1   as aforesaid, in which case the PUBLISHERS shall bear the reasonable expense of such examination;

h) permit the AUTHOR, upon written consent of the PUBLISHERS, to assign by written assignment all rights reserved by the AUTHOR in such work.

4. The AUTHOR does hereby grant, assign, transfer, and convey to the PUBLISHERS the sole and exclusive right, title, and interest in such work, including the right to arrange for, market, and contract for any first or second serialization, motion picture, television, radio production or transcription, or dramatic or musico-dramatic production of such work for the stage, and to arrange for, promote, or contract for any book club, reprint, or other selection of such work.

II. The AUTHOR hereby promises to:

1. Furnish to the PUBLISHERS, within a reasonable time after the execution of this contract and ready for publication, a manuscript, to the satisfaction of the PUBLISHERS;

2. Supply at his own expense all illustrations for such publication;

3. Make an index for said publication, if such be required by the PUBLISHERS;

4. Remit to the PUBLISHERS, within thirty (30) days following publication of such work, any costs or expense incurred on the part of the PUBLISHERS, which said PUBLISHERS are hereby expressly authorized to incur, arising from the typing or retyping of all or any portion of such manuscript furnished by said AUTHOR required to comply with the stipulation, hereby made, that it be typewritten, double-spaced, with no longhand insertions, on paper eight and one-half (8½) by eleven (11) inches in size, and to conform otherwise to the Manual of

OKLAHOMA whose signatures are affixed hereto, and the members of the BOARD OF REGENTS OF THE UNIVERSITY OF OKLAHOMA, in their individual capacities shall in no manner, individually or collectively, be liable for any damages to anyone, and that any suit or claim hereunder shall be filed against the BOARD OF REGENTS OF THE UNIVERSITY OF OKLAHOMA in a corporate capacity, or against the STATE OF OKLAHOMA, as duly provided by the laws of the STATE OF OKLAHOMA.

In witness hereof, the undersigned have hereunto affixed their signatures.

UNIVERSITY OF OKLAHOMA PRESS

By _____
                Director

By _____
                Service Manager

_____
                AUTHOR

Executed this ___30th___ day of ___August___, 19 _77_, at Norman, Oklahoma.

Style of the PUBLISHERS or to one designated by the PUBLISHERS, or arising from any changes, except typographical errors, made by the AUTHOR in the proofs thereof;

5. Return to said PUBLISHERS all proofs within five (5) days after the receipt thereof by the AUTHOR;

6. Accept as complete and full compensation under this contract for his work in preparing said literary work for publication the royalty and net profit payments to be made him by the said PUBLISHERS as provided in Part I, paragraph 3, subparagraphs c), d), and f) of this contract;

7. Co-operate with the said PUBLISHERS in expediting in every way possible the production and publication of the said literary work.

III. The AUTHOR does hereby warrant that:

1. The manuscript to be furnished by him hereunder when submitted will be complete and ready for publication, that he will be the sole author thereof, and that he has full power to enter into the within contract;

2. The manuscript to be furnished by him hereunder when submitted will be free from any and all libelous or otherwise unlawful or objectionable matter;

3. He will hold the said PUBLISHERS harmless against any suit, claim, or recovery upon any proprietary right, copyright, or libelous or other unlawful or objectionable matter as regards such literary work, and will, at his own expense defend any such suit, claim, or recovery in his own behalf and in behalf of the PUBLISHERS;

4. The manuscript to be furnished by him hereunder has not previously been published in whole or in part by anyone, and that it is therefore to be considered by the PUBLISHERS to be a new work and subject to copyright by the PUBLISHERS as a book now published for the first time in the United States of America.

IV. It is further mutually promised and agreed between the PUBLISHERS and the AUTHOR that:

1. The title of such manuscript to be produced and published hereunder shall be   NO TIME FOR HOUSEPLANTS

and such title shall be changed only by mutual consent of the parties expressed in writing;

2. Such changes may be made by the PUBLISHERS in the text of the manuscript submitted by the AUTHOR as may be required to conform to the PUBLISHERS' Manual of Style or one designated by the PUBLISHERS, and otherwise conform to the prerequisites of the PUBLISHERS for publication;

3. Notice of copyright or copyrights, if copyrightable, shall be imprinted in all copies of such work sold and distributed;

4. If, after three (3) years from date of publication, fewer than twenty-five (25) copies of such work shall have been sold in any one (1) year, to be computed as and from respective anniversaries of the publication date, the PUBLISHERS may offer, at a remainder price, free of royalties, to the AUTHOR, the remaining part of the edition, and in the event that the AUTHOR does not, within sixty (60) days from receipt of such offer, notify the PUBLISHERS in writing of his agreement to purchase same, the said remaining part of the edition may be destroyed by the PUBLISHERS or disposed of as waste paper, without payment of any royalty, as hereinbefore provided, on the portion thus destroyed;

5. In the event of any suit arising from publication of such work, the signatories and agents of the UNIVERSITY OF OKLAHOMA and the STATE OF

[Top form]

Date 3/9/78
Pub Date Fall 1978
House Ed. LW

Author (s) Jerry Minnich
Editor (s)
Translator (s)
Forwarder (s)
Prefacer (s) →
Introducer (s)
Illustrator (s) Dian Wehrle Hjertman
Other (s)

Title NO TIME FOR HOUSEPLANTS: A Busy Person's Guide to Indoor Gardening

Series _____ No. _____

MS pages (total) 180

Accents

Special Features Scientific names of plants. Following each plant there will appear four symbols (art) identifying the temperature, moisture, humidity, and sunlight needs of each plant. These will have to be photographed and stripped
Design Suggestions in for each cf about 80 plants.

Jacket Suggestions Cartoon of busy people rushing out of the house, briefcases in hand, watering a plant on the way.

Schedule rush.

Comments There are several items missing: dedication, acknowledgements page, explanation of symbols (which will appear in two places in the book), and some art.

	Editor	Director	Art Department
Print Order			
Text	5,000		
B&W Illustrations			
Color Illustrations			
Bind Order	3000		
Bind			
Leave flat sheets			
Leave sewn sheets			
List Price	4.95 paper		
Discount Price			
Mfg. Cost/Copy			
Margin			

[Bottom form]

REPORT ON CONTRACTED MANUSCRIPT RECEIVED

AUTHOR: Jerry Minnich   DATE CONTRACTED: 10-17-77
TITLE: "No Time for House Plants"   DATE RECEIVED: November 16, 1977

Physical inventory of the manuscript: 180 pp.

Prelims
Text
Appendix
Bibliography (alph. order under topics--may not be best--i.e., easiest to use--format)

Missing materials:

1. To be supplied by author: illustrations; explanation of plant key (see Chap. 3), index*

2. To be supplied by the Press (finished artwork, etc.):

Problems:

1. Editorial:

Light editing (check for mechanics, grammar). Au caps & ital genus when also common name (resolve w/au). Some sections have already been minimally edited. Resolve w/au organization of Bibliography.

2. Design and production:

Tables (few) 4 values subheads: 1 ctr, 1 run in, in plant-lists 2 sep-line side heads (1 for plant groups in list--see Chaps. 3 & 4)

Recommendations:

Print: _____ cloth; _____ paper
Bind: _____ cloth; _____ paper
Price: $ _____ (editor's recommended price)
Publication season: _____

Other comments: **Will need a good index.** Garden books often lacking good ones. Include both common and scientific names, types (e.g., "Ferns")

Date: _____   by: _____

Royalty rate: 10% List

AUTHOR: Midwich

Title: No Time For Houseplants

Format: 6 x 9   Print #: 5000   Price: $5.95 (6.50)

# of Pages: 128   cloth: paper:

(handwritten note, circled) Print 5,000 / Bind all / Price $5.95 / all PB

INCOME	$ 17,850	$5.95 — 29,850 / 50,000
Grant or Subsidy: $		
Composition, Paper and Printing	Unit Cost: $ 2.19 $ 10,945	10,945
Binding	Unit cost: $	
Freelance Costs	$ 183	183
TOTAL PLANT COSTS (Comp., ppb, freelance minus grant or subsidy)	$ 11,128	11,128
ROYALTIES	$ 2975	5475
TOTAL COSTS (Plant plus royalties)	$ 14,103	16,602
NET INCOME	% 21% $ 3747	13,248 (44%)
OVERHEAD	__ % of I $	
NET SURPLUS OR DEFICIT	% $	

COMMENTS: Needs help.

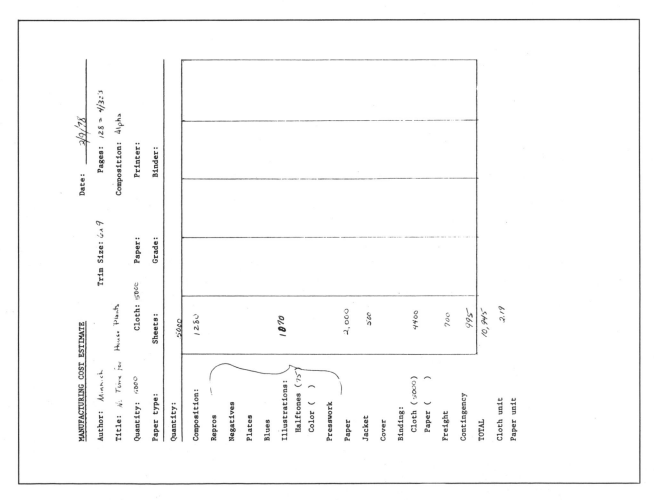

MANUFACTURING COST ESTIMATE

Author: Midwich

Title: No Time for House Plants

Date: 2/9/78

Trim Size: 6 x 9

Pages: 128 = 4/32's   Composition: Alpha

Quantity: 5000   Cloth: 5000   Paper: Printer:

Paper type: Sheets: Grade: Binder:

Quantity: 5000

Composition:	1280
Repros	
Negatives	
Plates	
Blues	
Illustrations: Halftones (75)	1870
Color ( )	
Presswork	
Paper	2,000
Jacket	500
Cover	
Binding: Cloth (5000)	4400
Paper ( )	
Freight	700
Contingency	995
TOTAL	10,945
Cloth unit	2.19
Paper unit	

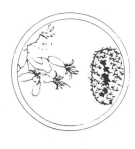

SPECIFICATIONS FOR MINNICH: NO TIME FOR HOUSEPLANTS

Trim size: 5½ x 8¼ inches.

Text type: 11/12 Patina on 24 picas.

Display type: Palatino Semibold and Arboret.

Runningheads: 7-point Patina caps.

Folios: 11-points Patina.

Type measure (overall page):   24 x 42 picas.

Head margins: 3 picas.

Inner margins: 4½ picas.

All composition by Alphatype and Phototypositor.

Cacti and Other Succulents

Many house plant fanciers are completely indifferent to cacti and the other succulents, and some express a distinct dislike for them. Still others are completely enthralled with these unusual and diverse plants, giving them attention to the exclusion of all others.

Whatever your individual preferences, there is no denying that the succulents (and cacti are but one group of succulents) are remarkably colorful and interesting subjects, easy to care for, and responsive to special attention. They are, further, ideal plants for the no-time gardener, since they require less attention than other plants. Most succulents ask little more than a sunny window, occasional water, and very occasional fertilizing. There is no pruning, no tying up, no staking, no repotting. They are slow growing and thoroughly dependable.

There are literally thousands of species in this plant category, including more than two thousand cacti alone. Of these, several hundred, both attractive and suitable for indoor culture, are bred and sold as house plants.

Although cacti are succulent plants, the two are treated as separate groups in common practice, and in these pages we will follow that practice. Botanists classify cacti according to their flower characteristics, although most of us recognize

may appear to die in colder months, but after an adequate rest period it will spring back to life. It is very sensitive to fertilizer burn and salt accumulation.

BLACK PEPPER (*Piper nigrum*)

This is not an especially attractive house plant, but it produces real peppercorns that you may use at the table and is a good conversation piece for that reason. The plant's green berries eventually turn red, then dry up and turn black. Pick the dried black corns, dry them thoroughly for several weeks in an open spot, and then use them in your pepper grinder. The care for black pepper is the same as that required for *Philodendron* (see below). It is not a demanding plant.

Note: Be sure that you have this plant and not one of the so-called black peppers of the deadly nightshade family!

BOXWOOD (*Buxus*)

The same plant that grows the most prized hedges outdoors can make a very attractive house plant. Boxwood, with its glossy, bright green leaves, is slow growing and dependable, a good subject for bonsai, the ancient oriental art of growing dwarf trees and shrubs. Japanese boxwood (*B. microphylla japonica*) and (*B. sempervirens*) are the two most popular species.

BROMELIADS

There are more than eighteen hundred varieties of this popular group, many of which are suitable for growing as house plants. Some of them produce attractive flowers, but most are grown for their striking and variegated leaf patterns. One distinctive feature of a bromeliad is the rosette of leaves

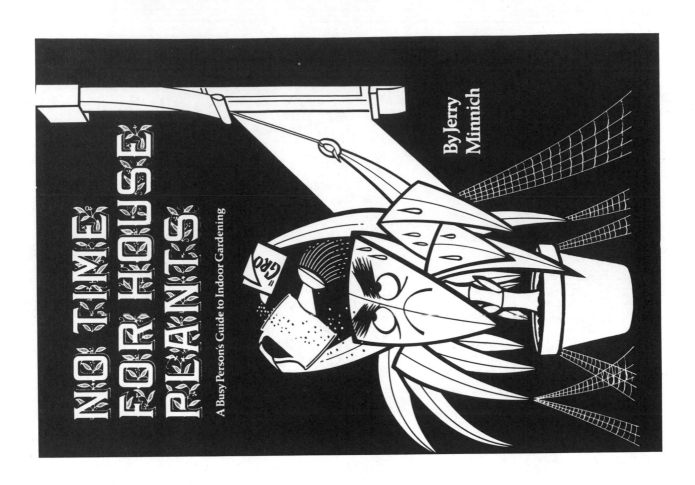

By Jerry Minnich

NO TIME FOR HOUSE PLANTS

A Busy Person's Guide to Indoor Gardening

CONTENTS	COPY Herewith	COPY To Come	PROOFS OF TO BE SHOWN IN OR WITH Galleys	Pages	Other
*FRONTMATTER					
halftitle	x				
title page	x				
copyright page	x	x			
dedication page		x			
acknowledgements	x				
Preface	x				
Contents	x				
Second halftit-e					
TEXT	x				
ILLUSTRATIONS	x	x			
Halftone					
Line	x				
Color					
Other					
ILLS., CAPTIONS **MAPS		x			
BIBLIOGRAPHY	x				
APPENDIX	x				
RUNNINGHEADS		x			
SERIES AD PAGE					
COLOPHON					
INDEX		x			
CLOTH COVER					
Spine					
Front					
PAPER COVER	xx				
Page 1					
Page 2					
Page 3					
Page 4		x			
Spine					
JACKET COPY	x*				
Front					
Back					
Flap					
Spine					
Inside					

PROOFS	NUMBER OF
Galleys	4
Pages	2
Illustrations	
Index	2

*List in sequence (series title, halftitle, frontis-
piece, title page, copyright page, card page, dedication, preface, foreword, introduction, contents, illustrations list, maps list, or whatever).
**Map art to be checked by editor before engraving.